外教社跨文化交际丛书 12

商务世界的跨文化沟通
THE INFLUENCE OF CULTURE IN THE WORLD OF BUSINESS

■ Michael B. Hinner 编
　万　华　导读

上海外语教育出版社
外教社 SHANGHAI FOREIGN LANGUAGE EDUCATION PRESS

图书在版编目(CIP)数据

商务世界的跨文化沟通/(美)赫纳(Hinner, M.B.)编;万华导读. —上海:上海外语教育出版社,2014
(外教社跨文化交际丛书)
ISBN 978−7−5446−3575−2

Ⅰ.①商⋯　Ⅱ.①赫⋯　②万⋯　Ⅲ.①商务−东西文化−文化交流−文集　Ⅳ.①G115−53

中国版本图书馆 CIP 数据核字(2013)第 313676 号

© by Peter Lang GmbH, Frankfurt/M., Germany, 2007.

This edition of *The Influence of Culture in the World of Business* is published by arrangement with Peter Lang GmbH.

Licensed for sale in the People's Republic of China.

本书由 Peter Lang 出版社授权上海外语教育出版社有限公司出版。
仅供在中华人民共和国境内销售。
图字:09−2012−840

出版发行：**上海外语教育出版社**
　　　　　（上海外国语大学内）　邮编：200083
电　　话：021−65425300（总机）
电子邮箱：bookinfo@sflep.com.cn
网　　址：http://www.sflep.com.cn　http://www.sflep.com
责任编辑：苗　杨

印　　刷：上海信老印刷厂
开　　本：787×965　1/16　印张 32.25　字数 653千字
版　　次：2014 年 4 月第 1 版　2014 年 4 月第 1 次印刷
印　　数：2 500 册

书　　号：ISBN 978−7−5446−3575−2 / G・1101
定　　价：68.00 元

本版图书如有印装质量问题，可向本社调换

外教社跨文化交际丛书编委会

主 任
胡文仲（北京外国语大学）
贾玉新（哈尔滨工业大学）

副主任
Bates Hoffer（三一大学）
Nobuyuki Honna（青山学院大学）
Steve Kulich（上海外国语大学）
陈　凌（香港浸会大学）
高一虹（北京大学）

委 员
Andy Kirkpatrick（科廷大学）
Michael Byram（杜伦大学）
Michael Prosser（上海外国语大学）
Richard Wiseman（加州州立大学福勒顿分校）
Robert N. St. Clair（路易斯维尔大学）
陈国明（罗得岛大学）
顾嘉祖（南京师范大学）
林大津（福建师范大学）
申惠中（悉尼大学）
宋　莉（哈尔滨工业大学）
孙有中（北京外国语大学）
许力生（浙江大学）
张红玲（上海外国语大学）
张惠晶（伊利诺大学芝加哥分校）
庄恩平（上海大学）
庄智象（上海外国语大学）

总　序

跨文化交际学是一门在传播学等学科理论的基础上，与人类学、心理学、语言学、文化学以及社会学等相互交叉而发展起来的学科。其实，不同文化间的交流古已有之，但是真正将文化交流进行理论研究进而发展成"跨文化交际学"，还只是近四五十年间的事情。想要深入探究这门学科，我们首先要了解它的起源。

20 世纪 60 年代是信息技术和交通技术高度发展的年代。随着科技的进步，空间距离大大缩短，各种文化间的交流日益频繁。但是空间距离的缩小并不意味着人们之间的文化距离或是心理距离可以瞬间缩短。与之相反的是，人们不能再用旧有的文化观念和思维方式来理解和解释日新月异的世界里出现的各种新问题。同时，文化差异滋生众多的交际失误、矛盾和冲突，反而使人们的心理距离加大。矛盾和冲突的背后不仅仅是利益或者领土的争夺，也不仅仅是政治和意识形态的分歧，而更多的是文化和价值观念上的巨大隔阂——正是这些隔阂使"地球村"中的人们虽然身在"咫尺"之间，却有如隔天涯之感。

美国作为一个多民族、多种族的国家自然而然成为跨文化交际研究的兴起之地，其中以美国人类学家 Edward T. Hall 为代表的一些学者在前人研究成果的基础上提出了跨文化交际的理论，现在学界也一致将他的著作 *The Silent Language*（Anchor Books，1959）当作是这一学科的奠基之作。

到了 20 世纪七八十年代，学者们把研究重点逐渐从对比和分析不同文化交际（Cross-cultural Communication）中的差异转到研究跨文化交际（Intercultural Communication）动态多变的过程中去。以此为基点，William B. Gudykunst 等一批学者建构了动态的跨文化交际理论。理论的突破带来了学科的快速发展，跨文化交际研究所涉及的学科越来越多，研究的内容更加丰富，研究方法日益科学。学科的发展引起了世界各国学者空前广泛的关注，跨文化交际学被引进大学课堂，相关的研究学会和专业学刊相继出现，各种国际学术研讨会也定期举行。现在只要在网上简单查询一下相关书目，我们就会发现此类专著多达几百种，在刊物上发表的论文更是不胜枚举。William B. Gudykunst 曾在其著作 *Cross-cultural and Intercultural Communication*（Sage Publications，2003）一书中总结了 15 种不同的跨文化交际理论。理论研究和探索上的巨大进步标志着跨文化交际学的学科发展日臻成熟。

进入新世纪，"地球村"每个角落的每个公民都不同程度地被卷入了经济一体化和全球化的浪潮。同时，人们清楚地意识到全球化不等于一元化。在多元文化并存的时代中，个人之间、社会全体之间、民族之间乃至国家之间，无不存在着文化差异甚至文化沟壑。培养对文化差异的敏感性，缩短文化距离，发展跨文化交际能力，已经成为新时代的迫切需求。由此，我们不难预见到跨文化交际研究会在 21 世纪被逐步推向高潮。

在关注国际学科发展趋势的同时,让我们把目光转向中国。虽然我国历史上早有注重语言与文化、语言与社会研究的传统,但是现代的跨文化交际研究在我国的起步还要追溯至20世纪的80年代。当时随着国内学界对于语言学和文化研究的不断重视,在"文化热"和"反思热"的影响下,语言研究入文化成为新的热点,这无疑为跨文化交际研究的兴起奠定了基础。改革开放扩大了国际间的学术交往,外语界的学者和教师成为国内首先接触到跨文化交际研究的一批人,他们理所当然地成为了这一学科的研究主力。我们可以这么说:20世纪80年代是跨文化交际学诞生、成长和发展的关键十年。一方面,海外归来的学者把西方有关跨文化交际理论、研究方法和教学实践介绍和引进到中国;另一方面,国内研究者在学习和借鉴的同时,在继承前人成果的基础上,结合中国实际,多方位、多角度地探索和开发我国跨文化交际的学科外延,开创了初步繁荣的研究局面。

外语教师和对外汉语教师是我国跨文化交际研究领域的主力军。他们在教学的过程中认识到跨文化交际能力的培养应当成为外语教育的重要内容,外语教学必须与文化相结合。在20世纪80年代末,国内一部分外语院校首先推出了跨文化交际学课程。时至今日,我国已有几十所大学的外语院系开设了这门课程。

1995年,首届中国跨文化交际国际研讨会在哈尔滨召开,来自世界20多个国家和地区的几百名学者进行了学术交流与探讨。中国跨文化交际研究会也在这次会议中正式成立——这标志着跨文化交际研究在中国迎来了一个新纪元。自学会成立以来,已定期组织了6次国际研讨会。同时有些院校也多次组织大型研讨会,广泛开展国内不同地区间和国际间的学术交流,跨文化交际研究得到了空前迅速的发展。

广大教师、语言学者们兼收并蓄,著书立说,撰写论文,编写教材。据不完全统计,目前出版的专著和教材多达几十本,发表的论文也有2000篇以上。他们研究和探讨的内容丰富多样,涵盖范围广泛;有些学者和教师的研究更是对西方学者的某些理论提出质疑,提出了自己的视角独特的观点。

由于学科性质所决定,跨文化交际研究比其他学科更需要不同文化间的交流。实际上,中国跨文化交际研究会已成为国际大家庭的一部分,并为推动跨文化交际研究在世界范围上的发展做出了应有的贡献。我们的研究会中有不少教师学者同时也是国际学会会员,他们或在国际学会组织和国际学刊中承担重要工作,或是经常受邀参加在海外举行的学术会议,在会上交流论文。不少论文受到国际学界的好评,并在国际学刊上发表。我国的跨文化交际研究学者也在国外出版他们的专著,传播中国在这一领域的研究成果。

回顾这20余年的学科发展,我们也应清楚地意识到前进路上存在着的诸多问题。首先,在理论研究方面,正如王宗炎先生所指出的,"收集采购之功多,提炼转化之功少",我们还没有形成具有中国文化特点的理论。William B. Gudykunst教授也曾指出亚洲学者需要创建适合自己文化的交际理论。只有学习和借鉴而没有发展和改造,没有结合自己文化特点的理论,是不可能把跨文化交际研究建成一门适合中国国情的学科的。其次,由于理论指导不足,我们的研究多集中在文化对比方面,对动态多变的交际过程的研究和探讨不够,在研究方法和研究内容上尚需要更多的探索和拓展,这些都影响了我们在这一领域的进一步发展。

在新的世纪,我们需要进一步开阔视野,发展我国的跨文化交际研究,推动此领域的学科建设,加强此领域的教学和教材建设,以满足广大教师、研究生以及各方面读者的需要。上海外语教育出版社出于推动我国跨文化交际研究的考虑,决定推出"外教社跨文化交际丛书"。丛书既引进国外权威力作,也出版我国学者的著述,还有中外专家的合力之作。我国读者可以通过这套丛书学习和借鉴来自不同文化背景的学者的真知灼见,在领略我国学者和专家的新思维和新成果的同时,还可以欣赏各种文化交流的结晶。我们相信"外教社跨文化交际丛书"对于今后我国跨文化交际学的发展将会起到极为重要的作用。在此,我们代表丛书编委会对上海外语教育出版社的大力支持表示诚挚的谢意。

胡文仲
北京外国语大学
贾玉新
哈尔滨工业大学
2006 年 4 月

导　　读

一、文化和跨文化交际

1. 文化与跨文化

　　文化有广义狭义两种概念。广义的文化包罗万象，是一种囊括传统、信仰、价值、规则和符号的稳定渐变的综合模式，这种模式从一代传到下一代，并通过相互交流和相互分享成为稳定的传统价值评判体系。文化也可分为物质文化和精神文化。人类交往可以受到物质文化的影响，更会受到诸如价值观、人生观、宗教信仰、风俗习惯等精神文化的影响。

　　Taylor (1920) 和 Herskovits (1955) 认为文化是一切包括知识、信仰、艺术、道德、法律、习俗以及社会成员个人所表现出来的能力和习惯的综合整体，即人们的一言一行。文化是社会群体中以价值观、信念、行为规范等为核心的观念体系，它会影响这个群体中个人的行为 (郑兴山，2010：9)。有人用冰山模型或洋葱模型来描述文化的结构和层次。从区域来分，有社区文化、南/北方文化、民族文化、欧洲文化、亚洲文化等；从类型来分，有社会人的个体文化、企业文化、政治文化、制度文化、汽车文化、饮食文化、婚丧文化、班级文化等；从时间来分，可有远古文化、中古文化、近代文化、当代文化等。因此，文化包括了人类所创造的一切软环境和硬环境。

　　文化的特点鲜明，它稳定不易变，为特定群体共享。不同文化均有自己的独特性，其群体或个体的行为有可预测性。因此，人们可以了解和把握不同地区、群体和组织的文化差异。

　　跨文化指的则是不同文化的交叉和跨越，是不同行为规范、价值观、隐含信念和基本假设的碰撞和交融。跨文化的前提是反映在不同层次上，如国家文化、组织文化或个人文化上的差异。

　　文化多样性有可能是生产力、创造力和决策力的原动力。然而处理不当，文化多样性也可能产生负面作用，如权力斗争。因此，欠缺文化知识和恰当的交际方式会导致冲突。冲突是指两个或多个对象在本质或关系问题上可观察到的或者实际存在的价值、期望、过程或者结果方面的不一致性。这也说明有效的跨文化交际对于解决争端的必要性。跨国企业的成功在于强大的生产能力和跨文化交际能力。

　　在经济全球化时代，跨文化交际能力的重要性得以凸显。文化反映了人的思维方式、决策过程、行为准则、信仰和价值，如果不了解文化对人类行为的影响，就会在交际中产生误解。在跨文化交际活动中，管理者们会面临着文化稳定不变的挑战和文化冲击和冲突的挑战。因此，理解文化是当今经济全球化背景下不可或缺的技能。

2. 跨文化交际

　　自从有了人类，就有了跨文化交际活动，因此人们对之习以为常而且常常忽略它的存在。什么是跨文化交际呢？跨文化交际指的是来自不同文化的个人之间的交际，交际的成功需要交际者拥有积极的情感、对文化差异的正确认识和合适的交际行为和技巧，即有效的和适当的跨文化交际能力，包括个人品行、交际技巧、心理调整能力和文化意识能力（陈国明，2007：244）。

跨文化交际能力直接影响着国际商务活动。跨国企业能否进入国际市场当然取决于其经济、技术和管理水平，同时也取决于其是否深刻理解了对象国的文化。因此经济的全球化更加需要跨国企业加深对多元文化的理解和提升跨文化交际能力。有效的跨文化交际必须克服陈旧观念、民族优越感以及偏见等消极假设的负面影响（John Oetzel and Adolfo José Garcia，详见本书第5篇文章）。跨文化交际意识影响企业在国际商务活动中与消费者的沟通、对市场的判断以及商务战略的制定。良好的沟通是成功商务活动的基石。

3. 跨文化交际研究

跨文化交际研究始于20世纪五六十年代，当时信息技术和交通技术迅猛发展，但人们意识到空间距离的缩短并不意味着于文化距离或心理距离的缩小，"地球村"也并不意味着一元化，多元文化下的交际无不存在着文化差异甚至沟壑（胡文仲，贾玉新：2006）。七八十年代跨文化交际研究实现理论突破，在国外发展成为比较成熟的学科。

跨文化交际的研究对象是交际行为，不同文化背景的人会采用完全不同的交际方式处理人际关系。跨文化交际研究是在传播学等学科理论的基础上，与人类学、心理学、语言学、文化学、社会学和管理学等相互交叉发展的学科。在世界全球化的过程中，文化观念的差异和思维方式的不同给人们日益频繁的交际带来了各种各样的问题，不断的交际失误、矛盾冲突反而加大人们的心理距离。跨文化交际研究因此得以快速发展，所涉及的学科越来越多，研究的内容越来越丰富，研究方法也日益科学。跨文化交际研究还被引入了大学课堂，相关的研究学会、专业学刊、国际研讨会不断涌现。

文化的差异也给国际商务合作造成摩擦和障碍，不同文化背景的企业经营者之间的文化冲突现象日益显著，合作双方在经营与管理时所产生的矛盾也日益增加，甚至导致合作失败。著名跨国文化差异研究专家David A. Ricks（2006）对此做了如下结论：大凡跨国公司大的失败，几乎都是忽略文化差异所导致的结果。因此，如何消除这些摩擦和障碍、提高跨文化沟通的有效性变得越来越重要，甚至成了决定国际商务活动成功与否的关键因素。整个社会迫切需要具有国际视野、跨文化意识、跨文化沟通能力，并且通晓国际规则的人才。于是，管理学者试图从管理角度分析跨文化管理失败的原因；跨文化研究学者也试图以跨文化视角探索产生文化冲突的根源。两种研究方法都有其道理，但实际上都难以解决企业所面临的实际问题。于是美国教授Iris Varner 和Linda Beamer（2007）提出了"跨文化商务沟通"的理论框架，将商务、文化与沟通三者融为一体，旨在分析与解决跨文化工作环境中的交流和管理问题。

我国的跨文化研究始于20世纪80年代的语言学研究，在研究者们的努力下发展迅速，这从每年全国跨文化研讨会召开的次数、出版的书和发表的文章的数量、高校专业的设置、从事跨文化交际的研究者和学者人数的增加等方面便可见一斑。但是，跨文化交际研究在我国起步较晚，相关理论及实证研究水平有待进一步提高，尤其是以中国商务文化为背景的跨文化交际研究具有重要的理论及现实指导意义。如今，众多外国企业纷纷涌入中国寻求发展，中国企业也争先跨出国门走向世界。由于我国政治文化、经济文化和社会文化的特殊性,国外大型的跨文化研究机构并不能完全解析中国跨国企业在跨文化管理上的复杂性,这因此要求我国学者在立足中国文化和中国跨国企业发展的特殊性的基础上,借鉴国外比较成熟的理论,提出适合中国国情的跨文化交际和管理理论。

二、本书的结构与特色

1. 本书结构

为了更好地解读商务沟通,人们不仅需要分析和研究商务规律,也同样需要研究商务沟通的原则及其应用,从而使人类的商务活动更加有效。本书以此为宗旨,共收入了论文20篇,根据内容可分为三大类:

1) 跨文化交际概念和理论

这部分的文章以综合的视角,对跨文化沟通、跨文化管理、跨文化交际的性别特点和语言特点等进行了研究。有研究强调从全球角度看跨文化沟通,认为经济实力并不等于文化实力,提醒人们在发展经济的同时别忘了文化的发展,否则本土文化、弱势文化、边缘文化会更加弱化(D. Ray Heisey)。也有研究主张对跨文化交际的适应性的研究不要把宏观的和微观的过程、长期的和短期的适应对立起来研究,否则必然走入歧途(Young Yun Kim)。对跨文化沟通效果的研究,陈国明先生认为首先要认清跨文化的本质,清楚跨文化交际的基本概念,怎样认识跨文化交际决定着对该领域进行怎样的研究。

这部分主要包括以下几篇文章:《全球社会的跨文化沟通》、《跨文化交际效果的概念综述》、《适应新文化:综合交际理论》、《交际能力的魅力:美日学生交际风格对比》、《中国文化背景下变革型领导的局限和前景》、《跨文化交际中的性别差异》、《文化在说服性演讲中的角色:以以色列和新西兰学生的视频交流为例》、《语用的多样性,语用的转移和文化认同》、《中国社会文化背景下的品牌建设:特点,趋势,问题》、《中国人的自我意识正在构建中吗?》。

2) 跨文化与企业管理

这部分主要概述的是商务活动中的跨文化管理,尤其是本书主编 Michael B. Hinner 本人对并购/合并现象的研究。他的研究发现合并和并购已是企业进入全球市场、扩大经营的首选战略。然而,并不是所有的并购都尽如人意,其成功率还不到一半。问题都在于人和文化差异。文化是人的价值观、信仰、行为规范等的集合和反映。在企业中文化可载舟亦可覆舟,能否管理好人、处理好文化,很大程度上决定着跨国经营的成与败。Hinner 提出了并购前、并购中和并购后的文化差异分析模型,以帮助并购企业认识和协调好并购后的文化差异,引导员工为共同目标协同作战,实现利益最大化,从宏观上为参与全球化的企业提供了解决问题的可行方案。

该部分的另一位突出的国际知名学者 Hofstede 用实地观察法研究美国管理学理论在全球的应用情况,指出人总是会受到自己成长环境的影响,这必然致使他的行为有其独特之处。正因为文化差异导致行为不同,人在跨文化交际中一定会面临着文化的冲击和冲突,这就需要跨文化商务人员去真诚解读和解码不同文化中的共同意义。

这部分的文章包括《并购和合并中的文化适应》、《管理理论中的文化约束力》、《管理跨文化冲突》、《决策过程中交际风格的对比》。

3) 跨文化商务活动

这部分的内容是从微观的视角研究国际商务中的跨文化交际,更加接近具体的市场行为和商务活动。研究者们展示给人们的是全球化时代里,跨文化经营者和管理者必须要懂得如何在不同的市场中通过市场定位、广告宣传和产品营销凸显产品的不同价值;懂得服务人员业绩考核机制,以了解服务人员的特质,尤其是他们跨文化沟通的技巧;懂得跨文化沟通中的语用变化,包括遣词造句和肢体语言;懂得文化导向下建立全球品牌的策略,从而彰显品牌价值;懂得全球化过程中如何读懂性别差异及其特色并在跨文化商务活动中发挥其作用;懂得全球化进程中如何确定自己的身份,找到自己的位置;还需要懂得旅游市场上的沟通原则、方法和策略。无论企业的大小,都能从这部分的研究中吸取营养。

这部分的文章主要包括《跨文化敏感度对跨文化服务员工绩效的影响——伦敦和佛罗里达两地研究》、《向金字塔底层投广告:与新兴市场的消费者沟通》、《跨国经营和营销策略的文化反思》、《跨文化视觉广告》、《西裔广告代理商:把握市场的脉搏》、《旅游文化:跨文化交流规则及跨国旅游》。

2. 本书特色

本书的出版对全球跨文化研究、全球化商务管理具有重大的意义,可有力地推动全球跨文化研究向纵深发展。

1) 研究既有科学的理性,又有经验的感性

本书的每篇文章或每个课题都展现了作者和研究者的理性思考和感性经验。例如,《并购和合并中的文化适应》就以戴姆勒—奔驰和克莱斯勒等的合并为例,根据 Schuler 和 Jackson 的并购理论、Hofstede 的文化理论、Berger 的沟通理论、Martin 和 Nakayama 的权力理论等,界定合并与并购的区别与意义,总结合并与并购的方法和步骤,并购和合并中可能存在的问题,造成问题的因素以及解决问题的策略。这对正在并购、即将并购、或正处于并购后迷茫和痛苦的企业来说有着重要的指导意义。

全球化形势下中国经济快速发展,中国企业走向世界必定会遇到许多跨文化交际问题,尤其在商务贸易界更是不可避免。《中国文化背景下变革型领导的局限和前景》指出了变革型领导在中国文化中的运筹方式,认为变革型领导与中国传统型领导有着相似之处。《中国社会文化背景下的品牌建设:特点,趋势,问题》一文则回顾了中国的品牌走向世界的经验和教训,为中国品牌的建设提供了借鉴。《中国人的自我意识正在构建中吗?》研究了中国人价值观的变化,它不仅为国内企业的发展,更为国际商业团体进入中国市场提供了参考。《跨文化敏感度对跨文化服务员工绩效的影响——伦敦和佛罗里达两地研究》以两地为例,分析了服务者和消费者之间的关系。《向金字塔底层投广告:与新兴市场的消费者沟通》分析了世界人口的变化与营销学策略的关系,从而为全球的商家指出了新的销售之路。《跨国经营和营销策略的文化反思》指出了针对不同文化群体应采用不同的营销策略,阐述了营销策略应与东道国的文化价值观相匹配,产品信息应与消费者的文化价值相符的观点。《跨文化视觉广告》重点研究跨文化视觉广告中的文化差异对信息诠释和评价的影响,讨论了如何利用图像来向特定的人群传递某种信息,以满足他们对产品的文化

期待,并帮助其对文化信息进行解读。《西裔广告代理商:把握市场的脉博》研究了在美国西裔移民越来越适应美国文化的背景下,面向西裔市场的广告代理商营销策略的演变。《旅游文化:跨文化交流规则及跨国旅游》一文研究了跨文化旅游的利与弊。跨文化旅游时,旅游者往往会强化原有的刻板印象,证明他们的先入为主之见是"正确"的;但跨文化旅游同时也确实具有积极意义,它使人们有机会了解他国文化,从而更加了解自身。这些研究为全球化尤其是国际商务铺平了道路,对中国走向海外、创造国际品牌、与国际接轨有着重大的意义。

此外,本书还有多篇文章研究了学生的交际风格、性别差异在跨文化交际中的作用和影响,如《交际能力的魅力:美日学生交际风格对比》通过测评和对比,指出美国学生在跨文化交际中表现得更加自信,而日本学生在与熟人和朋友的交际中更加自信,在与陌生人的交际中则缺乏自信。《跨文化交际中的性别差异》指出了在跨文化商务活动中,女性表现了更优秀的社交能力和更有效解决跨文化问题的潜质,在海外委派中获得更高的满意度。《文化在说服性演讲中的角色:以以色列和新西兰学生的视频交流为例》集中研究了跨文化交际中语言的表现力,分析了语速、语调等特定的语用规则在交际中被交际者忽略,导致跨文化交际失败的案例。《语用的多样性,语用的转移和文化认同》主要以中美师生交流为例,指出来自不同文化群体的人们以英语交流时,仍遵循本族语言的思维模式和价值判断,误解和沟通失败多因此而起。在教育国际化的今天,这些研究为各国留学生尽快适应新文化、融入新文化提供了良好的借鉴和佐证。

2) 作者均有很强的理论能力和实践能力

本书的第二个特点是作者中既有理论功底深厚的名家学者,又有一批直接从事跨文化商务活动和企业管理、并能够进一步充实和完善理论的实践者。他们自世界各地,代表着不同的文化,且年龄跨度大,视角新颖,共同就跨文化交际如何影响、引领甚至决定全球经济做了深入的诠释。主编 Michael B. Hinner 出生于德国,在美国长大,就读于纽约州立大学石溪分校(State University of New York at Stony Brook),研究人类学、对比研究、英语、德语、历史学、语言学,在圣约翰大学(St. John's University)法学院学习法律。他在德国弗莱贝格工业大学(TU Bergakademie Freiberg)和德累斯顿国际大学(Dresden International University)教授商务英语、商务交际和跨文化沟通。再如 Geert Hofstede 在跨文化研究领域影响巨大,D. Ray Heisey 对跨文化交际做了科学界定,陈国明和贾玉新两位学者也是中国国内跨文化研究领域的领军人物,还有 John Oetzel、Teruyuki Kume、Arvind Singhal、Vivian Sheer、Andrea Graf、Paul Messaris、Felipe Korzenny、Barbara Mueller、Nagesh Rao 都是大学或研究机构的教授、学者。另外,Steve Sizoo 在跨国公司做过市场总监,Andrea Graf 在德国一家跨国医药公司做过管理研发,De Mooij 为公司董事长,专门研究文化对市场、广告、消费行为的影响,Korzenny 是 Cheskin 高级顾问和联合创始人。他们都具有丰富的实践经验。

三、本书文章简介

1. 并购和合并中的文化适应

并购和合并是经济发展中的常见现象,已成为企业巩固其竞争地位或扩大市场的首选方式。合并或并购后的企业能否为共同目标协同作战,实现利益最大化?事实证明,50% - 70%的合并或并购以失败告终,失败的原因何在？研究表明,人是主要的因素。合并前的企业文化、价值观、行为准则将被带入合并后的新组织,来自不同企业文化的员工面对的是改变了的新环境,努力沟通是适应新环境的必要条件。但这种沟通问题往往会因为陌生感和不确定性变得尤为突出,有可能转化成合并后企业经营中的困难所在。人的因素不仅是企业中最重要的因素,也是最脆弱的资源。当然,民族文化也会影响跨国并购。

Schuler 和 Jackson 列出了合并或并购的三步模式:1.合并前、2.合并—伙伴关系的融合、3.巩固和发展—新的实体。合并后的新实体必将面临着以下跨文化沟通问题:不确定性、权力关系、冲突管理、文化冲击、文化适应、认可度的提高,以及新集体的形成。

Berger 认为文化差异会使个人在新的不同的文化环境里产生失落和痛苦。因为"失去熟悉的社会交往中的符号或代码。正是这些符号或代码使我们和我们的日常生活联系在一起"。失去了这一套熟悉的人际交往方式,交流也就受到阻碍,并引发个体的身份危机。文化失落感有好几种表现方式:角色的失落、过渡阶段的失落、适应过程中的紧张、文化差异。为了融入新的文化,参与者就必须适应新环境,接受新的企业文化。因此,在合并或并购前认真研究对方的文化会使后面的调整适应容易许多。当然,跨文化交际专家和人力资源专家都认为不是所有人都在适应过程中表现得同等熟练和有效。Martin 和 Nakayama, Lustig 和 Koester 提出了适应新文化的四种基本方式,而这四种方式正好与 McShane 和 Von Glinow 的合并理论重合了三项。

文化适应方式	合并理论
同化	同化
融合	融合
孤立	孤立
边缘化	去文化

同化意味着人们放弃许多原有文化的因素,对新的文化几乎全盘接受,包括新的信仰、价值观和规则。融合是指人们在保留原有文化的基础上接受部分新的文化。在文化适应方式和合并理论中唯一不同的就是最后的边缘化和去文化。边缘化指个体既不保留自己的文化也不和新的文化环境保持积极的接触,而去文化则指一公司把自己的文化强加于另一公司,因此,去文化很可能使被并购公司的员工抵制文化侵略并设法延迟或破坏合并。去文化和边缘化都容易使员工产生困惑和异化,因而给合并或并购带来阻碍。

本文中的某些观点在全球化的今天为理解某些经济问题提供了全新的视角,对读者寻求解决合并或并购中文化适应问题的方案提供了有益的信息。

2. 全球社会的跨文化沟通

本文专题论述商业语境下文化因素对交际的影响。Heisey 曾担任国际跨文化交际学会主席和全美传播学会跨文化传播研究组主席。

Heisey 认为全球化是一把双刃剑,而全球化的结果就是文化变革。他认为理解文化差异对经济、教育、军事、宗教和政治都至关重要。他观察到人们有误将经济实力看成是文化实力表现形式的倾向,因此督促人们发展经济的同时不要失去本族文化,因为强势文化会引领和同化边缘文化。为了帮助商界人士更好地理解商业语境下对话和交际的隐含意义,Heisey 致力于研究文化和交际的相互作用及其影响。他在本文中提出了研究跨文化交际的理论方法、实践方法、教学方法和训练方法。他还研究了口语和书面语的文化差异和意义上的区别,包括具体的语境下文化价值、文化信仰和文化认知等方面的差异,比如媒体、谈判、处理争议、对文化差异的反应、文化身份的建构、文化渗透以及发展跨文化能力等。Heisey的研究清晰地展示商务活动中跨文化交际的重要性。

3. 跨文化交际效果的概念综述

中华传播研究学会的创始人、美国罗得岛大学交际学教授陈国明(Guo-Ming Chen)先生的研究兴趣在于跨文化交际、组织架构、国际交往、中国交际行为等,著有大量的论文、专著和随笔。

陈国明在本文中提到,学术界已经花了几十年时间研究跨文化交际能力这个概念,但该领域的研究仍受到概念模糊以及操作不一致性的困扰。他认为跨文化交际能力包含三个相互关联但又相互独立的概念:跨文化敏感性、跨文化意识性以及跨文化有效性或者熟练性。正是这些不同但又相互联系的概念,使得大多数研究在概念上混淆不清。陈先生认为跨文化敏感性是跨文化交际能力的情感因素,即跨文化交际中理解和欣赏文化差异的能力;跨文化的意识性是跨文化交际能力的认知因素,即对影响人们思维和行为的文化规则的理解;跨文化有效性指的是正确判断交流的认知能力或情感能力或敏感性,并将其融入到不同文化语境下的交际中,以达到有效合理的跨文化交际。

在区分交际有效性和适合性时,陈国明指出人们可以通过各种手段达到有效交际的目的,包括强制的方法;而适合性指的是理解交际情景和对方的交际要求。适合性在跨文化交际中特别重要,因为一种文化一般包含一套严格的文化规则,从而规定着它的成员按照其信仰和价值体系来思考和行动。跨文化交际中要求其参与者熟知另一种文化的规则,并积极认同和接受文化差异,因此,熟练性或许更能描述这个概念。陈国明先生提出了跨文化有效性或熟练性的五个维度——信息能力、交际管理、行为灵活性、身份管理以及关系培养。尽管这些维度看起来是所有人际交流的共性,但每一个维度的重点或者在文化上可接受的成分会因为文化差异而不同。任何一个商业组织,无论其背景如何——市场营销还是人力资源管理,都应该重视交际的有效性和适合性。作者呼吁要对此做更加深入和细致的研究。

4. 适应新文化:综合交际理论

Young Yun Kim对不同的族群文化进行过研究,如亚洲移民、西裔移民、不同背景的本土美国人和欧洲裔美国人,她的研究旨在揭示在他们的文化适应过程中交流的作用和角色。

Kim在本文中阐述了关于文化适应性的综合理论。她提到自20世纪30年代,跨文化适应性的研究和理论成为各学科的研究课题并得到传播。研究者一般将适应过程中的各个方面分而治之,以满足不同学科和不同人群的兴趣要求,也因此导致了宏观和微观过程的分离、长期和短期适应性的对立。Kim认为对跨文化适应性研究受挫的部分原因是狭隘的理解,认为跨文化交际要么是一种独立的变体,要么是一种非独立的变体。据Kim观察,这种直接的因果观产生了许多不同而且不一致的定义、模型、指数和等级。正是在这种背景下,Kim决定发展一种宏观理论,将各种概念域联系起来,从而更加系统地认识跨文化活动。

Kim 的模式旨在探讨跨文化适应性的两个核心问题:1.定居者个人随着时间的流逝到底经历了怎样的适应过程? 2.为什么一些定居者在东道国环境里要比其他人更能获得心理的适应性? 第一个问题可在过程模型中找到答案。对个人而言,过程模式是寻求多功能适应性和心理健康以及渐现的跨文化身份变化的理论描述。第二个问题是通过一个结构模式来解答的,该模式能找寻出那些促进或阻碍适应过程的关键因素,并明确它们之间的关系。Kim 指出文化植入过程不是新文化简单接纳旧文化的过程。新的学习能弱化或取代旧文化或者旧文化因素,同时,产生新的反应。这个过程是动态辩证的,并伴随着压力,但压力会被适应性和成长所取代。

5. 管理跨文化冲突

　　John Oetzel 是新墨西哥大学交际和新闻系副教授、院长,教授跨文化、健康交流、组织交际以及定量研究方法等课程,研究兴趣是工作小组、机构中和健康交流背景下的文化和争端交际。Adolfo José Garcia 的研究兴趣为跨文化交际困难中的第三方角色。他曾在美国、法国、德国、西班牙和英国工作。

　　Oetzel 和 Garcia 认为当今的一个普遍现象是国际商务越来越多地需要接触他国文化,公司的员工也多有跨文化背景。文化差异造成的争端现今更为频繁,这些争端可能会因为处理不当而升级。有些问题在一种文化中可能被视为争端,而在另一种文化中却不是,人们有必要意识到潜在的问题并尝试解决它。因此,本文研究了以文化为基础的情景争端模式。研究结果显示有效的编译和解码会产生共同的意义,而共同的意义会产生可接受的跨文化理解。如果能清晰地认识和理解潜在的问题,争端升级的可能性就会减少。解决争端的关键是知识、动机、警觉和交际技能。Oetzel 和 Ting-Toomey 进一步发展了该模式。

6. 管理理论中的文化约束力

　　Geert Hofstede 是马斯特里赫特大学组织人类学、国际管理荣誉教授以及香港大学的名誉教授,著有《预算控制的游戏》、《文化的结果》、《文化和组织:思想软件》等。

　　Hofstede 认为那些被普遍接受的美国理论,如 Maslow, Herzberg, McClelland 等人的理论,在美国之外或许就不那么普遍。无论普通员工、经理人、管理科学家、理论家或作家,他们都是人,都是在特定的社会历史时期成长的,因此其思想一定会受到环境的影响。为了证明这一点,作者考察了当地的管理活动和全球的管理理论,尤其是德国、日本、法国、荷兰、海外华人聚居区、东南亚、非洲、俄罗斯和中国等地方,并且将它们和美国的管理活动和理论做了科学的比较,发现了全球不同的管理风格,并用他的文化模式对此做了深刻的解释。Hofstede 的文化模式包括五个独立的维度,以解释管理活动中的差异。当然,Hofstede 也指出他的文化模式并非万能,充其量只能解释 49% 的现象。但是,Hofstede 强调他至少有一种工具可以大大降低文化沟通的难度。他的文化模式解释了不同国家和地区管理理论和管理实践的差异,这也解释了为什么美国的管理实践和理论未能在其他文化环境里那么行之有效。

　　Hofstede 的文章提醒我们,在不同文化背景下不能完全奉行同样的管理理论。这种提醒在经济全球化背景下显得特别重要,因为在这种背景下,人们很容易倾向于借用其他国家的成功方法却不考虑其中的文化差异。

7. 决策过程中交际风格的对比

Teruyuki Kume 专门从事跨文化交际、人际交际和组织交际研究,研究兴趣是以任务为导向的多文化领导关系和日本人在国外的多文化冲突。

Kume 相信决策过程和行为是文化的产物,文化的差异必将导致争端。Kume 研究过美国和日本文化中的交际风格和决策过程,并确认了两种对立的原型风格,即 mawashi 风格和 tooshi 风格,第一种指信息在相关成员之间传播,第二种则是信息是通过相关成员直接传进的。

Kume 认为文化对交际风格有着巨大的影响,不管组织结构如何变化,这种风格都会保持不变。他的研究发现由于日本是集体主义社会,日本组织一般分工不明,常常是集体共同承担职责,这种情况下的交际备受语境影响,关注点是整体,多数日本经理不会自己做决定。相反,美国是个人主义的社会,美国的组织里个人工作领域清晰,交际风格受语境影响比较低,关注点通常在部分而非整体,美国经理们会在管辖范围内自己做决定。Kume 的研究发现即使日本公司里的美国经理接受了一些日本式的决策风格,他们仍然采用一种不同于日本同事的交际风格。

Kume 指出他的两分法(即 mawashi 风格和 tooshi 风格)只是强调交际方式的不同。那些适应了某种交际风格的人和不同交际风格的人交流时会非常困难。在 Kume 看来,交际可以反映人的不同思维方式和认知倾向。Kume 提醒人们必须记住,即使在同一个组织里也要根据领导风格和决定的性质综合利用两种风格,例如,当要迅速做决定时可以使用 tooshi 风格,当在作长期规划或一种新产品的研发时可以用 mawashi 风格。

8. 交际能力的魅力:美日学生交际风格对比

Arvind Singhal 的研究方向为革新的传播、引领变革、策略交际的设计和执行、娱乐教育交际策略。Motoko Nagao 的研究兴趣为交际能力和跨文化交际,著述颇丰。

Singhal 和 Nagao 认为了解不同文化背景的人际交际过程、理解文化和交际的关系有助于减少交际冲突。交际能力指人际交往中恰当并有效交际的能力,交际能力与多种因素相关。他们的研究旨在探索文化因素如何影响美国和日本学生的交际风格,集中探讨他们在自信行为态度上的差异。研究结果显示,美国学生的自信程度要高过日本学生,日本学生对组内和组外人的态度不同,也就是说,日本学生在朋友之间有更多的自信行为,而在陌生人、长辈和权威面前就表现得没那么自信。研究还显示性别在自信行为中也扮演着角色,但需进一步论证,这正说明以后的跨文化交际研究需要从多个角度来考虑。国际商务活动显示,不论在会议、谈判还是在广告中,交际风格和认知风格同样在发生变化。换句话说,在一个国家被认为是成功并且理想的交际技能在另一个国家可能被否定。因此,一方面我们必须接受不同的交际风格,另一方面又要意识到同一种交际风格在不同文化里的认识度是不同的。

9. 中国文化背景下变革型领导的局限和前景

Vivian Sheer 的研究范围包括技术对组织沟通的影响、上下级交际和跨文化领导沟通,2005年以后开始从事市场调查和管理咨询。

Sheer 更加关注交际和管理研究者的研究方法——变革型领导,它属于关系导向型和交际管理型风格,这使得它能激发更大的动机和生产力。Sheer 力图判定变革型领导是否在中国文化背景下也行之有效,她认为变革型领导和中国传统领导方式之间有着许多相似之处。首先,两者都能引导下属认识重要目标;其次,两者都力求使下属能够为了团队和组织超越个人利益;另外,两者都会尽力推动下属产生更高层次的需求,包括归属感、尊重、认可和全部潜能的发挥。中国领导方式在传统上被视为魅力型,中国文化也被归为集体主义型。因此,在 Sheer 看来,中国工作氛围是典型的以营造和谐为最高要义的关系导向型和团队导向型风格。

Sheer 认为中国社会和文化中存在许多因素阻碍变革型领导在中国组织中发挥作用,这些因素包括权力距离、集体关系导向和团队合作。中国文化所呈现的较大权力距离使得许多中国人将权力不平等视作公理。此外,中国文化的关系导向是垂直的集体主义,其中一个具有家长式作风的领导者居于最高位,他不受任何下属的质问。Sheer 指出,和谐的关系并不一定是高质量的关系。相对于开诚布公的交流,中国文化有史以来更重视安静的榜样效仿。此外,员工的充分授权是和中国文化背道而驰的。

Sheer 得出结论,包括在中国,变革型领导是一种普遍理想的方式,它之所以没有被广泛应用于中国文化是由于历史和文化的限制。Sheer 认为,如果传统中国领导方式就像中国蓬勃发展的经济一样,那么中国可能并不需要变革型领导。因此,将某种具体的管理方式从一种文化应用到另一种文化并不是简单的事情。此外,Sheer 的文章对于当今中国管理方式提出了深入有趣的见解。

10. 跨文化敏感度对跨文化服务员工绩效的影响——伦敦和佛罗里达两地研究

Steve Sizoo 的研究主要关注跨文化、商务教育和旅游。

Sizoo 指出全球服务业的发展使得商务学者开始关注服务接触——顾客和服务者之间的接触。跨文化服务接触也受到越来越多的关注,因为不同的文化范式和价值观常会导致交流者辞不达意,甚至发生冲突,结果是交易失败,顾客不愉快,服务者受挫。研究显示,有三分之二的消费者在接受服务时感觉不愉快并不会表达不满,而是更换服务者。研究显示可用工具来评估和提高服务人员的跨文化沟通技巧,但人们尚未明确跨文化服务胜任力评估的市场价值。Sizoo 开始着手在两个类似却又不同的服务型市场——伦敦和佛罗里达两家豪华酒店中的餐饮服务——进行实验,分析跨文化敏感度对于跨文化服务员工绩效的影响。

研究结果表明,在服务周到指数、收入贡献、人际交往技巧、工作满意度和社会满意度方面,具有高跨文化敏感度的员工比低跨文化敏感度的员工得分高。有趣的是,性别、外语流利程度和海外工作年限等社会人口特征并不能可靠地预测跨文化敏感度。服务工作者需要对来自其他不同文化的顾客更加留意。因此,提高员工跨文化敏感度可以给消费者营造更好的服务环境和服务体验,同时给企业带来更好的商业效益。

11. 跨文化交际中的性别差异

Andrea Graf 是德国雷根斯堡大学管理组织学教授,并在德国法兰克福一家跨国医药公司做过三年的管理开发,研究主要涉及国际人力资源管理、变革管理和跨文化能力。

Graf 指出国际委派人员的数量持续增长,而海外委派的失败率却居高不下,造成大量的金钱损失和组织内消极性影响,如生产迟滞、与本土员工关系紧张、公司名声败坏、外籍接任者遭遇问题和外派人员因表现不力被遣返回国等问题。研究表明,文化差异导致的交际困难是失败的主要原因。因此,跨文化交际能力被视为外派经理们的必备素质。Graf 指出,在国际委派中,男性受青睐,女性通常被忽略,尽管女性对国际委派工作很感兴趣,并在跨文化行为中表现出更优秀的社交能力,能更高效地解决跨文化项目中的问题,获得更高的满意度。因此,Graf 决定在德国和美国开展实证研究,测评性别是否会影响跨文化交际能力,包括评估跨文化交际效力、跨文化敏感度和人际交往能力。结果显示,性别在德国和美国跨文化交际能力中是一项突出独立的变量,最为明显是女性参与者具有较高的跨文化交际能力,胜任涉外职务。

12. 向金字塔底层投广告:与新兴市场的消费者沟通

Barbara Mueller 的研究方向是国际广告和消费者沟通,包括儿童营销和医疗产品广告等有争议性话题,著有多篇相关文章和多部专著。

Mueller 着眼于发展中国家的广告研究。人口变化使得许多西方国家正在老龄化或人口缩减,而发展中国家的人口年龄结构趋于年轻化;另一个趋势就是许多全球新兴市场拥有超过 17 亿人的消费群体,其中近一半在发展中国家,人均年购买力超过七千美元。虽然占世界人口的三分之二的 40 亿人仍处在全球经济金字塔的最底层,但这些处于贫困中的人群却展现出惊人的市场潜力,巨大的人口数量代表着数万亿的市场,已经有很多公司成功地从发展中市场获得了利益。但跨文化营销技巧和价值观的问题成为了关注的重点,如何在贫穷的坏境中投放广告推介产品,其有何利弊还不甚明了,这也必将是一个有价值的研究课题。

13. 跨国经营和营销策略的文化反思

De Mooij 系跨文化交际公司董事长,欧洲多国访问教授,专门研究文化对市场、广告、消费行为的作用。

本文研究显示许多全球公司因追求规模经济以及经营的统一性,在不同的国家采用相同的营销策略。在跨文化环境下的经营中,公司的使命、愿景和企业形象都反映了总公司东道国的文化价值观,也就是说,大部分的北美企业重视个人主义价值观,而日本企业则重视集体主义价值观。这些价值观通常被转化为公司品牌策略,因此,北美企业更加关注品牌的独特性,而日本企业则更关注建立信任和品牌与企业之间的联系。

在产品的使用上也存在同样的分歧,即不同的国家对于同种产品不仅看法不同,用法也不尽相同。因此,只有当广告中的信息与消费者的价值观相匹配,广告才能发挥作用。De Mooij 建议,广告应反映消费者的文化,而不是生产者的文化。所以品牌应该更加实际并适应消费者的文化思维模式,而不是保持所谓的统一性。

14. 跨文化视觉广告

Paul Messaris 专门研究和教授视觉文化和数字媒体,研究观众对形象的解读、观众对正式广告及其他视觉信息的反应、计算机对媒体的影响等。

Messaris 通过关注跨文化情景下的视觉广告来判定文化差异是否影响信息的诠释和评价。

视觉图像的全球普遍性和文化式植入性显然是个非常有趣的重要话题,对于所有跨国广告宣传都有重要意义。

Messaris 指出,有学者认为图像规则与文化息息相关,这正是有些广告能够在全球范围内经久不衰,获得成功的原因。有证据表明所有图像都期望向某些人群传递某种信息。问题是在不同的文化中意义是否都相同? 作者选择了二战期间硫磺岛升旗这一典型的美国图像,这是一个关于美国特殊体制——春假——的电影广告。Messaris 想要证明外国学生不能把升旗的意义和真实的历史事件联系起来,美国学生同样不能。结论是图像确实传达着某种意义,即使读者没能从图像中识别出真实事件。当一个基于视觉图像的广告投放到另一个文化环境中时,这个广告有可能不被人们理解,但这些困难也可能被其他一些因素所抵消,比如好莱坞电影,它为跨文化视觉传播奠定了基础。

Messaris 认为,绝大部分跨文化广告的研究只局限于广告的内容而忽视了广告对象的反应。如果一个广告产生的是消极的反馈,那就意味着观看者是将这消极反馈和广告的东道国文化联系了起来,而没能理解广告原本的意义。换句话说,穆斯林观众们会因看到猪肉和白酒的广告而不愉快,但这不意味着他们不认识猪肉和白酒这两种物质。事实上,穆斯林观众会对该公司不悦,是因为明知穆斯林不吃猪肉不喝白酒,还明知故犯。

当然,现代科技使得远程图像形象的分享成为可能。即使观众们知道广告所诉求的价值观与他们本国的不同,他们仍旧能够理解来自其他文化图像传达出的意义,这表明人们能够正确识别不同的价值观和情感。

15. 文化在说服性演讲中的角色:以以色列和新西兰学生的视频交流为例

Prue Holmes 的研究领域主要是国际学生,特别是高等教育和更广社区范围内的华裔的交流经历。最近,她集中研究多元文化课堂中的跨文化交际能力、信息技术在读写能力方面的应用和发展、跨文化交际和移民群体之间的社会文化适应和发展。Nurit Zaidman 的研究兴趣包括跨国公司中的知识转换、跨文化商务沟通、跨文化组织行为比较、组织精神、新时代、宗教商品的消费和销售等。

Holmes 和 Zaidman 认为,大多数商务活动都受关系驱动,这也是因为在国际竞争中跨文化交际处于一个非常重要的地位。核心问题是如何把当地文化融入到产品和服务中去。Holmes 和 Zaidman 研究了文化对视觉信息认知的影响。结果表明,文化确实在解释和评价视频信息上有着深刻的影响。本文研究对象主要是在以色列和新西兰攻读商学学位的学生,这些学生也修习跨文化交际课程。本项研究主要有两个目的:第一是通过对不同语言和文化背景学生的交流来提高他们的跨文化交际知识和技能;第二是鼓励学生去探索人们如何从另一种文化体验中了解自己的文化。所有小组都采用语言和图式信息,以帮助受众更好地了解彼此的研究内容和方向。然而,Holmes 和 Zaidman 的研究发现,语言被所有的实验小组低估了。作者指出,交际中要想获得清晰明确的信息,可以通过减弱口音、放慢语速,或利用视觉线索如字幕和标题来实现。当然,当受众遇到不熟悉的国际符号时,获得信息的能力会受到限制,使用象征性的符号不利于产品的销售。因此,有必要对目标市场的受众进行分析和市场研究,了解相似符号和象征符号的差异以及目标受众的价值观和信仰体系。Holmes 和 Zaidman 的研究也揭示了编辑技术的重要性,不同的风格对整个制作的评判有一定的影响。

16. 语用的多样性，语用的转移和文化认同

贾玉新（Yuxin Jia）被普遍认为是中国跨文化交际研究的奠基人之一，其专著《跨文化交际学》被用作中国高校外语学院的教科书或参考书。

贾教授认为，如今英语几乎是全球通用的交流工具。然而，文化价值观、社会准则和习俗都会决定一个人说话的方式，并使说话者判断什么样的行为是得体的。而各国文化价值观、准则、习俗又大相径庭，即存在文化差异或语用差异，这便使得文化背景不同的人倾向于使用本国的文化标准来评判他们的境遇。正是没有这种差异意识，才导致了跨文化交际的失败或误解。

贾教授指出，尽管语言或交际的社会功能以及要完成的任务是不言而喻的，但隐藏在语用准则下的话语却会因为文化的差异而不同。正如每种语言都有问候、道歉的功能，但每一种文化在特定的语境中都会有其特定的规则或语言策略。正是这些以文化为基础的语用规则决定了特定语境中的意义传递和解读方式。贾教授注意到，不同文化背景的人交流时，语用差异就会被转化成英语信息，从而导致理解上的困难或误解，即便是中美人互相用英语交流，情况亦是如此。研究表明中国人更倾向于隐晦地表达想法，而美国人却更直接。英语为第二语言的人倾向于把母语的思维转换成英语来交流。同时，人们也喜欢用自己的文化标准来评判其他的语言。母语为非英语或不同的文化背景的人一旦开始用英语交流时，这一点就显得尤为重要。

17. 西裔广告代理商：把握市场的脉博

Felipe Korzenny 是佛罗里达州立大学西裔市场交流中心主任、教授，该研究中心在美国属第一家，为西裔市场销售、项目调研、出版业等提供人才。Korzenny 也是 Cheskin 高级顾问和联合创始人。Maria Gracia Inglessis 精通古典哲学、语言学和符号学，现任佛罗里达州立大学西裔市场交流中心助理研究员，是西裔电视广告主要研究人员之一，研究兴趣为西裔市场和交流，包括艺术和文化产业市场、时尚和服装等。

两位作者认为西裔美国人的文化适应呈多样化趋势，广告代理市场亦错综复杂。西裔移民不知道如何去适应美国生活的时代已经一去不返了，即使是那些社会地位卑微的拉美移民也很清楚自己在美国可以找到什么样的产品。西裔美国人曾钟爱名牌，但如今，随着消费信息和知识的增加，他们会对自己的行为做更加全面的分析。同样，市场遍地都是，瞬息万变。对西裔美国人而言，英语变得触手可及。市场营销人员使用不同的方式与他们交流，移民人数不断地增加也使西班牙语的地位得到巩固，如今，人们使用英语和西班牙语向西裔美国人传递着信息。

作者发现，西裔广告代理商的客户可分为四大类：学习型，投资回报追求型，老手型和刻板型。学习型指的是第一次进入美国西裔市场，而且很大程度上依赖咨询客户和广告代理商才能寻求到自己的发展机遇。投资回报追求型是实用主义者，他们只求短期内能在西裔市场上得到回报。老手型是那些已学会如何在西裔市场上共事并也付出了许多精力的人。刻板型仍然使用传统文化进入到西裔市场。作者认为，随着市场的复杂化，理解西裔美国人之间的细微差别就显得尤为重要。

18. 中国社会文化背景下的品牌建设：特点，趋势，问题

洪俊豪(Junhao Hong)的研究方向为跨文化交流、媒体与社会、传媒与信息技术,著有多部专著,如《中国电视的国际化:改革开放以来意识形态,社会以及媒体的演变》等。陈先红(Xianhong Chen)为华中科技大学教授。

作者在研究中记录了中国品牌建设的心路历程。中国改革开放30年,经济快速发展,然而,中国产品的质量却始终上不去。中国的公司试图通过广告赞助商来提升产品的认可度,事实却不尽如人意,中国的品牌在发达国家的知名度难以拔高。直到最近中国的公司才开始转变策略,着手长期改善和提升品牌质量,并得到了中国政府的大力支持。

当然,中国企业的早期策略似乎与中华文化的渊源背道而驰。事实上,Hofstede的文化模式显示中国文化在长远定位上极具价值,尤其是在商务背景下。同时,中国的商务运作也在不断改善,以满足世界消费者的需求,明确地显示出中国公司的市场化特点。

19. 中国人的自我意识正在构建中吗？

Nagesh Rao是俄亥俄州大学传媒学院院长,出版过多部著作并发表过多篇论文。Arvind Singhal是俄亥俄州大学传媒学院教授、研究专员,研究涉及创新传媒、动态变革、战略交流的策划和实施,寓学于乐交流战略等,出版了八部专著。

Nagesh Rao等在研究中发现,中国文化正在发生变化,中国人开始重新认识自己,重新认识自己与他人的关系,例如如何对待权威、等级制度、群体内聚力、家庭责任等。他们的研究还涉及中国人的独立自我识解以及人际关系识解。自我识解就是个人施于他人的想法、情感、行为以及自我的独立存在。不同的文化类型如个人主义或集体主义对自我识解的研究具有良好的指导作用,而那些有效的认知工具却未能有效地解释为什么不同文化的个体可同时表现出个人主义或集体主义特性。独立的和相互依存的自我意识代表了个人素质,成为一个变量,融入包括个人主义、集体主义和人类行为等在内的文化领域。

研究人员采用量化手段如问卷、访谈等方式,对社会人口因素如年龄、性别以及城乡户籍等进行了研究。结果显示,中国人的自我识解因年龄、性别和城乡居所而有别,并受到中国不断变化的政治、经济和社会文化的影响。从文化的层面上看,集体主义在中国仍然盛行,传统的自我识解依旧深深地烙印在中国人集体的脑海中。改革开放以来中国人的自我意识更加显化,尤其是年轻一代。如今,中国人对自我意识的宽容度也比以前大有提高。事实上,中国人正处于儒家传统、共产主义意识以及新生的西方个人主义的混合体中,经受着思想文化的冲击。因此,大多数的中国人开始信奉一种弹性价值体系,以适应不断变化的环境。这也再次证明文化不是静止的。

本研究的结论应该会引起一些国际商业团体的兴趣,因为只要跟中国人做生意,不论是想寻找一个潜在的产品基地还是销售市场,该研究都会对他们有帮助,因为这些自我意识的变化会影响他们的谈判方式、动机及购买计划。

20. 旅游文化：跨文化交流规则及跨国旅游

Sundae R. Bean专攻旅游文化,专门研究旅游者和景点当地人的对话,以更好地了解跨国旅

游背景下身份认同感的确定。Judith N. Martin 的研究兴趣包括国际交流中沟通的作用、白人身份和跨种族关系,以及跨文化交际教学法。

Bean 和 Martin 探究了商业界跨文化交流最突出的领域——国际旅游。她们认为,跨文化旅游研究被忽略的程度出人意料。由于旅游是一个庞大的研究领域,因此她们把研究仅限于历史文化旅游。

两位研究者发现,旅游已成为世界上最大的一个行业。如今越来越多的人们涌入别国,接触当地文化,但这更强化了他们的文化偏见,进一步证明他们之前观点是"正确"的,从而令他们充满了民族优越感。这令旅游者期望与当地进行"真实的"文化接触,而这种接触往往歪曲了当地的文化事实。事实上,许多第三世界国家以此为耻。这种情况的主导力量,也就是花钱去体验这种"原始"文化的旅游者,令情况更难改变。因为当游客们不能够感受到他们所向往的体验时,他们必定会去别处寻找。

当然,跨国旅游大有好处,它让人们意识到文化差异的存在,进一步促进心灵沟通,使得人与人之间产生更多的共鸣。当文化再次碰撞的时候,人与人不再像以前那样无理、无知。人们开始更加经常地反省自己,学到更多的东西。因此,跨文化交流同时为游客及旅游目的地的当地人提供了有价值的启示。这种启示越早越好,因为跨国旅游已经变成研究跨文化交流的一个自然选择。

万 华(上海大学)

参考文献

Herskovits, M. J. (1955), *Cultural Anthropology*. New York: Knopf.
Ricks, D. A. (2006), *Blunders in International Business*: Blackwell Publishing Ltd.
Tylor, F. (1920), *Primitive Culture*. New York: J. P. Putnam's Sons, p.l.
Varner, I. & Beamer, L. (2007), *Intercultural Communication in the Global Workplace*. Shanghai: Shanghai Foreign Language Education Press.
陈国明(2007),跨文化交际学基础。上海:上海外语教育出版社。
胡文仲、贾玉新(2006),跨文化交际基础。上海:上海外语教育出版社。
郑兴山(2010),跨文化管理。北京:中国人民大学出版社。

Michael B. Hinner (ed.)

The Influence of Culture in the World of Business

Dedication

I would like to dedicate this fourth volume of the *Freiberger Beiträge* to William B. Gudykunst who was one of the contributors of the first volume. He was a very prolific writer who had a profound influence on the writings and research of many. Most of his books have become classics. I felt, therefore, greatly honored when he agreed to contribute a text to this series. So I was very shocked and deeply touched when his brother informed me of his untimely death. Bill Gudykunst's knowledge and insights as well as his broad range of knowledge will be sorely missed.

> "The purest treasure mortal times afford
> Is spotless reputation."
>
> William Shakespeare
> *Richard II*, 1.1.177-8

Michael B. Hinner

Acknowledgement

I would like to thank everyone who helped make the publication of this fourth volume of the *Freiberger Beiträge* possible.

First of all, I would like to thank Guo-Ming Chen for his invaluable support and help. He contacted a number of fellow researchers and asked them to participate in this project. Thanks to his efforts, all chose to participate. Guo-Ming also personally coordinated and edited his colleagues' texts prior to forwarding them to me.

I would also like to thank all contributing authors because without their work, this volume would not have been filled. I want to thank everyone for having participated in this project despite the fact that most of them did not know me prior to my contacting them. I am, therefore, very thankful for the fact that they decided to participate nonetheless.

And finally, I would like to thank the people who helped prepare the manuscript for publication. Their invaluable help and assistance as well as their adroit skills and talents helped make this publication possible. In particular, I want to thank Manja Otto and Christian Peter.

To everyone, therefore, my most heartfelt thanks! Without your support and assistance, we would never have gotten this unique endeavor off the ground.

"Vielen Dank!"

Michael B. Hinner

Preface

The *Freiberger Beiträge* evolved as a series dedicated to general and intercultural business communication. This series is designed to spotlight and highlight the role and importance of communication in the world of business. Communication is often taken for granted because it is so fundamental to human interaction that most people do not realize its importance or the fact that they are actually engaged in it. While people may muse over the wording of a particular statement or deliberate the specific meaning of a word, few consider the wider and deeper role and function of communication, both verbal and nonverbal, in human interaction. For without communication, no human interaction is possible which also means that no business is possible without communication since business revolves around interactions, e.g. interaction with other entities, with consumers, and with employees. Once one begins to contemplate any aspect of the world of business, one realizes that communication is also tied directly and indirectly to it. Hence, one needs to understand communication and its principles in order to fully understand the world of business. That is why one should not leave communication to chance. Communication must be studied, analyzed, and applied as deliberately as any other aspect of business if it is to be applied successfully. It is in this that the series seeks to help the interested business professional.

The contributing authors of this series are all acknowledged authorities in their field of expertise. The texts they have written for this volume all have relevance to the world of international business - either directly or indirectly. Each text is preceded by a brief introduction that also includes a short biographical sketch of the author or authors of the text. While some of the texts focus on specific business topics, others offer a more general perspective. The introductions to the texts also explain how the texts relate to the world of business if the texts do not contain a discussion of specific business topics. This explanation should help spotlight and clarify the text's business relevance.

This fourth volume is actually a fortuitous result of the many responses to the initial invitation to participate in this project. Because so many chose to answer this call with very interesting and insightful texts, their responses translated into more than eight hundred pages of manuscript. Hence, the publisher pointed out that a single volume with over eight hundred pages might be a bit too bulky for easy use. And a book that size would also end up costing too much on the retail market. So it was decided to split the submitted texts into two volumes: One containing primarily general communication texts, and one containing intercultural communication texts. This decision, however, also necessitated the writing of another introductory chapter for this fourth volume. Consequently, the date of the original publication had to be pushed back by a few months. But the slight delay was well worth the waiting period since the collection of texts offer interesting insights into how culture influences communication.

The texts of this fourth volume focus on a variety of intercultural communication issues that have direct relevance to the world of international business. The first text offers a broad introduction to intercultural communication. It is followed by a text that shows how local motivations can influence the understanding of global relations. The next texts review and discuss the concept of intercultural effectiveness as well as adaptation to a new culture. When different representatives of different cultures meet, the potential for conflict due to misunderstandings is great; hence, a method for de-escalating the potential conflict is quite helpful. Due to cultural differences, not every management method will work everywhere, though. The same is true for decision making processes which can also vary from culture to culture. Likewise, a particular communication style that is considered desirable in one cultural environment will not be as desirable in another context. So it is not surprising that Chinese management seems very different from Western management styles. Another study demonstrates that intercultural sensitivity has a positive effect in cross-cultural service encounters. Interestingly, gender seems to also have an impact on effective intercultural communication.

An often neglected realm of international business is the communication with consumers in developing markets which might be an error. This leads to a look at how culture influences business and marketing strategies. While one text comes to the conclusion that consumers around the globe generally understand visual advertising without too many difficulties, another text presents a cross-cultural study which comes to the conclusion that cultural differences do have an impact on the decoding of visual messages. Yet another text points out that even English messages will be decoded differently depending on the cultural background of the speaker. This is also why Hispanic ad agencies have to closely coordinate Spanish and English language ad campaigns directed at Hispanics in the USA. Interestingly, Chinese companies are still struggling with positive brand associations due cultural stereotypes and ineffective brand campaigns. So as Chinese companies are rethinking their marketing strategies, this might be reflective of a general change within Chinese culture that seems to be adjusting to a changing cultural environment. The volume ends with discussion of how travel to foreign countries is often the first and only contact most people have with other cultures and how this can influence or reinforce people's attitudes and stereotypes of other cultures.

This eclectic mix of texts, therefore, demonstrate how intercultural communication influences, directs, and affects international business.

> "We the globe can compass soon,
> Swifter than the wandering moon."
>
> William Shakespeare
> *A Midsummer Night's Dream,* 4.1.97-8.

Michael B. Hinner

Table of Contents

General Introduction:
Cultural Adaptation in Mergers and Acquisitions
Michael B. Hinner 13

Intercultural Communication for a Global Society
D. Ray Heisey 43

A Review of the Concept of Intercultural Effectiveness
Guo-Ming Chen 71

Adapting to a New Culture: An Integrative Communication Theory
Young Yun Kim 93

Managing Intercultural Conflict:
Applying the Culture-Based Situational Conflict Model
John Oetzel, Adolfo José Garcia 133

Cultural Constraints in Management Theories
Geert Hofstede 161

Contrastive Prototypes of Communication Styles in Decision-Making:
Mawashi Style vs. Tooshi Style
Teruyuki Kume 185

Assertiveness as Communication Competence: A Comparison of the
Communication Styles of American and Japanese Students
Arvind Singhal, Motoko Nagao 205

The Practice of Transformational Leadership in Chinese Culture:
Constraints and Promises
Vivian Sheer 225

The Effect of Intercultural Sensitivity on Employee Performance in
Cross-Cultural Service Encounters in London and Florida
Steve Sizoo 247

Gender- Related Differences in Intercultural Communication
Andrea Graf 273

Advertising to the Bottom of the Pyramid: Communicating with Consumers in Developing Markets
Barbara Mueller 293

The Reflection of Culture in Global Business and Marketing Strategy
Marieke De Mooij 317

Visual Advertising across Cultures
Paul Messaris 333

The Role of Culture in Persuasive Presentations:
An Israeli and New Zealand Student Video Exchange
Prue Holmes, Nurit Zaidman 367

Pragmatic Diversity, Pragmatic Transfer, and Cultural Identity
Yuxin Jia 389

Hispanic Ad Agencies: Taking the Pulse of Their Market
Felipe Korzenny, Maria Garcia Inglessis 411

Brand-Building in the Chinese Social and Cultural Contexts:
Characteristics, Trends, and Problems
Junhao Hong, Xianhong Chen 419

Is the Chinese Self-Construal in Transition?
Nagesh Rao, Arvind Singhal, Li Ren, Jianying Zhang 429

Touring Culture(s): Intercultural Communication Principles and International Tourism
Sundae R. Bean, Judith N. Martin 459

General Introduction:
Cultural Adaptation in Mergers and Acquisitions

Michael B. Hinner

Mergers and acquisitions have become a preferred method for corporations to consolidate and/or enlarge their business activities in order to safeguard themselves from competitors and/or expand their market position (Schuler & Jackson, 2001). Yet anywhere from fifty percent to seventy-five percent of all mergers and acquisitions fail to achieve their designated goals (Marks, 2000; Schuler & Jackson, 2001; Fischer & Steffens-Duch, 2002). Why is there such a high failure rate if on paper at least most of these mergers and acquisitions should have resulted in the exact opposite, i.e. create a synergy effect that actually multiplies the benefits of each corporation. After all, any well intending business manager would most likely not willingly want to destroy capital. What, then, are the possible causes for such failures? One of the primary causes seems to be the human factor (Imberman, 1985; Marks & Mirvis, 1992; Bourantas & Nikandrou, 1998; Gunders & Alpert, 2000; Schuler & Jackson, 2001). After all, when two corporations are joined, the employees of two distinct corporate cultures have to adapt to the changed environment and attempt to communicate and interact effectively and efficiently with one another. Yet this communication and interaction is often fraught with difficulties arising from the unfamiliarity of the participating parties with one another. And if there are difficulties in the adaptation process arising from the human factor, then difficulties are preprogrammed for the entire merger or acquisition process since human resources are not only the most important, but also the most fragile resources associated with any merger or acquisition (Imberman, 1985; Marks & Mirvis, 1992; Bourantas & Nikandrou, 1998; Gunders & Alpert, 2000; Jackson & Schuler, 2001). And if those resources do not function properly, then probably the entire cooperation may falter. Indeed, "numerous studies confirm the need for firms to systematically address a variety of human resource issues and activities in their merger and acquisition activities" (Schuler & Jackson, 2001, p. 239).

Mergers and acquisitions exhibit striking parallels to culture shock phases and adaptation to a new cultural environment, i.e. acculturation, when viewed from a cultural perspective. Approaching mergers and acquisitions from a cultural perspective might be a worthwhile effort in addition to traditional business analyses that focus on, for example, legal aspects, financial matters, production processes, products or services offered, distribution networks, or customers. In fact, a cultural analysis might be appropriate – or even necessary – since humans are the essential, core issue of any merger or acquisition as noted above (Imberman, 1985; Marks & Mirvis, 1992; Bourantas & Nikandrou, 1998; Gunders & Alpert, 2000; Jackson & Schuler, 2001). Yet, as Schuler and Jackson (2001) note, the human side of mergers and acquisitions "appears to be a somewhat neglected focus of the top management's attention" (p. 243) despite the fact that the major reason for failure in mergers and acquisitions is due the human factor (Schuler & Jackson, 2001). But if the discussion of mergers and acquisitions is to include the human factor, then it will also have to include a discussion of corporate culture. This discussion becomes necessary because whenever and wherever humans regulate their interaction in some standardized manner, i.e. as members of a corporation would have to do in order to function properly, culture becomes the regulator of this interaction, i.e. it determines how and in what manner one is to interact with others. Out of this interaction, accepted behavioral patterns and norms evolve which can then generate role models and values to further regulate and reinforce the acceptable patterns of interaction. Corporate culture, thus, refers to the intra-corporate values, norms, and behavior adopted by the employees to assure successful interaction within the corporation (Peters & Waterman, 1982). So when two separate and distinct corporate cultures come into direct contact with one another through mergers or acquisitions, inter-corporate cultural encounters occur. Consequently, it is possible to draw on parallels from other intercultural encounters when studying and analyzing mergers and acquisitions to see if there is anything of interest in intercultural research that might indicate why so many mergers and acquisitions fail and how such failures might be circumvented.

This discussion of mergers and acquisitions will focus primarily on mergers and acquisitions without considering the external, national macrocultural aspects and factors so as not to complicate this discussion further. Obviously, international mergers and acquisitions entail more complexity since different national macrocultures will also have a bearing on people's core beliefs and values which in turn can influence and/or determine microcultural corporate values. It is, for example, not surprising to note that many hierarchically organized corporations come from countries that also exhibit and respect hierarchies, e.g. France or China. In fact, Hofstede (1993) notes that national and organizational cultures overlap. An observation also made by Schreyögg et al (1995):

If the two perspectives, namely that of shaping by the national culture and that of shaping by corporate culture, are confronted, it can be seen very quickly that these are not parallel approaches which can be pursued separately. They are, in fact, overlapping influence patterns, or even competing theories, for shaping behavior in organizations. Both are assumed to have a lasting influence on the thinking and behavioral patterns of their members, so that behavior in organizations is essentially conditioned by them (p. 191).

Hofstede (1993), though, also notes that for some issues, such as dealing with authority, national culture is relevant while for other issues, such as dealing with innovation, organizational culture is more important. Consequently, external, national macrocultural aspects should generally not be ignored in international mergers and acquisitions. Yet as noted above, for the purpose of this discussion, the external, national macroculture of the companies involved in the merger or acquisition will be ignored so that it is possible to see how corporate culture influences mergers and acquisitions. One can well imagine, though, what influence external, national macroculture can have on international mergers and acquisitions.

What then are mergers and acquisitions? According to Schuler and Jackson (2001), "in a merger, two companies come together and create a new entity. In an acquisition, one company buys another one and manages it consistent with the acquirer's needs" (p. 240). Schuler and Jackson (2001) also point out that there are different types of mergers and acquisitions. Mergers, for example, can be of equals, where both companies are of approximately equal size, and of unequals, where they are not. "A merger of equals often compels the two companies to share in the staffing implications; whereas a merger of unequals results in the staffing implications being shared unequally" (Schuler & Jackson, 2001, p. 240). This essentially means is that the company which is the larger one in a merger will usually be the more dominant company in direct proportion to its size and the size of the other company. It is, thus, probable that power relationships play a considerable role in such a union of two distinct corporate cultures. As Martin and Nakayama (1997) observe, "power is pervasive in communication interactions" (p. 58). "Dominant cultural groups attempt to perpetuate their positions of privilege in many ways. However, subordinate groups can resist this domination in many ways, too" (Martin & Nakayama, 1997, p. 40). It, therefore, comes as no surprise that many mergers fail because "at the core of many of them [i.e. the failures] are people issues" (Schuler & Jackson, 2001, p. 242). Acquisitions also fall into two major categories, i.e. those involving acquisition and integration and those involving acquisition and separation. "An acquisition that involves integration has greater staffing implications than one that involves separation" (Schuler & Jackson, 2001, p. 240) because integration calls for the harmonization of two independent and distinct corporate cultures.

What are the steps of mergers and acquisitions? Schuler and Jackson (2001) propose a three-stage model of mergers and acquisitions:

1. Pre-combination
2. Combination – integration of the partners
3. Solidification and advancement – the new entity

It might be of interest and also very helpful to take a brief, closer look at these three stages to learn how mergers and acquisitions proceed because these insights might reveal areas where intercultural communication might offer potential understanding and/or solutions to the inherent problems of mergers and acquisitions.

During the first stage, one of the important tasks includes the identification of the reasons why a company decides to initiate a merger or acquisition. Another vital task is to find potential companies for the union. And finally, it is critical that the entire merger or acquisition process is well planned early enough for all three stages (Schuler & Jackson, 2001). It is also at this stage that a so-called cultural assessment is carried out. A cultural assessment describes and evaluates the "companies' philosophies and values regarding such issues as: leadership styles; time horizons; relative value of stakeholders; risk tolerance; and the value of teamwork versus individual performance and recognition" (Schuler & Jackson, 2001, p. 244). Anyone familiar with the work of Hall and Hofstede will recognize some of their cultural dimensions in this assessment. For example, time [i.e. Hall], power distance, uncertainty avoidance, and individualism vs. collectivism [i.e. Hofstede] (Chen & Starosta, 1998; Klopf, 1998; Samovar et al, 1998; Lustig & Koester, 1999). Thus, demonstrating again that there are sufficient reasons to study and analyze mergers and acquisitions from an intercultural perspective.

During the second stage of mergers and acquisitions, the companies are integrated. "In general, integration is the process by which two companies combine after a merger or an acquisition is announced and pre-combination activities are completed" (Schuler & Jackson, 2001, p. 245). This stage is usually the most extensive and complex in a merger or acquisition. According to Schuler and Jackson (2001), the second stage involves, for example, the creation of new teams, the development of new strategies, the retention of key employees, the motivation of employees, the management of the change process, the communication with the respective stakeholders as well as the establishment of a new culture, structure, policies, and practices. The second stage, therefore, involves power disparity, conflict management, identity preservation and development as well as community building. "It appears to be crucial that restructuring should be done early, fast, and at once. This minimizes the uncertainty" because uncertainty causes problems (Schuler & Jackson, 2001, p. 246). A supposition that is also raised and hypothesized in Berger's Uncertainty Reduction Theory and Gudykunst's Anxiety-Uncertainty Management Theory; both of which focus on the role and impact of uncertainty on communicating with strangers in new situations and unfamiliar environments (Littlejohn, 2002). Schuler and Jackson (2001) also note that mergers and acquisitions are not identical because there are mergers of equals and non-equals as well as acquisitions with inclusion and acquisitions with separation so that different strategies are called for during the different types of union.

During the third stage of mergers and acquisitions, a new entity is created. "As the new combination takes shape, it faces issues of readjusting, solidifying and fine-tuning" (Schuler & Jackson, 2001, p. 248). These issues include the assessing of the new strategies and structures, the new culture, and the concerns of the stakeholders as well as learning from the process which includes making necessary changes and adjustments (Schuler & Jackson, 2001). Any merger and acquisition requires time and resources which should not be underestimated. And a merger or acquisition will change the involved entities in some way, i.e. a new community is created, but an attempt must also be undertaken to save at least some element of each organization so that the employees of both companies can still identify themselves in some manner with the new entity and, thus, their workplace and themselves (Schuler & Jackson, 2001) as the new community is being formed.

What are the consequences of mergers and acquisitions? "In practice, the outcome of both a merger and an acquisition is some combination of the human, material, and financial assets of two or more organizations into a new legal and accounting entity" (Nicholson, 1997, p. 324). And the goal of such a union is the realization of synergetic advantages due to joint usage of existing resources such as plants, abilities, and knowledge (Schuler & Jackson, 2001; Müller-Stewens et al, 2002). However, very often uncertainty as to what will happen during and after a merger or acquisition has a negative impact on the general morale of the employees in both companies. This uncertainty results in, for example, increased stress, decreased satisfaction and commitment, and it has a negative impact on the perception of the organization's trustworthiness, honesty, and caring (Schweiger & Denisi, 1991). "These outcomes may have tremendous costs in terms of future productivity, turnover of valued personnel, and achieving the goals of the 'new' organization" (Ivancevich et al, 1987, p. 24). Schweiger and Denisi's (1991) empirical study revealed that "the negative effects of mergers and acquisitions activity do not seem to go away with time but seem, instead, to get more serious" (p. 127). These symptoms sound similar to those exhibited by people undergoing culture shock when entering, working in, and adapting to a new cultural environment.

This brief review of mergers and acquisitions, thus, identifies the following intercultural communication aspects: Uncertainty reduction, power relationships, conflict management, culture shock, adaptation and acculturation, identity development, community building. These intercultural aspects will be discussed below. First, the intercultural topic will be presented which will then be discussed within the context of mergers and acquisitions. When people are usually confronted with a new or strange situation, such as a new (corporate) cultural environment, most people need to reduce uncertainty in order to lower the degree of anxiety associated with the unknown. During the first contact with strangers, power relationships often play an important role as they do when different entities meet. The strangeness of the new situation coupled with an unequal power distribution – real or imagined – can result in conflict. Hence, conflict management is a vital consideration in preparation for an encounter with the new and strange both among individuals and corporations. This is followed by a brief look at the culture shock phenomenon to identify the phases associated with the contact with a new (corporate) cultural environment. Next follows a discussion of the different types of adaptation and acculturation to show how individuals and corporations adjust to the new environment. This, then, has direct relevance to identity development which in turn ties in with community building since humans are social creatures and usually need the assistance and assurance of other human beings in order to survive and thrive which, in turn, necessitates that individual differences be taken into consideration to assure harmonious and mutually beneficial interaction also at the corporate level. It will, therefore, be of interest to see how these cultural aspects might offer some useful insights into mergers and acquisitions.

Berger's Uncertainty Reduction Theory states that when strangers meet, their primary concern is to reduce uncertainty or to increase predictability about the behavior of everyone involved in the interaction. Uncertainty refers to the cognitive inability to explain one's own or the other party's behavior in interactions due to the ambiguity of such encounters which in turn creates anxiety. With successful communication, it is possible to reduce uncertainty while becoming familiar with the communication partner(s). This exchange of information can lead to the development of relationships among the people communicating extensively with one another. Berger postulates that people have difficulties with uncertainty and want to be able to predict the behavior of the communication partner. People are, therefore, constantly seeking to reduce the level of uncertainty by exchanging information. Higher levels of uncertainty seem to create distance between the communication partners. As the communication partners discover similarities, their attraction to one another increases and their apparent need for information goes down because initially people need to collect as much information as possible to reduce uncertainty; but as uncertainty is reduced, there is less need for gathering this information (Berger & Calabrese, 1975; Berger, 1979; Chen & Starosta, 1998; Samovar et al, 1998; Littlejohn, 2002).

According to Berger, there are three strategies for gathering information: Passive, active, and interactive strategies. Passive strategies reduce uncertainty by observing the target person interact with others to gather information on how the target person interacts in specific situations. Active strategies attempt to reduce uncertainty by asking others about the target person. Interactive strategies include interrogation and self-disclosure. By directly asking the target person specific questions and also divulging information about oneself, an atmosphere of trust is created so that a full exchange of information can be realized which reduces uncertainty (Berger, 1979; Chen & Starosta, 1998; Samovar et al, 1998; Littlejohn, 2002). Gudykunst's research has revealed that in intercultural contexts, different cultures reduce uncertainty in different ways. The degree of anxiety associated with uncertainty also depends on how close or distant another culture appears. The more familiar the stranger seems, the less anxious one will be to reveal information about oneself whereas anxiety will increase with greater cultural remoteness. The most effective communicators are those who, for example, have a flexible attitude and behavior, i.e. a tolerance for ambiguity and empathy, and who are not rigid in their categorization of others, i.e. are able to identify similarities and differences and avoid stereotypes (Gudykunst & Kim, 1997; Martin & Nakayama, 1997; Chen & Starosta, 1998; Littlejohn, 2002).

Clearly, avoiding uncertainty during mergers and acquisitions is of primary importance as well since uncertainty due to insufficient information can result in the failure of the merger or acquisition (Gunders & Alpert, 2000; Schuler & Jackson, 2001; Walther, 2001). In the absence of answers, negative speculations and rumor grow so that apprehension and anxiety begin to distract the employees of the organizations that are joining (Feldman & Murata, 1991). "Lack of trustworthy information is the principal source of fear, uncertainty, and lost productivity during a merger. Employees will seize upon every rumor and flawed piece of information to fill the void" (Slowinski et al, 2002, p. 27). Hence, Ivancevich et al (1987) recommend that accurate information is provided at all stages of the merger or acquisition, and that it is as comprehensive as possible. Gall (1991), therefore, advocates that communication planning must already commence during the first stage before the merger commences because it is at this stage that the positive or negative views of the merger are crystallized in the employees. A view echoed by others (Ivancevich et al, 1987; Slowinski et al, 2000; Young & Post, 1993; Schuler & Jackson, 2001; Wirtz, 2003).

The merger of Daimler-Benz and Chrysler may serve as an example of how insufficient communication resulted in frustration and anger among the workforce.[1] The merger was announced in May 1998 and officially approved in November 1998 which was called "Day One" of the new DaimlerChrysler corporation. The period of time between these two dates, i.e. six months, was officially called the "Silent Period." During the silent period, working contacts between both companies were limited to the Board of Management and several issues of strategy. Employees, executives, and managers on both sides of the Atlantic waited, not surprisingly, with tense expectations as well as curiosity and euphoria, on the one hand, and with anxiety and worries, on the other hand (*Unternehmensfusion Daimler Chrysler,* n.d.). Communication specialists from Daimler-Benz and Chrysler finally met in December 1998, i.e. one month *after* the official merger and seven months after announcing it to the public, to develop a common understanding for working together (Walther, 2001). This behavior might be one of the reasons why initially the DaimlerChrysler merger ended up destroying so much capital (Waller, 2001). "DaimlerChrysler believed two company cultures could simply be put in a blender and poured out as a new synergistic company. . . Either Daimler and Chrysler did not fully realize the implications of cultural differences or they chose to focus on the operational and business synergies hoping that culture would sort itself out"[2] (Schuler & Jackson, 2001, p. 241). Hence, clearly demonstrating how improper communication strategies, or worse, no communication strategy at all, lead to problems due to uncertainty and anxiety which actually call for increased and effective communication.

Consequently, a reduction of uncertainty and anxiety is of paramount importance, and the companies involved in the merger or acquisition should undertake all efforts to communicate as effectively and comprehensively as possible. In this, Berger's passive, active, and interactive strategies may prove useful in reducing uncertainty through building trust among the employees of the companies involved in the merger or acquisition irrespective of whether it is a merger of equals or unequals, or an acquisition that involves integration or separation. If one compares Berger's theory with some of the advice proposed by Schuler and Jackson (2001), one immediately notes a number of parallels since they, too, essentially seek to avoid uncertainty and reduce anxiety through gathering information from all sources and channels while interacting with all participants at all three stages of mergers and acquisitions. Schuler and Jackson (2001) also call for more flexibility and tolerance for ambiguity since unforeseen events are bound to happen which conforms to Gudykunst's theory.

Turning to power, Martin and Nakayama (1997) note that "power is pervasive in communication interactions" (p. 58). It is often assumed in communication models that the parties involved in the act of communication are equals, but this is rarely the case, Martin and Nakayama (1997) point out. Power usually comes from social institutions and the roles individuals occupy in those institutions. For example, a judge has certain powers that are vested in the court office by the constitution which give the judge certain powers inside the courtroom. However, this power is not vested in the individual person occupying that office, but rather the office the person holds. So outside the courtroom, the judge will not have that same power, but rather that of any other ordinary citizen. It should also be remembered that power is dynamic and not just one directional, Martin and Nakayama (1997) emphasize. Factory workers, for example, may assert their power in a slow-down or strike, and they may negotiate with the employer for higher wages either individually or collectively. It is also possible to abandon one individual or institution in favor of another. "Power is complex, especially in relation to institutions or social structure. Some inequities, such as gender, class, or race, are more rigid than those created by temporary roles such as student or teacher" (Martin & Nakayama, 1997, p. 59).

Power also plays a role in discourse. Martin and Nakayama (1997) note that the meaning of words depends not just on the context, but also on the social relationships that are part of social interactions. While the same words may be used, the meaning often depends on who says them. So if a boss and a worker both refer to the company personnel as a "family," both could attach a different meaning to the same term. For example, to the boss this could mean a "big, happy family" while it could mean a "problem family" to an unhappy worker (Martin & Nakayama, 1997). Society is structured so that all individuals occupy various social positions. These differences in social positions are central to understanding communication because not all positions within the social structure are equivalent or identical. So if the same statement were made by someone in power, it would carry a different weight than it would if the speaker did not have a position of power. For example, if at a press conference a person in power voices the opinion that all workers are generally lazy, it has a different impact than if two employees voice the same opinion while having a drink in a bar after work. "Discourse is tied closely to social structure, so the messages communicated through the use of labels depend greatly on the social position of the speaker" (Martin & Nakayama, 1997, p. 131).

Within the context of mergers and acquisitions, power plays also an important role. Schuler and Jackson (2001) point out that there are mergers of equals and unequals. They also note that failures of mergers and acquisitions can result from situations in which power and politics are the driving force and not the productive objectives. Thus, positions of power constantly play a role in mergers and acquisitions; especially if it is a merger of unequals or an acquisition.

According to Martin and Nakayama (1997), such differences in power can result in tension. The following example from the early phase of the Daimler Chrysler merger helps to illustrate this point clearly: "Chrysler marketing chief Jim Holden recalls his first meeting at the Mercedes-Benz US headquarters in Montvale, NJ. As the Germans presented their view of the brand hierarchy – Mercedes on top and everything else far, far below – the tension in the room was palpable" (Schuler & Jackson, 2001, p. 242). It is, therefore, crucial that power and its influence on communication be taken into consideration so that tension and anxiety can be reduced before it has serious consequences among the workforce. If it is not possible to reduce the tension and anxiety, people will find an outlet for their frustrations and dislikes. They may either decide to leave the company (Imberman, 1985; Ivancevich et al, 1987; Feldman & Murata, 1991; Schuler & Jackson, 2001), or they may decide to vent their frustration in public (Invancevich et al, 1987; Bourantas & Nikandrou, 1998; Cooper, 1998; Nikandrou et al, 2000).

These actions and reactions may only be minimized or kept in check if the power distance is reduced by embracing new partnership roles indicating that all are working together towards a common goal (Imberman, 1985; Schweiger & Denisi, 1991; Schuler & Jackson, 2001). After the initial difficulties of the Daimler Chrysler merger, the strategy and tactics were changed: "Along with this the culture changed, both to reflect the new strategy and the new leadership. Zetsche and his team are much more egalitarian" (Schuler & Jackson, 2001, p. 249). By reducing power distance, the CEO can become a role model in a positive sense (Young & Post, 1993; Wittwer, 1995). It is also crucial that the CEO be willing to address challenging questions, listen carefully, and respond quickly to sensitive topics to demonstrate behavioral commitment (Young & Post, 1993). One-directional communication, often an indicator of a top-down power hierarchy, is inappropriate to explain the background of a strategy, notes Kling (2003). One-sided communication often makes the affected employees feel like helpless victims during mergers and acquisitions (Scharfenkamp et al, 2002). According to Bragg (2001), it is essential to listen to the employees of the companies being united because they are the key to success. All of these examples illustrate the importance of attempting to reduce the power levels or inequality to a manageable level so that power does not become a reason per se for the failure of a merger or acquisition.

Since it seems inevitable that conflicts can and do arise during mergers and acquisitions, it might make sense to briefly look at intercultural conflict management. According to Martin and Nakayama (1997), "conflict is often exacerbated because of the unwillingness of partners to recognize style differences" (p. 257). Everyone involved in a conflict is often incapable of seeing the situation from the other party's perspective. People tend to see phenomena from their own perspective and will assume that their interpretation is the right one. If both parties persist in this type of behavior, the relationship can quickly become damaged and frozen in place because neither party is willing to move from their position. If in addition power also plays a role, then the person with a position of power will often attempt to use that power to force his or her interpretation on the weaker person. If the weaker person accepts the stronger party's interpretation, this does not mean, though, that the weaker will have abandoned his or her views, or that the interpretation of the more powerful party is right (Martin & Nakayama, 1997). It just compounds the situation in that frustration and anger are added to uncertainty and anxiety.

According to Martin and Nakayama (1997), the next aspect of conflict management focuses on identifying one's preferred style. Different people have adopted different styles, and often only one style. In order to successfully manage conflict, though, it is necessary to adopt different styles in different situations. It would, for example, not make much sense to persist in a confrontational style if the other party has signaled a willingness to compromise (Martin & Nakayama, 1997). Here, it might make sense to have developed a number of plans in advance in order to be prepared for such a situation. According to Berger (2005), people who do make such plans tend to resolve those situations better than those people who have not made any plans, or too few. Martin and Nakayama (1997) suggest that one practices self-restraint, joins the opponent in a team to find a solution to a common problem, and engages in a dialog so as to understand the other person's perspective.

Clearly, if there is no similar interpretation of the same event in a merger or acquisition, then such perceptual divergence can be problematic and may result in conflict. For example, if during a merger of equals, one of the companies perceives to be taken over by the other company, conflict seems preprogrammed (Vlasic & Stertz, 2000; *Unternehmensfusion DaimlerChrysler,* n.d.). At the time of the merger, Daimler-Benz and Chrysler looked back on different company histories, different characters, and different goals. Each side was protective of its identity while envying the other (Vlasic & Stertz, 2000; Schuler & Jackson, 2001). This difference in perspective most likely also played a role in the internal conflict observed during the early stages of the Daimler Chrysler merger. So it is crucial that both companies create a common perspective and communicate as one voice in a merger or acquisition (Invancevich et al, 1987; Young & Post, 1993; Slowinskiet al, 2000; Schuler & Jackson, 2001; Wirtz, 2003). If this strategy is applied successfully, it might counter the impression that one of the companies is the winner and the other the loser. This would, then, reduce the conflict potential of mergers and acquisitions (Bourantas & Nikandrou, 1998).

Imberman (1985) suggests that teams be built consisting of members from both companies so that representatives from both organizations get to know one another. "These teams have a vital role to play in bridging the gap between management and employees. Team members should keep tuned in to problems of morale, and the concerns people express" (Imberman, 1985, p. 37). According to Young and Post (1993), while many of such meetings initially encounter hostility, continued meetings usually improve the situation; in particular, when attempts are undertaken to answer all questions openly and addressing all worries. In fact, "the employees' sense of participation and the respect accorded their views and concerns, dramatically improved morale within the company" (Imberman, 1985, p. 37). This, in turn, usually results in improved productivity (Imberman, 1985; Bourantas & Nikandrou, 1998; Schuler & Jackson, 2001). So one can see how teams can contribute to improved communication within organizations which in turn reduces uncertainty and anxiety during mergers and acquisitions. Consequently, the management of conflicts ought to be improved if everyone knows how the other feels about the merger or acquisition so that inherent fears may be allayed.

Many of the problems and situations associated with mergers and acquisitions are reminiscent of culture shock as noted above. According to Oberg (1979), culture shock is the generalized trauma affecting individuals in a new and different culture. It is triggered "by the anxiety that results from losing the familiar signs and symbols for social intercourse. These signs or cues encompass the many ways by which we habituate ourselves to our daily routines" (Klopf, 1998, pp. 242-243). In other words, through the loss of familiar signs and signals, communication breakdowns can occur which can result in a personal identity crisis. Culture shock can assume a number of forms. According to Chen and Starosta (1998), six concepts have been used to describe culture shock. In this discussion of mergers and acquisitions, the following four concepts of culture shock may prove to be insightful:

- Role shock
- Transition shock
- Adjustment stress
- Culture distance

Role shock is the feeling of lost personal status in an ambiguous new environment and the efforts one undertakes to change one's role so as to fit into and function within the new culture. Transition shock is the experience people make when attempting to cope with the many changes one needs to undertake in order to cope in the new cultural environment. Adjustment stress is the physical tension that signals a person's readiness to meet the challenges of the new culture. And culture distance is the distance between the old and the new culture and the attendant estrangement and alienation one feels in the new environment (Chen & Starosta, 1998).

According to Klopf (1998), six stages of culture shock have been identified. Of these six stages, the first five should be of interest to the discussion of mergers and acquisitions:

- Preliminary stage
- Spectator stage
- Participant stage
- Shock stage
- Adaptation stage

The preliminary stage refers to the phase during which plans are made in anticipation of the journey. The spectator stage marks the arrival in the new cultural environment and the encounter with the new and strange sights and sounds. The participant stage denotes the period during which the traveler will have to get involved in the daily routines. It is at this point that the participant realizes that some of the usual methods and approaches do not seem to function as well in the new cultural environment as they do in the home culture. The shock stage begins when the problems begin to increase and become difficult to handle. Usually depression sets in and hostile feelings can arise due to the inability to cope with the strange situations. The adaptation stage is the phase during which the traveler has adjusted to the new environment, lost most of the anxiety, and accepted new customs (Klopf, 1998). Gudykunst and Kim (1997) point out, though, that not everyone passes through all five stages in the same manner. Some individuals cope better with the situation than other individuals, some handle some stages better than other stages, and many individuals seem to vacillate in their phases of adjustment. It also seems that prior cultural training helps reduce some of the stress and difficulties typically encountered when entering new cultural environments (Gudykunst & Kim, 1997; Chen & Starosta, 1998; Klopf, 1998; Lustig & Koester, 1999).

The problems encountered in mergers and acquisitions clearly indicate certain parallels to the culture shock phenomenon. The phases of anxiety and stress have been observed in many individuals involved in and/or affected by mergers and acquisitions (Imberman, 1985; Ivancevich et al, 1987; Schweiger & Denisi, 1991; Gutknecht & Keys, 1993; Bourantas & Nikandrou, 1998; Gunders & Alpert, 2000; Gunders & Alpert, 2000; Schuler & Jackson, 2001). And the causes are similar to those of culture shock in that employees of one or both companies may lose their familiar signs and signals because they have to cope with a new corporate culture in the aftermath of the merger or acquisition which also entails the use and adoption of new signs and symbols, values, and role models (Schuler & Jackson, 2001). This in turn can result in a personal identity crisis (Ivancevich et al, 1987; Schweiger & Denisi, 1991) similar to one encountered in culture shock.

Closer scrutiny reveals that the six stages of culture shock are also contained in Schuler and Jackson's (2001) three stage model of mergers and acquisitions as seen in the following table:

Table 1
The Stages of Culture Shock and Mergers and Acquisitions

Culture Shock Model	Schuler & Jackson's Model
Preliminary Stage Spectator Stage	Pre-combination Stage
Participation Stage Shock Stage	Combination-Integration Stage
Adaptation Stage	Solidification & Assessment Stage

The preliminary and spectator stages of culture shock parallel in many ways the pre-combination stage of the Schuler and Jackson model. Both consist of preparatory stages that encompass the gathering of information about the other culture/company and include attempts to observe, analyze, interpret, and evaluate what is being perceived. The participation and shock stage correspond to the combination-integration stage. It is acknowledged by Schuler and Jackson (2001) that this is the most difficult stage during which many things can go wrong; much of it due to false perception, communication, and/or interpretation. It is also a learning process that requires constant adjustment to newly emerging situations; and if the companies cannot make the right decisions in light of these experiences, the likelihood of failure is greatly enhanced. Something similar is observed in sojourners attempting to adjust to unusual situations encountered in the new cultural environment (Gudykunst & Kim, 1997; Lustig & Koester, 1999). And in both cases, i.e. sojourners and companies, individual talents can play a decisive role since some people/companies are better equipped to handle such situations than others (Gdykunst & Kim, 1997; Schuler & Jackson, 2001). The final stage of culture shock, i.e. the adaptation stage, shows remarkable similarities to stage three of the Schuler and Jackson model, i.e. solidification and assessment of the new entity. Both indicate that the participants will have adapted to the new environment and adopted new customs in this final stage – should the participants reach this stage.

With so many parallels existing between cultural encounters and mergers and acquisitions, it seems to make sense that the quality of preparation in anticipation of such encounters, i.e. a sojourn to another country or the merger with and/or acquisition of another company, will help make the adjustment easier. The assumption being, of course, that the involved parties are willing and capable of making the adjustment to the new environment. Both intercultural communication experts (Gudykunst & Kim, 1997; Chen & Starosta, 1998; Lustig & Koester, 1999) and human resource management experts (Schweiger & Denisi, 1991; Young & Post, 1993; Schuler & Jackson, 2001) note, however, that not everyone is equally proficient in this task. That having been noted, prior training, though, does seem to offer assistance and help in reducing stress and anxiety (Young & Post, 1993; Wittwer, 1995; Gudykunst & Kim, 1997; Chen & Starosta, 1998; Klopf, 1998; Lustig & Koester, 1999; Schewe et al, 2000; Schuler & Jackson, 2001). Prior training and preparation should, therefore, be carried out as comprehensively, effectively, and efficiently as possible. It should also continue after the merger or acquisition has taken place to assure continued success and to verify whether the acculturation process is proceeding as planned.

Adaptation and acculturation are important aspects of any long-term contact within a new cultural environment. Essentially, there are four basic ways in which people adapt to new cultures (Martin & Nakayama, 1997; Lustig & Koester, 1999):

- Assimilation
- Integration
- Separation
- Marginalization

Assimilation refers to the situation in which people give up many aspects of their old culture and assume the new culture almost entirely. This includes the assumption of new beliefs, values, and norms. The metaphor of the "melting pot" is often used in this context (Martin & Nakayama, 1997; Lustig & Koester, 1999). Integration is the situation in which people maintain their original culture and also adopt parts of the new culture to be able to interact successfully with other groups. Integration differs from assimilation "in that it involves a greater degree of interest in maintaining one's own cultural identity" (Martin & Nakayama, 1997, pp. 181-182). Separation consists of two forms. In one, persons are deliberately isolated by the dominant social group as in apartheid or Jewish ghettos. While in the other form, people deliberately choose to keep their original culture and isolate themselves from other groups as the Amish have done in parts of North America which is then also respected by the dominant social group (Martin & Nakayama, 1997; Lustig & Koester, 1999). Marginalization is the situation in which a person does not retain his or her cultural heritage nor has little interest in maintaining positive contacts with other groups in the new cultural environment. "This form of acculturation is characterized by confusion and alienation" (Lustig & Koester, 1999, p. 346). Reality, of course, is often not as clear cut as the above modes of acculturation seem to indicate and may consist of varying degrees of each type (Gudykunst & Kim, 1997; Chen & Starosta, 1998; Martin & Nakayama, 1998; Lustig & Koester, 1999).

Interestingly, McShane and Von Glinow (2002) have also identified four strategies for merging different companies:

- Assimilation
- Integration
- Separation
- Deculturation

Their categorization is actually more precise than Schuler and Jackson (2001) who only refer to integration. According to McShane and Von Glinow (2002), assimilation refers to the situation in which one company surrenders its corporate culture to be integrated into or replaced by the corporate culture of the other company. In fact, the employees of one company welcome and accept the cultural values of the other organization. This strategy works best when one company has a weak and dysfunctional culture. At the same time, the other company's culture has to be strong and focused on clearly defined values. McShane and Von Glinow (2002) point out that this strategy seems to work best if it is a union of unequals.

Integration refers to the attempts to combine the two cultures into a new culture and preserves the best features of the two previous corporate cultures. Integration, however, is slow and risky because there are many features that preserve the existing cultures. But McShane and Von Glinow (2002) recommend this strategy when the two companies have relatively weak cultures or when their corporate cultures include several overlapping values. It also works as a strategy when the employees realize that their existing cultures are ineffective and, thus, are motivated to adopt new values.

Separation occurs when the two companies agree to remain distinct entities with minimal changes in their corporate cultures or organizational practices. McShane and Von Glinow (2002) point out that this strategy is suitable for situations in which the two companies are in unrelated industries. In particular, distinct cultures within an organization can lead to the separation strategy.

Deculturation means that one company imposes its culture on the other company. This is usually done when a company has been acquired and the employees of that acquired company resist organizational change. McShane and Glinow (2002) recommend that the acquiring company remove the artifacts and reward systems of the old company and replace them with those of the acquiring organization. People who cannot adopt the acquiring company's culture, tend to be laid off. However, the deculturation strategy rarely works because when the employees of the acquired company resist the cultural intrusions of the acquiring firm, the employees would delay or undermine the whole merger process (McShane & Von Glinow, 2002).

These four merger strategies of McShane and Von Glinow (2002) appear to be quite similar to the four types of acculturation (Martin & Nakayama, 1997; Lustig & Koester, 1999):

Table 2
Acculturation and Merger Strategies

Stages of Acculturation	Strategies for Mergers
Assimilation	Assimilation
Integration	Integration
Separation	Separation
Marginalization	Deculturation

One of the differences is that in mergers assimilation seems to work best when one of the companies is weaker than the other, both in economic terms and in corporate culture, while one would not automatically assume that an immigrant is weaker; though, many people migrate due to economic reasons and are, thus, dependent on those who can and/or are willing to give them a job and/or money. Interestingly, assimilation was the strategy initially pursued by Daimler and Chrysler in their corporate merger. But it was not very successful (Vlasic & Stertz, 2000; Schuler & Jackson, 2001). Integration exhibits similarities in that some aspects of both cultures are retained. It seems as if DaimlerChrysler ultimately ended up with this merger strategy (Schuler & Jackson, 2001). Separation also shows similarities in both mergers and acculturation. It seems that DaimlerChrysler decided to opt for separation after encountering its initial difficulties while attempting to pursue the assimilation strategy. "Two separate operational headquarters were maintained; one in Michigan and one in Germany. Business operations continued to be separate. . . Daimler and Chrysler each had their own agenda focusing on different aspects of the automobile market" (Schuler & Jackson, 2001, p. 242) before ultimately pursuing an integration strategy. And finally, deculturation exhibits certain characteristics of marginalization; with one important difference, the acquiring company can impose its power and culture on the acquired company. Those who do not like the merger or acquisition, have to or can leave the companies. Both deculturation and marginalization entail problems since they are associated with confusion and alienation (Lustig & Koester, 1999; McShane & Von Glinow, 2002).

What the DaimlerChrysler example indicates is that in reality, the actual merger strategies are not as clear cut as they may appear in theory. Depending on the situations encountered during a merger or acquisition as well as in the aftermath, adjustments and/or changes have to be made. In this respect, the merger and acquisition of companies mirrors the adaptation and acculturation of people. When companies are deciding which strategy to pursue during a merger or acquisition, they should thoroughly analyze each other to determine the distinguishing and unique characteristics of one another so that they may be able to deliberate the advantages and disadvantages of each strategy on the basis of their status. Ideally, the right strategy, or combination of different strategies, will be selected that matches the identity and goals of the companies seeking to undertake a merger or acquisition.

From this discussion of how people and companies become acculturated, it becomes clear that identity development, whether it is an individual's identity or a company's identity, is also an important aspect that needs to be discussed in order to see how identity influences the behavior of individuals and corporations prior to, during, and after acculturation as well as mergers and acquisitions; and how identity may change as a result of such processes. People generally tend to have "multiple identities that come into play at different times, depending on the context" (Martin & Nakayama, 1997, p. 66). Identity is important because it links culture with communication. People communicate their identity to others, and they communicate on the basis of their identity. People also learn who they are through communication with others, i.e. perception. By communicating with others, people come to understand themselves and also form and shape their own identity. Conflicts can arise between who one thinks one is and who others think one is. If there is a discrepancy in those identities, problems can arise (Martin & Nakayama, 1997). For example, a child may think he or she is old enough to go out alone while the parents will not let the child out of the home alone at night since they think the child is too young or the destination is too dangerous so late at night. Such a scenario may create a conflict situation in that the child's self identity, i.e. to be old enough to go out alone, does not conform to the identity the parents have of the child, i.e. too young to go out alone to that destination at night.

This interrelationship of the self and others in forming and shaping identity is often called the social psychological perspective (Gudykunst & Kim, 1997; Martin & Nakayama, 1997; Lustig & Koester, 1999). "The social psychological perspective emphasizes that identity is created in part by the self and in part in relation to group membership" (Martin & Nakayama, 1997, p. 65). A person has, according to this perspective, multiple identities which are culturally bound. People belong to a number of groups that all help identify who one is. For example, one may be part of a particular gender group, such as females, and a particular age group, such as teenagers. Hence, the identity of female teenagers will be shaped and influenced by a number of characteristics typical of the group females and the group teenagers which can be quite different from another gender group, for example males, or other age groups, for example toddlers or seniors. These various groups are often also identifiable as microcultures, e.g. age, gender/sex, ethnic and national origin, religion, class/occupation, geographic region, urban/suburban/rural, and exceptionality (Klopf, 1998). Each individual can assume certain roles that are characteristic of a particular group, or combination of groups depending on the relevance of the situation. Thus, for example, female teenagers could exhibit certain behavioral traits typical of all teenagers, i.e. males and females, such as rebelling against their parents, as well as exhibiting certain behavioral traits typical of all females, i.e. female teenagers and female seniors, such as the use of cosmetics. These roles then also influence or determine the way a person communicates. In addition to the groups one is born into, for example one's biological sex, and selects in the course of one's life, for example political affiliation, people are also sometimes forced into certain groups by society which have a direct impact on who one is and how one may behave (Gudykunst & Kim, 1997; Martin & Nakayama, 1997; Lustig & Koester, 1999). For example, German Jews had to wear a yellow star on their clothing and could not hold public office in Germany under the Nazis. Obviously, such roles had a direct impact on the identity of a person and how that person communicates with others.

Obviously, there are a number of parallels between the identity of a person and that of a corporation. Just like a person's identity is composed of one's own perception and that of others, a company's identity is based on how the organization sees itself and how the public perceives it (Solomon et al, 1999; Kotler & Armstrong, 2001; Assael, 2004). Thus, a chemical company may think its plant is a very good factory since it has a very high production rate and is very profitable. The public, however, may think it is an environmental hazard. Likewise, the group or economic sector a company belongs to can have an influence on how a company communicates. Hence, a food company will behave and communicate differently than a mining company. Similarly, a company in the food branch can be a wholesaler or a retailer and will behave and communicate accordingly. For example, a food wholesaler will focus on other merchants who are either other wholesalers or retailers. These wholesalers and retailers are fellow merchants who will be able to understand the jargon and principles of commerce and trade which the general public, to whom the retailer caters, might not understand. Consequently, a retailer cannot not use the trade specific jargon the wholesaler uses, but instead will have use language the general public can understand; this makes the message content different from that used by wholesalers. Likewise, the wholesaler will sell food to other wholesalers and retailers in bulk quantities while the public generally does not make bulk purchases at the retailer. These examples demonstrate that the role and function of the company has direct relevance on the behavior and communication of the company with others.

The employees of a company identify themselves not just on the basis of the tasks they perform at their workplace, but also how their colleagues and supervisors interact with them and treat them which is often due to the employee's group affiliation and status, i.e. power. Likewise, the profession and gender of an employee can influence and determine the behavior and communication of an employee. Thus, a male construction worker and female nurse might both exhibit different behavior and use different language which can be indicative of a different identity perception since perceived identity can influence how one behaves and communicates with others.

Martin and Nakayama (1997) identify four stages of minority identity and five stages of majority identity. The four stages of minority identity are:

1. Unexamined identity
2. Conformity

3. Resistance and separation
4. Integration

Unexamined identity refers to the stage during which minority members may initially accept the values and norms of the majority culture. They may have a strong desire to assimilate into the dominant culture. Conformity is characterized by the internalization of values and norms of the majority members. This stage continues until the person runs into situations that may cause the person to question the values and norms of the majority. Resistance and separation can be characterized by a return to the values and norms of one's group and the rejection of the values and norms of the majority. Integration[3] is the ideal outcome of the identity process. A person who reaches this stage has a strong sense of his or her own group identity and an acceptance of other groups (Martin & Nakayama, 1997).

The five stages of majority identity are:

1. Unexamined identity
2. Acceptance
3. Resistance
4. Redefinition
5. Integration

Unexamined identity is the stage during which individuals accept the values and norms of society and may be aware of minorities, but do not question their role or existence. Acceptance is the internalization of certain roles, and individuals accept certain inequities as given without questioning their validity. Resistance is major paradigm shift. Individuals may begin to question the roles assigned to others and move away from acceptance of the given. Redefinition refers to the stage during which people begin to refocus or redirect their definitions of group roles. People realize that they do not have to accept the given. Integration is the stage during which people are able to integrate their role into those of other groups and accept them as equals (Martin & Nakayama, 1997).

Since individuals and corporations exhibit certain similarities to one another, a case might be made to transfer the stages of minority and majority identity development to mergers and acquisitions. Schuler and Jackson (2001) pointed out that mergers can be of equals and unequals, i.e. companies can hold a majority or minority share in the new organization. A look at the stages of minority and majority identity development from the perspective of mergers and acquisitions might, therefore, reveal some interesting insights into companies involved in mergers and acquisitions. The example of the Daimler Chrysler merger shall serve once again as an example. While the Daimler Chrysler merger is not representative of all mergers and acquisitions, it is an interesting case for minority and majority identity development. Though originally hailed as a merger of equals (Vlasic & Stertz, 2000; Waller, 2001), it quickly became apparent that Chrysler was the junior partner in the merger (Schuler & Jackson, 2001). This, therefore, will allow one to analyze the behavior exhibited by Chrysler, the minority, and Daimler, the majority, in the course of the merger from the perspective of identity development.

Originally, Daimler-Benz and Chrysler assumed that they could merge their companies and generate a positive synergy effect that would also have a positive impact on their overall profitability (Vlasic & Stertz, 2000; Schuler & Jackson, 2001; Waller, 2001). As Chrysler's CEO Robert Eaton said: "Consolidation is inevitable. Being among the first with the idea of doing a merger, we were able to pick our favorite partner" (Vlasic & Stertz, 2000, p. 250). This view is very reminiscent of the first stage of identity development, unexamined identity. Both companies apparently assumed that they could carry out the merger without major problems since they were similar companies in the same industrial branch (Schuler & Jackson, 2001).

After the merger, it seems that Chrysler sought conformity, i.e. the second stage of minority identity development, and Daimler acceptance, the second stage of majority identity development, because both companies thought they could and would share their knowledge and technology with one another equally. "During the initial stages of the merger, Chrysler President Thomas Stallkamp indicated that Daimler intended to adopt Chrysler's product development methods . . . [and] Chrysler would adopt Daimler practices" (Schuler & Jackson, 2001, p. 242).

But quite soon thereafter, problems arose and dissatisfaction with the status quo was voiced by Chrysler employees (Vlasic & Stertz, 2000; Schuler & Jackson, 2001; Waller, 2001). This parallels the third stage of minority identity development for Chrysler while Daimler remained in the second stage of majority identity development, i.e. Chrysler questioned its role in the merger, Daimler continued to conduct its business unchanged. "However, evidence of the lack of true sharing and cooperation was soon to emerge and could be demonstrated by Daimler executives' refusal to use Chrysler parts in Mercedes vehicles" (Schuler & Jackson, 2001, p. 242) because they did not want to compromise the quality of Mercedes cars.

After Chrysler's dissatisfaction became apparent to Daimler, Daimler seemed to have entered the third stage of majority identity development, resistance, i.e. a major paradigm shift. In other words, Daimler began to acknowledge Chrysler as a separate entity. "Business operations continued to be separate as evidenced by Daimler's decision to allow Chrysler more leeway in the design and production of its vehicles, which more closely emulated the practices of the old Chrysler" (Schuler & Jackson, 2001, p. 242).

Daimler then entered the fourth stage of majority identity development, redefinition. It began to refocus its goals and efforts which also included a reassessment and change of the corporate structure (Schuler & Jackson, 2001). "This new culture, combined with the new strategy and structure, is reshaping the thrust of performance appraisal and compensation to focus more on cost cutting objectives, supplier management, flexibility and employee morale" (Schuler & Jackson, 2001, p. 249).

Parallel to this development, Daimler literally forced Chrysler out of the third stage of minority identity development, resistance and separation. After a number of top Chrysler executives had headed Chrysler and left (Vlasic & Stertz, 2000; Schuler & Jackson, 2001; Waller, 2001), Daimler put one of its veteran executives, Dieter Zetsche, at the head of Chrysler. Probably due to the fact that Daimler was in the fourth stage of majority identity development, i.e. redefinition, it was ready to treat Chrysler with respect. Zetsche "created his own top management team composed of one Daimler veteran and five Chrysler veterans. . . Along with this the culture changed, both to reflect the new strategy and the new leadership. Zetsche and his team are much more egalitarian" (Schuler & Jackson, 2001, p. 249).

It would appear that Daimler and Chrysler are both headed towards integration, i.e. the fourth stage of minority identity development and the fifth stage of majority identity development, as personified by the change in leadership of DaimlerChrysler, i.e. Zetsche coming from Chrysler to replace Schrempp as CEO. Since having been appointed as DaimlerChrysler's CEO, Zetsche has participated in an ad campaign (2006) designed to promote DaimlerChrysler in North America under the heading "Ask Dr. Z" which includes TV commercials and an interactive website which proclaims "German engineering meets American design" (www.dodge.com, 2006). Thus, Zetsche as CEO of DaimlerChrysler seems to have become the icon of the new integrated organization.[4]

As the above discussion of the DaimlerChrysler merger illustrates, it is possible to draw certain parallels between identity development and mergers and acquisitions. Should this be the case for most mergers and acquisitions, then such an analogy might prove to be insightful and useful for the study and analysis of company roles in mergers and acquisitions.

The DaimlerChrysler example also demonstrates the importance of community building in mergers and acquisitions because through community building, it might be possible to optimize the merger and acquisition and minimize the conflict potential inherent to such transactions. According to Gudykunst and Kim (1997), a community is composed of diverse individuals who are open and honest with one another, trust one another, are engaged in ethical behavior, and are committed to living together. Community members respect one another, and they value diversity while, at the same time, searching for commonality. A community is inclusive. Gudykunst and Kim (1997) name seven community building principles:

1. Be committed
2. Be mindful
3. Be unconditionally accepting
4. Be concerned for both oneself and others
5. Be understanding
6. Be ethical
7. Be peaceful

These seven principles will be discussed below within the context of mergers and acquisitions.

People must be committed to the principle of building a community and building relationships with the other people who are also participants of that community. In order to achieve a community, people need to be committed to the idea of the community and committed to dialog as a means of solving problems. And finally, people need to be committed to the principles, not to insisting on being right (Gudykunst & Kim, 1997). The same is true for companies with their commitment to a merger or acquisition as studies have demonstrated (Gall, 1991; Gunders & Alpert, 2000; Schuler & Jackson, 2001). Likewise, comprehensive communication, i.e. establishing a functioning dialog, with everyone is crucial to making the merger or acquisition successful (Gall, 1991; Gutknecht & Keys, 1993; Young & Post, 1993; Nikandrou et al, 2000).

People must be mindful of what they say and do. It is important that one attempts to understand the others from their perspective, not just one's own. People should attempt to adapt their messages so that others can understand the message (Gudykunst & Kim, 1997). Once the merger or acquisition has been announced, employees need to know what will happen to them and their job, their colleagues, and their company. They need honest and useful information, not just any information, to feel secure and reduce their anxiety (Ivancevich et al, 1987; Young & Post, 1993; Nikandrou et al, 2000); and they need information that can be understood by everyone (Kling, 2003).

People must accept others as they are and not attempt to change or control them. It is important that the identities of all participants are respected and fostered (Gudykunst & Kim, 1997). According to Bragg (2001), it is essential for merging companies to really listen to the employees because this is very decisive for a successful merger. Force and coercion are actually counterproductive in mergers and acquisitions and seldom prove to be an effective instrument (Schweiger & Denisi, 1991; Bourantas & Nikandrou, 1998; Nikandrou et al, 2000). It is, therefore, very important that the identities of everyone involved in and affected by the merger or acquisition are retained and maintained (Ivancevich et al, 1987).

People should avoid polarization and express care and concern about others. Consultation with others is crucial as is an open mind to other ideas. People should take others into consideration when there is a conflict and fight gracefully if it proves necessary (Gudykunst & Kim, 1997). During mergers or acquisitions, it is important that companies communicate care and concern to the employees in order to maintain or even increase employee commitment to the merger or acquisition (Schweiger & Denisi, 1991). Holtzhausen (2000) believes that participation by everyone will increase a company's ability to deal with change. But mergers and acquisitions also create hostility and conflict which, though, can be profitable if managed properly (Marks, 1999).

People should strive to understand others as completely as possible. This also includes an understanding of the real differences of the various groups in addition to searching for and establishing commonality (Gudykusnt & Kim, 1997). According to Stahl (2001), differences are not per se a cause for failure in mergers and acquisitions because corporate cultural differences are not just risks but also offer opportunities. Diversity can, for example, spark creativity and productivity (Marks, 1999). And input by everyone can become a self-motivating force that will be beneficial to the organization (Robbins, 2001).

People should be engaged in behavior that is not a means to an end, but behavior that is ethical. This does not, though, mean that one should not make moral judgments, people cannot avoid doing so; but it is necessary that people understand the behavior of others before making any judgment (Gudykunst & Kim, 1997). Gall (1991) believes that is important for companies to create a positive climate because it will facilitate the management of a merger or acquisition.

The key to success is based on everyone pulling together in the same direction. This in turn calls for everyone to understand their mutual goals and for everyone to have a solid sense of how their efforts to achieve those goals relate to those of others (Nikandrou et al, 2000; Rusaw, 2000; Holtzhausen, 2002).

And finally, people must not be violent or deceitful, breach valid promises, or be secretive. People should strive for internal harmony. And if everyone acts according to these tenets, then everyone should benefit from such behavior (Gudykunst & Kim, 1997). Essentially everyone who studies and analyzes mergers and acquisitions comes to a similar conclusion, i.e. establishing balance and internal harmony within the united enterprises in order to create a positive environment that translates into profitability (Imberman, 1985; Feldman & Murata, 1991; Gall, 1991; Slowinski et al, 2000; Robbins, 2001; Schuler & Jackson, 2001; Wirtz, 2003).

If, therefore, a community can be established among the companies involved in a merger or acquisition, it should be possible to reduce uncertainty and anxiety due to the familiarity that has developed among the members of the new community in the course of the merger or acquisition. If such a community is properly established and maintained, it should also help lessen the abuse of power among the members of that community. This, in turn, could lead to the development of conflict management methods that would provide a just and fair means of dealing with conflict among the community's members. Consequently, the impact of culture shock may be lessened and the desire to become acculturated in the new organization is increased. Thus, a functional community can become a vehicle to develop and foster a strong and positive identification of employees with the new entity.

The reader will have probably realized from this discussion of mergers and acquisitions that intercultural communication is indeed able to offer useful information which mirrors, to some degree, the counsel of human resource management experts. But this should not come as a surprise because corporations consist of people; people who are also responsible for creating corporate culture. So who is better to analyze corporations and corporate cultures than cultural experts? The reader is, therefore, invited to peruse through the texts of this volume. The one or the other idea presented herein might be of interest and offer new or different perspectives to problems encountered in today's globalized economy and may, thus, offer useful, supplemental information in finding viable solutions to a variety of business problems.

Endnotes

[1] In this and subsequent discussions of the DaimlerChrysler merger, the issue of external, national macroculture will be ignored in order not to complicate the analysis further with another highly complex variable, i.e. national macroculture, as noted above. Thus, only the corporate microcultures will be addressed.

[2] Schuler and Jackson refer here to the *corporate* microcultures, not the national macroculture.

[3] The terminology used here is identical to that used in acculturation even though the meaning in this context is slightly different. Inconsistent use of terminology is often encountered in interdisciplinary studies.

[4] Quite interestingly, integration is also the apparent merger strategy pursued by DaimlerChrysler as noted above. Here, coincidentally, the terminology and meaning are similar even though the word refers to two different concepts.

References

Assael, H. (2004). *Consumer behavior: A strategic approach.* Boston: Houghton Mifflin.

Berger, C. R. (2005). Planning theory and strategic communication: Achieving goals through communicative action. In M. B. Hinner (Ed.), *Introduction to business communication*, pp. 97-113. Frankfurt am Main: Peter Lang Verlag.

Berger, C. R. (1979). Beyond initial interactions: Uncertainty, understanding, and the development of interpersonal relationships. In H. Giles & R. St. Clair (Eds.), *Language and social psychology.* Oxford: Basil Blackwell.

Berger, C. R., & Calabrese, R. (1975). Some explorations in initial interactions and beyond: Toward a developmental theory of interpersonal communication. *Human Communication Research* 1, pp. 99-112.

Bourantas, D., & Nikandrou, I. I. (1998). Modelling post-acquisition employee behavior: Typology and determining factors. *Employee Relations* 20 (1/2), pp. 73-92.

Bragg, T. (2001). Attitudes of employees can ruin prospects for a successful merger. *Hudson Valley Business Journal* 11 (26), pp. 6-8.

Chen, G. M., & Starosta, W. J. (1998). *Foundations of intercultural communication.* Boston: Allyn and Bacon.

Cooper, C. L. (1998). *Theories of Organizational Stress.* Oxford: Oxford University Press.

Felman, M. L., & Murata, D. K. (1991). Why mergers often go "pfft." *ABA Banking Journal* 83 (8), pp. 34-35.

Fischer, H., & Steffens-Duch, S. (2002). Die Bedeutung der Unternehmenskultur bei Akquisitionen und Fusionen – Das Beispiel Deutsche Bank und Bankers Trust. In U. Krysteck & E. Zur (Eds.), *Handbuch Internationalisierung. Globalisierung – eine Herausforderung für die Unternehmensführung.* Berlin: Springer Verlag, pp. 809-818.

Gall, E. A. (1991). Strategies for merger success. *The Journal of Business Strategy* 12 (2), pp. 26-29.

Gudykunst, W. B., & Kim, Y. Y. (1997). *Communicating with strangers: An approach to intercultural communication* (3rd ed). Boston: McGraw-Hill.

Gunders, S., & Alpert, A. (2000). Ensuring merger integration success: Instilling confidence, control and commitment throughout the integration process. *Euromoney's International Mergers & Acquisitions Review.*

Gutknecht, J. E., & Keys, J. B. (1993). Mergers, acquisitions and takeovers: Maintaining morale of survivors and protecting employees. *Academy of Management Executive* 7 (3), pp. 26-37.

Hofstede, G. (1993). Intercultural conflict and synergy in Europe. In D. J. Hickson (ed.), *Management in Western Europe.* Berlin: Walter de Gruyter & Co.

Holtzhausen, D. R. (2000). The effects of workplace democracy on employee communication behaviour: Implications for competitive advantage. *Competitiveness Review* 12 (2), pp. 30-48.

Imberman, A. J. (1985). The human element of mergers. *Management Review* 74 (6), pp. 35-37.

Ivancevich, J. M., Schweiger, D. M., Power, F. R. (1987). Strategies for managing human resources during mergers and acquisitions. *Human Resource Planning* 10 (1), pp.19-36.

Kling, L. (2003). *Change Marketing: Marketingbasierte interne Kommunikation im Change Management.* Aachen: Shaker Verlag.

Klopf, D. W. (1998). *Intercultural encounters: The fundamentals of intercultural communication* (4th ed). Englewood: Morton Publishing Company.

Kotler, P., & Armstrong, G. (2001). *Principles of marketing.* Upper Saddle River: Prentice-Hall.

Littlejohn, S. W. (2002). *Theories of human communication* (7th ed.). Belmont: Wadsworth/Thomson Learning.

Lustig, M. W., & Koester, J. (1999). *Intercultural competence: Interpersonal communication across cultures* (3rd ed.). New York: Longman.

Marks, M. L. (1999). Adding cultural fit to your diligence checklist. *Mergers & Acquisitions: The Dealmaker's Journal* 34 (3), pp. 14-21.

Marks, M. L. (2000). Mixed signals. *Across the Board.* 37, pp. 21-26.

Marks, L.M., & Mirvis, P. H. (1992). Rebuilding after the merger: Dealing with "survivor sickness." *Organizational Dynamics* 21 (2), pp. 18-33.

Martin, J. N., & Nakayama, T. K. (1997). *Intercultural communication in contexts.* Mountain View: Mayfield Publishing Company.

McShane, S. L., & Von Glinow, M. A. (2002). *Organizational behavior: Emerging realities fort he workplace revolution.* Boston: Irwin/McGraw-Hill.

Müller-Stewens, G., Willeitner, S., & Schäfer, M. (2002). Stand und Entwicklungstendenzen von Cross-Border-Aquisitionen. In U. Krysteck & E. Zur (Eds.), *Handbuch Internationalisierung. Globalisierung – eine Herausforderung für die Unternehmensführung.* Berlin: Springer Verlag, pp. 141-169.

Nicholson, N. (1997). *The Blackwell encyclopedic dictionary of finance.* Cambridge: Blackwell.

Nikandrou, I. I., Papalexandris, N., & Bourantas, D. (2000). Gaining employee trust after acquisition. *Employee Relations* 22 (4/5), pp. 334-355.

Oberg, K. (1979). Culture shock and the problems of adjustment in new cultural environments. In E. C. Smith and L. F. Luce (eds.), *Toward Internationalism: Readings in cross-cultural communication.* Rowley: Newbury House.

Peters, T. J., & Waterman, R. H. (1982). *In search of excellence.* New York: Harper & Row.

Robbins, S. P. (2001). *Organizational behaviour.* Upper Saddle River: Prentice-Hall.

Rusaw, A. C. (2000). The ethics of leadership trust. *International Journal of Organization Theory & Behavior* 3 (3/4), pp. 549-571.

Samovar, L. A., Porter, R. E., & Stefani, L. A. (1998). *Communicating between cultures* (3rd ed.). Belmont: Wadsworth Publishing Company.

Scharfenkamp, N., Armutat, S., Mielich, R., Becker, J., Baur, M., Sigl, H., & Malessa, G. (2002). Erfolgreiches Personalmanagement im M & A-Prozess. *Schriftreihe Deutsche Gesellschaft für Personalführung e. V.* Vol. 67.

Schewe, G., Schaecke, M., & Münstermann, M. (2000). Post Merger Integration: Der Fall Bayerische Vereinsbank / Bayerische Hypotheken- und Wechselbank. *Arbeitspapiere des Lehrstuhls für Betriebswirtschaftslehre, insb. Organisation, Personal und Innovation der Westfälischen Wilhelms-Universität Münster,* Vol. 13.

Schuler, R., & Jackson, S. (2001). HR issues and activities in mergers and acquisitions. *European Management Journal* 19 (3), pp. 239-253.

Schreyögg, G., Oechsler, W. A., & Wächter, H. (1995). *Managing in a European context: Human resources-corporate culture-industrial relation, text and cases.* Wiesbaden: Gabler Verlag.

Schweiger, D. M., & Denisi, A. S. (1991). Communication with employees following a merger: A longitudinal field experiment. *Academy of Management Journal* 34 (1), pp. 110-135.

Slowinski, G., Rafii, Z., Tao, J., Gollob, L., & Krishnamurthy, K. R. (2000). Integrating R & D organizations in a merger & acquisition. *Research Technology Management* 43 (5), pp. 11-13.

Solomon, M., Bamossy,G., & Askegaard, S. (1999). *Consumer behavior: A European perspective.* London: Prentice-Hall Europe.

Stahl, G. K. (2001). Management der sozio-kulturellen Integration bei Unternehmenszusammenschlüssen und –übernahmen. *Die Betriebswirtschaft: DBW* 61 (1), pp. 61-78.

Unternehmensfusion Daimler Chrysler. Ein Erfahrungsbericht aus interkultureller Perspektive. (n.d.).

Vlasic, B., & Stertz, B. A. (2000). *Taken for a ride: How Daimler-Benz drove off with Chrysler.* New York: Morrow.

Waller, D. (2001). *Wheels on fire: The amazing inside story of the Daimler-Chrysler merger.* London: Coronet.

Walther, C. (2001). Erfolgsstratgien für Unternehmensfusionen – die besondere Rolle der internen Kommunikation. In K. P. Johanssen & U. Steger (Eds.), *Lokal oder Global? Strategien und Konzepte von Kommunikations-Profis für internationale Märkte.* Frankfurt am Main: F.A.Z.-Institut.

Wirtz, B. W. (2003). *Mergers & Acquisitions Management. Strategie und Organisatin von Unternehmenszusammenschlüssen.* Wiesbaden: Gabler Verlag.

Wittwer, A. (1995). *Innerbetriebliche Kommunikation bei Unternehmenszusammenschlüssen: Eine Untersuchung über Strategien zur Mitarbeiter Integration.* Munich: Tuduv.

Young, M., & Post, J. E. (1993). Managing to communicate, communicating to manage: How leading companies communicate with employees. *Organizational Dynamics* 22 (1), pp. 31-43.

Introduction to

Intercultural Communication for a Global Society

By D. Ray Heisey

Heisey's text is a very good introduction to the subsequent texts of this fourth volume which is devoted to the influence of culture on communication in a business context.

Heisey notes that globalization is a phenomenon that has both positive and negative consequences. He goes on to state that cultural transformation is one of the consequences of globalization. When dominant cultures overtake and absorb marginal cultures in any part of the world, the danger of losing cultural integrity on part of each involved culture is evident. Heisey also observes that there is the temptation to view economic strength as being a manifestation of a superior culture to those less developed. He urges, though, that ways must be found to increase economic advancement without losing cultural authenticity in the process. That is why an understanding of cultural differences is vital to the advancement in all aspects of living – whether it be economic, educational, military, religious, or political, for example. Heisey, therefore, sets out to examine the ways in which culture and communication interact and impact each other so that those working in the business world better understand the implications of these dialogues and interactions for the business context.

In his overview of intercultural communication, Heisey looks at the different approaches that can be used in studying intercultural communication; noting also that there are theoretical, practical, methodological, and training approaches. He then examines cultural differences in language, both verbal and nonverbal; pointing out that differences exist in the meaning of words as well as in nonverbal communication. This is followed by a study of the differences in cultural values, beliefs, and perceptions; the author emphasizes that the perceptions of personality characteristics in other cultures often end up being stereotypes that can impact communication interaction. And finally, Heisey looks at cultural differences in specific contexts, such as media, negotiation, managing conflict, responses to cultural differences, construction of cultural identity, acculturation, and developing intercultural competence. He ends the text with an example of how one international corporation joined with the Business College of a local university to engage in a training program to improve cross-cultural communication practices. This program emphasized the importance of learning the factors of being able "to walk in the other nation's shoes," to use empathetic viewpoints to understand the strengths and advantages of each nation, and to utilize the strength of first person multicultural expertise. Heisey ends his dissemination with the advice that global companies wishing to improve their market share may want to consider using the principles discussed in this text. Thus, clearly showing how important an understanding of intercultural communication is in the world of international business.

Michael B. Hinner

D. Ray Heisey is Professor and Director Emeritus, School of Communication Studies, Kent State University, Kent, Ohio. He taught at Kent State from 1966 to 1996, with leaves of absence to serve as President of Damavand College, Teheran, Iran, and visiting professor at the University of Leuven in Belgium and at the University of Lund in Sweden, and has taught intercultural communication twice at Peking University in Beijing. He has published research on cultural values in political communication in communication journals and edited *Chinese Perspectives in Rhetoric and Communication* (Ablex, 2000), and co-edited several books on Chinese studies in communication. He served as president of the International Association for Intercultural Communication Studies (2001-2003), and as chair of the International and Intercultural Communication Division of the National Communication Association (2001-2002).

Intercultural Communication for a Global Society

D. Ray Heisey

The cultural globalization taking place in our world is a striking example of a phenomenon that has both positive and negative consequences. On the negative side, as cultures are propagated and advanced, share and mix with one another, and are exposed to one another in our fast-moving world of commerce, media and transportation, they are vulnerable in the ways that they may influence each other and become modified from their original and authentic form. Cultural transformation is one of the consequences of globalization. When dominant cultures overtake and absorb marginal cultures in any part of the world, the danger of losing cultural integrity on the part of each involved culture is evident.

In the interest of sharing our cultural strengths with others, we may lose sight of the importance of maintaining cultural integrity for the one being influenced. One of the prime examples of this is the temptation to view economic strength as being a manifestation of a superior culture to those less developed. In an effort to achieve modernization, sometimes societies fail to protect their own cultural integrity. This should not be allowed to happen. We must find ways to increase economic advancement without losing cultural authenticity in the process.

One of the ways of looking at the problem of globalization that I like is Chan and Ma's (2002) concept of "transcultural perspective". Instead of seeing the problem as either the "liberal" perspective which views cultural globalization as "the triumph of the market economy" or as the "critical" perspective which views it as "the domination by Western or American culture" (p. 3), they argue that cultural globalization should be seen as "the continual development of multiple modernities on a global scale" (p. 16). In this claim they believe "transculturation captures the historicity, multiplicity, power asymmetry, reciprocal dialectic, uneven hybridization, creative synthesis, transborder imagination, material embodiment, and sociopsychological inscription in the global expansion of modernity" (p. 16).

They want to see many modernities developing so that cultures can be true to their own indigenous strengths and not be swept into a similar pattern of only one type of transformation. This requires dialectical hybridizations that creatively combine "dominant global motifs and local preferences" (p. 16). Cultures and cultural/political leaders should engage in dialogue so that creative approaches can be negotiated and cultural identities maintained.

When President Jiang Zemin of China made his visit to the United States and gave his famous speech at Harvard University in November 1997 and President Clinton reciprocated by going to Beijing in June 1998, they were engaging in a dialogue that advanced each country's image of the other in more positive ways. When President Khatami, after his landslide victory in Iran in May 1997, gave a television interview with CNN's international correspondent, Christiane Amanpour, he was also engaging in an international dialogue on a people-to-people dimension that helped to advance the political relationship. It had a positive response on both sides of the conflict between Iran and the United States. As I argue elsewhere (Heisey, 2000a), these are examples of the international media playing a part in the transformation of public opinion by means of the process of human communication. This can be a positive aspect of globalization by cultural dialogue.

Understanding cultural differences in our world today is vital to advancement in all aspects of living—economic, medical, educational, military, religious, legal, governmental, and political. It is especially important in the business world because of the ways in which business connections are so global. The purpose of this chapter is to examine the ways in which culture and communication interact and impact each other so that those working in the business world better understand the implications of these dialogues and interactions for the business context. The chapter will include references to research studies to support the ideas as well as references to my intercultural experiences from visiting 40 countries over a lifetime of 40 years of teaching in higher education.

We will first look at the different approaches that can be used in studying intercultural communication. We will then look at the cultural differences in language, both verbal and nonverbal. This will be followed by an examination of the differences in cultural values, beliefs, and perceptions. Finally, we will look at cultural differences in specific contexts, such as media, negotiating, managing conflict, responding to culture shock, construction of cultural identity, acculturaton, and developing intercultural competence that results in becoming a multicultural person in a world of globalization.

Different Approaches for Studying Intercultural Communication

We may define culture as a set of expectations and behaviors common to a specific group of people who live together and share a common history and future. Porter and Samovar (1988) simply call it the "pattern for living" (p.19) while Hall (1959) says that culture is communication and communication is culture. The ways in which people from different cultures interact and relate to each other may be described as intercultural communication. Studying these interactions produces understanding and meaning for scholars as well as practitioners. As with the study of any phenomenon, there may be different approaches to studying that obviously produce different results. This is why we should keep an open mind to ways of studying. Each one has its own methodologies and advantages.

The Theoretical Approach

In the theoretical approach, the interest is in coming up with theories that help to explain how intercultural communication occurs and why it has the results it does. For example, Professor Young Kim from the University of Oklahoma believes that when a person goes to live in another culture or meets someone from another culture, that person experiences stress because of the unknown situation. But that is a good thing because the stress results in adaptation since humans are so able to adapt to new situations. Then the adaptation results in growth of the individual. The better the adaptation, the better the growth. This theory explains how an individual can grow in his/her competence in adapting to new and unfamiliar situations. The central focus is on adaptation as the key component of the communication process.

Another theory is media effects which focuses on the impact on television viewers of the media messages and images that they pay attention to. What happens to people's beliefs and behaviors as they put themselves in the way of selected media messages as compared to those who put themselves under the influence of different messages? Underwood (2006) says, "Uses and gratifications uses to the media emphasize the active use made of media by audience members to seek gratification of a variety of needs. The standard adage is that, where effects research asks 'what do the media do to audiences?', the uses and gratifications approach asks 'what do audiences do with the media?'. Audiences are said to *use* the media to *gratify* needs. The needs most commonly identified are: *surveillance* (i.e. monitoring what's going on in the world), *personal relationships*, *personal identity* and *diversion* (i.e. entertainment and escapism)."

Related to the media is the theory of cultural imperialism. Underwood (2006) claims that *"cultural imperialism* or *media imperialism* is the thesis that 'Western' (especially American) cultural values are being forced on non-Western societies, to which they are spread most especially by the mass media. Herbert Schiller argues forcefully that the US-inspired spread of 'free trade' and 'free speech' since the Second World War has, in view of the imbalance of economic power, worked to the advantage of the US. He quotes a number of official sources which make it clear that the establishment of US economic, military and cultural hegemony was deliberate US policy, which would depend crucially on US dominance of global communications. Schiller argues that the (mostly US-based) transnational media and communications corporations which now span the globe have reached the point where they pose a distinct threat to the sovereignty of the weaker nation-states. Clearly the US are dominant in the export of media products, as well as in the control of news agencies, and, even where the US originals are not purchased, the genres of US TV are closely copied. However, recent reception studies suggest that we cannot simply deduce the acceptance of American values from the prevalence of US media products."

In the area of business management, one of the theories is that if employers provide for an open communicative environment with their employees, giving them "worker's voice," the employees will have a higher degree of satisfaction in their work and be more positively disposed toward management. Related to this is the theory of external and internal rewards which are determinants of worker motivation conceived by Christensen, Rosethlisberger, & Zalesnick (1958). They wanted to be able to make predictions about productivity of workers based upon external reward characteristics that disclose internal reward characteristics.

Connected with rewards theory is the theory of leadership style in management and motivation theories, emphasizing what workers bring to the organization and "the degree of fulfillment one can derive from working in the organization" (Yu, 2000, p. 122). That these theories vary from culture to culture helps explain why some employees have difficulty in adapting to a different cultural work environment when they are assigned to another county. One who is accustomed to having a boss who invites feedback will have difficulty working with management who does not care what the workers think or what unique contributions they can bring to the workplace.

The Practical Approach

In addition to the theoretical approach, there is the practical approach to studying intercultural communication. In this approach the concern is primarily with studying actual cases from the real world in order to understand what is happening. For example, Professor Ken Cushner from Kent State University, offers with his colleague, Richard Brislin, a book (1986) of case situations for students to study what the best response should be in intercultural confrontations. These incidents have been constructed to show the results of responding in different ways to a given situation and how different cultures might choose different responses to the same situation. More on this is given under the topic of training.

The Methodological Approaches

There also are different methodological approaches to studying intercultural communication. This means that students might look at situations in the real world such as observing the process of communication in a different culture to see how the communicators behave, how the recipients respond, how the message gets conveyed, and how the interaction takes place. This is the participant observation approach used in ethnography. An example of personal ethnographic research is found in Mendoza (2005) where she moves in her classroom from a theory of certainty to a what she calls "a theory of challenge" in which students are confronted in transformative encounters.

Another approach is the experimental approach where the scientist sets up a controlled situation to test his/her hypothesis about the factors that are at play in determining a given outcome. The results are submitted to statistical analysis. For example, Fritz, Graf, Hentz, Mollenberg, & Chen (2005) replicated the Chen and Starosta Model of Intercultural Sensitivity to see if they would find the same results as previous researchers found. In this case they did not, which suggests further research is needed. This would be an example of the quantitative approach.

Another approach is content analysis, which is "the statistical analysis of a range of texts. The results are usually compared with a different set of results from the same range of texts - e.g. what proportion of reports about men in the tabloid press represents men as victims and what proportion represents women as victims? - or with some 'objective' standard, such as official statistics - e.g. what proportion of women in soaps is shown as housewives as against the proportion of women in the population who are housewives The most serious problem with content analysis is the initial selection of categories. The second most serious problem is where to find your objective standard" (Underwood, 2006).

The interpretive/critical approach is when the researcher uses his/her skills in interpreting data that need to be analyzed and criticized according to predetermined criteria. An example would be a study of the speeches of President George W. Bush compared with those of Chancellor Angela Merkle to see how each one uses metaphor from his/her own culture to persuade their audiences to believe that it is time to take Iran to the Security Council of the United Nations for considering sanctions for its violation of international agreements. I used this approach when I compared the use of narrative and metaphor in interventionist rhetoric by Margaret Thatcher, Ronald Reagan, Menachem Begin, Francois Mitterrand, and Leonid Brezhnev (Heisey, 1993).

The Training Approach

A final approach for studying intercultural communication is to examine the best ways to train people to engage effectively in communicating with people from other cultures. There are different ways of training that offer different results, depending on the circumstances of a particular situation. Trainers can use simulation techniques, play strategic games that demonstrate how people react in different situations, and set up cultural conditions for decision-making that require people to make choices. These trainers then debrief the participants to discuss the results that occurred and what cultural factors contributed to those results.

One of the well-known training techniques is the Culture General Assimilator by Kenneth Cushner and Richard W. Brislin. They offer 100 scenarios, or "critical incidents," around 18 themes which provide a framework for understanding intercultural interactions and for developing cross-cultural training programs. In these intercultural episodes there is a breakdown in communication. The episode is described and then four alternative answers are offered to explain what happened, and then detailed rationales are provided for why each response was not good or was the effective one. Here is an example, called "Learning the Ropes" (Cushner & Brislin, 1986, 220-222).

> Helen Connor had been working in a Japanese company involved in marketing cameras. She had been there for two years and was well-respected by her colleagues. In fact, she was so respected that she often was asked to work with new employees of the firm as these younger employees "learned the ropes." One recent and young employee, Hideo Tanaka, was assigned to develop a marketing scheme for a new model of camera. He worked quite hard on it, but his scheme was not accepted by his superiors because of industry-wide economic conditions. Helen Connor and Hideo Tanaka happened to be working at nearby desks when the news of the unacceptance was transmitted from company executives. Hideo Tanaka said very little at that point. That evening, however, Helen and Hideo

happened to be at the same bar. Hideo had been drinking and vigorously criticized his superiors at work. Helen concluded that Hideo was a very aggressive Japanese male and that she would have difficulty working with him again in the future.

Which alternative provides an accurate statement about Helen's conclusion?

1. Helen was making an inappropriate judgment about Hideo's traits based on behavior that she observed.

2. Since, in Japan, decorum in public is highly valued, Helen reasonably concluded that Hideo's vigorous criticisms in the bar marks him as a difficult coworker.

3. Company executives had failed to tell Helen and Hideo about economic conditions, and consequently Helen should be upset with the executives, not Hideo.

4. Helen felt that Hideo was attacking her personally.

Cushner and Brislin then provide a detailed rationale for each of the four alternatives, showing why number one was the best response and the other responses were not the best explanation. In this way the authors set up simulated experiences for discussion and deliberation, emphasizing the importance of being sensitive to other cultural situations and conditions.

The intercultural interactions in the Cushner and Brislin guide cover most areas of people's experiences, including a comprehensive list of 18 categories of cross cultural encounters, such as anxiety, prejudice, hierarchies, values, learning styles, and ambiguity. Companies preparing their employees for intercultural assignments do well to invest in training for overseas experience. At the conclusion of this chapter I offer another example of a training program in which I served as one of the presenters.

This variety of approaches provides an opportunity for a group to examine different methods and makes it possible for the participants to experience the different benefits.

Cultural Differences in Languages and Their Use

There are two types of language—verbal and nonverbal. We shall look at each of these to see how different cultures use language to communicate.

Verbal Language

In verbal language, we examine the ways cultures assign meaning to words, symbols, and the rules for using them. Even though we have dictionaries to provide meanings for words, it is more true that the meanings for words reside in the recipient of the message. Meaning is a product of experience, background, and culture. The word "terrorist," for example, might mean "freedom fighter" to one person and "murderer" to another. We can't always be sure how someone may take our words when we use them.

One of the views of language is that language is not only a means of reporting reality but more importantly, it is a means of actually determining what reality is for the speaker. The Sapir-Whorf hypothesis says that language "can be the shaper of one's experience in a given culture" (Wang, 2002, p.101) and helps determine how we perceive the real world. Language gives structure and meaning to what we observe and how we tend to communicate those observations. An example of how the structure of language differs in both Navajo and Chinese is that they have no plural form for words like in English. We say "he has a horse" and "she has three horses" while in Navajo or Mandarin, the structure of the sentence would indicate the plurality, not the form of the word horse or horses.

Another example of how language shapes reality comes from my experience in a former Soviet country. In Tallinn, Estonia, I had the opportunity of teaching a class in rhetorical analysis to a group of students at the Estonian School of Diplomacy. This was in 1992, soon after the fall of the Soviet Union, which, of course, had occupied Estonia from before the beginning of the Second World War. The Estonians were very sensitive to the fact that the Russian language had been forced upon them during this occupation. Now that they were independent, the use of the Russian language remained a controversial issue. The government took steps to soften the requirements for Estonian citizenship so that the many people who had grown up knowing only the Russian language could more easily take the Estonian language test for citizenship. And the government also made the testing of the Estonian language free to senior citizens, students and unemployed.

One of the truly fascinating things I discovered from my students was that in the early days of the independence movement in the late 1980s, the Estonian people used a cultural and historical tradition to communicate their unrest and opposition to the ruling Soviet (Russian) hierarchy. In June 1988 the people engaged in what they called "a singing revolution" that was based upon a tradition of the Estonian people singing together. To see and hear the impact of 30,000 people singing together, my students told me, was truly amazing to the officials. This singing revolution lasted for some time and in June of 1989, a year later, Gorbachev appointed the first Estonian communist leader who spoke to the people in their own Estonian language. Previous leaders had been Russian. There was no blood shed in this singing revolution, but they re-gained their independence, they told me, by singing. In the other Baltic states, Latvia and Lithuania, there had been the use of troops and killings, and they expected it in Estonia, but it never happened. This became a turning point for Estonia and made the independence movement secure from then on. The Estonian example is a striking example of how language can be used to create an independence movement as a symbol and as a reality. I first presented this Estonian example in a paper presented in Seattle, Washington in 2000 (Heisey, 2000b).

Some cultures are more explicit in the way they use words while others are more implicit in the use of words. An example would be the American culture versus the Chinese culture. Americans are more direct and explicit. If an American says to a colleague, "Come on over for a cup of coffee tomorrow," she most likely means this literally. If a Chinese says, "Let's get together to talk," she most likely means simply that she is favorably disposed toward that person and would like to have good relations in the future. She doesn't mean getting together literally.

Let me give an example of how different meanings to symbols made a difference in communication. I was lecturing at Peking University in English in the fall of 1996 and wanted the Chinese students to introduce themselves to the class. Since they had come from different regions of the country, I asked them to come up front and give their name and the province they were from and put an X on the blackboard to identify where their hometown was located on the map of China I had drawn on the board. Interestingly, not one student followed my instruction. They used other symbols or signs but would not use an X. The class monitor later explained to me why. The reason was that they had been brought up in school to associate an X with something that was wrong, or bad and they didn't want to use that symbol for their hometown. This dialogue between my student and me continued throughout the semester and ended with a joint paper we wrote and presented at an international convention on the symbols used in cultural dialogues (Qiu and Heisey, 1997).

When we choose certain words to communicate rather than others it makes a difference because words can offend, stir up emotions, make us laugh, make us cry, and in many ways make an impact on our responses. Words tell us a lot about the person who uses them and about the person who responds to them. Kenneth Burke, the twentieth-century American philosopher of language, said, "Language is the dancing of an attitude" (Burke, 1952). We disclose our attitudes toward the subject we are talking about, toward the listener, and toward ourselves when we talk. And it is good to remember that different cultures use language in different ways to communicate their ideas and feelings. We should be interested in learning how others use meanings for different purposes.

Sometimes language is used to express domination and superiority. Foucault has written much about how discourse exerts power in places we often don't expect. Rabinow (1984) writes, "In asking, 'How does discourse function,?' [Foucault's] aim has been to isolate techniques of power exactly in those places where this kind of analysis is rarely done" (p. 10). Using knowledge and discourse to exert power and influence over others takes on interesting dimensions in different cultures. Cultural imperialism, to be discussed later, where English and technology are used to dominate, is a good example of this. When we live in another country, the host language is dominant.

When we were living in Belgium where I was teaching at the University of Leuven, I had occasion to go the Brussels airport to pick up an air freight package that had been sent to me from home. I went to the counter and asked the clerk in English, since I did not know French, though all official business in Brussels was conducted in French, whether I could pick up my package. He did not pay any attention to me. I repeated my question. He still ignored me. I repeated it again. It was very disconcerting to be ignored by an official when I was there on official business. I kept my cool and after a long time the clerk came over to where I was standing and said, in English, "Are you telling me that you are a professor teaching here in my country and you cannot even speak to me in my own language?" With this appropriate reprimand, I acknowledged that I was deficient and expressed my sincere appreciation that he was getting my package for me. Such an incident underscores how language difference can obstruct effective communication but also be used as an agenda item to communicate certain feelings and attitudes when desired.

Problems of translation are important to consider when we are talking about people from different cultures communicating. One of these is to determine whether the translation is to be taken literally or generally. Some people expect a literal translation while others are satisfied with simply the spirit of the meaning. Another problem is the role of the translator. Does the translator exercise his/her judgment in softening the language used to protect the person from an undesirable response or does the translator actually change the meaning knowing that the original meaning used would be unacceptable in this context?

In addition to problems of directness and indirectness and problems of translation, there are problems of how language is used to communicate emotion versus fact. Some cultures like to use language to share emotional feelings, not just factual information. Of course, all languages have the ability to communicate both of these values but some languages are constructed to lean toward one way or another. Experts suggest that the Arabic language, for example, is conducive to flowery or emotionally laden meanings while English is given to explicit and factual meanings. Hitti claims, "No people in the world, perhaps, manifest such enthusiastic admiration for literary expression and are so moved by the word, spoken or written, as the Arabs" and so enjoy what they call "lawful magic" (Hitti, 1958, p. 90). Poetry and beautiful language are highly valued in Arabic-speaking countries while in English-speaking countries value is placed upon using language in concrete and matter-of-fact ways. Different cultures have different ways of using language to achieve different ends and for different purposes.

Differences in grammatical construction also need to be taken into consideration. In English we have past, present and future in our tenses. In Mandarin, there is no future tense. This suggests that the Chinese way of perceiving reality is more holistic than the Western way. In art, in medicine, in history, and in almost all aspects of life, the Chinese way of looking at something is to look at it as a whole, not in its parts, analyzing a reality into its disparate elements, such as is done in the West with its analytical approach. The Chinese language reflects this difference.

Another difference is in the importance of language for communicating. In China and Japan there is a historical tradition that can be traced to Confucius that puts a lesser importance on public communication and debate than in the West. There is a saying from *The Analects* by Confucius that "Heaven rules without language." This traditionally means that "he who knows does not speak," and "he who speaks does not know." This is why some experts have suggested that Chinese and Japanese students do not enjoy public speaking or easily enter into public debates and hearty argumentation. They are taught to listen to their masters rather than argue with them or confront them with difficult questions. When I was getting ready to go to Beijing to teach, I was told that I would have difficulty getting my students to discuss things in class and to have a lot of interaction like I was used to in my classes in the States. One of my Chinese students in Peking University, when I taught there several years ago, suggested to me that they don't like to engage their professors in dialogue and in expressing their own viewpoints by asking many questions, because the more they, the students, talk, the less time there is for their professors who know much more than they do.

Nonverbal Language

In nonverbal language, meaning is communicated in different channels. Time and space are means of communication as different cultures value these dimensions differently. Edward Hall brought these dimensions to our attention in his books, *The Silent Language* (the use of time) (1959) and *The Hidden Dimension* (the use of space) (1966). The study of the use of time is called chronemics. Orientation toward time, whether personal or societal, is an important consideration when people from different cultures are interacting Though airplanes must run on time and are judged to be better if they do, when it comes to personal behavior, time may take on a different meaning. Societies that emphasize doing one thing at a time, sequentially, are called monochronic. They are oriented toward completing tasks on time and following strict schedules. Polychronic societies emphasize being able to do many things at a time because they feel people are more important than time management. In these cases, personal relationships are considered more valuable than meeting a time schedule. In some cultures promptness is not important. It is perfectly acceptable to show up for an appointment ten or fifteen minutes late. In other cultures this behavior would be considered rude and an affront.

Space also communicates. This is the study of proxemics. Personal space is considered important and in western cultures, people may apologize if they happen to bump into another person while walking, as that person's intimate space has been violated. In some cultures, such as southern European or Latin countries, people stand very close together to talk, while in others, such as northern European or American, they maintain a discrete distance because of respect for personal space. Spatial arrangements of furniture and of objects communicate expectations for people's behavior. When people are asked to sit together around a table for a discussion rather than in rows of chairs, it means people are expected to talk freely with each other rather than direct their talk to a central location down front where a podium stands where one person is expected to talk.

Body language also needs to be considered in intercultural communication. Some cultures are very expressive in the ways people use gestures, hands, and motion while they speak. Some cultures tend to be loud in their talking while others maintain a very low-key volume in speaking, considering it rude to speak loudly in a group. I remember that while we were living in Sweden I was greatly impressed with how quiet people were in public meetings or on the train or bus. Also, high contact cultures tend to use a lot of touch in their speaking while low contact cultures refrain from this behavior. Eye contact differs also from culture to culture as a means of communicating important understandings.

When I was serving as president of a woman's college in Tehran, Iran, the heads of institutions were invited to the palace to meet the Shah of Iran at a ceremony. We all stood in a long line around the huge room while the Shah came to each one to address and be addressed by the delegations. I was told that it was the custom in Iran that when you stand face to face with the Shah one must look down as a sign of respect and not look the Shah directly in the eyes when he was addressing you. I had to make a cultural decision whether to conform to that custom or whether to be myself and behave toward the Shah as my culture suggests—looking a person directly in the eye shows personal respect and interest and attention. I decided that the Shah would understand my Western behavior and would actually expect me to behave as I was used to doing in my own culture. That is what I did and I never heard anything about it (Heisey, 2000b).

Sometimes body language such as a smile can be misinterpreted. Another example from my experience in Iran demonstrates this. The early stages of the Islamic revolution were beginning to be felt before we left in late 1978. Our college was holding a celebration ceremony on the campus to honor the unveiling of women. As part of this occasion, an older woman was showing the young students what the earlier chador looked like and was holding it up and trying it on one the students for all to see. A photographer's picture of the occasion published in the paper the next day showed the scene but one of the faculty members happened to be behind the women holding up the chador and her face was smiling. A local cleric interpreted the photo as an occasion where the chador was being ridiculed and made light of and was gravely offended. The college received a call with a threat that if an apology were not issued, the college would be closed down, not by the government which supported the college, but by the clerics.

I immediately contacted the government because the matter had considerable implications. The Shah's government supported the liberation of women and celebrating the unveiling of women was something they were not going to back down on. We had to go back and forth with the government's ministry of education officials in order to come up with language that would be acceptable to both the government's position of not apologizing and the clerics' position of apologizing. We finally managed it by taking the position that we were sorry for any misinterpretation that may have occurred in the publishing of the photo. This was one of the most delicate negotiation matters I have ever experienced—all based on the conflict of cultures expressed in linguistic form (Heisey, 2000b).

Sometimes vocal communication, beyond the words used, called paralanguage, says things that add to the meaning of the message. Vocal intonations, accents, voice tempo, resonance, range, intensity, and pitch, all serve as qualifiers that add meaning to the use of the voice. A study was reported at my university some years ago that found that TV talk show hosts actually defer to or direct their guests simply by using their voices with their intonations. Different cultures have different ways of expressing themselves in the sounds they use.

When I was visiting Sweden on one occasion, I happened to be standing next to a Swedish woman waiting to be served lunch at an international conference. As we were talking together very casually, I noticed that she often would give a vocal sound (like drawing in the breath) at the ends of her sentences that sounded different to my ears. I had noticed it also in other Swedes I had heard speaking. I decided to get bold and express an interest in this vocalization. I asked her if I could ask a question about her speaking. She said yes, so I asked her what that vocal sound meant. She said, "What vocal sound?" It was so much a part of her speaking that she did not know what I was talking about. I tried to mimic it for her and then she caught on. She said that no one had ever asked about that before. Further, she said it was very interesting to her that I would have the nerve to ask her about such a vocalization. She said the sound meant something like "yes," or "don't you see."

What happened as a result of my inquiry was that we struck up a closer relationship at that international conference and she ended up showing me around town, including the place where she does her research and giving me more information about her research on the importance of proper physical climate in the workplace. This contact then led to her joining my intercultural workshop in England the next summer and her inviting my university to send a workshop of students and faculty to her university the following summer. This led to a faculty exchange program between our two universities a couple years later. I share this story to suggest that in intercultural communication experiences, sometimes it is well to explore differences as a way of showing interest and an attitude of openness and learning from the other.

Related to sounds in nonverbal communication is the opposite—silence. Silence can be a powerful nonverbal means of communication that different cultures use differently. In interpersonal, small group, or social contexts, silence can be used to gain attention and control, demonstrate superiority and authority, and indicate reserve, disapproval and uncooperativeness. Indirect societies often use silence to show disapproval without having to say the word "no." Direct cultures would be more likely to use the language of "No, I don't agree with that." Silence is a softer way of saying the same thing. Then, too, silence may be used to show power. Ishii and Bruneau in their article on silence as viewed by Japanese and American, say, "Contrary to outspoken and often ego-driven Western women (even the milder ones), many women in Eastern cultures view their silent roles as very powerful.... There is a power of control in silence and in the outward show of reticence" (Ishii & Bruneau, 1988, p. 311).

It is important to learn the different ways that cultures communicate verbally and nonverbally and to observe ways in which they are similar. Ting-Toomey (1999) claims that "the core concepts of the intercultural communication process" are "cultural values," the features and functions of "language" and of "nonverbal communication." She continues, "While language is the key to the heart of a culture, nonverbal communication is the heartbeat of a culture" (p. viii).

Cultural Differences in Assumptions

The assumptions that different cultures hold and that play an important part in human interaction need to be examined. These assumptions are their values, their beliefs, and their perceptions. One of the most important ways that cultures communicate is with the expression of their values. Much research has been completed in this regard and we can learn much from the findings of these studies.

In Values

Cultural values were found to be important factors in the shaping of workers' motivations in China (Yu, 2000). He interviewed many factory workers there and concluded, "Strong interpersonal relationships in organizations not only make relationship partners more satisfied about their organizational life, but, more importantly, such relationships cultivate mutual obligation or indebtedness between relationship partners and stipulate the efforts of employees to accomplish organizational tasks." He found that obligations and indebtedness go together and interconnectedness and loyalty go together (p. 133). These cultural values add to our understanding of what motivates employees to perform their organizational tasks well in China. Yu argues that more research should be engaged to determine if other cultural values are at work in other cultures.

An important study by Hofstede (1980), the Dutch social scientist, was one where the researchers interviewed the workers in many different countries and found that they held values that differed. One of these was the continuum of individualism and collectivism. Countries that tend toward individualism, such as the United States, value much more the importance of thinking and behaving in ways that are important to that individual, not to the family or group or community. The personal thoughts and valuing the individual rights of that person are paramount. In collectivist societies, such as in China, the importance is placed on what the family or community thinks and thus conformity to those values is expected.

A powerful example of this difference was made clear to my wife and me in 1978 when we were one of the first groups of visitors to China, just two years following the death of Mao Zedong. When we visited a school room on one occasion, we asked the children what they wanted to be when they grew up. The answer given was, "Whatever the party wants me to be." This answer of course demonstrates a political climate as well as a cultural one, and the students we talk to today in China have an entirely different answer, showing that economic interests are now paramount. When we asked university students in 2000 what they wanted to do upon graduation, the answer was, "We want to get a good-paying job that uses our talents best." Many of them asked me to write letters of recommendation for their applications to get into American graduate schools in order to earn an advanced degree and thus improve their credentials for obtaining a high-level job. This suggests part of the change in some values that is taking place in China since the drive to economic reform has been a priority for the government.

Another value that needs to be considered is power distance identified by Hofstede (1980). Some cultures are very comfortable with a great power distance between employer and employee, meaning a high degree of inequality. The boss has complete control and authority over the workers without any input from them and little communication. Other cultures are not comfortable with this relationship and demand a short power distance between boss and worker. The worker wants to make input into his/her job and have a stake in the decision-making process. If the cultural climate in the society and in the particular organization encourages this, we call this an example of small power distance which makes a difference in the communication process between management and subordinates. He, Zhu, & Peng used the power distance value as one of the factors they studied in joint ventures in China to predict worker preferences for certain styles of conflict resolution (2002).

In Beliefs

Kluckhohn and Strodtbeck (1961) have argued that cultures have different beliefs about innate human nature, as to whether humans are basically evil, good, or evil and good. Then there is the belief in the relationship between humans and nature, whether humans are to be subject to nature, in harmony with, or be master over. Also, they claim that some cultures tend to believe more in an orientation toward the future, such as the United States, where the emphasis is on the future for progress, advancement, and improvement, not looking back. Other cultures are more oriented toward believing in the past and are interested in stressing the importance of history. Sometimes China is given as an example of this orientation.

Of course it is more likely that a country with thousands of years of history will emphasize its past more than one that is only a couple hundred years old. Whether one values more the past than the future depends upon a number of factors and the context of the situation. Even in the United States where future time and progress are highly valued, in the legal profession at the level of appeals courts and the Supreme Court, historical precedent is believed in to help guide the decision-making process in any given case. And in China, now the government and the people believe that economic reform should be highly valued, with progress and future advancement taking on more importance at the present time. The important point is that when we interact with and examine other cultures, we need to be careful to consider the beliefs toward which they are oriented compared with those of our own.

In Perceptions

Finally, perceptions of reality differ from culture to culture. We have already suggested that language plays a part in the way we see the world. As previously discussed, some cultures tend to see the world through the eyes of synthesis, emphasizing the importance of seeing things as a whole and as being related to each other in inseparable ways. Other cultures tend to see the world through the eyes of analysis, emphasizing the importance of analyzing things into their important individual components. Americans are known for their analytical skills and the Chinese are known for their synthesizing skills (Guan, 2000, p. 34). If one views reality from one of these orientations, it makes a difference when communicating with someone from the other orientation. Guan gives examples of the Chinese orientation in terms of traditional medicine where the whole body is taken into consideration rather than simply the individual part or organ under scrutiny. Another example Guan gives is the unique Peking Opera where the artistry is based on a whole scheme of integrated performances, such as singing, reciting, dancing, and fighting, unlike anything in the West (Guan, 2000, p. 35). A study by Xiao and Heisey (2005) concludes, as well, that Peking Opera, such as Tian Xian Pei, demonstrates "the Chinese holistic and interconnected view of reality" (p. 197).

One of the interesting phenomena in perception is the way we see ourselves in having certain cultural personality characteristics. When I was teaching at Peking University in the fall of 2000, I asked my Chinese graduate students how they saw themselves versus Americans as far as personality characteristics were concerned. I invited them to write down the characteristics they saw in Americans and then in Chinese people. The terms they used to describe Americans were "friendly," "curiosity," "independent," "self-content," "aggressive," "creative," and "talk straight." The terms for Chinese were "hard-working," "responsible," "industrious," "conservative," "harmony," "sensitive," "cautious," and "afraid of being different." Perceptions of personality characteristics in other cultures often end up being stereotypes that can impact communication interaction.

Cultural Differences in Specific Contexts

We will now look at selected contexts in which cultural differences may be observed. It is important to understand these differences and to become knowledgeable of how cultures view these.

In Media

The ways in which different cultures view and use the media should be considered in understanding intercultural communication. Freedom of the press is an important value in the United States as well as in other Western countries. The media depend upon this value for the expression, expansion, and success of their products—information and entertainment. Some countries have more restrictions on this freedom than others, depending upon how free they want their citizens and their media to be. With the coming of modern technology and the Internet, many problems arise in the meaning of this value and its implications. One of the problems is the dominance of one cultural expression over another. Globalization makes it easier for some cultures to share their values and products with others when they have the means and technological advances. This can result in cultural imperialism and domination, as suggested earlier.

Intercultural communicators should be knowledgeable of the role of the media in transformation of societies. One of the important roles the media play in cultural transformation is agenda setting. The media produce what they consider to be important and what will be accepted by the consumer. Chan and Ma (2002), referenced earlier, argue that this confrontation can be a good thing. "Encounters of distinct cultures can result in creative confrontations that may lead to cultural blending and recreation. Associated with the transcultural perspective is a concern with the ideas of cultural mixing and hybridization, rather than with direct cultural imposition from the West. During transculturation, modernity or other values are essentialized, appropriated, transfigured, decontextualized an recontextualized" (Chan and Ma, 2002, p.14).

In Negotiation and Managing Conflict

Cultures also differ in the ways in which they negotiate and manage conflict. Societies that are more direct in the way they communicate are more likely to be confrontational in conflict situations. Avoiding controversy is a mark of an indirect society. For example, the Chinese society values harmony over directness in communication. According to Chen (2002), "In order to pursue conflict-free interaction, Chinese have developed five communication rules that are regulated by the principles of ren, yi, and li: self-restraint-self-discipline, indirect expression of disapproval, saving or making face for counterparts, reciprocity, and the emphasis on particularistic relationships" (p. 8). These principles enable the Chinese to manage conflict in accord with their overriding value of harmony. Western communicators do not have harmony as the core value of their society, so they have developed different rules governing conflict management.

Emphasis on relationships are well-recognized in Chinese circles and are important in negotiations. When it comes to international relationships, other considerations need to be taken into account. Cai and Waks (2002) remind us, "Yet the commitment to interpersonal relationships within Chinese society may not translate to relationships across national boundaries. On one hand, Chinese negotiators may actually trust their foreign counterparts more than people from their own country, because of a reverence for foreigners and foreign products. But on the other hand, the benefits and commitments to in-group relationships may not apply to international partners" (p. 187).

Conflict can be examined from a societal viewpoint as well. How is conflict used by leaders to achieve their political ends? Social and political movements, such as the Anti-Slavery Movement and the Civil Rights Movement in the United States, the Islamic Revolution in Iran, and other important movements, offer fascinating examples of how political leaders use conflict to achieve their ends. What is important to cultures in how their leaders manage and use conflict may be seen emerging from a study of these cultural movements.

The study by Heisey and Trebing (1983) on the contrast between the Islamic Revolution by the Ayatollah and the White Revolution by the Shah of Iran is a stark example of how a leader used conflict with the authority in power by asserting a different, religious authority to gain the support of the people to overthrow the Shah. The Ayatollah was so able to identify the Shah's government with the evils of the West that it was rejected by the clerics and the people. What political leaders do in their countries, organizational leaders are sometimes able to do in their companies when they try to identify certain managers with negative consequences in order to remove them.

In Responding to Culture Shock

Responding to culture shock is a phenomenon that differs from culture to culture. The primary dimension of culture shock is the psychological reaction to different expectations and unexpected circumstances, rendering the person incapable of maintaining an equilibrium. Culture shock usually begins with the first reaction to the new culture being a touch of euphoria because everything is so new and different and exciting. As this wears off and experiences catapult upon the person, the feeling of being overwhelmed and incapable of taking it all in comes over one, causing a type of depression. After a period of negative reactions, then more and more understanding and acceptance take place which rehabilitates the person somewhat.

The degree of preparation for going to the new culture makes the difference in the ability to absorb the culture shock. This preparation can be in terms of information about the new country, information about what is to be expected about the job, and understanding about how to adapt to the new situations. This is why it is important for companies to prepare their employees adequately when being assigned to a position overseas. Being aware of the differences they can expect in language use, in values, in emotional expression, in how they respond to conflict, and in how business management is handled can be crucial in preparation.

In Constructing Cultural Identity

The concept of cultural identity is important to examine. We have all grown up thinking of ourselves in certain ways. We have a conception of who we are that was constructed out of our experiences in the family as we were growing up, in our schooling, and in the ways our society influenced us in shaping our attitudes and values. What is more true, however, is that we all have multiple identities, depending upon the situations we are in. As a male who is married, I see myself as a husband, as a father to my three sons, as a brother to my siblings, as a teacher who has been a mentor to my students, and as a friend to the people from other cultures whom I have met. We play different roles in different situations where different people are engaged. When I was greeting the Shah of Iran in his palace, I was subordinate to the king. When I met a student in my office who was requesting that I talk to a teacher to have her change her grade in that course so that she would be able to graduate, I was a superior who had the power to order a teacher to change a grade, so she thought. As a westerner, I was a guest in the country of these people and I was there to learn from them as much as I was there to share my expertise in their educational setting. These attitudes helped to shape how I reacted to their ideas, to their behaviors, and to their requests. I was changed by them in my attitudes and beliefs about them and their culture and thus was engaged in a process of identity modification.

Whenever people encounter other cultures, this process of identity modification takes place. We should view this process positively and look for ways in which we can absorb what is valuable and helpful to us in our growing understanding of others. Gudykunst and Kim (1984) offer a view of the "stranger" as one who has "face-to-face contact with the group for the first time" and thus has "the contradictory qualities of being near and far at the same time" (p. 19). This near and far perspective has the advantage of making the concept of distance a positive characteristic. We can see things differently when we get close and when we are far away.

In Acculturation and Developing Intercultural Communication Competence

A final concept of intercultural communication in contexts is the notion of achieving acculturation and becoming a multicultural person in the world of globalization. As leaders in business, in education, in government, in diplomacy, in medicine, or in religion, persons who are required to enter into intercultural encounters should be aware of the process of acculturation. This means having the ability to negotiate different cultures with grace and confidence without losing one's own identity. We call this ability having intercultural or multicultural communication compentence. Most researchers believe that this competence includes at least three things: knowledge, motivation, and behavior.

Competent multicultural persons possess adequate knowledge of interaction rules for the host country, language structure and vocabulary, culture specific information, history, cognitive styles, and cultural assumptions of the host country. Motivation refers to the attitudes, sensitivity, and awareness of the person toward the other culture. Being able to break out of one's own ethnocentrism and being able to consider other cultures as different but not inferior are important perceptions that help mold motivation. Behavior refers to the skills development in managing transitions, demonstrating survival skills, functioning according to the new cultural norms, dealing with ambiguity, displaying respect and tolerance and flexibility and empathy. One word that sums up most of what is meant by behavior is mindful. Being mindful in the new culture suggests that the person is attentive, responsive, and adaptive to everything that is encountered.

Conclusion

As a way of concluding this chapter, I offer an example of how one international corporation joined with the Business College of a local university to engage in a training program to improve cross cultural communication practices. I was personally involved as one of the experts. Bioproducts, Inc., of Ohio, sent 20 of its managers and executives to a week-long seminar to learn about global business strategies and intercultural communication for becoming more competitive in a global world. Each manager began by completing a personal inventory to obtain a self-assessment of personal skills and knowledge in the following topic areas: change management, cross cultural communication, relationship building, global ethics, leading globally, global strategy, global economics, and competitive intelligence. After listening to experts from the university in an interactive-lecture-learning environment for four days on these same topics, the group was addressed by university multicultural experts who represented each of the four countries to give a first-person background for that country.

On the final day the company managers were divided into four country teams (Japan, UK, Netherlands, and Egypt). Each of these country teams of four managers then prepared a public presentation to give to a Team Global Acquisition group who would decide which country team made the best case for its beginning a development program in that country. In this presentation the team was to present compelling reasons why that nation should be the selected choice for development. The team from the UK, for example, discussed its short-term and long-term objectives, identified the relevant factors that should be considered by the Team Global Acquisition group in making their decision. These factors were environmental, time, action-doing, space, power, individualism, competitiveness, thinking and structure. The team concluded with the economic benefits of sales cycle reduction and greater profits sooner that would result from a proper process of acculturation and adaptation by the development program being proposed.

In this global presentation program, the judging team, consisting of nine persons combined from the Bioproducts company and from the university, made its decision as to which country team had done the best job and why, of making its case for development in that country. A debriefing of the whole "game" experience emphasized the importance of considering the learning factors of being able (1) "to walk in the other nation's shoes," (2) to use an empathetic viewpoint to understand the strengths and advantages of each nation, and (3) to utilize the strength of first person multicultural expertise.

A good example of this type of empathic and multicultural approach may be seen in a joint venture in China as described by Tai Ping Chen, a Beijing business man now self-employed as an international business executive in New York. He reports that the Little Swan corporation was one of the largest automatic washing machine manufacturers in China. It had 58 stores around the country with many subsidiary markets and a market share of 40% in ten years. Siemens Germany noticed this point with importance, and decided to create a new joint venture with Little Swan, keeping the successful brand name. It bought 20% of the shares and made good profits. Chen writes, "The Chinese local manager showed good understanding of advanced management principles, and good leadership ability. Using more local persons in the joint venture than others had done, along with more foreign expertise and investment, it applied a localization policy in order to remove the conflicts between Chinese and Western culture. The locals and foreign investors worked together to create a new Over-pass culture." This "over-pass culture" produced cooperation, Chen concludes, and "resulted in increased tangible assets, thus making a proper joint venture, with good results for both sides" (Chen, 1999, p. 9)

Global companies wishing to improve their market share may want to consider using the principles discussed in this chapter. Perhaps the human resources department would want to have its groups develop their own projects of constructing a "strategic and creative game" for experiencing cross cultural communication for working effectively and competing successfully in a global world.

References

Burke, K. (1952), *The rhetoric of motives.* New York: Prentice-Hall.
Cai, D. A. & Waks, L. (2002). What we still need to know about Chinese negotiation. In W. Jia, X. Lu, & D. R. Heisey (eds.), *Chinese communication theory and research: Reflections, new frontiers, and new directions* (pp.177-193). Westport, CT: Ablex.
Cushner, K. & Brislin, R. (1986). *Intercultural interactions: A practical guide.* Thousand Oaks, CA: Sage.

Chan, J. M. & McIntyre, B. T. (2002) (eds.). *In search of boundaries: Communication, nation-states and cultural identities.* Westport, CT: Ablex.

Chen, G. M. & Ma, R. (2002) (eds.). *Chinese conflict management and resolution.* Westport, CT: Ablex.

Chen, T. P. (1999). Chinese approaches to resolving conflicts in joint ventures: Chinese and Western joint ventures. Paper presented at the National Communication Association convention, Chicago, November.

Christensen, C. R., Rusethlisberger, F. J., & Zaleznik, A. (1958). The motivation, productivity, and satisfaction of workers: A predictive study. Boston: Harvard Business School Press.

Fritz, W., Graf, A., Hentze, J., Mollenberg, A., & Chen, G. M. (2005). An examination of Chen and Starosta's Model of Intercultural Sensitivity in Germany and the United States. *Intercultural Communication Studies, XIV:1*, 53-65.

Ge, X. (1996). An application of Kenneth Burke's dramatistic order in analyzing China's Cultural Revolution. Paper presented to D. R. Heisey's Peking University intercultural communication class.

Guan, S. (2000). A comparison of Sino-American thinking patterns and the function of Chinese characters in the difference. In D. R. Heisey (ed.), *Chinese perspectives in rhetoric and communication* (pp. 25-44). Stamford, CT: Ablex.

Gudykunst, W. B. & Kim. Y. Y. (1984) *Communicating with strangers.* New York: Random House.

Hall, E. T. (1959). *The silent language.* New York: Prentice-Hall.

Hall, E. T. (1966). *The hidden dimension.* New York: Prentice-Hall.

He, Z., Zhu, J. H., & Peng, S. (2002). Cultural values and conflict resolution in enterprises in diverse cultural settings in China. In G. M. Chen & R. Ma (eds.), *Chinese conflict management and resolution* (pp. 129-147). Westport, CT: Ablex.

Heisey, D. R. (1993). The strategy of narrative and metaphor in interventionist rhetoric: International case studies. In David Zarefsky (ed.), *Rhetorical movement: Essays in honor of Leland M. Griffin* (pp. 186-209, 253-256). Evanston, IL: Northwestern University Press.

Heisey, D. R. (2000a). Global communication and human understanding. In G. M. Chen & William Starosta, *Communication and Global Society* (pp.193-214). New York: Peter Lang.

Heisey, D. R. (2000b). Language difference as a key component in intercultural communication. Paper presented at the National Communication Association convention, Seattle, WA, November.

Heisey, D. R. & Trebing, J. D. (1983). A comparison of the rhetorical visions and strategies of the Shah's White Revolution and the Ayatollah's Islamic

Revolution. *Communication Monographs, 50*, 158-174.

Hitti, P. K. (1958). *History of the Arabs*, quoted in Anwar G. Chejne, "Arabic: Its Significance and Place in Arab-Muslim Society," *The Middle East Journal, XIX*, 449.

Hofstede, G. (1980). *Culture's consequences: International differences in work-related values*. Beverly Hills, CA: Sage.

Ishii, S. & Bruneau, T. (1988). Silence and silences in cross-cultural perspective: Japan and the United States. In Larry A. Samovar & Richard E. Porter (eds.), *Intercultural communication: A reader* (pp. 310-315). Fifth edition. Belmont, CA: Wadsworth.

Kluckhohn, F. R. & Strodtbeck, F. L. (1961). *Variations in value orientations*. Evanston, IL: Row, Peterson.

Mendoza, S. L. (2005). From a theory of certainty to a theory of challenge: Ethnography of an intercultural communication class. *Intercultural Communication Studies, XIV:1*, 82-99.

Qiu, L. & Heisey, D. R. (1997). American-Chinese serendipity dialogues in intercultural communication. Paper presented at the National Communication Association convention. Chicago, Illinois, November.

Rabinow, P. (1984) (ed.). *The Foucault reader by Michel Foucault*. New York: Pantheon.

Ting-Toomey, S. (1999). *Communicating across cultures*. New York: The Guilford Press.

Underwood, R. (2006). *Communication, culture and media studies*. Available: www.ccms-infobase.com.

Wang, M. L. (2002). Humanism and human rights: A comparison between the Occidental and Oriental traditions. In X. Lu, W. Jia, & D. R. Heisey (eds.), *Chinese communication studies: Contexts and comparisons* (pp. 181-196). Westport, CT: Ablex.

Xiao, X. & Heisey, D. R. (2005). Shifting the perfomative characteristics of opera and the status quo for women in China. In Laura Lengel (ed.). *Intercultural communication and creative practice: Music, dance, and women's cultural identity* (pp. 199-210). Westport, CT: Praeger.

Yu, X. (2000), Examining the impact of cultural values and cultural assumptions on motivational factors in the Chinese organizational context: A cross-cultural perspective. In D. R. Heisey (ed.), Chinese perspectives in rhetoric and communication (pp. 119-138). Stamford, CT: Ablex.

Introduction to

A Review of the Concept of Intercultural Effectiveness

By Guo-Ming Chen

Chen notes that while scholars have studied the concept of intercultural communication competence for decades, conceptual ambiguity and operational inconsistency continue to plague this line of research. According to Chen, intercultural communication competence consists of three interrelated concepts: intercultural sensitivity, intercultural awareness, and intercultural effectiveness/ adroitness. He goes on to point out that even though these three dimensions are closely related, they represent three independent concepts. Unfortunately, it is these distinct, though related, concepts that most research usually mingles without clearly distinguishing these three dimensions from one another. Chen states that intercultural sensitivity is the affective aspect of intercultural communication competence, referring to the development of a readiness to understand and appreciate cultural differences in intercultural communication. Intercultural awareness is the cognitive aspect of intercultural communication competence referring to the understanding of cultural conventions that affect how people think and behave. And intercultural effectiveness/adroitness refers to the cognitive ability, or intercultural awareness, and the affective ability, or intercultural sensitivity, which individuals need to have in order to make accurate judgments of the communication exchange and further infuse these abilities to the behavioral level of interaction depending on different cultural contexts in order to achieve communication goals effectively and appropriately.

Chen makes this distinction of effectiveness and appropriateness because he points out that people can be effective in their communication by, for example, coercing or forcing others to carry out a particular action in a Machiavellian style while appropriateness refers to understanding situations and their requirement. Appropriateness is particularly important in intercultural communication because a culture always posses a very rigid and distinct set of cultural rules that stipulates how its members should think and act based on its belief and value system. Thus, to speak or act appropriately in intercultural communication requires interactants to be familiar with their counterparts' cultural rules and be able to project positive emotion that show acknowledgment, respect, or acceptance of cultural differences. Hence, effectiveness and appropriateness are the two sides of a coin, according to Chen, which is why adroitness is a better term to describe this concept. So while all three concepts, i.e. intercultural awareness, sensitivity, and effectiveness, are closely related concepts, they must be clearly distinguished in order to fully understand the concept of intercultural communication competence. Chen proceeds to propose five dimensions of intercultural effectiveness/adroitness: Message skills, interaction management, behavioral flexibility, identity management, and relationship cultivation. While these dimensions seem to be universal in human communication, the emphasis or the culturally acceptable components for each dimension may vary due to cultural differences. Chen calls for detailed research in this field.

This text is clearly of interest to any business organization that has contact with intercultural communication in any number of contexts, whether it be marketing or human resource management, where these observations would need to be considered.

Michael B. Hinner

Guo-Ming Chen is Professor of Communication at the University of Rhode Island, USA. Chen was the founding president of the Association for Chinese Communication Studies. He was the recipient of the 1987 outstanding dissertation award presented by the NCA International and Intercultural Communication Division. He served as Chair of the ECA Intercultural Communication Interest Group and at-large member of the SCA Legislative Council. His primary research interests include intercultural/organizational/ global communication and Chinese communication behaviors. Chen has published numerous papers, book chapters, and essays. He has also (co)authored and (co)edited more than 20 books and journal special issues, including *Foundations of Intercultural Communication, Communication and Global Society,* and *Chinese Conflict Management and Resolution.* Chen also served as the co-editor of *International and Intercultural Communication Annual,* 2003-2005.

A Review of the Concept of Intercultural Effectiveness

Guo-Ming Chen

The rapid globalizing trend has strongly demanded people to acquire the ability of intercultural communication competence in order to promote a peaceful and successful life in the new millennium. Scholars in different disciplines have begun to study the concept for decades, unfortunately conceptual ambiguity and operational inconsistency continue to plague this line of research. In an effort to improve the problem, this paper focuses on the examination of the behavioral aspect, i.e., intercultural effectiveness/adroitness, of intercultural communication competence. In addition to clarifying differences of the three dimensions of intercultural communication competence, this paper defines the meaning of intercultural effectiveness/adroitness, delineates its dimensions and components, and further provides directions for future research. It is hoped that through this effort, the concept of intercultural effectiveness can be demystified and further contribution can be made to improve the understanding of intercultural communication competence in the globalizing society.

A Review of the Concept of Intercultural Effectiveness

We live in time of rapid change. The change will continue for years ahead and its complexity will increase due to the on-going development of technology, globalization of economy, widespread population migration, and the emergence of multiculturalism or cultural diversity in modern societies. The development expedites the pace of globalization which impacts every aspect of human life and has made the world smaller. Globalization continues to redefine our identity in workplace, at home, and other arenas of our life by breaking down the stereotypical roles we played at previous weeks or years. Moreover, globalization demands a community where people of different cultural backgrounds must learn to be interdependent in order to survive. As a result, the need for intercultural communication competence in the globalizing society becomes indispensable for a peaceful and successful life in the new millennium (Chen 2000; Chen & Starosta, 2005).

Intercultural communication competence can be conceptualized as the ability to effectively and appropriately achieve one's goal by executing communication behaviors to negotiate both interactants' identity in a culturally diverse environment (Chen & Starosta, 1996). In other words, interculturally competent persons know how to elicit a desired response in interaction and to fulfill their own communication goals by respecting and affirming the worldview and cultural identities of the interactants. It is the ability to effectively and appropriately acknowledge, respect, tolerate, and integrate cultural differences that qualifies us for enlightened global citizenship. Chen and Starosta (1996) indicated that intercultural communication competence comprises three interrelated concepts: intercultural sensitivity, intercultural awareness, and intercultural effectiveness/adroitness.

Although the three dimensions of intercultural communication competence are closely related, they represent three independent concepts. Unfortunately, most research tends to mingle them without clearly distinguishing them from one another. Chen and Starosta (1997, 2000, 2003), in addition to criticizing the problem of conceptual ambiguity and confusion in the research of intercultural communication competence, have separately explored intercultural sensitivity and intercultural awareness in a great depth.

Intercultural sensitivity is the affective aspect of intercultural communication competence, referring to the development of a readiness to understand and appreciate cultural differences in intercultural communication. The concept focuses on one's emotions that are caused by particular situations, people, or environment (Triandis, 1977). With the readiness of dealing with cultural differences, interculturally sensitive persons are capable of projecting and receiving positive emotional responses in the process of interaction. Chen and Starosta (1997, 2000) and Fritz, Mollenberg, and Chen (2002) indicated that in order to foster a positive emotion for acknowledging, appreciating, and respecting cultural differences, an interculturally sensitive person must possess five personal attributes: (1) Self-esteem – to be able to show optimistic outlook and confidence in intercultural interaction. (2) Self-monitoring – to be able to consciously regulate one's behaviors in response to situational constraints in intercultural interaction. (3) Open-mindedness – to be able to openly and appropriately explain oneself and accept one's counterpart's explanation in intercultural interaction. (4) Empathy – to be able to project oneself to another person's point of view and to demonstrate reciprocity of affect displays and active listening in order to show understanding in intercultural interaction. And (5) Suspending judgment – to be able to avoid rash judgment about one's counterpart's inputs and foster a feeling of enjoyment of cultural differences in intercultural interaction.

Intercultural awareness is the cognitive aspect of intercultural communication competence referring to the understanding of cultural conventions that affect how we think and behave. In other words, intercultural awareness is a process of attitudinally internalizing insights about a group's predominant values, attitudes, and beliefs that dictate members' behaviors. It is the ability to draw an accurate "cultural map" (Kluckhohn, 1948), to sort out the "cultural theme" (Turner, 1968), or to understand "cultural grammars" (Colby, 1975).

The process of intercultural awareness is evolving in three stages (Hanvey, 1987). The first stage is to be aware of the superficial cultural traits that show the most visible characteristics of a culture and its people. The second stage is to be aware of significant and subtle cultural traits that contrast with ours. This stage includes two phases with the first approaches intercultural awareness through culture conflict situation and second through intellectual analysis. The last stage is to be aware of how another culture feels from the insider's perspective or empathy ability. Chen and Starosta (1998-9) pointed out that the main components that comprise "cultural map", "cultural theme", or "cultural grammars" include basic factual information and deep structured cultural values. The authors further identified models from Parsons (1951), Kluckhohn and Strodbeck (1961), Condon and Yousef (1975), Hall (1976), and Hofstede (1983, 1984) that can be used to study intercultural awareness.

Because no existing studies have been done to clarify the concept of "intercultural effectiveness", this paper aims to continue this line of research by demystifying the concept from four aspects: (1) Conceptualization of intercultural effectiveness, (2) intercultural effectiveness and intercultural training, (3) dimensions and components of intercultural effectiveness, and (4) discussion and directions for future research.

Conceptualization of Intercultural Effectiveness

Since half century ago, scholars in psychology and other disciplines have discussed the concept of effectiveness when trying to define the meaning of competence. For example, Foote and Cottrell (1955) conceptualized interpersonal competence as the acquired ability for effective interaction, and White (1959) considered competence as an inherent ability to interact effectively with its environment. The difference between the two is that Foote and Cottrell treated the "effectiveness" of interaction as a learning ability which is increased through socialization either by manipulation or incident; while White treated it as an organism's capacity which can be reached through behaviors instigated by drives in their own right.

Later, Weinstein (1969) extended the meaning of competence to include, in addition to the ability to control the responses of one's counterpart, one's ability to accomplish tasks. In other words, interaction effectiveness is comprised of two elements: manipulation and goal orientation. Moreover, this effective ability should be observable and recognized by one's counterpart (Bochner & Kelly, 1974). Bochner and Kelly (1974) also proposed another critical concept to delineate the meaning of interpersonal competence: appropriateness. A competent person not only is able to effectively formulate and achieve communication objectives and to effectively collaborate with others, but also need to appropriately adapt to situational or environmental variations.

The distinction between "effectiveness" and "appropriateness" is critical in understanding the meaning of communication competence. Individuals might be able to effectively achieve their goals or objectives in interaction by using an inappropriate or unacceptable means, such as using the Machiavellian style. Thus, "effectiveness" only represents one side of the coin of communication competence which refers to getting one wishes to get in the process of interaction, or in Phillips' (1983) words, is the "ability to accomplish specific goals" (p.33), and this ability requires behavioral skills to meet communication requirements.

"Appropriateness" refers to understanding situations and their requirements. It is the ability to maintain "the face and line of his fellow interactants within the constraints of the situation" (Wiemann, 1977, p. 198). As a result, appropriateness becomes the indispensable ability to regulate one's effective behaviors in order to be accounted as being competent. Wiemann and Backlund (1980) further stipulated that appropriateness generally refers to the ability of an individual to meet the basic contextual requirements of the situation in the process of communication, and these contextual requirements include: "(1) The verbal context, that is, making sense in terms of wording, of statements, and of topic; (2) The relationship context, that is, the structuring, type and style of messages so that they are consonant with the particular relationship at hand; and (3) The environmental context, that is, the consideration of constraints imposed on message making by the symbolic and physical environments" (p. 191).

Trenholm and Rose (1981) also pointed out that in order to recognize how context constrains communication or how to act and speak appropriately, an individual must understand that "different situations give rise to different sets of rules; compliance and noncompliance separate those who 'belong' from those who do not 'fit in'" (p. 13). More specifically, being appropriate in interaction is embedded in four elements: quantity, quality, relevancy, and manner (Allen & Wood, 1978). Quantity refers to saying just enough; quality refers to not saying something that's false; relevance refers to relating one's contribution to the topic and situation; and manner refers to being clear about one is saying.

Appropriateness is especially important in intercultural communication, because a culture always possess a very rigid and distinct set of cultural rules that stipulates how its members should think and act based on its belief and value systems. A single response in intercultural communication setting might lead to an unnecessarily abrasive, intense, or bizarre outcome that results in negative consequences due to the violation of cultural rule.

Thus, to speak or act appropriately in intercultural communication requires interactants to be familiar with their counterparts' cultural rules and be able to project positive emotion that show acknowledgment, respect, or acceptance of cultural differences. That is, the foundation of appropriate intercultural communication is built on the basis of intercultural awareness and intercultural sensitivity. Therefore, as indicated previously, although intercultural awareness, intercultural sensitivity, and intercultural effectiveness are three closely related concepts, they must be clearly distinguished in order to fully understand the concept intercultural communication competence. Unfortunately, the failure of distinguishing these three concepts continues to plague this line of research.

To avoid the confusion and ambiguity, Chen and Starosta (1996) conceptualized intercultural effectiveness as "the ability to get the job done and attain communication goals in intercultural interaction" (p. 367) through behavioral performance. They further suggested to use "intercultural adroitness" to replace "intercultural effectiveness" so that the problem of using "intercultural effectiveness" and "intercultural communication competence" interchangeably can be improved. In other words, to be interculturally competent individuals must hold cognitive ability or intercultural awareness and affective ability or intercultural sensitivity to make accurate judgments, and further infuse these abilities to behavioral level of interaction depending on different cultural contexts in order to achieve communication goals effectively and appropriately.

Dimensions and Components of Intercultural Effectiveness

The emphasis of behavioral skills of intercultural effectiveness/adroitness corresponds to communication skills that are comprised of those verbal and nonverbal behaviors enabling people to achieve their goals in intercultural interaction. Such communication behaviors form the content of intercultural effectiveness/adroitness. They include five dimensions: message skills, interaction management, behavioral flexibility, identity management, and relationship cultivation (Chen, 1989, 1990, 1992; Chen & Starosta, 1996; Cupach & Imahori, 1993; Gudykunst, 1993; Hammer, Gudykunst, & Wiseman, 1978; Hammer, 1987; Imahori & Lanigan, 1989; Lustig & Koester, 1999; Martin & Hammer, 1989; Ruben, 1977; Ruben & Kealey, 1979; Spitzberg, 1988, 1997; Wiseman, 2003).

Message Skills

Message skills demand the ability to exercise one's counterpart's verbal and nonverbal behaviors. Verbal skills refer to the ability to code skillfully and to create recognizable messages in the process of communication (Kim, 1994; Kim & Wilson, 1994; Milhouse, 1993; Parks, 1994; Weber, 1994). This is the so-called "linguistic competence" or "communicative competence" (Spitzberg & Cupach, 1984) which is concerned with language and messages in the interaction process. In addition, verbal skills also relate to the knowledge of rules underlying the use of language (Chomsky, 1965).

Messages skills are tempered by self-disclosure which refers to willingness of individuals to openly reveal information about themselves to their counterparts. In the process of communication self-disclosure may reflect the amount, depth, intent, accuracy, and valence of the message an individual delivers (Wheeless, Erickson, & Behrens, 1986; Wheeless & Grotz, 1976). Without self-disclosure human communication simply cannot happen. However, self-disclosure must be regulated by the principle of appropriateness in order to reach a successful outcome. This is especially important in intercultural communication setting, because the emphasis of self-disclosure varies among cultures, including the list of topics, the degree of intimacy, the level of hierarchy that are all sanctioned by the culture (Chen, 1995; Nakanishi, 1987; Nakanishi & Johnson, 1993).

Similar to verbal skills, nonverbal skills refer to the ability to code skillfully and to create recognizable nonverbal messages, including those cues in the areas of Kinesics, Proxemics, Paralanguage, and Chronemics (Burgoon, Buller, & Woodall, 1989; Chen & Starosta, 2005; Hall, 1959, 1966, 1976, 1984). However, nonverbal messages are much less systematized and more ambiguous than verbal communication (Chen & Starosta, 2005), they as well involve those humanly and environmentally generated stimuli that convey potential nonlinguistic message values to the interactant (Samovar & Porter, 1995). To acquire nonverbal skills, as Ricard (1993) suggested, individuals need to follow five steps: assess learning needs, observe similar situations, use appropriate resources, reach tentative conclusions, and reevaluate the conclusions as necessary.

Rubin (1982) organized message skills into four categories from the western cultural perspective: (1) communication codes – refer to using words, pronunciation, grammar, voice, and nonverbal signs appropriately; (2) oral message evaluation – refers to be able to identify main ideas in messages, distinguish facts from opinions, distinguish informative and persuasive messages, and to recognize when another does not understand your message; (3) basic speech communication skills – include the ability to express ideas clearly and concisely, express and defend one's point of view, organize understandable messages, ask, answer, and summarize questions effectively, and to give concise and accurate directions; and (4) human relations – include the ability to describe another's viewpoint, describe differences in opinion, express feelings to other, and to perform social rituals.

Interaction Management

Interaction management refers to the ability to initiate, terminate, and take turn in conversation "based on a reasonably accurate assessment of the needs and desires of others" (Ruben, 1976, p. 341). Ruben, for example, further stipulated that a low interaction management person often show the following behaviors: (1) Unconcern turn taking in conversation; (2) Either dominate or refuse to interact; (3) Unresponsiveness or unawareness towards counterparts' needs for involvement and time sharing; (4) Initiate and terminate discussion without regard for the wishes of other individuals; (5) Continue to talk long after obvious displays of disinterest and boredom by others; and (6) Terminate discussion or withhold information when there is clear interest expressed by others for further exchange.

In contrast, Ruben continued, a high interaction management person is extremely concerned with providing equal opportunity for all participants to share in contributions to discussion. In the initiation and termination of discussion, he or she always indicates concern for the interests, tolerances, and orientation of others who are party to discussion.

Spitzberg and Cupach (1984) indicated that interaction management deals with one's ability to structure and maintain the procedure of a conversation. Thus, individuals with interaction management skills always know how to develop a topic smoothly in interaction and give their counterparts an opportunity to contribute to the conversation. In addition to this, interaction management is also reflected in the ability of "double-emic listening" through which the interactants are able to develop a space-between and "move from their respective views to formulate an etic view of the other" (Starosta & Chen, 2000, p. 290). Through the process of an effective interaction management, not only can one gather information to improve the quality of interaction, but also play an important role in defining how the conversation will proceed. Interaction management has been found to be a major element for being competent in intercultural communication (Chen, 1989; Olebe & Koester, 1989; Ruben & Kealey, 1979; Spitzberg, 1994).

The fostering of interaction management skills is based on one's constant concern on the interests and orientations of others in interaction. This other-oriented ability or avoiding monopoly in conversation to display mutual dependency or reciprocity is embedded in the concept of "interaction involvement." According to Cegala (1981, 1984) and Cegala, Savage, Brunner, and Conrad (1982), interaction involvement is a kind of social behavior that is related to personal abilities of responsiveness, attentiveness and perceptiveness in interaction. The three elements, i.e., responsiveness, attentiveness and perceptiveness of interaction involvement, reflect that they are not only part of interaction or behavioral skills for an effective communication, but also founded on the ability of affective aspect or sensitivity of the person.

Finally, based on literature review, Wiemann (1977) summarized five components of interaction management: "(1) Interruptions of the speaker are not permitted, (2) One person talks at a time; (3) Speaker turns must interchange; (4) Frequent and lengthy pauses should be avoided; and (5) An interactant must be perceived as devoting full attention to the encounter" (pp. 198-199).

Behavioral Flexibility

Behavioral flexibility refers to an individual's ability to be accurate and "flexible in attending to information," and "in selecting strategies" in order to achieve personal goals in interaction (Parks, 1976, p. 16). In other words, it is the ability to select an appropriate behavior to fit different communication contexts (Bochner & Kelly, 1974). Duran (1983) and Wheeless and Duran (1982) proposed the concept of communication adaptability to indicate this behavioral flexibility that leads a person to feel comfortable with a variety of people in different situations. Several components of communication adaptability include being easy to get along with new people, being easy to fit in with different group of people, enjoying social gatherings where one can meet new people, and feeling relaxed in conversing with a new acquaintance.

Behavioral flexibility also refers to "environmental mobility" that requires a person to cope with different kinds of people at different levels of circumstance (Cleveland, Mangone, & Adams, 1960). From the perspective of message exchange, Argyle (1969) and Robinson (1972) pointed out that behavioral flexibility denotes the ability in making the alternation and co-occurrence of specific speech choices that mark the status and affiliative relationships of interactants.

In intercultural communication behavioral flexibility is an important component for being a "multicultural person" mentioned by Adler (1998). According to Adler, multicultural persons are always situational in interacting with others, are always in a state of "becoming" that shows continual personal transitions, and always maintain an open boundary of the self to allow change. In other words, behaviorally flexible or adaptive persons are able to integrate various communication demands in terms of culture, ethnicity, race, gender, and religion.

Finally, the development of behavioral flexibility is dependent on the cognitive awareness of cultural variations and affective ability in self-monitoring. Cultural variations represent the different features of cultural context. For example, Chung and Chen (2002) summarized the differences between high-context and low-context cultures by indicating that high-context cultures are characterized by the emphasis of group value orientation, indirect communication, feeling, permanent relationship, and spiral thinking pattern; while low-context cultures emphasize individualism, direct expression, logic, transitory relationship, and line reasoning logic. Self-monitoring is an individual's ability to detect the appropriateness of their social behaviors and self-presentation in response to situational constraints and to adjust their behaviors to fit the situation (Chen & Starosta, 1997; Snyder, 1974). Research has shown that high self-monitoring persons tend to more adaptable to diverse communication situation and more adept in the use of communication strategies (Smith, Cody, Lovette, & Canary, 1990; Spitzberg & Cupach, 1984)

Identity Management

Identity management allows individuals to maintain their counterpart's identity. Because human communication is partially prompted by a person's need to learn who he or she is, to reach a successful communication relies not only on the ability to know oneself or self-awareness, but also the ability to inform their counterparts who they are.

Although part of identity may be created by the self, but it is mainly co-created through communication with others. Through the process of negotiation, co-creation, challenge, and reinforcement between the interactants, identity formation reflects a dynamic and multifaceted process. Thus, the salience and intensity of identity varies in different spatial and temporal situations (Collier,

1994). In addition, identity also shows diverse faces in different contexts and is presented in affective, cognitive, and behavioral levels of human interaction (Lustig & Koester, 2000; Martin & Nakayama, 1997).

The diverse faces of identity refer to that an individual plays different roles in different contexts. In intercultural communication it is similar to Adler's "muliticultural identities" (1998) or Starosta's "dual consciousness" (2000) that shows identity is a social character that is fluid, mobile, colliding, susceptible to change, and open to variation. Moreover, identity requires the involvement of affection. In certain situation one might strongly claim one's identity to assure the psychological balance, such as in the crisis stage of intercultural adjustment. Identity as well relates to one's understanding and belief regarding identity itself. For example, people with different cultural identity might posses a similar belief in other issues. In this situation the similar belief often outstrips one's cultural or other identities. Lastly, in the behavioral level, identity is displayed in the exchange of verbal and nonverbal messages. In other words, identity is formed through the verbal and nonverbal interaction in which participants achieve mutual understanding. Thus, in terms of cultural identity, an individual's identity or group belonging can be identified through the analyses of verbal and nonverbal messages (Chen, 2004).

The characteristics of identity show that the use of identity management skills must vary with different situations and different personal goals, and with movement from one salient identity to another (Collier, 1989; Parks, 1985; Ting-Toomey, 1989; 1993). Intercultural communication competence is then demonstrated by one's ability to effectively and appropriately enact one's counterpart's cultural identity, which manifests the match between the avowed and ascribed identity, and reinforces different identities salient in the particular situation (Collier, 1994).

Relationship Cultivation

The last dimension of intercultural effectiveness/adroitness is relationship cultivation. The relational aspect of intercultural effectiveness/adroitness emphasizes the independent and reciprocal process of interaction (Spitzberg & Cupach, 1984). It refers to the ability to establish certain degree of relationship with one's partner in order to satisfy each other's needs and reach a positive outcome of interaction. As an affinity-seeking behavior, relationship cultivation can be achieved through being friendly or showing concern and interest in the interaction (Martin & Hammer, 1989), and such behaviors as courtesy and cooperativeness (Harris, 1973). Moreover, relationship cultivation is displayed in the degree of intimacy, relationship stability and commitment, and idiosyncratic rules created during the interaction (Imahari & Lanigan, 1989).

According to Ruben (1976), the ability of building, maintaining, or cultivating relationship is a functional flexibility in different kinds of role behaviors. In other words, individuals with the ability of relationship cultivation are able to lead the group to such outcomes as "harmonizing and mediating scraps and/or conflicts between group members, attempts to regulate evenness of contributions of group members," offer comments "relative to the group's dynamics," displays "indications of a willingness to compromise one's own position for the sake of group consensus" (p. 350), and displays interest. Although the application is in a group setting, it is generally applicable to different contexts of communication. In contrast, those individuals who are highly resistant to others' ideas or "attempt to manipulate the group by asserting authority through flattery, sarcasm, interrupting, etc.," will bring detrimental effect to relationship development. Finally, Hammer, Gudykunst, and Wiseman (1978) found that the ability to establish interpersonal relationships is a dimension of intercultural effectiveness/adroitness which leads to intercultural communication competence.

Discussion and Directions for Future Research

Questions regarding the study of intercultural communication competence have been raised by scholars from different disciplines (Chen & Starosta, 1996, 1998-9; Collier, 1989; Koester, Wiseman, & Sanders, 1993; Lustig & Spitzberg, 1993; Martin, 1993; Ruben, 1989). Among them, two issues including conceptualization and operationalization of intercultural communication competence are especially applicable to the study of intercultural effectiveness/adroitness.

Conceptually, first, although scholars continue to demystify the meaning of intercultural communication competence, very few of them made an effort to clarify the difference between competence and effectiveness. This conceptual confusion and ambiguity not only misleads people to treat both competence and effectiveness as interchangeable, but also leads to operational inconsistency and fragmentation of the concepts. As previously mentioned, intercultural communication competence is a multidimensional concept which is comprised of cognitive, affective, and behavioral aspects of human interaction. The cognitive aspect is represented by the concept of intercultural awareness; the affective aspect is by the concept of intercultural sensitivity; and the behavioral aspect is by the concept of intercultural effectiveness. In other words, intercultural effectiveness only represents one of the dimensions of intercultural communication competence. To treat intercultural effectiveness and intercultural communication competence interchangeably is inconceivable. Thus, as proposed by Chen and Starosta (1996), in order to avoid confusion, it is recommendable to use "intercultural adroitness" to replace "intercultural effectiveness" which portrays the behavioral or interactional skills of intercultural communication competence.

Second, since intercultural communication competence is a multidimensional concept comprising intercultural awareness, intercultural sensitivity, and intercultural effectiveness/adroitness, it is important for future research to investigate the relationship among the three dimensions. As Chen and Starosta (1996, 1999) argued, the three concepts are closed related but independent dimensions of intercultural communication competence. How to clearly conceptualize these concepts remains a significant task for scholars to further demystify the concept of intercultural communication competence. Moreover, do these three dimensions possess the same weight for accounting intercultural communication competence? Are they all sufficient and necessary elements for interactants to be interculturally competent in different cultural contexts or other situations? These questions deserve more future investigations in this line of research.

Finally, the distinction and relationship between intercultural effectiveness and intercultural appropriateness needs to be further elucidated. Obviously, individuals can be highly effective in achieving their task or goals in intercultural interaction by using an inappropriate means, such as a Machiavellian's style or intentionally violating communication rules discussed previously. Thus, it is necessary to treat appropriateness and effectiveness as two different concepts. In other words, effectiveness and appropriateness are the two sides of a coin of intercultural communication competence which cannot be achieved without either one of them. The previous analysis has indicated that appropriateness is more attached to the cognitive and affective aspects of intercultural communication competence. It is the understanding of cultural themes and the affective sensitivity of intercultural differences through acknowledging, respect, and accepting that help interactants act more appropriately while applying behavioral skills in intercultural communication. Here we can see the tight relationship among intercultural awareness, intercultural sensitivity, and intercultural effectiveness/adroitness, but how to project or integrate this appropriateness based on awareness and sensitivity into effectiveness by guiding interactants' behaviors is another area future research needs to examine.

The issue of operationalization mainly concerns the assessment of the concept which contains two tasks: What are the attributes of intercultural effectiveness/adroitness and how to assess them. First, the attributes of intercultural effectiveness/adroitness concern the content of the concept. This paper proposes five dimensions of intercultural effectiveness/adroitness, including messages skills, interaction management, behavioral flexibility, identity management, and relationship cultivation. The dimensions seem to be universal in human communication, while in intercultural communication setting, due to the involvement of cultural differences, the emphasis on each one or the culturally acceptable components for each dimension may vary. For instance, comparing to Westerners, the Chinese tend to be more restrained in interaction, more uneasy to directly show disapproval, more concerned on saving or making face for their counterparts, more reciprocal in social interaction, and place more emphasis on particularistic relationships (Chen, 2002).

How would these cultural values affect the content variations of the dimensions of intercultural effectiveness/adroitness? In other words, it might be suitable to adopt culture-general approach to conceptualize the more abstract-level dimensions of intercultural effectiveness/adroitness, but when trying to operationalize or empirically observe the elements of these dimensions, a culture-specific approach becomes more appropriate (Chen & Starosta, 1996; Lustig & Spitzberg, 1993).

Second and lastly, how do behavioral skills be observed or assessed? There is no doubt that intercultural effectiveness/adroitness is displayed through how the individual acts or behaves in the interaction. The problem is who should be the best person to evaluate or judge whether the interactants' external actions or behaviors account for being interculturally effective/adroit. Is it the actor the most suitable person to decide whether he or she is interculturally effective/adroit? In other words, should intercultural effectiveness/adroitness be observed or assessed based on the self-report process? Is it the actor's counterpart the best person to make the judgment? The counterpart can be more objectively observe the actor's behaviors, but this objectivity might be compromised due to his or her involvement in the interaction, and limitation might be caused by cultural myopia. Using the third party to observe the interacants' behaviors seems most likely to attain objectivity, however, the lack of interactional relationship between the third party and the interactants might jeopardize the reliability of the observation results. All these questions should be addressed in future research in this line of study.

References

Adler, P. S. (1998). Beyond cultural identity: Reflections on multiculturalism. In M. J. Bennett (Ed.), *Basic concepts of intercultural communication: Selected readings* (pp. 225-245). Yarmouth, ME: Intercultural Press.

Allen, R. R., & Wood, B. S. (1978). Beyond reading and writing to communication competence. *Communication Education, 27*, 286-292.

Argyle, M. (1969). *Social interaction*. London,: Tavostock.

Barna, L. M. (1994). Intercultural communication stumbling blocks. In R. E. Porter & L. A. Samovar (Eds.), *Intercultural communication: A reader* (pp. 337-346). Belmont, CA: Wadsworth.

Bochner, A. P., & Kelly, C. W. (1974). Interpersonal competence: Rational, philosophy, and implementation of a conceptual framework. *Speech Teacher, 23*, 279-301.

Brislin, R. W. (1979). Orientation programs for cross-cultural preparation. In A. J. Marsella, R. G. Tharp, & T. J. Ciborowski (Eds*.), Perspectives on cross-cultural psychology* (pp. 287-303). New York: Academic Press.

Brislin, R., & Yoshida, T. (1994). *Intercultural communication training: An introduction*. Thousand Oaks, CA: Sage.

Burgoon, J. K., Buller, D. B., & Woodall, W. G. (1989). *Nonverbal communication: The unspoken dialogue*. New York: Harper & Row.

Cegala, D. J. (1981). Interaction involvement: A cognitive dimension of communicative competence. *Communication Education, 30*, 109-121.

Cegala, D. J. (1984). Affective and cognitive manifestations of interaction involvement during unstructured and competitive interactions. *Communication Monographs, 51*, 320-338.

Cegala, D. J., Savage, G. T., Brunner, C. C., & Conrad, A. B. (1982). An elaboration of the meaning of interaction involvement: Toward the development of a theoretical concept. *Communication Monographs, 46*, 229-248.

Chen, G. M (1989). Relationships of the dimensions of intercultural communication competence. *Communication Quarterly, 37*, 118-133.

Chen, G. M. (1990). Intercultural communication Competence: Some perspectives of research. *The Howard Journal of Communications, 2*, 243-261.

Chen, G. M. (1992). A test of intercultural communication competence. *Intercultural Communication Studies, 2*, 63-82.

Chen, G. M. (1995). Differences in self-disclosure patterns among Americans versus Chinese: A comparative study. *Journal of Cross-Cultural Psychology, 26*, 84-91.

Chen, G. M. (2000). Globalization and intercultural communication competence. In *Shapes of future: Global communication in the 21st century - proceedings of the 2000 International Communication Conference* (pp. 51-64). Taipei: Tamkang University.

Chen, G. M. (2002). The impact of harmony on Chinese conflict management. In G. M. Chen & R. Ma (Eds.), *Chinese conflict management and resolution* (pp. 3-19). Westport, CT: Ablex.

Chen, G. M. (2004). *An introduction to intercultural communication*. Taipei: WuNan.

Chen, G. M., & Starosta, W. J. (1996). Intercultural communication competence: A synthesis. *Communication Yearbook, 19*, 353-384.

Chen, G. M., & Starosta, W. J. (1997). A review of the concept of intercultural sensitivity. *Human Communication, 1*, 1-16.

Chen, G. M., & Starosta, W. J. (1998-9). A review of the concept of intercultural awareness. *Human Communication, 2*, 27-54.

Chen, G. M., & Starosta, W. J. (2000). The development and validation of the intercultural communication sensitivity scale. *Human Communication, 3*, 1-15.

Chen, G. M., & Starosta, W. J. (2003). A review of the concept of intercultural awareness. In L. A. Samovar and R. E. Porter (Eds.), *Intercultural communication: A reader* (pp. 344-353). Belmont, CA: Wadsworth.

Chen, G. M., & Starosta, W. J. (2005). *Foundations of intercultural communication*. New York: University Press of America.

Chomsky, N. (1965). *Aspects of the theory of syntax*. Cambridge: MIT Press.

Chung, J. & Chen, G. M. (2002, July). *The Impacts of Media Contexts and Cultural Contexts on Media Choice*. Paper presented to the Pacific Asian Communication Association (PACA) bi-yearly meeting, Seoul, Korea.

Cleveland, H., Mangone, G. J., & Adams, J. C. (1960). *The overseas Americans*. NY: McGraw-Hill.

Colby, B. N. (1975). Culture grammars. *Science, 187*, 913-919.

Collier, M. J. (1989). Cultural and intercultural communication competence: Current approaches and directions for future research. *International Journal and Intercultural Relations, 13*, 287-302.

Collier, M. J. (1994). Cultural identity and intercultural communication. In L. A. Samovar & R. E. Porter (Eds.), *Intercultural communication: A reader* (pp. 36-44). Belmont, CA: Wadsworth.

Condon, J. C., & Yousef, F. (1975). *An introduction to intercultural communication*. Indianapolis: Bobbs-Merrill.

Cupach, W. R., & Imahori, T. T. (1993). Identity management theory: Communication competence in intercultural episodes and relationships. In R. L. Wiseman & J. Koester (Eds.), *Intercultural communication competence* (pp. 112-131). Newbury Park, CA: Sage.

David, K. (1972). Intercultural adjustment and applications of reinforcement theory to problems of culture shock. *Trends, 4*, 1-64.

Duran, R. L. (1983). Communicative adaptability: A measure of social communicative competence. *Communication Quarterly, 31*, 320-326.

Foote, N. N., & Cottrell, L. S. (1955). *Identity and interpersonal competence*. Chicago: University of Chicago Press.

Fritz, W., Mollenberg, A., & Chen, G. M. (2002). Measuring intercultural sensitivity in different cultural context. *Intercultural Communication Studies, 11*, 165-176.

Gudykunst, W. B. (1993). Toward a theory of effective interpersonal and intergroup communication: An anxiety/uncertainty management (AUM) perspective. In R. L. Wiseman & J. Koester (Eds.), *Intercultural communication competence* (pp. 33-71). Newbury Park, CA: Sage.

Gudykunst, W. B., Hammer, M. R., & Wiseman, R. L. (1977). An analysis of an integrated approach to cross-cultural training. *International Journal of intercultural Relations, 2*, 99-110.

Hall. E. T. (1959). *The silent language*. Garden city, NY: Doubleday.

Hall. E. T. (1966). *The hidden dimension*. Garden City, NY: Doubleday.

Hall, E. T. (1976). *Beyond culture*. Garden City, NY: Anchor.

Hall, E. T. (1984). *The dance of life: The other dimension of time*. Garden City, NY: Doubleday.

Hammer, M. R. (1987). Behavioral dimensions of intercultural effectiveness: A replication and extension. *International Journal of Intercultural Relations, 11*, 65-88.

Hammer, M. R., Gudykunst, W. B., & Wiseman, R. L. (1978). Dimensions of intercultural effectiveness: An exploratory study. *International Journal of Intercultural Relations, 2*, 382-392.

Hanvey, R. G. (1987). Cross-culture awareness. In L. F. Luce & E. C. Smith (Eds.), *Toward internationalism* (pp. 13-23). Cambridge, MA: Newbury.

Harris, J. G. (1973). A science of the South Pacific: An analysis of the character structure of the Peace Corp volunteer. *American Psychologist, 28*, 232-247.

Hofstede, G. (1983). National cultures in four dimensions. *International Studies of Management and Organization, 13,* 46-74.

Hofstede, G. (1984). *Culture's consequences*. Beverly Hills, CA: Sage.

Imahari, T. T., & Lanigan, M. l. (1989). Relational model of intercultural communication competence. *International Journal of Intercultural Relations, 13*, 269-286.

Kim, M. (1994). Cross-cultural comparisons of the perceived importance of conversational constraints. *Human Communication Research, 21*, 128-151.

Kim, M., & Wilson, S. R. (1994). A cross-cultural comparison of Kim, Y. Y. (1994b). Interethnic communication: The context and the behavior. In S. A. Deetz (Ed.), *Communication Yearbook 17* (pp. 511-538). London: Sage.

Kluckhohn, C. (1948). *Mirror of man*. New York: McGraw Hill.

Kluckhohn, C., & Strodbeck, F. (1961). *Variations in value orientations*. Evanston, IL: Row, Peterson.

Koester, J., Wiseman, R. L., & Sanders, J. A (1993). Multiple perspectives of intercultural communication competence. In R. L. Wiseman & J. Koester (Eds.), *Intercultural communication competence* (pp. 3-15). Newbury Park, CA: Sage.

Lustig, M. W., & Koester, J. (1999). *Intercultural competence: Interpersonal communication across cultures*. New York: Longman.

Lustig, M. W., & Koester, J. (2000). The nature of cultural identity. In M. W. Lustig & J. Koester (Eds.), *Among us: Essays on identity, belonging, and intercultural competence* (pp. 3-8). New York: Longman.

Lustig, M. W., & Spitzberg, B. H. (1993). Methodological issues in the study intercultural communication. In R. L. Wiseman & J. Koester (Eds.), *Intercultural communication competence* (pp. 153-167). Newbury Park, CA: Sage.

Martin, J. N. (1993). Intercultural communication competence: A review. In R. L. Wiseman & J. Koester (Eds.), *Intercultural communication competence* (pp. 16-29). Newbury Park, CA: Sage.

Martin, J. N., & Hammer, M. R. (1989). Behavioral categories of intercultural communication competence: Everyday communicators' perceptions. *International Journal of Intercultural Relations, 13*, 303-332.

Martin, J. N., & Nakayama, T. K. (1997). *Intercultural communication in contexts*. Mountain View, CA: Mayfield.

Milhouse, V. H. (1993). The applicability of interpersonal communication competence to the intercultural communication context. In R. L. Wiseman & J. Koester (Eds.), *Intercultural communication competence* (pp. 184-203). Newbury Park, CA: Sage.

Nakanishi, M. (1987). Perceptions of self-disclosure in initial interaction: A Japanese sample. *Human Communication Research, 13*, 167-190.

Nakanishi, M., & Johnson, K. M. (1993). Implications of self-disclosure on conversational logics, perceived communication competence, and social attraction. In R. L. Wiseman & J. Koester (Eds.), *Intercultural communication competence* (pp. 204-221). Newbury Park, CA: Sage.

Olebe, , M., & Koester, J. (1989). Exploring the cross-cultural equivalence of the Behavioral Assessment Scale for intercultural communication. *International Journal of Intercultural Relations, 13*, 333-347.

Parks, M. R. (1976, December). *Communication competence*. Paper presented at the meeting of the Speech Communication Association. San Francisco, California.

Parks, M. R. (1985). Interpersonal communication and the quest for personal competence. In M. L. Knapp & G. R. Miller (Eds.), *Handbook of interpersonal communication* (pp. 171-201). Beverly Hills, CA: Sage.

Parks, M. R. (1994). Communication competence and interpersonal control. In M. L. Knapp & G. R. Miller (Eds.), *Handbook of interpersonal communication* (pp. 589-618). Thousand Oaks, CA: Sage.

Parsons, T. (1951). *The social system*. Glencoe, IL: Free Press.

Phillips, G. M. (1984). A competent view of "competence." *Communication Education, 33*, 25-36.

Ricard, V. B. (1992). *Developing intercultural communication skills*. Malabar, FL: Krieger.

Robinson, W. P. (1972). *Language and social behavior*. Baltimore: Penguin.

Ruben, B. D. (1976). Assessing communication competency for intercultural adaptation. *Group & Organization Studies, 1*, 334-354.

Ruben, B. D. (1977). Guidelines for cross-cultural communication effectiveness. *Group & Organization Studies, 2*, 470-479.

Ruben, B. D. (1989). The study of cross-cultural competence: Traditions and contemporary issues. *International Journal and Intercultural Relations, 13*, 287-302.

Ruben, B. D., & Kealey, D. J. (1979). Behavioral assessment of communication competency and the prediction of cross-cultural adaptation. *International Journal of intercultural Relations, 3*, 15-47.

Rubin, R. B. (1982). Assessing speaking and listening competence at college level: The Communication Competency Assessment Instrument. *Communication Education, 31*, 19-32.

Samovar, L. A., & Porter, R. E. (1995). *Communication between cultures*. Belmont, CA: Wadsworth.

Seidel, G. (1981). Cross-cultural training procedures: Their theoretical framework and evaluation. In S. Bochner (Ed.). *The mediating person: Bridge between cultures*. Cambridge: Schenhman.

Shirts, G. (1973). *BAFA BAFA: A cross-cultural simulation*. Delmar, CA: Simile.

Smith, S. W., Cody, M. J., Lovette, S., & Canary, D. J. (1990). Self-monitoring, gender and compliance-gaining goals. In M. J. Cody & M. L. McLaughlin (Eds.), *The psychology of tactical communication* (pp. 91-134). Clevedon, England: Multilingual Matters.

Snyder, M. (1974). Self-monitoring of expressive behavior. *Journal of Personality and Social Psychology, 30*, 528.

Spitzberg, B. H. (1988). Communication competence: Measures of perceived efectiveness. In C. H. Tardy (Ed.), *A handbook for the study of human communication: Methods and instruments for observing, measuring, and assessing communication processes* (pp. 67-106). Norwood, NJ: Ablex.

Spitzberg, B. H. (1994). A model of Intercultural communication competence. In L. A. Samovar & R. E. Porter (Eds.), *Intercultural communication: A reader* (pp. 347-359). Belmont, CA: Wadsworth.

Spitzberg, B. H. (1997). A model of Intercultural communication competence. In L. A. Samovar & R. E. Porter (Eds.), *Intercultural communication: A reader* (pp. 379-391). Belmont, CA: Wadsworth.

Spitzberg, B. H., & Cupach, W. R. (1984). *Interpersonal communication competence*. Beverly Hills, CA: Sage.

Starosta, W. J. (2000). Dual_consciousness@USAmerican.white.male. In M. W. Lustig & J. Koester (Eds.), *Among us: Essays on identity, belonging, and intercultural competence* (pp. 107-115). New York: Longman.

Starosta, W. J., & Chen, G. M. (2000). Listening across diversity in global society. In G. M. Chen & W. J. Starosta (Eds.), *Communication and global society* (pp. 279-293). New York: Peter Lang.

Thiagarajan, S. & Steinwachs, B. (1990). *Barnga: A simulation game on cultural clashes*. Yarmouth, ME: Intercultural Press.

Ting-Toomey, S. (1989). Identity and interpersonal bond. In M. K. Asante & Gudykunst (Eds.), *Handbook of international and intercultural communication* (pp. 351-373). Newbury Park, CA: Sage.

Ting-Toomey, S. (1993). Communication resourcefulness: An identity negotiation perspective. In R. L. Wiseman & Koester, J. (Eds.), *Intercultural communication competence* (pp. 72-111). Newbury Park, CA: Sage.

Trenholm, S., & Rose, T. (1981). The compliant communicator: Teacher perceptions of classroom behavior. *Western Journal of Speech Communication, 45*, 13-26.

Turner, C. V. (1968). The Sinasina "big man" complex: A central cultural theme. *Practical Anthropology, 15,* 16 - 22.

Weber, S. N. (1994). The need to be: The socio-cultural significance of black language. In L. A. Samovar & R. E. Porter (Eds.), *Intercultural communication: A reader* (pp. 221-226). Belmont, CA: Wadsworth.

Weinstein, E. A. (1969). The development of interpersonal competence. In D. A. Goslin (Ed.), *Handbook of socialization theory and research* (pp. 753-775). Chicago: Rand McNally.

Wheeless, E. W., Erickson, K. V, & Behrens, J. S. (1986). Cultural differences in disclosiveness as a function of locus of control. *Communication Monographs, 53*, 36-46.

Wheeless, E. W., & Grotz, J. (1976). Conceptualization and measurement of reported self-disclosure. *Human Communication Research, 2*, 238-346.

White, R. W. (1959). Motivation reconsidered: The concept of competence. *Psychological Review, 66*, 297-333.

Wiemann, J. M. (1977). Explication and test of model of communication competence. *Human Communication Research, 3*, 195-213.

Wiemann, J. M., & Backlund, P. (1980). Current theory and research in communicative competence. *Review of Educational Research, 50*, 185-199.

Wiseman, R. L. (2003). Intercultural communication competence. In W. B. Gudykunst (Ed.), *Cross-cultural and intercultural communication* (pp. 191-208). Thousand Oaks, CA: Sage.

Wright, A. (1970). *Experiential cross-cultural training*. Mimeo produced by Center for Research and education, Estes Park, Colorado.

Introduction to

Adapting to a New Culture:
An Integrative Communication Theory

By Young Yun Kim

Kim presents her integrative theory on cultural adaptation in this text. She notes that many studies and theories exist already on cross-cultural adaptation which have been undertaken and promulgated in various scientific disciplines since the 1930s. Researchers typically isolate segments of the adaptation process specific to disciplinary and individual interests which have resulted in the dichotomous distinction drawn between macro- and micro-level processes and between short- and long-term adaptation. Kim also points out that a more realistic understanding of cross-cultural adaptation has, in part, been frustrated by the narrowly based linear-causal understanding of cross-cultural adaptation as either a "dependent" variable, or an "independent" variable of something. This one directional cause-and-effect notion, observes Kim, has produced many different and often inconsistent definitions, models, indices, and scales. It is against this backdrop that Kim has decided to develop a broadly based general theory that attempts to link the various conceptual domains to gain a systematic insight into what happens when someone crosses cultural boundaries.

Kim's model seeks to address the two central questions of cross-cultural adaptation: 1. What is the essential nature of the adaptation process individual settlers undergo over time? and 2. Why are some settlers more successful than others in attaining a level of psychosocial fitness in the host environment? The first question is answered in a process model – a theoretical representation of the process of personal evolution toward increased functional fitness and psychological health, and a gradual emergence of intercultural identity. The second question is addressed by a structural model in which key dimensions of factors that facilitate or impede the adaptation process are identified and their interrelationships articulated. Kim notes that the acculturation process is not a process in which new cultural elements are simply added to prior internal conditions. As new learning occurs, deculturation or unlearning of some old cultural elements has to occur; at least in the sense that new responses are adopted in situations that previously would have evoked old responses. And this is a dynamic, dialectic process that is accompanied by stress which in turn is replaced by adaptation and growth.

According to Kim, the successful adaptation of strangers is realized only when their personal communication systems sufficiently overlap with those of the natives. So personal communication skills can determine the degree of success or failure during adaptation. But in addition, it is also important to what degree the host social communication is open to the stranger at both the interpersonal and mass media level. Also, the environment is crucial which is affected by host receptivity, host conformity pressure, and ethnic group strength. Kim then lists personal factors such as predisposition and individual personality which includes openness, strength, and positivity. As strangers experience a progression of internal change, they undergo a set of identifiable changes in their habitual patterns of cognitive, affective, and behavioral responses. But one undeniable reality of cross-cultural adaptation also exists: The real choice is left to each individual as to what degree of change a person is willing to undergo. By accelerating one's efforts to cultivate host communication competence and engaging oneself actively in host social communication processes, one can maximize one's adaptation.

These insights ought to be also of interest to international businesses because it offers some interesting and illuminating insights into the integration of foreign employees in an existing organizational structure as well as the integration process of two corporate cultures during a merger or acquisition.

Michael B. Hinner

Young Yun Kim is Professor of Communication at the University of Oklahoma. She has conducted original research among various Asian and Hispanic immigrant groups as well as native-born Americans of different ethnic backgrounds including Native Americans and European Americans. Kim's research has been aimed primarily at explaining the role of communication in the cross-cultural adaptation process of immigrants, sojourners, and native-born ethnic minorities. Recently, she has expanded her research domain to investigating the associative and dissociative interethnic communication behaviors among citizens of the United States. Kim has published over seventy journal articles and book chapters, and has authored or edited eleven books including *Becoming Intercultural* and *Communicating with Strangers* (with William B. Gudykunst). Kim has served leadership roles in a number of academic organizations including the National Communication Association, International Communication Association, and International Academy for Intercultural Relations. She is currently on the editorial boards of *Journal of Communication, Communication Research,* and *International Journal of Intercultural Relations*. She is a Fellow of the International Communication Association.

Adapting to a New Culture:
An Integrative Communication Theory

Young Yun Kim

"When the skies grow dark, the stars begin to shine."

Charles Austin Beard (1874-1948)

Millions of people change homes each year crossing cultural boundaries. Immigrants and refugees resettle in search of a new life, side by side with temporary sojourners finding employment overseas as artists, musicians, writers, accountants, teachers, and construction workers. Diplomats and other governmental agency employees, business managers, Peace Corps volunteers, researchers, professors, students, military personnel, and missionaries likewise carry out their work overseas for varying lengths of time. Individuals such as these are the contemporary pioneers venturing into an unfamiliar cultural terrain where many of the "business-as-usual" ways of doing things lose their relevance. Even relatively short-term sojourners must be at least minimally concerned with building a healthy functional relationship to the host environment in ways similar to the native population. As they confront their predicaments as strangers and engage in new learning for an improved "goodness-of-fit," they begin to undergo a gradual process of personal transformation beyond the original cultural perimeters and toward a more inclusive and less categorical self-conception and self-other orientation. This description, in a nutshell, points to the cross-cultural adaptation phenomenon being theorized in this essay.

Background

Cross-cultural adaptation has been investigated extensively across social science disciplines since the 1930s in the United States, a nation that has dealt with a

---

Young Yun Kim, Adapting to a New Culture: An Integrative Communication Theory, In *Theorizing about Intercultural Communication* pp 375-400, Copyright 2005, Reprinted by permission of Sage Publications Inc. and of the author.

large and continuous influx of immigrants (e.g., Spicer, 1968; Stonequist, 1937). More recently, significant research attention has been given to adaptation-related phenomena throughout Northern and Western European countries, Canada, Australia, New Zealand, and Israel, among others (e.g., Berry, 1980; Jasinskaja-Lahti, Liebkind, Horenczyk, & Schmitz, 2003; Ward & Kennedy, 1993).

Approaches to Cross-Cultural Adaptation: Richness and Fragmentation

Although the field has benefited from an extensive amount of information and insights, it suffers from disconnectedness, making it difficult for individual investigators to gain a clear and cohesive picture of the body of knowledge accumulated over the decades. Couched in various terms such as culture shock, acculturation, adjustment, assimilation, integration, and adaptation, the field is fractionated by differing perspectives and foci. Researchers typically isolate segments of the adaptation phenomenon specific to disciplinary and individual interests, which have resulted in the dichotomous distinction drawn between macro-and micro-level processes and between short- and long-term adaptation. A fuller, and thus more realistic, understanding of cross-cultural adaptation has been frustrated, in part, by the narrowly-based linear-causal reasoning that conceives cross-cultural adaptation as either a "dependent" variable or an "independent" variable of something. This one-directional cause-and-effect notion has produced many different and often inconsistent definitions, models, indices, and scales. (For a review, see Ady, 1995; Ward & Kennedy, 1999.)

Further complicating the adaptation inquiry are the ideological shift in the United States since the 1960s when the "new ethnicity" movement began prompted by the civil rights movement (Gordon, 1981). The traditional social scientific conceptions of cross-cultural adaptation as a desirable goal for individual settlers and immigrant groups, as well as for the cohesion of a given host society over time (Gordon, 1973), were challenged by more pluralistic conceptions. Berry's (1980, 1990) model, for example identifies four different "acculturation modes," relying on two key questions concerning the subjective identity orientation: "Are cultural identity and customs of value to be retained?" and "Are positive relations with the larger society of value and to be sought?" By combining the response types (yes, no) to these two questions, Berry and associates identify four modes of psychological acculturation: "integration" (yes, yes), "assimilation" (no, yes), "separation" (yes, no), and "marginality" (no, no). A modified version of this model is offered by an interactive model proposed by Bourhis, Moiese, Perreault, and Senecal (1997), replacing "marginality" with "anomie" and "individualism." What distinguishes pluralistic models such as these from traditional models is the implicit assumption that adaptation is a matter of conscious choice individuals make for themselves, and not a matter of necessity.

The trend toward pluralistic conceptions of cross-cultural adaptation has been further spurred by recent works by "critical" or "postmodern" scholars (e.g., Hedge, 1998; Young, 1996). These scholars have questioned the legitimacy of the traditional normative-representational social scientific theories for their inherent "flaw" of not stressing cultural diversity, not highlighting the predicaments in which immigrant groups and ethnic minorities find themselves as "victims" of "systematic cultural oppression," and thereby serving to reproduce the status quo of the dominant cultural ideology of assimilationism and its "melting pot" vision of society. Based on interviews with a small group of Asian Indian immigrant women in the United States, for example, Hedge (1998) approaches the experiences of these women from the perspective of critical-feminist scholarship and emphasize the challenges they face employing such terms as "displacement" and "struggle" of having to deal with the contradictions between their internal identity and external "world in which hegemonic structures systematically marginalize certain types of difference" (p. 36). (For a more extensive discussion of ideological divergence, see Kim, 2001 and Kim, 2002.)

In Search of a Big Picture

Against this vast and fragmented backdrop of the field, the main driving force behind this author's work has been a search for a "big picture," a broadly-based general theory that can help cross-pollinates various probes of limited conceptual domains with one another to gain a systemic insight into what happens when someone crosses cultural boundaries. Such a theory would offer an integrated system of description and explanation, in which common themes addressed in the existing approaches, concepts, and models can be identified with their interrelationships clarified and many of the existing divisions in the field bridged. With this aim, the author has sought to address in her theory the following five key missing links in the cross-cultural adaptation literature:

(1) In investigating cross-cultural adaptation of individuals, little attention has been given to macro-level factors such as the cultural and institutional patterns of the host environment and the ethnic community within it, or to micro-level factors such as the background and psychological characteristics of the individual. Both macro- and micro-level factors need to be taken into account for a fuller understanding of the cross-cultural adaptation process.

(2) The two traditionally separate areas of investigation of long-term and short-term adaptation need to be integrated. These two areas have common conceptual issues that inform each other.

(3) The problematic nature of cross-cultural adaptation must be viewed in the context of new learning and psychological growth. Both of these aspects of adaptation, taken together, provide a more balanced and complete interpretation of the experiences of individuals in an unfamiliar environment.

(4) Different sets of factors have been identified as constituting and/or explaining (influencing) the cross-cultural adaptation process of individuals. Efforts must be made to sort and consolidate these factors, so as to achieve a greater coherence in describing and explaining differing levels or rates of adaptive change in individuals.

(5) The divergent ideological premises of assimilationism and pluralism need to be recognized and incorporated into a pragmatic conception of cross-cultural adaptation as a condition of the host environment as well as of the individual adapting to that environment.

A Trajectory of Theorizing and Researching

The author began a scientific investigation of cross-cultural adaptation over two and half decades ago. As a graduate student from South Korea, she was drawn to this field partly prompted by a keen personal interest in understanding the adaptive struggles and successes that she and those around her were experiencing. The doctoral research began to address these issues through a survey among Korean immigrants in the Chicago area (Kim, 1976, 1977a, 1977b, 1978a). The author has since conducted studies among other immigrant and refugee groups in the United States, including Japanese Americans (Kim, 1978b), Mexican Americans (Kim, 1978b), and Southeast Asian refugees from Vietnam, Cambodia, and Laos (Kim, 1980, 1989, 1990). The research subjects and contexts have been extended to American Indians living in a predominantly Anglo milieu (Kim, Lujan, & Dixon, 1998a, 1998b). The author also has worked with a number of doctoral students investigating the adaptation patterns of Malaysian students in the United States (Tamam, 1993), Western and non-Western international university students in Japan (Maruyama, 1998; Maruyama & Kim, 1997), Turkish employees of an American military organization in Germany (Braun, 2002; Kim & Brown, 2002), and Korean expatriates in the United States and American expatriates in South Korea (Y. S. Kim, 2003; Kim & Y.S. Kim, in press).

While the basic research issues stated above have remained the same throughout these studies, the author's methodological perspective has undergone a change-- from the initial linear-causal approach exemplified in the "path model" developed through the doctoral research (Kim, 1976, 1977a), to a more interactive and integrative general systems perspective with a special emphasis on an "open systems" perspective (Bertalanffy, 1956; Jantsch, 1980) incorporated into her subsequent work. The systems approach is predicated on a set of assumptions, based on which cross-cultural adaptation is conceived of as a case of "organized complexity" and the unfolding of the natural human tendency to struggle for an internal equilibrium in the face of often adversarial environmental conditions. Focusing on the communication activities linking the individual (the "figure") and the environment (the "ground"), this open-systems perspective renders itself to a consolidation of previously separate theoretical foci such as the person, the group, and the society, and has enabled the author to find a way to integrate the existing approaches into a broadly-based general theory in which communication occupies the central place.

The initial groundwork for development of a comprehensive, integrative theory was laid in 1979 in an article entitled, "Toward an interactive theory of communication-acculturation" (Kim, 1979), followed by a full theory presentation in Communication and cross-cultural adaptation: An integrative theory (Kim, 1988). This theory has since been further elaborated and refined in "Becoming intercultural: An integrative theory of communication and cross-cultural adaptation" (Kim, 2001), and is briefly described below.

Organizing Principles

The author's theory is rooted in a number of open-systems premises with respect to the basic nature of cross-cultural adaptation and of the scientific approach to theorizing about the phenomenon. Taken together, these premises render the present theory a distinct character, differentiating it from other existing theories that address issues related to cross-cultural adaptation.

Adaptation as a Natural and Universal Phenomenon

The author intends this theory to serve not as an advocacy of any particular ideological position, but as an accurate representation and abstraction of regularities found in the reality of individuals adapting to a new and unfamiliar culture wherever it may be taking place. This theoretical aim hinges on the open-systems principle that adaptation manifests the natural human instinct to struggle for an internal equilibrium in the face of adversarial environmental conditions. Cross-cultural adaptation is a case of "a common process of environmental adaptation" (Anderson, 1994, p.293), as it entails the totality of a complex, dynamic, and evolutionary process an individual undergoes. This conception elevates the ontological status of adaptation to the level of a pan-human universal phenomenon--a basic human tendency that accompanies the internal struggle of individuals to regain control over their life chances in the face of environmental challenges.

Adaptation as an All-Encompassing Phenomenon

The author regards cross-cultural adaptation not as a specific analytic unit (or variable), but as the entirety of the evolutionary process an individual undergoes vis-à-vis a new and unfamiliar environment. This process "moves" with a structure of multidimensional and multifaceted forces operating simultaneously and interactively. Some of these forces are external to the individual setting limits on the adaptive behavior of the stranger; Other forces are internally located within the individual's predispositions and behaviors. Cross-cultural adaptation is, therefore, to be understood in terms of a dynamic interplay of the person and the environment. This conception counters the reductionist strategies of explanation commonly employed in the existing theoretical models, and instead emphasizes the unitary nature of psychological and social processes and the reciprocal functional person-environment interdependence. In this view, the micro-psychological and macro-social factors are taken together into a theoretical fusion or "vertical integration" (Berkowitz, 1982; Fielding & Fielding, 1986). This systemic approach is consistent with the perspective taken in the philosophical pragmatism (Givon, 1989; Joas, 1993) and with such methodological schools as "contextualism," "ecological psychology," and "evolutionary social psychology reflected in the works of Bateson (1972), Ruesch and Bateson (1951/1968), Watzlawick, Beavin, and Jackson (1967), and Buss & Kenrick (1998).

Adaptation as a Communication-Based Phenomenon

By placing adaptation at the intersection of the person and the environment, the present approach views cross-cultural adaptation as a process that occurs in and through communication activities. Underscored in this view is that communication is the necessary vehicle without which adaptation cannot take place, and that cross-cultural adaptation occurs as long as the individual remains in interaction with the host environment. The only situation in which adaptation cannot take place would be under the condition of complete insularity from the host environment. This interactive communication-based conception echoes the view of Ruesch and Bateson (1951/1968), who regard "all actions and events [having] communicative aspects, as soon as they are perceived by a human being . . . . Where the relatedness of entities is considered, we deal with problems of communication" (pp. 5-6). It allows the author to move beyond the linear-causal assumption underlying most existing models in which cross-cultural adaptation is treated as an independent or dependent variable.

Theory as a System of Description and Explanation

Consistent with the systems-theoretic view of the fundamental goal of science as "pattern recognizing" (Monge, 1990), the present theory is designed to identify the patterns that are commonly present within a clearly defined set of individual cases and to translate these patterns into a set of generalizable and interrelated statements. Given that adaptation is something natural and universal to all living systems, and given that communication activities serve as the very vehicle for adaptation, the author's main concern is not whether individuals adapt, but how and why they adapt when they relocate in a new and unfamiliar environment. In addressing this basic question, the author has sought to achieve a balance between the two distinct goals for social science: understanding and prediction" (Dubin, 1978, pp. 9-10). Understanding is to be achieved via a thorough and accurate system of description and explanation of how cross-cultural adaptation plays out in reality, what key elements constitute the phenomenon, and how these elements interact and evolve together over time. The degree to which such understanding is provided by the present theory is assessed in terms of its descriptive power. At the same time, the present theory allows prediction of adaptive changes in individuals over time, and of the role that each identified element plays in influencing the change.

Theorizing at the Interface of Deduction and Induction

The author's theorizing process has taken a back-and-forth movement between deductive and inductive processes—between the conceptual realm of logical development of ideas from a set of basic open systems assumptions about human adaptation and empirical substantiation of the ideas based on proofs available in social science literature. Following Blalock (1989) and Dubin (1978), the present theory has been developed without being restricted by empirical evidence. At the same time, it is firmly grounded in and strengthened by the extensive research evidence that has been made available across disciplines. Also utilized in the theorizing process are anecdotal stories and testimonials of immigrants and sojourners available in non-technical sources such as reports, biographies, letters, diaries, dialogues, commentaries, and a host of other materials in magazines, newspapers, fiction and non-fiction books, radio programs, and television programs.

Although these individual stories do not render themselves to the prerequisites of scientific data, they serve as a vital source of insights into the "lived experiences" of cross-cultural adaptation. The practical and participatory experiences expressed in these stories offer credible, sensitive, and close-up witness to what is actually occurring in reality (see Kim, 2001).

Focal Concepts and Boundary Conditions

The author has strived to achieve maximum generality of this theory by employing concepts of higher-order abstraction and, thus, of greater integrative power and parsimony. Among the various general concepts employed in the present theory are the two central terms, adaptation and stranger. These two terms are chosen for their broad generality and as a "master concept" or "superordinate category" (White, 1976, p. 18) that help define the domain of the theory.

The term "cross-cultural adaptation" is defined in this theory as the entirety of the phenomenon of individuals who, upon relocating to an unfamiliar sociocultural environment, strive to establish and maintain a relatively stable, reciprocal, and functional relationship with the environment. At the core of this definition is the goal of achieving an overall person-environment "fit" (Mechanic, 1974; Moos, 1976) between their internal conditions and the conditions of the new environment. Adaptation, thus, is an activity that is "almost always a compromise, a vector in the internal structure of culture and the external pressure of environment" (Sahlins, 1964, p. 136). Placed at the intersection of the person and the environment, adaptation is essentially an interactive communication process and embraces other similar but narrower terms, from "assimilation" (the acceptance of mainstream cultural elements of the host society by the individual) and "acculturation" (the process commonly defined as the acquisition of some, but not all, aspects of the host cultural elements), to "coping" and "adjustment" (both of which are often used to refer to the psychological responses to cross-cultural challenges), as well as to "integration" (often defined as social participation in the host society). The concept, "stranger," incorporates in it all individuals who enter and resettle in a new cultural or subcultural environment. Initially employed by Simmel (1908/1950), this concept has served as one of the most ubiquitous and heuristic concepts for analyzing the social processes involving individuals who confront an unfamiliar milieu. The notion of strangers integrates other more specific terms such as immigrants, refugees, and sojourners who resettle for various lengths of time, as well as members of ethnic groups who cross subcultural boundaries within a society. All of these individuals are included in the present definition of strangers, as they commonly share the experience of beginning their adaptation experience as cultural "outsiders" and of moving in the direction of cultural "insiders" over time. (See Gudykunst & Kim, 2003, for a more detailed examination of this concept.)

As such, the present theoretical domain is broadly defined, limited only by three boundary conditions: (1) the strangers must have had a primary socialization in one culture (or subculture) and have moved into a different and unfamiliar culture (or subculture); (2) the strangers are at least minimally dependent on the host environment for meeting their personal and social needs; and (3) the strangers are engaged in continuous, first-hand communication experiences with that environment. These boundary conditions offer a domain that is broad and general without being delimited by either the specific reasons for or the lengths of contact with the new environment (e.g., long-term or short-term exchange students, business employees, immigrants, and refugees). Included in this domain is the adaptive experience of anyone who faces significant changes in domestic sociocultural environment, either through a voluntary relocation (e.g., American Indians leaving a tribal reservation to find employment in a predominantly Anglo urban environment) or through the demographic changes in the surrounding environment through incoming and outgoing population movements (e.g., a significant increase in Asians and Hispanics in Los Angeles). Also included in the present domain are the situations of re-entry into one's original culture. Generally, the process of re-adapting to one's original culture is less demanding of new cultural/language learning as the process of adapting to a foreign culture. Yet, to the extent that the returnee has been changed by the sojourn experience, and to the extent that the original cultural milieu has changed during the sojourn, he/she must, once again, go through the cross-adaptation process upon returning home.

Based on the two focal terms, adaptation and stranger, and the related boundary conditions described above, the theory addresses two central questions: (1) What is the essential nature of the adaptation process individual settlers undergo over time?; and (2) Why are some settlers more successful than others in attaining a level of psychosocial fitness in the host environment? The first question is addressed in the form of a process model—a theoretical representation of the process of personal evolution toward increased functional fitness and psychological health, and a gradual emergence of intercultural identity. The second question is addressed by a structural model in which key dimensions of factors that facilitate or impede the adaptation process are identified and their interrelationships articulated.

The Process of Cross-Cultural Adaptation

All of us are born into this world knowing little of what we need to know to function acceptably in a given culture. Nor are we born prepared to engage in the various activities out of which our sense of reality and self is constructed. Instead, we learn to relate to our social environment and its culture; that is, the universe of information and operative linguistic and nonlinguistic communication rituals that gives coherence, continuity, and distinction to a communal way of life. The familiar culture is the "home world," which is associated closely with the family or significant others. The unwritten task of every culture is to organize, integrate, and maintain the home world of the individual primarily in the formative years of childhood. Through continuous interaction with the various aspects of the cultural environment, our internal systems undergo a progression of changes as we integrate culturally acceptable concepts, attitudes, and actions. We thus become fit to live in the company of others around us who share a similar image of reality and self.

This process is commonly called enculturation. The continuous enculturation process occurs in and through communication, the pillar of all human learning. We learn to speak, listen, read, interpret, and understand verbal and nonverbal messages in such a fashion that the messages will be recognized and responded to by the individuals with whom we interact. Once acquired, communicative abilities serve us as an instrumental, interpretive, and expressive means of coming to terms with our environment. Crucial features of this communication-enculturation process are the relational bonding between individuals, the forming of groups, and a cultural identity.

Entering a New Culture

In many ways, entering a new culture is like starting an enculturation process all over again. Only this time, strangers are faced with situations that deviate from the familiar and internalized original culturalscript. They become more aware of the previously taken-for-granted habits of mind because, as Boulding (1956/1977) notes, the human nervous system is structured in such a way that "the patterns that govern behavior and perception come into consciousness only when there is a deviation from the familiar" (p. 13). Now, strangers discover that they lack a level of understanding of the new communication system of the host society, and must learn and acquire many of its symbols and patterns of activities. They may be forced to suspend or even abandon our identification with the cultural patterns that have symbolized who we are and what we are. The situation generates "crises" in which our mental and behavioral habits are brought into awareness and called into question.

Such inner conflicts, in turn, make us susceptible to external influence and compel us to learn the new cultural system. This activity of new learning is the essence of acculturation (Shibutani & Kwan, 1965), the acquisition of the host cultural practices in wide-ranging areas. But new learning and adaptive change is not random (Wheatley, 1999, p. 84). Consciously or unconsciously, an individual stranger's need to maintain himself or herself influences the selection of new information. At least in early stages of cross-cultural adaptation, predisposition and self-interest influence the specific nature of acculturation as each individual tends to be more ready or willing to embrace those host cultural elements that serve his or he own needs. The selectivity in acculturation reflects the ego-protective and ego-centric psychological principle, and is demonstrated in Bogner's (2001) finding of uneven development in gender role change between male and female immigrants, and in Chang's (2001) finding among Asian immigrants in Singapore of relatively higher levels of acculturation in workplace-related and public norms and values compared to private realms and home life.

Acculturation is not a process in which new cultural elements are simply added to prior internal conditions. As new learning occurs, deculturation or unlearning of some of the old cultural elements has to occur, at least in the sense that new responses are adopted in situations that previously would have evoked old ones. "No construction without destruction," in the words of Burke (1974). The cost of acquiring something new is inevitably the "losing" of something old in much the same way as "being someone requires the forfeiture of being someone else" (Thayer, 1975, p. 240). The act of acquiring something new is the "suspending" and, over a prolonged period, "losing" some of the old habits. As the interplay of acculturation and deculturation continues, we may undergo an internal transformation—from changes in superficial areas such as overt role behavior to more profound changes in fundamental values. We are susceptible to conformity pressure from the host environment, often in the form of simple and routine cultural assumptions and expectations extended to us. To the extent that there are discrepancies between the demands of the host environment and our internal capacity to meet those demands, and as long as there are pressures to conform, we are compelled to learn and make changes in our customary habits.

The ultimate theoretical directionality of adaptive change is toward assimilation, a state of the maximum possible convergence of our internal and external conditions to those of the natives (see Figure 1). For most settlers, assimilation remains a lifetime goal than an obtainable goal that often requires the efforts of multiple generations. Whether by choice or by circumstance, individual settlers also vary in the level of overall adaptation level achieved during any given period, falling at different points on a continuum ranging from minimal acculturation and deculturation to maximum acculturation and deculturation.

The Stress-Adaptation-Growth Dynamic

Each experience of adaptive change inevitably accompanies stress in the individual psyche--a kind of identity conflict rooted in resistance to change, the desire to retain old customs in keeping with the original identity, on the one hand, and the desire to change behavior in seeking harmony with the new milieu, on the other. This conflict is essentially between the need for acculturation and the resistance to deculturation—the push of the new culture and the pull of the old. The internal turmoil created by such conflicting forces produces a state of disequilibrium, manifested in emotional "lows" of uncertainty, confusion, and anxiety. *Stress*, a broad concept measured by researchers variously in terms of "difficulties" or "culture shock" people experience (e.g., Ward, Bochner, & Furnham, 2001), is a manifestation of the generic process that occurs whenever an individual's internal capabilities are not adequate to the demands of the environment. It is an expression of the instinctive human desire to restore homeostasis, that is, to hold constant a variety of variables in internal structure to achieve an integrated whole.

Figure 1
Relationships among Key Terms Associated With Cross- Cultural Adaptation

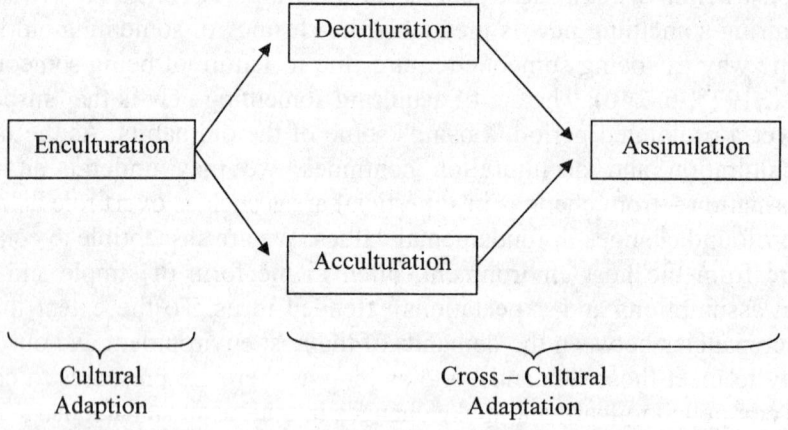

Source: Kim, 2001, p. 53

The natural tendency of an open system is to resist change and perpetuate the state of maladaptation and work against its own adaptive change. This tendency manifests itself in various forms of psychological resistance. Some people may attempt to avoid or minimize the anticipated or actual "pain" of disequilibrium by selective attention, denial, avoidance, and withdrawal, as well as by compulsively altruistic behavior, cynicism, and hostility toward the host environment (Lazarus, 1966, p. 262). Others may seek to regress to an earlier state of existence in the original culture, a state in which there is no feeling of isolation, no feeling of separation. Although stress is universal, few have an easy time accepting it. Yet, no open system can stabilize itself forever. If it were so, nothing would come of evolution. The state of misfit and a heightened awareness in the state of stress serve as the very forces that propel individuals to overcome the predicament and partake in the act of adaptation through the active development of new habits. This is possible as they engage in forward-looking moves, striving to meet the challenge by acting on and responding to the environment (Piaget, 1963). Out of these activities, some aspects of the environment may be incorporated into an individual's internal structure, gradually increasing its overall fitness to the external realities.

What follows the dynamic stress-adaptation disequilibrium is a subtle growth. Periods of stress pass as we work out new ways of handling problems, owing to the creative forces of self-reflexivity of human mentation. Stress, adaptation, and growth thus highlight the core of the changes individuals undergo over time. Together these forces constitute a three-pronged stress-adaptation-growth dynamic of psychological movement in the forward and upward direction of increased chances of success in meeting the demands of the host environment. Stress, in this regard, is intrinsic to complex open systems and essential in the adaptation process--one that allows for self-(re)organization and self-renewal. The stress-adaptation-growth dynamic does not play out in a smooth, steady, and linear progression, but in a dialectic, cyclic, and continual "draw-back-to-leap" pattern. Each stressful experience is responded to with a "draw back," which, in turn, activates adaptive energy to help individuals reorganize themselves and "leap forward." As growth of some units always occurs at the expense of others, the adaptation process follows a pattern that juxtaposes integration and disintegration, progression and regression, novelty and confirmation, and creativity and depression (Kirschner, 1994). This explanation of the adaptation process echoes Dubos' (1965) view of human adaptation as "a dialectic between permanence and change" (p. 2). It also converges with Hall's (1976) conception of "identity-separation-growth" syndrome and with Jourard's (1974) account of "integration-disintegration-reintegration."

The stress-adpataion-growth process continues as long as there are new environmental challenges, with the overall forward and upward movement in the direction of greater adaptation and growth. In this process, large and sudden changes are more likely to occur during the initial phase of exposure to a new culture. Such drastic changes are themselves indicative of the severity of difficulties and disruptions, as have been demonstrated in many culture shock studies (Ward, Bochner, & Furnham, 2003). Over a prolonged period of undergoing internal change, the fluctuations of stress and adaptation are likely to become less intense or severe, leading to an overall "calming" of our internal condition, as depicted in Figure 2. In Jantsch's (1980) words,

The higher the resistance against structural change, the more powerful the fluctuations which ultimately break through--the richer and more varied also the unfolding of self-organization dynamic at the platform of a resilient structure. The more splendid unfolding of mind, as we may also put it. (p. 255)

Figure 2
The Stress- Adaptation- Growth Dynamic

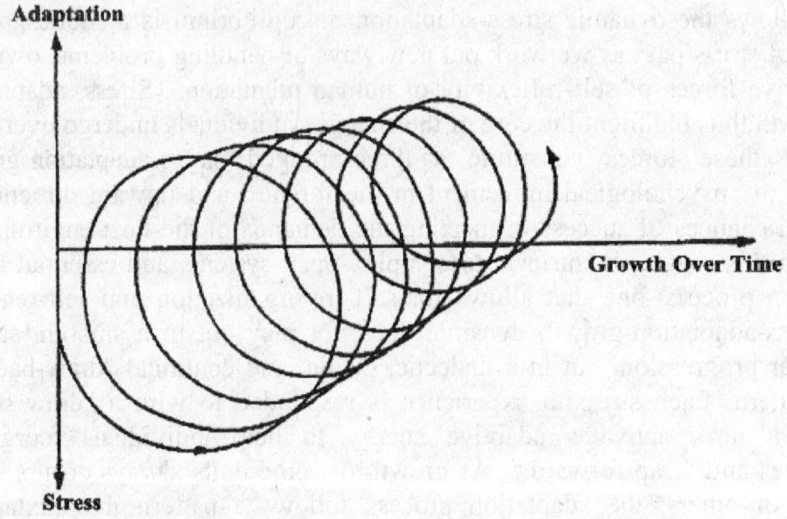

Source: Kim, 2001, p.59

The Structure of Cross-Cultural Adaptation

Building on the above description and explanation of the cross-cultural adaptation process, the theory now moves to address the second theoretical aim, that is, identifying the structure of interlocking adaptive changes and thus help explain the differential rates (or speeds) at which this process plays out across different individuals.

Once again, the metatheoretical perspective of open systems helps to locate relevant explanatory factors within the communicative interface of the stranger and the environment. In this communication framework, strangers' communication activities are conceptualized, following Ruben (1975), in two basic, interdependent dimensions: (1) personal communication, or "private symbolization" and all the internal mental activities that occur in individuals that dispose and prepare them to act and react in certain ways in actual social situations); and (2) social communication, or "public symbolization" that underlies "intersubjectivization" and occurs whenever two or more individuals interact with one another, knowingly or not.

Personal Communication: Host Communication Competence

The successful adaptation of strangers is realized only when their personal communication systems sufficiently overlap with those of the natives. The capacity of strangers to appropriately and effectively receive and process information (decoding) and to design and execute mental plans in initiating or responding to messages (encoding) is labeled in the present theory as host communication competence. By definition, host communication competence facilitates the cross-cultural adaptation process in a most direct and significant way. It serves as an instrumental, interpretive, and expressive means of coming to terms with the host environment. It enables strangers to understand the way things are carried out in the host society and the way they themselves need to think, feel, and act in that environment

The key elements that generally constitute the concept of communication competence, including the present conceptualization of host communication competence, are grouped into three commonly recognized categories: (1) cognitive, (2) affective, and (3) operational. Cognitive Competence includes such internal capabilities as the knowledge of the host culture and language including the history, institutions, worldviews, beliefs, mores, norms, and rules of interpersonal conduct, among others. Language/culture learning is accompanied by a development of "cognitive complexity," that is, the structural refinement in an individual's internal information processing ability. Along with cognitive competence, affective competence facilitates cross-cultural adaptation by providing an motivational capacity to deal with various challenges of living in the host environment, the openness to new learning, and the willingness to participate in the natives' aesthetic and emotional sensibilities in their experiences of beauty, fun, joy, as well as despair, anger, and the like. Relatedly, affective competence further is reflected in one's willingness for making necessary changes in the original cultural habits so as to incorporate some of the new habits in one's repertoire.

Among the recent studies addressing some of the affective components of host communication competence is Gong's (2003) study of international students in the United States, in which strong motivation ("leaning goal orientation") is found to be positively associated with measures of both academic and social adaptation. In a study of ethnic repatriates in Findland, Israel, and Germany, Jasinskaja-Lahti, Liebkind, Horenczyk, and Schmitz (2003) observe that those expatriates objecting to acculturation in the host society perceived more discrimination or reported more stress than other immigrants. This finding suggests a functional relationship between adaptive motivation and psychological health vis-à-vis the host environment.

Closely linked with the cognitive and affective components of host communication competence is operational competence (Taft, 1977), otherwise referred to as "behavioral competence" or the "enactment tendencies" (Buck, 1984). This competence facilitates the strangers to enact, or express, their cognitive and affective experiences outwardly. As they try to come up with a mental plan for action, therefore, they must base the decision on their current knowledge and cognitive capacity to process information about the host culture as well as their motivational and attitudinal capacity to meaningfully appreciate and join in the natives' emotional and aesthetic experiences. The strangers' operational competence, thus, enables them to choose a "right" combination of verbal and nonverbal behaviors, so as to achieve smooth and harmonious interface with the host milieu.

Host Social Communication

Host communication competence is directly and reciprocally linked to participation in the interpersonal and mass communication activities of the host environment. A stranger's host social communication experiences are constrained by his/her host communication competence. At the same time, every host social communication event offers the stranger an opportunity for cultural learning.

Host interpersonal communication, in particular, helps strangers to secure vital information and insight into the mindsets and behaviors of the local people, thereby providing them with points of reference for a check and validation of their own behaviors. Most strangers in a new culture must begin to form a new set of relationships as they find themselves without an adequate support system when they are confronted with highly uncertain and stressful situations. Participation in either or both of the host and ethnic social communication activities is an expression of the fundamental human need to belong (Baumeister & Leary, 1995). The crucial importance of host interpersonal communication activities in facilitating cross-cultural adaptation has been acknowledged and demonstrated widely and repeatedly across social sciences.

Host mass communication facilitates the adaptation of strangers by exposing strangers to the larger environment. Serving this function are various mediated forms of communication such as radio and television programs, magazine and newspaper articles, movies, museum exhibits, theater performances, Internet websites, audiotapes, videotapes, and posters. While the interpersonal channel of communication offers opportunities for more personalized and, thus, meaningful involvement with members of the host culture, mass communication channels help them participate in vicarious learning through "para-social interactions" with the host environment at large beyond the ordinary reaches of their daily life (Horton & Wohl, 1979, p. 32). Compared to interpersonal communication activities, mediated communication activities may be governed by a lesser sense of mutual obligation and effort. Whereas host mass communication renders less opportunity for feedback than do interpersonal situations where a quick exchange of information is maximal, it serves as an important source of cultural and language learning, particularly during early phases of the adaptation process when strangers have less direct access to and less likelihood to succeed in communicating with the natives face-to-face.

Ethnic Social Communication

In many societies and communities today, strangers' interpersonal and mass communication activities involve their co-ethnics or co-nationals and home cultural experiences as well. Whether we speak of American military posts in West Germany, Puerto Rican barrios in New York city, Chinatown in Tokyo, or a Japanese student association in a Canadian university, ethnic communities provide strangers with access to their original cultural experiences. Many aliens have organized some form of mutual-aid or self-help organizations that render assistance to those who need material, informational, emotional, and other forms of social support. In the case of many larger ethnic communities, mass media (including newspapers, radio stations, and television programs that are made accessible via the Internet or in pre-recorded audio- and videotapes and computer disks) perform various informational, educational, entertainment, and social services.

These ethnic interpersonal and mass communication systems serve adaptation-facilitating functions during the initial phase of their adaptation process. Because many strangers initially lack host communication competence and do not have access to resources to become self-reliant, they tend to seek and depend heavily on ethnic sources of informational, material, and emotional help and thereby compensate for the lack of support they are capable of obtaining from host nationals. Due to the relatively stress-free communication experience in dealing with their own ethnic individuals and media, ethnic communication experiences may offer temporary refuge and a support system. In the case of relatively short-term residents, such as American military personnel stationed overseas, their daily duties confine their social communication activities almost exclusively to other Americans at the military base.

Beyond the initial phase, however, ethnic social communication serves the function of original cultural identity maintenance (Boekestijn, 1988) and negatively associated with adaptation into the host culture. Whether by choice or by circumstance, the strangers' heavy and prolonged reliance on co-ethnics sustain their original cultural identity and limit their opportunities to participate in the social communication activities of the host society. Implied in this observation is that strangers cannot remain exclusively ethnic in their communication activities and, at the same time, become highly adapted to the host environment. Among the extensive empirical evidence supporting this observation is Cui's (1998) finding from a study of Chinese graduate students enrolled in various academic programs in an American University indicate that ethnic communication has negative relationships with host communication competence and host interpersonal communication activities. Another recent study by Nesdale & Mak (2003) report that immigrants' level of ethnic identification is positively associated with "ethnic self-esteem," but not with either "personal self-esteem" or "psychological health."

Environment

To the extent that strangers participate in host social (interpersonal, mass) communication activities, the host society exerts influence on their adaptation process. The nature of such influence, in turn, is shaped by the various characteristics of the host society. For many, their social environment includes fellow co-ethnics as well. Given the mixed nature of the environment in which many strangers find themselves, three environmental conditions are identified in the present theory as affecting the individual stranger's adaptation process: (1) host receptivity; (2) host conformity pressure; and (3) ethnic group strength.

The term, *host receptivity*, incorporates the meaning of other similar terms such as "interaction potential" (Blau & Schwartz, 1984; Hallinan & Smith, 1985) or "acquaintance potential" (Cook, 1962), and refers to the degree to which a given environment is structurally and psychologically accessible and open to strangers. Different locations in a given society may offer different levels of receptivity toward different groups of strangers. For example, Canadian visitors arriving in a small town in the United States are likely to find a largely receptive host environment. On the other hand, the same small town may show less receptivity toward visitors from a lesser known and vastly different culture such as Turkey or Kenya.

Along with receptivity, *host conformity pressure* varies as well across societies and communities. Host conformity pressure refers to the extent to which the environment challenges strangers to act in accordance with the normative patterns of the host culture and its communication system. In particular, the conformity pressure of a host environment is often reflected in the expectations the natives routinely have about how strangers should think and act, thereby exerting a pressure on the strangers to adapt to the host cultural milieu. Different host environments show different levels of tolerance to strangers and their ethnic/cultural characteristics. For example, heterogeneous and open host environments such as the United States generally tend to hold a more pluralistic political ideology concerning cultural/ethnic differences and exert less pressure on strangers to change their habitual ways. Within the United States, ethnically heterogeneous metropolitan areas such as Los Angeles, Miami, and New York City tend to demand less that strangers conform to the dominant Anglo-white cultural practices than do small, ethnically homogeneous rural towns. Even within a city, certain neighborhoods may be more homogeneous and expect more conformity from strangers.

The degree to which a given host environment exerts receptivity and conformity pressure on a stranger is closely influenced by the overall *ethnic group strength*, that is, a given stranger's ethnic group's capacity to influence the surrounding host environment at large. An insight into ethnic group strength has been provided by sociologists Clarke and Obler (1976), who describe ethnic communities developing from the stages of initial economic adjustment and community building, to the subsequent stage of aggressive self assertion and promotion of identity. Additional insights are offered in Breton's (1964) model of "institutional completeness" and the social psychological concept of "ethnolinguistic vitality" (Giles, Bourhis & Taylor, 1977). These and related theoretical descriptions point to an observation that a strong ethnic group offers its members a strong informational, emotional, and material support system within the larger environment facilitating the cross-cultural adaptation of strangers during the initial phase. In the long run, however, a strong ethnic community is likely to exert a stronger social pressure to conform to its own cultural practices and to maintain the stranger's ethnic group identity and discourages their participation in host social communication activities that are necessary for successful adaptation to the host society at large.

Supporting this theoretical observation is Braun's (Braun, 2002, Kim & Braun, 2002) finding that Turkish workers in an American military organization in Germany perceive the Americans to be more receptive toward them than the Germans they encounter. This difference between the two host environments is found to be linked to the extent to which the Turkish workers have formed American and German interpersonal relationships Americans, as well as to the degree of psychological health they profess in relating to the two groups. Likewise, Maruyama's study (Maruyama, 1998; Maruyama & Kim, 1997) of international university students in Japan reports that students from other Asian countries (e.g., China, Korea, and India) report lower levels of perceived host receptivity among Japanese people they encounter than their American and Western European counterparts, affecting the two groups' psychological health differentially. (See, also, Y. S. Kim, 2003; Kim & Y. S. Kim, in press).

Predisposition

Along with the above-described host and ethnic environmental conditions, the process of cross-cultural adaptation is affected by the internal conditions of the strangers themselves prior to resettlement in the host society. To the extent that strangers differ in their backgrounds, such differences help set the perimeters for their own subsequent adaptive changes.

Strangers come to their new environment with differing levels of preparedness, that is, the mental, emotional, and motivational readiness to deal with the new cultural environment including the understanding of the host language and culture. Affecting their preparedness is a wide range of formal and informal learning activities they have had prior to moving to the host society. Included in such activities are the schooling and training in, and the media exposure to, the host language and culture, and the direct and indirect experiences in dealing with members of the host society, as well as their prior cross-cultural adaptation experiences in general. In addition, the strangers' preparedness is often influenced by the level of positive expectations toward the host society and of willingness to participate in it voluntarily. Voluntary, long-term immigrants, for example, are more likely to enter the host environment with a greater readiness for making adaptive changes in themselves compared to temporary sojourners who unwillingly relocate for reasons imposed on them.

Strangers also differ in cultural, racial, and linguistic backgrounds. The term, ethnic proximity (or ethnic distance), is employed in the theory as a relational concept comparing a given individual stranger's ethnicity and the predominant ethnicity of the host environment. Now all individuals from a given culture share similar extrinsic ethnic markers. Jewish immigrants in Israel, for example, differ significantly among themselves, from dark-skinned Ethiopian immigrants to light-skinned Russian immigrants (Abbink, 1984). What is commonly known in the United States as the "Hispanic community" is, in fact, a loose federation of individuals of widely varying racial, national, linguistic, religious, and cultural backgrounds. Given the substantial intraethnic variations, the present theory deals with extrinsic ethnic markers as a set of individual-level ethnicity-related characteristics as bearing on the cross-cultural adaptation process.

The theory identifies two facets of ethnic proximity: (1) the degree of similarity (or difference) in "extrinsic ethnic markers such as ethnic-group related physical and facial features and material artifacts such as food, dress, decorative objects, and religious practices, as well as certain noticeable behaviors such as unique gestures and paralinguistic patterns reflected in distinct accents, tempos of utterance, intonations, and pitch levels.; and (2) compatibility (or incompatibility) of "intrinsic ethnic markers" such internalized beliefs, value orientations, and norms closely associated with a particular ethnic group (Nash, 1989). Low ethnic proximity that a given stranger brings to the host environment serves as a kind of handicap in their adaptive effort. Conversely, strangers with many ethnic characteristics that are close to those of the native population are likely to enjoy a smoother transition.

An extensive amount of direct and indirect empirical evidence has been made available to support the theoretical relationship that links the salience of a stranger's ethnic markers and the difficulty he or she experiences in cross-cultural adaptation. In reviewing literature on the adaptation of Hispanic adolescents in the United States, Montalvo (1991) reports a number of studies that link darker skin color to greater "phenotyping" and thus greater adaptive stress. Other studies examining the interpersonal relationship patterns of international students report that European students interact with Americans more extensively than do students from Asia (Selltiz et al., 1963). Similar results are presented in a study of international students in England (Furnham & Bochner, 1982) , and in a comparative study of Asian Americans and Hispanic Americans (Stephan & Stephan, 1989) , and of Malaysian and Singaporean students in New Zealandand in Singapore (Ward & Kennedy, 1993) .

With respect to the adaptation-facilitating or impeding function of intrinsic ethnic markers, David Mura, a third-generation Japanese-American, write in his book, *Turning Japanese: Memoirs of a Sansei* (1991), about the discomfort he experienced when sojourning in Japan despite his Japanese physical appearance. Research findings also support the link between the cultural compatibility of strangers and their integration in host social communication networks. Various forms of psychological distress (e.g., depression, escapism, neurosis, and psychosis) have been witnessed among those whose native culture radically departs from that of the host community (e.g., David, 1969; Krau, 1991; Searle & Ward, 1990). Studies of Southeast Asian refugee groups (e.g., Goza, 1987; Kim, 1980, 1989, 1990; Ryan, 1987) have shown that Vietnamese and Laotian refugees are economically adapting to the American environment more quickly than Cambodians and Hmongs. Such differential adaptation is attributable, at lest in part, to the cultural and economic background of the first two groups that is more comparable to that of the American society.

Personality. Along with ethnic backgrounds, strangers enter a host environment with a set of more or less enduring personality traits. They begin and continue to face the challenge of the new environment within the context of their personality, which serves as the basis upon which they pursue and internalize new experiences with varying degrees of success. Of particular interest to the present theory are those personality resources that would help facilitate the strangers' adaptation by enabling them to endure stressful events and to maximize new learning, both of which are essential to their intercultural transformation. The present theory identifies three such personality resources: openness, strength, and positivity.

Openness is such a personality construct. In the systems perspective, openness is defined as an internal posture that is receptive to new information (Gendlin, 1962). Openness minimizes resistance and maximizes a willingness to attend to new and changed circumstances, and enables strangers to perceive and interpret various events and situations in the new environment as they occur with less rigid, ethnocentric judgments As Wheatley (1999) notes, "Openness to the environment over time spawns a stronger personal system....Because it [the system] partners with the environment, the system develops increasing autonomy from the environment and also develops new capacities that make it increasingly resourceful" (p. 84). As a theoretical concept, openness is employed in the present theory as varying in degrees among strangers. It is a broad term which incorporates other similar but more specific concepts such as "open-mindedness," "intercultural sensitivity," "empathy," and "tolerance for ambiguity" (e.g., Ali & Sanders, 2003; Matsumoto et al., 2003; Van der Zee & Van Oudenhoven, 2000).

Coupled with openness, the *strength* of personality allows individuals to face new challenges and remain supple, effervescent, and confident (Lifton, 1993). As the inner quality that absorbs "shocks" from the environment and bounces back without being seriously damaged by them, high levels of personality strength are reflected in the tendencies of a range of more specific, interrelated personality attributes such as "resilience," "risk-taking," "hardiness," "persistence," "patience," "elasticity," "resourcefulness," and "emotion regulation" (e.g., Matsumoto et al., 2003). Also important to the adaptation process is the personality attribute of positivity, or the proclivity for optimism and affirmative orientation in the strangers' basic outlook on life, as well as a fundamental "self-trust" in the face of adverse circumstances. It is a dimension of personality that enables strangers to continually seek to acquire new cultural knowledge, and to cultivate greater intellectual, emotional/aesthetic, and behavioral compatibility with the natives.

The three broad concepts--openness, strength, and positivity-- help define the strangers' overall personal predisposition to "push" themselves in their adaptation process. Strangers with greater openness and strength are less likely to succumb and more likely to take on the challenging situations. Together, they serve as an inner resource for working toward developing the host communication competence, so as to facilitate their own intercultural growth. A serious lack of openness and strength, on the other hand, would weaken their adaptive capacity and would serve as self-imposed psychological barriers against their own adaptation.

Intercultural Transformation

As strangers experience a progression of internal change, they undergo a set of identifiable changes in their habitual patterns of cognitive, affective, and behavioral responses. Through deculturation and acculturation, some of the "old" cultural habits are replaced by new cultural habits. They acquire increasing proficiency in self-expression and in fulfilling their various social needs. The present theory identify three interrelated aspects of the strangers' intercultural transformation as the key outcomes of cross-cultural adaptation. These outcomes, in turn, facilitate the further development of their host communication competence and participation in host interpersonal and mass communication activities.

The first aspect is an increased *functional fitness*. Through the repeated activities resulting in new cultural learning and self organizing and re-organizing, strangers in time achieve an increasing "synchrony" (Hall, 1976; Kim, 1992) between their internal responses and the external demands in the host environment. Successfully adapted strangers have accomplished a desired level of proficiency in communicating and developing a satisfactory relationship with the host environment--particularly with those individuals and situations that are of direct relevance to their daily activities. The development of the strangers' functional fitness in the host society has been documented extensively. The studies of both sojourners and immigrants have shown an increase over time in various subjective indicators of functional fitness such as life satisfaction, positive feelings toward one's life in the host environment, sense of belonging, and greater congruence in subjective meaning systems (e.g., Szalay & Inn, 1987), as well as such objective socioeconomic indicators as occupational and income status (e.g., Kim, Lujan, & Dixon, 1998b).

Closely associated with the increased functional fitness is the increased psychological health vis-a-vis their host environment. Extensive data in support of this increasing trend in the strangers' psychological well-being are documented in "culture shock" studies and similarly in the studies of mental health/illnesses among immigrants and refugees in the United States (e.g., David, 1969; Dyal & Dyal, 1981; Huhr & K. Kim, 1988; Kino, 1973). The development of functional fitness and psychological health in strangers further accompanies an emergent intercultural identity. Adversarial cross-cultural experiences bring about the experiences of what Zaharna (1989) calls "self-shock," a "shake-up" of the strangers' sense of connection to their original cultural group and an accompanying growth beyond the perimeters of the original culture. The psychological movement of strangers into new dimensions produce "boundary-ambiguity syndromes" (Hall, 1976, p. 227), in which the original cultural identity begins to lose its distinctiveness and rigidity while an expanded and more flexible definition of self emerges (Adler, 1976; Kim, 1995; Kim & Ruben, 1988). The process is far from smooth, as has been shown in the upward-downward-forward-backward movement of the stress-adaptation-growth dynamic. Intense stress can reverse the process at any time, and strangers may, indeed, regress toward re-affirming and re-identifying with their ethnic origins, having found the alienation and malaise involved in maintaining a new identity too much of a strain (De Vos & Suarez-Orozco, 1990, p. 254).

As such, the emergence of an intercultural identity is a continuous search for the authenticity in self and others across group boundaries. An important element of intercultural identity development is an emerging self-other orientation that is increasingly individualized. Individualization allows strangers to practice life that comes with diminishing grips of conventional categories. Individualization of one's self-other orientation involves a clearer self-definition and definition of the other that reflects a capacity to see the connectedness of oneself to humanity without being restricted by categories of social grouping. The resulting selfhood is one that generates a heightened self-awareness and self-identity. With this capacity, one can see oneself and others on the basis of unique individual qualities rather than categorical stereotypes, reflecting a mental outlook that exibits greater cognitive differentiation and particularization (cf. Boekestijn,1988; Hansel, 1993).

Accompanying the individualization of self-other orientation is universalization--a parallel development of a synergistic cognition "of a new consciousness, born out of an awareness of the relative nature of values and of the universal aspect of human nature" (Yoshikawa, 1978, p. 220). As people advance in their intercultural transformation process, they are better able to see the oneness and unity of humanity, and locate the points of consent and complementarity beyond the points of difference and contention. As such, they are on the way to overcoming cultural parochialism and forming a wider circle of identification. Universalization frees one's mind from the exclusive parochial viewpoint, so as to attain a perspective of a larger, more inclusive whole. A universalistic outlook underlies a mindset that integrates, rather than separates, all the perspectives represented in a communication transaction.

Research findings offer some evidence for the present theoretical claim of the emergence of an intercultural identity and its main features of individualization and universalization of self-other orientation. Amerikaner (1978) observes, in a study of military cadets, seminarians, and college fraternity members, that subjects of a high degree of personality integration (measured by the ability "to deal effectively with everyday tensions and anxieties") exhibit greater cognitive differentiation and integration, less categorical and simplistic self-identity, and greater openness to new social experiences. The author's study (Kim, Lujan, & Dixon, 1998a, 1998b) has found that Native Americans in Oklahoma who are highly integrated into the predominantly Anglo-American milieu reveal a self-other orientation that transcends ethnic categories. A more recent study by Milstein (2003) indicates that the sojourn experience in Japan among exchange students from the United States and a number of other countries has resulted in increased levels of "self-efficacy." The study also shows that the increase in self-efficacy is linked positively to the self-reported level of challenge the students experience as well as to the self-reported success of sojourn.

The Structural Model and Theorems

The six dimensions of factors identified above and summarized in Table 1 help explain the fact that not everyone is equally successful in making cross-cultural transitions. The dimension of personal communication or the cognitive, affective, and operational components of host communication competence (Dimension 1) serves as the very engine that pushes individual strangers along the adaptation process. Inseparably linked with host communication competence are the activities of host social communication (Dimension 2), through which strangers participate in the interpersonal and mass communication activities of the host environment. The dimension of ethnic social communication (Dimension 3) provides distinct, subcultural experiences of interpersonal and mass communication with fellow co-ethnics. Interacting with the personal and social (host, ethnic) communication are the conditions of the host environment (Dimension 4), including the degree of the receptivity and conformity pressure of the local population as well as the strength of the stranger's ethnic group. The stranger's predisposition (Dimension 5), consisting of preparedness for the new environment, proximity (or distance) of the stranger's ethnicity to that of the natives, and the adaptive personality attributes of openness, strength, and positivity, influences the subsequent development in the stranger's personal and social communication activities.

Each of these factors directly or indirectly facilitates or impedes the adaptation process of an individual. Like a locomotive engine, the workings of each unit operating in this process affect, and are affected by, the workings of all other units. Out of this dynamic interface among the dimensions and factors arise the fluctuating experiences of stress, adaptation, and growth—an emerging development accompanying an increasing level of congruence and ease with respect to the host environment, the original culture, and, indeed, the on-going transformation itself. Together, all of the factors directly contribute to explaining and predicting differential rates or levels of intercultural transformation with a given time period manifested in increased functional fitness, psychological health, and the emergence of an intercultural identity orientation (Dimension 6). The level of intercultural transformation, in turn, helps to explain and predict the levels of all other dimensions that constitute the overall structure of cross-cultural adaptation represented in Figure 3 [see Figure 3 on p. 145].

The six dimensions of factors identified above constitute an interactive and functional model, in which all the linkages indicate mutual stimulations (and not unidirectional causations). These linkages emphasize reciprocal functional relationships between factors internal to a stranger and the new environment, as well as the changes the stranger undergo over time. Unlike many existing models in which time length is included as an "independent" variable, time is a given background against which the present model identifies those dimensions of factors that contribute a facilitative or impeding function to the overall adaptation process.

Time, by itself, Does Not Play Such a Role

The interlocking relationships identified in the structural model are formally specified in 21 theorems. The nature of each theoretical linkage in the model is specified as a theorem, that is, a generalizable and predictive statement of a functional relationship such as: "The greater the host communication competence, the greater the participation in host social (interpersonal, mass)

Figure 3
Factors Influencing Cross-Cultural Adaptation: A Structural Model

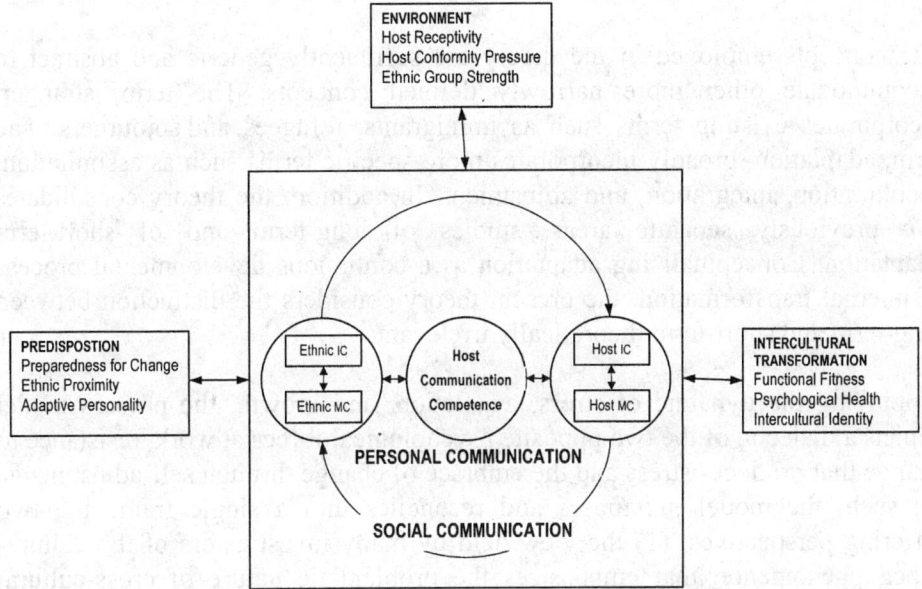

Note: IC = Interpersonal communication, MC = mass communication

Source: Kim, 2001, p. 87

communication" (Theorem 1); "The greater the host interpersonal and mass communication, the greater the intercultural transformation" (Theorem 4); and "The greater the host receptivity and host conformity pressure, the greater the host communication competence" (Theorem 8). (See Kim, 2001, pp. 91-92, for a complete list of the 21 theorems.)

Discussion

Building on the open-systems principle pointing to the natural drive of human beings to adapt whenever new environmental challenges threaten their internal equilibrium, the theory illuminates the process of adapting to a new cultural environment. This dynamic process acts as the prime mover of the journey of intercultural transformation, in which they achieve an increasing levels of functional fitness, psychological health, and intercultural identity development. This cross-cultural adaptation process is influenced by a multitude of factors identified in the structural model, including the factors of the environment and of the predisposition of a stranger influencing and being influenced by the host communication competence, interpersonal communication activities, and mass communication activities of an individual stranger within and outside his or her ethnic community.

The concepts employed in the theory are sufficiently generic and abstract to accommodate other more narrowly defined concepts. The term, stranger, incorporates existing terms such as immigrants, refugees, and sojourners. The term, adaptation, broadly incorporates more specific terms such as assimilation, acculturation, integration, and adjustment. In addition, the theory consolidates two previously separate areas—studies of long-term and of short-term adaptation. Conceptualizing adaptation as a continuous developmental process of internal transformation, the present theory considers the distinction between long-term and short-term theoretically irrelevant.

Employing the dynamic of stress, adaptation, and growth, the process model depicts a dialectic of the two opposite psychological forces at work, resistance to change that produces stress and the embrace of change through self-adjustments. As such, the model juxtaposes and reconciles into a single frame the two differing perspectives: (1) the view held by many investigators of the culture-shock phenomenon that emphasizes the problematic nature of cross-cultural adaptation experiences; and (2) the contrary view that emphasizes the aspect of cross-cultural learning and growth. These two approaches are joined in the present theory in which both stressful and growth-promoting functions are identified and linked together as two competing but complementary psychological forces intrinsic to the adaptation process.

The multidimensional and multifaceted structure model reflects the open systems perspective on human communication that emphasizes the principal features of the inseparable and interactive relationship between an individual and the environment. This holistic perspective on adaptation serves to integrate sociological and anthropological factors and psychological factors in explaining the cross-cultural adaptation of individual strangers. It brings together the macro-level analyses that have long investigated the issues of ethnic community, interethnic relations, social integration, and ethnicity into the micro-level analyses that have been typically taken in social psychology and communication for exclusively intrapersonal issues such as culture shock reactions, psychological adjustment, attitude toward the host society, and culture learning.

In addition, the present structural model bridges the division between the two opposing ideological views, assimilationism and pluralism. It does so by taking the systems-theoretic premise that cross-cultural adaptation (and, indeed, all other aspects of human adaptation) is something that occurs naturally and inevitably through communication, as strangers achieve new learning (acculturation) while some of the original cultural habits subside into the background and lose their relevance to their everyday life activities (deculturation). The assumption that adaptation is a natural and inevitable phenomenon by no means denies the fact that the ideological climate of the host environment is consequential to individual strangers' adaptation processes. To the contrary, the structural model incorporates such ideological influence in two ways. On the individual level, a given stranger's personal ideological position has to be a part of the affective-motivational component of his or her host communication competence. Strangers with an assimilative orientation are more likely to be determined to partake in the host social communication processes than others with a pluralist orientation. On the macro-level of the environment, the assimilative or pluralistic ideological climate is clearly a defining element of its receptivity and conformity pressure toward strangers.

In the end, the goodness of a theory is to be determined when the logical system of ideas correspond with the empirical reality. To the present theory, the reality is the experiences and accompanying changes in individuals who, at this very moment and at all corners of the world, are forging a new life away from their familiar grounds. There is no denying that cross-cultural adaptation occurs. The present theory affirms this reality. Once the undeniable reality of cross-cultural adaptation is understood, the real choice left for us is the degree of change that we are willing to undergo. By accelerating our efforts to cultivate host communication competence and engage ourselves actively in host social communication processes, we can maximize our own adaptation. By refusing to do so, we can minimize it. As we keep our sight on the goal of successful adaptation in the host society, we will experience a gradual transformation--a subtle and largely unconscious change that leads to an increasingly intercultural personhood. Of significance in this growth process is the development of a perceptual and emotional maturity and a deepened understanding of human conditions. Despite, and because of, the many unpredictable vicissitudes of the new life, we are challenged to step into a domain that reaches beyond the original cultural perimeters. Along with increased functional fitness and psychological health, an increasingly intercultural identity and selfhood emerges from extensive experiences of stress and adaptation. In this process, we are likely to see a blurring of lines between "us" and "them." Our old identity is never completely replaced by a new one. Instead, our identity is transformed into something that will always contain the old and the new side by side, to form a perspective that allows more openness and acceptance of differences in people, an understanding of "both-and" and a capacity to participate in the depth of aesthetic and emotional experience of others. Our true strength will be no longer found in rigidly insisting on who we were in the past and who we are at the moment, but in affirming our capacity for change and in embracing what we may yet become.

References

Abbink, J. (1984). The changing identity of Ethiopian immigrants (Falashas) in Israel. *Anthropological Quarterly*, 57(4), 139-153.

Adler. P. (1976). Beyond cultural identity: Reflections on cultural and multi-cultural man. In L. Samovar & R. Porter (Eds.), *Intercultural communication: A reader* (pp. 389-408). Belmont, CA: Wadsworth.

Ady, J. C. (1995). Toward a differential demand model of sojourner adjustment. In R. Wiseman (Ed.), *Intercultural communication theory* (pp. 92-114). Thousand Oaks, CA: Sage.

Amerikaner, M. (1978). *Personality integration and the theory of open systems: A cross-subcultural approach.* Unpublished doctoral dissertation, University of Florida, Gainesville.

Ali, A., Van der Zee, K., & Sanders, G. (2003). Determinants of intercultural adjustment among expatriate spouses. *International Journal of Intercultural Relations*, 27(5), 563-580.

Anderson, L. (1994). A new look at an old construct: Cross-cultural adaptation. *International Journal of Intercultural Relations*, 18, 293-328.

Bateson, G. (1972). *Steps to an ecology of mind: Collected essays in anthropology, psychiatry, evolution and epistemology*. New York: Ballantine. (Original work published 1951).

Baumeister, R. F., & Leary, M. R. (1995). The need to belong: Desire for interpersonal attachments as a fundamental human motivation. *Psychological Bulletin*, 117, 497-529.

Belay, G. (1993). Toward a paradigm shift for intercultural and international communication: New research directions. In S. Deetz (Ed.), *Communication yearbook 6* (pp. 437-457). Newbury Park, CA: Sage.

Berkowitz, S. (1982). *An introduction to structural analysis: The network approach to social research.* Toronto: Butterworth.

Berry, J. W. (1980). Marginality, stress and ethnic identification in an acculturated aboriginal community. *Journal of Cross-Cultural Psychology*, 1, 239-252.

Berry, J. W. (1990). Psychology of acculturation: Understanding individuals moving between cultures. In R. Brislin (Ed.), *Applied cross-cultural psychology* (pp. 232-253). Newbury Park, CA: Sage.

Bertalanffy, L. (1956). *Robots, men, and minds.* New York: Braziller.

Blalock, H. M. Jr. (1989). *Power and conflict: Toward a general theory*. Newbury Park, CA: Sage.

Blau, P., & Schwartz, B. (1984). *Cross-cutting social circles.* New York: Academic Press.

Boekestijn, C. (1988). Intercultural migration and the development of personal identity. *International Journal of Intercultural Relations*, 12(2), 83-105.

Bognar, N. (2001, April). Cross-cultural adjustment and gender-related norms: A study of Eastern Europeans in the United States. Paper presented at the 2nd biennial congress of the International Academy for Intercultural Research, Oxford, MS.

Boulding, K. (1956/1977). *The images: Knowledge in life and society.* Ann Arbor: The University of Michigan.

Bourhis, R., Moiese, L., Perreault, S., & Senecal, S. (1997). Towards an interactive acculturation model: A social psychological approach. *International Journal of Psychology*, 32, 369-386.

Braun, V. (2002, May). *Intercultural communication and psychological health of Turkish workers in an American workplace in Germany*. Unpublished doctoral dissertation, University of Oklahoma, Norman.

Breton, R. (1964). Institutional completeness of ethnic communities and the personal relations of immigrants. *American Journal of Sociology*, 70(2), 193-205.

Buck, R. (1984). *The communication of emotion*. New York: Guilford.

Burke, K. (1974). *Communication and the human condition. Communication, 1.* United Kingdom: Gordon and Breach Science Publishers, 135-52

Buss. D. M., & Kenrick, D. T. (1998). Evolutionary social psychology. In D. T. Gilbert, S. T. Fiske, & G. Lindzey (Eds.), *Handbook of social psychology*, Vol. 2 (4th ed., pp. 982-1026). New York: Oxford University Press.

Chang, W. C. (2001, April). A model of situation-specific multiculturalism of Asian immigrants in Singapore. Paper presented at the 2nd biennial congress of the International Academy for Intercultural Research, Oxford, MS.

Clarke, S., & Obler, J. (1976). Ethnic conflict, community-building, and the emergence of ethnic political traditions in the United States. In S. Clarke & J. Obler (Eds.), *Urban ethnic conflicts: A comparative perspective* (pp. 1-34). Chapel Hill: University of North Carolina Press.

Cook, W. (1962). The systematic analysis of socially significant events: A strategy for social research. *Journal of Social Issues*, 18(2), 66-88.

Cui, G. (1998). Cross-cultural adaptation and ethnic communication: Two structural equation models. *Howard Journal of Communication*, 9, 69-85.

David, H. (1969). Involuntary international migration: Adaptation of refugees. In E. Brody (Ed.), *Behavior in new environments: Adaptation of migrant populations* (pp. 73-95). Beverly Hills, CA: Sage.

De Vos, G. A., & Suarez-Orozco, M. M. (1990). *Status inequality: The self in culture.* Newbury Park, CA: Sage.

Dubin, R. (1978). *Theory building* (Rev. ed.). New York: Free Press.

Dubos, R. (1965). *Man adapting.* New Haven, CT: Yale University Press.

Dyal, J., & Dyal, R. (1981). Acculturation, stress and coping. *International Journal of Intercultural Relations*, 5(4), 301-328.

Fielding, N., & Fielding, J. (1986). *Linking data*. Newbury Park, CA: Sage.

Furnham, A., & Bochner, S. (1982). Social difficulty in a foreign culture: An empirical analysis of culture shock. In S. Bochner (Ed.), *Cultures in contact: Studies in cross-cultural interaction* (pp. 161-198). New York: Pergamon.

Furnham, A., & Bochner, S. (1986). *Culture shock: Psychological reactions to unfamiliar environments*. New York: Routledge.

Gendlin, E. (1962). *Experiencing and the creation of meaning*. New York: The Free Press.

Giles, H., Bourhis, R., & Taylor, D. (1977). Toward a theory of second language acquisition. *Journal of Multilingual and Multicultural Development, 3*, 17-40.

Givon, T. (1989). *Mind, code and context: Essays in pragmatics*. Hillsdale, NJ: Lawrence Erlbaum.

Gong, Y. (2003). Goal orientations and cross-cultural adjustment: An exploratory study. *International Journal of Intercultural Relations, 27*(3), 297-305.

Gordon, M. (1973). Assimilation in America: Theory and reality. In P. Rose (Ed.), *The study of society* (pp. 350-365). New York: Random House.

Gordon, M. (1981). Models of pluralism: The new American dilemma. *Annals of the American Academy of Political and Social Science, 454*, 178-188.

Goza, F. (1987). Adjustment and adaptation among Southeast Asian refugees in the United States. *Dissertation Abstract International, 48*(02), 486B. (University Microfilms No. AAC87-08086).

Gudykunst, W. B., & Kim, Y. Y. (2003). *Communicating with strangers: An approach to intercultural communication (4th ed.)*. New York: McGraw-Hill.

Hall, E. (1976). *Beyond culture*. Garden City, NY: Anchor.

Hallinan, M., & Smith, S. (1985). The effects of classroom racial composition on students' interracial friendliness. *Social Psychology Quarterly, 48*, 3-16.

Hansel, B. (1993). *An investigation of the re-entry adjustment of Indians who studied in the U.S.A.* (Occasional Papers in Intercultural Learning No. 17). New York: AFS Center for the Study of Intercultural Learning.

Hedge, R. S. (1998). Swinging the trapeze: The negotiation of identity among Asian Indian immigrant women in the United States. In D. V. Tanno & A. Gonzalez (Eds.), *Communication and identity across cultures* (pp. 34-55). Thousand Oaks, CA: Sage.

Horton, D., & Wohl, R. (1979). Mass communication and para-social interaction. In G. Gumpert & R. Cathcart (Eds.), *Inter/Media: Interpersonal communication in a media world* (pp. 32-55). New York: Oxford University Press.

Hurh, W., & Kim, K. (1988). Uprooting and adjustment: A sociological study of Korean immigrants' mental health. Final report submitted to National Institute of Mental Health, U.S. Department of Health and Human Services (Grant No. 1 R01 MH40312-01/5 MH40312-02).

Jantsch, E. (1980). *The self-organizing universe: Scientific and human implications of the emerging paradigm of evolution*. New York: Pergamon.

Jasinskaja-Lahti, I., Liebkind, K., Horenczyk, G., & Schmitz, P. (2003). The interactive nature of acculturation: Perceived discrimination, acculturation attitudes and stress among ethnic repatriates in Finland, Israel and Germany. *International Journal of Intercultural Relations*, 27(1), 79-97.

Joas, H. (1993). *Pragmatism and social theory*. Chicago: University of Chicago Press.

Jourard, S. (1974). Growing awareness and the awareness of growth. In B. Patton & K. Griffin (Eds.), *Interpersonal communication* (pp. 456-465). New York: Harper & Row.

Kim, Y. S. (2003, May). Host communication competence and psychological health: A study of cross-cultural adaptation of Korean expatriate employees in the United States. Paper presented at the annual conference of the International Communication Association, San Diego.

Kim, Y. Y. (1976). *Communication patterns of foreign immigrants in the process of acculturation: A survey among the Korean population in Chicago*. Unpublished doctoral dissertation, Northwestern University, Evanston, IL.

Kim, Y. Y. (1977a). Communication patterns of foreign immigrants in the process of acculturation. *Human Communication Research*, 4(1), 66-77.

Kim, Y. Y. (1977b). Inter-ethnic and intra-ethnic communication: A study of Korean immigrants in Chicago. *International and Intercultural Communication Annual*, 4, 53-68.

Kim, Y. Y. (1978a). A communication approach to acculturation processes: Korean immigrants in Chicago. *International Journal of Intercultural Relations*, 2(2), 197-224.

Kim, Y. Y. (1978b, November). Acculturation and patterns of interpersonal communication relationships: A study of Japanese, Mexican, and Korean communities in the Chicago area. Paper presented at the Speech Communication Association Conference, Minneapolis, MN.

Kim, Y. Y. (1979). Toward an interactive theory of communication-acculturation. In B. Ruben (Ed.), *Communication Yearbook 3* (pp. 435-453). New Brunswick, NJ: Transaction Books.

Kim, Y. Y. (1980). *Research project report on Indochinese refugees in Illinois. Vol. 1: Introduction, summary and recommendations. Vol. 2: Methods and procedures. Vol. 3: Population characteristics and service needs. Vol. 4: Psychological, social and cultural adjustment of Indochinese refugees. Vol. 5: Survey of agencies serving Indochinese refugees* . (Based on a grant from the Department of Health, Education and Welfare Region V, P: 95-549). Chicago: Travelers Aid Society.

Kim, Y. Y. (1988). *Communication and cross-cultural adaptation: An integrative theory* . Clevedon, United Kingdom: Multilingual Matters.

Kim, Y. Y. (1989). Personal, social, and economic adaptation: The case of 1975-1979 arrivals in Illinois. In D. Haines (Ed.), *Refugees as immigrants: Survey research on Cambodians, Laotians, and Vietnamese in America.* Totowa, NJ: Rowman & Littlefield.

Kim, Y. Y. (1990). Communication and adaptation of Asian Pacific refugees in the United States. *Journal of Pacific Rim Communication*, 1, 191-207.

Kim, Y. Y. (1992). Synchrony and intercultural communication. In D. Crookall & K. Arai (Eds.), *Global interdependent: Simulation and gaming perspectives* (pp. 99-105). New York: Springer-Verlag.

Kim, Y. Y. (1995). Identity development: From cultural to intercultural. In H. Mokros (Ed.), *Information and behavior, Vol. 6. Interaction and identity* (pp. 347-369). New Brunswick, NJ: Transactions.

Kim, Y. Y. (2001). *Becoming intercultural: An integrative theory of communication and cross-cultural adaptation* . Thousand Oaks, CA: Sage.

Kim, Y. Y. (2002). Unum vs. Pluribus: Ideology and differing academic conceptions of ethnic identity. In W. Gudykunst (Ed.), *Communication yearbook 26* (pp. 298-325). Mahwah, NJ: Lawrence Erlbaum Associates.

Kim, Y. Y. (in press). Long-term cross-cultural adaptation: Training implications of an integrative theory. In D. Landis, J. Bennett, & M. Bennett (Eds.), *Handbook of intercultural training (3rd ed.)*. Thousand Oaks, CA: Sage.

Kim, Y. Y. & Braun, V. (2002, July). Host communication competence and psychological health: A study of Turkish workers' adaptation to an American-German host environment. Paper presented at the annual conference of the International Communication Association, Seoul, South Korea.

Kim, Y. Y. & Kim, Y. S. (in press). Patterns of communication and adaptation: A comparative study of Korean expatriates in the United States and American expatriates in Korea. *Asian Communication Research* 1.

Kim, Y. Y., Lujan, P., & Dixon, L. (1998a). Patterns of communication and interethnic integration: A study of American Indians in Oklahoma. *Canadian Journal of Native Education*, 22(1), 120-137.

Kim, Y. Y., Lujan, P., & Dixon, L. (1998b). "I can walk both ways": Identity integration of American Indians in Oklahoma. *Human Communication Research*, 25(2), 252-274.

Kim, Y. Y., & Ruben, B. (1988). Intercultural transformation: A systems theory. In Y. Kim & W. Gudykunst (Eds.), *International and intercultural communication annual 12. Theories in intercultural communication* (pp. 299-321). Newbury Park, CA: Sage.

Kino, F. (1973). Aliens' paranoid reaction. In C. Zwingmann & M. Pfister-Ammende (Eds.), *Uprooting and after* (pp. 60-66). New York: Springer-Verlag.

Kirschner, G. (1994). Equilibrium processes: Creativity and depression. *Mind and Human Interaction*, 5(4), 165-171.

Krau, E. (1991). *The contradictory immigrant problem: A sociopsychological analysis.* New York: Peter Lang.

Lazarus, R. (1966). *Psychological stress and the coping process.* St. Louis: McGraw-Hill.

Lifton, R. (1993). *The protean self: Human resilience in an age of fragmentation.* New York: Basic Books.

Maruyama, M. (1998). *Cross-cultural adaptation and host environment: A study of international Students in apan.* Unpublished doctoral dissertation, University of Oklahoma, Norman.

Maruyama, M., & Kim, Y. Y. (1997). Cross-cultural adaptation of international students in Japan: An exploratory study. Paper presented at the annual conference of the International Communication Association, Montreal.

Matsumoto, D., ReRoux, J. A., Iwanoto, M., Choi, J. W., Rogers, D., Tatani, H., & Uchida, H. (2003). The robustness of the intercultural adjustment potential scale (ICAPS): The search for a universal psychological engine of adjustment. *International Journal of Intercultural Relations*, 27(5), 543-562.

Mechanic, D. (1974). Social structure and personal adaptation: Some neglected dimensions. In G. Coelho, D. Hamburg, & J. Adams (Eds.), *Coping and adaptation* (pp. 32-44). New York: Basic Books.

Mernard, S. (1991). *Longitudinal research.* Newbury Park, CA: Sage.

Milstein, T. J. (2003, May). Transformation abroad: Communication self-efficacy via sojourning. Paper presented at the annual conference of the International Communication Association, San Diego.

Monge, P. R. (1990). Theoretical and analytical issues in studying organizational processes. *Organization Science*, 1, 406-430.

Montalvo, F. (1991). Phenotyping, acculturation, and biracial assimilation of Mexican Americans. In M. Sotomayor (Ed.), *Empowering Hispanic families: A critical issue for the '90s* (pp. 97-119). Milwaukee, WI: Family Service America.

Moos, R. (Ed.). *Human adaptation: Coping with life crises.* Lexington, MA: D.C. Heath.

Mura, D. (1991). *Turning Japanese: Memoirs of a sansei*. New York: Atlantic Monthly Press.

Nash, M. (1989). *The cauldron of ethnicity in the modern world*. Chicago: University of Chicago Press.

Nesdale, D., & Mak, A. S. (2003). Ethnic identification, self-esteem and immigrant psychological health. *International Journal of Intercultural Relations*, 27(1), 23-40.

Piaget, J. (1963). *The origins of intelligence in children*. New York: W. W. Norton.

Ruben, B. D. (1975). Intrapersonal, interpersonal, and mass communication processes in individual and multi-person systems. In B. Ruben & J. Kim (Eds.), *General systems theory and human communication* (pp. 120-144). Rochelle Park, NJ: Hayden.

Ruesch, J., & Bateson, G. (1951/1968). *Communication: The social matrix of psychiatry*. New York: W. W. Norton.

Ryan, C. (1987). Indochinese refugees in the U. S.: Background characteristics, initial adjustment patterns, and the role of policy. *Dissertation Abstracts International*, 48(04), 1025B. (University Microfilms No. AAC87-15554).

Sahlins, M. (1964). Culture and environment: The study of cultural ecology. In S. Tax (Ed.), *Horizons of anthropology* (pp. 132-147). Chicago: Aldine.

Searle, W., & Ward, C. (1990). The prediction of psychological and socio-cultural adjustment during cross-cultural transitions. *International Journal of Intercultural Relations*, 14, 449-464.

Selltiz, C., Christ, J. R., Havel, J., & Cook, S. W. (1963). *Attitudes and social relations of foreign students in the United States*. Minneapolis: University of Minnesota Press.

Shibutani, T., & Kwan, K. M. (1965). *Ethnic stratification: A comparative approach*. New York: Macmillan.

Simmel, G. (1908/1950). The stranger. In K. Wolff (Ed. and trans.), *The sociology of Georg Simmel*. New York: Free Press.

Spicer, E. (1968). Acculturation. In D. Sills (Ed.), *International encyclopedia of the social sciences* (pp. 21-27). New York: Macmillan.

Stephan, W., & Stephan, C. (1989). Antecedents of intergroup anxiety in Asian Americans and Hispanic Americans. *International Journal of Intercultural Relations*, 13, 203-219.

Stonequist, E. (1937). *The marginal man*. New York: Scribner's.

Szalay, L., & Inn, A. (1987). Cross-cultural adaptation and diversity: Hispanic Americans. In Y. Kim & W. Gudykunst (Eds.), *Cross-cultural adaptation: Current approaches* (pp. 212-232). Newbury Park, CA: Sage.

Taft, R. (1977). Coping with unfamiliar cultures. In N. Warren (Ed.), *Studies in cross-cultural psychology* (Vol. I, pp. 121-153). London: Academic Press.

Tamam, E. (1993, December). *The influence of ambiguity tolerance, open-mindedness, and empathy on sojourners' psychological adaptation and perceived intercultural communication effectiveness.* Unpublished doctoral dissertation, University of Oklahoma, Norman, OK.

Thayer, L. (1975). Knowledge, order, and communication. In B. Ruben & J. Kim (Eds.), *General systems theory and human communication* (pp. 237-245). Rochelle Park, NJ: Hayden.

Van der Zee, K. I., & Van Oudenhoven, J. P. (2000). Psychometric qualities of the multicultural personality questionnaire: A multidimensional instrument of multicultural effectiveness. *European Journal of Personality*, 14, 291-309.

Ward, C., Bochner, S., & Furnham, A. (2001). *The psychology of culture shock (2nd ed.).* Philadelphia: Routledge.

Ward, C., & Kennedy, A. (1993). Where's the culture in cross-cultural transition. Comparative studies of sojourner adjustment. *Journal of Cross-Cultural Psychology*, 24, 221-249.

Ward, C. & Kennedy, A. (1999). The measurement of sociocultural adaptation. *International Journal of Intercultural Relations*, 23, 659-677.

Watzlawick, P., Beavin, J., & Jackson, D. (1967). *Pragmatics of human communication.* New York: Norton.

Wheatley, M. J. (1999). *Leadership and the new science: Discovering order in a chaotic world.* San Francisco: Berrett-Koehler Publishers.

White, R. (1976). Strategies of adaptation: An attempt at systematic description. In R. Moos (Ed.), *Human adaptation: Coping with life crises* (pp. 17-32). Lexington, MA: D.C. Heath & Co.

Young, R. (1996). *Intercultural communication: Pragmatics, genealogy, deconstruction.* Philadelphia: Multilingual Matters.

Yoshikawa, M. (1978). Some Japanese and American cultural characteristics. In M. Prosser (Ed.), *The cultural dialogue: An introduction to intercultural communication* (pp. 220-239). Boston: Houghton Mifflin.

Zaharna, R. (1989). Self-shock: The double-binding challenges of identity. *International Journal of Intercultural Relations*, 13(4), 501-525.

Introduction to

Managing Intercultural Conflict:
Applying the Culture-Based Situational Conflict Model

By John Oetzel and Adolfo José Garcia

Oetzel and Garcia point out that today it is quite common for international businesses to not only negotiate with representatives from other cultures, but also for employees of a company to be of diverse intercultural background. Consequently, the probability of conflict situations due to cultural differences is more likely today than ever before. And these conflicts can and do arise due to different approaches to and resolutions of conflicts. In other words, even though representatives of different cultures may be attempting to resolve a conflict situation, they may not be perceived as doing so by the others and vice versa. It, therefore, becomes essential for people to be aware of this potential problem and to attempt to overcome it. Hence, the authors point to the "Culture-Based Situational Conflict Model," developed by Oetzel and Ting-Toomey, which helps overcome these problems.

It turns out that studies indicate that effective encoding and decoding lead to mutually shared meanings and mutually shared meanings lead to perceived intercultural understanding. So with better and clearer understanding of what may be happening in a given situation, the likelihood of escalating a misunderstanding to a conflict is reduced. Critical in overcoming these problems is knowledge, motivation, and mindfulness as well as interaction skills.

These aspects are helpful for any intercultural encounter in a business context because conflicts that are avoided due to better understanding of everyone involved in the situation are more beneficial and profitable to both sides. This is very useful for intercultural encounters - whether it be encounters between organizations or within organizations.

Michael B. Hinner

John Oetzel is an Associate Professor and Chair in the Department of Communication and Journalism at the University of New Mexico. He teaches courses in intercultural, health, and organizational communication as well as quantitative research methods. His research interests focus on culture and conflict communication in work groups, organizations, and health settings. His work has appeared in journals such as *Psychologische Beiträge, Human Communication Research, Communication Monographs, Communication Research,* and the *International Journal of Intercultural Relations.* He is co-author (with Stella Ting-Toomey) of *The Sage Handbook of Conflict Communication* (2006). He is also on the editorial board of several journals including *Communication Education, Journal of Intercultural Communication Research, Communication Reports,* and *The International and Intercultural Communication Annual.*

Adolfo José Garcia is a lecturer at the University of Wisconsin-Green Bay and expects to finish Ph.D. work (University of New Mexico) in 2007. Before receiving his Master's degree, Garcia worked in the manufacturing, software, and distribution industries in the United States, France, Germany, Spain, and England. He teaches courses in interpersonal, public speaking, intercultural, mediation, small group communication, mass communication, research methods, and communication theory. His research interests center on the role of third parties in intercultural communication difficulties.

Managing Intercultural Conflict:
Applying the Culture-Based Situational Conflict Model

John Oetzel
Adolfo José Garcia

Conducting business today often necessitates an international perspective that incorporates cultural differences. On a daily basis business people communicate in airports, in business meetings, and through electronic means and must negotiate business without necessarily being culturally proficient. Culture is defined as "a learned meaning system that consists of patterns of traditions, beliefs, values, norms, and symbols that are passed on from one generation to the next and are shared to varying degrees by interacting members of a community (Ting-Toomey, 1999, p. 10).

Many countries have recognized the monetary benefits of cultural integration but companies are starting to recognize that integration and immigration also change the way that people relate and work together (e.g., see Kurthen, 1995). At an organizational level, culturally diverse teams come together to solve problems but with varied understanding of each other's cultures. Nonetheless, cultural diversity can enhance the bottom line with improved productivity, creativity and decision making (Cox, 1994; McLeod, Lobel, & Cox, 1996; Oetzel, 2005). However, cultural diversity also leads to increased negative interactions including power struggles and conflict (Cox, 1994; Oetzel, 2005). Not surprisingly, lack of cultural knowledge coupled with ineffective communication can lead to conflict (Ting-Toomey & Oetzel, 2001). Conflict is "the perceived and/or actual incompatibility of values, expectations, processes, or outcomes between two or more parties over substantive and/or relational issues" (Ting-Toomey, 1994, p. 360). Effective intercultural communication is essential for navigating conflict. Intercultural communication is the study of interaction created through communication that defines relationships of individuals from diverse cultural backgrounds (Ting-Toomey, 2005). Effective intercultural communication also must address stereotypes, ethnocentrism, and prejudice since the dynamics created by these negative assumptions has implications on innovation, growth, and conflict (Ting-Toomey & Oetzel, 2001).

Organizations and business people are productive when conflicts are resolved in appropriate ways. Unfortunately, cultural integration does not equate to competent intercultural communication. In many cases, integration as a result of demographic changes and fueled by economic change can exacerbate conflict. Models of conflict behavior can help practitioners, academics, and business people understand the dynamics of intercultural conflict. The purpose of this manuscript is to describe the Culture-Based Situational Conflict Model (CBSCM), which illuminates many of the factors of culture and conflict. (Ting-Toomey, 2005). After presenting the CBSCM, we provide four suggestions that can aid business people in competently and peacefully managing intercultural conflict.

We chose four countries to illustrate cultural diversity evident across the globe, which illustrates the need for the CBSCM: Germany, the United States, China, and Japan. These countries have different immigration policies, value systems, political systems, histories, and economic approaches. However, all four are active in global business and serve as illustrative of how culture and other factors influence conflict in business. Further, these profiles illustrate that there is within country diversity as well as intercultural diversity in business communication. Finally, there is sufficient research describing the conflict approaches in members from these cultures (Clackworthy, 1996; Elsayed-Ekhouly & Buda, 1996; Gao & Ting-Toomey, 1998; Oetzel et al., 2001; Oetzel et al., 2003; Oetzel & Ting-Toomey, 2003; Ohbuchi, Fukishima, & Tedeschi, 1999).

Germany, the United States, China, and Japan show the changing cultural makeup evident by immigration. Germany's relative prosperity, its involvement in the European Union, and the unification in 1990 with the former German Democratic Republic have made this country a prime destination for many immigrants (Federal Statistics Office - Germany, 2005). Most notably, Turkey, the countries formerly represented under Yugoslavia, and Greece constitute 43% of the immigrant population residing in Germany in 2004 (Federal Statistics Office - Germany, 2005). In the United States, the North American Free Trade Agreement (NAFTA) contributes to immigration from Central and South America. Hispanics (mainly from Mexico) accounted for 50% of the overall U.S. population growth in 2004 and currently represent 14% of the overall population (U.S. Census Bureau, 2005). For China, their accession into the World Trade Organization (WTO) in 2001 has dramatically increased trade, making the country the world's third largest trading nation, second only to the United States and Germany (Allen, 2003). As a result, in 2002, China became the second largest net sender of migrants to other countries totaling 230,000 people and second only to Mexico (Allen, 2003). Finally Japan, a highly urban and industrialized society with only 6% of the labor force in agriculture, continues to rely heavily on foreign countries for food, clothing, travel and a wide variety of other goods and services (Number of Japanese Living Abroad, 2005). From 2000 to 2004 the total number of Japanese living abroad has increased by 16% to almost one million people (Number of Japanese Living Abroad, 2005). The apparent diversity across the globe evident by these four countries and the potential misunderstanding caused by close integration is the ideal reason to propose our model, the CBSCM, which describes conflict situations in the workplace.

The Culture-Based Situational Conflict Model

The CBSCM is a contextual model to describe intercultural conflict and can be used as a guide for individuals in everyday business encounters. To be competent in situations of intercultural conflict means communicating in such a way that is inclusive, yet aware of our own ethnocentric lenses. There are many factors that affect our competent management of an intercultural conflict episode. In order to explain these factors, Ting-Toomey and Oetzel (2001) created the CBSCM to organize, relate, and explain concepts in a coherent fashion. This chapter examines some of the cultural, personal, and situational factors that shape face-to-face intercultural conflict. Ting-Toomey and Oetzel (2001) identified four clusters of factors in this model: (a) primary orientation factors: cultural value patterns, personal attributes, conflict norms, and face concerns; (b) situational and relationship boundary features: intergroup boundaries, rela-

Figure 1
Culture-Based Situational Conflict Model

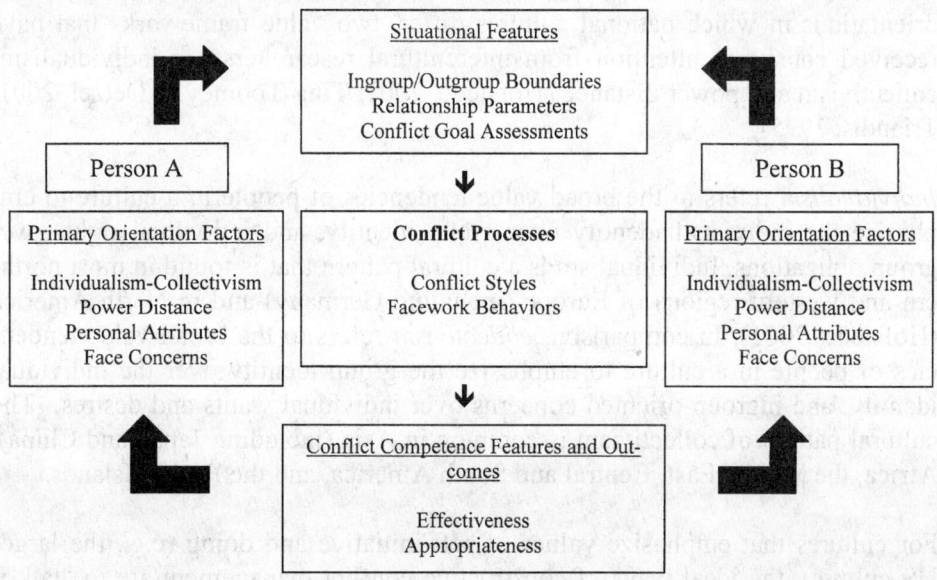

tionship parameters, conflict goal assessments, and conflict intensity; (c) conflict communication process factors: conflict styles, facework strategies, emotional expressions, and conflict rhythms; and (d) conflict competence features (see Figure 1).

The primary orientation factors refer to factors that create primary differences between cultural members in an intercultural conflict episode. Additionally, because of these primary orientation factors, our interpretations of different situational and relationship features may differ across cultures and individuals. Situational and relationship features, in turn, serve as moderating variables that influence our conflict communication process. As a result of these processes, individuals evaluate the conflict in terms of satisfaction, productivity, effectiveness, and appropriateness. In order to develop our competencies in managing differences in an intercultural conflict episode, we should learn to attune to the primary orientation factors that create the initial conflict conditions.

Primary Orientation Factors. In conflict episodes that include two polarized intercultural parties, the participants often carry with them different cultural values, personality orientation, and face concerns. These different cultural values and patterns often affect the fundamental expectations and attitudes indicating how an intercultural conflict should be approached, managed, and resolved.

Cultural value patterns. Differences in cultural values often give rise to the different ideals of how conflicts should be managed. While there are many value orientations in which national cultures differ, two value frameworks that have received consistent attention from intercultural researchers are individualism-collectivism and power distance (Hofstede, 2001; Ting-Toomey & Oetzel, 2001; Triandis, 1995).

Individualism refers to the broad value tendencies of people in a culture to emphasize the individual identity over group identity, and individual rights over group obligations. Individualism is a cultural pattern that is found in most northern and western regions of Europe (including Germany) and in North America (Hofstede, 2001). In comparison, *collectivism* refers to the broad value tendencies of people in a culture to emphasize the group identity over the individual identity, and ingroup-oriented concerns over individual wants and desires. The cultural pattern of collectivism is common in Asia (including Japan and China), Africa, the Middle East, Central and South America, and the Pacific Islands.

For cultures that emphasize values of self-initiative and doing (e.g., the larger US culture), the ideal ways of constructive conflict management are to "talk it out" and perhaps "brainstorm creative solutions" to the problem. In comparison, for cultures that emphasize values of relational harmony and uncertainty avoidance (e.g., the larger Japanese culture), the ideal ways of competent conflict management are to "talk around the point" for the sake of preserving relational harmony, and perhaps even avoid the conflict altogether.

Another value framework that national cultures differ on is power distance (Hofstede, 2001). *Small power distance* refers to broad value tendencies of people in a culture to emphasize individual credibility and expertise, democratic decision-making process, equal rights and relations, and equitable rewards and punishments based on performance. Small to moderate power distance index values are found in Germany and the United States (Hofstede, 2001). *Large power distance* refers to broad value tendencies of people in a culture to emphasize status-based credibility and experience, benevolent autocratic decision-making process, asymmetrical role-based relations, and rewards and punishments based on age, rank, status, title, and seniority. Large power distance index values are found in Japan and China (Hofstede, 2001). Power is distributed relatively evenly in small power distance work situations. Subordinates expect to be consulted, and the ideal boss is a resourceful democrat. In contrast, in large power distance work situations, the power of an organization is centralized at the upper management level. Subordinates expect and prefer, to some extent, to be told what to do, and the ideal boss plays the benevolent autocratic role (Ting-Toomey & Oetzel, 2001).

Intercultural conflicts often arise between members who subscribe different meanings to respect and power. Small power distance members respect self-empowered individuals who actively seek solutions to the conflict problem and activate individual resourcefulness in solving the problem. On the other hand, large power distance members respect individuals who are well connected in their networks and are able to find the proper individuals in the proper channels to resolve the conflict problem.

Personal Attributes. An alternative way to understand individualism and collectivism and power distance focuses on how individuals within a culture conceptualize the sense of "self." We must remember that within-cultures variations exist in each culture. In individualistic cultures, there are individuals who act just like collectivists. Likewise, in collectivistic cultures, there are persons who behave just like individualists. We must also keep in mind that behavior is only a partial indicator of a person's identity. To understand a "full-fledged" independent or interdependent person, we must also examine the thinking and affective pattern of this individual rather than just their cultural value tendencies. Markus and Kitayama (1991) argued that our self-conception within our culture profoundly influences our communication with others: individuals with a strongly *independent sense of self* tend to see self as autonomous, self-reliant, unencumbered, and as rational choice-makers; individuals with a strongly *interdependent sense of self* tend to see themselves as ingroup-bound, obligatory agents, and as relational harmony seekers. Both types of self-construal exist within a culture. Overall, however, independent concepts of self are more common in individualistic cultures, and interdependent concepts of self are more common in collectivistic cultures (Ting-Toomey, 2005). However, some research indicates change in cultures and self. For example, Oetzel et al. (2001) found that independent types were more common in the U.S. than Germany, China, and Japan, but that there was no significant difference in the prevalence of interdependent types.

Independent-self types tend to worry about whether they present their unique self credibly and competently in front of others. Interdependent-self types tend to be more attune to what others think of their face image in the context of ingroup/outgroup relations. When communicating with others, high independents believe in voicing their personal opinions, striving for personal goals, and expressing their conflict needs assertively. On the other hand, high interdependents tend to be more circumspective in an interpersonal conflict situation. They prefer self-restraint and self-monitoring strategies in approaching a conflict in order not to bring relational chaos, disharmony, or shame to their perceived ingroup. They tend to practice other-centered communication in anticipating the thoughts and feelings of the other person in the conflict situation.

Parallel to the above self-construal idea, we can examine power distance from a personal-level. Individuals and their behaviors can be conceptualized as either moving toward the "horizontal self" spectrum or the "vertical self" spectrum. Individuals who endorse horizontal self-construals prefer informal-symmetrical interactions (i.e., equal treatment) regardless of people's position, status, rank, or age. In comparison, individuals who emphasize vertical self-construals prefer formal-asymmetrical interactions (i.e., differential treatment) with due respect to people's position, titles, and age. As Triandis (1995) observed, "This [conceptualization] means that people will seek different kinds of relationships and when possible 'convert' a relationship to the kind that they are most comfortable with. Thus, a professor from a horizontal-based self may convert a professor-student relationship to a friend-friend relationship, which may well confuse a student from a vertical-based self" (p. 164). While horizontal selves tend to predominate in small power distance cultures, vertical selves tend to predominate in large power distance cultures. Oetzel et al. (2001) found that vertical selves were more prevalent in China and Japan than Germany, which had more vertical selves than in US. Thus, it is important to reiterate that while prior research has found certain trends among national cultures, cultures do change, certain samples may not reflect overall cultural populations, and there is significant within-culture diversity.

Face concerns. Hu (1944) provided one of the earliest definitions of face when he argued that there are two types of face in Chinese culture: *lien* and *mianzi*. *Lien* refers to the moral character of an individual while *mianzi* refers to the social status achieved through success in life. Face is an important social-self concept in China (Gao & Ting-Toomey, 1998), Japan (Morisaki & Gudykunst, 1994), Korea (Lim & Choi, 1996), Colombia (Fitch, 1998), Mexico (Garcia, 1996), and many Arab countries (Katriel, 1986).

Although the concept of face originated in Eastern cultures, people in all cultures share aspects of face. Face can be lost, saved, and protected. Every member of a society wants to present and protect his/her own public images (Brown & Levinson, 1987; Goffman, 1959). Previous studies indicate that the concept of face is used across cultures; however, the meanings and usages are different depending on the culture (Condon, 1984; Ting-Toomey, 1988).

Face is the claimed sense of favorable social self-worth and/or projected other-worth in a public situation (Ting-Toomey & Kurogi, 1998). It is a vulnerable resource especially in conflict situations because this resource can be threatened, enhanced, maintained, and bargained over. Since face is vulnerable, recovering it becomes a primary goal and can supersede any other concern in conflict. Face is associated with respect, honor, status, reputation, credibility, competence, network connection, and relational obligation issues. Face has simultaneous affective (e.g., feelings of shame and pride), cognitive (e.g., calculating how much to give and receive face), and behavioral levels (e.g., appropriate language use or nonverbal displays).

Face consists of three dimensions: (a) locus of face—concern for self, other or both; (b) face valence—whether face is being defended, maintained, or honored, and (c) temporality—whether face is being restored or proactively protected (Rogan & Hammer, 1994). Locus of face is the primary dimension of face and determines the direction of the subsequent conflict messages (Ting-Toomey, 1988). *Self-face* is the protective concern for one's own image when one's own face is threatened in the conflict situation. *Other-face*, on the other hand, is the concern for accommodating the other conflict party's image in the conflict crisis situation. *Mutual-face* is the concern for both parties' images and/or the "image" of the relationship (Ting-Toomey & Kurogi, 1998).

The majority of research investigations indicate that individualistic cultures and independent types have more self-face concern and less other and mutual-face concerns than collectivistic cultures and interdependent types (Gao & Ting-Toomey, 1998; Lim & Choi, 1996). In a study of Germany, U.S., Japan, and China, Oetzel et al. (2001) found that the best predictor for face concern was self-construal. Specifically, people with an interdependent self-construal will more likely be concerned with the other's face (no relationship was found to mutual face concern in this study) while individuals with independent self-construal will most likely be concerned with self-face preservation. In terms of national cultural differences for other-face, China and Japan had greater concerns than the U.S. and Germany (as expected). For self-face, China and Germany had more self-face concern than the U.S., which had more concern than Japan.

Situational and Relational Features

Situational and relationship boundary features refer to two aspects: (a) the physical setting and work activity in a particular interaction; and (b) the nature of the relationship that you have with the other party. In order to manage intercultural conflict mindfully, we have to understand the features that mediate between the primary orientation factors on one hand, and the conflict communication process factors on the other. Even though there are numerous features (e.g., see for example Ting-Toomey, 2005), how individuals draw ingroup-outgroup boundaries, how they perceive the nature of their relationship, and how they evaluate the different goal types of the conflict will have a profound influence on the conflict behaviors exhibited in an intercultural conflict episode. We discuss each of these features in this subsection.

Ingroup-outgroup boundaries. *Ingroups* are groups of individuals "about whose welfare a person is concerned, with whom that person is willing to cooperate without demanding equitable returns, and separation from whom leads to anxiety" (Triandis, 1995, p. 9). Ingroups are usually characterized by members who perceive a "common fate" or shared attributes among them. *Outgroups* are groups of individuals "with which one has something to divide, perhaps unequally, or are harmful in some way, groups that disagree on valued attributes, or groups with which one is in conflict" (Triandis, 1995, p. 9).

Members of collectivistic cultures make a greater distinction between ingroups and outgroups than members of individualistic cultures (Triandis, 1995). Collectivists tend to have greater self-face concerns with outgroup members and greater other-face concerns with ingroup members. In contrast, individualists have greater self-face concerns in dealing with both ingroup and outgroup members. For highly important conflicts, both collectivists and individualists prefer the use of the equity norm when competing with outgroup members for needed resources. For example, both individualistic and collectivistic managers from different companies would compete with each other for a contract by showing that they deserve it more than other bidders. However, for less important conflicts, collectivists prefer the use of the communal norm with either ingroup or outgroup members (Leung & Iwawaki, 1988) opting for maintaining surface relational harmony over getting too "worked up" dealing with irritants.

Relationship parameters. Another feature of situational and relationship boundary features is relationship parameters. *Relationship parameters* can be understood in terms of three dimensions: competition-cooperation, affiliation-control, and trust-distrust (Lewicki & Bunker, 1995; Rubin & Levinger, 1995). In an intercultural conflict episode, conflict combatants may emphasize different features of the perceived relationship parameters. Relationship parameters affect how we frame a conflict. Framing is critical to how two conflict parties view one another and how they view their relationship and the conflict task. Framing directs our attention and steers our focus to what is at stake in a conflict.

The first set of relationship parameters concerns the competitive-cooperative dimension. If members frame the relationship as "purely" *competitive*, they are likely to use conflict and facework strategies that enhance individual (or ingroup) gains and minimize individual (or ingroup) loss. If members frame the relationship as somewhat *cooperative* in nature, they are more likely to maximize mutual gains and less likely to "push away" the other conflict party in their negotiation behavior.

The second set of relationship parameters concerns the affiliation-control dimension. *Affiliation* involves social ties and intimacy issues, as well as relational rapport and support. On the other hand, *control* involves social dominance and submission issues, as well as respect and deference orientations. Depending on the culture, relationship affiliation can be expressed via a variety of behaviors. For example, some individuals may perceive direct eye gaze or close personal space as affiliative, while in other cultures these may be considered as "aggressive and intrusive." Likewise, what is considered as a decisive power move by one party, such as a loud and "take charge" tone of voice can be viewed as "overbearing and insulting" by another party in an intercultural conflict episode.

A third set of relationship parameters is the trust-distrust dimension. Trust is often viewed as the single most important element of a good working relationship (Fisher & Brown, 1988). While *trust* is about reliability and sustained faith issues, *distrust* is about reliability violations and sustained skepticism issues. In an intercultural conflict episode, adversaries will often view the relationship with distrust and skepticism because of competition for resources or the fact that the other party is from an outgroup. Trust building depends heavily on repeated reliable words and actions, promises that are kept, and the sustained faith that the other conflict party will come through (Rubin & Levinger, 1995). For individualists, trust may be tested in a short-term basis (e.g., one meeting). For collectivists, however, trust may entail a long-term trial (e.g., many meetings).

In high power-distance cultures, the spoken words of the high-powered person (e.g. the manager) constitute their "face." Therefore words are chosen carefully so that when the agreement is made each side will carry out their respective tasks based on solid relational foundations. High power-distance individual tend to distrust "wordy" individuals and sign contracts only after safe consideration of the relationship with the other person (Ting-Toomey & Kurogi, 1998).

Conflict goal assessments. A third situational feature is conflict goal assessments. People experience conflict in intimate and non-intimate relationships across a diverse range of cultures. How we perceive the conflict, whether we choose to engage in or disengage from it, and how we attribute different weights to the different goals in a conflict episode can vary greatly across cultural lines. The perceived or actual conflict differences often rotate around the following goal issues: content, relational, and identity (Wilmot & Hocker, 1998).

Content conflict goals are the substantive issues that are external to the individual involved. For example, intercultural business partners might argue about whether they should hold their business meetings in Mexico City or Los Angeles. Recurrent content conflict issues often go hand-in-hand with relational conflict goals.

Relational conflict goals refer to how individuals define, or would like to define, the particular relationship (e.g., nonintimate vs. intimate, formal vs. informal) in that conflict episode. For example, in a business setting, one business partner from the U.S. might opt to scribble a note and fax it to another international partner from Japan. The latter might well view this hastily prepared communication as a cavalier and unfriendly gesture. The Japanese partner may have perceived and experienced face threat and relationship threat. However, the U.S. business partner may not even realize that he or she has committed a relational error by sending this offhand message. S/he perceived the informal note as signaling "affiliation" or "friendliness" to minimize the formal relationship distance.

Identity-based goals revolve around issues of validation-rejection, approval-disapproval, respect-disrespect, and valuing-disconfirming of the individuals in the conflict episode. In a given interaction, identity goals are directly linked to face-saving and face-honoring issues. Over the course of many interactions, identity goals are broadly linked to the underlying beliefs and value patterns of the culture and the individuals. Thus, to reject someone's proposal or idea in a conflict can mean rejecting that person's deeply held beliefs and convictions. For example, in the case of deciding where an international business meeting should take place, the conflicting parties may be arguing over a concrete topic such as a location site; however, they are also testing their "self-images" or "face" in front of the other. The decision to hold the business meeting in country X may be interpreted as enhanced power or increased status for the business representatives of that country. In this way, identity goals are tied closely to culture-based "face orientation" factors. Identity-based conflict goals often underlie content-based and relational-based conflict issues. On the overt level, people may be arguing or disagreeing over content or relational issues; however, identity conflict problems lie beneath the surface.

Conflict Communication Processes. The process-based factors of conflict styles and facework behaviors are drawn from the conceptual explanations of Ting-Toomey's (1988; see also Ting-Toomey & Kurogi, 1998) face-negotiation theory. Influence of primary orientation factors and situational features are discussed in the context of the four cultures considered.

Conflict interaction styles. Conflict interaction style refers to patterned responses to conflict in a variety of dissenting conflict situations (Ting-Toomey, 1994). Findings in many past studies indicate that people display consistent styles across a variety of conflict situations in different cultures. Conflict style is learned within the primary socialization process of one's cultural or ethnic group.

Many researchers conceptualize conflict styles along two dimensions (Blake & Mouton, 1964; Thomas & Kilmann, 1974). For example, Rahim (1983, 2001) based his classification of conflict styles on the two conceptual dimensions of concern for self and concern for others. The first dimension illustrates the degree (high or low) to which a person seeks to satisfy her/his own interest or own face need. The second dimension represents the degree (high or low) to which a person desires to incorporate the other's conflict interest. The two dimensions are combined resulting in five styles of handling interpersonal conflict: integrating, compromising, dominating, obliging, and avoiding. Briefly, the *integrating* style reflects a need for solution closure in conflict and involves high concern for self and high concern for other in conflict substantive negotiation. The *compromising* style involves a give-and-take concession approach in order to reach a mid-point agreement concerning the conflict issue. The *dominating* style emphasizes conflict tactics that push for one's own position or goal above and beyond the other person's conflict interest. The *obliging* style is characterized by a high concern for the other person's conflict interest above and beyond one's own conflict interest. Finally, the *avoiding* style involves eluding the conflict topic, the conflict party, or the conflict situation altogether. In the U.S. conflict management literature, obliging and avoiding styles often take on a Western slant of being negatively disengaged (i.e., "placating" or "flight" from the conflict scene). However, collectivists do not perceive obliging and avoiding conflict styles as negative. These two styles are typically employed to maintain mutual-face interests and relational network interests (Ting-Toomey, 1988).

Face-negotiation theory helps to explain how individualism-collectivism, power distance, and self-construals influence conflict style (Ting-Toomey 1988; Ting-Toomey & Kurogi, 1998). The premise of the theory is that members who subscribe to individualistic values tend to be more self-face oriented and members who subscribe to group-oriented values tend to be more other- or mutual-face oriented in conflict negotiation. In addition, cultural members who subscribe to small power distance values tend to be more sensitive to "horizontal face" treatment, and cultural members who subscribe to large power distance values tend to be more attune to "vertical face" treatment (Ting-Toomey & Kurogi, 1998). Parallel to the cultural-level predictions, personal attributes such as independent/interdependent self and horizontal/vertical self also assert a strong influence on conflict styles. Different situational contexts and goals call for different rituals of conflict styles and facework appropriateness and effectiveness.

The face-orientations, influenced by the various cultural and individual influences, affect conflict styles. Research across cultures (e.g., in Germany, China, Japan, Korea, Mexico, and the United States) clearly indicates that individualists tend to use more self-defensive, dominating, and competitive styles in managing conflict than do collectivists. In comparison, collectivists tend to use more integrative and compromising styles in dealing with conflict than do individualists. Furthermore, collectivists tend to use more obliging and avoiding styles in task-related conflicts more so than do individualists (Chua & Gudykunst, 1987; Oetzel & Ting-Toomey, 2003; Oetzel et al., 2001; Ting-Toomey et al., 1991; Ting-Toomey et al., 2000; Trubisky, Ting-Toomey, & Lin, 1991). On the personal attributes level, independent-self individuals tend to use more dominating conflict styles than interdependent-self individuals, while interdependent-self individuals tend to use more avoiding, obliging, integrating, and compromising styles than independent-self individuals (Oetzel, 1998; Oetzel & Ting-Toomey, 2003).

Conflict facework behaviors. A closely related concept to conflict style is facework behavior. *Facework* is the communication strategies used to uphold, support, and challenge self- and other-face. Facework is linked closely with identity and relationship conflict goal issues. Facework can be specific behaviors of a broad conflict style, but unlike conflict styles can be manifest before, during, or after conflict situations. Three types of facework have been identified: dominating, integrating, and avoiding (Oetzel, Ting-Toomey, Yokochi, Masumoto, & Takai, 2000). Dominating facework includes being aggressive, defending a position, and expressing an opinion. Integrating facework includes problem-solving, displaying respect, privately discussing the conflict, apologizing, and remaining calm during the conflict. Avoiding facework includes pretending that the conflict does not exist, giving in to the other's position, and utilizing a third-party to help managing the conflict (Oetzel et al., 2000; Oetzel et al., 2001).

Prior research has found that individualists (e.g., U.S. Americans or Germans) tend to use more dominating and integrating facework than collectivists, whereas collectivists (e.g., Chinese or Japanese) tend to use more avoiding facework than individualists (Cocroft & Ting-Toomey, 1994; Ting-Toomey et al., 1991). However, the patterns are a bit more complex than this generalization, particularly for integrating facework. Oetzel et al. (2001) found that individualists (Germans and U.S. Americans) reported using dominating facework more than collectivists (Chinese and Japanese) (defending and expression, but not aggression). For avoiding, collectivists reported using more avoiding facework (pretend and give in) than individualists. For integrating, individualists reported using more problem-solving, respect, and private discussion than collectivists, but collectivists reported using more apologizing and remain calm than individualists.

Additionally, there are differences within individualistic cultures and collectivistic cultures. Germans reported using defending more and giving in and remaining calm less than U.S. Americans. Chinese reporting using a third-party and defending more and giving in and remaining calm less than Japanese. These findings enhance our understanding of cultural differences in facework, particularly within the general categories of individualism and collectivism.

Conflict Competence Features. Conflict processes affect the rating of intercultural conflict competence. Intercultural conflict competence refers to applying the intercultural knowledge we have learned in a skillful manner (Ting-Toomey & Oetzel, 2001). It refers to a transformative learning process in connecting intercultural knowledge with competent conflict practice. To be a competent conflict communicator, we need to internalize and be motivated to adapt our knowledge of intercultural theories into appropriate and effective application.

Perceived appropriateness and effectiveness are inferred through the exchange of messages between persons of different cultures and the outcome that is generated as a result of such exchange. Competent exchange of messages means that both intercultural communicators perceive that they and their messages are being understood in the proper context and with the desirable effects. When interested conflict parties experience communication appropriateness and effectiveness, the experience can impact satisfaction and productivity at work.

Appropriateness refers to the degree to which the exchanged conflict behaviors are regarded as proper and match the expectations generated by the insiders of the culture. Individuals typically use their own cultural expectations and scripts to approach an intercultural interaction scene. They also formulate their impressions of a competent conflict communicator based on their perceptions of the other's verbal and nonverbal behaviors in the particular conflict setting. While insiders have worked out a smooth script of how to approach a conflict episode, outsiders may be completely baffled by what seems like a "dishonest" or "hypocritical" way of conflict expression.

Appropriate conflict behaviors can be assessed through understanding the underlying values, norms, social roles, expectations, and scripts that govern the conflict episode. The criterion of communication appropriateness works concurrently with the criterion of communication effectiveness. When we act appropriately in a conflict scene, our culturally proper behaviors can facilitate communication effectiveness. By signaling to the other party that we are willing to adapt our behaviors in a culture-sensitive manner, we convey our respect for the other's cultural frame of reference.

Effectiveness refers to the degree to which conflict adversaries achieve mutually shared meaning and integrative goal-related outcomes. Effective encoding and decoding processes lead to mutually shared meanings. Mutually shared meanings lead to perceived intercultural understanding. During a conflict episode, perceptual filters and "noises" often distort our ability to comprehend what transpires in a conflict scene. Ineffective encoding and decoding by one of the two communicators can lead to further intercultural or intergroup polarization. Interaction effectiveness has been achieved when multiple conflict meanings are attended to with accuracy, and mutually desired interaction goals have been reached. Interaction ineffectiveness occurs when content or relational meanings are mismatched, and intercultural noises and clashes jam the communication channels.

Effective and appropriate conflict interactions tend to be productive in that they lead to the generation of new ideas, new plans, new momentum, and new directions in resolving the conflict problem. In productive conflict, both sides feel that they have influence over the conflict process, and they both think that they have gained something as a result of the conflict. In an unproductive conflict, both sides feel that they have wasted their time and energy in being involved in the conflict in the first place, and that both sides have lost sight of the original goals in the conflict episode. While a productive conflict discussion leads to a win-win outcome orientation, an unproductive conflict discussion reflects a lose-lose or win-lose outcome orientation. Conflict parties who perceive a win-win outcome often feel that their conflict goals have been fully addressed, and salient issues in the conflict have been dealt with affirmatively. In contrast, conflict parties who perceive a lose-lose outcome often feel that their conflict goals have been bypassed or ignored, tangential issues have been exchanged, the conflict process is devitalized, and conflict burnout is the only outcome. In the next section, we discuss how to apply the above information by localizing competence within the three facets that constitutes appropriateness and effectiveness; cultural knowledge, motivation and mindfulness, and interaction skills.

Building Intercultural Communication Competence

Cultural exchanges in conflict can be a difficult, complicated, and perhaps the most taxing communication endeavor (Canary, 2003). Our concern in this essay was to explain the conflict interaction with (a) the preceding dispositions of each person or the primary orientation factors, (b) the situational and relational boundaries framing an interaction, (c) the in-the-moment exchange of messages or the conflict process factors, and (d) the proximal outcomes of the exchange or the conflict competence criteria and outcomes.

Successfully attaining competence reflects enhancing knowledge, motivation/ mindfulness, and skill (Cupach & Canary, 1997; Cupach & Canary, 1997; Spitzberg & Cupach W. R., 1989; Ting-Toomey, 2005; Ting-Toomey & Kurogi, 1998; Ting-Toomey & Oetzel, 2001). Spitzberg and Cupach (1989) and Cupach and Canary (1997) provided three dimensions salient to the formation of communication competence: knowledge, motivation/mindfulness, and interaction skills. Knowledge is the basis for performing skills necessary for competence in a consistent and repeatable manner. Motivation is related to the meaning that an actor associates with a situation and is critical to whether the person will participate in the situation. Motivation therefore determines to what extent the actor will use skills and knowledge in a conflict situation. In this way, motivation is similar to mindfulness since we "attend to one's internal assumptions, cognitions and emotions" of the self and other individual (Ting-Toomey & Oetzel, 2001, p. 177). Interaction skills are the overt behaviors displayed during interaction. In this section, we also provide four concrete suggestions for organizations looking to build intercultural conflict competence. These suggestions are organized around knowledge, motivation/ mindfulness, and skill as framed by the CBSCM.

Knowledge. The knowledge dimension of intercultural competence supercedes the other two dimensions in that "disputants cannot learn to uncover the implicit ethnocentric lenses they use to evaluate behaviors" without specific knowledge of the other culture (Ting-Toomey & Oetzel, 2001, p. 174). Knowledge about primary orientation factors, situational and relational boundaries, and conflict processes can help prepare individuals for intercultural conflict interactions. These factors help to illustrate basic cultural differences, but also make us aware of our own ethnocentric lenses.

> *Suggestion #1:* Monitor stereotyping and all the while attending to "face" issues. Within-culture similarities exist but individuals can often diverge from cultural expectations. Therefore, expectations cannot rely only on cultural value dimensions.

This first suggestion is a knowledge issue because we cannot learn to uncover our implicit assumptions used to evaluate another without understanding the culture of the other. In this way, managing cultural knowledge appropriately specifies that an individual is knowledgeable of their own culture and thereby their cultural bias (Hall, 1976), and information relevant to the other's culture (Hall, 1959).

In organizations, people adhere to varying styles of handling conflict. Tendencies toward individualism or collectivism can help inform what conflict strategies will be used, but as we have shown, inconsistencies within individualist and collectivist countries exist. For example, Ting-Toomey and Oetzel (2001) illustrated that Germans and Americans have different strategies for handling conflict:

> Germans take a great deal of time to focus through issues and to hammer out differences. They disagree very honestly and clearly (many U.S. Americans label it as blunt). U.S. Americans, on the other hand, tend to focus on future visions during conflict and are action oriented. [U.S. Americans] want to come up with solutions and propose compromises (Ting-Toomey & Oetzel, 2001, p. 123-124).

The differences between Germans and Americans could be attributed to individual self-construal differences and even though Germans and U.S. Americans differ, certain similarities also exist. Independent selves share concern for confronting the issue openly and quickly and conflict outcomes are seen as productive when there are tangible goals, which often includes formulating a plan of action. Conflict produces protective, self-face reactions.

Interdependent types, conversely, share concerns for face threatening acts with specific ingroup/outgroup situational factors, which highlights relational aspects of conflict rather than goal oriented outcomes. For interdependent types, conflict communication is more productive when parties preserve mutual-face issues and attend to verbal and nonverbal exchanges before tasks are discussed. Interdependent types may perceive direct confrontation of substantive issues (e.g. "how do we get the order delivered on time?") inappropriately unless relational goals are given attention (e.g. "How can we work on this if we don't know each other better?"). Similarly, independent types may feel that time is being wasted if the most "obvious" tasks are not completed expediently.

Since many encounters are familiar, some knowledge is processed without much consideration. In intercultural encounters, cultural knowledge awareness is particularly important in difficult situations and can serve to inform skills necessary for communication (Chen, 1990). Making stereotypical generalizations about cultural values can create identity threatening situations. Cultural knowledge helps us to navigate the delicate dance played by each social actor in real time, but only if we have the willingness and sensitivity to take on such tasks. Consequently, knowledge supports the need for the second competence dimension, motivation/mindfulness.

Motivation/Mindfulness. The motivation/mindfulness dimension of intercultural communicative competence is a creative process that requires daily practice. Ting-Toomey and Oetzel (2001) proposed two ways to view mindfulness holistically (a) see behavior or information in conflict as fresh or novel, and (b) attend to the conflict context and the conflict partner's behavior. Finding the motivation to envision conflict information with novelty with separation from one's own emotion-laden response is difficult. However, "the practice of analytical empathy enables disputants to see both differences and similarities between each other's cultural and personal perspectives" (p. 178) and attach less negativity to other's behavior or even appearance. Suitably, motivation/mindfulness directs us to think about situational constraints.

Suggestion #2: Create opportunities that increase contact and familiarity between co-workers thereby encouraging motivation/mindfulness. If necessary, introduce a cultural coach or official third party. If individuals consider themselves part of each other's ingroup, the likelihood increases that conflict will be handled more cooperatively. However, care should be taken in assuming that building motivation toward ingroup inclusion ends conflict.

This suggestion is a motivation/mindfulness issue because co-workers need to separate themselves from their emotional reactions by "stepping back" while allowing certain conditions to form that allow outgroup members to be incorporated in specific ways. It is easy to assume that being inclusive will create opportunities for conflict to subside. Open communication may diminish some conflicts but research has shown that underlying prejudice may linger toward outgroup members. Gaertner and Dovidio (2000) stated, the "ambivalence associated with aversive racism is rooted in the conflict between feelings and values" (p. 14). People who consider themselves to be egalitarian, non-prejudice, and culturally aware may unconsciously hold negative associations toward other cultural groups. Therefore, even though creating inclusion is positive, subtle and seemingly unobtrusive bias like aversive prejudice can create barriers to resolving the root causes of conflict and undermine motivation toward resolving conflict. Care should be taken in creating motivation and mindfulness may be subverted by subtle forms of resistance to true cultural understanding.

Gaertner and Dovidio's (2000) research provides valuable evidence that intergroup bias can be diminished when certain conditions are met. The conditions include equal status between members, cooperative interdependence, the opportunity for self-revealing interactions, and egalitarian norms. These conditions help to establish a common "superordinate identity" while simultaneously maintaining the identity of the subgroups that each party belongs. According to their common ingroup identity theory, improving ingroup/outgroup relations across cultures is partly accomplished by creating the environment for intergroup cooperation with common goals, supportive norms, and equal status. If ingroup and outgroup members seem to be working on the "same team" while retaining their own separate identities, it can predict more positive intergroup relations and tolerance. The key, then, is to create motivation and mindfulness, by supporting activities and tasks that generate the formation of a new ingroup while not suppressing individual cultural differences. Creating these conditions can be difficult during conflict, which creates opportunities for outside, experienced cultural coaches or third party interveners.

Third parties can be integral in facilitating positive change by intervening with processes that support Gaertner and Dovidio's (2000) prescriptions for intergroup cooperation. Third party intervention has been documented as useful international disputes between different cultural groups (Crocker, Hampson, & Aall, 1999; Lederach, 1995) and with interpersonal disputes (Brown, 1977; Bush & Folger, 1994; Folger & Jones, 1994; Moore, 1996). Third party approaches have been found to be useful in culturally specific ways, for example collectivist cultures seem to prefer third party intervention to direct confrontation (Ma, 1992; Ogawa, 1999; Smith, 2000).

Creating motivation and mindfulness in conflict situations is a difficult and demanding task. The strategies presented above can be used by individuals within conflicts and by managers that are searching for ways to subside conflict within groups. With care, providing opportunities to diminish ingroup/outgroup differences can aid in reducing conflict. Competence interactions skills allow parties to put knowledge, motivation and mindfulness into action.

Interaction Skills. The third dimension of intercultural communicative competence, interaction skills, is skills used to "manage the process of conflict adaptively and reach important goals for all parties amicably" (Ting-Toomey & Oetzel, 2001, p. 179). Interaction skills ground the knowledge and motivation/mindfulness dimensions through action. Unfortunately, inappropriate skills "fuel the flames" of conflict as parties engage in, it may seem, irresistible reactions to each other's behaviors. Appropriate behavioral skills include mindful listening and facework management (Ting-Toomey & Kurogi, 1998, p. 204). *Mindful listening* is when we "mindfully listen to the identity, relational, content, and socio-historical meaning of the messages that are being exchanged" (Ting-Toomey & Kurogi, 1998, p. 204). Facework management, or the behavioral display of face concern (Ting-Toomey, 2005), is the "use of culture-sensitive identity support messages that enhance self-face and/or other-face" (Ting-Toomey & Kurogi, 1998, p. 205) and allows each party to respect the social-identity of the other person. Enacting facework management means not humiliating or embarrassing each other and leaving enough room for each person to stabilize their face concern by "giving face."

Suggestion #3:   Display mindful listening behavior to help avoid conflict from happening and from managing conflict when it does happen.

Mindful listening means that both individuals need to behave in ways that shows respectful and responsible listening with our ears, eyes, and one heart, or *ting* in Chinese (Ting-Toomey & Kurogi, 1998, p. 204). Also, we must attend to the sounds, tones, gestures, movements, nonverbal nuances, pauses and silence that accompany the exchange of words (p. 204). For example, the *paraphrasing skill* helps the other person see that mindful listening is in progress. When paraphrasing, each person intentionally restates the message heard without evaluation while providing supportive nonverbal queues. When paraphrasing collectivistic statements more care can be taken to ask in a relational building, deferential way such as "I may be mistaken but…" One can be more direct with paraphrasing individualistic statements: "What I am hearing is…" Mindful listening incorporates more than just the conventional meaning of "listening." A person mindfully and respectfully incorporates the words heard without evaluation or disrespect.

Mindful listening can rapidly deescalate repeated negative conflict messages by allowing a break in the "face damaging battlefield." If one party can successfully disengage from the "apparent" intent of the other party and, instead, engage mindful listening, one of the first and most important hurdles of conflict communication can be overcome. The escalation of competitive messages is one of the most damaging, conflict situations (Spitzberg & Cupach, 1989). Therefore, finding internal strength to sidetrack tendencies to hurdle a quick succession of hurtful, face damaging messages can help parties to begin to repair relations.

Suggestion #4: Use culturally appropriate facework management skills to manage conflict situations. Every conflict threatens "face" and therefore managing threats to identity can address the root cause of conflict.

As with mindful listening, facework management is another way to competently interact during conflict. Facework management means that each individual must be conscious of each others' individual- and cultural-level tendencies and attempt to use strategies to enhance "face-saving" approaches. Ting-Toomey and Kurogi (1998) stated

> Both independent-individualist and interdependent-collectivists may want to learn to "give face" to each other in the conflict negotiation process. Giving face means not humiliating or embarrassing each other in the public arena. It means leaving room enough for the other to retrieve his or her social dignity [and] respecting or even enhancing the other's favorable identity claims if [toward] positive relational interdependence (p. 205).

In "giving face" individualists can be especially careful to uphold the perceived public image of the collectivist by verbalizing and recognizing the connection with ingroups and obligations to them. In turn, collectivists can pay special attention to sending credibility messages related to the other's individualistic, goal oriented pride.

Facework management is also important between German and U.S. Americans. "Germans are well known for 'compartmentalizing' their lives, not only in the separation of work and personal time but in the distinction between professional and personal acquaintances. One U.S. traveler working overseas was taken aback to find that friends are made with caution and over time at work, whereas U.S. Americans favor working with friends" (Hooker, 2003, p. 103). Of course, as with all rules, there are exceptions but Germans could be said to control relationships more carefully in this way. Therefore facework management may be needed to uphold the ingroup/outgroup differences within work partner settings distinct from friends.

Intercultural conflict parties should learn to cultivate appropriate and effective face-management skills in dealing with intergroup conflicts. Face-management skills basically address the fundamental core issue of identity respect before, during, and after a conflict episode. All human beings prefer to be respected and be approved of in their daily interactions. However, what constitutes respectful and disrespectful behaviors, or approval and disapproval facework actions differ from one culture to the next. One study (Jaing Bresnahan, Morinaga Shearman, Lee, Ohari, & Mosher, 2002) tested the level of assertiveness or avoidance that an individual would respond to when faced with personal criticism. This study showed that U.S. Americans responded more assertively while Chinese or Japanese individuals used apologies or agreement when met with criticism. The findings point to the affiliation/control relational dimension discussed earlier in that U.S. Americans displayed social dominance while the Chinese were more submissive when criticized.

Interestingly, the study also found that U.S. Americans used silence to mean anger while for the Chinese silence showed embarrassment. Silence, it seems, is used differently by each group and therefore supports the need to use interaction skills that can be explicitly understood by both parties. The U.S. Americans used silence to potentially control the interaction while the Chinese used silence to give away control to the other person.

Conclusion

Drawing from the CBSCM, we have seen that primary orientation factors and situational features influence conflict process factors. In turn, these factors influence the perception of competent outcomes. Since competence mediates the relationship between conflict style and relational outcomes, it is no surprise that integrating strategies are instrumental in viewing relations with more trust, higher intimacy, and relational satisfaction (Oetzel et al., 2000). Cultural knowledge, motivation/mindfulness, and interaction skills form the basis for assessing competent intercultural communication. Organizations today compete for varying resources, have divergent goals, struggle with diversity management and weigh the potential benefits of integration. Cultural integration, through demographic shifts, ensures the inevitability that culturally dissimilar people will work together and will likely experience conflict. Our hope is that the CBSCM aids disputants with the peaceful exchange of productive messages and thus limits conflict in organizations.

References

Allen, C. (2003). *China CCG FY 2004 - executive summary.* STAT-USA, U.S. Department of State.
Blake, R. R., & Mouton, J. S. (1964). *The managerial grid.* Houston, TX: Gulf Publishing.

Brown, B. R. (1977). Face-saving and face-restoration in negotiation. In D. Druckman (Ed), *Negotiations: social-psychological perspectives* . Beverly Hills, CA: Sage.

Brown, P., & Levinson, S. (1987). *Politeness: Some universals in language usage.* Cambridge, UK: Cambridge University Press.

Bush, R. A. B., & Folger, J. P. (1994). *The promise of mediation responding to conflict through empowerment and recognition.* San Francisco, CA: Jossey-Bass.

Canary, D. J. (2003). Managing interpersonal conflict, a model of events related to strategic choices. In J. O. Greene, & B. R. Burleson *Handbook of communication and social interaction skills* (pp. 515-549). Mahwah, NJ: Lawrence Erlbaum Associates.

Chen, G. M. (1990). Intercultural communication competence: some perspectives of research. *The Howard Journal of Communication, 2*(3), 243-361.

Chua, E., & Gudykunst, W. (1987). Conflict resolution styles in low and high context cultures. *Communication Research Reports, 5*, 32-37.

Clackworthy, D. (1996). Training Germans and Americans in conflict management. In M. Berger (Ed.), *Cross-cultural team building: Guidelines for more effective communication and negotiation.* (pp. 91-100). London: McGraw-Hill.

Cocroft, B., & Ting-Toomey, S. (1994). Facework in Japan and the United States. *International Journal of Intercultural Relations, 18*(4), 469-506.

Condon, J. (1984). *With respect to the Japanese: A guide for Americans.* Yarmouth, ME: Intercultural Press.

Cox, T. (1994). *Cultural diversity in organizations theory, research, & practice* (1st ed.). San Francisco: Berrett-Koehler.

Crocker, C. A., Hampson, F. O., & Aall, P. R. (1999). *Herding cats multiparty mediation in a complex world.* Washington, D.C: United States Institute of Peace Press.

Cupach, W. R., & Canary, D. J. (1997). *Competence in interpersonal conflict.* Prospect Heights, IL: Waveland Press.

Elsayed-Ekhouly, S. M., & Buda, R. (1996). Organizational conflict: A comparative analysis of conflict style across cultures. *The International Journal of Conflict Management, 7*, 71-81.

Federal Statistics Office - Germany. (2005). *Population by sex and citizenship.* Germany.

Fisher, R., & Brown, S. (1988). *Getting together: Building relationships as we negotiate.* New York: Penguin.

Fitch, K. (1998). *Speaking relationally: Culture, communication, and interpersonal communication.* New York: Guildford.

Folger, J. P., & Jones, T. S. (1994). *New directions in mediation communication research and perspectives.* Thousand Oaks: Sage Publications.

Gao, G., & Ting-Toomey, S. (1998). *Communicating effectively with the Chinese.* Thousand Oaks, CA: Sage.

Garcia, W. R. (1996). *Respeto*: A Mexican base for interpersonal relationships. In W. B. Gudykunst, S. Ting-Toomey, & T. Nishida (Eds.), *Communication in personal relationships across cultures.* (pp. 137-155). Thousand Oaks, CA: Sage.

Goffman, E. (1959). *The presentation of self in everyday life.* Garden City, N.Y: Doubleday.

Hall, E. T. (1959). *The silent language.* Garden City, N.Y: Doubleday.

Hall, E. T. (1976). *Beyond culture.* Garden City, N.Y: Anchor Press.

Hofstede, G. (2001). *Culture's consequences: Comparing values, behaviors, institutions, and organizations across nations.* Thousand Oaks, CA: Sage.

Hooker, J. (2003). *Working across cultures.* Stanford, CA: Stanford University Press.

Hu, H. C. (1944). The Chinese concept of "face.". *American Anthropologist, 46*, 45-64.

Jaing Bresnahan, M., Morinaga Shearman, S., Lee, S. Y., Ohari, R., & Mosher, D. (2002). Personal and cultural differences in responding to criticism in three countries. *Asian Journal of Social Psychology, 5*, 93-105.

Katriel, T. (1986). *Talking straight: Dugri speech in Israeli Sabra culture.* Cambridge, UK: Cambridge University Press.

Kurthen, H. (1995). Germany at the crossroads: National identity and the challenges of immigration. *International Migration Review, 4*, 914-938.

Lederach, J. P. (1995). *Preparing for peace conflict transformation across cultures.* Syracuse studies on peace and conflict resolution. Syracuse, NY: Syracuse University Press.

Leung, K., & Iwawaki, S. (1988). Cultural collectivism and distributive behavior. *Journal of Cross-Cultural Psychology, 19*, 35-49.

Lewicki, R. J., & Bunker, B. B. (1995). Trust in relationships: A model of development and decline. In B. Bunker, J. Rubin, & Associates (Eds.), *Conflict, cooperation and justice* (pp. 39-57). San Francisco: Jossey-Bass.

Lim, T. S., & Choi, S. (1996). Interpersonal relationships in Korea. In W. B. Gudykunst, S. Ting-Toomey, & T. Nishida (Eds.), *Communication in personal relationships across cultures.* (pp. 122-136). Thousand Oaks, CA: Sage.

Ma, R. (1992). The role of unofficial intermediaries in interpersonal conflict in the Chinese culture. *Communication Quarterly, 40*(3), 269-278.

Markus, H. R., & Kitayama, S. (1991). Culture and the self: implications for cognition, emotion and motivation. *Psychological Review, 98*(2), 224-253.

McLeod, P. L., Lobel, S. A., & Cox, T. H. (1996). Ethnic diversity and creativity in small groups. *Small Group Research, 27*, 248-264.

Moore, C. W. (1996). *The mediation process practical strategies for resolving conflict.* San Francisco: Jossey-Bass.

Morisaki, S., & Gudykunst, W. B. (1994). Face in Japan and the United States. In S. Ting-Toomey (Ed.), *The challenge of facework.* (pp. 47-94). Albany: State University of New York Press.

Number of Japanese living abroad (1986-2004). (n.d.) Retrieved November 6, 2005, from http://web-japan.org/stat/stats/21MIG31.html.

Oetzel, J. (1998). The effects of self-construal and ethnicity on self-reported conflict styles. *Communication Reports, 11*(2), 133-144.

Oetzel, J. (2005). Effective intercultural workgroup communication. In W. B. Gudykunst (Ed.), *Theorizing about intercultural communication* . Thousand Oaks, CA: Sage.

Oetzel, J., & Ting-Toomey, S. (2003). Face concerns in interpersonal conflict: A cross-cultural empirical test of the face negotiation theory. *Communication Research, 30*(6), 599-624.

Oetzel, J., Ting-Toomey, S., Masumoto, T., Yokochi, Y., Pan, X., Takai, J. et al. (2001). Face and facework in conflict: a cross-cultural comparison of China, Germany, Japan, and the United States. *Communication Monographs, 68*(3), 235-258.

Oetzel, J. G., Ting-Toomey, S., Yokochi, Y., Masumoto, T., & Takai, J. (2000). A typology of facework behaviors in conflicts with best friends and relative strangers. *Communication Quarterly, 48*, 397-419.

Ogawa, N. (1999). The concept of facework: its functions in the Hawaii model of mediation. *Mediation Quarterly, 17*, 5-20.

Ohbuchi, K., Fukushima, O., & Tedeschi, J. T. (1999). Cultural values in conflict management: Goal orientation, goal attainment, and tactical decision. *Journal of Cross-Cultural Psychology, 30*, 51-71.

Rahim, M. A. (1983). A measure of styles of handling interpersonal conflict. *Academy of Management Journal, 26*, 368-376.

Rahim, M. A. (2001). *Managing conflict in organizations* (3rd ed.). Westport, Conn: Quorum Books.

Rogan, R. G., & Hammer, M. R. (1994). Crisis negotiations: A preliminary investigation of facework in naturalistic conflict discourse. *Journal of Applied Communication Research, 22* , 216-231.

Rubin, J. Z., & Levinger, G. (1995). Levels of analysis: In search of generalizable knowledge. In B. Bunker, J. Rubin, & Associates (Eds.), *Conflict, cooperation, and justice* (pp. 13-38). San Francisco: Jossey-Bass.

Smith, M. (2000). Diversity in community mediation: A conversation with Janice Tudy-Jackson and Roberto Chene. *Mediation Quarterly, 17*, 369-376.

Spitzberg, B. H., & Cupach W. R. (1989). *Handbook of interpersonal competence research*. New York: Springer-Verlag.

Thomas, K. W., & Kilmann, R. H. (1974). *Thomas-Kilmann conflict MODE instrument*. Tuxedo, NY: Xicom.

Ting-Toomey, S., Gao, G., Trubisky, P., Yang, Z., Kim, H. S., Lin, SL. et al. (1991). Culture, face maintenance, and styles of handling interpersonal conflict: a study of five cultures. *The International Journal of Conflict Management, 2*, 275-296.

Ting-Toomey, S. (1988). Intercultural conflict styles: a face negotiation theory. In Y. Y. Kim, & W. Gudykunst *Theories in intercultural communication*. Newbury Park, CA: Sage.

Ting-Toomey, S. (1994). Managing intercultural conflicts effectively. In L. Samovar, & Porter R. (Eds.), *Intercultural communication: A reader* (7th ed., pp. 360-372). Belmont, CA: Wadsworth.

Ting-Toomey, S. (1999). *Communicating across cultures*. New York: Guildford.

Ting-Toomey, S. (2005). The matrix of face: An updated face-negotiation theory. In W. Gudykunst (Ed.), *Theorizing about Intercultural Communication* (pp. 71-92). Thousand Oaks, CA: Sage.

Ting-Toomey, S., & Kurogi, A. (1998). Facework competence in intercultural conflict: an updated face-negotiation theory. *International Journal of Intercultural Relations, 22*, 187-225.

Ting-Toomey, S., & Oetzel, J. G. (2001). *Managing intercultural conflict effectively*. Thousand Oaks, CA: Sage.

Ting-Toomey, S., Yee-Jung, K. K., Shapiro, R. B., Garcia, W., Wright, T. T., & Oetzel, J. G. (2000). Ethnic/cultural identity salience and conflict styles in four US ethnic groups. *International Journal of Intercultural Relations, 24*, 47-81.

Triandis, H. C. (1995). *Individualism and collectivism*. Boulder: Westview Press.

Trubisky, P., Ting-Toomey, S., & Lin, S. L. (1991). The influence of individualism-collectivism and self-monitoring on conflict styles. *International Journal of Intercultural Relations, 15*, 65-84.

U.S. Census Bureau. (2005). *Global Population Profile: 2002*. March, 2002.

Wilmot, W., & Hocker, J. (1998). *Interpersonal conflict*. Boston: McGraw-Hill.

Introduction to

Cultural Constraints in Management Theories

By Geert Hofstede

Hofstede points out that management in its current definition is essentially an American invention and if culture is added, it will become obvious that there are no such things as universal management theories. Hofstede also argues that generally accepted US theories like those of Maslow, Herzberg, McClelland, and others may not or only partly apply outside the borders of their country of origin. Hofstede argues that not only are employees and managers human, but also management scientists, theorists, and writers. They all grew up in a particular society in a particular period of time, and their ideas cannot but reflect the constraints of the environment they know. To support his argumentation, the author looks at local management practices and local management theories around the globe – in particular, Germany, Japan, France, Holland, South-East Asia, Africa, Russia, and China (including Hong Kong, Taiwan and the Chinese mainland) and the Chinese enterprises in foreign countries, and compares them with US management practices and theories.

After having demonstrated that differences in management styles do exist around the world, Hofstede proceeds to explain the different styles with the help of his cultural model of national cultures. Hofstede's model consists of five independent dimensions that explain, in part, the differences in management practices. Interestingly, the model's dimensions coincide with dimensions predicted in an anthropological article dating back to 1954. Hofstede goes on to point out, though, that there are also unique characteristics in each country or region that no model can account for. In fact, the statistical analysis of the empirical data of the first four dimensions explains 49% of the variance in the data. The other 51% remain specific to individual countries. But, Hofstede notes, he now has at least a tool that allows him to reduce the complexity of culture by half. His model helps to explain the differences in management practices and theories around the globe, including those of the USA. But it also becomes apparent that this is the reason why US management practices and theories cannot work as effectively in other cultural contexts as they do in the USA.

Hofstede's text, therefore, ought to caution the wholesale adoption of *any* management theory in another cultural context. This caution is of particular importance in today's globalized economy in which one may easily be tempted to borrow successful methods from around the globe without considering the cultural differences.

Michael B. Hinner

Geert Hofstede is Professor Emeritus of Organizational Anthropology and International Management at Maastricht University and Honorary Professor at the University of Hong Kong. He worked in industry in roles varying from production worker to Director of Human Resources. Hofstede founded and managed the Personal Research department of IBM Europe and was a faculty member at IMD, Lausanne, Switzerland; INSEAD, Fountainebleau, France; the European Institute for Advanced Studies in Management, Brussels, Belgium; and IIASA, Laxenburg Castle, Austria. His best known books are *The Game of Budget Control, Culture's Consequences,* and *Culture and Organizations: Software of the Mind.* He is a Senior Fellow of the Institute for Research on Intercultural Cooperation and a Fellow of the Center for Economic Research at Tilburg University in the Netherlands.

Cultural Constraints in Management Theories

Geert Hofstede

Management Theorists Are Human

Lewis Carroll's *Alice in Wonderland* contains the famous story of Alice's croquet game with the Queen of Hearts. Let me quote from it:

> Alice thought she had never seen such a curious croquet-ground in all her life; it was all ridges and furrows; the balls were live hedgehogs, the mallets live flamingoes, and the soldiers had to double themselves up and to stand on their hands and feet, to make the arches. (Carroll, 1955 [1865]: 110)

You probably know how the story goes: Alice's flamingo mallet turns its head whenever she wants to strike with it; her hedgehog ball runs away; and the doubled-up soldier arches walk around all the time. The only rule seems to be that the Queen of Hearts always wins.

Alice's croquet playing problems are a suitable parabole for any attempts to build culture-free theories of management: any concepts available for this purpose are themselves alive with culture, having been developed within a particular cultural context, and they have a will of their own in guiding our thinking towards the conclusion we wanted to arrive at in the first place.

As the same reasoning may also be applied to the arguments I am about to present, I better tell you my conclusion before I continue my speech, so that you know the rule of my game in advance. I plan to take you on a trip around the world and demonstrate that there are no such things as universal management theories.

Diversity in management theories seems a suitable contribution to an Annual Meeting labelled "The Management of Diversity". The diversity in management *practices* as we go around the world has been recognized in this country's management literature since more than thirty years (Harbison and Myers, *Management in the Industrial World,* 1959), and the term "comparative management" has been in use since the 1960s (Farmer and Richman, *Comparative Management and Economic Progress,* 1965). However, it has taken much longer for the U.S. academic community to accept that not only practices but also the validity of *theories* may stop at national borders, and I wonder whether even today everybody would agree with this statement. An article I published in *Organizational Dynamics* in 1980 and which carries the subtitle "Do American Theories Apply Abroad?" raised an upheaval way beyond what I had expected. The article argued, with empirical support, that generally accepted US theories like those of Maslow, Herzberg, McClelland, Vroom, McGregor, Likert, Blake and Mouton may not or only very partly apply outside the borders of their country of origin - assuming they do apply within those borders. Among the requests for reprints, by the way, a larger number were from Canada than from the USA itself.

My argument is that not only employees are human - a discovery from the 1930s, with the Human Relations school (Mayo, 1933), and managers are human, an idea introduced in the late 40s by Herbert Simon's "bounded rationality" (Simon, 1947) and elaborated in Richard Cyert and James March's *Behavioral Theory of the Firm* (1963, and recently re-published in a second edition). Management scientists, theorists, and writers are human too: they grew up in a particular society in a particular period, and their ideas cannot but reflect the constraints of the environment they know.

The idea that the validity of a theory is constrained by national borders is more obvious in Europe, with all its borders, than in a huge borderless country like this one. Already in the sixteenth century Michel de Montaigne from France wrote a statement which was made famous by Blaise Pascal about a century later: *"Vérite en-deça des Pyrenées, erreur au-delà"*: "There are truths on this side of the Pyrenées which are falsehoods on the other": the Pyrenées being the border mountains between France and Spain. In present-day France this sense of relativity has been applied to the borders between disciplines in the work of Pierre Bourdieu, who in his book *Homo Academicus* has dealt with the sociology of social scientists (Bourdieu, 1984, 1988). Surprisingly, he has not (yet ?) referred explicitly to national differences.

From Don Armado's Love to Taylor's Science

According to the comprehensive ten-volume *Oxford English Dictionary* (1971), the words "manage", "management" and "manager" appeared in the English language in the 16th century. The oldest recorded use of the word "manager" is in Shakespeare's "Love's Labour's Lost", dating from 1588, in which Don Adriano de Armado, "a fantastical Spaniard", exclaims (Act I, scene ii, 188):

"Adieu, valour! rust, rapier! be still, drum! for your manager is in love; yea, he loveth".

The linguistic origin of the word is from Latin *manus,* hand, via the Italian *maneggiare,* which is the training of horses in the *manege;* subsequently its meaning was extended to skillful handling in general, like of arms and musical instruments, as Don Armado illustrates. However, the word also became associated with the French *menage,* household, as an equivalent of "husbandry" in its sense of the art of running a household (Oxford English Dictionary, 1971; Mant, 1977:20). The theatre of present-day management contains elements of both *manege* and *menage* and different managers and cultures may put different accents.

The founder of the science of economics, the Scot Adam Smith, in his 1776 book on "The Wealth of Nations", used "manage", "management" (even "bad management") and "manager" when dealing with the process and the persons involved in operating joint stock companies (Smith, V.i.e.). British economist John Stuart Mill (1806-1873) followed Smith in this use and clearly expressed his distrust of such hired people who were not driven by ownership. Since the 1880s the word "management" appeared occasionally in writings by American engineers, until it was canonized as a modern science by Frederick W. Taylor in *Shop Management* in 1903 and in *The Principles of Scientific Management* in 1911.

While Smith and Mill used "management" to describe a process and "managers" for the persons involved, "management" in the American sense - which has since been taken back by the British - refers not only to the process but also to the managers as a class of people. This class (1) does not own a business but sells its skills to act on behalf of the owners and (2) does not produce personally but is indispensable for making others (workers) produce, through a process called "motivation". Members of this class carry a high status, and many American boys (as well as quite a few girls) aspire to joining it. In the USA, the manager is a culture hero.

You are now invited to follow me on our trip around the world. We will look at management in its context in other successful modern economies: subsequently in Germany, Japan, France, Holland, and among the Overseas Chinese. Then we will also pay some attention to management in the much larger part of the world that is still poor, especially in South-East Asia and Africa, and in the new political configurations of Eastern Europe, in particular in Russia, returning to the USA via the Chinese mainland.

Germany

One could hardly say that the manager is a culture hero in Germany. If anybody, it is the engineer rather than the manager who plays the hero role here. Frederick Taylor invented his Scientific Management in a society of immigrants: one in which large number of workers with quite diverse backgrounds and skills had to be put to work together. In Germany this heterogeneity never existed. Elements of the mediaeval guild system have survived in historical continuity until the present day: in particular, a very effective apprenticeship system both on the shop floor and in the office, in which practical work and classroom courses alternate. At the end of the apprenticeship the worker receives a certificate, the *Facharbeiterbrief*, which is recognized throughout the country. About two thirds of the German worker population holds such a certificate and the corresponding occupational pride. For comparison sake, in Britain two thirds of the worker population has no occupational qualification at all. Quite a few German company presidents have worked their way up from the ranks through an apprenticeship.

These highly skilled and responsible German workers do not necessarily need a manager, American style, to "motivate" them. They expect their boss or *Meister* to assign their task and to be a superior expert in order to resolve their technical problems. Comparisons of matched German, British and French organizations have shown the Germans have the highest rate of personnel in productive roles and the lowest both in leading and in staff roles (Maurice, Sorge and Warner, 1981). Business schools are virtually unknown in Germany. Native German management theories concentrate on formal systems (Kieser and Kubicek, 1983). The inapplicability of American concepts of management in this situation became quite apparent when in 1973 the US consulting firm of Booz, Allen and Hamilton, commissioned by the German Ministry of Economic Affairs, wrote a study of German management from an American point of view. The report is highly critical and writes among other things that "Germans simply do not have a very strong concept of management" (Lawrence, 1980:88-93). Since 1973, according to my personal experience, the situation has not changed much. However, during this period in comparison with the USA the German economy has performed in a superior fashion in virtually all respects, so a strong concept of management might have been a liability rather than an asset.

Japan

The manager, US style, is equally missing in Japan. In the USA the core of the enterprise can be said to be its managerial class. The core of the Japanese enterprise consists of its permanent worker group; workers who for all practical purposes are tenured and who aspire at life-long employment. They are distinct from the non-permanent employees, that is most women as well as sub-contracted teams led by gang bosses, to be laid off in slack periods. University graduates in Japan first join the permanent worker group and subsequently fill various positions, moving from line to staff as the need occurs while paid according to seniority rather than position. They take part in Japanese-style group consultation sessions for important decisions, which extend the decision-making period but guarantee fast implementation afterwards. Japanese are to a large extent controlled by their peer group rather than by their manager.

Three researchers from the East-West Center of the University of Hawaii, Joseph Tobin, David Wu and Dana Danielson, did an observation study of typical preschools in three countries: China, Japan and the USA. Their results have been published both as a book and as a video (Tobin et al., 1989). In the Japanese preschool, one teacher handled twenty-eight four-year olds. The video shows one particularly obnoxious boy, Hiroki, who fights with other children and throws teaching materials down from the balcony. When a little girl tries to alarm the teacher, the latter answers "what are you calling me for? Do something about it!" In the US preschool, there is one adult for every nine children. This class has its problem child too, Glen, who refuses to clear away his toys. One of the teachers has a long talk with him and isolates him in a corner, until he changes his mind. It doesn't take much imagination to realize that managing Hiroki thirty years later will be a different process from managing Glen.

American theories of leadership are ill-suited for the Japanese group-controlled situation. The Japanese have over two decades developed their own "PM" theory of leadership, in which P stands for Performance and M for Maintenance. The latter is less a concern for individual employees than for maintaining social stability (Misumi and Peterson, 1987). In view of the amazing success of the Japanese economy in the past thirty years, many Americans have sought for the secrets of Japanese management (e.g. Pascale and Athos, 1981; Ouchi, 1981), hoping to be able to copy them. There are no secrets of Japanese management, however; it is even doubtful whether there is such a thing as management, in the American sense, in Japan at all. The secret is in Japanese society; and if any group in society should be singled out as carriers of the secret, it is the workers, not the managers.

France

The manager, U.S. style, does not exist in France either. In a very enlightening book, unfortunately not yet translated into English, the French researcher

Philippe d'Iribarne (1989) describes the results of in-depth observation and interview studies of management methods in three subsidiary plants of the same French multinational: in France, in the USA, and in Holland; and he relates what he finds to information about the three societies in general, where necessary going back in history to trace the roots of the strikingly different behaviors in the completion of the same tasks. He identifies three kinds of basic principles (*logiques*) of management. In the USA, the principle is the *fair contract* between employer and employee, which gives the manager considerable prerogatives, but within its limits. This is really a labor *market* in which the worker sells his or her labor for a price. In France, the principle is the *honor* of each class in a society which has always been and remains extremely stratified, in which superiors behave as superior beings and subordinates accept and expect this, conscious of their own lower level in the national hierarchy but also of the honor of their own class. The French do not think in terms of managers versus nonmanagers but in terms of *cadres* versus *non-cadres*; one becomes cadre by attending the proper schools and one remains it forever; regardless of their actual task, cadres have the privileges of a higher social class, and it is very rare for a non-cadre to cross the ranks.

The conflict between French and American theories of management became apparent already in the beginning of the twentieth century, in a criticism by the great French management pioneer Henri Fayol (1841-1925) on his US colleague and contemporary Frederick W. Taylor (1856-1915). The difference in career paths of the two men is striking. Fayol was a French engineer whose career as a *cadre supérieur* culminated in the position of Président-Directeur-Général of a mining company. After his retirement he formulated his experiences in a pathbreaking text on organization: *Administration industrielle et générale*, in which he focussed on the sources of authority. Taylor was an American engineer who had started his career in industry as a worker and attained his academic qualifications through evening studies. From Chief Engineer in a steel company he became one of the first management consultants. Taylor was not really concerned with the issue of authority at all; his focus was on efficiency. He proposed to split the task of the first-line boss into eight specialisms, each exercised by a different person; an idea which eventually led to the idea of a matrix organization.

Taylor's work appeared in a French translation in 1913, and Fayol read it and showed himself generally impressed but shocked by Taylor's "denial of the principle of the Unity of Command" in the case of the eight-boss-system (Fayol, 1916:85). However, this principle was and is much holier in France than in the USA.

Seventy years later André Laurent, another of Fayol's compatriots, found that French managers in a survey reacted very strongly against a suggestion that one employee could report to two different bosses, while U.S. managers in the same survey showed fewer misgivings in this respect (Laurent, 1981). Matrix organization has never become popular in France as it has in the U.S.A.

Holland

In my own country, Holland or as it is officially called, the Netherlands, the study by Philippe d'Iribarne found the management principle to be a need for *consensus* between all parties, neither predetermined by a contractual relationship nor by class distinctions, but based on an open-ended exchange of views and a balancing of interests. In terms of the different origins of the word "manager", the organization in Holland is more *menage* (household) while in the USA it is more *manege* (horse drill).

At my university, the University of Limburg at Maastricht, we receive every semester a class of American business junior students who take a Program in European Studies. We asked both the Americans and a matched group of Dutch students to describe their ideal job after graduation, using a list of twenty-two job characteristics (Hofstede and Vunderink, 1992). The Americans attached significantly more importance than the Dutch to earnings, advancement, benefits, a good working relationship with their boss, and security of employment. The Dutch attached significantly more importance than the Americans to freedom to adopt their own approach to the job, being consulted by their boss in his or her decisions, training opportunities, contributing to the success of their organization, fully using their skills and abilities, and helping others. This list confirms d'Iribarne's findings of a contractual employment relationship in the USA, based on earnings and career opportunities, against a consensual relationship in Holland. The latter has centuries-old roots; it should be remembered that the Netherlands were the first republic in Western Europe (1609-1810), and a model for the American republic. The country has been and still is governed by a careful balancing of interests in a multi-party system.

In terms of management theories, both motivation and leadership in Holland are different from what they are in the USA. In Abraham Maslow's Hierarchy of Needs, for example, he puts self-actualization above esteem above belongingness and love. In Holland self-actualization presupposes consensus which carries elements of both esteem and belongingness; but this is a logic that simply does not figure in Maslow's categorization (Maslow, 1970). Leadership in Holland presupposes modesty, as opposed to assertiveness in the USA. No US leadership theory known to me has room for that. I hope you don't interpret me as claiming that working in Holland is a constant feast; there is a built-in premium on mediocrity and jealousy, as well as time-consuming ritual consultations in order to maintain the apperance of consensus and the pretense of modesty. There is unfortunately another side to every coin. The perceptive observer will have recognized an expression of Dutch modesty in what I just said.

The Overseas Chinese and Chinese in Hong Kong and Taiwan of China

Among the champions of economic development in the past thirty years we find three areas mainly populated by Chinese living outside the Chinese mainland: Hong Kong, Taiwan of China and Singapore. Moreover, overseas Chinese play a very important role in the economies of Indonesia, Malaysia, the Philippines and Thailand, where they form an ethnic minority. If anything, the "little dragons" Hong Kong, Taiwan of China and Singapore have even been more economically successful than Japan, moving from rags to riches and now counting among the world's wealthy industrial economies. Yet very little attention has been paid to the way in which their enterprises have been managed. I can highly recommend a recent book *The Spirit of Chinese Capitalism* by Gordon Redding (1990), the British dean of the Hong Kong Business School, who bases his insights on personal acquaintance and in-depth discussions with a large number of Chinese business people, especially overseas ones. The title of his book is obviously a paraphrase on Max Weber's *The Protestant Ethic and the Spirit of Capitalism* (1930). Few of Redding's interviewees are protestants, but they are possessed by a strong ethic.

The Chinese enterperises in Hong Kong and Taiwan of China and in other countries lack almost all characteristics of modern management, American style. They tend to be small, cooperating for essential functions with other small organizations through networks based on personal relations. They are family-owned, without the separation between ownership and management typical in the West, or even in Japan and Korea. They normally focus on one product or market, with growth by opportunistic diversification; in this, they are extremely flexible. Decision making is centralized in the hands of one dominant family member, but other family members may be given new ventures to try their skills on. They are low-profile and extremely cost-conscious, applying the Confucian virtues of thrift and persistence. Their size is kept small by the assumed lack of loyalty of nonfamily employees, who, if they are any good, will just wait and save until they can start their own family business. They prefer economic activities in which great gains can be made with little manpower, like commodity trading and real estate. They employ few professional managers, except their sons and sometimes daughters who have been sent to prestigious business schools abroad, but who upon return continue to run the family business the Chinese way.

The origin of this system, or - in Western eyes - this lack of system is found in the history of Chinese society, in which there were no formal laws, only formal networks of powerful people guided by general principles of Confucian virtue; in which the favors of the authorities could change from one day to another, so that nobody could be trusted except one's kinfolk - of whom, fortunately, there used to be many, in an extended family structure. This way of doing business is also very well adapted to their position in the areas in which they form ethnic minorities, often envied and threatened by ethnic violence.

This kind of businesses following this unprofessional approach command a collective Gross National Product of some 200 to 300 billion US dollars, exceeding the GNP of Australia. There is no denying that it works.

Management Transfer to Poor Countries

So far we have visited five countries or areas in the industrially developed, that is rich, part of the world: Germany, Japan, France, Holland, and the little dragons of East Asia. In none of these areas organizations and businesses are run according to the American management theory book, although elements of the theories can be fruitfully used here and there; but different elements in different places.

Four-fifths of the world population live in countries that are not rich but poor. After World War II and decolonization, the stated purpose of the United Nations and the World Bank has been to promote the development of all the world's countries in a War on Poverty. After forty years it looks very much like we are losing this war. If one thing has become clear, it is that the export of Western - mostly American - management practices **and** theories to poor countries has contributed little to nothing to their development. There has been no lack of effort and money spent for this purpose: students from poor countries have been trained in this country, and teachers and Peace Corps workers have been sent to the poor countries. If nothing else, the general lack of success in economic development of other countries should be a sufficient argument to doubt the validity of Western management theories in non-Western environments.

If we take a closer look at different parts of the world, the development picture is not equally bleak all over, and history is often a better predictor than economic factors for what happens today. There is a broad regional pecking order with East Asia leading: the little dragons having passed into the camp of the wealthy; then follow South-East Asia (with its overseas Chinese minorities), Latin America (in spite of the debt crisis), South Asia, and Africa always trails behind. Several African countries have only become poorer since decolonization. Regions of the world with a history of large-scale political integration and civilization generally have done better than regions in which no large-scale political and cultural infrastructure existed, even if the old civilations had decayed or been suppressed by colonizers. It has become painfully clear that development cannot be pressure-cooked; it presumes a cultural infrastructure that takes time to grow. Local management is part of this infrastructure; it cannot be imported in package form. Assuming that with so-called modern management techniques and theories outsiders can develop a country has proven a deplorable arrogance. At best, one can hope for a dialogue between equals with the locals, in which the Western partner acts as the expert in Western technology and the local partner as the expert in local culture, habits, and feelings.

Russia and China

The crumbling of the former Eastern block has left us with a scattering of states and would-be states the political and economic future of which is extremely uncertain. The best predictions are those based on a knowledge of history, because historical trends have taken revenge on the arrogance of the Soviet rulers who believed they could turn them around by brute power. One obvious fact is that the former block is internally extremely heterogeneous, including countries traditionally closely linked with the West by trade and travel, like Czechia, Hungary, Slovenia and the Baltic states, as well as others with a Byzantine or Turkish past; some having been prosperous, others always extremely poor.

The industrialized Western world and the World Bank, from what I read in the newspapers, seem committed to helping the ex-Eastern block countries develop, but with the same technocratic neglect for local cultural factors that proved so unsuccessful in the development assistance to other poor countries. Free market capitalism, introduced by Western style management, is supposed to be the answer from Albania to Russia. Is it? What are the chances of success of this philosophy?

Let me limit myself to the Russian republic, a huge territory with some 140 million inhabitants, mainly Russians. We know quite a bit about the Russians as their country was a World Power for several hundreds of year before Communism, and in the nineteenth century it has produced some of the greatest writers in the world literature. If I want to understand the Russians - including how they could so long support the Soviet regime - I tend to re-read Lev Nikolayevich Tolstoy (1828-1910). In his most famous novel *Anna Karenina* (1876) one of the main characters is a landowner, Levin, whom Tolstoy uses to express his own views and convictions about his people. Russian peasants used to be serfs; serfdom had been abolished in 1861, but the peasants, now tenants, remained as passive as before. Levin wanted to break this passivity by dividing the land among his peasants in exchange for a share of the crops; but the peasants only let the land deteriorate further. Here follows a quote:

> (Levin) read political economy and socialistic works ... but, as he had expected, found nothing in them related to his undertaking. In the political economy books - in (John Stuart) Mill, for instance, whom he studied first and with great ardour, hoping every minute to find an answer to the questions that were engrossing him - he found only certain laws deduced from the state of agriculture in Europe; but he could not for the life of him see why these laws, which did not apply to Russia, should be considered universal.... Political economy told him that the laws by which Europe had developed and was developing her wealth were universal and absolute. Socialist teaching told him that development along those lines leads to ruin. And neither of them offered the smallest enlightenment as to what he, Levin, and all the Russian peasants and landowners were to do with their millions of hands and millions of acres, to make them as productive as possible for the common good. (Tolstoy, 1978 [1876]:366-67)

In the summer of 1991, the Russian lands yielded a record harvest, but a large share of it rotted on the fields because no people were to be found for harvesting. The passivity is still there, and not only among the peasants. And the heirs of John Stuart Mill (whom we met before as one of the early analysts of "management") again present their universal recipes which simply do not apply.

In the summer of 1990 my wife and I travelled by train through Russia and China. The Russian railways are wide gauge, contrary to those in Europe and in China, and we twice had the bogies under the carriages changed, at the Polish-White Russian border and at the Mongolian-Chinese border. When this happens the carriages are pulled into a shed, disconnected, lifted, and the old wheels are rolled away and replaced by a new set; all of this with the passengers inside the carriages. The ways in which the wheels changing process at the two borders was carried out were incredibly different. At Brest-Litowsk, on the Polish-White Russian border, dirty Russian men in an even dirtier shed worked slowly at their routine. At Erlian, on the Chinese-Mongolian border, our Chinese female carriage attendants got out, put an apron on, and with some help from local operators performed the job in a clean shed and in record time.

Citing Tolstoy, I implicitly suggest that management theorists cannot neglect the great literature of the countries they want their ideas to apply to. The greatest novel in the Chinese literature is considered Cao Xueqin's *The Story of the Stone*, also known as *The Dream of the Red Chamber* which appeared around 1760. It describes the rise and fall of two branches of an aristocratic family in Beijing, who live in adjacent plots in the capital. Their plots are joined by a magnificent garden with several pavillions in it, and the young, mostly female members of both families are allowed to live in them. One day the management of the garden is taken over by a young woman, Tan-Chun, who states:

> "I think we ought to pick out a few experienced trustworthy old women from among the ones who work in the Garden - women who know something about gardening already - and put the upkeep of the Garden into their hands. We needn't ask them to pay us rent; all we need ask them for is an annual share of the produce. There would be four advantages in this arrangement. In the first place, if we have people whose sole occupation is to look after trees and flowers and so on, the condition of the Garden will improve gradually year after year and there will be no more of those long periods of neglect followed by bursts of feverish activity when things have been allowed to get out of hand. Secondly there won't be the spoiling and wastage we get at present. Thirdly the women themselves will gain a little extra to add to their incomes which will compensate them for the hard work they put in throughout the year. And fourthly, there's no reason why we shouldn't use the money we should otherwise have spent on nurserymen, rockery specialists, horticultural cleaners and so on for other purposes."(Cao, 1980[1760], Vol.3:69)

As the story goes on, the capitalist privatization - because that is what it is - of the Garden is carried through, and it works. When in the 1980s Deng Xiaoping allowed privatization in the Chinese villages, it also worked. But what works in China - and worked two centuries ago - does not have to work in Russia, not in Tolstoy's days and not today. I am not offering a solution; I only protest against a naive universalism that knows only one recipe for development, the one supposed to have worked in this country.

A Theory of Culture in Management

Our trip around the world is over and we are back in the USA. What have we learned? There is something in all the countries we visited that can be called "management", but its meaning differs to a larger or smaller extent from one country to the other, and it takes considerable historical and cultural insight into local conditions to understand its processes, philosophies, and problems. If already the word may mean so many different things, how can we expect one country's theories of management to apply abroad? One should be extremely careful in making this assumption, and test it before considering it proven. "Management" is not a phenomenon that can be isolated from other processes taking place in a society. During our trip around the world we saw that it interacts with what happens in the family, at school, in politics and government. It is obviously also related to religion and to beliefs about science. Theories of management always had to be interdisciplinary, but if we cross national borders they should become more interdisciplinary than ever.

The reason I was invited for this speech is that I published an empirically derived theory of culture applicable to management (Hofstede, 1980, 1991). The theory states, briefly, that cultural differences between nations can be to some extent described using first four, and now five, bipolar *dimensions*. The position of a country on these dimensions allows to make some predictions on the way the national societies operate, including their processes of management and the kind of theories applicable to their management.

As the word "culture" plays such an important role in my theory, let me give you, or remind you of, my definition, which differs from some other very respectable definitions. Culture to me is *the collective programming of the mind which distinguishes one group or category of people from another*. In the part of my work I am referring to now, the category of people is the nation.

Culture is a *construct,* that means it is "not directly accessible to observation but inferable from verbal statements and other behaviors and useful in predicting still other observable and measurable verbal and nonverbal behavior" (Levitin, 1973:492). It should not be reified; it is an auxiliary concept that should be used as long it proves useful but bypassed where we can predict behaviors without it.

The same applies to the *dimensions* I introduced. They are constructs too that should not be reified. They do not "exist"; they are tools for analysis which may or may not clarify a situation. In my statistical analysis of empirical data the first four dimensions together explain 49% of the variance in the data. The other 51% remain specific to individual countries. But at least I have a tool that allowed me to reduce the complexity by half.

The first four dimensions were initially detected through a comparison of the values of similar people (employees and managers) in 64 different national subsidiaries of the IBM Corporation. People working for the same multinational, but in different countries, represent very well-matched samples from the populations of their countries, similar in all respects except nationality. The same dimensions have later on been found in multi-country studies of other matched populations (Hofstede and Bond, 1984; Hoppe, 1990). What gave me confidence initially that I was on the right track, is that very similar dimensions had been predicted in a review article of the anthropological literature (Inkeles and Levinson, as far back as 1954), as common basic problems worldwide, with consequences for the functioning of societies, of groups within those societies, and of individuals within those groups. If one really finds something fundamental in the social sciences, there must be others who found it before.

The first dimension has been labelled *Power Distance*, and it can be defined as the degree of inequality among people which the population of a country considers as normal: from relatively equal (that is, small power distance) to extremely unequal (large power distance). All societies are unequal, but some are more unequal than others.

The second dimension is labelled *Individualism*, and it is the degree to which people in a country prefer to act as individuals rather than as members of groups. The opposite of individualism can be called *Collectivism*, so collectivism is low individualism. The way I use the word it has no political connotations. In collectivist societies a child learns to respect the group to which it belongs, usually the family, and to differentiate between in-group members and out-group members (that is, all other people). When children grow up they remain members of their group, and they expect the group to protect them when they are in trouble. In return, they have to remain loyal to their group throughout life. In individualist societies, a child learns very early to think of itself as "I" instead of as part of "we". It expects one day to have to stand on its own feet and not to get protection from its group any more; and therefore it also does not feel a need for strong loyalty.

The third dimension has been called *Masculinity* and its opposite pole *Femininity*. It is the degree to which "tough" values like assertiveness, performance, success and competition, which in nearly all societies are associated with the role of men, prevail over "tender" values like the quality of life, maintaining warm personal relationships, service, care for the weak, and solidarity, which in nearly all societies are more associated with the role of women. Women's roles differ from men's roles in all countries; but in tough societies, the differences are larger than in tender ones.

The fourth dimension has been labelled *Uncertainty Avoidance,* and it can be defined as the degree to which people in a country prefer structured over unstructured situations. Structured situations are those in which there are clear rules as to how one should behave. These rules can be written down, but they can also been unwritten and imposed by tradition. In countries which score high on uncertainty avoidance, people tend to show more nervous energy, while in countries which score low, people are more easy-going. A (national) society with strong uncertainty avoidance can be called rigid; one with weak uncertainty avoidance, flexible. One way of describing countries where uncertainty avoidance is strong, is to say that in these countries a feeling prevails of "what is different, is dangerous". In weak uncertainty avoidance societies, the feeling would rather be "what is different, is curious".

The fifth dimension was added on the basis of a study of the values of students in 23 countries carried out by Michael Harris Bond, a Canadian working in Hong Kong of China. He and I had cooperated in another study of students' values which had yielded the same four dimensions as the IBM data. However, we wondered to what extent our common findings in two studies could be the effect of a Western bias introduced by the common Western background of the researchers: remember Alice's croquet game. Michael Bond resolved this dilemma by deliberately introducing an Eastern bias. He used a questionnaire prepared at his request by his Chinese colleagues, the *Chinese Value Survey* (CVS), which was translated from Chinese into different languages and answered by fifty male and fifty female students in each of twenty-three countries in all five continents. Analysis of the CVS data produced three dimensions significantly correlated with the three IBM dimensions of power distance, individualism, and masculinity (*The Chinese Culture Connection,* 1987; Hofstede and Bond, 1988). There was also a fourth dimension, but it did not resemble uncertainty avoidance. It was composed, both on the positive and on the negative side, from items that had not been included in the IBM studies but were present in the Chinese Value Survey because they were rooted in the teachings of Confucius, the great Chinese philosopher of 500 BC. I labelled this dimension: *Long-term* versus *Short-term Orientation* (Hofstede, 1991). On the long-term side one finds values oriented towards the future, like thrift (saving) and persistence. On the short-term side one finds values rather oriented towards the past and present, like respect for tradition and fulfilling social obligations.

Table 1 lists the scores on all five dimensions for the USA and for the other countries we just visited on our world trip. The table shows that each country has its own configuration on the four dimensions. Some of the values in the table have been estimated based on imperfect replications or personal impressions. The different dimension scores do not "explain" all the differences in management I described earlier; in order to understand management in a country, one should have both knowledge of and empathy with the entire local scene. However, the scores should suffice to make us aware that people in other countries may think, feel and act very differently from us when confronted with basic problems of society.

Table 1
Culture Dimension Scores for Nine Countries

	PD	ID	MA	UA	LT
USA	40 l	91 h	62 h	46 l	29 l
Germany	35 l	67 h	66 h	65 m	31 m
Japan	54 m	46 m	95 h	92 h	80 h
France	68 h	71 h	43 m	86 h	39 m
Netherlands	38 l	80 h	14 l	53 m	44 m
Indonesia	78 h	14 l	46 m	48 l	25*l
West Africa	77 h	20 l	46 m	54 m	16 l
Russia	93 h	39 m	36 m	95 h	20*l
China	80 h	20 l	66 m	30 m	118 h

* estimated

PD = Power Distance; ID = Individualism; MA = Masculinity;
UA = Uncertainty Avoidance; LT = Long Term Orientation;
H = top third, M = medium third, L = bottom third (among 53 countries and regions for the first four dimensions; among 23 countries for the fifth)

Idiosyncrasies of American Management Theories

In comparison to other countries, the US culture profile as I found it presents itself as below average on Power Distance and Uncertainty Avoidance, highly individualistic, fairly masculine, and short-term oriented. The Germans show a stronger Uncertainty Avoidance and less extreme Individualism; the Japanese are different on all dimensions, least on Power Distance; the French show larger Power Distance and Uncertainty Avoidance, but are less individualistic and somewhat feminine; the Dutch resemble the Americans on the first three dimensions, but score extremely feminine and relatively long-term oriented; and so on.

The American culture profile is reflected in American management theories. I will just mention three elements not necessarily present in other countries: the stress on market processes, the stress on the individual, and the focus on managers rather than on workers.

1. The Stress on Market Processes

In the U.S.A. in the 1970s and 80s it has become fashionable to look at organizations from a point of view of "transaction costs". Economist Oliver Williamson has opposed "hierarchies" to "markets" (Williamson, 1975). The reasoning is that human social life consists of economic transactions between individuals. We found the same in d'Iribarne's description of the US principle of the contract between employer and employee, the labor market in which the worker sells his or her labor for a price. These individuals will form hierarchical organizations when the cost of the economic transactions (such as getting information, finding out whom to trust etc.) is lower in a hierarchy than when all transactions would take place on a free market. From a cultural perspective the important point is that the *"market" is the point of departure or base model*, and the organization is explained from market failure. A culture that produces such a theory is likely to prefer organizations that internally resemble markets to organizations that internally resemble more structured models, like those in Germany or France. The ideal principle of control in organizations in the market philosophy is competition between individuals. This philosophy fits a society that combines a not-too-large Power Distance with a not-too-strong Uncertainty Avoidance and Individualism; besides the USA, it will fit all other Anglo countries.

2. The Stress on the Individual

I find this again and again in the design of research projects and hypotheses; also in the fact that in this country psychology is clearly a more respectable discipline in management circles than sociology. Culture however is a collective phenomenon. Although we may get our information about culture from individuals, we have to interpret it at the level of collectivities. There are snags here known as the "ecological fallacy" and the "reverse ecological fallacy" (Hofstede, 1980; Hofstede et al., forthcoming); none of the US college textbooks on methodology I know deals sufficiently with the problem of multilevel analysis. Culture can be compared to a forest, while individuals are trees. A forest is not just a bunch of trees: it is a symbiosis of different trees, bushes, plants, insects, animals and micro-organisms, and we miss the essence of the forest if we only describe its most typical trees. In the same way, a culture cannot be satisfactorily described in terms of the characteristics of a typical individual. There is a tendency in the US management literature to overlook the forest for the trees and to ascribe cultural differences to interactions among individuals. A striking example is found in the otherwise excellent book "Organizational Culture and Leadership" by Edgar H. Schein (1985). On the basis of his consulting experience he compares two large companies, nicknamed

"Action" and "Multi". He explains the differences in culture between these companies by the group dynamics in their respective Boardrooms. Nowhere in the book are any conclusions drawn from the fact that the first company is an American based computer firm, and the second a Swiss based pharmaceutics firm; this information is not even mentioned. A stress on interactions among individuals obviously fits a culture identified as the most individualistic in the world, but it will not so well be understood by the four-fifths of the world population for whom the group prevails over the individual.

One of the conclusions of my own multilevel research has been that "culture" at the national level and "culture" at the organizational level - corporate culture - are two very different phenomena, and that the use of a common term for both is confusing (Hofstede et al., 1990; Hofstede, 1991). If we do use the common term, we should also pay attention to the occupational and the gender level of culture. National cultures differ primarily in the fundamental, invisible values held by a majority of their members, acquired in early childhood, whereas organizational cultures are a much more superficial phenomenon residing mainly in the visible practices of the organization, acquired by socialization of the new members who join as young adults. National cultures change only very slowly if at all; organizational cultures may be consciously changed, although this isn't necessarily easy. This difference between the two types of culture is the secret of the existence of multinational corporations that employ, as I showed in the IBM case, employees with extremely different national cultural values. What keeps them together is a corporate culture based on common practices.

3. *The Stress on Managers Rather than Workers*

The core element of a work organization, the world round, is the people who do the work. All the rest is superstructure, and I hope to have demonstrated to you in our trip around the world that it may take many different shapes. In the US literature on work organization, however, the core element, if not explicitly then implicitly, is considered the manager. This may well be the result of the combination of extreme individualism with fairly strong masculinity, which has turned the manager into a culture hero of almost mythical proportions. For example, he - not really she - is supposed to make decisions all the time. Those of you who are or have been managers must know that this is a fable. Very few management decisions are just "made" as the myth suggests it. Managers are much more involved in maintaining networks; if anything, it is the rank-and-file worker who can really make decisions on his or her own, albeit on a relatively simple level.

An amusing effect of the US focus on managers is that in at least ten American books and articles on management I have been misquoted as having studied IBM *managers* in my research, whereas the book clearly describes that the answers were from IBM *employees*. My observation may be biased, but I get the impression that compared to twenty or thirty years ago less research in this country is done among employees and more on managers. But managers derive their *raison d'être* from the people managed: culturally, they are the followers of the people they lead, and their effectiveness depends on the latter. In other parts of the world, this exclusive focus on the manager is less strong, with Japan as the supreme example.

Conclusion

This speech started with *Alice in Wonderland*. In fact, the management theorist who ventures outside his or her own country into other parts of the world is like Alice in Wonderland. He or she will meet strange beings, customs, ways of organizing or disorganizing and theories that are clearly stupid, old fashioned or even immoral - yet they may work, or at least they may not fail more frequently than corresponding theories do at home. Then, after the first culture shock, the traveller to Wonderland will feel enlightened, and may be able to take his or her experiences home and use them advantageously. All great ideas in science, politics and management have travelled from one country to another, and been enriched by foreign influences. The roots of American management theories are mainly in Europe: with Adam Smith, John Stuart Mill, Lev Tolstoy, Max Weber, Henri Fayol, Sigmund Freud, Kurt Lewin and many others. These theories were re-planted here and they developed and bore fruit. The same may happen again. The last thing we need is a Monroe doctrine for management ideas.

References

Bourdieu, Pierre. *Homo academicus*. Paris: Éditions de Minuit, 1984. English translation Cambridge Polity Press and Stanford University Press, 1988.

Bourdieu, Pierre. "Vive la crise ! For heterodoxy in social science". *Theory and Society*, 1988, Vol.17.

Cao, Xueqin. *The Story of the Stone*, translated by David Hawkes, Volume 3. Harmondsworth Mddx: Penguin,1980 [1760].

Carroll, Lewis. *Alice in Wonderland*. Harmondsworth Mddx: Penguin, 1946 [1865].

Cyert, Richard M. and James G. March. *A Behavioral Theory of the Firm*. Englewood Cliffs NJ: Prentice-Hall, 1963.

d'Iribarne, Philippe. *La logique de l' honneur: Gestion des entreprises et traditions nationales*. Paris: Éditions du Seuil, 1989.

Farmer, Richard N. and Barry M. Richman. *Comparative Management and Economic Progress*. Homewood IL: Irwin, 1965.

Fayol, Henri. *Administration industrielle et générale*. Paris: Dunod, 1970 [1916].

Harbison, Frederick and Charles A. Myers. *Management in the Industrial World: An International Analysis*. New York NY: McGraw Hill, 1959.

Hofstede, Geert. "Motivation, leadership and organization: Do American theories apply abroad ?". *Organizational Dynamics*, 1980, Vol.9 no.1, 42-63.

Hofstede, Geert. *Culture's Consequences: International Differences in Work-Related Values*. Beverly Hills CA: Sage Publications, 1980.

Hofstede, Geert. *Cultures and Organizations: Software of the Mind*. London: McGraw Hill, 1991.

Hofstede, Geert and Michael Harris Bond. "Hofstede's culture dimensions : an independent validation using Rokeach's Value Survey". *Journal of Cross-Cultural Psychology*, 1984, Vol.15 no.4, 417-433.

Hofstede, Geert and Michael Harris Bond. "The Confucius connection: from cultural roots to economic growth". *Organizational Dynamics*, Spring 1988, Vol.16 no.4, 4-21.

Hofstede, Geert and Mieke Vunderink. *A Comparison of Goals and Gender Roles between American and Dutch University Students*, paper presented at the XIth Congress of Cross-Cultural Psychology, Liège, Belgium, July 1992.

Hofstede, Geert, Bram Neuijen, Denise D. Ohayv and Geert Sanders. "Measuring organizational cultures". *Administrative Science Quarterly*, 1990, Vol.35, 286-316.

Hofstede, Geert, Michael Harris Bond and Chung-Leung Luk. "Individual perceptions of organizational cultures: a methodological treatise on levels of analysis". Forthcoming in *Organization Studies*, 1993.

Hoppe, Michael H. *A Comparative Study of Country Elites: International Differences in Work-related Values and Learning and their Implications for Management Training and Development*. Unpublished Ph.D. dissertation, University of North Carolina at Chapel Hill, 1990.

Inkeles, Alex and Daniel J. Levinson. "National character: the study of modal personality and sociocultural systems". In G. Lindsey & E. Aronson (eds.), *The Handbook of Social Psychology*, 2nd ed., Vol.4. Reading MA : Addison-Wesley, 1969 [1954].

Kieser, Alfred and Herbert Kubicek. *Organisation*. Berlin: Walter de Gruyter, 1983.

Laurent, André. "Matrix organizations and Latin cultures". In *International Studies of Management and Organization*, Winter 1981, Vol.10 no.4, 101-114.

Lawrence, Peter. *Managers and Management in West Germany*. London: Croom Helm, 1980.

Levitin, Teresa. "Values", in J.P. Robinson and P.R. Shaver (eds.), *Measures of Social Psychological Attitudes*. Ann Arbor MI: Institute for Social Research, University of Michigan, 1973, 489-502.

Mant, Alistair. *The Rise and Fall of the British Manager*. London UK: Pan Books, 1979 [1977].

Maslow, Abraham H. *Motivation and Personality*. New York NY : Harper & Row, second edition 1970.

Maurice, Marc, Arndt M. Sorge and Malcolm Warner. "Societal differences in organizing manufacturing units: a comparison of France, West Germany, and Great Britain". *Organization Studies*, 1980, Vol.1 no.1, 59-86.

Mayo, G. Elton. *The Human Problems of an Industrial Civilization*. Boston MA: Division of Research, Harvard Business School, 1933.

Misumi, Jyuji and Mark F. Peterson. "Supervision and leadership", Chapter 17 in B.M. Bass and P.J.D. Drenth, *Advances in Organizational Psychology: An International Review*. Newbury Park CA: Sage, 1987.

Ouchi, William G. *Theory Z*. New York NY: Addison-Wesley, 1981.

Oxford English Dictionary. *The Compact Edition of the Oxford English Dictionary,* Oxford UK: Oxford University Press, 1971 [1933].

Pascale, Richard and Anthony G. Athos. *The Art of Japanese Management*. New York NY: Simon & Schuster, 1981.

Redding, S. Gordon. *The Spirit of Chinese Capitalism*. Berlin: Walter de Gruyter, 1990.

Schein, Edgar H. *Organizational Culture and Leadership*. San Francisco CA: Jossey-Bass, 1985.

Shakespeare, William. *The Complete Works*, edited by W,J, Craig. Oxford UK: Oxford University Press, 1955 [1616].

Simon, Herbert A. *Administrative Behavior: A Study of Decision-Making Processes in Administrative Organization*. Third Edition. New York NY: Free Press, 1976 [1945].

Smith, Adam. *An Inquiry into the Nature and Causes of the Wealth of Nations*, edited by R.H. Campbell, A.S. Skinner and W.B. Todd. Oxford UK: Clarendon Press, 1979 [1776].

Taylor, Frederick W. *Shop Management*. New York NY: Harper & Bros, 1903.

Taylor, Frederick W. *The Principles of Scientific Management*. New York NY: Harper & Bros, 1911.

The Chinese Culture Connection (a team of 24 researchers). Chinese values and the search for culture-free dimensions of culture". *Journal of Cross-Cultural Psychology*, 1987, Vol.18 no.2, 143-164.

Tobin, Joseph J, David Y.H. Wu and Dana H. Danielson. *Preschool in Three Cultures: Japan, China and the United States*. New Haven CT: Yale University Press, 1989.

Tolstoy, Lev Nikolayevich. *Anna Karenin*, translated by Rosemary Edmonds. Harmondsworth Mddx: Penguin, 1978 [1876].

Weber, Max. *Essays in Sociology* (H.H. Gerth and C.W. Mills, eds.). London: Routledge & Kegan Paul, 1970 [1948].

Weber, Max. *The Protestant Ethic and the Spirit of Capitalism*. London: George Allen & Unwin, 1976 [1930].

Williamson, Oliver E. *Markets and Hierarchies: Analysis and Antitrust Implications*. New York NY: Free Press, 1975.

Introduction to

Contrastive Prototypes of Communication Styles in Decision-Making: Mawashi Style vs. Tooshi Style

By Teruyuki Kume

Kume assumes that decision making processes and behaviors are products of culture which can result in conflicts since differences in those processes and behaviors can result in misunderstandings. Kume has studied communication styles and decision making processes in a number of cultures and identified two contrastive prototypes which he terms *mawashi* style, which means that messages are circulated among the involved members, and *tooshi* style, which means that messages are pushed directly through the involved members.

Kume bases his *mawashi* and *tooshi* prototypes of communication styles in decision making on a number of studies that have been carried out in Japan and the USA. It seems that Japanese organizations generally do not have jobs of individual members clearly defined; in fact, there is even room for ongoing operations that are shared by several members who work nearby or who happen to be available. The communication style is high-context oriented, and perception is focused on seeing the whole rather than a part of an organization. In contrast, American organizations clearly define everyone's job with no room for ambiguity as far as job territory is concerned. The communication style is low-context oriented, and perception is focused analytically on a part of the whole organization. When it comes to decision making, most Japanese managers do not make decisions by themselves which, in contrast, most American managers do. This is, in part, due to the collectivistic society of Japan and the individualistic society of the USA. And Kume's study shows that even though American managers of Japanese companies in the USA adopted some of the Japanese decision-making styles, they use a different style for communicating ideas than their Japanese colleagues use. Hence, indicating the great influence culture has on one's communication style; a style which tends to remain unchanged no matter how rapidly organizational structures change.

Kume notes, though, that his simplistic dichotomy of the *mawashi* style and *tooshi* style is merely intended to emphasize that there might be profound differences in the manner people of different cultural background communicate. And people who are accustomed to a particular communication style have difficulties understanding people who are using a drastically different communication style. According to Kume, communication is a reflection of people's patterns of thinking as well as their perceptual mindsets. But it must also be remembered, so Kume, that even within the same organization, the two styles can be employed depending on the nature of leadership and decision. For example, the *tooshi* style may be used when immediate action must be taken whereas the *mawashi* style might be used for formulating long-range strategies or the development of a new product.

This text clearly demonstrates that differences in communication styles and decision making processes exist around the world. One, therefore, has to be aware of those differences and attempt to overcome them on the basis of this understanding.

Michael B. Hinner

Teruyuki Kume is Professor of Communication in the Graduate School of Intercultural Communication at Rikkyo (St. Paul's) University in Tokyo. His major teaching and research interests are in intercultural, interpersonal, and organizational communication. His article "Managerial Attitudes toward Decision-Making: North America and Japan" appeared in *International and Intercultural Communication Annual,* (1985), Vol. IX. His Japanese co-authored publications include *Intercultural Communication* (1996), *Intercultural Communication Handbook* (1997), *Intercultural Communication Keywords* (2001), *Intercultural Communication Theories* (2001), *Intercultural Communication Research Methods* (2005), and *The Empathic Communicator* (1992 with William S. Howell). He translated Edward C. Stewart's book *American Cultural Patterns: From Cross-Cultural Perspectives* into Japanese in 1982. Currently, he is working on the book entitled *Learning Intercultural Communication through Case Studies.* He is the Vice President of the Japan Society for Multicultural Relations. His research interest is leadership in task-oriented multicultural teams and intercultural conflict of Japanese abroad.

Contrastive Prototypes of Communication Styles in Decision-Making: Mawashi Style vs. Tooshi Style

Teruyuki Kume

Organizations in the present world are becoming increasingly multicultural. Workers, managers, as well as professionals are crossing national boundaries and many complex intercultural communication problems among people from various backgrounds often result. Japanese organizations are not an exception. Most of the large Japanese companies that had been composed of predominantly Japanese nationals have undergone rapid globalization since the 1970s by expanding their activities overseas and inviting managers and workers from overseas. A similar thing can be said about organizations in Europe, North America, Asia, and the world over.

Under such circumstances, intercultural conflict or friction within such multicultural organizations is likely to occur. While there are a number of factors creating such conflicts, differences in the nature and style of communication of members are certainly a major factor. In order to see these differences more clearly, this chapter focuses on communication style in the process of decision-making in organizations.

Two contrastive prototypes of communication style, mawashi and tooshi, have emerged as a result of the review of the relevant literature and two kinds of research the author has done. One was a study on decision-making in Japanese companies operating in the United States, and the other was a cross-cultural study of communication style in task-oriented small group discussions in China, Japan, and the United States. The basic features of the two prototypes will be briefly described in four areas: 1) leadership style, 2) process of discussion, 3) temporal orientation of decision-making, and 4) mode of arriving at a decision.

Then, three cases will be introduced to illustrate intercultural friction attributable to the sharp differences in communication style. I will conclude this chapter by suggesting ways to minimize the friction arising from the interaction between and among people in multicultural settings.

Organization and Communication

What is essential for organizations is input of capital, materials, and human resources. With these resources, organizations engage in various activities making full use of the input, and finally produce something valuable or necessary for our society as an output. In this connection, communication among the members of an organization plays an increasingly key role in the above-mentioned organizational activities. Communication is defined here as a dynamic process involving exchange of symbols between people.

Communication within organizations is multi-layered and multi-dimensional. Downward and upward communication, as well as formal and informal communication is constantly going on within an organization. For example, in formal communication, leaders communicate with their members through command, persuasion, request, guidance, instruction, and so forth, while members communicate with their leaders through acceptance, reporting, consultation, inquiry, and so on. In informal communication, not only exchange of personal information and transmission of rumors, but also feelings or emotions are expressed among members during or after business hours, which is considered to be important for an organization to function.

With regard to the basic concepts about organization, there are a variety of views ranging from the idea that organizations are nothing but mechanical containers to the idea that organizations are organic, living creatures. Similarly, there are a variety of views and opinions on how we should develop, maintain, and manage organizations. In other words, when members of different backgrounds join an organization, we can expect discrepancies and gaps of understanding among the members about the ways that organizations should be operated.

By examining the organizing principle for many multinational organizations, Hayashi (1994) termed an organization where high-context oriented communication is the norm as, an "O-type" (organic) organization, whereas he termed an organization where low-context oriented communication is the norm as, an "M-type" (mechanical) organization. According to him, in an O-type organization, it is necessary for the members to understand the context under which the organization is operating. The context mainly consists of such analog information as customs and habits, the nature of human relations, tacit understanding, and organizational climate.

In an M-type organization, it is important for the members to communicate verbally with each other, because the level of context is low, and information is not often shared by the members. In this type of organization, people are trained to use such digital information as contracts, rules and regulations, policies, job descriptions, skills, and techniques. To put it differently, people of this type of organization have a tendency to rely on classified and categorized information through the use of language and other codes.

The notable difference between O-type and M-type organizations is that in an O-type organization, an individual member's job is not clearly defined. One's job is composed of the area of individually assigned work, in addition to the area outside one's assigned job that is called green area by Hayashi (1994). The green area that covers the kind of work born out of necessity from ongoing daily operations is usually shared by several members who work nearby or by those members who are available. In contrast, in an M-type organization, everyone's job is clearly defined, and there is no room for ambiguity as far as job territory is concerned. Hayashi (1994) asserts that most Japanese organizations belong to the O-type, whereas most of the western organizations are of the M-type. The figures of the two types of organizations are shown below:

Figure 1
Organizing Principle[1]

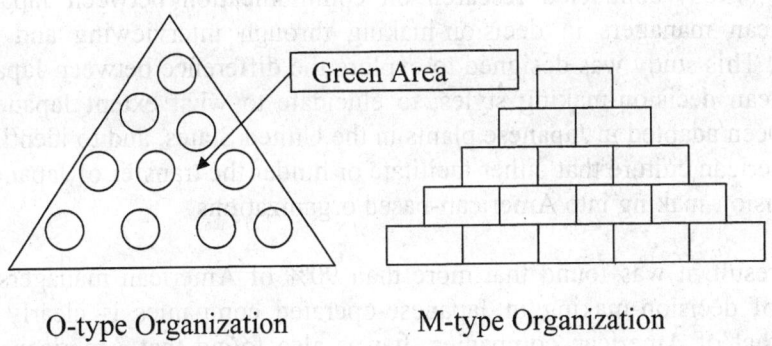

O-type Organization   M-type Organization

Having done research on multinational corporations of various countries for more than twenty years, Hayashi (1994) concluded that there are at least two types of perceptual mindsets among business people. One is analog perception and the other is digital perception. According to him, those business people with analog perception are apt to view the whole rather than a part of an organization, to rely on such soft data as personal impression, emotion, and experience, and to value interpersonal relations, whereas those with digital perception are inclined to focus on a part of the whole organization analytically, to rely on such hard data as number, classification, categorization, definition, language, and theory, and also to be oriented toward achievement. He asserts that most of the Japanese business people are analog, whereas most of the western business people are digital. Since the concept of organization and the perceptual mindset will surface in the style of communication, cultural differences can be detected clearly when we focus on communication in a specific situation.

Stewart (1985) claims that decision-making is a process or form bridging the gap between internal mental process and action. His claim indicates that values and assumptions embodied in different cultures affect the manner and rationality of decision-making, and thus decision-making can manifest cultural differences and similarities most clearly. Moreover, he suggests that decision-making must be examined in relation to American culture, because many ideas about decision-making are common for Americans, but rare for some non-westerners. Hayashi (1989) asserts that decision-making cannot be separated from communication. Hence, the author will identify communication styles of those involved in decision-making as a way of understanding cultural difference and intercultural communication in organizations.

Communication Styles in the Decision-Making Process

Kume (1985) conducted research on communication between Japanese and American managers in decision-making through interviewing and questionnaires. This study was designed to explore the difference between Japanese and American decision-making styles, to elucidate to what extent Japanese styles have been adapted in Japanese plants in the United States, and to identify factors in American culture that either facilitate or hinder the transfer of Japanese styles of decision-making into American-based organizations.

As a result, it was found that more than 90% of American managers said the style of decision-making in Japanese-operated companies is clearly different from that of American companies. It was also found that American decision-making is regarded as internal mental activities that take place in each individual manager including judgment of the situation, and selection of solutions available. In contrast, most Japanese do not make decisions by themselves. Rather, Japanese managers take decision-making as broad activities including exploration of solutions, ways of collecting information, various kinds of meetings and networking, and even examination of methods to put into practice based on the assumption that a certain decision will be made soon. In order to transplant this kind of decision-making style, every Japanese company the author surveyed in the United States has a top management committee as ultimate decision-making body, and holds interdepartmental meetings that emphasize horizontal coordination and the consensus style of group decision-making.

Even though several features of Japanese decision-making styles have been adapted to a certain degree in the United States, the research result reveals that American cultural factors such as individualism and self-reliance tend to hinder the transfer of Japanese styles. More specifically, Americans' tendency to control, dominate, and compete in various group situations is likely to create conflicts with Japanese approaches. Another American tendency to specialize and a sense of urgency are also likely to inhibit them from adopting the Japanese style of intense horizontal as well as vertical coordination and exchange of information. American individualism and self-reliance are vastly different from the attitudes the Japanese assume toward self and others.

While every person in an organization is recognized fully as an important person contributing to the organizational goal in Japanese companies, what is emphasized more is a sense of commitment, shared responsibility, interdependence, and close coordination. These results indicate that even though American managers adopt some of the Japanese decision-making styles, they differ greatly in styles of communicating their ideas on such occasions as task-oriented small group discussion. Reflecting one's deep-rooted culture, communication style tends to remain unchanged no matter how rapidly organizational structure changes.

A cross-cultural study was made by Kume, Tokui, and Xu (2000) on communication styles in task-oriented small group discussion among Japanese, American, and Chinese business people. An analysis of small group discussion by each national group was made through modifying the frame originally developed by Bales (1951). The results will be briefly described below.

The Japanese participants usually spend some time on procedural matters such as who should be the first speaker and how to discuss the topic. Very few utterances are made to navigate the direction of discussion. They seem to be very much concerned about how other members of the group are reacting to their own opinions, and how they should express their disagreement. They show disagreement indirectly and softly after agreeing with the previous speaker or by asking rhetorical, self-referenced questions. All in all, Japanese participants do not look necessarily concerned about achieving their tasks. They take special care about the nature of interpersonal relations with those who are older and higher in position and status. When discussion is sidetracked from the topic, they tend to get excited about what they are talking about, with frequent turn-taking. They seem to be comfortable in inviting others to join the conversation and to be just a listener.

American participants seem to be active or forward-looking in group discussion. In the initial stage of the discussion, they immediately go into the subject matter and get into active discussion. The flow of discussion is sequential: it follows a "proposal-response-additional comments" pattern. They seldom hesitate to speak up. Expression of views seems to be considered as something very important for them, regardless of whether they agree or disagree with others. They look adept at interrupting others and in taking turns, losing no time in expressing their views and opinions. They are task-oriented, trying hard to move toward achievement of the goal. When disagreeing with another person, they tend to express disagreement frankly and directly, while respecting the view of that person. They sometimes ask for information or make sure if they understand others correctly, so that conversation seems to move smoothly and interactively.

The Chinese participants seem to be task-oriented, without any sidetracking from the topic. When a speaker expresses his opinion with confidence, he has a tendency to dominate the conversation by making a long speech. During the discussion, listeners rarely ask questions but often give supportive feedback or expressions of agreement such as "yes, yes". There are very few instances when participants leave their sentences incomplete unlike the cases of the Japanese. Overall, opinions are expressed clearly and in some cases very assertively.

Watanabe (2006) studied intercultural corporate business discourse in Japan to explore differences between German and Japanese managers' communication styles using frame analysis. According to Watanabe, the Japanese sequence of frame is prelude—story telling—short expression of key message, while that of Germans is headline/title—rationale—recapitulation. Moreover, she reports that the Japanese initial frames tend to show backward orientation, consistently referring to previous speakers' remarks, while German initial frames demonstrated forward orientation, guiding the audience through the rest of the utterances. She asserts that these differences may indicate rather contrastive cultural knowledge schemas and interactive frames between the two groups. In conclusion, she assumes that the two groups have different perceptions and approaches to a meeting itself: the Japanese view of meeting is rather "people and process first," while the Germans prioritize "getting ideas understood with clarity" (p.80)

Based on the above-mentioned research findings, the author can speculate that while Japanese and American styles of discussion in task-oriented small groups are radically different, German style of discussion is quite close to that of Americans. The Chinese style of communication can be located in between the Japanese and American ones, but somewhat closer to that of Americans.

From the review of the relevant literature, the two kinds of research the author has done as well as the research of Watanabe (2006), two contrastive prototypes in the process of decision-making have emerged. I would like to term them *mawashi* style which is closer to that used in Japanese organizations and *tooshi* style closer to what characterizes western organizations. Needless to say, pure mawashi-type or tooshi-type communication does not exist in any organization. Most of the organizations in the world might be located somewhere along the continuum between mawashi and tooshi. Thus, this dichotomy is merely a theoretical model for understanding cultural differences.

Maywashi Style vs. Tooshi Style

I would define mawashi as a way of reaching consensus by passing around views almost endlessly among members of a group. Mawashi is the noun form of the verb mawasu (to circulate or rotate). The verb mawasu is in everyone's daily vocabulary in Japan. In contrast, I would define tooshi as a direct communication style of an individual expressing one's view clearly so that one's idea is accepted by the members concerned as such. Tooshi is the noun form of the verb toosu (to push through or have one's own way). The verb toosu is another word in daily use in Japan.

Let me illustrate these two prototypes more concretely. In mawashi style, people communicate by circulating their ideas or hinting something indirectly, while in tooshi style, someone's idea is adopted when that idea can convince everyone concerned. For example, when you are invited to your friend's house and asked if you prefer tea or coffee, you might say, "Whichever is convenient for you." This is an example of mawashi in that you are circulating your message to see how the other person is reacting. However, in the similar situation you might say, "Coffee, please." This is an example of tooshi, stating one's preference clearly and having it accepted. In the mawashi style, you will figure out how your message is interpreted by the other person. By circulating your idea in such forms as indirectness, polite expressions, or self-deprecatory expressions, the two persons are engaged, so to speak, in synchronization of thoughts and feelings. This is in sharp contrast to tooshi style in which conversational partners find meanings in interaction by appreciating the differences of views between the two participants. To put it simply, mawashii style is listener-oriented while tooshi style is speaker-oriented in conversation. Ramsey and Birk (1983) illustrate a sharp contrast between Japanese and American interaction patterns as seen below.

There are at least four areas to be discussed in contrasting mawashi and tooshi style as communication styles in the process of decision-making. Those four areas will be briefly introduced in the order of 1) the leader's role, 2) process of discussion, 3) temporal orientation of decision-making, and 4) mode of arriving at a decision.

Figure 2
Interaction Patterns between Japanese (Person A) and Americans (Person B)[2]

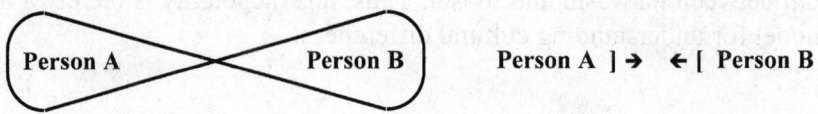

(1) The Leader's Role

The leader in mawashi style is a facilitator. The role of the leader is to bring up the proposed idea and facilitate the discussion so that everyone directly and indirectly affected by the decision can unanimously agree. If there is any disagreement or difference of opinion along the way, the leader is expected to encourage someone to explain so that eventually everyone comes to an agreement. The leader does not have to have profound professional or technical knowledge about the subject matter. Rather, what is needed as a leader is to grasp the flow of discussion by being sensitive to the emotional aspects of the participants. The leader is usually selected based on characteristics such as friendly personality and long years of contribution to the organization. He or she is rather symbolic as a leader without much substantial power. Thus, the responsibility for the decision is either shared by the decision-makers or can be avoided as much as possible. If the result of the decision turns out to be very unfavorable to the organization, the leader may retire from his or her position based on a strong sense of responsibility for the outcome.

The leader in tooshi style has a driving approach. The role of the leader is to collect information necessary for solving problems and to select one out of the alternative plans for solution. The leader is expected to have strong willpower to lead the group, to take initiative in leading discussion, and to propose an idea for solution. Moreover, the leader is expected to have a powerful decision-making capacity by being assertive and persuasive, explaining matters clearly when necessary. For this purpose, a leader may need a few professionals or specialists as advisers. The responsibility of the leader for the outcome of the decision is overall. If the result is favorable, he or she can get more power, but when the result is unfavorable, he or she needs to explain why such a result was brought about or he or she might have to resign from the leadership position.

(2) Process of Discussion

Discussion in mawashi style could be considered as an occasion for ceremony or ritual. The proposal, mostly agreed upon through prior consultation among some of members concerned, will be presented to the meeting. The participants consider the proposed idea, based on the assumption that everyone is an insider with a sense of mutual interest. In order to avoid possible discrepancies or widening in gaps of opinions, each member of the group is expected to consider the issue even before the meeting and to hold small informal meetings. In case the group cannot reach any agreement in prior discussion, the leader will not put the proposed idea on the agenda in the formal meeting.

In meetings of tooshi style, usually the leader has a powerful position. The meeting is the place where the leader proposes an idea, explains the background leading to the proposal, and then persuades the members concerned. Needless to say, participants are given a proper amount of time to examine the issue. In this regard, a question and answer session is quite important for arriving at a decision. The discussion is focused on whether the proposal is good enough to be approved. In other words, discussion continues along the given agenda and agreement is reached after frank exchange of opinions.

(3) Temporal Orientation of Decision-Making

In mawashi style, the general trend is that the meeting will continue on and on and on until agreement is reached. What is valued in the meeting is that everyone spends some time together sitting face-to-face to consider the proposal. Participants are expected to understand in which direction the discussion is flowing. Usually, they keep silent while making proper judgment about the general flow of discussion. The participants may disclose their own opinion with much reservation. Besides, the meeting will sometimes be sidetracked. In that case, it takes an extremely long time until a decision is reached. However, as everyone concerned is well aware of how to carry out the proposed decision, its execution is swift and thorough once the decision is finalized.

In sharp contrast, in tooshi-style, promptness is the utmost concern of members. Before the meeting is held, the agenda will be sent out in advance to the members concerned either through documents or e-mails, including the time of beginning and ending. In meetings, time will be spent sequentially from proposal to explanation, and then to questions and answers, to be followed by voting for decision-making. What is important here is that the group will be able to make a decision as efficiently as possible. They do not see any necessity in spending time together with other members of the group outside the conference room, as is often the case with people involved in mawashi style.

(4) Mode of Arriving at a Decision

The basic mode of arriving at a decision in mawashi style is unanimous agreement. All possible efforts will be made to achieve this goal before and during the meeting. At the meeting, there might be some people who express controversial views or disagreement, but usually it will proceed along a certain line of argument. When the leader as a moderator tries hard to preside over the meeting and reach consensus on the proposal, the participants might say that the meeting went well and the will of all of the members will be solidified to implement a proposal.

In a tooshi style meeting on the contrary, the basic mode of decision-making is either one-way announcement by the leader or majority voting. The leader tries his or her best to push through the proposal. The leader often needs to describe the background against which the particular proposal was made, explain why such a proposal is presented for decision, and tell them what had been discussed between the leader and some other members on the given proposal. The deliberation is focused on whether the proposal can be either supported or rejected. In other words, the meeting will concentrate on a given proposal and a certain amount of time will be spent for discussion, and the agreement will be reached usually within a limited time frame. The following is a schematic drawing of the two prototypes of mawashi and tooshi style.

Figure 3
Contrastive Prototypes of Mawashi and Tooshi[3]

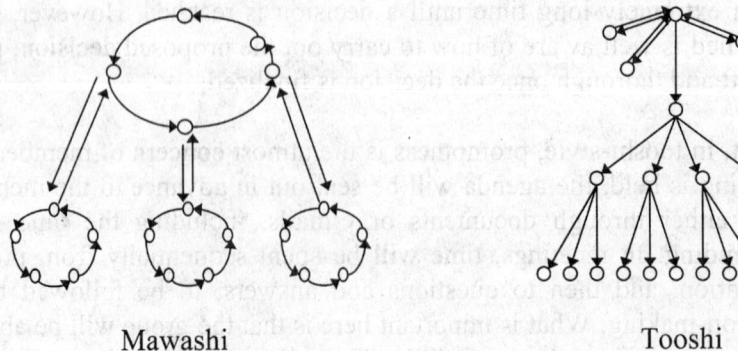

Mawashi　　　　　　　　　　　Tooshi

Case Studies

The following are three cases that actually happened: one in Europe and the second and third ones cross-culturally between Japan and the United States. The first one is in a business organization, the second one in media, while the third one is in diplomatic relations. While not all of these cases took place in multicultural organizational settings, the author is convinced that they are relevant to what was discussed so far. After introducing each case briefly, some analyses will be made for each one.

Case 1: Mr. K. Sugiyama (pseudonym) is the newly assigned president of the Japanese company in Europe. His company is located in the downtown section of a big city, just a few blocks away from the main street. The company's location is not easily found by their clients and consumers. Under such circumstances, Mr. Sugiyama suggested to Mr. J. Smith (pseudonym), manager of public relations, to make a sign for the company so that people walking in the main street can easily find their way to their company. Mr. Smith started to get in touch with various sections of the company concerning the making of the sign. Mr. Sugiyama was convinced that he could get a proposed idea from Mr. Smith sooner or later. Mr. Smith vigorously negotiated with several firms on such conditions as design, color, and cost of making the sign. He finalized the contract with one company. Mr. Smith looked very proud of what he had done so far. Then, he reported to Mr. Sugiyama that the company is going to put up a beautiful neon sign of their company name in the main street. Mr. Sugiyama was so surprised, and shouted "Neon sign?" He was also surprised by the extremely high expenditure that was different from his expectation. However, Mr. Smith went on to say, "Is anything wrong? They will be ready to start their work even from tomorrow." (Japan Overseas Enterprises Association, 1996)

Case 2: In 1992, the Japan Imperial Household Agency requested the Japanese mass media to strictly control reporting of who was going to be the candidate for crown princess in Japan, even though media people were almost certain that she was Masako Owada. In compliance with the request by the Imperial Household Agency, more than 400 companies in mass media reporting accepted this request and had firmly adhered to this policy of controlling coverage of this issue. However, a very small article titled, Prince Chose Masako as Princess, was featured in the Washington Post on January 5, 1993. Tom Reid, Tokyo Bureau chief of the Washington Post and his colleague Kazuhiko Togo decided to send this news to the headquarters of the Washington Post on the grounds that this news could be disclosed outside Japan, even though it was prohibited in Japan. The majority of Japanese TV stations started to broadcast this news at 8 o'clock in the evening of January 6 throughout Japan as an "extra, extra" (Kume, 1993).

Case 3: On August 2, 1990, Iraq invaded Kuwait. The United States immediately asked the United Nations to open the Emergency Security Council, and decided to declare economic sanctions on Iraq including freezing of assets. Together with some European nations, Japan also embarked on economic sanctions. However, Iraq had no intention to bring their army back to their own country. This was the beginning of the Gulf Crisis. In response to this crisis, the United States requested the United Nations to form the Multinational Forces. President Bush obtained a support rate of more than 96% of the American people. The Japanese Prime Minister Kaifu canceled his plan of visiting the Middle East during the middle of August. President Bush called the Prime Minister over and over again, requesting Japan to make as much contribution as possible. The items of request included participation in the multinational forces, sending of an ocean cleaning vessel, provision of medicines and doctors. It turned out to be clear later that the current law did not allow Japan to send any military forces. Then, President Bush requested financial assistance from Japan. The initial contribution of 1 billion dollars was not adequate. Later, the Japanese government announced that they added another billion dollars. The Japanese government decided to take this opportunity to open the congress so that the Japanese self-defense forces could be sent over to foreign countries. However, the proposed act did not pass the congress. The Gulf War broke out on January 15, 1991, and ended within two months. The Japanese government decided to give another additional gift of 9 billion dollars to the Multinational Forces. Also, the ocean cleaning ship was dispatched. However, the United Sates did not express much appreciation for this Japanese contribution. (Kume, 1993)

Analysis of the Three Cases

Case 1: Mr. Sugiyama, the Japanese president, used the mawashi style when he asked Mr. Smith to come up with a proposal regarding the sign. So, he was waiting for Mr. Smith to give a good proposal that could have been discussed by the top-ranking discussion meeting. However, Mr. Smith interpreted what was told by the president to be an order to do something about it. With this understanding, Mr. Smith thought he had total control over the making of the sign including the spending of the necessary expenditure. The question was what kind of sign he could make. That is the reason why Mr. Smith decided to negotiate with some makers to order the production of the neon sign which he thought was very appealing. Since Mr. Smith was the manager in charge of public relations, he had been convinced that he was in total control over this matter of advertisement. Thus, he used tooshi style in creating this plan. The conflict between the president and the manager was brought about by different communication styles in the process of decision-making.

Case 2: Curiosity about who was going to be the crown princess had been very intense in Japan for a few years, and actually a number of candidates had been seriously injured psychologically by the mass media reporting. As a result, the Imperial Household Agency requested the companies of the mass media in Japan to control reporting of this issue. In response to this request, all the mass media companies throughout Japan accepted this with a strong sense of respecting the will of the esteemed Imperial Household Agency. In Japanese society, no company was allowed to violate such an agreement for fear of heavy social sanctions. In a way, the Imperial Household Agency's policy had been successfully executed. However, Mr. Tom Reid of the Washington Post employed the tooshi style in scooping this news on the grounds that he just wanted to report this news to the United States because they are free from the control of the Imperial Household Agency.

Case 3: U.S. President Bush used the tooshi style in communicating his policy directly to the American people on TV by declaring he would send American troops to Saudi Arabia to exert the utmost pressure on Saddam Hussein. But at the same time, Bush had to cope with the financial difficulty of retaining the force in Saudi Arabia. Consequently, Bush telephoned Kaifu over and over again to get help from Japan. It was obvious that during the process of arriving at decisions, leaders in various segments of the Japanese government constantly employed the mawashi style. For instance, the Foreign Minister instructed the top officials of the his Ministry to come up with specific proposal of Japan's contribution whereas the Finance Minister instructed the top officials of his Ministry to explore ways to procure the necessary funds.

In the mean time, Kaifu had been swinging back and forth in his judgment because he had been bombarded with various conflicting elements—strong urge by the United States versus the Japanese constitutional restriction on the dispatch of personnel overseas, hawkish views of several leaders of the ruling party versus pacifist views of the opposition parties on the dispatch of the Self-Defense Forces. Above all, he was concerned about the national sentiment-the general reluctance of Japan to get involved in a military operation. Another factor regarding his long and serious consideration was Kaifu's personal relationship with President Bush. He relied heavily on strong public support of President Bush to retain his post.

One can speculate that during the process of formulating Japan's policy during the Gulf Crisis, the demand from the United States was a big shaping factor. Curiously enough, President Bush might have been perceived as a leader in the Japanese circle of mawashi. In the mawashi style, a leader's feeling must be given due account. Kaifu was overly concerned about the feeling of Bush, but was not able to decide quickly.

Conclusion

In this chapter, the features of the mawashi and tooshi styles as two contrastive modes of communication style in the process of decision-making were introduced and discussed. As was indicated earlier, they are hypothetical presentations of a model of two radically different communication styles in organizations. This simplistic dichotomy was intended to emphasize that there might be profound differences in the manners of communication between people who are from different cultural backgrounds.

While communication is playing a pivotal role in organizations, people are employing their own particular modes of communication even though they join multinational organizations. Those people who are so accustomed to a particular communication style simply cannot understand people who are using a drastically different communication style. I would say that communication is a reflection of people's patterns of thinking as well as perceptual mindsets. Since people's perception and ways of thinking are regarded as aspects of deep culture, communication style is also a reflection of deep culture. Thus, I would argue that it is usually quite difficult for anyone to change his or her communication style, because it may involve a paradigmatic change. Thus, one can expect that people in multicultural organizations might suffer from a variety of conflicts and problems in communicating with their associates or leaders who are culturally different from them.

The author is of an opinion that the mawashi style is prevalent in most Japanese organizations, while the tooshi style is prevalent in most western organizations. The mawashi style is not necessarily limited to Japan. It may be seen in such Asian countries as Thailand and Indonesia where analog orientation is the norm (Hayashi, 1994). As a matter of fact, however, some Japanese organizations can be categorized as much closer to tooshi when their leaders are very powerful and charismatic.

It seems that even within the same organization, the above-mentioned two styles are being employed depending on the nature of leadership and decision. For instance, the tooshi style may be used when immediate actions must be taken, whereas the mawashi style is employed for the formulation of long- range strategies, or development of a new product and so forth.

What is important is that a given style of decision-making must be consistent with the sense of fairness and appropriateness in the mind of people working in organizations. For example, if the leader in a mawashi-oriented organization fails to have sufficient prior discussion with some members, the organization might not work well, because some members of the organization might be very much frustrated. Similarly, if the leader in a tooshi-oriented organization immediately takes an action without sufficiently explaining the reasons for his or her decision to the members, this style will not work well, because those people affected by the decision cannot understand the leader.

Despite the fact that various organizations in the world are undergoing a drastic change in structure and procedure to globalize, one can still speculate that people will continue to communicate in their own particular ways. In this connection, we need to sensitize ourselves to different cultures and undergo various kinds of training to appreciate the perspective of the others so that we can flexibly shift ourselves to the diversity of different styles. This paradigm shift will be of the first and foremost importance in minimizing intercultural misunderstandings and frictions in multicultural organizational settings.

Endnotes

[1] From Intercultural Interface Management by K. Hayashi, 1994, p. 57.
[2] From "Preparation of North Americans for interaction with Japanese: Considerations of language and communication style." by S. Ramsey & J. Birk in *Handbook of Intercultural Training*. 1983, p. 242;
[3] From *Theories of Intercultural Communication*, p. 181, by T. Kume, 2001;

References

Adler, N. J. (2002). *International dimensions of organizational behavior* (4th ed.). Cincinnati, OH: South-Western.
Blaker, M. (1977). *Japanese international negotiating style*. New York: Columbia University Press.
Bales, R. F. (1951). *Interaction process analysis: A method for the study of small groups*. Cambridge, MA: Addition-Wesley Press.
Davidson, W. H. (1982). Small group activity at Matsushita Semiconductor Works. *Sloan Management Review, 23*(3), 3-14.
Hall, E. T. (1976*). Beyond culture*. New York: Doubleday.
Hayashi, K. (1994). *Ibunka intaafesisu keiei (Intercultural Interface Management)*. Tokyo: Yuhikaku.
Hayashi, K. (1994). O-gata keieino kokusaika genchika: Tai indoneshia wo chuushinni (Internationalization and localization of O-type management: Centering around Thailand and Indonesia.) *Aoyama International Politics and Economy Review. 29,* 31-53.

Hayashi, K. (1995). Komyunikeishon no shinten karamita nihontekikeieino yukue (Prospects of Japanese management from the perspective of communication), *Aoyama International Politics and Economy Review. 32*, 49-67.

Hayashi, K. (2002). Current intercultural issues and challenges in Japanese business interfaces: Blending theory and practice. *Intercultural Communication. 5*, 23-32. Aichi Shukutoku University.

Hofstede, G.(1980). *Culture's consequences: International differences in work related values*. Beverly Hills, CA: Sage.

Japan Overseas Enterprises Association. (1996). *Kaigaihakensha Handobukku: Yooroppa Hen* (Handbook for Those People Assigned Overseas: Europe Edition). 58-59.

Kume, T. (1985). Managerial attitudes toward decision-making: North America and Japan. In W. B. Gudykunst et al. (Ed.), *Communication, culture and organizational processes* (pp.231-251). Beverly Hills, CA: Sage.

Kume, T. (1986). Percpetion of time of Japanese and Americans in intercultural setting. *Kobe City University Journal, 37*(1-3).

Kume, T. (1993). Kimekatano bunkamasatsu: Ibunka komyunikeishon kenkyuueno ichishiron (Intercultural friction on decision-making: An ecological approach to the study of intercultural communication). *Intercultural Communication Studies, 5*, 61-93. Intercultural Communication Institute, Kanda University of International Studies.

Kume, T. (1996). The mawashi style in Japanese decision-making: A case study. *Japanese Society, 1*, 41-60.

Kume, T., Tokui, A., & Xu, Y. (2000). Komynikeishonyoushikino Nichibeichu Hikaku Kenkyuu: Shoushuudantooronno shitsutekibunnsekiwotooshite (A comparative study among Japanese, American, and Chinese communication styles: Through qualitative analysis of small group discussion.). Grant-in-Aid for COE Research Report (4) (No. 08CE1001) Researching and Verifying as Advanced Theory of Human Language, Research Leader: Kazuko Inoue, Graduate School of Language Sciences, *Kanda University of International Studies*, 625-672.

Kume, T. (2001). Shuudansoshikinaino ishikeisei shiron (An exploratory study of decision emergence?). In S. Ishii, T. Kume, & J. Tooyama (Eds.), *Theories of intercultural communication*. Tokyo: Yuuhikaku.

Kume, T., Tokui, A., Hasegawa, N., & Kodama, K. (2001). A comparative study of communication style among Japanese, Americans, and Chinese: Toward an understanding of intercultural friction. Grant-in-Aid for COE Research Report (5) (No. 08CE1001) Researching and Verifying as Advanced Theory of Human Language, Research Leader: Kazuko Inoue, Graduate School of Language Sciences, *Kanda University of International Studies*, 361-401.

Midooka, K.(1990). Characteristics of Japanese-style communication. Media, *Culture and Society, 12,* 477-489. Beverly Hills, CA: Sage.

Miyamoto, T. (1984). *Wasurerareta Nihonjin*, (The forgotten Japanese). Tokyo: Iwanami Publishing.

Moran, R. T., & Harris, P. R. (1981). *Managing cultural synergy*. Houston, TX: Gulf Publishing Company.

Mushakoji, K. (1976). The current premises of Japanese diplomacy. In Japan Center for International Exchange (Ed.) *The silent power: Japan's identity and world role.* Tokyo: Simul Press.

Nakane, C. (1970). *Japanese society*. Berkley, CA: University of California Press.

Nishiyama, K. (2000). *Doing business with Japan*. Honolulu, HI: The University of Hawaii Press.

Pascale, R. T. (1978). Communication and decision-making across cultures: Japanese and American comparisons. *Administrative Science Quarterly, 23*, 91-110.

Pascale, R. T., & Athos, A. G. (1981). *The art of Japanese management*. N.Y: Simon and Schuster.

Ramsey, S., & Birk, J. (1983). Preparation of North Americans for interaction with Japanese: Considerations of language and communication style. In *Handbook of Intercultural Training*. (pp. 227-259): Pergamon Press.

Stewart, E. C. (1985). Culture and decision-making. In W. B. Gudykunst, et al. (Eds.) *Communication, culture organizational processes* (pp. 231-251). Beverly Hills, CA: Sage.

Stewart, E. C., & Bennett, M. (1992). *American cultural patterns: A cross-cultural perspective*. Yarmouth, ME: Intercultural Press.

Takamiya, S. (1972). Group decision-making in Japanese management. *International Studies of Management and Organization, 12*(4), 139-169.

Takasugi, T. (1992). Wangansensou to nihonno taiou. (An Analysis of the Japanese Response to the Gulf War). *Intercultural Communication Studies, 4*, Intercultural Communication Institute, Kanda University of International Studies. 67-81.

Watanabe, K. (2006). Framing in intercultural business discourse: With focus on differences between German and Japanese managers, *Rikkyo Intercultural Communication Review, 4,* 81-96.

Watanabe, S. (1993). *Cultural differences in framing: American and Japanese group discussion.* In Framing in discourse. Oxford.

von Wolfren, K. (1989). *The enigma of Japanese power*. London: Macmillan.

Introduction to

Assertiveness as Communication Competence
A Comparison of the Communication Styles of American and Japanese Students

By Arvind Singhal and Motoko Nagao

Singhal and Nagao note that it is important to be aware of and to understand communication processes between people of different cultures because a better understanding of the relationship between culture and communication can help reduce the possibility of conflict between individuals of different cultures. And here, communication competence as well as those aspects which constitutes communication competence, have assumed greater relevance. Communication competence represents the notion of appropriate and effective communication in an interpersonal interaction. Singhal and Nagao point out that assertiveness is generally associated with communication competence in the USA, but not in Japan. Their study seeks to explore how cultural factors might influence communication styles of American and Japanese students. The study focuses on the differences in attitudes toward performing assertive behavior, the perception of assertiveness as communication behavior, and what role, if any, gender plays in all of this.

Data were gathered from college students in the USA and Japan. The scores of American students in their attitudes toward performance of assertive behaviors and their perceptions of assertiveness as communication competence were higher than those of Japanese students. Japanese students discriminated more between ingroup and outgroup members in their attitudes toward performing assertive behaviors, i.e. they tend to exhibit more assertive behavior among friends than in front of strangers or elders and authority figures. Both American and Japanese students exhibited gender differences in their attitudes towards the performance of assertive behavior, with the Japanese students exhibiting greater gender divergence than American respondents, but no significant culture and gender interaction was found. This would require further study to determine if there are indeed differences; but, unfortunately, the wrong questions were asked which in turn did not address those situations under which women would tend to be more assertive than men and vice versa. What this study has, though, shown is that future intercultural communication studies need to consider multiple perspectives of interpersonal communication processes.

This study has also demonstrated that communication styles do vary as do their perception, an important lesson for the international business context – whether it be meetings, negotiations, or advertisements. In other words, that what may be considered competent communication and desirable communication techniques in one country may not necessarily be considered so in another country. So one will have to, on the one hand, adapt a different communication style, and, on the other hand, realize that the same communication style will be perceived differently in different cultures. Hence, careful study and analysis of communication styles needs to be undertaken prior to interaction with another culture.

Michael B. Hinner

Arvind Singhal is Professor and Presidential Research Scholar in the School of Communication Studies, Ohio University, where he teaches and conducts research in the areas of diffusion of innovations, mobilizing for change, design and implementation of strategic communication campaigns, and the entertainment-education communication strategy. He is author or editor of eight books: *Communication of Innovations: A Journey with Everett M. Rogers* (Sage Publications, forthcoming), *Organizing for Social Change* (Sage Publications, 2006), *Entertainment-Education Worldwide: History, Research, and Practice* (Lawrence Erlbaum Associates, 2004), *Combating AIDS: Communication Strategies in Action* (Sage Publications, 2003), *The Children of Africa Confront AIDS: From Vulnerability to Possibility* (Ohio University Press, 2003), *India's Communication Revolution: From Bullock Carts to Cyber Marts* (Sage Publications, 2001), *Entertainment-Education: A Communication Strategy for Social Change* (Lawrence Erlbaum Associates, 1999), *India's Information Revolution* (Sage Publications, 1989). Two of Singhal's books, *Combating AIDS: Communication Strategies in Action* and *Entertainment-Education: A Communication Strategy for Social Change,* received the National Communication Association's Applied Communication Division's Distinguished Book Award for 2004 and 2000 respectively. Furthermore, his book *India's Communication Revolution: Bullock Carts to Cyber Marts* received the CHOICE 2002 Outstanding Academic Title Award.

Motoko Nagao is Associate Professor of interpersonal communication at Takusyoku University Faculty of Commerce, Department of International Business and the author and co-author of numerous journals articles and books. Dr. Nagao's current research interests are in the study of interpersonal communication competence and intercultural communication apprehension.

Assertiveness as Communication Competence
A Comparison of the Communication Styles of American and Japanese Students

Arvind Singhal
Motoko Nagao

While the interest in studying the influence of culture on communication processes dates back many decades, scholarly interest in this topic is on the rise. The increased mobility of people across national and cultural boundaries, and the push towards globalization of business, has made it especially important to be aware of and to understand communication processes between people of different cultures. A better understanding of the relationship between culture and communication can help reduce the possibility of conflict between individuals of different cultures.

In recent years, intercultural communication scholars have become increasingly interested in communication competence issues. *Communication competence* represents the notion of appropriate and effective communication in an interpersonal interaction (Spitzberg and Cupach, 1984). In intercultural settings, an appropriate communicative behaviour in one culture may not be appropriate in another culture. For example, eye contact is a sign of a competent communicator in the US, but does not convey the same meaning to Japanese people. Arabs, on the other hand, tend to engage in more eye contact than Americans (Samovar, 1991).

While assertiveness is associated with communication competence in the US (Zakahi, 1985), such is not the case in Japan. Consider what an American student, who was studying in Japan said (cited in Ramsey and Birk, 1983:238):

> .... whenever I get into a group discussion with Japanese [people], the questions I ask and the timing of my statements seem to cause them to clam up. I am the only one left speaking, even when I sincerely try to encourage others to speak. . . . Apparently many Japanese people place a high value on non-assertiveness when speaking or writing. I, too, consider it rather rude to

blatantly assert disagreements, or to boorishly assert my own ideas without regard for others. But to thoughtfully ask another Person questions and to logically analyze their Statements would seem to me not in the least bit selfish or assertive, but rather, it would be considered the heart and soul of intellectual discussion.

Clearly, the Americans student differed from his Japanese counterparts in his attitude towards performing assertive behaviours and in his perceptions of assertiveness as communication competence.

The purpose of the present study is to explore how cultural factors might influence communication styles of Arnerican and Japanese students. The study especially focuses on the differences between American and Japanese students' (1) attitudes towards performing assertive behaviours, and (2) their perceptions of assertiveness as communication competence.

Culture and Communication in the US and Japan

In the past few decades, an increased number of tourists, students, and business people have begun to travel back-and-forth between the US and Japan. This increased intercultural interaction has encouraged both American and Japanese people to pay more attention to the intercultural dimensions of interpersonal communication.

The influence of cultural factors on the communication styles of American and Japanese people may be conceptualized along four general dimensions (Nagao, 1991) (Figure 1). First, communication styles may be influenced by the 'individualistic' or 'collectivistic' orientation of the culture. Western industrialized cultures are often characterized by a value of individualism, and Asian cultures by a value of collectivism. In individualistic cultures, 'people are supposed to look after themselves and their immediate family only', whereas in collectivistic cultures, 'people belong to ingroups, that is, collectivities which are supposed to look after them in exchange for loyalty' (Hofstede and Bond, 1984:419). Collectivistic cultures value group goals over individual goals. The primary distinction between collectivistic and individualistic cultures is that members of collectivistic cultures make relatively clear distinctions between members of ingroups (groups to which they feel they belong) and outgroups (groups to which they feel they do not belong) than members of individualistic cultures (Tkiandis, 1986). Members of collectivistic cultures also perceive ingroup relationships to be more intimate than members of individualistic cultures.

Figure 1
Cultural Factors that Influence Communication Styles of American and Japanese people

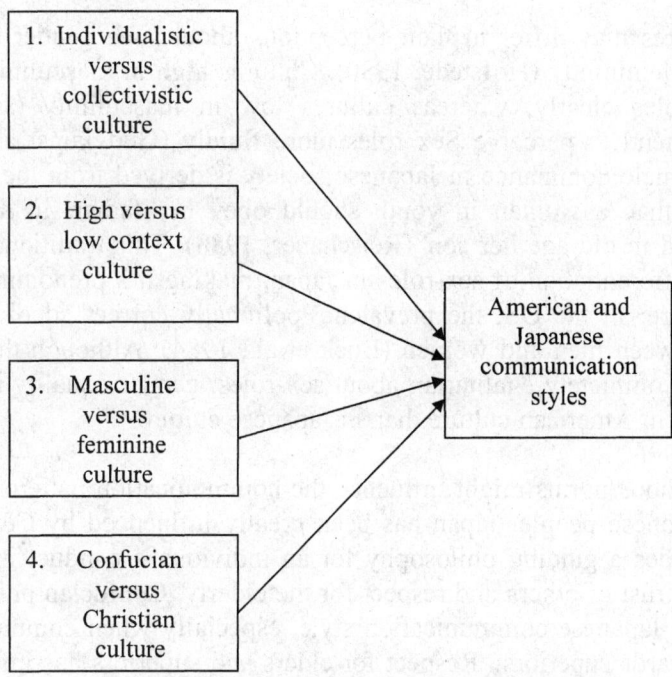

The second cultural dimension which may influence communication styles of American and Japanese people is represented by Hall's (1976) classification of low and high-context communication. Hall (1976:7) explains:

> A high-context (HC) communication or message is one in which more of the information is either in the physical context or internalized in the Person, while very little is in the coded, explicit part of the message. A low-context communication is just the opposite; ie, the mass of information is vested in the explicit code.

Verbal skills are more necessary and more highly prized in low-context cultures while nonverbal aspects of communication are more emphasized in high-context cultures (Okabe, 1983). Gudykunst and Nishida (1986) found significant differences between people of the US (a low-context culture) and Japan (a high-context culture) in the way they reduced uncertainty through the process of communication. The frequency of direct communication was found to be important for reducing uncertainty in low-context cultures, whereas indirect forms of communication such as shared communication networks, interaction with others' friends, and spending free time with others were more emphasized in high-context cultures.

Third, cultures may differ in their perceptions about such gender concepts as masculinity-femininity (Hofstede, 1980). Cultures high in masculinity differentiate Sex roles clearly, whereas cultures low in masculinity (and high in femininity) tend to perceive Sex roles more fluidly (Gudykunst and Nishida, 1986). The male dominance in Japanese society is derived from the old Confucian adage that 'a woman in youth should obey her father, in maturity her husband, and in old age her son' (Reischauer, 1988). This traditional spirit has led to the differentiation of sex-roles in Japan, making it a predominantly 'masculine' culture. In the US, the prevalent, 'politically correct' ideology stresses equality between men and women (Buck et al., 1984). Although the US is far from being completely egalitarian about sex-roles, gender equality is relatively more valued in American culture than in Japanese culture.

Fourth, religious norms might influence the communication patterns of American and Japanese people. Japan has been greatly influenced by Confucianism, which provides a guiding philosophy for an individual's conduct in society. It emphasizes trust of others and respect for the elderly. Confucian philosophy influences the Japanese communication style, especially when communication is directed towards superiors: 'Respect for elders and superiors has influenced the expression of opinion in public. To avoid offending elders or superiors, dissenting opinions are more often than not withheld' (Chu, 1988:128). On the other hand, Christianity, an actively practiced religion in the US, encourages its members to more actively engage in exchanging opinions, even with elders and superiors.

In Summary, past research suggests that American culture exhibits the following characteristics. It is generally:

1. individualistic,
2. low-context,
3. relatively low in masculinity, and
4. influenced by Christianity.

Japanese culture exhibits the following characteristics. It is generally:

1. collectivistic,
2. high-context,
3. relatively high in masculinity, and
4. influenced by Confucian ethics.

Further, in the US, a more verbal, explicit, and direct communication style is encouraged, regardless of the age-group across which communication occurs. In Japan, more nonverbal, implicit, and indirect communication patterns are preferred, especially when communicating with elders or superiors.

Assertiveness and Communication Competence

There is a wide body of literature on assertiveness and assertiveness training. *Assertiveness* is defined as the practice of behaviours which enables individuals to act in their best interest, or stand up for themselves without undue anxiety, or to express their rights without denying the rights of others (Alberti and Emmons, 1970; Wolpe, 1969).

More recently, assertiveness has been viewed as a measure of social competence or as an indicator of interpersonal communication competence. Communication competence is defined as the ability of interactants to choose among available communication behaviours in order that they may successfully accomplish their interpersonal goals during an encounter, while maintaining the face and line of their fellow interactants within the constraints of their Situation (Wieman, 1975). In the US, assertive behaviours are perceived as being more competent and attractive than unassertive behaviours (Cook and St. Lawrence, 1990; Henderson and Furnham, 1982; Rose, 1975); and assertiveness is viewed as a characteristic of a competent communicator (Zakahi, 1985).

As perceptions of assertiveness are influenced by such factors as the level of assertion, gender of the Person, culture, and situational context (Cook and St. Lawrence, 1990), communication competence may also be perceived differently in different cultural contexts (Spitzberg and Cupach, 1984). As assertive behaviours generally value individual events, beliefs, and feelings above those of groups, assertiveness is often regarded as more of an individualistic interpersonal-oriented behaviour as opposed to a collectivistic interpersonal-oriented behaviour (Shoemaker and Satterfield, 1977). Previous studies have reported that Asians are less assertive than Caucasians (Fukuyama and Greenfield, 1983; Johnson and Marsella, 1978); and the Japanese are less assertive than Americans (Thompson and Ishii, 1990).

Also, assertiveness is generally perceived as a masculine trait (Galassi et al., 1974). Assertiveness is considered as a sex-role violation for women, who are less positively evaluated for similar assertive behaviours than men (Gervasio and Crawford, 1989).

Rationale and Hypotheses

The purpose of the present study is to investigate the differences between American and Japanese students' (1) attitudes towards performing assertive behaviours, and (2) their perceptions of assertiveness as communication competence. While past research studies have focused on differences in the performance of assertive behaviours between people of different cultures, none have investigated the differing perceptions of assertiveness as communication competence.

As discussed previously, assertiveness is a behavioural social skill which is related to communication competence. However, since the perception of being competent is contextually-derived (for instance, between individualistic and collectivistic cultures), assertiveness can be perceived as a characteristic of a competent communicator in a certain culture, and as aggressive and inappropriate in another culture.

The review of literature suggests that American people generally believe in behaving more assertively than Japanese people. Since their beliefs are derived from their socio-cultural norms, should Americans also rate assertiveness as communication competence more highly than the Japanese?

> Hypothesis one: *American students will score more highly in their attitudes towards performing assertive behaviours than Japanese students, and American students will also exceed Japanese students in their perceptions of assertiveness as communication competence.*

While assertiveness is valued in individualistic cultures such as the US, such is not the case in such collectivistic cultures as Japan. Collectivistic cultures emphasize distinctions in behaviours between members of ingroups and outgroups. So one can hypothesize that:

> Hypothesis two: *Japanese students will exhibit greater differences in their attitudes towards performing assertive behaviours and in their perceptions of assertiveness as communication competence between ingroup and outgroup members than American students.*

Assertiveness is generally considered more of a masculine trait rather than a feminine one. The extent of gender differences varies across cultures: For instance, the US is relatively a more egalitarian society (in terms of Sex roles) as compared to Japan, which is relatively a more male-dominant society. More so than Christianity, Confucianism emphasizes a greater differentiation of Sex roles between men and women. So greater gender differences can be expected among Japanese people (who hail from a 'masculine' and 'Confucian culture') than Americans in their attitudes towards performing assertive behaviours, and in their perceptions of assertiveness as communication competence.

> Hypothesis three: *Japanese students will exhibit greater gender differences in their attitudes towards performing assertive behaviours and in their perceptions of assertiveness as communication competence than American students.*

Decision-Rule

The decision rule to reject or fail to reject a hypothesis was set at p 0.05. As all the hypotheses were directional, a one-tailed probability test was employed.

Methodology and Data Collection

A random sample of 118 American students was selected from a general education class of 400 students at Ohio University, Athens, Ohio. The sample included 59 male and 59 female respondents. A random sample of 109 Japanese students was selected from two general education classes at Kyoto University of Foreign Studies, Kyoto, Japan. The Japanese sample included 55 male and 54 female students.

The instrument

A modified version of the College Self-Expression Scale, developed by Galassi et al. (1974), was employed to measure American and Japanese attitudes towards performing assertive behaviours and their perceptions of assertiveness as communication competence. The reliability and validity of the College Self-Expression Scale to measure assertiveness was established by Galassi et al. (1974). The test-retest reliability coefficients for the Self-Expression Scale for two samples were found to be 0.89 and 0.90 (Galassi et al., 1974). The scale correlated positively and significantly with various measures that typify assertiveness: Self-confidence, achievement, dominance, exhibition, and autonomy.

Of the 50 questions in the original scale, 15 were carefully selected to fit the purpose of the present study. The selected questions focused on interactions with members of ingroup, outgroup, and superiors. The questionnaire was structured in two parts: Part one measured the attitudes of respondents towards performing assertive behaviours in certain communication situations, including interactions with friends (ingroup), strangers (outgroup), and superiors and elders; part two measured their perceptions of assertiveness as communication competence in similar situations.

For part one, respondents were asked to rate their attitudes toward performing assertive behaviours by choosing a five point Likert-type scale ranging from (1) never or rarely, (2) seldom, (3) sometimes, (4) usually, to (5) always or almost always. Examples of questions included: 'If a friend who has borrowed $5.00 from you seems to have forgotten about it, would you remind this person?'; and 'Do you call attention to the person who barges in front of you when you are standing in line?'; and 'If you were in a small Seminar and the professor made a statement that you considered untrue, would you question it?'

Questions in part two were repeated from the first part. However, in part two, the wording of the questions was modified such that the respondents were being asked how they would perceive a competent communicator. For example, the same questions of part one became: 'Competent communicators should remind a friend if that person who has borrowed $5.00 from them seems to have forgotten about it'; and 'Competent communicators should call attention to the person who barges in front of them when they are standing in line'; and 'Competent communicators should question a professor if they were in a small seminar and the professor made a Statement that they considered untrue'. Responses ranged from: (1) strongly disagree, (2) disagree, (3) undecided, (4) agree, to (5) strongly agree. A total score for the scale, ranging from 15 to 75, was obtained by summing all worded items. In order to eliminate ordering effects in the respondents' answers, the questions in part one and two were randomly reordered.

The questionnaire was carefully translated into Japanese, pretested on a small sample jN=20) of Japanese students at Ohio University, before it was administered to the students in Japan. The pretest was highly useful: The respondents provided suggestions about how to better convey the implicit meanings of certain questionnaire terms.

Results

Scale reliability

Since the scale used in this study was a modified version of the original Self-Expression Scale, Cronbach's alpha was computed to measure its reliability. The reliability of the 15-item scale used to measure students' attitudes towards performance of assertive behaviours was found to be 0.82. The reliability of the 15-item scale used to measure students' perceptions of assertiveness as communication competence was found to be 0.79.

Respondents' characteristics

Both the American and Japanese respondents were similar in age and education: Some 86 per cent of American respondents and 91 per cent of Japanese respondents were less than 21 years of age. Some 53 per cent of American students and 83 per cent of Japanese students were first-year college students.

Tests of hypotheses

A t-test was employed to test hypothesis one:

> *American students will score more highly in their attitudes towards performing assertive behaviours than Japanese students, and American students will also exceed Japanese students in their perceptions of assertiveness as communication competence.*

The average Scores for American students on their attitudes towards performing assertive behaviours were higher than that of Japanese students (Table 1). The t-test showed a significant difference between the two groups in their attitudes towards performing assertive behaviours ($t=7.89$, $df=223$, $p \leq .00025$, $w^2=.21$). The average scores for American students on their perceptions of assertiveness as communication competence were higher than Japanese students (see Table 1). The t-test showed significant difference between American and Japanese perceptions of assertiveness as communication competence ($t=3.22$, $df=191.48$, $p \leq .0005$, $w^2= .04$) (see Table 1 [on p. 241]).

In addition to determining significance, w^2 scores were estimated to measure the extent of differences between American and Japanese students in their attitudes towards performing assertive behaviours, and in their perceptions of assertiveness as communication competence. The difference between American and Japanese students' attitudes towards performing assertive behaviours ($w^2=.2\ 1$) was found to be much greater than that of their perceptions of assertiveness as communication competence ($w^2= .04$).

A gain score approach was employed to assess hypothesis two:

Japanese students will exhibit greater differences in their attitudes towards performing assertive behaviours and in their perceptions of assertiveness as communication competence between ingroup and outgroup members than American students.

The average gain score of American students was less than that of Japanese students in their attitudes towards performance of assertive behaviours (Table 2). The t-value showed a significant difference between American and Japanese respondents in their attitudes towards performing assertive behaviours in front of ingroup and outgroup members (t = -6.29, df=223, p $\leq$ .00035, w^2= .15) (see Table 2 [on p. 241]). The Japanese students discriminated more between ingroup and outgroup members in their attitudes towards performance of assertive behaviours than did the American students.

In measuring the perceptions of assertiveness as communication competence, the average gain Score of American students was less than that of Japanese students (see Table 2). However, the t-value did not show significant differences between the American and Japanese students in their perceptions of assertiveness as communication competence (t= -1.18, df=173, p $\leq$ .121, w^2= ,001) (see Table 2). Thus hypothesis two was only partially supported.

A two-way ANOVA was conducted to examine hypothesis three:

Japanese students will exhibit greater gender differences in their attitudes towards performing assertive behaviours and in their perceptions of assertiveness as communication competence than American students.

The results of the two-way ANOVA assessing attitudes towards performance of assertive behaviours indicated that there were main effects for both culture (F=64.17 [1,221], p $\leq$ .00025) and gender (F=6.35 [1,221], p $\leq$ .006). The cell means in Table 3 [see Table 3 on p. 242] indicate that cultural differences and gender differences were found among both American and Japanese students in their attitudes towards performance of assertive behaviours.

Japanese respondents exhibited greater gender differences than American respondents. However, no significant culture and gender interaction (F=1.63 [1,221], p $\leq$ .102) were found (Table 4).

In measuring the perceptions of assertiveness as communication competence, there was a main effect for culture (F=10.64 [1,221], p $\leq$ .0005) but no effect for gender (F= .80 [1,221], p $\leq$ .186). The cell means indicate that the size of the cultural differences were somewhat greater than the gender differences (see Table 3). Also, female respondents in both

Table 1
Cross-cultural Attitudes and Perceptions of Assertiveness

Cultural group	Attitudes towards performance of assertive behaviours		Perception of assertiveness as communication competence	
	Mean	SD	Mean	SD
American Students	57.2	7.0	58.2	5.5
Japanese Students	49.2	8.2	55.3	7.6
T-value Significance	7.89* 0.00025		3.22* 0.0005	

* $p \leq Q.05$ (according to decision-rule)

American and Japanese cultures obtained relatively higher scores on their perceptions of assertiveness as communication competence compared to their male counterparts. However, no significant culture and gender interactions (F= .40 [1,221], $p \leq .263$) were found (see Table 4 [on p.]).

Table 2
Cross-cultural Differences for Ingroups and Outgroups

Cultural group	Attitudes towards performance of assertive behaviours		Perception of assertiveness as communication competence	
	Mean	SD	Mean	SD
American Students	0.48	3.05	0.65	2.47
Japanese Students	3.25	3.55	1.18	3.98
T-value Significance	- 6.29* 0.00025		- 1.18* 0.121	

* $p \leq .0.5$, (according to decision-rule)

Table 3
Cell Means for Cross-Cultural Gender Differences

Cultural group	Attitudes towards performance of assertive behaviours		Perception of assertiveness as communication competence	
	Gender			
	Male	Female	Male	Female
American Students	57.83	56.53	62.05	62.27
Japanese Students	51.07	47.21	58.50	60.25

Table 4
Cross-cultural Gender Differences

Source	Attitudes towards performance of assertive behaviours			Perception of assertiveness as communication competence		
	Mean	F-value	SD	Mean	F-value	SD
Main Effects	2/221	35.17*	.0005	2/221	5.73*	.002
Culture	1/221	64.17*	.0005	1/221	10.64*	.0005
Gender	1/221	6.35*	.006	1/221	.80	.186
Two-way Interaction						
Culture X Gender	1/221	1.63	.102	1/221	.40	.263

* $p \leq .05$ [according to decision-rule]

Discussion

The present study investigated the communication styles of American and Japanese students, especially focusing on the differences (1) in their attitudes about performing assertive behaviours, and (2) in their perceptions of assertiveness as communication competence.

Significant differences were found between American and Japanese students' attitudes towards performing assertive behaviours. This result is consistent with Thompson and Ishii's (1990) study that American students are generally more assertive than their Japanese counterparts. Significant differences were also found between American and Japanese students' perceptions of assertiveness as communication competence. For instance, Japanese students perceive it to be inappropriate to question a professor if they disagreed with a professor's statement (at least more so than American students). The Japanese communication style is geared to maintaining group harmony. Differences of opinion must not be openly stated, especially in front of elders and authoritative figures (Austin, 1975; Chu, 1988). On the other hand, American culture encourages its members to actively engage in exchanging opinions.

A wider gap was observed between the American and Japanese students in their attitudes towards performance of assertive behaviours than in their perceptions of assertiveness as communication competence. A possible explanation for this finding might be that even though Japan is a collectivistically-oriented culture, it has no doubt been somewhat influenced by Western individualism (Ito, 1989). So while Japanese students might hold as an 'ideal' certain tenets of individualism (such as assertiveness), they in reality still feel uncomfortable about performing assertive behaviours.

Triandis (1986) argues that members of collectivistic cultures make relatively clearer distinctions between members of ingroups and outgroups than members of individualistic cultures. In the present study, Japanese students reported that they were more likely to behave assertively among friends than in front of strangers, whereas American students reported that their assertive behaviours were likely to be more consistent, regardless of whether or not they were with friends or strangers.

This Japanese communication style can be understood by considering their twofold structure of consciousness: *Omote* is the pattern one would show to others, and *Ura* describes those private intimate thoughts that are generally not to be shown to others, that is, to be shown only to intimate friends (Ramsey and Birk, 1983). *Omote* is related to a formal front acceptable to others for the sake of group harmony regardless of one's real feeling. *Ura* is related to the honest and private feelings about a matter. While Doi (1973) admits that these are universal traits, he stresses that they are more highly emphasized in Japanese culture than in any other culture.

The concepts of *Omote* and *Ura* can shed further light on why the Japanese respondents rated perceptions of assertiveness as communication competence more highly than their attitudes towards performance of assertive behaviours. Japanese students ideally understand that a competent communicator should display assertiveness, but in their own behaviour, they are careful not to be assertive. This Japanese response may be explained by their distinctive attitude called *Honne* and *Tatemae* which are related to *Ura* and *Omote*. *Honne* is the real feeling or intention expressed only in informal settings, and *Tatemae* is the official stance shown in formal or unfamiliar situations (Midooka, 1990). Japanese students' *Honne* is to perceive assertiveness as a desirable behaviour, but their *Tatemae* is not to break group harmony, that is, not to make other people lose face by actually being assertive.

Hypothesis three was not supported by the results of the present study. While it is possible that a type II error might have occurred, the power of the statistical test for the interaction indicates that a type II error is unlikely. The power of this test, determined from tables provided by Cohen (1988), was approximately 0.80, given a moderate effect size at an alpha level of 0.05. There are several possible explanations for rejection of this hypothesis. First, the absence of interaction effects between culture and gender does not necessarily preclude the presence of some additive effects. College students are generally more aware of egalitarian gender roles than are subjects of other populations. While still far from being egalitarian, Japanese society has been steadily moving towards gender equality. Women students in Japan are especially sensitive to this matter. This fact may point to the presence of additive effects from Japanese women respondents in regard to their attitudes towards the performance of assertive behaviours, which perhaps resulted in no interaction effects between culture and gender.

Another explanation might lie in the nature of the instrument used in the present study. Each question measured attitudes towards performance of assertive behaviours in a certain social situation. There might be situations other than the 15 covered by our questionnaire under which women tend to be more assertive than men or vice versa. Communication competence is contextual and situational (Spitzberg and Cupach, 1984). It may vary from situation to situation depending on the man or woman. Although the results showed that there was no interaction between culture and gender, the means of each group showed that a somewhat greater gender difference existed between Japanese men and women than their American counterparts.

The results of this study indicate the need for further investigation of assertiveness as a measure of communication competence in intercultural settings. First, observation of assertive behaviours in naturalistic settings should be employed in order to compare assertiveness of American and Japanese groups in their actual behaviours. In the present study, American students obtained much higher Scores than Japanese students in their attitudes towards performance of assertive behaviours, and in their perceptions of assertiveness as communication competence. However, a gap might exist between attitudes about performing assertive behaviours and the actual performance of assertive behaviours. Observation of assertive behaviours in naturalistic settings can provide additional insights.

Second, respondents from non-college populations should be used. Japanese students rated perceptions of assertiveness as communication competence more highly than their attitudes towards performance of assertive behaviours. American students did not show as large a gap as the Japanese students between their perceptions of assertiveness as communication competence and their attitudes towards performing assertive behaviours. College years are highly influential in shaping people's perceptions, attitudes, and behaviours related to assertiveness. Non-college populations might yield additional insights.

Finally, situational matters should be considered. Spitzberg and Cupach (1984) suggest that communication competence is contextual. Ayabe (1971) found that Asian Americans displayed differential assertiveness depending on the specific situation at hand. The present study showed that American students scored higher than Japanese students in their attitudes towards performing assertive behaviours and in their Perceptions of assertiveness as communication competence. Perhaps under certain social Situations, Japanese students would have scored higher.

While a number of intercultural communication studies compared one perspective of assertiveness across cultural groups, the strength of the present study lies in that it compared two perspectives: (1) attitudes towards performance of assertive behaviours, and (2) perceptions of assertiveness as communication competence. Future intercultural communication studies need to consider multiple perspectives of interpersonal communication processes.

References

Alberti, R.E. and M.L. Emmons (1970). *Your perfect right: A guide to assertive behavior.* San Luis Obispo, CA: Impact.
Austin, L. (1975). *Saints and samurai: The political culture of the American and Japanese elites.* New Haven: Yale University Press.
Ayabe, H.I. (1971). 'Deference and ethnic differences in voice levels', *Journal of Social Psychology* 85, 181-85.
Buck, E.B., B.J. Newton, and Y. Muramatsu (1984). 'Independence and obedience in the United States and Japan', *International Journal of Intercultural Relations* 8, 279-300.

Chu, L.L. (1988). 'Mass communication theory: A Chinese perspective', pp. 126-38 in W. Dissanayake (ed.), *Communication theory: An Asian perspective*. Singapore: The Asian Mass Communication Research and Information Centre.

Cohen, J. (1988). *Statistical power analysis for the behavioural sciences* (2nd ed.). Hillsdale, NJ: Lawrence.

Cook, D.J. and J.S. St. Lawrence (1990). 'Variations in presentation format: Effect on interpersonal evaluations of assertive and unassertive behavior', *Behavior Modification* 14(1), 21-36.

Doi, T.L. (1973). 'Omote and ura: Concepts derived from the Japanese two-fold structure of consciousness', *Journal of Nervous and Mental Diseuse* 157(4), 258-61.

Fukuyama, M.A. and T.K. Greenfield (1983). 'Dimensions of assertiveness in an Asian-American student population', *Journal of Counseling Psychology* 30, 429-32.

Galassi, J.P., J.S. Delo, M.D. Galassi, and S. Bastien, (1974). 'The college Selfexpression scale: A measure of assertiveness', *Behaviour Therapy* 5, 165-71.

Gervasio, A.H. and M. Crawford (1989). 'Social evaluations of assertiveness: A critique and speech act reformulation', *Psychology of Women Quarterly* 13, 1-25.

Gudykunst, W.B. and T. Nishida, (1986). 'The influence of cultural variability on perceptions of communication behaviour associated with relationship terms', *Human Communication Research* 13(2), 147-66.

Hall, E.T. (1976). *Beyond culture*. New York: Doubleday.

Henderson, M. and A. Furnham j1982). 'Self-reported and self-attributed Scores on personality, social skills, and attitudinal measures as compared between high and low nominated friends and acquaintances', *Psychological Reports* 50, 88-90.

Hofstede, G. (1980). *Culture's consequences*. Beverly Hills, CA: Sage.

Hofstede, G., and M. Bond (1984). 'Hofstede's culture dimensions: An independent validation using Rokeack's value survey', *Journal of Cross-Cultural Psychology* 15, 417-33.

Ito, Y. (1989). 'Socio-cultural backgrounds of Japanese interpersonal communication style', *Civilizations* 39(1), 101-27.

Johnson, F.A., and A.J. Marsella (1978). 'Differential attitudes toward verbal behaviour in students of Japanese and European ancestry', *Genetic Psychology Monographs* 97, 43-76.

Midooka, K. (1990). 'Characteristics of Japanese-style communication', *Media, Culture and Society* 12, 477-89.

Nagao, M. (1991). *Assertive behaviours and perceptions of assertiveness as Communication competence: A comparative study of American and Japanese students*. Unpublished master's thesis, Ohio University, Athens, Ohio.

Nagao, M. and A. Singhal (1992). 'Comparing the communication styles of American and Japanese students in terms of their assertive behaviours and perceptions of assertiveness as communication competence'. Paper presented to the Annual Conference of the Communication Association of Japan, June.

Okabe, R. (1983). 'Cultural assumptions of East and West: Japan and the United States', pp. 21-44 in W. Gudykunst jed.), *Intercultural communication theory: Current perspectives,* Beverly Hill, CA: Sage.

Ramsey, S. and J. Birk (1983). 'Preparation of North Americans for interaction with Japanese: Considerations of language and communication style', pp. 227-59 in D. Landis, and W. Brislin (eds.), *Handbook of Intercultural naining* Vol. 3. New York: Pergamon.

Reischauer, E.O. (1988).*The Japanese today.* Cambridge, MA: Harvard University Press.

Rose, S.D. (1975). 'In pursuit of social competence', *Social Work* 20, 33-39.

Samovar, L.A. and R.E. Porter (1991). *Communication between cultures.* Belmont, CA: Wadsworth.

Shoemaker, M. and D.O. Satterfield (1977). 'Assertion training: An identity crisis that's coming on strong', pp. 49-58 in R.E. Alberti (ed.), *Assertiveness: Innovations, application, issues.* San Luis Obispo, CA: Impact.

Spitzberg, B.H. and W.R. Cupach (1984). *Interpersonal communication competence.* Beverly Hills, CA: Sage.

Thompson, C.A. and Ishii, S. (1990). 'Japanese arid Americans conlpared on assertivenesslresponsiveness', *Psychological Reports* 66, 829-30.

Triandis, H.C. (1986) . 'Collectivism vs. individualism: A reconceptualization of a basic concept in cross-cultural psychology', pp. 47-89 in C. Bagley and G. Verma (eds.)*Personality, cognition, and values.* London: Macmillan.

Wieman, J.M. (1975). An exploration of communicative competence in initial interactions: An experimental study [Doctoral dissertation, Purdue University, 1975). *Dissertation Abstracts International* 36, 639A-37A.

Wolpe, J. (1969). *The practice of behaviour therapy.* New York: Pergamon.

Zakahi, W.R. (1985). 'The relationship of assertiveness to communication competence and communication satisfaction: A dyadic assessment', *Communication Research Reports* 2(i), 36-40.

Introduction to

The Practice of Transformational Leadership in Chinese Culture: Constraints and Promises

By Vivian Sheer

Sheer takes a closer look at transformational leadership which is a method that is often scrutinized and studied by communication and management researchers because it promised greater motivation and productivity due to its relationship oriented, communicative management style. Sheer seeks to determine whether transformational leadership would also work in Chinese culture. She notes that on the surface a number of similarities seem to exist between transformational leadership and traditional Chinese leadership styles because both attempt to (a) raise the followers' understanding of important goals, both try to (b) get followers to transcend their own self interest for the sake of the team or organization, and both seek to (c) move followers to address higher level needs such as affiliation, respect and recognition, and the realization of full potential. Traditionally, Chinese leadership has been deemed charismatic, and Chinese culture has been classified as being collectivistic. Consequently, Chinese work environments are typically said to be relationship oriented with a high priority directed at establishing harmony while also being group oriented, Sheer notes. However, closer inspection also reveals certain discrepancies.

Sheer points out that transformational practice is not common in Chinese organizations which raises the question why that is. The author notes that there are a number of barriers in Chinese societies and culture that lead to transformational leadership not being implemented in Chinese organizations. These cultural factors include power distance, collective relationship orientation, and collective teamwork. Chinese culture traditionally exhibits great power distance which makes many Chinese accept power inequality as a given. Furthermore, the relationship orientation in Chinese culture is vertically collective with a paternalistic leader at the top who is not questioned by the subordinates. Sheer also notes that harmonious relationships do not necessarily symbolize quality relationships. And finally, in Chinese culture, historically, silent role-modeling is valued over open communication. Moreover, the concept of employee empowerment is alien to Chinese culture.

Consequently, Sheer concludes that while transformational leadership is a universally desired style, including in Chinese culture, this desirability has not translated into a common practice in Chinese culture due to constraints that stem from cultural and historic reasons. And, Sheer comments, one may contend that transformational leadership may not even be needed if traditional Chinese leadership styles have been working successfully which seems to be the case as the booming Chinese economy demonstrates. Thus, illustrating once again that it is not so easy to import a specific management style from one culture to another. In addition, Sheer's text also offers an interesting, closer look at current Chinese management styles.

Michael B. Hinner

Vivian Sheer is Associate Professor in the Department of Communication Studies at Hong Kong Baptist University (HKBU). Upon earning her Ph.D. in Communication Studies at the University of Florida in 1995, she immediately took her first academic appointment as Assistant Professor in the Department of Communication Studies, St. Louis University. She joined HKBU faculty in 1997 for the first time, and again in 2005 after spending five years in market research and management consulting. She teaches organizational communication, organizational communication audits, leadership communication, conflict and negotiation, consumer behavior, research methods, and persuasion psychology. Her research areas entail technological impact on organizational communication, supervisor-subordinate interaction, and intercultural leadership communication. Dr. Sheer's research has been widely published in various academic journals, among which are *Management Communication Quarterly, The Journal of Business Communication, Human Communication Research, Communication Research,* and *Journal of Applied Communication.*

The Practice of Transformational Leadership in Chinese Culture: Constraints and Promises

Vivian Sheer

Transformational leadership (TL), much studied in organizational communication and management sciences, is a relationship-oriented, communicative management style. TL is hailed as a modern leadership approach for effective organizational managers, possibly across various cultures (e.g., Bass, 1997; Kang & Chang, 2001; Koh, Terborg & Steer, 1991). Does TL fit Chinese culture? Is TL widely practiced in Chinese organizations? This chapter attempts to answer these questions through an extensive critical literature review.

Transformational Leadership as a Communicative Style

Transformational leadership in early writings refers to the process in which an individual engages and connects with others, which inspires motivation in both the leader and the follower (e.g., Burns, 1978; Downton, 1973). Bass (1985) expands transformational leadership into a follower-oriented model. He argues that transformational leaders motivate followers to exert high performance by (a) raising followers' understanding of important goals, (b) getting followers to transcend their own-self interest for the sake of the team or organization, and (c) moving followers to address higher-level needs such as affiliation, respect and recognition, and realization of full potential. Transformational leadership is typically conceptualized and operationalized via four dimensions: idealized influence, inspirational motivation, intellectual stimulation and individualized consideration (e.g., Bass, 1985, 1997; Bass, & Avolio, 1990, 1992).

Idealized influence, also called charisma, describes leaders who exhibit strong role model behaviors, make others feel like following them and are capable of communicating vision and sense of mission. *Inspirational motivation* characterizes leaders who use persuasion such as rational arguments and particularly emotional talks to inspire followers to become committed to the tasks and the organization, and articulate a vision in such a way that is convincingly shared by followers. *Intellectual stimulation* refers to leadership that stimulates followers to be creative, innovative and participate in problem-solving and decision-making.

Individualized consideration showcases leaders who are concerned with followers' individual needs and feelings, engage in supportive communication with them and give them individualized attention. Empathy is clearly stressed over sympathy in understanding and solving subordinates problems.

In contrast with typical transactional or authoritative leadership that focuses on command, coordination, delegation, resource acquisition, the transaction of reward and punishment (e.g., Zhu, Chew, & Spangler, 2005), transformational leadership brings communication to the foreground. As a matter of fact, persuasion, vision articulation, supportive communication and participation encouragement are the built-in elements for all four transformational dimensions. The emphasis on communication was clearly evidenced in Leung and Bozionelos' (2004) study that discovered that extraversion, a communicative personality, as TL leaders' strongest trait. An individual who shows actions silently does not emerge to be the leader as quickly as someone who has the desire and skills to communicate a clear vision, one that others can understand and agree with. Rafferty and Griffin (2004) explicitly gave a new label "inspirational communication" to inspirational motivation and intellectual stimulation to highlight the communicative elements inherent in the process of transformational leadership.

The communicative nature of transformational leadership enables organizational managers to be sensitive, nurturing and developmentally oriented to followers and their needs (Rosner, 1990). As such, TL is deemed an empowering style that motivates subordinates to achieve goals beyond the call of duty (Kark & Isreal, 2004). In essence, transformational leaders see employees as those with free choice and develop follower autonomy within the realm of the vision. Thus true transformational leadership requires employee empowerment, not employee dependence.

Transformational Leadership and Effects and Effectiveness

Transformational leadership has been consistently linked to positive organizational outcomes and is considered an effective style able to meet the challenge of our modern-day organizations. Rafferty and Griffin (2004) found that TL was positively related to employee commitment and negatively to bureaucracy (see also Basu & Green, 1997). Regarding managerial effectiveness, TL was positively predictive of employee performance, affective commitment and organizational citizen behavior (Whittington, Goodwin & Murray 2004). With a sample of 400 fire rescue workers, Pillai and Williams (2004) discovered that transformational leaders built committed work groups by enhancing employee self-efficacy and cohesiveness, which in turn directly enhanced unit performance. TL's impact on group performance was further evidenced in DeGroot, Kiker and

Cross' (2000) meta-analysis which showed that TL's effect size on group performance was rather large. Further, transformational leadership is positively related to subordinate satisfaction (Ross & Offermann, 1997), work unit effectiveness (Lowe, Kroeck, & Sivasubramaniam, 1996) and follower commitment to the organization.

The findings cited here are merely a small portion of the available published studies that have found TL to have positive impact on organizations, with the majority of those studies using samples from Western countries. TL appears to have a good fit with modern Western organizations that are characterized by complexity, constant change and uncertainty.

Transformational Leadership and Its Universal Appeal

The discoveries of positive impact of transformational leadership on organizational processes, however, are not limited to Western countries. TL has generally been endorsed universally and regarded desirable. Based on a large data set, collected from more than 17,000 middle managers in 951 organizations in 62 countries, Dorfman, Hanges, and Brodbeck (2004) reported that Charismatic, team-orientation and follower-participation were the three strongest culturally endorsed leadership dimensions in the famed Global Leadership and Organizational Behavior Effectiveness research program (GLOBE) that span the years beginning in the mid-1990s. These three universal traits are very much the essence of transformational leadership. As is known, transformational leadership is charismatic, spurs team work and encourages follower participation, these strongest culturally invariant factors argue for TL as a universally desired leadership. TL's positive effects as illustrated in the preceding section, as a matter of fact, have held true across samples and cultures, with limited studies conducted in collective countries (e.g., Howell & Avolio, 1993; Koh, Terborg & Steer, 1991, Wafford, Whittington & Goodwin, 2001). Transformational leadership thus sometimes is viewed as an unbounded "universal" theory (Bass, 1997). Consequently, most studies examining TL in collective societies have taken TL as a given without questioning whether TL fits collective cultures on a broad scale.

The "Natural" Fit of Transformational Leadership and Chinese Culture

The position that TL is universal contends that TL fits Chinese culture as well as any other. Some may even argue that TL fits Chinese culture better than more others. Three arguments are presented below.

First, Chinese leadership has long been deemed one of the charismatic or transformational style. In analyzing traditional Chinese ideas, writings by ancient Chinese philosophers such as Confucian and Laotzu, about leadership, Rindova and Starbuck (1997) concluded that these idea resemble both contemporary transformational and charismatic leadership styles. They discovered that ancient Chinese rulers encouraged their advisors to use past events and history to create visions for their regime and military missions. Vision, of course, is the required element for TL's idealized influence. Thus, as charismatic leadership has been historically praised in China, so fitting in Chinese organizations is transformational leadership that has a charisma dimension.

The second argument is about transformational leadership being a relational style (e.g., Kark & Isael, 2004), appropriate in collective cultures. Transformational managers care about subordinates and desire to maintain a good relationship with them. They listen to subordinates and give them individualized consideration. The relationship orientation is a strong trait of a collective culture. Chinese, who value others' evaluation of self (i.e., the matter of face), often are oriented toward others than to self. Thus, paying attention to subordinates is a Chinese way. Further, as the Confucian value of harmony directs, managers should be motivated to maintain a harmonious relationship with subordinates. They are likely to be attentive to followers' needs and wants, as a transformational leaders would. With a sample of education workers from Taiwan of China, Kang and Chang (2001) reported that subjects considered giving respect and consideration, listening to suggestions, being humble, accepting criticism and showing trust and support to be highly desirable traits for their supervisors. This finding can be translated to that the respondents from Taiwan of China liked the behaviors similar to those of a transformational leader.

A third argument about a natural fit of TL in Chinese culture is group relationship-orientation. Collectivism stresses relatedness in that individuals are supposed to conform to the relatedness within groups (Kim, 1994). TL's interpersonal focus is thus believed to constitute an ideal style that can enhance team cohesion and effectively resolve group conflict (Atwater & Bass, 1994), which in turn boosts team performance. Jung, Bass, and Sosik (1995) propose that transformational leadership would emerge more easily and could be more effective in collective cultures due to TL's strong emphasis on group orientation, work centrality and respect for authority. Likewise Meindl (1995) argues that charismatic leaders could emerge rather more easily in work groups in collectivist rather than individualistic organizations. Additionally, the connection between team orientation and transformational leadership has been documented in several studies, among which, Pillai and Meindl (1998) gleaned a positive correlation between work group collectivism and charismatic leadership. In facing the empirical evidence of positive impact of TL on teams, scholars (e.g., Dionne,

Yammarino, Atwater & Spangler, 2004) conclude that team performance is the result of the quality of interpersonal relationships. Good relationships among group members nurtured by transformational leaders become a enabling factor for satisfaction, cohesion, and group output. In short, TL is believed to enhance teamwork and team interactions facilitate the emergence of transformational leaders. Chinese stress group activities more than do people in individualistic countries, thus TL naturally fits Chinese culture.

Thus far, TL's charismatic style, relational focus, team orientation characteristics seem to point to its high desirability in collective Chinese societies. Next, one would like to find out whether the highly desirably transformational approach would have positive effects on organizational processes and outcomes.

Positive Impact of Transformational Leadership in Chinese Organizations

Studies probing transformation leadership using Chinese respondents or within Chinese organizations have not been many. The more than a dozen published ones reported TL's positive impact on interpersonal relationships, managerial effectiveness and other organizational outcomes, which is consistent with findings from individualist countries (e.g., Jung, Chow & Wu, 2003; Leung & Bozionelos, 2004). It appears that TL's four dimensions, idealized influence or charisma, inspirational motivation, intellectual situation and idealized influence, were all well received in Chinese samples either in the original four-factor form or with other measures similar to these four dimensions. In other words, Chinese respondents considered TL behaviors or the likes desirable (Leung & Bozionelos, 2004,). In other words, Chinese respondents rated TL items highly in terms of these items being characteristic of a good leader.

In addition, transformational leadership predicted managerial effectiveness and positive organizational outcomes. Kang and Chang (2001) reported that respondents favored administrators who exhibited a high degree of TL-like communicative behaviors such as listening to suggestions, being cooperative, expressing appreciation, showing empathy, using reason to persuade, serving as a mentor, sharing and participating. Further, the more TL-like behaviors a supervisor displayed, the more effective, he/she was rated. With a sample of managers in thirty-two companies from Taiwan of China, Jung, Chow and Wu (2003)'s study showed that transformational leadership was positively correlated to organizational support for innovation, a requirement for a modern corporate to survive and grow. Further, the scores on the TL dimensions of HR managers and CEOs in a Singapore sample positively predicted the firm's past three year performance in planning, selecting, training (Zhu, Chew, & Spangler, 2005).

The findings reviewed here cast little doubt that transformation leadership has positive impact on organizational processes and outcomes. One might assume that TL's "natural fit" could may be a natural, and perhaps a wide-spread practice in Chinese organizations. If TL were broadly practiced, employees' in Chinese organizations would likely experience a great degree of autonomy and relational satisfaction with each and with their supervisors, demonstrate a strong organizational commitment and achieve high unit/team performance, just to mention a few possible positive outcomes. A reality check of the transformational practice is rather warranted to help provide a better gauge of leadership in Chinese culture.

Transformational Reality in Chinese Culture

The reality of transformational practice in Chinese organizations, however, remains bleak. Despite TL's high desirability and likely positive effects, the actual use of it is low. In Sheer and Chen (2003)'s study of TL and intranet use among HK managers of China, the respondents' ratings of their supervisors hovered slightly below 3, the mid-point of a six-point scale. Likewise, Zhu, Chew, and Spangler's (2005) HR manager and CEO subjects scored below the mid-point of their TL scales. Jung, Chow and Wu (2003), too, gleaned similar findings regarding the ratings of managers' TL. It appears that TL can enhance organizational processes and outcomes and is liked and desired by employees in Chinese culture and societies. Although the more TL is used, the more positive effects, as in indicated consistently in research, TL is nonetheless not widely practiced in societies. High level managers, even at the CEO positions, on average display low transformational leadership. In a study of 115 mid-level managers in Singapore and 96 in Australia, Harrison (1995) discovered that job satisfaction was lower, job tension higher and interpersonal relations poorer perceived by Singaporean managers than by the Australian counterparts. If TL practice increases relational satisfaction, Harrison's findings may have lent some credence to possibly a lack of TL practice by Chinese managers.

A further look at leadership in a larger collective context leads back to the GLOBE program. In GLOBE, the two TL-relative leadership dimensions, charisma and team-orientation are the most highly universally endorsed. Yet, some variability exists. Interestingly, the Confucian Asia, which included China, Korea, Japan and Singapore, scored toward the middle pack on these two dimensions, lower than some typical individualistic cultural groupings such as Anglo, Eastern Europe and Nordic Europe (Dorfman, Hanges, & Brodbeck, 2004). This could harbinger an initial question mark regard the assertion that collective culture has a more natural fit with TL than does individualistic culture.

These findings, coupled with the empirical evidence that TL is universally desirable and has positive effects on organizations (Chinese ones included), raise a question as to why TL is not widely practiced in Chinese organizations. The positive association between TL and organizational processes and outcomes can simply be interpreted as "the more TL is used, the better the effects." This however, does not translated into how popular TL is exhibited. An examination of barriers to TL practice begins with cultural values.

Possible Cultural Barriers to Transformational Leadership Practice

Barriers to the wide-practice of transformational leadership in Chinese culture come from many aspects of Chinese societies and culture. Managerial practices at various organizations, individual differences, manager personal background can become reactive to the use of TL. Yet the cultural aspects are the ones that serve as the beginning point when systemic patterns are found to be different in one culture than another. Three deep-rooted Chinese cultural constraints are identified here.

Cultural Constraint 1: Power Distance

Power distance in the cultural context derives from Hofstede's (2001, 1980) notion to refer to the degree to which members of an organization or society expect and agree that power should be shared unequally. Individual countries see small power distance while collective cultures embody a large one. In low power distance societies, subordinates and superiors regard each as equivalent people with equal rights and representation. Organizational members generally enjoy psychological freedom without fearing retaliation in case they beg to differ from superiors. Managers, on the other hand, are used to treat different opinions as a matter of organizational norm, and do not take subordinates' different views as a sign of disrespect. High power-distance organizations operate on quite dissimilar doctrines. Chinese, who are predisposed to the five Confucian cardinal relationships that stipulates a vertical, age- and seniority- based hierarchy, tend to accept power inequality. In a Chinese organization, the senior person is expected to provide support and encouragement for the lower-status persons whereas the later is expected to return with loyalty and respect (Carl, Gupta & Javidan, 2004). In practice, superiors are expected to lead to make decisions autocratically and paternalistically while subordinates generally are afraid and unwilling to disagree with their superiors (Harrison, 1995). Superiors may take subordinate disagreement personally and get defensive in an effort to maintain face. Harrison (1995) draws upon Hofstede's (1908) work and comes up with a comparative table that reveals the major organizational implications of high- versus low- distance societies (see Table 1).

Table 1.
Selected Connotations of Power Distance (PD) Contrasting Low and High PD Societies

---

Low power distance
People at various levels feel less threatened and more prepared to trust others
Latent harmony between the powerful and the powerless
Employees less afraid of disagreeing with their boss
Managers seen as showing more consideration
Employees show more co-operation
Co-operation among the powerless can be based on solidarity
Stronger perceived work ethic; strong disbelief that people dislike work

High power distance
Other people are a potential threat to one's power and rarely can be trusted
Latent conflict between the powerful and the powerless
Employees fear to disagree with their boss
Managers seen as showing less consideration
Employees reluctant to trust one another
Co-operation among the powerless is difficult because of the low faith in people norm
Weaker perceived work ethic: more frequent belief that people dislike work

---

Harrison empirically tested the distinctions conceptualized above and found that job satisfaction was lower, job tension higher and interpersonal relations poorer for managers in the high power distance, collectivist cultures of East Asian nations than for managers in the low power distance, individualist cultures of Anglo-American nations (Harrison, 1995). Likewise, Huff and Kelley (2003) discovered that the propensity to trust and general trust level were lower in Asia than in the US in their sample. Moreover, lack of autonomy in high power distance has consistently predicted low job satisfaction while empowerment has enhanced both job satisfaction and performance (Bowen, 1995; Hui, Au & & Fock, 2004; Spreitzer, 1995).

Does the power distance analysis shatter the seeming fit of the collective culture and transformational leadership? To answer this question, one would need to examine the first seeming fit that comes from historic writings of the charismatic leader. A charismatic leadership was praised and advocated historically for top or high-ranking state and military leaders. When applied to modern management, a charismatic middle manager or frontline supervisor certainly is ideal and highly desired. But to require an average manager to become charismatic could be a bit over the head. Further, the pervasive high power distance cultural norms give managers little motivation to be transformational, which would require them to spend time and use the means of persuasion to empower subordinates who would accept task commands obediently anyway. However, it is entirely possible that some individual differences such as personality, democratic organizational culture and special management training might drive certain managers to practice transformational leadership. But high power distance surely inhibits the emergence of transformational leaders.

Furthermore, the examination of high distance thus far raise the issue of comparative effectiveness of a transformational leader nurtured by lower power distance versus an authoritative of leader fostered by high power distance. Widely known is that fact that TL that gives employees more autonomy is universally desired, but is it needed to get a job done in the high power distance Chinese culture? The literature has taken for granted that TL is more effective, few, next to none, studies have been conducted to compare TL against the traditional authoritative leadership on same organizational process and outcome variables. Such research is needed to shed light on the degree to which TL is applicable in Chinese organizations.

Cultural Constraint 2: Collective Relationship Orientation

Another alleged natural fit comes from TL's imbedded relationship orientation and the human relationship focus in the collective Chinese culture. Such superficial equating of relationship based on the same word label has commits a fallacy. The relationship orientation in Chinese culture appears quite divergent from what is construed and understood in the TL literature.

Due to the inherent high power distance element, Chinese culture is vertically collective (cf., horizontal collectivism as in Eskimo culture where members view each other similar and share collective goals) (Triandis & Gelfand, 1998). Chinese collectivism stresses relatedness over rationality with priority given to relationships and accommodation to the needs of others (Kim, 1994). In the organizational setting, members are expected to view themselves as highly interdependent with the organization. Organizational identity supercedes and becomes part of the individual one. Employees would assume that their relationships, duties and obligations are central to their employment, not merely their unique attributes such as competence and capability. Managers, on the other hand, assume that employees are willing to make personal sacrifices for organizational goals—generally with persuasion. In turn, employees would expect that the organization stand by them in hard economic times; and if not, resentment breeds. They would also expect reward to be allocated for group performance rather than individual merit and thus may not have the motivation to outperform. Employees consequently view their job more as a matter of long-term relational exchange rather than a short-term performance-reward transaction (Gelfand, Bhawuk, Nishi & Bechhold, 2004; Hofstede, Neuijen, Ohayv, Sanders, 1991).

Primarily, the norms of a collective organization describe a paternal relationship between the manager and subordinates. This paternal relationship, to a limited degree, converges with TL's individualized consideration in that managers attend to subordinates' personal needs—but only when such needs are not in conflict with organizational goals. Otherwise, managers must persuade or tell employees to sacrifice. A transformational leader would try to meet subordinate needs and give explanations and choices in case such needs can not be met; in turn, the subordinate makes the ultimate decision live with the consequences. The paternal mentality always demands loyalty and obedience without guaranteeing to repay employees' sacrifice. Such mentality discourages intellectual stimulation that inspires commitment, which is thought as an obligation rather than a volition in collective culture. Paternal leaders play no part in empowering employees by raising their personal capacity; neither would leaders entrust employees with autonomy or high responsibility. Rather, they keep responsibility away from employee, who are expected to depend on managers. This, can be backed by Sarros and Santora's (2001) study which found that Chinese managers allowed little self-direction for their subordinates. In general, there is very little empirical evidence as to which, paternal or transformational style, is preferred by Chinese employees as the majority of the studies have not tested one against the other. Nonetheless, a valid argument can be made that paternal mentality can hinder the practice of transformational leadership.

Further, collective relationship orientation is exemplified by the value of harmony, an overarching goal of human interaction among Chinese people (Chen & Starosta, 1997). Harmony exits in mutual dependency. In organizations, harmony often is advocated to avoid conflict as collective culture has a conflict-aversive tendency (Sheer, 2000). As long as organizational members can work and live in peace with each other, harmony is considered preserved even though differences are a matter of undercurrents flowing silently beneath the surface. Harmonious relationships do not necessarily symbolize quality relationships. A key issue here is whether the relationship between the supervisor and the subordinator is generally better in Chinese culture that values unconditional harmony than in individualistic culture where communicating the difference is key to a trusting relationship. Whichever leadership, paternal or transformational, leads to better interpersonal relationship is the one to be commended. Harrison (1995) argues that individualistic leadership often is more egalitarian, more considerate than is paternal authority; and individualistic leadership should contribute to better relationships across hierarchical levels, particularly in contrast to vertically collective societies. This argument has received empirical evidence in that relationships between supervisor and subordinates would be worse in high power distance collective culture than in low power distance individualistic culture (Harrison, 1995; Hofstede, 1980; 1988).

The emphasis on harmony gives Chinese managers little incentive to engage in transformational communication with subordinates to explain and iron out differences for the sake of achieving a mutual understanding—since the unwritten rule is "keep quite". A harmonious surface (i.e., peace but no trust) in Chinese organizations could feed cynicism and cultivate a defensive climate, which could alienate employees from supervisors and draw wedges among employee themselves. In-groups probably are the ones that have true harmony, peace and trust. Ye understandably, most work units are not in-groups due to varied task assignments and personnel turnovers. Thus, plausible is that emphasis on harmony suppresses motivation to communicate openly and reduces and opportunities for communication, required of transformational leadership.

A third salient characteristic of collective relationship orientation resides in the concept of *Guanxi,* which refers to the interconnections of people in a network. Those who belong to a network are in-group members who trust and depend on each other for material resources and service. Those who fall out of a network are out-group members. In-groupers are protective of each other against outside threats (Kim, 1994). For self-protection and job security, Chinese managers may resort to building strategic *Guanxi*-often people who rank higher in an organization. Such upward *Guanxi* is assumed to be helpful to managers in getting promoted. As a matter of fact, hiring and promoting people in a Guanxi network is considered a norm in a collective culture like China (Gelfand, Bhawuk, Nishi & Bechhold, 2004). When managers are promoted through *Guanxi*, they often lack the training or skills a modern business schools give. Transformational leadership, extolled by modern management and organizational communication scholars and practitioners, thus has less of a chance to be applied in an actual Chinese organization. Further, *Guanxi*-propelled promotions could lead the newly promoted managers to feel personally indebted to the superior who made the advancement possible. Consequently the new managers feel more accountable to the superior than to the subordinates. As long as *Guanxi* is the primary mode for promotion in a given organization, then the majority of the managers are not very likely to exhibit transformational behaviors.

Cultural Constraint 3: Collective Teamwork Mode

Team participation is central to the theories of transformational leadership. Transformational leaders encourage autonomy and personal responsibility, reward team members' unique contribution, and subsequently raise subordinates' job and relationship satisfaction and increase their commitment to the organization. thus leading to satisfaction in job and work relationships and commitment to organizations. In Chinese culture, team or group work is much emphasized as collectivism is all about relationship, group identity, group task and group performance. The seeming natural fit of TL's team focus and Chinese' group orientation has been unquestioned. Even studies with Chinese samples took for granted that TL's team participation is equivalent to Chinese group work. As a result, these studies simply examined the relationship, oftentimes correlations, between degree to which TL is exhibited and group performance, without questioning whether TL's team concept and Chinese group notion are compatible.

A transformational team process requires managers to engage in open and candid communication with subordinates and instill a sense of pride in their work. Transformational managers, who believe that the whole of a system is greater than the sum of all parts, stimulate creativity and innovation and welcome members' individual contribution to team tasks and goals. They empower members by encouraging personal responsibility and self-direction. Members are reward as individuals and team players. To that end, Pillai and Williams (2004) discovered that transformational leaders built committed work groups by enhancing employee self-efficacy and cohesiveness, which in turn directly enhanced unit performance.

In Chinese culture, historically, silent role-modeling is valued over open communication. Confucius once taught his students to keep silent when in disagreement and use only actions to show the real intention (Chan, 1963; Lau, 1979). The tendency of tolerating uncertainty among Chinese and the prevalent lack of management transparency produce a work environment where communication and persuasion is not high on managers' agenda. Even though Chinese employees prefer more communication, they nonetheless have not problem tolerating the lack of it. The communication ingredient in a transformational leader is weak, if not missing, among managers in collective team work within Chinese organizations.

Moreover, the concept of employee empowerment is alien in Chinese culture. Employees are supposed to be "children" to depend on managers and the organization, and managers often do not identify self-direction as a key corporate value (Sarros & Santora, 2001). In practice, unless a work team/unit is an in-group, which is becoming rarer due to modern job mobility, managers often are defensive regarding giving autonomy or decision making responsibility to employees. They could feel threatened by empowered subordinates. Individuals in out-groups often notoriously display mistrust among each other while in-group members normally show a high degree of trust for each other (Huff & Kelley, 2003). One the flip side of the coin, Chinese employees, who are used to paternal and authoritative management style, are not comfortable with responsibility. Chinese, particularly mainlanders, tend to behave passively and would rather receive commands than taking the initiatives for fear to risks (Selmer, Ling, Shiu, & de Leon, 2003). It seems that people in collective cultures are not quite comfortable about taking personal responsibility on the job (Gelfand, Bhawuk, Nishi, & Bechhold, 2004). They would rather work in a work without having their own performance evaluated individually. The unwillingness to break the paternal/authoritative equilibrium of responsibility by both the superior and the subordiate may suggest possible resistance against full-scale application of transformational leadership in the team setting.

The Chinese parenting management philosophy does not believe in employee participation and unique contribution. Instead of stimulating subordinates intellectually and giving them opportunities to grow, and instilling confidence, Chinese managers opt to spend much more time, than their individualistic counterparts, juggling interpersonal relationships, maintaining the cohesion of the group, and avoiding conflict (e.g., Bass, Burger, Doktor & Barret, 1979; Dorfman, Hanges & Brodbeck, 2004). Group maintenance serves to clarify and solidify each member's group role responsibilities in orienting toward and ultimately meeting the collective goals. In addition, Chinese managers often endeavor to cultivate subordinates' personal loyalty to get the job done (Sheer & Chen, 2003b). To put it plainly, teamwork means doing what is told without getting too creative or extending to extra-role behaviors. As is explained here, team participation and performance propelled by transformational leadership is quite different from how the same label is conceived in Chinese culture. Until individual contribution and creativity is valued, the participative teamwork will not be encouraged. Thus, group behaviors and strong managerial control will continue to take precedence over the practice of transformational leadership that solicits individual participation in team tasks.

Group orientation in the collective Chinese culture can result in social loafing, the phenomenon that persons make less effort to achieve a goal when they work in a group than when alone. Unless in a in-group situation where tight-knit, motivated members exert concerted effort to achieve group goals, individuals in out-groups often exhibit loafing behaviors (Earley, 1993). As long as individuals' identity is buried in the group identity with their performance not being evaluated individually, out-group members do not have to be motivated and give their best effort (also see Francesco & Chen, 2004). If social loafing is inevitable in a collective, paternal environment, transformational leadership, however, may offer a remedy (Dionne, Yammarino, Atwater & Spangler, 2004). TL has been found to be effective in evoking self-motivation, taking personal responsibility and enhancing organizational commitment, thereby boosting individual performance. The problem of social loafing would render TL an effective practice in collective culture, yet implementing TL may meet obstacles discussed early on.

Future of Transformational Leadership in Chinese Culture

Transformational leadership is a universally desired style, including in Chinese culture, as TL appeals to human fundamental needs for autonomy and trusting relationships. However, TL's desirability has not translated into a common practice in Chinese culture due to constraints that stem from cultural and historic reasons. The three constraints, power distance, collective relationship orientation and collective teamwork mode, can all amount to obstacles to the implementation of transformational leadership in Chinese organizations. The cultural constraints may be able to explain why the current TL scores are rather low among Chinese managers. The most important question regarding the future of TL in Chinese culture must address these: (1) Do Chinese organizations need TL? and (2) Will TL work? The valid approach to answer that question is via empirical examination, a challenge to be taken by organizational communication and management scholars and researchers.

One may contend that TL may not even be needed if traditional Chinese leadership styles have been working, as is true the fact that Chinese organizations, corporations included, are obviously producing and sustaining China's booming economy. The place for TL in Chinese culture can be justified only when TL is better than traditional Chinese leadership. To that end, researchers can begin by clearly identifying the dominant Chinese leadership styles, among many that exit (Tsui, Wang, Xin, Zhang & Fu 2004). As a matter of fact, Confucian values, Western influence and economic reform may result in a hybrid of various styles. Nonetheless, dominant leadership approaches likely hold strong the traditional elements (Tsui, etal., 2004). Generally speaking, paternal leadership is regarded as the most effective and widely practiced approach, compared to others such as authoritarian or moral- and exchange- based *renqi* orientation.

Researchers can conduct comparative studies that contrast paternal with transformational leadership in terms their effects on the organizational processes and outcomes. Key variables can include perceived leadership desirability, levels of communication, communication content, performance level, subordinate-supervisor relationship quality, employee relationship, organizational commitment, organizational citizenship behavior, sense of pride and job satisfaction. Comparative studies must also control for typical key contextual factors such as organizational ownership (e.g., government agency, foreign subsidiaries, multi-national, state-owned, or Chinese private owner) and industry type (e.g., service, manufacturing, sales, and trading), and organization size. Based on the existing empirical evidence, transformational leadership likely will have positive impact on Chinese organizations. Also likely, a combination of a few TL dimensions and several paternal leadership aspect may constitute the most effective leadership in Chinese culture. Such hybrid leadership styles might meet less resistance from the traditional value holders. Findings through those comparative studies should be able to offer substantive directions, if not solutions.

To look into the future, the market economy is likely to drive Chinese organizations to become less hierarchical, more flexible, team-oriented, and participative (Fondas, 1997; Rosener, 1995). As a result, management will be required to meet the economic challenge by offering pragmatic, flexible and motivational approach that maximizes human resources, thus comes the breeding ground for transformational leadership.

References

Atwater, D., & Bass, B. M. (1994). Transformational leadership in teams. In B. Bass and B. Avilio (Eds.), *Improving organizational effectiveness through transformational leadership*, pp. 48-83. Thousand Oaks, CA: Sage.

Bandura, A. (1997). Exercise of personal and collective control in changing societies. In A. Bandura (Ed.), *Efficacy in Changing Societies*, pp. 1-45. Cambridge: Cambridge University Press.

Bass, B. M. (1997). Does the transformational leadership paradigm transcend organizational and national boundaries? *American Psychologist, 52,* 130-139.

Bass, B. M. (1985). *Leadership and performance beyond expectations*. New York: Free Press.

Bass, B. M., & Avolio, B. J. (1992). *Multifactor leadership questionnaire-Short Form 6S*. Binghamton, NY: Center for leadership Studies.

Bass, B. M., Burger, P.C., DoKtor, R., & Barret, G. V. (1979). *Assessment of managers: an international comparison*. New York: Free Press.

Basu, R., & Green, S. G. (1997). Leader-member exchange and transformational leadership: An empirical examination of innovative behaviors in leader-member dyads. *Journal of Applied Social Psychology, 27(6),* 447-499.

Bowen, D.E. (1995). Empowering service employees, *Sloan Management Review, 36,* 73-84.

Burns, J. M. (1978). *Leadership*. New York: Harper & Row.

Carl, D., Gupta, V., & Javidan, M. (2004). Power distance. In . In R. J. House, P. J., Hanges, M. Javidan, P. W. Dorfman, and V. Gupta (Eds.), *Culture, leadership, and organizations: The GLOBE study of 62 societies* (pp.523-563). Thousand Oaks, CA: Sage

Chan, W. T. (1963). *Source book in Chinese philosophy*. Princeton, NJ: Princeton University Press.

Chen, G. M., & Starosta, W. J. (1997). Chinese conflict management and resolution: Overview and implications. *Intercultural Communication Studies, 7*, 1-16

DeGroot, T., Kiker, D. S., & Cross, T. C. (2000). A meta-analysis to review organizational outcomes related to charismatic leadership. *Canadian of Administrative Sciences, 17*, 356-371.

Dionne, S. D., Yammarino, F. J., Atwater, L. E., & Spangler, W. D. (2004). Transformational leadership and team performance. *Journal of Organizational Change Management, 17(2)*, 177-193.

Dorfman, P. W., Hanges, P.J., & Brodbeck, F. C. (2004). Leadership and cultural variation: The identification of culturally endorsed leadership profile. In R. J. House, P. J., Hanges, M. Javidan, P. W. Dorfman, and V. Gupta (Eds.) *Culture, leadership, and organizations: The GLOBE study of 62 societies* (pp.669-710). Thousand Oaks, CA: Sage

Downton, J. V. (1973). *Rebel leadership: Commitment and charisma in a revolutionary process*. New York: Free Press.

Earley, P. C., (1993). East meets West meets Mideast: Further explorations of collectivistic and individualistic work groups. *Academy of Management Journal, 36*, 319-348.

Fondas, N. (1997). Feminization unveiled: Management qualities in contemporary writings. *Academy of Management Review, 22*, 257-282.

Francesco, A. M., & Chen, Z. X. (2004). Collectivism in action: Its moderating effects on the relationship between organizational commitment and employee performance in China. *Group & Organizational Management, 29*, 425-441.

Gelfand, M. J., Bhawuk, D. P. S., Nishi, L. H., & Bechhold, D. J. (2004). Individualism and collectivism. In R. J. House, P. J., Hanges, M. Javidan, P. W. Dorfman, and V. Gupta (Eds.) *Culture, leadership, and organizations: The GLOBE study of 62 societies* (pp.437-512).

Harrison, G. L. (1995). Satisfaction, tension and interpersonal relations: a cross-cultural comparison of managers in Singapore and Australia. *Journal of Managerial Psychology, 10(8)*, 13-19.

Hofstede, G (2001). *Culture's consequences: Comparing values, behaviors, institutions and organizations across nations*. (2nd ed.) Thousand oaks, CA: Sage.

Hofstede, G.H. & Bond, M.H. (1988). The Confucius connection: from cultural roots to economic growth. *Organizational Dynamics, 16(4),* 5-21.

Hofstede, G.H., *Culture's Consequences: International Differences in Work-Related Values,* Beverly Hills, CA: Sage, 1980.

Hofstede, G., Neuijen, B., Ohayv, D. D., & Sanders, G. (1991). Measuring organizational cultures. *Administrative Science Quarterly, 35,* 286-316

Howell, J., & Avolio, B. (1993). Transformational leadership, transactional leadership, locus of control, and support for innovation: Key predictors of consolidated-business-unit performance. *Journal of Applied Psychology, 78,* 891-902.

Huff, L., & Kelley, L. (2003). Levels of organizational trust in individualist versus collectivist societies: A seven-nation study. *Organization Science,* 14(1), 81-90.

Hui, M. K., Au, K. & Fock, H (2004). Empowerment effects across cultures. *Journal of International Business Studies, 35(1),* 46-77.

Jung, D. I., Chow, C., & Wu, A. (2003). The role of transformational leadership in enhancing organizational innovation: Hypotheses and some preliminary findings. *The Leadership Quarterly, 14,* 525-544.

Jung, D., Bass, B., & Sosik, J. (1995). Bridging leadership and culture: A theoretical consideration of transformational leadership and collectivistic cultures. *Journal of Leadership Studies, 2,* 3-18

Kang, T. L., & Chang, S.H. (2001). Development of a new three-dimensional leadership mode in technological and vocational education in Taiwan. *Global Journal of Engineering Education, 5(2),* 139-146.

Kark, R., & Isael, R. G. (2004). The transformational leader: who is (s)he? A feminist perspective. *Journal of Organizational Change Management, 17(2),* 160-176.

Kim, U. (1994). Individualism and collectivism: Conceptual clarification and elaboration. In U. Kim, H. C. Triandis, C Kagitcibasi, S. C. Choi, & G. Yoon (Eds.). Individualism and collectivism: Theory, method, and applications (pp. 19-40). Thousand Oaks, CA: Sage.

Koh, W. Terborg, J., & Steer, R. (1991). *The impact of transformational leadership on organizational commitment, organizational citizenship behavior, teacher satisfaction, and student performance in Singapore.* Paper presented at the Academy of Management annual meeting, Miam, FL.

Lau, D. C. (1979). *Confucius: The analects.* Harmondsworth: Penguin.

Leung, S. L. & Bozionelos, N. (2004). Five-factor model traits and the prototypical image of the effective leader in the Confucian culture. *Employee Relations, 26(1/2),* 62-71.

Lowe, K. B., Kroeck, K. G., & Sivasubramaniam, N. (1996). Effectiveness correlates of transformational and transactional leadership: A meta-analytic review of the MLQ literature. *Leadership Quarterly, 7(3),* 384-426.

Meindl, J. R. (1995). The romance of leadership as a follower-centric theory: A social constructionist approach. *Leadership Quarterly, 6(3)*, 329-341.

Pillai R. & Meindl, J. R. (1998). Context and charisma: A "meso" level examination of the relationship or organic structure, collectivism, and crisis to charismatic leadership. *Journal of Management, 24(5),* 643-671.

Pillai, R., & Williams., E. A. (2004). Transformational leadership, self-efficay, group cohesiveness, commitment, and performance. *Journal of Organizational Change Management, 17(2),* 144-159.

Raffferty, A. E., & Griffin, M. A. (2004). Dimensions of transformational leadership: Conceptual and empirical extensions. *Leadership Quarterly, 15,* 329-354.

Rindova, V. P., & Starbuck, W. H. (1997). Ancinet Chinese Theories of control. *Journal of Management Inquiry, 6*, 144-159.

Rosener, J. B. (1995). *America's competitive secret: Women managers.* New York: Oxford University Press.

Roser, J. B. (1990). Ways women lead. *Harvard Business Review, 68,* 119-125.

Ross, S. M., & Offermann, L. R. (1997). Transformational leadership: Measures of personality attributes and work group performance. *Personality and Social Psychology Bulletin, 23,* 1078-1086.

Sarros, J. C., & Santora, J. C. (2001). Leaders and values: A cross-cultural study. *Leadership & Organization Development Journal, 22(5/6),* 243-248.

Selmer, J., Ling, E. S. H., Shiu, L. S., & de Leon. C. C.T. (2003). Reciprocal adjustment? Mainland Chinese managers in Hong Kong vs. Hong Kong Chinese managers on the mainland. *Cross Cultural Management, 10(3),* 58-79.

Sheer, V. C. (2000). Conflict Processes in China's International Export Trading: Impact of the Chinese Culture and the Trading Culture. *Intercultural Communication Studies, 9(2),* 47-69.

Sheer, V. C., & Chen, L. (2003a). Do supervisors' intranet use predict their transformational leadership? *Asian Journal of Communication, 13(1),* 120-136.

Sheer V. C., & Chen, L. (2003b). Successful Sino-Western business negotiation: Participants' accounts of national and professional cultures. *The Journal of Business Communication, 40(1),* 50-85.

Spreitzer, G.M. (1995) Psychological empowerment in the workplace: dimensions, measurement, and validation. *Academy of Management Journal, 38(5),* 1442-1465.

Triandis, H. C., & Gelfand, M. J. (1998). Converging measurement of horizontal and vertical individualism and collectivism. *Journal of Personality and Social Psychology, 74,* 118-128.

Tsui, A. S., Wang, H. X., Xin, K., Zhang, L., & Fu, P. (2004). "Let a thousand flowers bloom": Variation of leadership styles among Chinese CEOs. *Organizational Dynamics, 33,* 5-20.

Wafford, J.C., Whittington, J. L., & Goodwin, V. L., (2001). Follower motive patterns as moderators of transformational leadership. *Journal of Managerial Issues, 9,* 196-211.

Whittington, J. L., Goodwin, V.L., & Murray, B. (2004). Transformational leadership, goal difficulty, and job design: Independent and interactive effects on employee outcomes. *Leadership Quarterly, 15,* 593-606.

Zhu, W., Chew, I. K. H., Spangler, W. D. (2005). CEO transformational leadership and organizational outcomes: The mediating role of human-capital-enhancing human resource management. *Leadership Quarterly, 16,* 39-52.

Introduction to

The Effect of Intercultural Sensitivity on Employee Performance in Cross-Cultural Service Encounters in London and Florida

By Steve Sizoo

Sizoo notes that the significant increase in service offerings throughout the world has caused business scholars to focus their attention on the problems and characteristics of the service encounter, i.e. the interaction between a customer and a service provider. Hence, also more attention is paid to cross-culture service encounters. It is in these encounters, Sizoo points out, that differing cultural norms and values often result in miscommunication and conflict that can result in unhappy customers, a frustrated service provider, and lost business. Indeed, studies show that when customers are unhappy with the encounter, up to two-thirds will not report their dissatisfaction, but simply switch to another provider. Other studies indicate that when the employees do not know their roles, as is the case in an unfamiliar situation such a cross-cultural encounter, the result is tension, frustration, dissatisfaction, and role conflict. However, these problems are unnecessary, Sizoo states. Although there is evidence that tools exist to measure and develop the intercultural communication skills of service personnel, managers are unlikely to make this investment since the value of having an interculturally competent service employee has not been sufficiently tested in the marketplace. Sizoo, therefore, set out to test and analyze the effect of intercultural sensitivity on employee performance in cross-cultural service encounters in two similar, but distinct service dependent markets, food servers in luxury hotels located in London and Florida.

The results of the study indicate that employees with high intercultural sensitivity scored significantly higher than employees with low intercultural sensitivity in terms of service attentiveness, revenue contribution, interpersonal skills, job satisfaction, and social satisfaction as they relate to cross-cultural encounters. Interestingly, socio-demographic characteristics such as gender, fluency in foreign languages, years worked abroad, etc. did not turn out to be reliable predictors for intercultural sensitivity. But what Sizoo's study does indicate is that interculturally sensitive employees provide international customers with better service, and they provide their managers with better results. Specifically, these service employees will be more attentive to the needs of customers from other cultures. Thus, service managers who hire and develop interculturally sensitive employees will be providing their foreign customers with a better service environment and their organization with better business results.

The results of this study, therefore, ought to make all internationally active companies look very closely at how well their employees are sensitized for such encounters.

Michael B. Hinner

Steve Sizoo is Associate Professor at Eckerd College. He has a B.S. and M.B.A. degrees from the University of Southern California as well as a Doctor of Business Administration from Nova Southeastern University in Florida. He has been teaching International Business courses at Eckerd College for 15 years. He spent an equal length of time working as a marketing executive with multinational corporations. His research interests focus on cross-cultural issues, business education, and tourism.

The Effect of Intercultural Sensitivity on Employee Performance in Cross-Cultural Service Encounters in London and Florida

Steve Sizoo

Globalization allows managers to look worldwide for customers, suppliers, and other business collaborators. The opportunities these partnerships create are particularly important in service industries, which are becoming increasingly essential to advanced "industrialized" economies (OECD, 2005). Icons of manufacturing such as IBM and Rolls Royce now depend on their global service operations (consulting, technical support, etc.) to generate the majority of their income (Friedman, 2005).

Yet, as globalization presents opportunities for business, it creates unique and formidable challenges as well. By their nature, these relationships--particularly service relationships--lead to cross-cultural interactions, during which differing cultural norms and values often create misunderstandings and conflict that can result in unhappy customers, frustrated employees, and lost business (Cushner & Brislin, 1996).

These business failures are unnecessary. Research shows that management has the tools available to measure and develop the cross-cultural skills of their service personnel (Bhawuk, 1998; Sizoo & Serrie, 2004). Still, although the value of having interculturally competent employees may make sense, the concept has not been sufficiently tested in the marketplace. As a result, managers are unlikely to make the investment in developing the cross-cultural skills of their customer-contact employees until they see evidence of the benefit. Therefore, the focus of this study was to test the effect of intercultural sensitivity on employee performance in cross-cultural service encounters in two similar but distinct service-dependent markets: greater London (England) and the state of Florida.

London is one of the leading centers of global business, with the service sector dominating the city's economy. Key services include international finance and business service, tourism and hospitality, and creative and cultural industries. London's inhabitants are global as well: over 300 languages are spoken by its seven million residents, 29% of whom are in the ethnic minority (London: Overview, 2005).

Florida, on the other hand, is even more dependent on services--particularly tourism. In 2004, nearly 77 million people visited the state, spent $57 billion, and resulted in over one million persons being directly employed by the tourism industry. In addition, seven million of those visitors were from outside the U.S. As is the case with London, international visitors spend significantly more as tourists than do their domestic counterparts (Office of National Statistics, 2005; Visit Florida Research, 2005).

For the purposes of comparison, the research design involved employees in similar positions, working for similar organizations, in similar but distinct service-based markets. If the relationship between employee performance and intercultural sensitivity was found to be positive and significant, it could help justify an investment in testing and training service employees who are involved in cross-cultural encounters.

Literature Review

The foundation of these growing service economies is the service encounter, the time when the consumer interacts directly with the service (Shostack, 1985). These are the "critical moments of truth in which customers often develop indelible impressions of a firm" (Bitner, Brown, & Meuter, 2000, p. 138). When customers are unhappy with the encounter, up to two-thirds will not report their dissatisfaction, but will simply switch to another provider (Bebko, 2001). As a result, the management of service encounters has become an important issue with service organizations, as have the measurement, analysis, and continued improvement of these interactions (Zeithaml & Bitner, 1996).

The theoretical basis for the service encounter is found in role and script theory (Broderick, 1999). These theories view people as social actors who learn behaviors appropriate to the positions they occupy (Biddle, 1979). Role theory is based on a "dramaturgical metaphor," that considers the participants as actors in a performance (Grove, Fisk, & Dorsch, 1998). When the actors do not know their roles, the result is tension, frustration, dissatisfaction, and role conflict (Kahn, Wolfe, Quinn, Diedrick-Snoek, & Rosenthal, 1964).

Consumer dissatisfaction occurs when service providers do not meet the culture-based expectations of their international customers (Stauss & Mang, 1999). The result is participants reading from different "scripts" and performing mismatched "roles." It is not surprising then that culture's influence in the service encounter has received increasing interest as reflected in articles by Winsted (1999), Donthu and Yoo (1998), Mattila (1999), and Furrer, Liu, and Sudharshan (2000).

These authors have examined culture's effect on customer behavior and evaluations. Winsted (1999) found that Japanese customers evaluate service encounters in the U.S. by dimensions that are different from those used by Americans. Donthu and Yoo (1998) examined the influence of culture on a customer's service quality expectations. Mattila's (1999) research indicates that a customer's evaluation and a service provider's performance are influenced by culture. Furrer, Liu, and Sudharshan (2000) showed that the relative importance of service quality dimensions of a service encounter varies from culture to culture.

While these studies have appropriately examined the cross-cultural service encounter from the customer's perspective, less research has been devoted to how employees--the service providers--perform during these encounters. This research attempts to close part of that gap by examining whether some employees are better able to adapt their role behavior during cross-cultural service encounters in order to contribute to a more successful interaction.

This is an important skill since international visitors, such as tourists, often expect the service provider to accommodate their values by demonstrating some degree of cross-cultural competence (Stauss & Meng, 2001). If the provider is reading from a different script, the result is role conflict and behavior that will likely lead to a service encounter failure: an unhappy consumer, frustrated employee, and lost business (Solomon et al. 1985).

As mentioned above, these failures are unnecessary since service managers have tools available that can reduce the likelihood of cross-cultural conflicts. Unfortunately, while these tools exist and their benefit to the service firm is intuitively appealing, the empirical support is limited. Until management sees evidence of the benefits of having interculturally adept employees, they are unlikely to invest the time and money to develop the skill in their service employees and therefore continue to run the risk of alienating their international customers through dysfunctional service encounters. Because of this limited empirical support, this study sought to measure the impact of intercultural sensitivity on employee performance in cross-cultural service interactions in London and compare the results to a comparable study for the state of Florida.

Method

The focus of this exploratory study was to measure whether or not service industry employees with higher levels of intercultural sensitivity would provide their foreign customers with a higher level of service. The research settings were luxury hotels in the Mayfair district in London and in the state of Florida. According to the management of these properties, international guests at the London hotels were largely from Europe and North America, and were traveling on business. The international guests in the Florida hotels were principally from Europe and Latin America, and mostly on vacation. The research participants were food servers working in the fine-dining restaurants of those hotels.

Czepiel, Solomon, Surprenant, & Gutman (1985) determined that the *INPUT* to a service encounter is influenced by the customer's and service employee's behavior. In a simplified representation of this research, see Figure 1. [see Figure 1 on p. 277] (The elements examined in this paper are in ***bold italics***):

The *customer's behavior* was affected by the

- character of the service (motivation, cost, etc.)
- customer's expectations
- characteristics of the customer, including socio-cultural factors and norms

The *service employee's behavior* was affected by the

- employee's expectations
- employees characteristics, including the employee's
  - expertise
  - Socio/demographic factors, including cultural norms
  - attitude, including ***intercultural sensitivity***

The independent variable in this study is the employee's intercultural sensitivity.

Research by Czepiel et al. (1985), Iskat (1995), and Samenfink (1994) indicate that the *OUTPUTS* of service encounter could be evaluated from the perspective of the customer, the management of the firm, and the service provider--the employee (see Figure 1).

Customer's evaluation would consider what was delivered and how it was delivered.

Management's evaluation would include

- Customer element: did the encounter lead to repeat purchase? increased usage? positive word-of-mouth?
- Competitive element: did the encounter produce added value? differentiation?
- Employee element:
  - how had the employees performed in terms of their *service attentiveness*? *revenue contribution*? *interpersonal interactions* (with co-workers)?
  - how do encounters effect employee *motivation*? *tenure*?

Service Provider's evaluation would include the

- task elements: did the encounters contribute to *primary rewards* (pay, promotion, recognition)? secondary rewards (increased *job satisfaction*)?
- were the encounters with the customers *socially satisfying*?

Figure 1
Output of a Service Encounter (elements examined in this paper in *bold italics*)

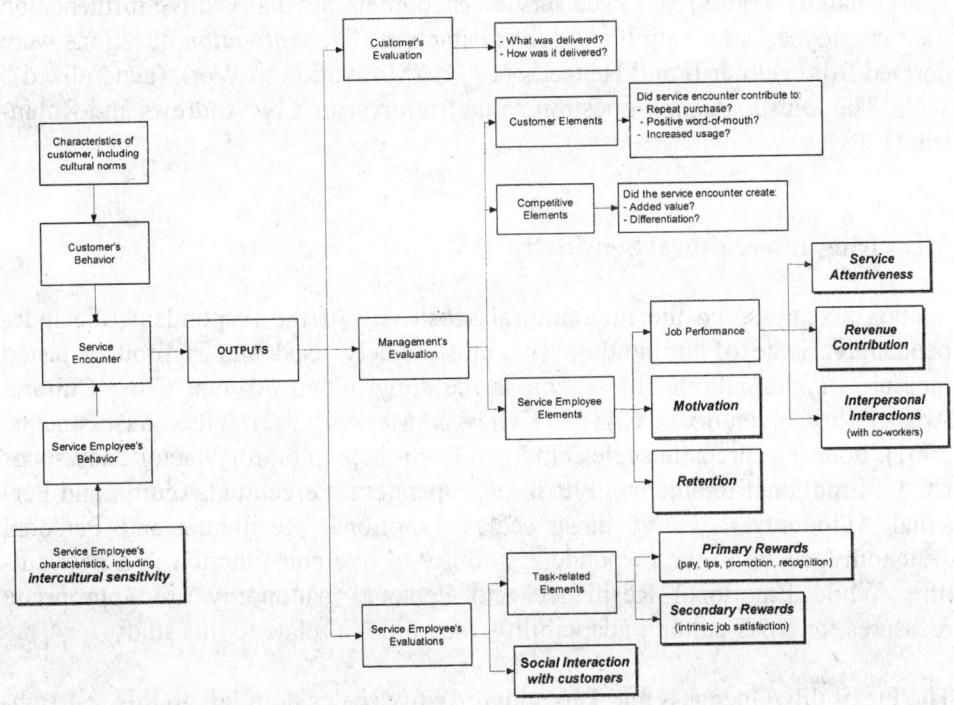

Research Instrument

A 60-item questionnaire was developed to measure the significance of intercultural sensitivity on the dependent variables described above. The instrument was divided into seven sections, with the first section consisting of ten background questions (one of which asked about the food server's *length of employment* at the hotel). Sections two through six consisted of 5-item, Likert-style questions (see *Appendix, Summary of Questions*). To keep from forcing inappropriate responses, the questions contained "does not apply to me" and "not sure" options. Section two (seven questions) was designed to determine the *service attentiveness* of the employee toward his or her foreign customers. The server was also asked (one question) to evaluate how the *gratuities received* from his or her foreign customers compared to those received by fellow employees. The questions were based on a study of food-server behavior in the hotel industry (Samenfink, 1994).

Section three addressed the *interpersonal interactions* of the food servers (three questions) and whether or not they enjoyed interacting with customers who were culturally different from themselves (one question). Section four (two questions) dealt with the *suggestive-selling skills* of the server. Section five (three questions) related to the server's motivation and job satisfaction. Research indicates that managers would like to see service encounters have a positive influence on their employees' motivation and job satisfaction. The *motivation* questions were derived from Burner II and Hensel's (1994) "Motivation to Work (generalized)" scale. The *job satisfaction* question came from research by Andrews and Robinson (1991).

Measuring Intercultural Sensitivity

Section six measured the intercultural sensitivity of the respondent (the independent variable of the study). The most widely used and rigorously tested measure of intercultural interaction is the copyrighted 50-item Cross-Cultural Adaptability Inventory, CCAI™ (Kelley & Meyers, 2001; NCS Assessments, 2001). Four interpretable scales emerged from the exploratory factor analysis of CCAI: Emotional Resilience, Flexibility/Openness, Perceptual Acuity, and Personal Autonomy. Two of those scales--Emotional Resilience and Personal Autonomy--relate to the respondent's ability to live and function in a new culture. While Emotional Resilience and Personal Autonomy are appropriate measures for cross-cultural adaptability, they did not relate to this study.

The Flexibility/Openness and Perceptual Acuity scales do relate to this research, in that they can be used to measure intercultural sensitivity. Chen and Starosta

(1997) described intercultural sensitivity as a person's ability to develop a positive emotion towards understanding and appreciating cultural differences that promotes appropriate and effective behavior in intercultural communications (p. 5). Graf and Harland (2005) added that "intercultural and interpersonal competence emphasize the fundamental ability to show consideration for others' needs while also fulfilling one's own rights, requirements, satisfactions, or obligations to a reasonable degree" (p. 47). According to Kelley and Meyers (2001), the 14-item Flexibility/Openness (FO) scale measures "the extent to which a person enjoys the different ways of thinking and behaving that are typically encountered in cross-cultural experiences" (p. 15). The FO-items could be subgrouped according to content focus: "liking for unfamiliar people and ideas," "tolerance toward others," and "flexibility with regard to experience" (p. 15). The 10-item Perceptual Acuity (PAC) scale, on the other hand, "focuses on communication cues and skills, and the accurate interpretation of those cues across cultures" (p. 16). In addition to reflecting intercultural sensitivity, the two scales are statistically sound in their own right. The scales have internal consistencies of .80 (FO) and .78 (PAC). Their high factor loadings are also a strong determinant of the construct validity of the two scales (Kelley & Meyers, 2001).

To control for self-flattering answers from the respondents, the final section of the instrument consisted of elements of the Marlowe-Crowne Social Desirability Scale (Crowne & Marlowe, 1964).

Results

Response Rates

Twelve luxury hotels in the Mayfair district of London and 26 luxury hotels in the state of Florida agreed to participate in the study. The study produced 85 and 306 responses respectively (Table 1).

Table 1
Participating Hotels and Employees

Hotel rating	London Hotels	Employees	Florida Hotels	Employees
Four star	4	21	23	282
Five star	8	64	3	24
Total	12	85	26	306

Food servers in fine-dining restaurants of these luxury hotels were the participants in this study. Supervisors in the London restaurants reported that 50% of their food servers returned their questionnaire. Supervisors in Florida reported a 61% response rate.

Employees and their supervisors were asked also to estimate what percent of their customers were from outside Britain and the U.S. respectively. The response was 60% from the London employees/supervisors, and 38% from their Florida counterparts.

Intercultural Sensitivity Results

The Flexibility/Openness (FO) and Perceptual Acuity (PAC) scales of the Cross-Cultural Adaptability Inventory were used to determine the intercultural sensitivity of the food servers, the independent variable of this study. Principal axis factor analysis with varimax rotation was conducted to assess the underlying structure for the 24 items of the FO and PAC scales. The sample generated four factors that parallel Kelley and Meyers' (2001) earlier findings. The first three factors reflected FO-subgroups mentioned above: Factor 1, "liking for unfamiliar people and ideas;" Factor 2, "tolerance toward others;" and Factor 3 "flexibility with regard to experiences." Factor 4 reflected the PAC-scale focusing on communication skills across cultures.

Cronbach's estimate of reliability was .76 for FO and .77 for PAC. This coincides with Kelley & Meyers' (2001) .80 and .78 result. The FO-PAC combined was .84, exceeding Nunnally's (1978) recommended minimum of .70. These findings suggest that FO and PAC make a satisfactory measure of intercultural sensitivity.

Social Desirability

To control for self-flattering responses, items from the Social Desirability Scale (SDS) were used. The significance (2-tailed) of the Pearson Correlation between intercultural sensitivity and the self-flattering items was 0.385 for London and 0.913 for Florida, which are both low according to Churchill (1979).

Correlation with Intercultural Sensitivity

A correlation analysis was also conducted to determine if certain socio-demographic characteristics were significantly related to an employee's intercultural sensitivity. For London, the results show no significant correlations. For Florida, the results show strong correlations (p≤0.01) between intercultural sensitivity and (1) gender type (R=-.151, p=0.010), (2) whether or not an employee had lived or worked outside his or her home country (R=-.204, p=0.000), (3) the years they had worked abroad (R=-.151, p=0.010), (4) and whether or not he or she was fluent in a foreign language (R=-0.224, p=0.000). Simple regression was conducted to investigate how well these variables predicted intercultural sensitivity. The adjusted R squared was .019 for gender, .038 for living and working abroad, .019 for working abroad, and .047 for fluency in a foreign language. According to Cohen (1988), the effect for each was small, indicating that--for this study--they were not reliable predictors of intercultural sensitivity.

Testing Intercultural Sensitivity and Dependent Variables

Two methods were used to assess the impact of intercultural sensitivity on a service employee's performance for their international customers. First, the correlation between intercultural sensitivity and the eight performance variables was analyzed for London and Florida separately. Second, the median split procedure was used to determine the level of intercultural sensitivity. Subjects with scores above the median for the FO-PAC scales were categorized as having high intercultural sensitivity. One-way analysis of variance (ANOVA) was then used to test the effect of intercultural sensitivity on the dependent variables. Both of these approaches are widely used in behavioral and intercultural research (Bhawuk, 1998; Harrison, Chadwick & Scales, 1996). Finally, *t* tests were conducted to investigate the difference between results for London and Florida.

Correlation Analysis

First, Pearson's Correlation was used to test the relationship between intercultural sensitivity and the dependent variables. Results were considered significant if the 2-tailed test was less than 0.05 (Sig.<0.05).

Research shows that employees with higher levels of intercultural sensitivity are better able to "read" their international customers and adjust their serving style to meet their needs--a fundamental aspect of quality service. The results in Table 2 show a very strong relationship (Sig.<0.01) between intercultural sensitivity and *service attentiveness* (Sig.=0.000) for both London and Florida.

Suggestive selling is frequently used to increase sales in the hospitality industry, and employees who effectively utilize suggestive selling techniques produce ad-

Table 2
Correlation of Variables

Performance Variables	Intercultural Sensitivity	
	London	Florida
a. *Service Attentiveness*		
Pearson Correlation	.418**	.532**
Sig. (2-tailed)	.000	.000
N	82	264
b. *Revenue Contribution (suggestive selling)*		
Pearson Correlation	.413**	.422**
Sig. (2-tailed)	.000	.000
N	82	260
c. *Interpersonal Skills (with co-workers)*		
Pearson Correlation	.439**	.443**
Sig. (2-tailed)	.000	.000
N	82	290
d. *Motivation to Work*		
Pearson Correlation	.119	.012
Sig. (2-tailed)	.281	.834
N	84	289
e. *Tenure (years at present organization)*		
Pearson Correlation	.046	.111
Sig. (2-tailed)	.679	.060
N	83	289
f. *Gratuities/Tips Received (primary rewards)*		
Pearson Correlation	-.039	.052
Sig. (2-tailed)	.744	.426
N	73	235
g. *Job Satisfaction (secondary reward)*		
Pearson Correlation	.188	.271**
Sig. (2-tailed)	.087	.000
N	84	289
h. *Social Interaction (social satisfaction)*		
Pearson Correlation	.401**	.424**
Sig. (2-tailed)	.000	.000
N	83	288

* Correlation is significant at 0.05 (2-tailed)   ** Correlation is significant at 0.01 (2-tailed)

ded *revenue* for their organization. For both London and Florida, there was a significant correlation (Sig.=0.000) between intercultural sensitivity and suggestive selling skills (revenue contribution).

In the less-structured environment of a restaurant (the setting of this research), managers need food servers to interact effectively with their co-workers as well as their customers. For this sample, there were very strong correlations (Sig.=0.000) for both London and Florida between intercultural sensitivity and *interpersonal interactions (with co-workers)*.

As reported earlier, service industry managers would like to see encounters between employees and their customers contribute to the *motivation (to work)* of those employees. In this study, however, the correlation was not significant for either the London (Sig.=0.281) or Florida (Sig.=0.834) samples. This result will be discussed later.

Service industry managers would also like to see that these service encounters are positive and that they contribute to the *tenure* (or retention) of their employees. In this study, the correlation between intercultural sensitivity and years at the present organization was not significant for London (Sig.=0.679), but was close to significance (Sig.=0.060) for Florida.

Some in the hospitality industry believe gratuities/tips are not only an important part of a food server's compensation (their *primary rewards*), but they are also thought to be a good index of service received by the customers (Lynn, 1996). Since there was a very strong correlation between intercultural sensitivity and service attentiveness (Sig.=0.000), one would also expect significant correlation between intercultural sensitivity and gratuities/tips received. Data in Table 2, however, show that this was not the case for London (Sig.=0.744) nor for Florida (Sig.=0.426).

The question addressing "primary rewards" was asked somewhat differently in each location. In Florida, where tipping is customary and food servers are reported to have an impressive ability to predict their own tips (Barkan, 2004), food servers were asked: "In my opinion, the tips I receive from *my* **foreign customers** are much more than the tips my fellow servers receive from *their* foreign customers." A form of this question had been used before in hospitality industry research (Samenfink, 1994) and it did not prove to be a problem in pilot tests of the questionnaire.

For London, where a Continental-style service charge and "tip pooling" are more common (Shaw, 2005), food servers were asked: "In my opinion, the gratuities and compensation I receive from my customers are much more than my fellow servers receive from theirs." (Since 60% of the customers in the London study were international, the question was simplified.) Again, there seemed to be little confusion about this question when it was asked in a pilot test in London. And recent studies indicate that food servers in Europe can indeed influence the size of their tips (van Baaren, 2005).

Even with these differences, the result is confusing in light of the fact that intercultural skills were not only significantly correlated to service attentiveness, they were significantly correlated to suggestive selling skills as well. Since suggestive selling skills can increase the revenue from each customer, it would seem to follow that this increased revenue would result in larger tips.

Since employees were asked to compare the gratuities/tips they received with those received by their fellow servers, it is possible that employees were simply unable to make this comparison (although very few employees marked the "not sure" responses in the survey). Also, some suggest that income tax considerations--particularly in the U.S.--may keep hospitality employees from discussing tips, even anonymously (Fullen, 2005).

Still, another consideration could be culture (Fernandez, 2004). Some cultures (and domestic *sub*cultures) are not accustomed to the practice of tipping for service, no matter how good the service is. This topic obviously deserves further exploration in terms of (1) the relationship between primary rewards in a service encounter and intercultural sensitivity, and (2) tipping, culture, and service.

Since these employees spend a major part of their working lives involved in service encounters, they need to receive some level of satisfaction from the job they do. Table 2 shows a correlation between intercultural sensitivity and *job satisfaction* for London of only Sig.=0.087, but Sig.=0.000 for Florida. These results will be discussed later.

In addition, research cited earlier indicates that it was important for a service provider to receive *social satisfaction* from interacting with his or her customers. As expected, Table 2 shows very strong correlations between intercultural sensitivity and satisfaction with workplace social interactions (with customers of other cultures) for both London (Sig.=0.000) and Florida (Sig.=0.000).

Median Split and Analysis of Variance

Next, the sample was divided between those respondents who had high and low intercultural sensitivity scores using the median split technique discussed earlier. One-way analysis of variance (ANOVA) was then used to test the effect of intercultural sensitivity on the dependent variables. Differences were considered significant if the F-value (Sig. of F) was less than 0.050 ($p<0.05$).

Similar to the correlation analysis, results in Table 3 show that for both London and Florida, service employees with high intercultural sensitivity demonstrated significantly ($p=0.000$) greater *service attentiveness*, they were more effective at using suggestive selling (*revenue contribution*) techniques with their foreign customers, and their *interpersonal interactions with co-workers* more positive than their fellow employees with low sensitivity.

Table 3
Management's Evaluation of a Service Encounter

a. *Service Attentiveness*

Location	Intercultural Sensitivity	N	Mean	Standard Deviation	F-Value
London	High	39	1.619	.4239	
	Low	43	1.960	.4679	
		82			11.88**
Florida	High	149	1.593	.3901	
	Low	115	1.962	.7534	
		264			26.40**

b. *Revenue Contribution (suggestive selling)*

Location	Intercultural Sensitivity	N	Mean	Standard Deviation	F-Value
London	High	41	1.756	.7863	
	Low	43	2.209	.7886	
		84			6.98**
Florida	High	148	1.645	.6449	
	Low	112	2.013	.9091	
		260			14.58**

c. *Interpersonal Interaction (with co-workers)*

Location	Intercultural Sensitivity	N	Mean	Standard Deviation	F-Value
London	High	39	1.479	.4244	
	Low	43	1.923	5484	
		82			16.55**
Florida	High	161	1.603	.4370	
	Low	129	1.894	.7917	
		290			15.83**

d. *Motivation to Work*

Location	Intercultural Sensitivity	N	Mean	Standard Deviation	F-Value
London	High	41	3.476	1.1399	
	Low	43	3.326	1.1067	
		84			0.38
Florida	High	160	3.659	.9473	
	Low	129	3.791	.9935	
		289			1.31

e. *Tenure (years at present organization)*

Location	Intercultural Sensitivity	N	Mean	Standard Deviation	F-Value
London	High	41	4.46	3.3682	
	Low	42	3.76	3.2300	
		83			0.853
Florida	High	160	3.17	3.037	
	Low	129	3.74	4.532	
		289			1.613

* Correlation is significant at 0.05 (2-tailed)   ** Correlation is significant at 0.01 (2-tailed)

Also, similar to the results of the correlation analysis, there was no significant difference between employees with high or low intercultural sensitivity and their *motivation (to work)* for either London or Florida. As with the results of the correlation analysis, the difference between high and low intercultural sensitivity for London and Florida was not significant for *tenure*--years at present organization.

Data in Table 4 show that like the correlation analysis, there was no difference for London. But unlike those earlier results, the difference for Florida between the gratuities/tips received (*primary rewards*) by food servers with high or low intercultural sensitivity was significant ($p<0.05$). As in the correlation analysis, there was a significant relationship between *job satisfaction* and high intercultural sensitivity for Florida ($p<0.01$), but not for London. Again, this contrast will be discussed later. Finally, employees with higher intercultural sensitivity in both London and Florida received significantly ($p<0.01$) more *social satisfaction* from interacting with customers who were culturally different from themselves. This is consistent with the results of the correlation analysis.

In summary, comparisons of the correlation analysis and median-split results for London and Florida (Table 5) show no differences for the five "Management Evaluations." Results for the three "Employee Evaluations" were the same for *social interaction* and similar for *gratuities/tips received*, but very different for *job satisfaction*. These differences will be discussed later.

Finally, a post hoc comparison of the influence of location on the results showed that, for both London and Florida, the effect of intercultural sensitivity on employee performance in cross-cultural services encounters is similar.

Discussion

Given the importance of international business to a country's economy, it is not surprising that managers and scholars in both Europe and the U.S. are devoting more attention to cross-cultural interactions. For the luxury hotels participating in this study, 60% of the London customers and 38% of the Florida customers were international guests. These are particularly valuable patrons to the respective hotels because they spend more money during their stay than their domestic counterparts.

In addition, the significance of these cross-cultural encounters is not limited to service organizations. "Service encounters are critical in all industries, including those that have not been traditionally defined as service industries," (Bitner et al., 2000). These issues may be equally important for employees outside of "service" industries--domestic employees (in manufacturing, educational, health care, or governmental organizations) who serve people from other cultures. These are what Tharenou (2002) described as "Domestic Jobs with International Responsibilities."

Table 4
Employees' Evaluation of a Service Encounter

a. *Gratuities/Tips Received (primary rewards)*					
Location	Intercultural Sensitivity	N	Mean	Standard Deviation	F-Value
London	High	34	2.850	.7840	
	Low	49	2.670	.8380	
		73			0.95
Florida	High	131	2.760	.8780	
	Low	104	3.000	.9030	
		235			4.38*

b. *Job Satisfaction (secondary reward)*					
Location	Intercultural Sensitivity	N	Mean	Standard Deviation	F-Value
London	High	41	2.020	1.1290	
	Low	43	2.120	.7620	
		84			0.19
Florida	High	162	2.190	.8740	
	Low	127	2.670	1.047	
		289			17.87**

c. *Social Interaction (social satisfaction)*					
Location	Intercultural Sensitivity	N	Mean	Standard Deviation	F-Value
London	High	41	1.290	.5590	
	Low	42	1.880	.7720	
		83			15.76**
Florida	High	161	1.620	.7070	
	Low	127	2.060	.8850	
		288			21.43**

* Correlation is significant at 0.05 (2-tailed)   ** Correlation is significant at 0.01 (2-tailed)

Table 5.
Summary of Significance of Results

Variable/Measure	London	Florida
Management Evaluations		
Service Attentiveness		
Correlation	.000**	.000**
Median-Split	.001**	.000**
Revenue Contribution		
Correlation	.000**	.000**
Median-Split	.010**	.000**
Interpersonal Interaction		
Correlation	.000**	.000**
Median-Split	.000**	.000**
Motivation-to-Work		
Correlation	.281	.834
Median-Split	.542	.253
Tenure		
Correlation	.679	.060
Median-Split	.359	.205
Employee Evaluations		
Tips Received		
Correlation	.744	.426
Median-Split	.332	.038*
Job Satisfaction		
Correlation	.087	.000**
Median-Split	.662	.000**
Social Interaction		
Correlation	.000**	.000**
Median-Split	.000**	.000**

* Significance at 0.05   ** Significance at 0.01

However, research has also shown that service encounters between customers of one culture and employees of another often result in misunderstanding and conflict because of differing cultural values, norms. The consequence can be an unhappy customer, a frustrated employee, and a loss of business for the organization.

For both London and Florida, the study shows that these conflicts are unnecessary, and that these interactions provide an opportunity for service organizations to differentiate the quality of their service. The research indicates that interculturally sensitive employees provide their international customers with better service and their managers with better results. Specifically, these service employees will be more attentive to the needs of customers from other cultures. They will make greater use of suggestive selling, thereby creating opportunities to generate more revenue per foreign customer. Their interpersonal skills in a multicultural workplace will be more appropriate. They will also get more satisfaction from interacting with foreign customers. According to this study, service managers who hire and develop interculturally sensitive employees will be providing their foreign customers with a better service environment and their organization with better results.

This research, however, did not show that interculturally sensitive service providers were necessarily more motivated-to-work, that would stay with the organization longer, felt they receive greater primary rewards (in this case, gratuities/tips) than employees with low sensitivity, or felt more satisfied with their jobs.

Regarding motivation-to-work, Zeithaml and Bitner (1996) report that an enthusiastic, committed workforce was on of the hallmarks of successful service organization. Furthermore, literature indicates that interculturally sensitive employees would be more enthusiastic and committed in a cross-cultural service setting (Bianchi, 2001). In this study, however, employees with higher intercultural sensitivity were no more motivated about work than employees with lower intercultural sensitivity. This result seems somewhat puzzling when compared to the results for the job satisfaction and social satisfaction the employees received from their jobs. Both measures and both approaches produced significantly stronger scores for employees with higher intercultural sensitivity. The question used in this study--from Brunner II and Hensel's (1994) "Motivation to Work (Generalized)" scale--measures the employee's motivation to engage in work rather than in other activities. It seems that while the employees in this sample (with higher intercultural sensitivity) were generally more satisfied with their job, work was not more important to their lives than other activities. Note, however, that the motivation-to-work results for *all* employees was significantly " better" in London than for Florida. It simply means that intercultural sensitivity did not significantly influence the results. In any case, this issue should be explored with other measures and approaches.

As mentioned earlier, the measure for primary rewards (in this study, "gratuities/tips received") needs further attention. Before this study, industry professionals and pilot tests indicated that food servers could form strong perceptions of how the tips they received from their customers compared to those their fellow servers received from theirs. In the end, very few respondents marked the "not sure" option to the question. The relationship between primary rewards in a service encounter and intercultural sensitivity, as well as the issues of tipping, culture, and service need further exploration. Nevertheless, from the perspective of the management of British and American organizations, as well as from the employees themselves, intercultural sensitivity appears to be a valuable attribute for employees working in businesses that cater to international customers.

The sharpest contrast between these London and Florida results was for intercultural sensitivity and employee job satisfaction. For the Florida sample, significance was reported for both the correlation and median-split analysis at $p<0.000$. For London, the results were not significant using either technique. Note, however, that this result does not mean that the employees in the London sample were particularly dissatisfied with their jobs. It is simply that intercultural sensitivity did not have a significant influence on the results in London.

The one item measure for job satisfaction--"taking all things together, I am satisfied with my job"--was based on research by Andrews and Robinson (1991). Different measures could be considered for any future research.

In summary, these results indicate that it would be useful for human resource managers in both markets to consider testing for and training in intercultural sensitivity for employees involved in cross-cultural service encounters. The long-term benefits from such an investment could be more satisfied customers (and employees), positive word-of-mouth, repeat business, and increased revenue.

Since this exploratory study emphasized one group (food servers in fine-dining restaurants) in a single segment of an industry (luxury hotels) in two markets (London and Florida), the generalizability of the findings is limited. (In addition, given the difficulty collecting data in foreign markets, the samples were lopsided: more than twice as many hotels and over three times as many employees participated in Florida than in London. Still, statistical measures indicate that the difference was accounted for in the results.) As with any limited investigation, it would be valuable to replicate and extend the research. It would be particularly important to test the research thesis (that interculturally sensitive service providers perform better in cross-cultural service encounters) in different service businesses and in different locales.

The most important limitation of the study, however, was probably the fact that international customers themselves were not interviewed for their reaction to the service they received. This was a function of the intimate nature of the service encounter and the limits of a field-study research design. Mattila (2000) recommends the use of controlled laboratory experiments to validate findings on cross-cultural service encounters. Such an experiment would allow researchers to measure the reaction of a customer from one culture to the service provided by an employee from another culture. At the same time, the socio-demographics and intercultural sensitivity of the employee could be measured, as well as the cultural norms and values of the customer.

Replicating and extending the research thesis would also allow investigators to further test the elements of the service employees, especially motivation and primary rewards. Different measures of these constructs may be necessary.

Again, due to the limited theoretical developments and empirical data available on intercultural sensitivity in cross-cultural service encounters, some of the above explanations must be regarded as intuitive and speculative. Furthermore, the results of the study cannot be readily generalized beyond the context of the luxury hotel industry in London and Florida.

Nevertheless, since there is evidence to show that intercultural sensitivity is a skill that can be learned as well as measured, organizations in Europe and North America that serve foreign customers should give serious consideration to providing their customer-contact employees with this valuable skill. The results could be more satisfied customers and service providers, as well as a more successful organization.

References

Andrews, F. M., & Robinson, J. P. (1991). Measures of subjective well-being. In J. P. Robinson, P. R. Shaver, & L. S. Wrightsman (Eds.) *Measures of personality and social psychological attitudes* (pp. 1-15). San Diego: Academic Press, Inc.

Barkan, R. (2004). Testing servers' roles as experts and managers of tipping. *Service Industries Journal, 24(6)*, 91-109.

Bebko, C. P. (2001). Service encounter problems: which service providers are more likely to be blamed? *Journal of Services Marketing, 15 (6)*, 480-495.

Bhawuk, D. P. S. (1998). The role of culture theory in cross-cultural training. *Journal of Cross-Cultural Psychology 39(5)*, 630-655.

Bianchi, C. C. (2001). The effect of cultural differences on service encounter satisfaction. *American Marketing Association, Conference Proceedings, 12*, 46-52.

Biddle, B. (1979). *Role theory: Expectation, identities, and behaviors.* New York: Academic Press.

Bitner, M. J., Brown, S. W., & Meuter, M. L. (2000). Technology infusion in service encounters. *Journal of the Academy of Marketing Services, 28(1),* 138-149.

Broderick, A. J. (1999). Role theory and the management of service encounters. *Services Industry Journal, 19 (2),* 117-131.

Bruner, G. C. II, & Hensel, P. J. (1994). Motivation to work (Generalized). *Marketing scales handbook: A compilation of multi-item measures* (pp. 1020-1021). Chicago: American Marketing Association.

Chen, G. M., & Starosta, W. J. (1997). A review of the concept of intercultural sensitivity. *Human Communication, 1,* 1-16.

Churchill, G. A., Jr. (1979, February). A paradigm for developing better measures of marketing constructs. *Journal of Marketing Research, 16,* 64-73.

Crowne, D. P., & Marlowe, D. (1964). *The approval motive: Studies in evaluative dependence.* New York: Wiley.

Cushner, K. H., & Brislin, R. W. (1996). *Intercultural interactions: A practical guide.* Thousand Oaks, CA: SAGE Publications.

Czepiel, J.A., Solomon, M. R., Suprenant, C. F., & Gutman, E. G. (1985). Service encounter: An overview. In J. A. Czepiel, M. R. Solomon, & C. F. Suprenant (Eds.), *The service encounter* (pp. 3-16). New York: Lexington Books.

Dontha, N. & Yoo, B. (1998). Cultural influences on service quality expectations. *Journal of Service Research, 1 (2),* 178-186.

Fernandez, G. A. (2004). The tipping point-gratuities, culture and politics. *Cornell Hotel and Restaurant Administration Quarterly, 45(1),* 48-52.

Friedman, T. L. (2005). *The world is flat.* New York: Farrar, Straus & Giroux.

Fullen, S. L. (2005). *The Complete Guide to Tips & Gratuities.* Ocala, FL: Atlantic Publication Group.

Furrer, O., Liu, B. S.-C., & Sudharshan, D. (2000). The relationships between culture and service quality perceptions. *Journal of Service Research, 2 (4),* 355-371.

Graf, A., & Harland, L. K. (2005). Expatriate selection: Evaluating the discriminant, convergent, and predictive validity of five measures of interpersonal and intercultural competence. *Journal of Leadership & Organizational Studies, 11(2),* 46-62.

Grove, S. J., Fisk, R. P., & Dorsch, M. J. (1998). Assessing the theatrical components of the service encounters: A cluster analysis examination. *Service Industries Journal 18(3),* 116-134.

Harrison, J. K., Chadwick, M., & Scales, M. (1996). The relationship between cross-cultural adjustment and the personality variables of self-efficacy and self-monitoring. *International Journal of Intercultural Relations, 20(2)*, 167-188.

Iskat, W. W. O. (1995). A thematic analysis of the service delivery act as applied to the hospitality industry: 1968-1993. Unpublished doctoral dissertation. New York University, New York City.

Kahn, R. L., Wolfe, D. M., Quinn, R. P., Diedrick Snoek, J., & Rosenthal, R. A. (1964). *Organizational stress: Studies in role conflict and ambiguity.* New York: Wiley.

Kelley, C., & Meyers, J. (2001). *CCAI: Cross-cultural adaptability inventory.* Minneapolis, MN: National Computer Systems, Inc.

London: Overview. (2005). *National Statistic Online.* Retrieved from the world wide web.

Lynn, M. (1996). Seven ways to increase servers' tips. *Cornell Hotel and Restaurant Administration Quarterly, 37(3)*, 24-29.

Mattila, A. S. (1999). The role of culture in the service evaluation process. *Journal of Service Research, 1(3)*, 250-261.

Mattila, A. S. (2000). The impact of culture and gender on customer evaluations of service encounters. *Journal of Hospitality & Tourism Research, 24(2)*, 263-273.

NCS Assessments (2001). *2001 NCS (Volume II).* Minneapolis, MN: National Computer Science, Inc.

Nunnally, J. C. (1978). *Psychometric theory.* New York: McGraw-Hill.

OECD: Statistical portal. (2005). *Organization for Economic Cooperation & Development, Paris.* Retrieved from the world wide web.

Office of National Statistics, UK. (2005). *United Kingdom tourism survey.* Retrieved from the world wide web.

Samenfink, W. H. (1994). A quantitative analysis of certain interpersonal skills required in the service encounter. *Hospitality Research Journal, 17(2)*, 3-15.

Shaw, S. A. (2005). *Turing the Tables: Restaurants from the Inside Out.* New York: Morrow.

Sizoo, S. L., & Serrie, H. (2004). Developing cross-cultural skills of international business students: An experiment. *Journal of Instructional Psychology, 31(2)*, 160-166.

Solomon, M. R., Surprenant, C., Czepiel, J. A., & Gutman, E.G. (1985, Winter). A role theory perspective on dyadic interactions: The service encounter. *Journal of Marketing, 49,* 99-111.

Strauss, B., & Mang, P. (1999). Culture shocks in intercultural service encounters? *Journal of Service Marketing, 13*.

Tharenou, P. (2002). Understanding participation in domestic jobs with international responsibilities. *National Academy of Management Conference Proceedings*.

Van Baaren, R. B. (2005). The parrot effect: How to increase tip size. *Cornell Hotel & Restaurant Administration Quarterly, 46(1)*, 79-85.

Visit Florida research.(2005). *FLA USA Visit Florida*. Retrieved from the world wide web.

Winsted, K. F. (1999). Evaluating service encounters: A cross-cultural and cross-industry exploration. *Journal of Marketing Theory and Practice, 7(2)*, 106-123.

Zeithaml, V. A., & Bitner, M. J. (1996). *Services marketing*. New York: McGraw-Hill Company.

Appendix - Summary of Questions

Service Attentiveness

When serving foreign customers, I adjust my serving style depending on the needs of the guests. (I modify my behavior depending on the situation.)

Does not – Always – Often – Sometimes – Rarely – Never – Not Sure Apply to me.

When serving foreign customers, I make a special effort that results in the guest feeling comfortable.

When serving foreign customers, I recognize and deal effectively with the special needs of the guest.

When serving foreign customers, I have the ability to anticipate the guest's needs and fulfill those needs (I bring refills of water, coffee, tea without excessive trips.)

When serving foreign customers, I have the ability to handle guest problems and complaints in a tactful and calm manner.

When serving foreign customers, I react personably and correctly when dealing with the guest.

When serving foreign customers, I deal effectively with unexpected situations.

In my opinion, the tips I receive from *my* foreign customers are much more than the tips my fellow workers receive from *their* foreign customers.

Revenue Contribution (suggestive selling skills)

When serving foreign customers, I use the appropriate table side sales techniques.

When serving foreign customers, I do an effective job of using suggestive-selling techniques to promote products like beverages, entrees, and desserts.

Interpersonal Interaction (with co-workers)

I get along well with other employees.

I control my emotions while at work.

I do not let personal problems interfere with work.

Motivation to Work

The work I do is one of the most satisfying parts of my life.

I enjoy my spare-time actives much more than my work.

Tenure (years at present organization)

Primary Rewards (tips received)

In my opinion, the gratuities and compensation I receive from my customers are much more than my fellow servers receive from theirs. (If uncertain, indicate "*Not Sure*.")

Job Satisfaction

Taking all things together, I am satisfied with my job.

Social Satisfaction

I enjoy interacting with customers who are culturally different from me.

Introduction to

Gender-Related Differences in Intercultural Communication

By Andrea Graf

Graf notes that the number of international assignees is expected to continue to increase. At the same time, however, the failure rates of overseas assignments are quite large. These failures encompass substantial monetary losses and negative organizational outcomes such as delayed productivity, poor relationships with local nationals, negative perceptions of the company, problems for expatriate successors, and ineffective repatriation. Studies have revealed, Graf observes, that difficulties with the host national culture are the main reason for these failures. Hence, intercultural communication competence is often seen as a critical qualification for managers working abroad. Graf points to the fact that women are generally underrepresented in international assignments; in fact, studies indicate that men are often preferred for international assignments even though women managers have also expressed interest in overseas assignments. At the same time, Graf mentions, other studies indicate that women seem to be able to show more social abilities in intercultural actions and, consequently, solve problems in international projects more effectively. Indeed, it would even seem that women expatriates possess more intercultural abilities than their male colleagues. And women derive more satisfaction from foreign assignments than men. So Graf decided to test whether gender might play a role in intercultural communication competence. She, therefore, carried out an empirical study in Germany and the USA to evaluate gender related aspects of intercultural communication competence. The study evaluated intercultural communication effectiveness, intercultural sensitivity, and interpersonal competence.

According to Graf's study, gender proved to be a significant independent variable of intercultural communication competence in Germany and the USA. Interestingly, the significant impact is exclusively caused by a higher communication capability of the female participants. So it would make sense, for a number of reasons, to send female managers on foreign assignments, Graf argues. Clearly an interesting empirical result that ought to be noted by human resource management departments of international corporations when considering the next overseas assignment.

Michael B. Hinner

Andrea Graf is Professor of Management and Organization at the Faculty of Business, Economics, and Information Systems at the University of Regensburg, Germany. She worked in management development for a large international pharmaceutical firm in Frankfurt on the Main, Germany, for three years. After having worked as Assistant Professor at the University of Braunschweig, Germany, Professor Graf achieved her habilitation (postdoctoral lecture qualification) in 2004. In 2005 she was Professor of Management at the University of Vienna, Austria. She has teaching experience in the USA, Australia, Bulgaria, Austria, and Germany. In her research, she focuses on International Human Resource Management, intercultural competence, and change management.

Gender-related Differences in Intercultural Communication

Andrea Graf

Increased global competition has been the most influential trend in economics during the last decade (Adler, 2002). Explosive growth in globalisation has led to a growing number of individuals with international assignments, cooperation of companies from different nations, and people moving to other countries to find work and prosperity. As a consequence, the concept of intercultural communication competence has become increasingly important in business management.

Worldwide, the number of international assignees is expected to continue increasing according to a global relocation survey (Windham International, 2001). However, when using a broad definition of failure (i.e., the expatriate assignment did not accomplish the goals of the company or the expatriate broke off the assignment), global failure rates have been estimated at 16-40% (Shaffer, Harrison and Gilley, 1999), 20-40% (Solomon, 1996), 30-50% (Black, Mendenhall and Oddou, 1991), and 50% (Allerton, 1997). The average monetary cost of an expatriate failure is placed at anywhere from 200,000 to 1.2 million dollars (Solomon, 1996; Swaak, 1995). In addition to monetary costs, failed expatriate efforts can also lead to negative organizational outcomes such as delayed productivity, poor relationships with local nationals, negative perceptions of the company, problems for expatriate successors, and ineffective repatriation (Bennett, Aston and Colquhoun, 2000). Indeed, difficulties with the host national culture have been identified as the main reason for the lack of success in the majority of analysed expatriate failures (Bennett, Aston and Colquhoun, 2000; Forster, 2000).

Intercultural communication competence is considered to be a decisive key qualification of managers working abroad (e.g., Gelbrich, 2004; Ingelfinger, 1995; Schneidewind, 1996; Karmasin and Karmasin 1997, p.192; Fritz et.al., 1999) and consequently as one of the most important selection criteria for expatriates (see e.g., Deller, 1996; Bolino and Feldmann, 2000; Graf, 2004b,c,d; Müller and Gelbrich, 2001; Bergemann and Sourisseaux, 2003; Wirth, 2003). However, there is no accepted definition of intercultural communication competence (Bradford, Allen and Beisser, 1998). For the purpose of this chapter, intercultural communication competence is very broadly considered as a cluster of abilities as well as characteristics, which facilitate - in a normative social sense - competent interaction with a person from a different national culture.

Traditionally, women have been underrepresented in international assigments (Domsch and Lichtenberger, 1992; Scholz, 1993; Tung, 1998; Domsch and, Lieberum 2004). Different studies show hereto that the number of women is low not only in comparison to men, but also to the percental part of women in managerial jobs (Hartl, 2003, p. 29). Accordingly, Harris notes "one of the few verifiable facts in the field of expatriate management research is the paucity of women expatriate managers" (1995, p. 229). Furthermore, Domsch and Lieberum (1996, p.12) show in an empirical analysis that men are generally preferred for international assignments in spite of the availability as well as the interest of female managers to go abroad (Stroh et al., 2000; Domsch and Lieberum, 2004).

The majority of authors assume gender specific attitudes and behaviors in an organizational context (Aaltio and Mills, 2002; Borisoff and Merril, 2004). Several studies have been conducted to evaluate gender specific aspects of management skills in an international context (see e.g., Friedel-Howe, 1990; Rosener, 1990; Macha, 1998). In general, studies indicate that women possess an at least equivalent potential of management know-how than men. For instance, Adler (1994) reports that female expatriates show more social abilities in intercultural actions and consequently solve problems in international projects more effectively. Similarly, Taylor and Napier (1996, p. 80) found in their empirical study that female expatriates possess more intercultural abilities than their male colleagues. Finally, Domsch and Liebermann (2004) identified more satisfaction of female expatriates during foreign assignments. Concerning intercultural communication competence no gender specific research could be found. However, it would be essential for business managers as well as for scholars to get to know whether the low percentage of female expatriates may be caused by a minor intercultural qualification of women - that is to say by a lack of intercultural communication competence. For example, in the case of an equal qualification of male and female managers opportunity costs due to the low employment of women have to be considered.

The purpose of this chapter is to evaluate gender-related aspects of intercultural communication competence. In an empirical study in Germany and the USA intercultural communication competence is assessed in a sample which is matched by the criteria of gender. Based on the results recommendations for international selection procedures are discussed. Finally, the limitations of the study are pointed out.

Method

Procedure of the Study

In research there is no agreement, which abilities and characteristics constitute intercultural communication competence (Bradford, Allen and Beisser, 1998). There are several lists of competencies, instead both from literature research and empirical studies, which are described to be important in intercultural interactions (as an overview see Kealey and Ruben, 1983). These lists will be the basis for identifying intercultural communication competencies to be evaluated in the studies.

An international literature research is conducted to identify which capabilities, skills and characteristics are significant variables for a successful intercultural communication. In the following sections the abilities and characteristics, which have been evaluated to be intercultural communication competencies, are specified. Moreover, for every intercultural communication competency the questionnaire utilized in the study is described. It was a prerequisite for the measures to be based on a sound theoretical foundation and to be valid for the US-American culture and language as well as for the German ones. In an empirical study in Germany and the USA the identified constructs are assessed with the selected questionnaires.

Instruments

Intercultural communication effectiveness. The capability to show efficiency in an interaction with a person from a foreign national culture has been identified as an important aspect in intercultual communication (e.g., Bradford, Allen and Beisser, 1998; Cui and Awa, 1992; Dean and Popp, 1990; Gudykunst and Lee, 2002; Martin and Hammer, 1989; Wiseman, Hammer and Nishida, 1989).

The Behavioural Assessment Scale for Intercultural Communication Effectiveness (BASIC), developed by Koester and Olebe (1988), was used to assess intercultural communication effectiveness in the study. According to Spitzberg (1989, p. 246), the BASIC is one of the most commonly used measures for intercultural effectiveness; for instance, Nishida (1985) and Ruben and Kealey (1979) utilized it in their studies. A German version of the BASIC was developed and validated for the German samples (Graf, 2004a). The BASIC assesses seven dimensions of intercultural communication effectiveness. Those seven dimensions were developed by Ruben (1976) and are as follows: 1) Display of Respect - the ability to express respect for another person, 2) Interaction Posture - the ability to respond to others in a non-judgemental way, 3) Orientation to Knowledge – how one explains the world, 4) Empathy - the capacity to "put oneself in another's shoes" in a communication, 5) Task Role Behaviours – verbal and nonverbal behaviours contributing to group problem-solving activities, 6) Relational Role Behaviours – verbal and nonverbal behaviours contributing to building or maintaining relationships in a group, 7) Interaction Behaviour/Management – communication skill in governing interactions to meet the needs and desires of group members, and 8) Tolerance of Ambiguity - the ability to react to new and ambiguous situations with little visible discomfort.

Each of the eight BASIC dimensions is assessed by one item. For example, the item measuring "Display of Respect" is as follows:

> Individuals express respect or positive regard for other people around them to different degrees. This is shown through their behaviour, which can take many forms. These range from spoken and unspoken expressions of low interest and regard to statements, gestures and tones of voice that are very supportive and show high regard and respect. Listed below are five descriptions of patterns of expression. Please indicate on the rating scale shownbelow which of these five describes your communication best. One response option for the above item includes "I show *deep respect* for the worth of others as persons of high potential and worth. I indicate (through eye contact, general attentiveness, appropriate tone of voice, and general interest) a clear respect for the thoughts and feelings of others. I am committed to supporting and encouraging their development."

Intercultural sensitivity. The emotional capability to be sensitive towards individuals from a different national culture has been identified to be crucial for competent intercultural communication by several authors (e.g., Abe and Wiseman, 1983; Chen and Starosta, 1996; Cui and Awa, 1992; Fritz, Möllenberg and Chen, 2002; Koester and Olebe, 1988; Martin, 1987).

The Intercultural Sensitivity Scale (ISS) by Chen and Starosta (2000) was selected to assess this intercultural communication competency in the study. The German version by Fritz and Möllenberg (1999) was utilized for the German sample. The ISS is based on the authors' concept of Intercultural Sensitivity (Chen and Starosta, 1996, 1997). The ISS consists of 24 items and uses a five-point Likert-type response scale. Scale anchors range from "strongly agree" to "strongly disagree". The ISS is composed of five scales: 1) Engagement in Intercultural Interactions (e.g., "I enjoy interacting with people from different cultures."), 2) Respect for Cultural Differences (e.g., "I respect the values of people from different cultures"), 3) Self-Confidence in Intercultural Interactions (e.g., "I am pretty sure of myself in interacting with people from different cultures"), 4) Enjoyment of Intercultural Interactions (e.g., "I get upset easily when interacting with people from different cultures" [reverse-coded]), and 5) Attentiveness in Intercultural Interactions (e.g., "I try to obtain as much information as I can when interacting with people from different cultures").

Interpersonal competence. The majority of studies concerning intercultural (communication) competence emphasizes the importance of interpersonal competence (e.g. Abe and Wiseman, 1983; Cui and Awa, 1992; Dean and Popp, 1990; Hammer, 1987; Hammer, Gudykunst and Wiseman, 1978; Hawes and Kealey, 1979; Kealey, 1989; Spitzberg and Cupach, 1989).

For the study the Interpersonal Competence Questionnaire (ICQ), which was developed by Buhrmester, Furman, Wittenberg, and Reis (1988), was selected to evaluate interpersonal competence. The German version of the questionnaire by Riemann and Allgöwer (1993) was utilized for the German sample. The ICQ contains 40 items assessing the following five domains of interpersonal competence: 1) Initiation of Interactions and Relationships (e.g., "Asking or suggesting to someone new that you get together and do something, e.g., go out together"), 2) Assertion of Personal Rights and Displeasure with Others (e.g., "Telling a companion you don't like a certain way he or she has been treating you"), 3) Self-Disclosure of Personal Information (e.g., "Confiding in a new friend/date and letting him or her see your softer, more sensitive side"), 4) Emotional Support of Others (e.g., "Helping a close companion work through his or her thoughts or feelings about a major life decision, e.g. a career choice") and 5) Management of Interpersonal Conflicts (e.g., "Being able to take a companion's perspective in a fight and really understand his or her point of view"). Respondents use a five-point rating scale to indicate their levels of success and comfort when engaging in the described behaviours. Scale anchors range from "I usually succeed rather badly acting in the described way. I feel very uneasy in such a situation" to "I usually succeed well acting in the described way. I feel very well in such situations."

Sample

Evaluating intercultural communication competence requires data in more than one nation respectively culture in order to reduce the (potential) influence of cultural specifics on the dependent variables (England and Neghandi, 1979; Hofstede, 1992; Helfrich, 1999). The decision for selecting data in Germany and the USA was made due to methodological reasons. So, two of the three selected questionnaires (namely the ISS assessing intercultural sensitivity and the ICQ assessing interpersonal competence) have been available in a US-American as well as in a German version. However, the BASIC assessing intercultural communication effectiveness was only available in an American version.

In the study, matched samples were used. In international studies non-random samples are accepted, because random samples cannot always be compared due to various influences (e.g. age of subjects, level of education; see e.g. Brislin and Baumgardner, 1971; Lonner and Berry, 1986). Holzmüller (1995, p. 242) recommends the use of matched samples in order to reduce the error of variance. Therefore, matched samples in the USA and Germany are chosen in order to be able to attribute resulting differences to national differences.

The population in the study are MBA students. Students were chosen as participants for different reasons. First, students are the type of employees (e.g., educated professionals) likely to be sent on expatriate assignments. Secondly, student samples can be matched very well according to the criteria of gender (see Table 1).

Of course, sex and gender (e.g., gender related attitudes and behaviors) must not be equated, but they represent narrowly corresponding phenomenons (Wicks and Bradshaw, 2002, p.140; Wood and Reich, 2004, p.145). In the study, gender related aspects are evaluated by differentiating between men and women, that is to say between the biological sex. Further matching criteria were age, education, subject and size of university.

Table 1
Data of the Two Partial Samples and the Population

	sample USA	sample Germany	overall sample
size of sample	188	179	367
age average	28	26	27
percentage of women	66 (36.8 %)	56 (31.2 %)	131 (35.6 %)
level of education	final exam	Abitur (comparable to final exam)	final exam
study subject	MBA	MBA	MBA
specialization	Management	Management	Management
size of the visited university	14.300	14.500	14.400

Table 2
Multivariate Tests Based on Pallai-Spur-Criterion (factor: "sex")[1]

	F	Sig.
Intercultural Communication Effectiveness	4.41	.000 ***
Intercultural Sensitivity	2.81	.016 *
Interpersonal Competence	3.81	.002 **
Total	3.23	.000 ***

Results

For the analyses whether the factor "sex" is a significant independent variable of the evaluated dimension of intercultural communication competence multivariate tests are conducted according to the Pallai-Spur-Criteria. Table 2 shows a significant result concerning each of the evaluated constructs and all dimensions. In other words, men and women significantly differ in intercultural communication effectiveness, intercultural sensitivity and interpersonal competence.

U-Tests by Mann-Whitney are calculated to test in which dimensions of intercultural communication competence gender-related differences exist (see Table 3 for descriptive statistics and results of U-Tests by Mann-Whitney). For the eighteen evaluated dimensions different average values between male and female participants can be found in seven scales. The significant differences are exclusively caused by higher scores of women: Regarding intercultural communication effectiveness female participants name more respect to individuals from another culture, a less descriptive evaluation of interaction partners and more empathy than men. Turning to the construct of intercultural sensitivity, women indicate a stronger engagement in intercultural interactions, a distinct respect for cultural differences and an increased attention. Concerning interpersonal competence women state a higher emotional support of their interaction partners.

Discussion

Starting point of this study were two matters of fact which have been confirmed in a high number of research projects: The first fact is that intercultural communication competence is a key qualification for foreign assignees. The second actuality is that women are clearly underrepresented in international assignments. Deduced from these findings the purpose of this study was to find out if

Table 3
Descriptive Statistics and Results of U-Tests by Mann-Whitney[2]

		M	SD	min.	max.	z	Sig.
1. BASIC- Respect	W	4.20	.61	2	5	4.78	.000 ***
	M	3.83	.52	1	5		
2. BASIC- Posture	W	2.90	.75	1	4	-2.58	.010 **
	M	2.69	.76	1	4		
3. BASIC-Knowledge	W	3.25	.55	1	4	-1.50	.134
	M	3.11	.69	1	4		
4. BASIC-Empathy	W	3.83	.77	2	5	-2.18	.029 *
	M	3.60	.96	1	5		
5. BASIC- Task	W	3.89	.61	2	5	-1.72	.084
	M	3.76	.75	2	5		
6. BASIC-Relational	W	3.72	.68	2	5	-.62	.531
	M	3.65	.74	2	5		
7. BASIC- Interaction	W	3.40	.91	1	5	-.15	.877
	M	3.37	.94	1	5		
8. BASIC- Ambiguity	W	3.55	.79	2	5	-.86	.387
	M	3.63	.89	1	5		
9. ISS-Engagement	W	3.88	.42	1.71	4.86	-2.35	.019 *
	M	3.77	.45	1.29	5.00		
10. ISS-Respevz	W	4.24	.25	1.83	5.00	-2.72	.006 **
	M	4.08	.31	2.00	5.00		
11. ISS-Confidence	W	3.42	.29	2.20	4.80	-1.40	.160
	M	3.34	.57	1.80	4.80		
12. ISS- Enjoyment	W	4.19	.61	1.00	5.00	-.09	.923
	M	4.20	.57	2.33	5.00		
13. ISS-Attentiveness	W	3.70	.54	2.33	5.00	-2.27	.023 *
	M	3.55	.61	2.00	5.00		
14. ICQ-Initiation	W	3.39	.73	1.50	5.00	-1.19	.233
	M	3.29	.75	1.13	5.00		
15. ICQ-Assertion	W	3.24	.75	1.38	4.88	-.07	.937
	M	3.22	.63	1.38	4.88		
16. ICQ-Disclosure	W	3.28	.71	1.38	4.88		.387
	M	3.21	.68	1.00	4.88		
17. ICQ-Support	W	4.11	.49	2.75	5.00		.002 **
	M	3.89	.59	1.50	5.00		
18. ICQ- Conflict	W	3.39	.57	2.00	4.63		.541
	M	3.43	.55	1.50	4.75		

the extent of intercultural communication competence of women might be the reason for the gender-related imbalance in international assignments. Intercultural communication competence was evaluated with the help of three constructs: intercultural communication effectiveness, intercultural sensitivity and interpersonal competence. Summed up, gender proved to be a significant independent variable of intercultural communication competence. Significant differences in the extent of the competencies were identified in seven of the scales. Interestingly, the differences were exclusively based on higher values of female participants. Consequently, women indicate to have better intercultural communication competence and therefore possess an advantage for international tasks.

Referring to international personnel selection criteria organisations should draw increased attention on one of the findings: women stated a higher respect for interaction partners from foreign cultures in the BASIC (evaluating intercultural communication effectiveness) as well as in the ISS (analysing intercultural sensitivity). On the one hand studies have indicated that the characteristic "respect" for cultural differences is an essential factor for a successful intercultural cooperation (see e.g., Gelbrich, 2004; Graf, 2004c; Ruben, 1979). On the other hand respect shows a high resistance against changes (Markus, 1996) because "Our biases, prejudices and stereotypes run deep and die hard!" (Sue, 1991, p.104). In other words, respect towards other cultures cannot be developed in a short period of time and therefore plays an important role when selecting applicants for international tasks.

However, a lot of companies are not sure whether women are perceived to be as competent as men in other cultures. And in fact, Foschi (1992) as well as Biernat and Kobrynowicz (1997) found in empirical studies that women have more difficulties than men to be acknowledged to be a competent manager in national context. Having said that, Adler (1987, 1995) could prove in various studies that this disadvantage for women in international assignments is compensated by the tendency of managers to judge female business partners from other countries mainly as foreigners who accidentally are women and not vice versa as women who accidentally are foreigners ("A Gaijin, Not a Woman"; Adler, 1987). Of course, this can not be generalized and there may be prejudices against women in several cultures: for example, younger women are often confronted with biased behaviour of host nationals in the Japanese (Taylor and Napier, 1996, p.79), Chinese (Westwood and Leung, 1994) and Arabic culture (Pezeshkpur, 1978).

Summing up, higher intercultural communication competence can be expected by women expatriates than by their male counterparts. Especially the resistant characteristic to feel and to show respect for individuals from another cultures is obviously shown more distinct by women. The question if the merely utilized female potential for foreign assignments is caused by an incorrect judgement of women's qualification or by other reasons such as discriminating attitudes of managers to women in respect to international objectives (Davison and Punett, 1995, p. 418; Stroh, 2000), or an insufficiently noticed availability of women for foreign assignments (Domsch and Lieberum, 2004) respectively the limited carreer-chances for women in general (Linehan, 2000, p. 13), cannot be answered with the help of this study. However, on the basis of the empiric results it can be concluded that remarkable opportunity costs may be assumed by the unbalanced ratio of female managers in foreign assignments.

Finally, it is important to note the limitations of this study. One limitation is that only two (western) nations are included in the study. Therefore, the gender-related differences in intercultural communication competence cannot be generalized to further cultures. Furthermore, a selection of dimensions of intercultural communication capability was evaluated; though it may be possible that the selection of constructs has created a bias for or against any of the dependent variables. Finally, a potential limitation of this research project concerns the use of self-report measures facing the threats to validity associated with self-report measures. The major threat is a potential systematic bias, which occurs when individuals misrepresent or misinterpret their own behaviour (Paulhus, 1986).

Endnotes

[1]*$p \leq 0.05$; **$p \leq 0.01$; ***$p \leq 0.001$
[2]W = results of women; M = reslts of men; *$p \leq 0.05$; **$p \leq 0.01$; ***$p \leq 0.001$

References

Aaltio, I., & Mills, A. J. (2002). *Gender, Identity and the Culture of Organizations*, London.

Abe, H., & Wiseman, R. (1983). A Cross-Cultural Confirmation of the Dimensions of Intercultural Effectiveness. *International Journal of Intercultural Relations, 10*(7), 53-67.

Adler, N. J. (1987). Pacific Basin Managers: A Gaijin, Not a Woman. *Human Resource Management, 26*(2), 169-191.

Adler, N. J. (1994). Competitive Frontiers: Women Managing Across Borders. In N. J. Adler & D. N. Izraeli (Eds.), *Competitive Frontiers: Women Managers in a Global Economy* (pp. 23-42). London.

Adler, R. B., & Towne, N. (2002). *Looking Out / Looking In*, 10. Ed., Forth Worth.

Allerton, H. (1997). Expatriate Gaps. *Training & Development, 51* (7), 7-8.

Bennett, M. J. (2001). Developing Intercultural Competence for Global Leadership. In R.-D. Reineke, & Ch. Fußinger (Eds.), *Interkulturelles Management: Konzeption - Beratung – Training* (pp. 205-226). Wiesbaden.

Bennett, R., Aston, A., & Colquhoun, T. (2000). Cross-Cultural Training: A Critical Step in Ensuring the Success of International Assignments. *Human Resource Management, 39*(2-3), 239-250.

Bergemann N., & Sourisseaux, A. L. (2003). Internationale Personalauswahl. In N. Bergemann, & A. L. Sourisseaux (Eds.), *Interkulturelles Management* (pp. 181-235), 3. Ed.. Berlin.

Bhawuk, D. P., & Brislin, R. (1992). The Measurement of Intercultural Sensitivity Using the Concepts of Individualism and Collectivism. *International Journal of Intercultural Relations, 16*(4), 413-435.

Biernat, M., & Kobrynowicz, D. (1997). Gender- and Race-Based Standards of Competence: Lower Minimum Standards but Higher Ability Standards for Devalued Groups. *Journal of Personality and Social Psychology, 72*, 544-557.

Birdseye, M., & Hill, J. (1995). Individual, Organizational/Work and Environmental Influences on Expatriate Turnover Tendencies: An Empirical Study. *Journal of International Business Studies, 26*(4), 787-813.

Black, J., Mendenhall, M., & Oddou, G. (1991). Toward a Comprehensive Model of International Adjustment: An Integration of Multiple Theoretical Perspectives. *Academy of Management Review, 16*(2), 291-317.

Bolino, M., & Feldman, D. (2000). Increasing the Skill Utilization of Expatriates. *Human Resource Management, 39*(4), 367-379.

Borishoff, D., & Merrill, L. (2004). Gender and Nonverbal Communication. In L. A. Samovar, & R. E. Porter (Eds.), *Intercultural Communication* (pp. 269-278), 10. Ed., Belmont.

Bradford, L., Allen, M., & Beisser, K. (1998). An Evaluation and Meta-Analysis of Intercultural Competence Research. In *Forschungsbericht: University of Wisconsin-Milwaukee.*

Brislin, R. (1981). *Cross-Cultural Encounters: Face-to-Face Encounters*. New York.

Brislin, R. W., & Baumgardner, S. R. (1971). Non-Random Sampling of Individuals in Cross-Cultural Research. *Journal of Cross-Cultural Psychology 4*, 397-400.

Buhrmester, D., Furman, W., Wittenberg, M., & Reis, H. (1988). Five Domains of Interpersonal Competence in Peer Relationships. *Journal of Personality and Social Psychology, 55* (6), 991-1008.

Chen, G.-M., & Starosta, W. J. (1996). Intercultural Communication Competence: A Synthesis. In B. Burleson (Ed.), *Communication Yearbook 19* (pp. 353-383), Thousand Oaks.

Chen, G.-M., & Starosta, W. J. (1997). A Review of the Concept of Intercultural Sensitivity. *Human Communication, 1*, 1-16.

Chen, G.-M., & Starosta, W. J. (2000). The Development and Validation of the Intercultural Communication Sensitivity Scale. *Human Communication, 3*, 1-15.

Copeland, L., & Griggs, L. (1986). *Going International: How to Make Friends and Deal Effecitvely in the Global Marketplace*. New York.

Craig, S. C., & Douglas, S. P. (2000). *International Marketing Research*. 2. Ed., Chichester et al..

Cui, G., & Awa, N. E. (1992). Measuring Intercultural Effectiveness: an Integrative Approach. *International Journal of Intercultural Relations, 16*, 311-328.

Davison, E., & Punnett, B. J. (1995). International Assignments: Is there a Role for Gender and Race in Decisions? *International Journal of Human Resource Management, 6* (2), 411-441.

Dean, O., & Popp, G. E. (1990). Intercultural Communication Effectiveness as Perceived by American Managers in Saudi Arabia and French Managers in the U.S.. *International Journal of Intercultural Relations, 14*, 405-424.

Deller, J. (1996). Interkulturelle Eignungsdiagnostik. In A. Thomas (Ed.), *Psychologie interkulturellen Handelns* (pp. 283-316). Göttingen.

Dinges, N. G., & Baldwin, K. D. (1996). Intercultural Competence. A Research Perspective. In D. Landis, & R. S. Bhagat (Eds.), *Handbook of Intercultural Training* (pp. 106-123). Thousand Oaks.

Domsch, M. (1997). Weibliche Führungskräfte im Ausland. *Personalwirtschaft, 9*, 18-21.

Domsch, M., & Lichtenberger, B. (1992). Foreign Assignment for Female German Managers. *The International Executive, 34*(4), 345-355.

Domsch, M., & Lieberum, U. (1996). *Möglichkeiten für Frauen im Management*. Hamburg.

Domsch, M., & Lieberum, U. (2004). Auslandseinsatz weiblicher Führungskräfte. In G. Krell (Ed.), *Chancengleichheit durch Personalpolitik* (pp. 231-242), Wiesbaden.

Domsch, M., Macke, H., & Schöne, K. (1996). *Weibliche Angestellte im deutschen Transformationsprozess*. München et al.

England, G. W., & Negandhi, A. R. (1979). National Contexts and Technology as Determinants of Employee's Perceptions. In G. England; A. Negandhi, & B. Wilpert, (Eds.), *Organizational Functioning in a Cross-Cultural Perspective* (pp. 175-190). Kent.

Forster, N. (2000). Expatriates and the Impact of Cross-Cultural Training. *Human Resource Management Journal, 10*(3), 63-78.

Foschi, M. (1992). Gender and Double Standards for Competence. In C. L. Ridgeway (Ed.), *Gender, Interaction and Inequality* (pp. 181-207). New York.

Friedel-Howe, H. (1990). Ergebnisse und offene Fragen der geschlechtsvergleichenden Führungsforschung. *Zeitschrift für Arbeits- und Organisationspsychologie, 34*(1), 3-16.

Fritz, W. (2001). Die interkulturelle Kompetenz von Managern – ein Schlüsselfaktor für den Erfolg auf Auslandsmärkten. In D. Oelsnitz von der, & A. Kammel (Eds.), *Kompetenzen moderner Unternehmensführung* (pp. 87-101). Bern at al.

Fritz, W., & Möllenberg, A. (1999). *Die Messung der interkulturellen Sensibilität in verschiedenen Kulturen – eine internationale Vergleichsstudie.* Braunschweig.

Fritz, W., Möllenberg, A., & Chen, G.-M. (2002). Measuring Intercultural Sensitivity in Different Cultural Contexts. *Intercultural Communication Studies, 11* (2), 165-176.

Fritz, W., Möllenberg, A., & Werner, T. (1999*). Die interkulturelle Kompetenz von Managern – Ihre Bedeutung für die Managementpraxis und Perspektiven für die Forschung.* Braunschweig.

Gelbrich, K. (2004). The Relationship between Intercultural Competence and Expatriate Success: A Structural Equation Model. *Die Unternehmung, 58*(3/4), 261-277.

Goldfried, M. R., & D'Zurilla, T. J. (1969). A Behavioral-Analytical Model for Assessing Competence. In C. D. Spielberger (Ed.), *Current Topics in Clinical and Community Psychology* (pp. 151-196), Vol. 1. New York,.

Graf, A. (2004a). *Interkulturelle Kompetenzen im Human Resource Management.* Wiesbaden.

Graf, A. (2004b). Expatriate Selection: An Empirical Study Identifying Significant Skill Profiles. *Thunderbird International Business Review, 46*(6), 667-685.

Graf, A. (2004c). Screening and Training Intercultural Competencies. *International Journal of Human Resource Management, 15*(6), 1124-1148.

Graf, A. (2004d). Assessing Intercultural Training Designs. *Journal of European Industrial Training, 28*(2/3/4), 199-214.

Graf, A., & Harland, L. (2004). Expatriate Selection: Evaluating the Convergent and Predictive Validity of Five Measures of Interpersonal and Intercultural Competence. *Journal of Leadership and Organizational Studies, 11*(2), 46-62.

Gudykunst, W. B., & Kim, Y. Y. (2003). *Communicating with Strangers: An Approach to Intercultural Communication,* 4. Ed.. London.

Gudykunst, W. B., & Lee, C. M. (2002). Cross-Cultural Communication Theories. In W. B. Gudykunst, & B. Mody (Eds.), *Handbook of International and Intercultural Communication* (pp. 25-50). Thousand Oaks.

Gudykunst, W. B.; Ting-Toomey, S., & Wiseman, R. (1991). Taming the Beast: Designing a Course in Intercultural Communication. *Communication Quarterly, 40,* 272-286.

Gudykunst, W. B.; Wiseman, R. L., & Hammer, M. R. (1977). Determinants of a Sojourner's Attitudinal Satisfaction: A Path Model. In B. D. Ruben (Ed.), *Communication Yearbook 1 (*pp. 415-425). Thousand Oaks,.

Hammer, M. R.; Gudykunst, W. B., & Wiseman, R. L. (1978). Dimensions of Intercultural Effectiveness: An Exploratory Study. *International Journal of Intercultural Relations, 2,* 382-392.

Harris, H. (1995). Women's Role in (International) Management. In A.-W. Harzing, & J. Van Ruysseveldet (Eds.), *International Human Resource Management* (pp. 229-252). London.

Hartl, K. (2003). *Expatriate Women Managers. Gender, Culture and Career.* München et al.

Hawes, F., & Kealey, D. J. (1979). Canadians in Development: An Empirical Study of Adaptation and Effectiveness on Overseas Assignment. *Technical Report, Ottawa.*

Helfrich, H. (1999). Beyond the Dilemma of Cross-Cultural Psychology: Resolving the Tension between Etic and Emic Approaches. *Culture & Psychology, 5* (2), 131-153.

Hofstede, G. (1992). Cultural Dimensions in People Management. The Socialization Perspective. In V. Pucik; N. M. Tichy, & C. K. Barnett (Eds.), *Globalizing Management: Creating and Leading the Competitive Organization* (pp. 139-158). New York.

Holzmüller, H. H. (1995). *Konzeptionelle und methodische Probleme in der interkulturellen Management- und Marketingforschung.* Stuttgart.

Ingelfinger, T. (1995). Interkulturelle Kompetenz als Notwendigkeit der Internationalisierung. *Marktforschung und Management, 39,* 103-106.

Karmasin, H., & Karmasin, M. (1997). *Cultural Theory: ein neuer Ansatz für Kommunikation, Marketing und Management.*Wien.

Kealey, D. J. (1989). A Study of Cross-Cultural Effectiveness: Theoretical Issues, Practical Applications. *International Journal of Intercultural Relations, 13,* 233-246.

Kealey, D. J., & Ruben, B. D. (1983). Cross-Cultural Personnel Selection: Criteria, Issues and Methods. In D. Landis, & R. W. Brislin (Eds.), *Handbook of Intercultural Training* (pp. 155-175), 1, New York.

Knapp, K. (1995). Interkulturelle Kommunikationfähigkeit als Qualifikationsmerkmal für die Wirtschaft. In J. Bolten (Ed.), *Cross-Culture – Interkulturelles Handeln in der Wirtschaft* (pp. 9-24). Sternenfels.

Koester, J., & Olebe, M. (1988). The Behavioral Assessment Scale for Intercultural Communication Effectiveness. *International Journal of Intercultural Relations, 12,* 233-246.

Lindner, D. (1999). Bestimmungsfaktoren der "Abbruchbereitschaft" von Auslands-entsandten: Eine theoretische und forschungspragmatische Analyse. *Zeitschrift für Personalforschung, 13*, 246-268.

Linehan, M. (2000). *Senior Female International Managers*. Aldershot.

Macha, H. (1998). Frauen und Macht – die andere Stimme der Wissenshaft. *Aus Politik und Zeitgeschichte, 48* (22-23), 12-21.

Markus, H. R., Kitayama, S., & Heiman, R. J. (1996). Culture and "Basic" Psychological Principles. In T. E. Higgins (Ed.), *Social Psychology. Handbook of Basic Principles* (pp. 857-913). New York.

Martin, J. N. (1987). The Relationships between Student Sojourner Perceptions of Intercultural Competencies and Previous Sojourn Experience. *International Journal of Intercultural Relations, 11*, 337-355.

McFall, R. M. (1982). A Review and Reformulation of the Concept of Social Skills. *Journal of Behavioral Assessment, 4*, 1-33.

Müller, S., & Gelbrich, K. (2001). Interkulturelle Kompetenz als neuartige Anforderung an Entsandte: Status quo und Perspektiven der Forschung. *Zeitschrift für betriebswirtschaftliche Forschung, 53* (5), 246-272.

Neuberger, O. (2002). *Führen und führen lassen: Ansätze, Ergebnisse und Kritik der Führungsforschung*. Stuttgart.

Paulhus, D. L. (1986). Self-Deception and Impression Management in Test Responses. In A. Angleitner, & J. S. Wiggins, (Eds.), *Personality Assessment via Questionnaires* (pp. 143-165), Berlin.

Pezeshkpur, C. (1978). Challenges to Management in the Arab World. *Business Horizons (Mai-Juni)*, 69-78.

Riemann, R., & Allgöwer, A. (1993). Eine deutschsprachige Fassung des „Interpersonal Competence Questionnaire" (ICQ). *Zeitschrift für Differentielle und Diagnostische Psychologie, 14* (3), 153-163.

Rosener, J. (1990). Ways Women lead. *Havard Business Review, 68* (11/12), 119-125.

Ruben, B. D. (1976). Assessing Communication Competency for Intercultural Adaptation. *Group & Organization Studies, 1*(3), 334-354.

Ruben, B. D., & Kealey, D. J. (1979). Behavioral Assessment of Communication Competency and the Prediction of Cross-Cultural Adaptation. *International Journal of Intercultural Relations, 3*, 15-47.

Schneidewind, D. K. (1996). Eine neue Kompetenz. *Gablers Magazin, 10*, 34-37.

Scholz, Ch. (1993). *Personalmanagement*. München.

Shaffer, M., Harrison, D., & Gilley, K. (1999). Dimensions, Determinants and Differences in the Expatriate Adjustment Process. *Journal of International Business Studies, 30*(3), 557-581.

Shay, J., & Tracey, J. (1997). Expatriate Managers: Reasons for Failure and Implications for Training. *Cornell Hotel and Restaurant Administration Quarterly*, February 19, 30-35.

Solomon, C. (1996). Danger Below! Spot Failing Global Assignments. *Personnel Journal, 75* (11), 78-83.

Spitzberg, B. H. (1989). Issues in the Development of a Theory of Interpersonal Competence in the Intercultural Context. *International Journal of Intercultural Relations, 13,* 241-268.

Spitzberg, B. H. (2000). A Model of Intercultural Communication Competence. In L. Samovar, & R. Porter (Eds.), *Intercultural Communication: A Reader* (pp. 375-387), Belmont et al.

Spitzberg, B. H., & Cupach, W. R. (1989). *Handbook of Interpersonal Competence Research.* New York et al..

Steenkamp, J.-B., & Baumgartner, H. (1998). Assessing Measurement Invariance in Cross-National Consumer Research. *Journal of Consumer Research, 25,* 78-90.

Stroh, L. K., Varma, A., & Valy-Durbin, S. J. (2000). Why are Women Left at Home: Are they Unwilling to Go on International Assignment? *Journal of World Business, 53*(3), 241-255.

Sue, D. W. (1991). A Model for Cultural Diversity Training. *Journal of Counselling and Development, 70,* 99-105.

Swaak, R. (1995). Expatriate failures: Too Many, Too Much Cost, Too Little Planning. *Compensation and Benefits Review, 27*(6), 47-55.

Taylor, S., & Napier, N. (1996). Working in Japan: Lessons from Women Expatriates. *Sloan Management Review, Spring,* 76-84.

Tung, R. L. (1998). American Expatriates Abroad: From Neophytes to Cosmopolitans. *Journal of World Business, 33*(2), 125-144.

Weber, W.; Festing, M.; Dowling, P. J., & Schuler, R. S. (2001). *Internationales Personalmanagement,* 2. Ed.. Wiesbaden.

Westwood, R., & Leung, S. (1994). The Female Expatriate Manager Experience: Coping with Gender and Culture. *International Studies of Management and Organization, 24*(3), 64-85.

Wicks, D., & Bradshaw, P. (2002). Investigating Gender and Organizational Culture: Gendered Value Foundations that Reproduce Discrimination and Inhibit Organizational Change. In I. Aaltion, & A. Mills (Eds.), *Gender, Identitiy and the Culture of Organizations* (pp. 137-159). London.

Windham International (2001). *Global Relocation Trends: 2000.* New York.

Wirth, E. (1992). *Mitarbeiter im Auslandseinsatz. Planung und Gestaltung.* Wiesbaden.

Wirth, E. (2003). International orientierte Personalentwicklung. In N. Bergemann, & A. Sourisseaux (Eds.), *Interkulturelles Management* (pp. 336-362). Berlin.

Wiseman, R. L. (2002). Intercultural Communication Competence. In W. B. Gudykunst, & B. Mody (Eds.), *Handbook of International and Intercultural Communication* (pp. 207-224). Thousand Oaks.

Wood, J. T., & Reich, N. M. (2004). Gendered Speech Communities. In L. A. Samovar, & R. E. Porter (Eds.), *Intercultural Communication* (pp. 144-154). Belmont.

Introduction to

Advertising to the Bottom of the Pyramid: Communicating with Consumers in Developing Markets

By Barbara Mueller

Mueller looks at advertising in developing countries. Due to demographical changes, most Western countries are aging and shrinking while developing countries are becoming younger and larger. Another appealing trend is that many of the developing markets have a growing consumer class, i.e. individuals whose purchasing power parity is more than $7,000 per year. This consumer class now includes already more than 1.7 billion people with nearly half of them in developing nations. Nevertheless, four billion people, i.e. two-thirds of the world population, are still at the bottom of the global economic pyramid. But even these "poorest of the poor" represent a market potential since this group represents a multi-trillion dollar market due to the large population size. And a number of companies have already demonstrated successfully that an ever growing share of their profits come from developing markets. Despite all of this information, relatively little is still known about how advertising operates in situations of comparative scarcity and poverty, Mueller notes.

While critics claim that international marketers are attempting to re-create Western style consumer cultures in countries outside the USA and Western Europe, little empirical evidence actually exists. Another criticism leveled against international marketers is that they are typically composed of Westerners who brought along not only their marketing skills but also their personal and professional values. Separating skills from values is difficult if not impossible, and much tension has developed when host countries want some of the skills but not the foreign values and styles. Mueller, therefore, sets out to disseminate the advantages and disadvantages of advertising and product promotion in the developing world. Due to the developing world's increasing importance in the global economy, this is a very valuable study because Mueller discusses all relevant aspects and weighs both sides of the arguments noting that the presence of transnational advertising agencies in any Third World society does generate some tension and conflict. In the end, however, the author urges companies to consider entering the markets of the developing world since a good many products have already proven to be both of value to consumers in those markets and profitable to international marketers.

Michael B. Hinner

Barbara Mueller is Professor of Advertising in the School of Communication at San Diego State University. She received her Ph.D. in Communications from the University of Washington. Her research focuses on international advertising, and communicating with the ethnic consumer. An additional stream of research focuses on controversial advertising practices such as marketing to children and the advertising of pharmaceutical products. In addition to numerous articles in professional journals, she is the author of *Dynamics of International Advertising: Theoretical and Practical Perspectives* (Peter Lang Publishing, 2004), and co-author (with Katherine Toland Frith) of *Advertising and Societies* (Peter Lang Publishing, 2003). She is currently working on her latest textbook: *Communicating with the Ethnic Consumer: Theoretical and Practical Perspectives* (Peter Lang Publishing, forthcoming).

Advertising to the Bottom of the Pyramid: Communicating with Consumers in Developing Markets

Barbara Mueller

Throughout the Western world, populations are aging, and also, often shrinking. While consumers in the United States and Europe are both graying, Europe is getting older even faster. According to United Nations forecasts, by 2050 the average age will go up from 39 to 48.5 in the European Union, and from 35.6 to 41.3 in the U.S. (De La Dehesa, 2004). Recent reports reveal that the dependency ratio – defined as the number of people over 65 as a percentage of the number of people 20 to 64 years old – will rise by 2050 to 37 percent from 22 percent in the United States, but it will jump to 52 percent from 26 percent in the EU (Brooks, 2005). This reflects, in part, the increase in life expectancy as a result of higher living standards and dramatic progress in the medical sciences. However, in many countries, it also reflects a fall in birthrates. As recently as the mid 1960s, every developed country was at, or above the 2.1 children-per-mother replacement rate needed to maintain a stable population from one generation to the next. Today, every developed country is below it and some are far below it. In Germany, the fertility rate is 1.3 and in southern and central Europe, 1.2. Only the United States remains near the replacement rate – but just barely (Jackson, 2003).

These demographic trends have caused many advertisers to look to developing countries for both larger and more youthful markets. According to World Bank estimates, over three-quarters of the world's population live in developing areas, and women in many of these regions still have between five and seven children. As Table 1 reveals, a significantly larger percentage of the population in many lower income countries falls into the 0-14 age grouping than in the higher income ones. However, even within these groupings, variation exists. Nearly half of Uganda's population is currently under 14 years of age. For India, the percentage is one-third, and one-fourth of China's population is currently 14 years or younger. In fifteen to twenty years, these citizens will be in their late 20s to

---

Barbara Mueller, *Dynamics of International Advertising: Theoretical and Practical Perspectives*, Copyright 2004, Reprinted by permission of Peter Lang Publishing Inc. and of the author.

late 30s, the prime earning and spending years – making these countries particularly attractive to international marketers.

Table 1
Economic Development and Age Structure (percentage between 0-14 years)

Low-Income Economies (36.9%)		*Upper-Middle Income Economies* (29.1%)	
Uganda	49.2%	Venezuela	36.5%
Kenya	43.5%	Brazil	28.8%
India	33.5%	Hungary	19.9%
China	24.8%	Portugal	16.7%
Lower-Middle Income Economies (26.9%)		*High-Income Economies* (18.5%)	
Algeria	34.8%	United States	21.5%
Peru	33.4%	France	18.7%
Thailand	26.7%	Germany	15.4%
Poland	19.2%	Japan	14.7%

Source: World Bank 2002 World Development Indicators.

Another appealing trend to international marketers is that many of these developing markets have a growing "consumer class" – defined as individuals whose purchasing power parity in local currency is more than $7,000 a year (roughly the poverty level in Western Europe). The consumer class now includes more than 1.7 billion people. High percentages in North America, Western Europe and Japan (85 to 90 percent) are no surprise. But nearly half of the consumer class is now in developing nations. India and China alone account for 362 million of these consumers, more than all of Western Europe combined (Knickerbocker, 2004). Chinese teens and young adults are one group marketers are particularly eager to reach. Although the majority of this group does not work, they are considered highly affluent because of the mainland's one-child policy. With two sets of grandparents as well as parents, there are typically six adults supplying money to one child. Indeed, this growing army of "little emperors" is usually flush with cash and ready to spend it. Clearly, available income has a direct influence on what consumers are capable of purchasing. Table 2 reveals the varying degrees to which consumers possess goods in both developed and developing countries.

Table 2
Possession of Goods (per 100 Households)

	Shower	Washing Machine	Refrigerator	Auto	Phone	CD Player
Argentina	93.6	49.5	83.8	58.9	69.8	25.3
Canada	99.5	85.6	99.0	86.4	88.6	81.0
China	42.6	2.5	6.7	2.9	27.1	2.2
France	84.3	98.2	85.7	78.7	89.0	24.1
Germany	99.6	98.7	88.9	90.7	99.2	85.4
Hungary	73.0	32.5	98.7	46.3	94.6	30.1
India	42.6	4.8	14.7	0.6	17.3	1.4
Italy	78.9	97.9	86.0	74.6	97.0	13.0
Japan	99.7	99.3	97.7	81.7	87.4	68.5
Mexico	68.7	41.9	68.7	23.0	31.0	9.9
Philippines	84.1	8.1	43.8	7.7	12.1	3.8
Poland	76.7	53.7	99.5	57.0	71.2	14.3
Singapore	99.6	95.4	99.3	43.4	96.7	56.5
Spain	78.9	97.9	88.1	74.6	97.0	39.8
South Africa	59.7	26.2	80.3	8.9	29.3	6.5
Thailand	66.9	5.0	70.4	35.4	26.8	5.4
U.K.	89.0	94.9	98.7	74.1	93.7	84.1
U.S.	99.7	82.3	99.4	93.1	85.6	59.6
Venezuela	92.3	39.6	83.0	47.5	42.7	9.8

Source: International Marketing Forecasts, *Euromonitor,* (2004/2005), Data and Statistics, *Euromonitor,* (2004)

As can be seen from the figures above, there is tremendous variation in the ownership of durable goods. For example, automobile ownership ranges from 93 cars for every 100 households in the U.S., to fewer than three cars per 100 households in China. For years, most cars in China were sold to state institutions and companies, or ended up in taxi fleets. Until recently, cars were out of reach of ordinary Chinese, including even members of the new middle class. This is now changing. As tariffs on imported cars dropped in the wake of China's accession to the World Trade Organization, and a slew of new models came on the market, domestic auto manufacturers were forced to drop their prices. Currently, the price for a small domestic vehicle is about $4,700. Private citizens, armed with savings and aided by a variety of installment plans are flocking to dealerships. According to Automotive Resources in Asia, a Beijing consultancy, car sales will grow 15 percent annually and could more than double to 2.5 million by 2010. Clearly, this has whet the appetite of foreign manufacturers – Ford Motor Co. and Volkswagen are just two of the firms actively wooing Chinese consumers (Roberts and Webb, 2002).

Research has shown that it is precisely during the recent period of increased globalization of the world economy, that poverty rates and global income inequality have most diminished (Globalization is Narrowing the Poverty Gap, 2003). Data reveals that both absolute poverty and poverty rates have substantially declined over the last 30 years. Australian Department of Foreign Affairs and Trade reports that the number of undernourished people in the world has been reduced from 920 million in 1970 to 810 million today (Burtless, 2002). Measures of income equality show that many developing countries (with Africa as a serious exception) are actually converging toward the richest countries' living standards. Nonetheless, four billion people – nearly two-thirds of the globe's population -- are still at the bottom of the world's economic pyramid. Yet, even these "poorest of the poor" represent market potential, notes University of Michigan Business School professor, C.K. Prahalad (2004). Because of their vast numbers, this group represents a multi-trillion-dollar market. According to World Bank projections, the population at the bottom of the pyramid could swell to more than 6 billion people over the next 40 years. Prahalad argues that for companies with the resources and persistence to compete for the aspiring poor who are joining the market economy for the first time, prospective rewards include growth, profits and incalculable contributions to humankind.

According to Prahalad, Hindustan Lever Ltd. (HLL), a subsidiary of Great Britain's Unilever PLC has been a pioneer among multinational corporations exploring markets at the bottom of the pyramid. While HLL has served India's small elite – those who could afford to purchase multinational's products -- for over half a century, in the 1990s, the firm drastically altered its traditional business model and began wooing a market that it had previously disregarded. HLL introduced a new detergent, called Wheel, which was specifically formulated to substantially reduce the ratio of oil to water in the product, responding to the fact that the poor often wash their clothes in rivers and other public water systems. The firm also changed the cost structure of its detergent business so it could introduce Wheel at a low price point. Finally, it created sales channels through the thousands of small outlets where people at the bottom of the pyramid are most likely to shop. Today, as a result of these efforts, HLL has an impressive 38 percent share of India's detergent market. Unilever benefited from its subsidiary's experience in the Indian market, and has adopted the bottom of the pyramid as a corporate strategic priority in India, as well as other developing markets. For example, Unilever's Rexona brand mini-size deodorant sticks, which sell for just 16 cents, are a huge hit in India, but also in the Philippines, Bolivia and Peru. Other companies have followed suit. For an increasing number of firms, an ever-growing share of their profits is coming from developing markets (See Table 3).

Table 3
Estimated Sales Distribution by Region for Major Multinationals/Products

Company	North America	Latin America	Western Europe	Eastern Europe	Asia/ Africa
Avon	38%	32%	11%	5%	14%
Colgate	33	26	21	3	17
Clorox	88	10	0	0	2
Gillette	43	11	30	4	12
Kimberly-Clark	59	11	19	1	10
P & G	51	8	22	5	14

Source: Neff, Jack (2002, March 4). Submerged. *Advertising Age*, 73(9), 14.

Table 4.
Advertising Spending Worldwide, by Region, 2003-2007 (as a % increase vs. prior year)

	2003	2004	2005	2006	2007
Africa, Middle East, Rest of World	19.1%	25.5%	17.1%	16.5%	13.0%
Asia-Pacific	5.4%	8.2%	5.5%	6.4%	8.2%
Europe	1.4%	6.1%	3.1%	4.4%	4.5
Latin America	3.5%	12.9%	19.3%	8.8%	10.2%
North America US	1.9%	6.0%	3.6%	5.6%	4.5%
US	3.1%	7.5%	5.2%	6.2%	6.1%
World Wide	3.1%	7.5%	5.2%	6.2%	6.1%

Note: includes newspapers, magazines, television, radio, cinema, outdoor, and Internet.
Source: ZenithOptimedia, October 2005.

Indeed, citing growth in emerging markets, ZenithOptimedia recently increased its growth projections for global ad spending. The media buying firm said it now expects global ad spending to increase 5.2 percent in 2005, up from its previous estimate of 4.7 percent. It estimates that worldwide advertising spending will rise to $406 billion in 2005, up from $386 billion in 2004. ZenithOptimedia also expects growth of more than 6 percent in both 2006 and 2007 (eMarketer, 2005). Table 4 shows advertising spending worldwide, by region, between 2003 and 2007, as a percentage increase over the previous year.

It has only been in the past few decades that manufacturers and distributors have begun to aggressively target consumers in these developing markets. As a result, while a good deal is known about the role of marketing and advertising in countries with economic systems based on plenty, still relatively little is known about how advertising operates in situations of comparative scarcity and poverty. Yet, the debate regarding advertising's effects on developing nations is a heated one. On the positive side, advertising can serve to educate consumers by informing them of what goods are available and where they may be obtained. Recent research (*Business Wire,* 2005, September 27) shows that 55 percent of young people in Mexico, 54 percent in China and 68 percent in India agree that advertising is a good way to learn about trends and things to buy. In fact, young consumers in developing countries appear to be even more receptive to advertising than those in developed countries – where only 30 percent in France, 32 percent in Germany and 35 percent in the United States agreed that advertising was a good source of information about products. Advertising can also enable consumers to compare goods, which often results in lower prices and improved product quality. Advertising may stimulate the local economy by encouraging consumption. Agencies often offer employment to locals, as well as providing career training. And, it has the potential to improve living standards. Many of the messages aired in developing countries serve to promote desirable social aims—such as increased savings, reduced illiteracy, lower birth rates, and improved nutrition and hygiene. Advertising has even been successfully employed in the fight against AIDS. For example, in conjunction with UNIFCEF, Clear Channel Outdoor mounted a global HIV/AIDS awareness campaign that will run in more than 50 countries on six continents. The goal of the campaign is to help the world's estimated 15 million children who are affected and infected by HIV and AIDS. More than 2 million of children are HIV-positive and more than 500,000 died in 2004 from AIDS-related causes. The chilling creative – a hand-drawn family portrait of a young girl standing beside the graves of her mother and father -- was developed by BesterBurke of Cape Town, South Africa. The image was selected from more than 300 entries from advertising agencies worldwide. Clear Channel Outdoor offices in both developed and developing countries are donating more than $5 million in advertising space for the campaign. The ad will be translated into local languages and accommodate local customs in each country. (*Business Wire,* 2005, October 27).

A good deal more attention has been paid to the negatives associated with the efforts of international advertisers in developing countries. Charles Frazer (1990) points out that "the idea that marketing, and particularly advertising, activities come to have disruptive, perverse and subversive effects in other cultures, especially the Third World, travels under a variety of labels, including cultural dependence, social mobilization...and cultural imperialism." The dependency approach, claims Michael H. Anderson (1984), suggests that "imported western institutions and values intentionally or unintentionally generate dependency and function as a hindrance to the development of genuinely independent nations."

According to social mobilization theory, writes John McGinnis (1988), "It is not economic development or modernization that leads to political instability, but the rate of rising expectations and the failure to satisfy those expectations." With regard to cultural imperialism, Herbert I. Schiller (1973) notes:

No part of the globe...avoids the penetration of the internationally active American advertising agency. These transnational advertising agencies have made deep inroads into most of the already industrialized states, and many of the third world nations are experiencing the same loss of national control of the image-making apparatus and internal communications systems. Advertising, and the mass media that it eventually transduces are, therefore, the leading agents in the business of culture, and the culture of business.

Regardless of the label, at the heart of the matter is the charge that international marketers attempt to re-create Western-style consumer cultures in countries outside the United States and Western Europe. Critics claim that consumers in these countries are particularly vulnerable to the efforts of international advertisers because they likely are poor and illiterate, lack experience with consumer goods, and have not been exposed to decades of media messages common in more developed markets. In addition, many developing countries lack legal systems for consumer protection. While there is much speculation on the possible impact of both multinational corporations and advertising agencies on developing countries, there exists little empirical evidence of these effects (Del Toro, 1986).

Charges Against and Arguments for Advertising in Developing Markets

International Advertising Agencies' Influence on Local Advertising Institutions.

Critics claim that international advertising agencies have the ability to dominate advertising in ways that small, local advertising agencies in weak, poor nations cannot. They suggest that powerful global agencies have a direct impact on a nation's efforts to build autonomous advertising institutions. In the 1960s many advertising agencies opened shop in the Third World—generally by setting up subsidiaries or purchasing local advertising firms. Further, these multinational agencies were often the driving force behind the creation of national and regional advertising associations, responsible for setting the criteria for agency accreditation (Fejes, 1990). These multinational agencies were typically staffed with Westerners who brought along not only their marketing skills but also their personal and professional values. Separating skills from values is difficult if not impossible, and tensions developed when host countries wanted some of the skills but not the full package of foreign professional values and styles (Anderson, 1984).

Because of their high levels of creative sophistication and innovation, multinational agencies more or less set the standard by which all advertising was measured. Local agencies were forced to provide similar services (such as audience research) and were also expected to reproduce the quality and style of multinational advertising in order to remain competitive. This remains a problem to this date. For example, for a number of years now, South African agencies have been receiving a large share of the awards at international advertising competitions. "Much of the work loses nothing in comparison to that of the best U.K. or U.S. agencies: it could as easily have been made in LA as SA. And that is the problem. For all the high production values and professional polish, there is nothing very African about South African advertising. The idea seems to have been to prove that 'look, we can do this stuff as well as anyone' – an attitude which is by no means particular to South Africa. Brazil, India, Eastern Europe – much of the work in what might be called advertising's 'developing world' is fixated with proving an ability to ape Western mores rather than tapping in to local culture. And you can't blame advertising alone for that. Clients and consumers look up to Western brands and Western media" (*Creative Review,* 2005). One agency, however, is seeking to break out of this mold. Copywriter Stuart Stobbs of Netpound Tork, a Johannesburg outpost of BBDO, observed that "There is a great desire among much of the South African advertising, design and communications industry to promote and use local concepts, thinking and visual culture in our work. Many people are talking about it and trying to push for it, but hardly anyone is doing it." To that end, the agency has begun using some of the talent at its doorstep, adopting South Africa's rich indigenous visual culture, from traditions of African art to vernacular trends such as barbershop signs and the decoration of township shacks. Netpound Tork's goal is to produce work with a specifically African flavor (*Creative Review,* 2005).

Many developing nations, which at one time welcomed foreign agencies with open arms, have begun to pass regulations limiting ownership and investment in domestic agencies. The advertising agency is increasingly seen as a national communications system that should not be handed over to foreigners. For example, in Latin America, foreign investment is limited to 19 percent, and in India it is limited to 40 percent. In addition to ensuring that the majority of an agency's ownership rests in the hands of locals, many nations are taking steps to ensure that agency personnel are also nationals and, as a result, are more likely to be familiar with the indigenous culture of the country. Unfortunately, all too often, foreigners are hired in decision-making roles, while locals are employed for the more routine tasks. In China, until quite recently, international agencies were required to have a local joint-venture partner before they could directly purchase media. As a result, locally hired people made up 80 – 90 percent of the staff at international agencies (Kloss, 2002). However, at the end of 2005, China's advertising sector was fully opened to the outside world. This meant that overseas agencies were able to set up wholly-owned advertising firms. It will be interesting to see if and how this will impact staffing in Chinese agencies in the future.

In an attempt to support local advertising institutions, a number of countries have passed a variety of laws. Among the strictest are those in Malaysia. In this country, all commercials require the Made-in Malaysia (MIM) certificate. The certification is proof that a particular commercial fulfills policy requirements, which state that all or a majority of the production crew are to consist of Malaysians, the location shoot shall be in Malaysia, negative or print processing is to be done in Malaysia, the music and voice over must be done in Malaysia, and at least 80 percent of production cost is to be spent locally. If foreign footage is to be used, approval from the Ministry of Information must be obtained. The country's guidelines have contributed tremendously to developing local production activities and local practitioners are now noted for their high level of technical competency (Bani, 1999).

Advertising's Influence on the Domestic Media Scene

A major criticism of international advertising is that it promotes commercialism of the media, as well as introducing Western media content. Wherever international corporations operate, the local mass media have been summoned to promote sales of consumer goods. As a result, the structure of national communications systems, as well as the programming offered, has been transformed according to the specifications of international marketers. In terms of media structure, many developing countries shifted away from public- or state-financing models to the U.S. model whereby the media are supported by advertising. The broadcast media appear to be particularly susceptible to the lure of advertising dollars. Today, the overwhelming number of radio and television stations in developing markets, both government-owned and private, are financed through advertising revenue. This model typically favors amassing profits over serving public needs. In Latin America, for example, 30–50 percent of newspaper content, over 33 percent of magazine content, and as much as 18 percent of television content is advertising. Not surprisingly, advertising clutter in many developing markets is even worse than in the United States.

With regard to media vehicles, multinational corporations generally prefer Western programming in which to air their messages. Because such reliance on imported foreign programming reduces opportunities for locals, governments increasingly are taking steps to ensure that a certain percentage of programming remains domestically produced. However, foreign styles and production standards are often copied while traditional styles are abandoned. For example, the popularity of reality TV in the United States has spawned similar programming in many developing markets. "Mentor" and "Malaysian Idol" are among the 26 reality TV programs broadcast in that country. In response to the proliferation of such reality shows, there has been a call for television stations in Malaysia to be more creative and innovative in producing programs. Deputy Prime Minister Datuk Seri Najib Tun Razak noted that local television stations should not blindly follow western TV programs because they could pose a threat to eastern values and the identity of Malaysian society (Ali, 2005). Even when multinationals utilize local programs, they typically prefer entertainment-oriented programming over more culturally oriented offerings. Further, they tend to prefer broadcast media over print, so that advertising revenues tend to flow to the broadcast media rather than to print. The end result may well be ever-increasing costs for print media and ever-decreasing levels of readership, which does not bode particularly well for literacy levels. Finally, multinational corporations have been accused of attempting to influence media content by threatening withdrawal—thus exerting powerful pressure on local media.

It should be noted that some researchers have, in fact, emphasized the beneficial effects of advertising on the local media scene. Supporters claim that, given the limited governmental funding available in many developing countries, advertising support is indeed essential to the health of local media. For instance, international advertising revenues may help to make the media autonomous from politics (Pollay, 1986).

Advertising's Influence on Competition

Critics claim that firms which advertise heavily make it impossible for competitors in developing countries to enter the marketplace because of the enormous sums spent on advertising. In contrast, supporters claim that by encouraging competition among producers, advertising actually stimulates the economy. Because there is little consensus as to the impact of advertising on competition in developed markets, not surprisingly, there is also a good deal of debate over its role in evolving economies. Although no significant studies document advertising's effect on competition, some interesting statistics suggest there may be some validity to this criticism. For example, multinational corporations outspend local firms by six to one in advertising. With so much exposure, international brands generally have substantially higher recall levels among consumers than do local brands. For example, to gauge the promise of Africa as an advertising market, Leo Burnett recently conducted a survey of consumers in eight countries: South Africa, Nigeria, Zimbabwe, Ghana, Cameroon, Ivory Coast, Mozambique and Kenya. Asked to name their favorite brands – local or international – African consumers picked big names and, interestingly enough, chose mobile phone names among their top four: Sony, Ericsson, Samsung and Nokia. They were followed by Nike, Coca-Cola, Mercedes-Benz, Toyota, Panasonic and Philips. Local brands had a hard time cracking the list in any country, though Tusker beer popped up at No. 3 in Kenya (Pfanner, 2005). Clearly, significant status is associated with foreign brands of consumer goods.

Advertising's Influence on Consumerism

Critics claim that international marketers promote commercialism and consumerism in developing markets. For example, Malaysia's Consumer Association of Penang describes the situation as follows: "A worrying trend is the growing influence of negative aspects of Western fashion and culture on the people of the Third World countries, including Malaysia. The advertising industry has created the consumer culture, which has in fact become our national culture. Within this cultural system people measure their worth by the size of their house, the make of their car and the possession of the latest household equipment, clothes and gadgets " (Consumer Association of Penang, 1986).

International advertising messages are said to stimulate artificial wants and needs and to encourage consumers to demand goods inappropriate for their level of development. Such charges are difficult to answer empirically. Distinguishing between what is a real and an artificial want or need is no easy task. Even in markets where there are no active selling and promotional efforts, demand for Western-style products appears to be widespread. For example, despite the nineteen-year trade embargo imposed on Vietnam (which was finally lifted in 1994), Coca-Cola was extremely popular in this, one of the poorest countries in the world. Apparently, brand-conscious and America-loving Vietnamese consumers had been purchasing Coca-Cola on the black market for years (Saporito, 1993).

It is of interest to note that the concern over commercialization and consumerism tends to be greatest in the developed – rather than the developing -- nations. The Pew Global Attitudes study, which surveyed some 66,000 people in 44 nations, found that while 63 percent of the French say both are threats to their culture, the poorest countries, on the whole, didn't see it that way. The survey reported that consumers in Lebanon (65 percent), Uzbekistan (57 percent), and Jordan (54 percent) say commercialism is no threat to their culture. Consumers in Turkey, Egypt and Pakistan agreed. In Vietnam, 66 percent said commercialism was not a threat. In Nigeria, the figure was 65 percent, and in Angola, 56 percent (Peron, 2004).

While consumerism is generally attacked as a negative consequence of advertising, it may also benefit a host society. Advertisements may, for example, convey messages about higher standards of living to a society and, as such, be viewed as a force contributing to the betterment and advancement of people's lives (Kaynak, 1989). For example, every society has a need for clean laundry. In many developing nations clothing was typically laundered in a stream of running water or on a rock. To meet the needs of such consumers, a small, plastic, hand-powered washing machine was developed, marketed, and widely accepted (Keegan, 1984). More recently, researchers at the Massachusetts Institute of Technology Media Laboratory, led by founding chairman Nicholas Negroponte, developed an economy laptop (less than US $100). Having witnessed first-hand in Cambodia how computers can transform children's learning, Negroponte plans to distribute 15 million "clockwork laptop" computers to children in the developing world during 2006, and another 150 million by 2007. Beyond the low price, the unique feature of this computer is its retractable winder used to generate electricity – vital given that the majority of children in the developing world do not have access to electricity or batteries (Rutter, 2005).

Multinationals note that even the poorest of the poor can be choosy about brands. Executives at Hindustan Lever note that poor people can become just as discerning about brands as rich consumers. If brands exist as a store of value – a promise about the products distinctive qualities and features -- then offering poor consumers a real choice of brands means offering them a slightly better quality of life. Marketing well-made products to the poor is not just a business opportunity, it is a sign of commercial respect for people whose needs are usually overlooked (Balu, 2002).

Advertising and the Allocation of Precious Resources

The criticism here is that scarce national resources are squandered for the production, promotion, and consumption of products that simply are not needed by consumers in developing markets. International businesses are accused of engaging in advertising to shift consumer behavior from rational consumption of locally produced goods to conspicuous consumption of foreign-made goods (Del Toro, 1986). To compete with foreign advertisers, local firms increasingly must also employ promotional techniques. These monies, it is argued, could be better spent assisting the local population via health and welfare programs. For example, in Kenya, one study has documented that expenditures for soap advertising are higher than government expenditures for rural health care. Not only do businesses spend unnecessarily, but so do consumers in these countries, because the cost of many international products is significantly higher than that of local goods. U.S. products, in particular, carry a premium price. For instance, in India,

Camay soap costs 27 cents while local soaps are priced at 19 cents; Head & Shoulders shampoo sells for $4.77 while local shampoos are priced at $2.00 (Khan, 1994). Clearly, the poor can ill afford such items, because the majority of their income is spent on sustenance. The counterargument here is that while multinational corporations and their advertising agencies may change the patterns of consumption, they do not impact levels of consumption (Tansey and Hyman, 1994). Regardless of perspective, the question remains, who is to decide which expenditures are wasteful and which are not? From the viewpoint of many international marketers, this is a decision best left to consumers themselves. Critics argue, however, that local governments in developing countries must consciously decide where valuable resources are to be spent.

Advertising's Influence on Rising Frustrations

In a related criticism, it's claimed that advertising creates demand for goods consumers cannot possibly afford. The concern here is that the associated dissatisfaction and frustration might possibly lead to social unrest or even political destabilization. In selling goods in developing countries, advertisers may communicate with three major markets: (1) the urban-center dwellers, consisting of foreign expatriates as well as sizable pockets of both high- and middle-income locals who often are as sophisticated in their tastes as their counterparts in developed markets; (2) suburbanites living in outlying areas some ten to fifteen miles from the urban centers; and (3) the rural population, whose life styles remain quite provincial and whose incomes are quite meager (Hill, 1984). Note that nearly 80 percent of the population in most less developed countries lives outside the cities and that the cultural and economic gap between the urban centers on the one hand and the villages or rural areas on the other is quite substantial (Hill and Hill, 1984). The problem lies in targeting promotional messages only to the most appropriate market segment. For example, international marketers may decide to offer a product to those consumers who are relatively well off with sufficient disposable income—primarily those in urban centers. This creates a taste for Western life styles and values that often trickles down to the lower classes. Inevitably, consumers in rural areas will seek ways to expend their limited resources to obtain these very same items. Ultimately, the lower sectors are perceived not simply as passive bystanders but as potential consumers of these very same products (Del Toro, 1986). Philippine author Renato Constantino (1986) voiced his concern: "In the Philippines for example, where estimates placed fully 70 percent of families below the poverty line, money sorely needed for food, shelter and basic health is often squandered on tobacco, cosmetics, soft drinks and the latest fashion jeans. Although the targets of transnational corporation sales are the elite and middle classes, their advertising is 'democratically' heard via transistor radios, seen on billboards and to a lesser extent on television."

Further, in many Third World countries upward mobility is virtually nonexistent. Generally, less than 10 percent of the population owns 60 percent or more of a nation's wealth. Many consumers in these countries do develop a desire—whether through advertising or other stimuli—for goods they can ill afford. In Mexico, for example, U.S. soft drinks control over 75 percent of the market, and schoolchildren will save money to purchase Pepsi, which costs three to five times what a local soft drink would cost. However, little evidence indicates that consumer frustrations have resulted in demands for radical change. Nonetheless, governmental bodies in some developing markets have undertaken steps to avoid the potential social or political unrest. For example, as early as 1981, the Indonesian government exerted a ban on commercial television in order to reduce the negative impact of advertising in remote villages where purchasing power is quite limited.

Advertising's Influence on Indigenous Culture

Advertising was heavily criticized in UNESCO's 1980 report, "Many Voices, One World: Communication & Society Today and Tomorrow," in which the McBride Commission took advertising to task for its uninvited cultural intervention in Third World countries. Paulo Freire (1970), a philosopher from Chile, argues: "The invaders penetrate the cultural context of another group, in disrespect of the latter's potentialities; they impose their own view of the world upon those they invade and inhibit the creativity of the invaded by curbing their expression." Note Katherine and Michael Frith (1989): "While multinational marketers and advertisers might consider a western-style global marketing campaign to be an efficient way to reach new audiences in the developing countries, critics like Freire would characterize this as an act of violence against the persons of the invaded culture." Much of the criticism of foreign messages asserts that the advertisements project non-indigenous values and beliefs. For example, in the mid 1990s Tony Koenderman (1994) pointed out that although over 85 percent of South Africa's population is black, advertising continues to focus on the white minority and advertising is largely fashioned by whites, for whites. Creative concepts tend to be Western with little relevance for local lifestyles and values, according to the head of the country's only black-owned advertising agency. They use white models even when the main market for a product is black. Until recently, advertisers could justify this Euro-centric approach on the grounds that whites accounted for most of the buying power in the South African market, which spends $1.2 billion annually on advertising. But official statistics show that the white share of total household expenditures fell from 57 percent in 1978 to 49.5 percent in 1988. Today it is closer to 40 percent.

In 2002, the South African government held its first round of hearings on racism in marketing and advertising. Resentment is increasing because although white people represent only 12 percent of the population, most of the people in ad agencies today are white, media ownership is white dominated and media targeted at the generally more affluent white community tend to be favored by advertisers. Critics argue that the advertising business in South Africa commands huge budgets which determine who creates, develops, packages and distributes content on TV, radio and print. As a result of this first meeting, a task force was established to eliminate racism in South African advertising. Only 31 percent of agency employees are black and it is estimated that only 16 percent of ad expenditures went to black media. Critics argue that an ideal model is one where the racial mix of consumers is exactly mirrored by the placement of ads (Advertising Age, 2002).

Western advertising clearly presents Western values, particularly when standardized campaigns are employed. What it means to be successful or attractive, what roles men, women, and children should play, are all outlined for consumers in developing markets in thirty-second messages, radio jingles, and outdoor billboards. Sales messages are overlaid on cultural messages glamorizing Western lifestyles. To counter this, many countries have taken protective steps. The governments of some developing countries demand messages that are created exclusively for their local consumers—messages designed to preserve and strengthen their own culture rather than reflect imported values. In Peru, for example, advertising must be locally produced in order to ensure that local values are projected. The Malaysian advertising code stipulates that advertisements must project the Malaysian culture, and identity, as well as reflect the multiracial character of the population. Advertisements that highlight western values are forbidden. Further, scenes of an amorous, intimate or suggestive nature are forbidden on Malaysian television. In addition, provocative scenes that show naked or scantily clad models are also not allowed to be shown (Kloss, 2002). Real or imagined, fears of cultural imperialism have spurred numerous governments to take preventive action.

Advertising's Potential to Exaggerate Claims and Deceive Consumers

That advertising often exaggerates claims and deceives consumers is widely accepted as a valid concern by both consumers and the advertising industry. This problem has always been associated with advertising, but in developed countries regulatory bodies developed alongside the advertising industry, offering consumers some degree of protection. In contrast, more than half of developing nations have no regulatory agencies to speak of. This leaves consumers in developing nations open to misleading advertising. In addition, there is little self-regulation of advertising in Third World markets, resulting in numerous instances of less than scrupulous advertising. For example, increased public awareness of the health risks of smoking, along with increasing regulation have taken their toll on cigarette smoking in the U.S., where sales volume has dropped by almost 10 percent since 1999. And smoking rates in other industrialized countries are decreasing at a rate of 1-2 percent annually. In contrast, thanks to aggressive marketing tactics, smoking in developing countries is increasing at a rate of about 3 percent a year. While multinational tobacco companies market high tar and nicotine cigarettes worldwide, in developing countries, they advertise their products with techniques that are banned in their home markets (Bettcher and Subramaniam, 2001). For example, a Public Citizen's Health Research Group study shows that cigarettes sold in Asia, Africa, South America and Eastern Europe give consumers less warning about the risks of smoking. The study suggests that non-Americans are being denied vital information readily available in the U.S. Further, it appears the providers of such information – the media – are also being manipulated. British-American Tobacco, which is owned by B.A.T. Industries held seminars at luxury resorts worldwide at which it offered foreign journalists data that play down the health risks of smoking. And advertising agencies, like Leo Burnett Inc, the creator of the legendary Marlboro Man campaign, have used their talents on behalf of tobacco producers to thwart anti-smoking campaigns outside the United States (Meier, 1998). Of the 8.4 million deaths that tobacco is expected to cause by 2020, 70 percent will occur in developing countries. Clearly, it is imperative that global legislation hold tobacco companies to the same standards of safety in developing markets that they are held to in their industrialized home markets. The same can be said for the marketing of both over-the-counter and prescription drugs. For these kinds of product categories, the lack of information, or worse yet, misleading information, is particularly harmful to poor, uneducated consumers in developing markets.

Problems in Assessing Advertising's Effects in Developing Markets

The most striking factor in the preceding discussion is the lack of empirical evidence regarding the effects of marketing and advertising in developing countries. The claims made are complex—and not easily substantiated or refuted. More often than not, arguments are based on anecdotal or scanty evidence, and conclusions clash depending on whose perspective is embraced (Del Torro, 1986).

Several problems are associated with assessing the influence of promotional efforts. First, in the debate regarding advertising's effects, the type of advertising often is not clearly defined. Criticisms are levied against advertising in general, yet advertising for specific product categories tends to generate more objections than others. For example, retail advertising, which brings together buyers and sellers and provides consumers with information about the local market, is generally not the target of criticism. Similarly, industrial advertising, directed not at the consumer population but rather at businesses, has received little criticism. This type of advertising also tends to be high in information content. On the other hand, advertising for brand-name products, such as soft drinks, sweets, alcoholic beverages, and, in particular, cigarettes, has received the greatest amount of criticism.

Second, in assessing advertising's effects, oversimplified models of buying behavior often are employed. Critics of advertising in developing countries ascribe great power to advertising, assuming advertising directly causes purchase behavior. Clearly, many additional factors come into play in stimulating buyer behavior. Conceivably, a variety of underlying social and environmental factors (such as church and school) play a more significant role in stimulating wants and needs than does advertising.

Finally, advertising is a process in which a great many intervening variables—some of which are not all that clearly defined—play a role. For example, research regarding the impact of international advertising on indigenous culture is complicated by the methodological problems associated with identifying exactly what indigenous culture is. A multitude of factors may impact the culture of a society, and each must be taken into consideration when analyzing both positive and negative claims against advertising. Charles Frazer (1990) notes that, unfortunately, advertising effects are not separable from those of other social forces: "How advertising effects might be disentangled from marketing, mass media, social, political, cultural and individual impetus is indeed a staggeringly complex undertaking."

Promotional Strategies in Developing Markets

The promotional strategies destined for developing countries often require significant changes from those used in more advanced or industrialized countries, for several reasons:

- The illiteracy rate in many developing countries is often very high, so written communication may be of limited value.
- The media infrastructure is often underdeveloped, so that the media frequently used elsewhere, such as television, may have limited uses for advertising purposes.
- Some countries may be multilingual, making translation quite costly.

- The company's products, brands, and so on may be unknown.
- The markets may be narrow because of wide variations in income and extremes in income distribution.
- The markets may be geographically diverse and dispersed and therefore difficult and expensive to reach (Toyne and Walters, 1989).

Yet, despite such differences, campaign adaptation is more common for developed markets than for developing markets. Research conducted by Hill and James (1990) revealed changes in sales platforms and creative contexts were more likely to occur in more affluent markets than in less affluent markets. This may well be a primary reason that international advertising messages targeted to consumers in developing markets are so heavily criticized. International marketers wishing to avoid further regulation and vicious social criticism would be well advised to create advertisements that:

1. Express local social values and needs (an admittedly difficult task because local values are complex and often in conflict with one another).

2. Encourage the economic austerity and personal savings needed to create domestic investment capital.

3. Foster greater awareness of the effect of personal consumption on the local environment (Tansey and Hyman, 1994).

The Future of Advertising in Developing Markets

Advertising in the Third World can have both positive and negative effects. It is, in many ways, a sword that cuts both ways. On the one hand, host nations obviously realize that international marketers and their agencies do make contributions to host societies, which is why they allow them to operate within their borders in the first place. Indeed, in numerous instances corporations and agencies are invited to enter these markets and are even offered concessions, incentives for foreign investment, and tax exemptions (Del Toro, 1986). A good many products have proven to be both of value to consumers in developing nations, and profitable for international marketers. And, as noted, advertising has been employed in combating social ills and improving health any hygiene in many less developed markets.

On the other hand, there are real dangers associated with the use of marketing and advertising in developing countries. Over-commercialization of the media may well result in the decline of local programming unless protective steps are taken. Deceptive campaigns and the promotion of undesirable or dangerous products pose potential health and other risks for Third World consumers. Additional regulatory bodies are needed to fulfill a watchdog function. It is indeed possible to limit the negative effects with planning and regulation. Scholars and researchers must continue to attempt to understand the effects of advertising in developing markets. Michael H. Anderson (1984) summarizes:

Generalizations about the precise costs and benefits that the transnational advertising agencies bring to their host nations are difficult to make. This is because nations and their development policies and patterns, problems and pressures are in a constant state of flux and are products of various interwoven factors operating within and between nations. What can be said with some certainty, however, is that the presence of the transnational advertising agencies in any Third World society *does* generate some tensions and conflict.

References

Advertising Age. (2002, November 18). Hearings on racism in South African advertising show little progress. Retrieved from the world wide web.

Ali, Syed Azwan Syed (2005, August 15). Call for TV programmes portraying Malaysian values. *Malaysian General News,* 1.

Anderson, Michael H. (1984). *Madison Avenue in Asia,* Cranbury, NJ: Associated University Press, 42.

Balu, Rekha (2002, June). Strategic innovation: Hindustan Lever. *Fast Company*, Boston, 120-136.

Bani, Eirmalasare. (1999, September 15). Ad guidelines helping local productions gain expertise. *Business Times,* Kuala Lumpur, 15.

Bettcher, Douglas and Subramaniam, Chitra. (2001, December 5). The necessity of global tobacco regulations. *Journal of the American Medical Association,* 286(21), 2737.

Brooks, David (2005, January 4) "A tale of two systems," *New York Times,* A-19.

Burtless, Gary. (2002, June), Is the global gap between rich and poor getting wider? The Brookings Institution.

Business Wire (2005, September 27). From "my generation" to "my media generation:" Yahoo! And OMD Global Study find youth love personalized media. New York, 1.

Business Wire (2005, October 27). Clear Channel mounts first-ever global outdoor advertising campaign. New York, 1.

Constantino, Renato (1986). Mass culture: Communication and development. *Philippine Journal of Communication,* 13–26, as quoted in Frith and Frith, "The Stranger at the Gate."

Consumer Association of Penang. (1986). *Selling dreams: How advertising misleads us,* Penang, Malaysia: CAP, as quoted in Katherine Toland Frith and Michael Frith, "The Stranger at the Gate: Western Advertising and Eastern Cultural Communications Values," paper presented at the International Communication Association Conference, San Francisco, 1989, 4.

Creative Review (2005, May 3). Made in Africa. London. 41.

De La Dehesa, Guillermo (2004, September 15) "Europe's social model will crumble without reform," *Financial Times,* London, 21.

Del Toro, Wanda. (1986, May 22-26). Cultural penetration in Latin America through multinational advertising agencies. Paper presented at the Annual meeting of the International Communication Association, Chicago.

EMarketer (2005, October 25). Worldwide ad spending to top$400 billion. Retrieved from the world wide web.

Euromonitor (2002). International Marketing Forecasts.

Fejes, Fred (1990, August 9-13). Multinational advertising agencies in Latin America. Paper presented at the annual meeting of the Association for Education in Journalism and Mass Communication, Boston.

Frazer, Charles (1990). Issues and evidence in international advertising. *Current Issues and Research in Advertising,* 12(1, 2), 75–90.

Freire, Paulo. (1970). *Pedagogy of the oppressed,* New York: Continuum.

Frith, Katherine Toland, and Frith, Michael (1989). Advertising as cultural invasion. *Media Asia,* 179–184.

Globalization is narrowing the poverty gap (2003.) Retrieved from the world wide web.

Hill, John S. (1984). Targeting promotions in lesser-developed countries: A study of multinational corporation strategies. *Journal of Advertising,* 13(4), 39–48.

Hill, John S., and Hill, Richard R. (1984, Summer). Effects of urbanization on multinational product planning: Markets in lesser-developed countries. *Columbia Journal of World Business,* 19, 62–67.

Hill, John S., and James, William L. (1990). Effects of selected environmental and structural factors on international advertising strategy: An exploratory study. *Current Issues and Research in Advertising,* 12 (1,2), 135-153.

Jackson, Richard (2003, Winter). The real threat to world stability, *American Outlook,* http://www.hudson.org/American_Outlook/index.cfm?fuseaction=article_detail&id=2767.

Kaynak, Erdener. (1989). *The management of international advertising: A handbook and guide for professionals,* New York: Quorum Books, 26.

Keegan, Warren J. (1984). *Multinational marketing management.* Englewood Cliffs, N.J.: Prentice Hall.

Kloss, Ingomar. (2002). *More advertising worldwide,* Berlin, Germany: Springer.

Knickerbocker, Brad (2004, January 22). If poor get riches, does world see progress? *The Christian Science Monitor,* Boston, Mass, 16.

Koenderman, Tony (1994, January 3). S. African marketers take new direction. *ADWEEK,* 16.

McGinnis, John. (1988). Advertising and social mobilization. Paper presented to the Association for Education in Journalism and Mass Communication, Portland, Oregon, 14.

Meier, Barry (1998, January 18). Tobacco industry, conciliatory in U.S., goes on the attack in the Third World. *New York Times,* 14.

Neff, Jack (2002, March 4). Submerged. *Advertising Age,* 73(9), 14.

Peron, Jim (2004, June). Antiglobalists are scarce in poor countries. *Freeman,* Irvington-on-Hudson, 54(5), 37.

Pfanner, Eric (2005, January 17). Marketers looking at Sub-Sahara on advertising. *International Herald Tribune,* Paris, 11.

Pollay, Richard W. (1986, April). The distorted mirror: Reflections on the unintended consequences of advertising. *Journal of Marketing,* 50, 18–36.

Prahalad, C. K. (2004). *The Fortune at the Bottom of the Pyramid.* Pearson PTR Publishing.

Roberts, Dexter and Webb, Alysha. (2002, June 17). Motor nation: Finally, China's middle classes can afford the family car. *Business Week,* 44-48.

Rutter, Mark (2005, October 12). Kids will power own computers: Third World students will get clockwork laptops. *The Toronto Sun,* 95.

Saporito, Bill (1993/1994, Autumn/Winter). Where the global action is. *Fortune,* Special Issue, 128(13), 63-65.

Schiller, Herbert I. (1973). *The mind managers,* Boston: Beacon Press, 129–133.

Tansey, Richard, and Hyman, Michael R. (1994, March). Dependency theory and the effects of advertising by foreign-based multinational corporations in Latin America. *Journal of Advertising,* 23(1), 27–42.

Toyne, Brian, and Walters, Peter G. P. (1989). *Global marketing management: A strategic perspective,* Boston: Allyn & Bacon, 549.

World Bank Group (2002). *World Development Indicators.* http://www.world bank. org. annualreport/2002/chap0300. htm.

Introduction to

The Reflection of Culture in Global Business and Marketing Strategy

By Marieke De Mooij

De Mooij notes that many companies apply the same marketing strategy around the world. This is, in part, due to an attempt to apply economies of scale and to be consistent. In an intercultural context, however, this may not always be a wise decision. The author points out that a company's mission and vision as well as corporate identity tend to actually reflect the values of the culture of origin of the company. Thus, most North American corporations tend to identify and outline individualistic values whereas Japanese corporations tend to refer to collectivistic values. These values are then also transferred to the brand strategy of the company. Consequently, North American companies tend to focus on the uniqueness of their brands whereas Japanese companies seek to establish trust and a link of the brand to the corporation that offers these brands.

The same divergence can be found in how products are used. This means that the same products may not only be perceived differently, but also used differently around the globe. Thus, advertising is effective when the values in the message match the values of the consumer. It is the culture of the consumer that should be reflected in advertising, not the culture of the producer De Mooij advises. So instead of being consistent, brands should be pragmatic and adapted to the cultural mindset of the consumer.

Clearly, valuable advise to businesses in an age of globalization, on the one hand, and standardization and homogenization, on the other hand.

Michael B. Hinner

Marieke De Mooij is President of the Cross Cultural Communications Company. She is a visiting professor at various universities in Europe: University of Navarra, Spain, Vaasa University, Finland, and the European University Viadrina, Germany. She is the author of several publications on the influence of culture on marketing, advertising, and consumer behavior. The titles of her major books include *Global Marketing and Advertising* and *Consumer Behavior and Culture*.

The Reflection of Culture in Global Business and Marketing Strategy[1]

Marieke De Mooij

When companies go global they often don't realize that their strategies are a product of their own culture and that they cannot turn a national strategy into a global strategy without reviewing the various elements. At the core of strategy is culture. Both mission statements and brand positioning statements appear to be culture-bound because they reflect the cultural values of a company's origin and its leaders. Any global corporate or brand strategy, to be effective, must incorporate not the values of its leaders but the values of all stake holders of the brand in all countries where the company operates, of which consumers are the most important. Already at the first levels of strategy development, a company's mission and vision, culture is involved. This article sums up the various aspects of global strategy, from a company's mission and vision to its communication strategy. Hofstede's[2] dimensions of national culture are used to explain the relationship between culture and the strategic issues.

A Company's Mission and Vision

Worldwide it is agreed that the *mission statement* is a crucial element in the strategic planning of a business organization. It is an explicit formulation of what the company stands for. In addition, the *vision* of a company states where the company wants to be some time in the future. Some companies include *strategic intent* in the vision. Vision and mission should give focus to everyone who is involved with the company, be it directly (employees) or indirectly (e.g. shareholders).

The Western origin of the mission statement concept can be recognized in the focus on uniqueness in a definition by North American author Christopher Bart:[3]

> A good mission statement captures an organization's unique and enduring reason for being, and energizes stakeholders to pursue common goals ..... It compels a firm to address questions like "What is our business? Why do we exist? What are we trying to accomplish?"

Although the concept of the mission and vision are Western inventions, the practice has been embraced by companies worldwide. It has become global management practice to provide statements expressing a company's strategic intent, its philosophy, values and ethics, or operational effectiveness. Analysis of such statements shows differences in content and form of such statements across the world. The mission statement of American companies is an abstract statement of what the company stands for, its identity. This reflects the values of an individualistic culture, where individuals grow up with the notion that they should be unique, be consistent in their attitudes and behaviour, stand out and be explicit in their communication. In collectivistic cultures individuals learn to live in harmony with others and communication is not explicit[4]. Companies function like families, and what the company stands for is not necessarily made explicit. Its content is less specific.

Any corporate mission or vision, in both form and content, reflects the worldview of its management, which usually represents the values of the culture of origin of the company.

An example of Asian *form* and *content* is formulating the company statement as a *Message from Top Management*, as on Toyota's website. The subtitle of this message forms the content: "Harmony with people, Society and the Environment."[5]

American statements tend to include hype, for example explicitly stating that a company is the best in the world, like American advertising does. This is a reflection of the values of individualistic/masculine cultures. Ford Motor Company[6] says "We anticipate consumer need and deliver outstanding products". The U.S. company DDI[7] (Data Direction Inc.) states that it "will continue to staff the finest data processing professionals available, ... use the highest standards ....., use the best design and programming techniques ....., attract and retain the best possible professionals." Microsoft's mission is "To enable people and business throughout the world to realize their full potential". This mission reflects the Anglo-Saxon value of self-actualization.

The corporate philosophy of Canon is *kyosei*, or "All people, regardless of race, religion or culture, harmoniously living and working together into the future".[8] Korean Samsung's management philosophy is "We will devote our human resources and technology to create superior products and services, thereby contributing to a better global society..... Our management philosophy represents our strong determination to contribute directly to the mutual prosperity of people all over the world. ..... We challenge the world to create the future with our customers".[9] Two elements of Toyota's *Vision 2010* – a long-term perspective that is characteristic of East-Asian cultures as opposed to the short-term orientation of most north-American companies – is to realize a large increase in the number of Toyota fans, and to be a truly global company that is trusted and respected by all peoples in the world.[10]

A global company that goes beyond universal statements and balances cultural values is Honda who says

> It is our mission to improve the lives of customers and communities where we all live, work and play. We will continue to develop and build products in local markets around the world to create value for all of our customers. Our established directions for the 21st century provide a balance of fun for the customer and responsibility for society and the environment. This is demonstrated through advanced technologies.[11]

Corporate Identity

From the vision and mission, a corporate identity can be distilled, which includes the core values of a company. This practice is also of Western origin. This is reflected in definitions of *corporate identity* that are based on the Western identity concept. The British communication consultant Nicholas Ind[12], for example, defines *corporate identity* as "an organization's identity in its *sense of self,* much like our own individual sense of identity. Consequently, it is unique." Uniqueness and consistency of corporate identity in individualistic cultures is opposed to a collectivist's identity, which can change according to varying social positions and situations. When global companies define their corporate identities they might consider to include variations for the different cultural contexts in which they operate instead of single-minded focus on consistency.

Usually the task of creating a corporate identity begins with the selection of an appropriate corporate name. Other factors that contribute to corporate identity include the logo of the organization and marketing communications. All this, including language, lettering, and associations, is logically a reflection of the home country of the organization. Many Western organizations prefer worldwide consistency of all these elements without realizing that this can be counterproductive, as not all elements are equally effective in all countries.

Some American companies in China have learned to adapt. Coca-Cola, for example has changed its name to adapt to the visual orientation of the Chinese. The company renamed its brand into 'Kokou kole', which also translates into 'happiness in the mouth'.

The basis of the western concept of corporate identity is that it should be perceived universally, but in reality it translates differently in different parts of the world.

Global Brand Strategy

Perception of a corporate identity is also dependent on the use of the company name as a corporate brand. For example, Unilever and Procter & Gamble are large companies, but hardly known to the general public because historically they have mainly marketed product brands without using their corporate name. Other companies, such as Nestlé, Heineken, Yakult, Sony, Mitsubishi, and Daewoo are world players who use their corporate name on (almost) all of their products. Some Western companies such as Heineken (Amstel, Tiger) and Nestlé (Perrier, Nestea, Kitkat), in addition to the corporate brand name, keep using other brand names of companies that they acquired. East-Asian companies tend to stick to one corporate brand name.

Until recently, Unilever has chosen not to use its corporate name on its different brands and products. The reason for this was that a scandal (such as nitrite in their Iglo's frozen foods in 1980 in the Netherlands) could easily transfer consumer scare to other Unilever products. Driven by cultural specifics of collectivistic cultures like Russia, Japan and China, Unilever has chosen to include its corporate name on all its brands. The very least that should be added to product brands in Asian advertising is the company's name. For some time, P&G in China has done so by adding a P&G signature to, for example, Head & Shoulders in TV commercials, and Nippon Lever in Japan has done so for its Japanese products. For sweet biscuits Danone uses the brand name Lu in Europe, but in Asia the corporate name Danone is also on this type of product[13]. The reason for this is the different sales process in individualistic and collectivistic cultures. Whereas the sales process is direct and based on argumentation and persuasion in individualistic cultures, in collectivistic cultures the sales process starts with building trust between seller and buyer. Also consumer decision making in collectivistic cultures is based on trust in the company and not on uniqueness of the brand. Therefore, knowing the company behind the brand is of utmost importance to consumers. Developing strong company brands is a better strategy for this purpose than developing a portfolio of competitive product brands. Therefore, few East-Asian companies carry more than one brand. Because in Asia brands are most successful if they are linked to companies with a successful image, all sorts of products that in the West would not be considered fit for use under one brand name can be linked to a company brand name in Asia. Whereas in the West, a diaper by the Japanese cosmetics company Shiseido would be judged primarily in terms of whether cosmetics and diapers go together, in Asia the image of Shiseido would provide enough justification for giving the product a try.[14]

In collectivistic cultures, people associate best with concrete product features. Consider for example, the Yakult products. In Western Europe it is sold under the name Yakult (or Yakult Light), containing specific live bacteria (the lactobacillus *casei shirota*) that are supposed to be good for your intestinal flora. Yakult has many more products (e.g. Yakult Ace 80, Yakult Bansoreicha) on the market in Japan, all of them with bacteria or other ingredients that are supposed to be good for your body. Each of the Yakult products has some specific ingredient, and Japanese consumers know very much about all these different ingredients. Moreover, they trust the Yakult Honsha Company to deliver good and beneficial products. It is Yakult they trust, and they therefore consume their products.

Global marketers need to realize that both branding and marketing theory originated in the United States. These theories reflect values of individualistic cultures. Companies should *differentiate* products and brands and *position* them vis-à-vis competing brands. A brand should be positioned as a *unique* entity with a clear *identity*, like human beings. This metaphor is not easy to understand for marketers of East Asian and other companies that originate in collectivistic cultures where *harmony* and *trust* is the basis of business.

Brand Positioning across Cultures

In Western marketing a brand position is what the brand stands for in a world of brands, what makes it unique. This position includes the associations it has in the mind of the consumer. It includes all aspects of a brand: the product attributes, consumer benefits and values. When developing brand strategies companies tend to formulate the desired brand position in a brand positioning statement.

The *brand positioning statement* links the external aspects of the brand with the internal aspects. With the description of these two aspects the most used set of terms of western branding theory are covered. The *internal* aspects of a brand are the brand elements injected into the brand by the company. They include the brand *identity* and *values* attached to the brand by which people should be able to recognize its identity. The identity is what the sender (company, organization) wants to convey about the brand, which includes the brand's characteristics in terms of *personality*.

The *external* aspects of a brand include the take-out by the consumer, its *image*, or how the consumer perceives the brand, and *usage*, or how the brand's products are used in daily life. The role of the brands and products in daily life contributes to the desired brand identity.

A brand is well positioned if there is a proper link between the external and internal aspects. This is visualized in the figure below.

Several marketing mix elements contribute to transferring the identity to an image, of which the *product* itself and the *communication* are the most visible and culturally-sensitive elements.

External Aspects: Product Usage and Brand Image

To enable the formulation of a brand identity, knowledge of the current brand image is needed as well as how consumers deal with the brand and its product(s). These are the tools of the marketer. The *image* is what a consumer sees of the brand, and how she consequently perceives and mentally integrates all messages. It is the association network in the mind of the consumer. Ideally the *image* matches the *identity*, what the sender wants to convey about the brand.

Figure 1
Elements Brand Positioning Statement

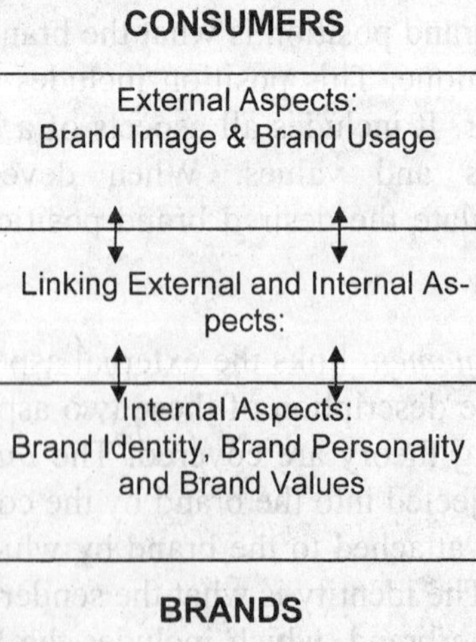

CONSUMERS

External Aspects:
Brand Image & Brand Usage

↕ ↕

Linking External and Internal Aspects:

↕ ↕

Internal Aspects:
Brand Identity, Brand Personality
and Brand Values

BRANDS

Product usage

Understanding how a global brand is perceived needs in-depth consumer research in many countries, to really understand all the situations in which the brand is used. It not only includes talking with consumers but also walking with consumers: Go into their houses, see what they are doing and how the brand fits (or could fit) their needs. For years, Western companies have been selling their irons to Japanese and Korean consumers only to discover at a very late stage that they do not iron standing up but sitting down. This obviously asks for different ergonomic requirements.

Knowledge of how a brand is perceived and how the brand's products are used is essential for defining the brand identity. In general, product usage does not change overnight although marketing and advertising people tend to think it does. People's behavior is quite stable and it is changing less than one is led to believe from the media. Much of new behavior is only a new format of existing behavior. Even new technologies find their way to consumers through already existing habits. At the start, the mobile phone penetrated fastest in countries that already had advanced telephone infrastructure.

Because people's behavior is stable, past or current behavior can often explain future behavior. When developing and marketing new products it is useful to analyze past behavior to predict the future.

When predicting product usage in developing countries, one should not expect people to copy behavior of the developed world, in particular American behavior. They may copy some behavior because it delivers social status, but after some time people will return to behavior that fits their old values. Right after World War II the Japanese adopted western clothing. At the start of the 21st century young Japanese rediscovered the kimono.

People increasingly identify with their local or regional communities. We have yet to hear anyone from a European country say to me, "I am from Europe"; they always state their nationality. Increased wealth doesn't lead to convergence of behavior across cultures. The wealthier countries become, the more manifest is the influence of culture on consumption and consumer behavior. Neither wealth nor new technology produces "new values." In post-scarcity societies "old" values become manifest in consumption and consumer behavior. More discretionary income gives people more freedom to express themselves, and that expression will be based in part on their national value system. Wealth brings choice. It enables people to choose leisure time or buy status products or devote free time to self-education. These choices are historically and culturally defined. The more money people possess, the easier it is for them to stick to or refine their culturally determined behavior. People will select brands that comply with this cultural behavior. This means that the brand position should be multifaceted because a brand will mean something else to a Portuguese woman than a Vietnamese man.

Brand Image

Brand image is the representation of the brand in the mind of the consumer. In Western cultures, the image can be like a human being with unique characteristics. In collectivistic cultures it can be the quality of the product and the representation of trust in a supplier - the product is part of a trusted family of products.

Ideally, the brand identity, the values the marketer puts into the brand, should be reflected in the image, which is the take-out of the consumer. Within cultures discrepancies between identity and image occur, but across cultures the gap between identity and image is likely to be wider. Many marketing research agencies offer positioning models that help define brands in terms of human personality traits or values that are suggested to be universal, but the characteristics of their own culture often can be recognized in the descriptions.

Consumers are driven by their own cultural values. They will attribute to the brand characteristics that fit their own mental maps and from there develop a brand image. This does not necessarily reflect the intended brand identity. So what is in the mind of the consumer, the brand image, is not necessarily the same as the brand characteristics the marketer uses to build the brand identity. Many global brands that desire a consistent brand identity and hope this will result in a consistent brand image end up with different brand images across cultures. Findings from a brand value study[15] of 2003 show that consumers of different cultures attribute different, culturally relevant brand characteristics to strong global brands. Successful global brands like Coca-Cola are viewed as *trustworthy* in high uncertainty avoidance cultures, where people want to reduce anxiety; as *prestigious* in high power distance cultures, where people need status symbols; and as *different* in low uncertainty avoidance cultures where people like change. The cause of success of many global brands has not been global advertising, but continuous innovation and intensive distribution. Coca-Cola was already a global brand when they started their global advertising. Many successful global brands are old. They have become part of daily life of consumers and as a result consumers attribute their own local values to these brands that are culturally relevant to them, although the companies have different brand identities in their own mind.

Internal Aspects: Brand Identity & Personality and Brand values

The internal aspects are the brand characteristics that the company inserts into the brand by advertising or other means of communication. Western global companies try to inject personality characteristics and values that are consistent across target groups and across countries. The innate need for consistency makes Western global companies want to develop consistent global strategies that are not necessarily equally successful in all countries.

In national segmentation studies, brands often appear to have different meanings for different target groups or subcultures. The same approach should be applied to international segmentation. Different brand values can be selected for different cultures. As long as the brand values selected for international exposure are not contradicting with the brand values used in specific countries, several may well exist next to each other. In a similar way, it should be possible to develop an international, but locally culturally relevant brand identity. After all, how many consumers notice that a brand is communicating different values in different countries? The only consumers who do are probably your own employees.

Brand Identity and Personality

What has been said regarding corporate identity also pertains to brand identity. The western wish to develop a consistent brand identity leads toward labeling the brand personality with concepts that may mean different things in different languages or cultures. Instead, a better option is to find what is meaningful with respect to the brand and its role in people's lives in different cultures and to load the brand with different core values, even though the product may be the same worldwide. International brands succeed when consumers in each market believe they are being spoken to by somebody who understands them, somebody who knows their needs and who talks and feels just as they do[16]. In cultures in which trust in the company and long-term relationships between consumers and companies are important, focus on the company brand will be a more effective strategy than developing strong product brands. Corporate branding and endorsement strategies will be more effective in Asian markets than a product-brand approach of strongly positioned brand values. On the other hand, now that Asian products are increasingly entering Western markets, Asian companies may do better in Western markets by developing more differentiated product brands.

Because personal traits vary across cultures personality descriptors for brand positioning across cultures will not lead to equal success in all countries. *First,* there are culture-specific personality dimensions, such as Ruggedness in the

United States and Peacefulness in Japan[17]. Brand personalities fitting in such indigenous dimensions are not likely to be as successful in other countries as they are in the home country. The Crocus study found that a brand characteristic like "friendly" is most attributed to strong brands in individualistic and low power distance cultures. "Trustworthy" was most attributed to strong brands in high uncertainty avoidance cultures. *Second,* similar trait labels can have different associations, so the meaning of seemingly similar trait descriptions can be very different. This poses a problem when brand personality traits are used for global brand positioning and particularly when they are used as a basis for marketing communications concepts.

Brand Values

Brand communication tends to be at three levels: Product attributes, consumer benefits and values. Many international companies want to go beyond presenting product attributes or benefits, and add values to the product to position the brand in the mind of the consumer. In particular Anglo-American companies have propagated this approach to global advertising because of their belief in universal, global values. Thus, *happiness* is used to sell fast food, *success* to sell cars or wristwatch brands, *unlimited human potential* ('just do it') to sell running shoes and *freedom* to sell jeans. Such values are not of equal importance to all cultures which makes such global advertising messages more effective in some cultures than in others.

Many global advertising campaigns of American origin reflect American values. Levi's, for example, focused on freedom (of movement) in international advertising. One commercial showed two people running fast, as if in competition. The take-out of Spanish viewers was competition (which they don't like), not freedom.

One of the reasons for desired cross-cultural consistency in global branding strategies is the need for *control.* Companies want to be sure that their brand values are consistently similar across countries. Usually these are the brand values that fit their own culture. If consumers elsewhere perceive these global brands as having different values than the company intended, the process is *out of control,* and to keep control, it may be better to define specific brand characteristics (values, traits) for each of the cultures where the company operates.

The lesson of all this is that a company that wants to work globally should consider the culture-specifics of its brands. When formulating a brand identity, be aware that Asian consumers are not so interested in an abstract brand identity or personality. They are more interested in what a company stands for, how reliable it is. A global company should align its corporate and brand identity in a way that both North Europeans/Americans (brand identity) and Asians (corporate identity) can be addressed.

Global Advertising Strategy and Stage of Market Development

The ideal of global companies is global, standardized advertising because of the benefits of economies of scale. However, what they gain by economies of scale is lost by loss of effectiveness.

Advertising is effective when the values in the message match the values of the receiver. It is the culture of the consumer that should be reflected in advertising, not the culture of the producer. Analysis of advertisements in international media such as *Newsweek, Business Week,* and CNN shows that, in reality, international advertisers target international audiences with their home country's value system. Thus, the full potential of cross-border media is not used.

For a long time international advertising strategists in the United States have thought that emotional or "feeling" appeals would travel better than "thinking" appeals because of the assumed universality of human values. Thus, much standardized international advertising has included appeals like happiness and love. Analysis of international advertising shows that this practice of using values in global advertising is mainly a US practice. European companies focus more on innovative product attributes that are communicated in a culturally relevant way.

Only when introducing a new product with product attributes that are innovative, appealing and distinct, standardized advertising can be effective. Such products are rare and they will not remain new and distinctive for a long time as competition will be quickly introducing similar products. Soon after introduction of new products, successful further penetration will depend on the products ability to satisfy the different needs and motives of consumers in different cultures. Knowledge of these differences helps to structure global marketing-communications programs.

Conclusion

One standard strategy has been assumed to reduce costs because of economies of scale. However, what is gained by cost reduction is lost by loss of effectiveness. Consistency in presentation is another frequently heard argument for standardization. This reflects a western frame of mind that is not shared glob ally. If you want to reach consumers in different parts of the world speak to them in a way they understand.

The new paradigm is cultural segmentation - defining markets based on their cultural specifics and developing culture-fit strategies. A strong corporate identity can go together with cultural sensitivity. Instead of being consistent, brands should be pragmatic and adapt to the cultural mindsets of consumers. This will be the future of global strategy.

Endnotes

[1] The content of this article is based on the final chapter of my book *Global Marketing and Advertising, Understanding Cultural Paradoxes*, second edition. Sage Publications, USA. 2005

[2] Hofstede, G. (2001) *Culture's Consequences*, second edition. Thousand Oaks, Sage Publications.

Hofstede distinguishes five dimensions of national culture: power distance (PDI), individualism/collectivism (IDV), masculinity/femininity (MAS), uncertainty avoidance (UAI) and long-term orientation (LTO). For those who are unfamiliar with the model, a short description follows of the five dimensions. *Power Distance* is the extent to which less powerful members of a society accept that power is distributed unequally. In large power-distance cultures (e.g. France, Belgium, Portugal, Poland) everybody has his/her rightful place in society and status to demonstrate this position is more important than in cultures of small power distance (e.g. Great Britain, Germany, the Netherlands and Scandinavia). In *individualistic* cultures people look after themselves and their immediate family only; in *collectivistic* cultures people belong to in-groups who look after them in exchange for loyalty. In individualist cultures people want to differentiate themselves from others, they develop unique personalities. In collectivist cultures the need for harmony makes people want to conform to others. Americans and North-Europeans are individualists, in the South of Europe people are moderately collectivistic. All of Asia, South-America and Africa is collectivistic. In *masculine* cultures the dominant values are achievement and success. The dominant values in *feminine* cultures are caring for others and quality of life. In masculine cultures performance and achievement are important. Status is important to show success. Feminine cultures have a people orientation, small is beautiful and status is not so important. Examples of masculine cultures are the US, Great Britain, Germany and Italy. Examples of feminine cultures are the Netherlands, the Scandinavian countries, Portugal and Spain. *Uncertainty avoidance* is the extent to which people feel threatened by uncertainty and ambiguity and try to avoid these situations. In cultures of strong uncertainty avoidance, there is a need for rules and formality to structure life. In weak uncertainty avoidance cultures people tend to be more innovative and entrepreneurial. The countries of South and East-Europe score high on uncertainty avoidance, England and Scandinavia low. *Long Term Orientation* versus *Short Term Orientation*. This fifth dimension distinguishes long-term thinking versus short-term thinking. Other elements are pragmatism, perseverance and thrift. This dimension distinguishes mainly between Western and East Asian cultures.

[3]Bart, Christopher (1998) Mission Matters. *The CPA Journal* (8) 56-57 www.web1.infotrac.galegroup.com

[4]De Mooij, M. (2003). *Consumer Behavior and Culture: Consequences for Global Marketing and Advertising*. Thousand Oaks, CA: Sage

[5]www.toyota.co.jp/en/about_toyota/message/index.htm. Downloaded August 3, 2004

[6]www.ford.com   August 3, 2004

[7]www.data-directions.com   August 3, 2004

[8]www.canon.com   August 8, 2004

[9]www.samsung.com   August 8, 2004

[10]www.toyota.co.jp   August 3, 2004

[11]www.hondacorporate.com   August 3, 2004

[12]Ind, Nicholas. (1992) *The corporate image. Strategies for effective identity programmes*. London: Kogan Page

[13]A C Nielsen. Global Mega Brand Franchise. Extending brands within a global marketplace. www.acnielsen.com/download/html/Global_Mega_Brand_Franchises.htm. Downloaded June 25, 2004

[14]Schmitt, Bernd H. and Pan, Yigang. (1994) Managing corporate and brand identities in the Asia-Pacific region. *California Management Review,* 36. pp. 32–48.

[15]The Crocus (Cross-Cultural Solutions) study was conducted by the advertising agency Interpartners and the market research agency Euronet, is a cross-cultural study that measures brand value (called *brand pull*), and provides a cultural explanation of strong or weak brand value in different countries. It was conducted in 2003 among Internet users in 17 countries: The US, Turkey, Russia and Ukraine as well as 13 Western-European countries. A set of value questions was combined with questions that measure consumers' relationships with brands as well as buying intentions and brand characteristics attributed to a large number of brands, both local and global. Factor analysis of the data resulting from the value questions delivered four robust and meaningful cultural factors explaining differences in consumer relations with international brands across countries. These factors are related to Hofstede's dimensions.

[16] Anholt, S. (2000). *Another one bites the grass: Making sense of international advertising*. New York: Wiley.

[17]Aaker, Jennifer Lynn; Benet-Martínez, Verónica; and Garolera, Jordi. (2001) Consumption symbols as carriers of culture: A study of Japanese and Spanish

brand personality constructs. *Journal of Personality and Social Psychology,* 81. pp. 492–508.

Introduction to Visual Advertising across Cultures

By Paul Messaris

Messaris takes a closer look at visual advertising in a global context to determine whether cultural differences influence the interpretation and evaluation of messages. The world of advertising seems to be split on the issue whether visual images are universal or culturally embedded. This is, obviously, a very interesting and important issue that could have serious consequences for all international ad campaigns.

Messaris notes that some ad campaigns have proven to be quite successful around the world for many years. Yet some scholars still insist that the conventions of pictorial representations are culture bound. The question, therefore, is whether some images might convey no meaning whatsoever to people of different cultures. But here, evidence is quite consistent that all images convey some meaning to everyone. So the next question is whether that meaning is the same across cultures. By selecting a very American image, the flag raising on Iwo Jima during World War II, in an ad for a movie about a very uniquely American institution, spring break in college, Messaris is able to demonstrate that even though foreign students could not identify the flag raising allusion to the real historical event, neither could the American students. Thus, demonstrating that the image itself can still convey a meaning even if the viewer is not able to identify the real event to which the allusion is made. It was likewise possible for foreign students to grasp the general idea being conveyed by the reference to the spring break even though they were not familiar with the American college ritual. It would seem that visual references to specific images can make an ad difficult to understand when it is exported to another culture. However, this difficulty is often counterbalanced by other factors such as the cross-cultural experience of Hollywood cinema which has paved the way for a common international visual culture.

Messaris also points out that most studies on cross-cultural advertising have often focused exclusively on the content of ads, without analyzing the viewers' responses. So if there is a negative response to an ad, it might actually be that the viewers are responding to the association that may be made to the country of origin of the ad instead of comprehending the intended message. In other words, Muslim viewers may be upset about an ad depicting pork or alcohol, but this does not mean they do not know what pork or alcohol is. They may in actual fact be upset about the American company that is so insensitive as to include pork and alcohol in its ad despite the fact that Muslims are forbidden from eating or drinking it.

So even though there are barriers to the cross-cultural reception of advertising images, these factors are often mitigated by countervailing circumstances so that someone will be able to understand the images even if that someone is unfamiliar with the original context. Modern technology has made the sharing of visual images possible. Receptivity to images from other cultures can also be possible even if the viewer identifies beliefs that are different from his or her home culture – demonstrating that people can correctly identify different beliefs and emotions.

Michael B. Hinner

Paul Messaris is the Lev Kuleshov Professor of Communication at the Annenberg School for Communication, University of Pennsylvania. He teaches and does research in the areas of visual communication and digital media. His publications have dealt with viewers' interpretations of images (*Visual 'Literacy': Image, Mind, and Reality*, winner of the National Communication Association's Diamond Anniversary Book Award in 1996); viewers' responses to the formal devices of advertising and other types of visual persuasion or manipulation (*Visual Persuasion: The Use of Images in Advertising*, 1998); and ways in which the media have been affected by the advent of computers (*Digital Media: Transformations in Human Communication*, 2006, co-edited with Lee Humphreys). His most recent research deals with digital special effects in fiction film, and he is working on a book about viewers' reactions to the style and content of movies.

Visual Advertising across Cultures

Paul Messaris

In thinking about the role of images in cross-cultural advertising, a useful starting point is the concept of "iconicity." In the vocabulary of communications theory, a mode of communication can be termed "iconic" if there is an analogical relationship between its constituent signs or symbols and the things that they represent (Sebeok, 2001; see also Peirce, 1991). For example, in the case of verbal onomatopoeia, a word contains an analogy to a real-world sound. In music, it can be argued that certain compositions – such as classical "program music" – contain analogies to human moods or emotions. However, the mode of communication that is most pervasively characterized by iconicity is pictorial communication. Indeed, iconicity is one of the defining aspects of visual images. Even relatively "unrealistic" images such as stick figures or cartoons are based on some degree of analogy to the visible structure of real-world objects and spaces.

If images can bring us closer to the appearance of reality than other communicational modes can, are they also an effective means of communicating across cultural boundaries? Does the iconicity of visual communication make it a vehicle for the sharing of meaning between people who are separated by linguistic or cultural differences? These are increasingly important questions in the world of advertising. Because of the growing globalization of economic activity, commercial advertising is directed to an ever greater variety of linguistic and cultural communities. Among advertisers as well as researchers, this situation has led to a recurring concern about the degree to which it is necessary to tailor advertising messages to the characteristics of each specific community. Should different ads be produced for different languages and cultures, or can pictures be relied upon to transcend such differences?

Paul Messaris, Chapter 3: Can Pictures Bridge Cultures, In *Visual Persuasion: The Role of Images in Advertising*, Reprinted by permission of Sage Publications Inc. and of the author.

Advertising across Cultures

In a survey of long-term trends affecting the foreseeable future, Hamish McRae argued that "The single greatest change in the world economy since the Second World War has been the extent to which it has gone international" (McRae, 1994, p. 141). Indeed, it has been estimated that, in the second half of the twentieth century, the dollar value of world trade increased by a factor of 90 (Gabel & Bruner, 2003, p. 12). Accordingly, advertising that crosses national boundaries is not a new development. Products such as Coca-Cola have been marketed internationally since before the Second World War (Quelch & Hoff, 1986, p. 59), and discussions of the feasibility of standardized international campaigns have been appearing in scholarly journals for several decades (e.g., Dunn, 1966; Elinder, 1965; Fatt, 1967; Hill & Shao, 1994; Lorimer & Dunn, 1967; Rosenthal, 1994). Increasingly, advertisers have come to see their target audience as spanning entire regions -- e.g., east Asia (Babyak, 1995; Javalgi et al., 1994) or western Europe (Halliburton & Huenenberg, 1993) -- or, indeed, the entire globe. More than twnty years ago, a prominent observer of these trends was arguing that "Companies must learn to operate as if the world were one large market -- ignoring superficial regional and national differences" (Levitt, 1983, p. 92).

In response to these imperatives, a number of writers have argued that advertisers need to place greater emphasis on the visual aspects of ads. In an article subtitled "To globalize, visualize," Kernan & Domzal (1993) claim that "effective global ads are never predominantly verbal" because "Anyone can interpret a visual execution" of an advertising theme, whereas "a verbal ad requires that the consumer understand the language in which it is written and, if the ad is ambiguous, the subtleties of that language as well" (p. 55). Similarly, Bourgery & Guimaraes (1993) make the following point:

> Advertising agencies today are trying to create a "visual esperanto": a universal language that will make global advertising possible for virtually any product or service. The new visual esperanto is based on the idea that visual imagery is more powerful and precise than verbal description (which leaves too much room for personal interpretation). Moreover, all people can comprehend the messages of visual imagery (p. 24).

But the central premise of these statements -- the idea that anyone can understand a picture -- is not without controversy. Academic writers have long insisted that the conventions of pictorial representation are culture-bound (Scott, 1990), and critics of international advertising can point to a variety of visual campaigns that did not travel very well from one culture to another. Arguing that "There are significant cultural differences in pictorial perception," de Mooij cites a Korean ad for LG which uses a fish to symbolize prosperity. As she points out, the significance of this symbol "is not understood in most of the Western world" (de Mooij, 2005, p. 47). Similarly, in their early, groundbreaking catalog of failures in cross-cultural advertising, Ricks et al. (1974) note that a picture of the emperor Nero in an Italian lipstick ad "struck no accord" when it was shown to Japanese consumers because "Nero was alien to them," while Exxon's famous tiger "failed to elicit favorable reaction in Thailand" where tigers are "simply not symbols of power and strength" (p.49). As a result of such concerns, advertisers have become cautious about standardization in their international campaigns. Since the 1980s, the proportion of "fully standardized" campaigns has fallen to a low of 10 percent, while the majority of international campaigns are now blends of both standardized and localized elements (Jones, 2000, p. 5). As one advertising consultant has put it, "Ads that are shoehorned into an alien environment really do no one any favors" (White, 2000, p. 39). More starkly, the director of a Russian advertising agency once said that certain "Western" TV commercials "would be incomprehensible for us" (quoted in Wells, 1994, p. 89), while an academic analysis warned that an excessive dedication to standardized global advertising is "not unlike being dedicated to committing economic suicide" (Onkvisit & Shaw, 1990, p. 110).

In addressing the theoretical issues raised by these arguments, it will be useful to distinguish between three different ways in which cross-cultural visual advertising could possibly go awry. First of all, it is conceivable -- in principle, at least -- that members of a culture to which an ad is exported might actually find the ad's images completely meaningless. In other words, in this situation we would be dealing with an inability to perform the fundamental mental act of connecting the shapes on a page or TV screen to real-world objects. If, as some academic writers have assumed (e.g., Goodman, 1976), pictures were a language that had to be learned just as much as any verbal language does, then we should certainly expect images to mean nothing to viewers who were not familiar with the particular representational conventions through which those images were created. Although variants of this hypothesis are not uncommon in the academic world, this type of misinterpretation is not something that advertisers are concerned about (or even aware of), partly because a base-level exposure to a common stock of visual media can probably be taken for granted in almost any culture today (Crane, 2002; Lull, 1995; Olson, 1999; Perlmutter, 2006; White, 2005). More importantly, there is considerable scholarly evidence that the iconicity of visual images makes them a relatively unproblematic medium for cross-cultural communication about the surface appearance of reality – i.e., what things look like, as opposed to what their underlying cultural significance might be (cf. Hecht et al., 2003). Accordingly, our discussion of potential problems in cross-cultural advertising will look elsewhere. We will consider two possibilities: on the one hand, a viewer might correctly perceive the contents of an image (people, objects, places) but misinterpret the intended cultural implications of those contents; on the other hand, a viewer might be aware of the cultural implications but unresponsive to the values behind them.

Cultural Allusions in Images

What kind of advertisement might lead to the former of these two potential scenarios? Consider a print ad for the film *Spring Break,* a 1983 Columbia production (Figure 1) . The ad portrays a group of young men raising a flag with the film's name on it. From that name and their appearance, the viewer may be able to infer that they are vacationing college students. They are standing on – and planting the flag in -- a bikini-clad woman's thigh (depicted on a much larger scale than they are). This picture is a visual parody. The men's poses and the position of the flag are based on a celebrated image from the Second World War, Joe Rosenthal's photograph of U.S. troops raising the Stars and Stripes on their way to victory during the battle of Iwo Jima. This photograph later became the model for a monumental statue honoring the U.S. Marine Corps at Arlington National Cemetary, and it has been the subject of numerous parodies both before and after its use in the *Spring Break* ad. For example, on the cover of the March 2006 issue of *Digit*, a magazine devoted to "The Future of Digital Design," a group of soldiers struggle to raise a flag bearing the initials "DR," symbolic of the magazine's cover story on "The Design Revolution."

In the context of American visual media, the cultural references of the *Spring Break* ad and other such parodies are anything but abstruse. However, it is easy to imagine a viewer from another country missing some of those references. Although the Iwo Jima flag-raising has occasionally been featured in movies or other media with an international audience (as, indeed, is the case with *Digit*, which is a British publication), its status as a recurring symbol is associated more narrowly with the U.S. furthermore, the concept of spring break as major party time is also distinctively American, although it may of course have equivalents in other parts of the world. So a viewer from outside the U.S. might well find the ad's meaning somewhat opaque, and this example would certainly seem to support the views of those writers who are skeptical about the viability of cross-cultural advertising.

But it is important not to overstate the case here. True, the *Spring Break* ad does contain layers of meaning that our hypothetical non-American viewer might not share. But this observation begs the question of how broadly those layers of meaning are shared by viewers within the United States itself (cf. Peebles, 1989). Even if we assume that the significance of spring break looms as large in the minds of all Americans as it does in those of some college students, when it comes to the Iwo Jima image things are very different. In a test of visual-culture knowledge conducted with a class of 29 undergraduates (Messaris, 1994, pp. 179-180), only 14 students were able to give even an approximate place and time (e.g., a World War II battle) for Joe Rosenthal's original photograph of the flag raising. Others mentioned Vietnam, Korea, and even the American Civil War. Recognition rates were similarly low among U.S.-born graduate students in visual communication, some of whom placed the flag raising as far back as the American Revolution or the War of 1812.

Furthermore, almost none of these students had any detailed knowledge about the actual circumstances memorialized in Rosenthal's photograph. Historians commonly describe Iwo Jima as one of the most horrific battles ever fought by U.S. troops, a relentless 36-day ordeal in which 6,821 marines were killed, 19,217 were wounded, and some 20,000 Japanese lost their lives, many of the latter being buried alive in underground tunnels or incinerated by flamethrowers (Ross, 1985; Wheeler, 1980). It is hard to believe that anyone familiar with such details could find the *Spring Break* ad amusing -- or, indeed, could have designed such an ad in the first place. Of course, it might be objected that these historical circumstances are irrelevant to the ad's meaning. But that is precisely the point. What this ad demonstrates is that the *intended* cultural references in advertising are often relatively shallow. There may be a gap in relevant cultural knowledge between viewers in an ad's country of origin and their counterparts in other places, but in many, if not most, cases that gap is not very profound.

These words of caution should be kept in mind as we proceed with our examination of cross-cultural interpretations of advertising. As we have just seen, the cultural knowledge required for the interpretation of an ad can involve both specific images (such as the Iwo Jima flag raising) and more diffuse cultural practices (such as the rituals of spring break). This is not always a hard-and-fast distinction, but it provides a convenient framework for thinking about the potential sources of cross-cultural misunderstandings of visual advertising. When an ad incorporates an allusion to, or replica of, a specific earlier image, a viewer's ability to comprehend that part of the ad's message can only come from previous media experience. However, references to more general cultural practices may make sense to viewers from other countries purely on the basis of cross-cultural parallels, without any prior exposure to the originating country's media or way of life. Because of this difference, we will discuss these two aspects of cultural content separately.

Figure 1

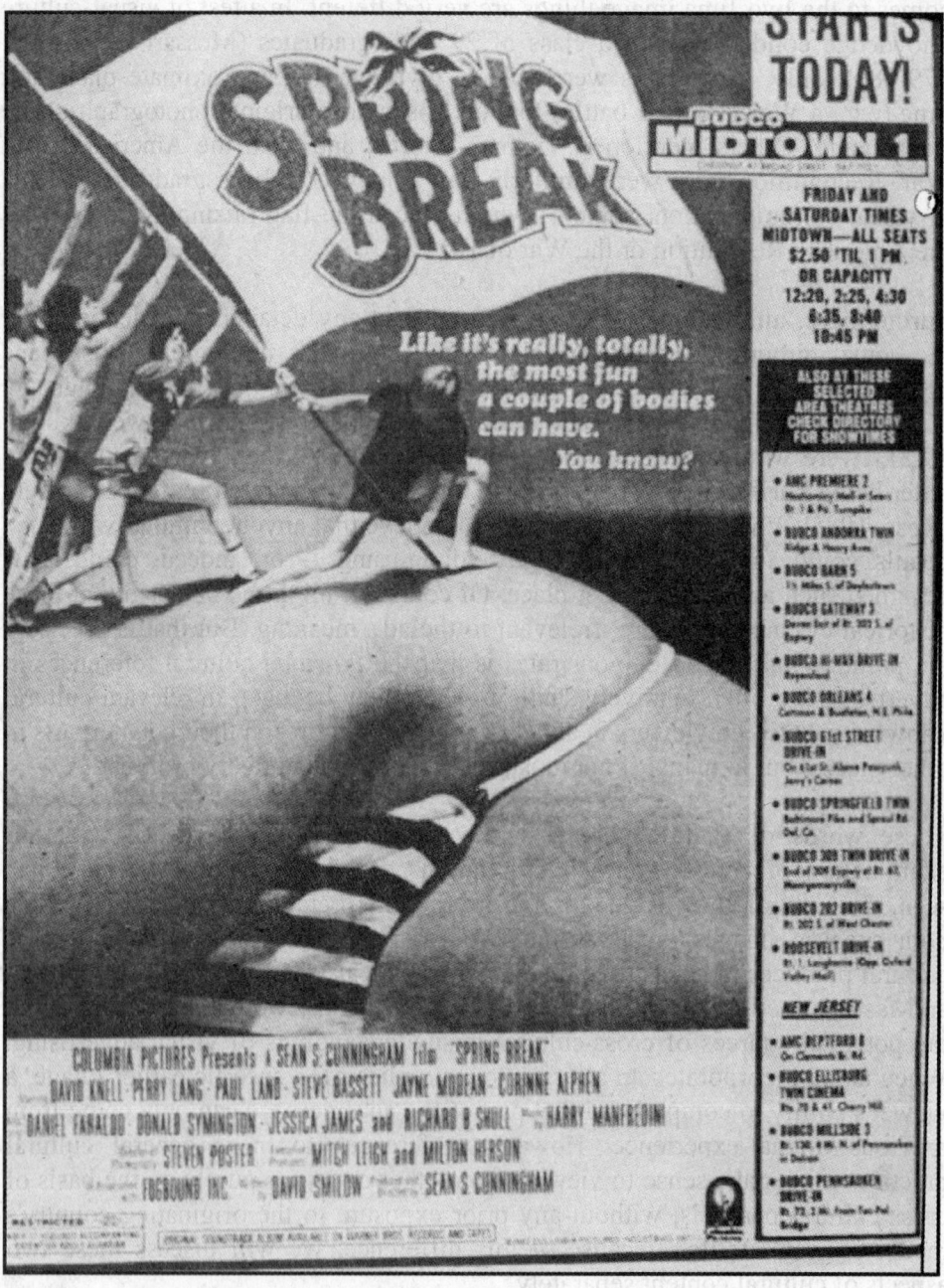

Allusions to Specific Images

In addition to testing students' knowledge of Joe Rosenthal's Iwo Jima photograph, the study mentioned above also assessed their familiarity with two classic American images that were presented in the form of advertising parodies: James McNeill Whistler's "Arrangement in Grey and Black, No. 1" (commonly referred to as "Whistler's Mother") and Saul Steinberg's *New Yorker* magazine cover in which radically diminishing perspective is used to give a Manhattanite's view of the rest of the country. In the parodies that were used in this study, the former image appeared in a newspaper advertisement for a department-store sale under the caption "A sale to make a mother whistle" (Figure 2), while the latter served as the template for a magazine ad about business opportunities in Pewaukee, Wisconsin (Figure 3).

Figure 2

With regard to the parody of Whistler's mother, the students were asked "Who is this?" (in a written questionnaire). In the case of the Pewaukee ad, the question was "What's the city in the original version of this picture?"

The study included a group of 12 international graduate students, who were tested in tandem with 23 grad students born in the U.S. Only two of the inter-

Figure 3

national students were able to name Whistler's mother, and three knew that New York was the city in the original version of the Pewaukee image. (Likewise, only two had recognized the Iwo Jima flag raising.) These numbers may appear to offer an unambiguous demonstration of the potential interpretational obstacles faced by advertising when it crosses cultural boundaries. Both the Whistler painting and the *New Yorker* cover are subjects of frequent parodies in the U.S., and yet these highly educated international students were evidently almost completely unfamiliar with either of the original images. Once again, though, one should be cautious in one's interpretation of these facts. As it happens, substantial numbers of the U.S.-born students (seven and ten, respectively) were also unable to identify these two images.

As in the *Spring Break* case, then, these additional numbers remind us that, when it comes to specific images, advertisers cannot take viewers' knowledge for granted even in the cultures from which those images originated, no matter how widely the images may have been reproduced. Of course, some kinds of ads deliberately use images that only a limited segment of the population can be expected to recognize. This practice is particularly common in advertising that incorporates references to high-art imagery in order to convey a sense of superior status. But when ads are addressed to a wider audience, the ability to make visual references that viewers can actually grasp will always be threatened by the fragmentary nature of visual culture and by the speed with which succeeding generations lose sight of the cultural imagery of the past.

Since advertisers are well aware of these circumstances, ads that borrow previously existing images are often designed to make some sense even to viewers who are not aware of the visual reference. This principle is clearly at work in an ad for Kennedy Funding, a commercial real-estate lending company specializing in "bridge loans" (i.e., short-term loans that allow borrowers to "bridge the gap" until permanent financing is secured). The ad's tagline reads, "WHEN YOU'RE UP AGAINST THE CLOCK YOU CAN GET MILLIONS FAST." These words appear over a photograph of a man dangling precariously from the hands of a clock on the side of a tall building, high above a city street (Figure 4). Fans of silent cinema will recognize the ineffable Harold Lloyd in a scene from *Safety Last* (1927). Much of that film is taken up by Lloyd's gravity-defying stunts as he climbs up the outside of a building, and the image used in the ad comes from the culminating moments of this scene. So, for someone who has seen the movie, the ad serves as a trigger for a host of hair-raising memories, and those memories undoubtedly increase the ad's impact. At the same time, though, the ad's picture of Lloyd is surely an arresting image in its own right. A viewer who had never heard of Harold Lloyd or seen *Safety Last* could still find

Figure 4

the ad enjoyable and should certainly be able to get the ad's point, since the relationship between the headline and the picture does not depend on any knowledge of the picture's source. Consequently, we can also imagine an image such as this crossing cultural boundaries with ease.

In fact, even though this image comes from a quintessentially American movie, it may seem strange to refer to it as an example of American visual culture. Unlike most photographs or paintings produced in the United States, Hollywood movies have achieved a certain universality, even when they deal with American society and American themes (Olson, 1999). To put it differently: In most parts of the world, there is already a substantial transplanted visual culture composed of Hollywood movies. A particularly telling demonstration of this point occurred in a political campaign poster that appeared in Warsaw on June 4, 1989, the day of the elections that signalled Poland's transition from communism to democracy (Weschler, 1989, p. 66) (Figure 5). Against a backdrop of the word "Solidarity," we see a tall man in Western garb striding confidently toward us. In place of a gun he is holding a ballot. Except for that metaphorical substitution, this is a picture straight out of another Hollywood movie, *High Noon* (1952), and the man is the classic Western star, Gary Cooper. Evidently, the image of the Westerner was as potent a symbol of freedom in post-communist Poland as it is in the United States.

So, more generally, this example adds a further complication to our evolving view of the limitations of cross-cultural advertising. In principle, visual references to specific images, such as the Iwo Jima flag-raising, can make an ad difficult to understand when it is exported to another culture. In practice, however, this kind of difficulty is often counterbalanced by other factors. Ads that focus mainly on the surface meanings of borrowed images, as in the case of our *Safety Last* example, can appeal to viewers regardless of any previous knowledge of those images. But even when previous knowledge does make a difference, as in Solidarity's Gary Cooper poster, that knowledge can often come from the cross-cultural experience of Hollywood cinema, which has paved the way for a substantially common international visual culture.

Allusions to General Cultural Practices

Hollywood cinema and television can also provide a basis for cross-cultural interpretation of American ads that make references to more diffuse cultural practices or values, as opposed to specific images. For instance, international viewers who had seen such earlier Hollywood movies as *National Lampoon's Animal House* (1978) or *Porky's* (1982) would presumably have been in a better

Figure 5

position to understand the values expressed in the ad for *Spring Break*, which appeared in 1983. Of course, being able to understand a certain set of values does not mean that one shares them, but that observation is as true of American viewers as of people in other countries. Indeed, it could even be argued that American movies and TV programs provide international viewers with an especially appropriate background for the understanding of American advertising, because the portrait of American culture that ads are based on is much closer to the fabrications of Hollywood than to the actual way of life of real Americans. But what about viewers who are not familiar with American media and are being exposed to American advertising for the first time?

Although such viewers might not be able to make much sense of references to specific images, their ability to interpret more general cultural depictions cannot be ruled out a priori. In the absence of either first-hand or mediated experience, a person may still be able to form an intuitive understanding of selected aspects of an unfamiliar culture through extrapolation from the known features of familiar ones.

In an attempt to address this topic, Anne Dumas (1988) performed a study with two groups of graduate students attending a university in the United States. One group consisted of students who had grown up in China and were recent arrivals in the U.S. The other group consisted of U.S.-born students. The time frame of this study – the late 1980s – is significant. At that time, students coming to the U.S. from China were still relatively unfamiliar with American mass media. Consequently, while the Chinese students in Dumas's study were certainly not first-time viewers of American advertising, their previous experience was quite limited compared with that of the U.S.-born group. The participants in the study were all interviewed individually regarding their responses to a set of print ads taken from American magazines. Each ad was initially shown with all text and other product information masked, in order to assess the viewer's interpretation of the image by itself.

The students' responses to these images were open-ended and were presented by Dumas in considerable detail, but for our purposes the following general findings stand out. To begin with, the Chinese respondents made it clear that they found most of the social situations depicted in the ads culturally remote from their own experiences. Their interpretations of these social situations were explicitly based on conjectures, rather than immediate recognition of familiar circumstances. It turned out, though, that these conjectures often coincided with the interpretations of the American respondents. In particular, the Chinese students' guesses about family relationships (or their absence) were generally similar to the guesses of the U.S.-born students. On the other hand, the one as-

Figure 6

pect of the ads that the Chinese respondents were consistently unable to interpret along American lines was the display of social status.

One of the clearest examples of an image that appeared culturally alien to the Chinese was an ad for Bulova watches (Figure 6). The ad portrays a tight embrace between a man in a military uniform and a woman. The text, which was withheld from the respondents until the end of the interview, explained that this was a homecoming scene from the Vietnam War era and that the man's watch had been a parting gift. This image drew immediate and warm praise from most of the U.S.-born students, who lauded its emotional power and its authenticity (e.g., "it really shows a moment of reality," "it's very genuine, I can believe it"). Among the Chinese, however, the first reactions were very different. Virtually all of them expressed some form of puzzlement or difficulty in making sense of what they were seeing (e.g., "it's hard to see what's happening," "it's hard to understand who is what"). And yet, despite this sharp discrepancy in the initial responses, the Chinese students' interpretations of what was going on in the image were closely parallel to the interpretations of their U.S.-born counterparts. Both groups were much more likely to view the scene as a homecoming than as a departure (a judgment that was subsequently confirmed by the text), and both groups were evenly divided in seeing the woman (whose face was hidden from the viewer) as either a mother or a wife/lover. Dumas noted that the percentages for these various responses were just about identical in the two groups (p. 46).

If the Chinese students' view of what was actually happening in the image was not substantially different from the view of their American counterparts, what are we to make of their initial statements of puzzlement or confusion? The students themselves provided the answer to this question. In part, what they were reacting to was the fact that the faces of the people in the image were not clearly visible, something that no U.S.-born viewer complained about. But the need to see the faces may have been largely symptomatic of a more fundamental lack of familiarity with the situation depicted in the image. In particular, what evidently seemed remote from the experiences of many of the Chinese viewers was the image's open, very physical display of emotion. As one viewer put it,

> Chinese people wouldn't express their feeling like this, they're very quiet people. Until maybe five or even two years ago, nobody could have done that. (quoted in Dumas, 1988, p. 49)

This kind of response to emotional expression was a recurring theme in the Chinese students' interviews, and the Bulova ad was not the only image that elicited such remarks. Similar comments were made about a Korbel champagne ad featuring a romantic couple strolling on a beach, as well as a Cutty Sark

Figure 7

whisky ad in which an older man affectionately places his hand on a younger man's shoulder (Figure 7). With regard to the former case, the Chinese students noted that the public display of affection between a man and a woman would have been frowned upon in China at the time of the study. As for the latter image, students pointed out that it would have been considered unusual in China because of its violation of traditional standards of formality in interactions between fathers and sons. This point was expressed as follows by one of the male respondents:

> Friendship between a father and a son! I like this relationship [i.e., the image in the ad] very much, it's very different from what one sees in China! In China, fathers give serious faces to their sons, they think they're superior. Usually they just give orders or advice, but their relationship is not like friends. Here, they're not just father and son, [they] can talk to each other, [they] can have a drink, [they] can be happy.... I like this, but this is not something I see too much in China (quoted in Dumas, 1988, p. 24).

Note the implied divergence between traditional Chinese cultural norms and this respondent's own professed values. This too was a recurring feature in the Chinese students' statements about the ads. Speaking of the romantic couple in the Korbel ad, a female respondent observed that such behavior outside of marriage would have been considered unseemly back home, and she went on to complain about the status of unmarried women in China:

> Here in America, if you're a single woman, it's fine, people don't blame you. People say, "It's a career woman, that's O.K." But if I go back to China and I don't get married before I'm thirty, people'll say, "Oh, she must have some problems, mental or maybe ... physical." Sometimes, it's really that they care about you, but sometimes, that kind of care, you don't want it! (quoted in Dumas, 1988, p. 41)

Another aspect of this tension between received norms and personal inclinations was voiced by a young woman who was commenting about the emotional embrace in the Bulova ad:

> This reminds me of my leaving.... In China we usually don't hold each other too much, but when I leave, I hold my mother.... Or when I see her again.... I can't help! (rising intonation) This is the first time I left her! (quoted in Dumas, 1988, p. 50)

These remarks are arguably one of the most important aspects of Dumas's findings. In talking about culture, we sometimes tend to think of it as a uniform set of practices or beliefs that everyone in a society subscribes to unquestioningly. But the statements quoted above remind us that the range of behavior that people view as natural or desirable can be considerably broader than the norms prescribed by their traditional culture. So, for many of Dumas's Chinese respondents, incompatibility between the advertising images and the canonical culture of their homeland was ultimately not an obstacle to comprehension. In fact, as these quotations suggest, the Chinese students were often highly receptive to the values implied in the images.

This is not to say that there were no instances whatsoever in which the Chinese missed some message that seemed perfectly obvious to the U.S.-born respondents. One situation in which this kind of thing happened repeatedly was the display of social status. Both the Cutty Sark and the Korbel ad featured men wearing tuxedos. To most of the U.S.-born viewers, this attire was a clear symbol of superior wealth and status. Many of the Chinese, however, were apparently uncertain about, or even unaware of, these upper-class connotations. The Chinese also differed markedly from the U.S.-born viewers in their inferences about a man in jeans, who was shown explaining a toy to a little boy in a Fischer Price ad (Figure 8). Whereas the overwhelming majority of the U.S.-born viewers saw this man as a member of the upper-middle class (e.g., "He is probably a yuppy, like the rest of us" -- from Dumas, 1988, p. 66), every one of the Chinese assigned the man to the working class, and half of them explicitly cited the jeans as evidence. As Dumas pointed out, the American concept of jeans as casual leisure wear was evidently unfamiliar to these Chinese respondents; instead, they treated the man's clothes as a sign that he was a manual laborer (p. 63). Despite these interpretational differences, though, the two groups of respondents were both very enthusiastic about the Fisher Price ad. As in the Cutty Sark case, they applauded the ad's positive father-son image, and this time many of the Chinese said that the scene was typical of their own culture as well, since the ad's emphasis was on the father as teacher.

More generally, then, Dumas's findings point to a somewhat bifurcated conclusion about the possibilities for cross-cultural comprehension of advertising images. As our discussion of jeans and tuxedos demonstrates, and as some other studies have shown (e.g., Farley, 1986, p. 20; Tansey et al., 1990, p. 32), there can be no doubt that individual cultural symbols may be meaningless or may have discrepant meanings outside their original settings.

However, when it comes to the fundamental relationships from which social bonds are constructed (nurturance, sexuality, etc.), the cases we have discussed here suggest that there is greater scope for cross-cultural empathy and understanding, even when the conventional values of two cultures differ

Figure 8

considerably. Cultures may selectively sanction one mode of social interaction or another (intimacy vs. reticence, privacy vs. display, etc.). But the range of relational tendencies within a society as a whole and within a single person's psychological repertoire is inevitably broader than the confines of any one culture. Where such breadth exists, cross-cultural communication may be possible, as Dumas's data indicate.

Cross-Cultural Differences in Values

Our examination of Dumas's findings has already given us a preview of our concluding topic in this discussion of potential interpretational barriers in cross-cultural advertising. It was noted earlier that many of Dumas's Chinese respondents not only understood but also approved of the cultural values implied in some of the ads they were shown. However, the connection between comprehension and approval is by no means inevitable. A viewer could understand these ads perfectly and yet be unmoved or even repelled by the values in them. It is this aspect of miscommunication, i.e., lack of receptivity to implied values, that we will examine next.

This topic has been the primary concern of much of the formal research on communicational problems in cross-cultural advertising. Typically, studies in this area deal with samples of ads from two or more countries. On the basis of systematic analyses of the strategies employed in these ads, the researchers look for differences in the implicit values behind the strategies. A common theme of these comparisons is the contrast in advertising styles between the United States and other parts of the world. According to a study by Han (1990), for instance, U.S. ads were more likely to use individualistic appeals, and less likely to use collectivistic appeals, than ads from Korea. Han interpreted these findings as reflections of a more fundamental cultural difference between Koreans' emphasis on group responsibility and Americans' emphasis on personal independence. The contrast between collectivism and individualism was also a focus of a study by Choi et al. (2005), who investigated differences between Korea and the U.S. regarding uses of, and reactions to, celebrity endorsers. Applying a similar analytical framework to a comparison between the United States and Japan, Hasegawa (1995) argued that the collectivist tendency of Japanese culture makes Japan an unsuitable venue for comparative advertising (i.e., direct references to competing brands), whereas such ads are quite common in the United States. Hasegawa's argument has been supported in research by Mueller (1987, 1992) and Gross (1993), who found that Japanese advertising was less likely than U.S. advertising to contain hard-sell techniques, including direct brand comparisons. In contrast to these Asian trends, however, more recent data by Jeong & Beatty (2002) indicate a growing acceptance of comparative advertising in Korea, and also perhaps among Thai consumers, although not by that country's regulatory authorities (Polyorat & Alden, 2005). The greater prevalence of comparative advertising in the United States has also been the focus of studies that have examined the differences between the U.S. and various European nations (Appelbaum & Halliburton, 1993; Cutler & Javalgi, 1992; Nevett, 1992). An additional finding of these studies has been that U.S. advertising is relatively more likely to convey information about the product, whereas European advertising has a relatively greater tendency to take an indirect approach, entertaining rather than explicitly informing the viewer. In general, then, both the Asian and the European comparisons lead to a characterization of U.S. advertising as more direct and openly commercial than the advertising of other countries. However, it should not be assumed automatically that these differences are reflections of irreconcilable disparities in cultural outlook. Especially with respect to Europe, diverging advertising styles may not correspond to any fundamental underlying cultural divergences. In fact, a related point has even been made with regard to Japan. According to Johansson (1994), the soft-sell approach, which has been considered a characteristic trait of Japanese advertising, may have been a product of institutional arrangements in Japanese advertising agencies (i.e., the fact that a single agency commonly handles ads for competing brands), rather than a direct result of Japanese culture.

Even where advertising strategy does stem from culture, though, it would be premature to conclude that the differences recorded in this kind of research are necessarily impediments to the cross-cultural reception of ads. A small example: Biswas et al. (1992) found that French advertising contained more sex than U.S. advertising; it could be argued that this difference mirrors a more relaxed attitude toward sex on the part of French culture (p. 75); but that does not mean that consumers in the U.S. are unresponsive to sexual appeals. Systematic research on cross-cultural advertising has often focused exclusively on the content of ads, without analyzing viewers' responses, and studies that have actually looked at viewers have been likely to investigate general attitudes towards advertising (e.g., Andrews, 1989; Somasundaram & Light, 1994), rather than responses to specific strategies. However, considerable information on the cross-cultural reception of ads is available in the form of anecdotal evidence.

Perhaps the most comprehensive source of this kind of information is David Ricks's *Blunders in International Business* (1993), a book-length compilation of stories illustrating various things that can go wrong when a company tries to conduct business in an unfamiliar culture. Many of Ricks's stories are about the pitfalls of incompetent translation, as when the Frank Perdue Company's slogan, "It takes a tough man to make a tender chicken," was turned into the Spanish equivalent of "It takes a sexually excited man to make a chicken affectionate"

(p. 74). Not surprisingly, such anecdotes have attracted a great deal of attention in advertising circles. An earlier edition of Rick's book has become a standard reference in discussions of cross-cultural advertising errors, and advertising agencies are now much more likely to check verbal copy for possible cross-cultural double-meanings, especially sexual ones.

Although Ricks's emphasis tended to be on verbal malapropisms rather than visual ones, his book describes a substantial number of cases involving visual material, and it is instructive to look at some of these in search of an overarching pattern. The following incidents are representative of Ricks's major themes. A refrigerator manufacturer trying to do business in the Middle East unwittingly offended local viewers by including a chunk of ham -- forbidden to Muslims -- in a picture of the product (pp. 60-61). An airline was almost banned from Saudi Arabia when its ads showed passengers consuming alcoholic drinks, which are also forbidden to Muslims (p. 61). Another airline managed to generate irate newspaper headlines in Japan when it inadvertently omitted a major Japanese island from a promotional map publicizing a new route (pp. 50-51). Some customers in other (unnamed) Asian countries object to a red circle on product labels because it reminded them of the Japanese flag (p. 31). Protests by citizens' groups in Ontario led to the termination of an advertising campaign which had used the Canadian flag in an attempt to create a local image for a new imported beer (p. 55). An aircraft manufacturer attempting to make sales in India experienced difficulties with a promotional brochure whose images of turbaned men turned out to be old *National Geographic* photographs of Pakistanis (p. 50). An ad highlighting the fact that a certain brand of toothpaste whitens teeth was received poorly in some regions of Southeast Asia where the local population valued darkly stained teeth as a mark of prestige (p. 60). An Irish-themed beer ad featuring a man in a green hat was ridiculed in Hong Kong of China because the green hat is allegedly a Chinese symbol for a cuckold (p. 62). A U.S. corporation's efforts to promote its name through fake billion-dollar currency bearing the company logo backfired at a German trade show, because "the Germans felt that the company was trying to show off American wealth, and they resented this impression" (p. 48).

What do these tales tell us about potential impediments to cross-cultural communication in advertising? With one or two exceptions, these episodes are not about viewers' lack of knowledge concerning the cultures in which the ads or other promotional materials were originally produced. (For example, Muslims know all too well that non-believers eat pork and drink alcohol.) Instead, the problem in most of these cases has to do with cultural ignorance in the opposite direction, i.e., the advertiser's lack of awareness or sensitivity regarding the culture that the ad is addressed to. This ignorance can give rise to ads that inadvertently offend the target audience's cultural values -- e.g., religious restrictions, patriotic sentiments, etc. -- but it is not just culture clash that accounts for the problems described in Ricks's anecdotes. Rather, it is likely that viewers' negative reactions to culturally inappropriate advertising are exacerbated by resentment at being treated with indifference by the advertiser. For instance, while a Japanese citizen might realize that the omission of a Japanese island from a U.S. airline's promotional map was not deliberate, she or he could still feel insulted at the thought that the airline didn't bother to learn more about Japanese geography or consult with a Japanese viewer before issuing the map.

The problem of potential resentment of the advertiser raises a related issue. As the Japanese example may suggest, a viewer's response to a culturally insensitive ad undoubtedly depends to a large extent on the ad's specific country of origin. The same geographical error that angered the Japanese when it was committed by Americans might not have caused as much resentment if its perpetrators had been of some other nationality. But the role of country of origin as a factor in viewers' responses is not confined to cases of cross-cultural misunderstanding. The place in which a certain product was made is frequently a significant aspect of the way in which that product is perceived by people in other countries (Parameswaran & Pisharodi, 1994; Suzuki, 1980). When country of origin is an asset, ads are likely to feature it. In the United States, French fashions, cosmetics, and fragrances (but not cars) are routinely advertised with pictures of Parisian street scenes. Conversely, in France and elsewhere, ads for American cars, liquor, and cigarettes commonly feature Western scenery or other images with an American flavor (e.g., Figure 9). To a certain extent, these national emblems may serve as certificates of quality, but their meaning clearly goes beyond that. When an American consumer buys a French perfume, we can probably take it for granted that "Frenchness" itself is part of the appeal. Likewise, to some people in some countries outside the U.S., the Marlboro man is not just a representation of masculinity; he also represents America.

In other words, nationality itself is often an important part of the meaning of international advertising. How an ad from one country will be received in another may depend to a large extent on the economic and/or ideological relationships between the two countries. In many parts of the world, images of the United States have traditionally been seen as potent symbols of political freedom and material well-being (Messaris & Woo, 1991). These perceptions affect people's attitudes toward American ads and products, and, by extension, they can also be appropriated in local advertising. We have already seen how the picture of Gary Cooper from *High Noon* was put to use in a Polish election poster. Similarly, Shay Sayre (1994) has describes several importations of "Western" imagery into Hungarian political ads, including a Tom and Jerry

Figure 9

cartoon clip that was used as a metaphor for the triumph of democracy over communism. A somewhat different use of "Western" images can be found in Japan and some other Asian nations. There, ads for local products have sometimes incorporated pictures of Americans (mostly white, but occasionally also black) in connection with themes of innovation, individualism and freedom from traditional social constraints (Creighton, 1995; Larrabee, 1994).

Of course, even within a single country reactions to such images are bound to vary widely. It has been argued that international advertising originating in the U.S. or other "Western" countries is particularly likely to find a receptive audience among younger, more fashion-oriented consumers (Domzal & Kernan, 1993). By the same token, however, people with a more traditional orientation often see American advertising as a threat. This kind of concern is expressed very poignantly in a letter to an Indian business journal quoted by Simon Chapman (1986):

> What advertising genius ... decided that "the all American" was a suitable copy-line to promote Chesterfield cigarettes in India? How are the connotations relevant here? All-American, the blonde, blue-eyed six-footer raised on grandma's apple pie...? Presumably [the advertiser is] counting on the good old Indian sense of inferiority in the face of anything foreign.... I am wondering why this sort of self-demeaning message should be deemed a likely winner by one of our advertising agencies.... Can we not take ourselves seriously?... The homogenization of the world by American multinationals is hardly a new phenomenon, but ... this particular assault of Americanization is one of its crudest manifestations yet -- in India (in Chapman, p. 124).

There is some evidence that such concerns are having tangible consequences. Both in India and elsewhere in the "non-Western" world, some observers have noted a reactive trend toward greater use of local models or actors in ads as well as in other media (Landler, 1994; Oyelele, 1990, p. 204; see also Rothacher, 2004). And there is another side to this coin. The United States itself occasionally goes through period of increasingly negative attitudes toward the outside world and, in particular, toward those countries which are perceived as posing an economic threat. In response to such sentiments, some foreign corporations doing business in the U.S. have felt a need to resort to advertising that attempts to overturn negative perceptions and to create a more welcoming attitude. For example, the Fuji Corporation (which has a history of trade disputes with Kodak) has run ads that featured its sponsorship of the U.S. Olympic team; ads by Toyota have used the map of the United States to show all the places where the company is hiring or buying from Americans (Figure 10); and an ad

Figure 10

for Mitsubishi contained a photograph of Albert Einstein as a reminder of the contributions that immigrants (including, by implication, immigrating companies) have made to the United States.

We began this chapter by asking whether the iconicity of visual communication makes pictures a particularly effective mode of advertising across cultural boundaries. The conclusions of our discussion may be summarized as follows. On the one hand, there are several factors that can pose barriers to the cross-cultural reception of advertising images. These factors include: the presence of culture-specific imagery (e.g., the Iwo Jima flag-raising); references to local cultural practices (e.g., the use of jeans as leisure wear by affluent Americans); and incompatibility of cultural values (e.g., American individualism vs. the more collectivist orientation of many other cultures).

On the other hand, however, the impact of these factors is often mitigated by countervailing circumstances. When images are appropriated for advertising purposes, they are often used in such a way as to facilitate comprehension even by someone who is unfamiliar with the original context (e.g., the shot of Harold Lloyd in *Safety Last*). Moreover, the global distribution of pictures through movies, TV, and the Web has created a substantial basis of shared images in parts of the world that differ considerably from one another with respect to current social conditions (e.g., the picture of Gary Cooper that was used as an election poster in Poland). Receptivity to images from other cultures can also be heightened by conflicts between individuals' personal beliefs and their society's official values (as in the case of some of Anne Dumas's Chinese respondents). Finally, acceptance or rejection of transnational advertising images can be affected crucially by general attitudes toward the ads' country of origin (e.g., American admiration of French sophistication vs. resentment of Chinese economic growth).

References

Andrews, J. C. (1989). The dimensionality of beliefs toward advertising in general. *Journal of Advertising, 18(1),* 26-35.

Appelbaum, U., & Halliburton, C. (1993). How to develop international advertising campaigns that work: The example of the European food and beverage sector. *International Journal of Advertising, 12,* 223-233.

Babyak, R. J. (1995). Demystifying the Asian consumer. *Appliance Manufacturer, 43(2),* 25-27.

Biswas, A., Olsen, J. E., & Carlet, V. (1992). A comparison of print advertisements from the United States and France. *Journal of Advertising, 21(4),* 73-81.

Bourgery, M., & Guimaraes, G. (1993, May-June). Global ads: Say it with pictures. *The Journal of European Business,* 22-26.

Bruner, H., & Gable, M. (2003). *Global Inc.: An atlas of the multinational corporation.* New York: The New Press.

Chapman, S. (1986). *Great expectorations: Advertising and the tobacco industry.* London: Comedia.

Choi, S.M., Lee, W.N., & Kim, H.J. (2005). Lessons from the rich and famous: A cross-cultural comparison of celebrity endorsement in advertising. *Journal of Advertising, 34(2),* 85-98.

Crane, D. (2002). *Global culture: Media, arts, policy, and globalization.* New York: Routledge.

Creighton, M. R. (1995). Imaging the other in Japanese advertising campaigns. In J. G. Carrier (Ed.), *Occidentalism: Images of the West* (pp. 135-160). New York: Oxford University Press.

Cutler, B. D., & Javalgi, R. G. (1992). A cross-cultural analysis of the visual components of print advertising: The United States and the European Community. *Journal of Advertising Research, 32(1),* 71-79.

De Mooij, M. (2005). *Global marketing and advertising: Understanding cultural paradoxes.* 2n ed. Thousand Oaks, CA: Sage.

Domzal, T. J., & Kernan, J. B. (1993). Mirror, mirror: Some postmodern reflections on global advertising. *Journal of Advertising, 22(4),* 1-20.

Dumas, A. A. (1988). *Cross-cultural analysis of people's interpretation of advertising visual cliches.* M.A. thesis, Annenberg School for Communication, University of Pennsylvania.

Dunn, S. W. (1966). The case study approach in cross-cultural research. *Journal of Marketing Research, 3,* 26-31.

Elinder, E. (1965). How international can European advertising be? *Journal of Marketing, 29,* 7-11.

Farley, J. U. (1986). Are there truly international products -- and prime prospects for them? *Journal of Advertising Research, 26(5),* 17-20.

Fatt, A. C. (1967). The danger of "local" international advertising. *Journal of Marketing, 31,* 60-62.

Goodman, N. (1976). *Languages of art: An approach to a theory of symbols.* Indianapolis: Bobbs-Merrill.

Gross, R. (1993, June 18). "Why is the gorilla flushing the toilet?" or Japanese advertising: Sights that tickle the eyes. Paper presented at the Seventh Annual Visual Communication Conference, Jackson Hole, WY.

Halliburton, C., & Huenerberg, R. (1993). Pan-European marketing -- myth or reality. *Journal of International Marketing, 1(3),* 77-92.

Han, S.-P. (1990). *Individualism and collectivism: Its implications for cross-cultural advertising.* Ph.D. dissertation, University of Illinois at Urbana-Champaign.

Hasegawa, K. (1995). Does the U.S. comparative advertising TV practice work abroad? The case of Japan and the United States. Paper presented to the International Communication Association, Albuquerque, NM.

Hecht, H., Schwartz, R., & Atherton, M. (Eds.) (2003). *Looking into pictures: An interdisciplinary approach to pictorial space.* Cambridge, MA: MIT.

Hill, J. S., & Shao, A. T. (1994). Agency participants in multicountry advertising: A preliminary examination of affiliate characteristics and environments. *Journal of International Marketing, 2(2),* 29-48.

Javalgi, R., Cutler, B. D., & White, D. S. (1994). Print advertising in the Pacific basin: An empirical investigation. *International Marketing Review, 11(6),* 48-64.

Jeon, J. O., & Beatty, S. E. (2002). Comparative advertising effectiveness in different national cultures. *Journal of Business Research,* 55 (November), 907-913

Johansson, J. K. (1994). The sense of "nonsense": Japanese TV advertising. *Journal of Advertising, 23(1),* 17-26.

Jones, J. P. (2000). Introduction: The vicissitudes of international advertising. In J. P. Jones (Ed.), *International advertising: Realities and myths* (pp. 1-10). Thousand Oaks, CA: Sage.

Kernan, J. K., & Domzal, T. J. (1993). International advertising: To globalize, visualize. *Journal of International Consumer Marketing, 5(4),* 51-71.

Landler, M. (1994, November 18). Think globally, program locally. *Business Week,* 186-189.

Larrabee, M. H. (1994). *Orthography and affect: Roman text in Japanese magazine advertisements.* M.A. thesis, Annenberg School for Communication, University of Pennsylvania.

Levitt, T. (1983, May-June). The globalization of markets. *Harvard Business Review,* pp. 92-102.

Lorimer, E. S., & Dunn, S. W. (1967). Four measures of cross-cultural advertising effectiveness. *Journal of Advertising Research, 7(4),* 11-13.

Lull, J. (1995). *Media, communication, culture: A global approach.* New York: Columbia University Press.

McRae, H. (1994). *The world in 2020: Power, culture and prosperity.* Boston: Harvard Business School Press.

Messaris, P. (1994). *Visual "literacy": Image, mind, and reality.* Boulder, CO: Westview Press.

Messaris, P., & Woo, J. (1991). Image vs. reality in Korean-Americans' responses to mass-mediated depictions of the United States. *Critical Studies in Mass Communication, 8,* 74-90.

Mueller, B. (1987). Reflections of culture: An analysis of Japanese and American advertising appeals. *Journal of Advertising Research, 27(3),* 51-59.

Mueller, B. (1992). Standardization vs. specialization: An examination of Westernization in Japanese advertising. *Journal of Advertising Research, 32(1),* 15-24.

Nevett, T. (1992). Differences between American and British Television Advertising: Explanations and implications. *Journal of Advertising, 21(4),* 61-71.

Olson, S. R. (1999). *Hollywood planet: Global media and the competitive advantage of narrative transparency.* Erlbaum.

Onkvisit, S., & Shaw, J. J. (1990). Global advertising: Revolution or myopia? *Journal of International Consumer Marketing, 2(3),* 97-112.

Oyeleye, A. A. (1990). *Advertising and commodity fetishism: Praxis in a peripheral theatre of consumption. A study of advertising in Nigeria.* Ph.D. dissertation: University of Leicester.

Parameswaran, R., & Pisharodi, R. M. (1994). Facets of country of origin image: An empirical assessment. *Journal of Advertising, 23(1),* 43-56.

Peebles, D. M. (1989). Don't write off global advertising: A commentary. *International Marketing Review, 6(1),* 73-78.

Peirce, C. S. (1991). *Peirce on signs: Writings on semiotic by Charles Sanders Peirce.* Ed. J. Hoopes. Chapel Hill: The University of North Carolina Press.

Perlmutter, D. (2006). Hypericons: Famous news images in the internet-digital-satellite age. In P. Messaris & L. Humphreys (Eds.), *Digital media: Transformations in human communication* (pp. 51-64). New York: Peter Lang.

Polyorat, K., & Alden, D. L. (2005). Self-construal and need-for-cognition effects on brand attitudes and purchase intentions in response to comparative advertising in Thailand and the United States. *Journal of Advertising,* 34(1), 37-48.

Quelch, J. A., & Hoff, E. J. (1986, May-June). Customized global marketing. *Harvard Business Review,* pp. 59-68.

Ricks, D. A. (1993). *Blunders in international business.* Cambridge, MA: Blackwell.

Ricks, D. A., Arpan, J. S., & Fu, M. Y. (1974). Pitfalls in overseas advertising. *Journal of Advertising Research, 14(6),* 47-51.

Rosenthal, W. (1994). Standardized international advertising: A view from the agency side. *Journal of International Consumer Marketing, 7(1),* 39-59.

Ross, Bill D. (1985). *Iwo Jima: Legacy of valor.* New York: Vintage Books.

Rothacher, A. (Ed.). (2004). Corporate cultures and global brands. Singapore: World Scientific Publishing.

Sayre, S. (1994). Images of freedom and equality: A value analysis of Hungarian political commercials. *Journal of Advertising, 23(1),* 97-106.

Scott, L. (1990). Toward visual rhetoric. Paper presented at the American Academy of Advertising Conference, Orlando, FL.

Sebeok, T. A. (2001). *Signs: An introduction to semiotics .* 2d ed. Toronto: University of Toronto Press.

Somasundaram, T. N., & Light, C. D. (1994). Rethinking a global media strategy: A four country comparison of young adults' perceptions of media-specific advertising. *Journal of International Consumer Marketing, 7(1),* 23-38.

Suzuki, N. (1980). The changing pattern of advertising strategy by Japanese business firms in the U.S. market: Content analysis. *Journal of International Business Studies, 11(3),* 63-72.

Tansey, R., Hyman, M. R., & Zinkhan, G. M. (1990). Cultural themes in Brazilian and U.S. auto ads: A cross-cultural comparison. *Journal of Advertising, 19(2),* 30-39.

Wells, L. G. (1994). Western concepts, Russian perspectives: Meanings of advertising in the former Soviet Union. *Journal of Advertising, 23,* 83-95.

Weschler, L. (1989, November 13). A grand experiment. *The New Yorker,* 59-104.

Wheeler, R. (1980). *Iwo.* Annapolis, MD: Naval Institute Press.

White, J. D. (2005). *Global media: The television revolution in Asia.* New York: Routledge.

White, R. (2000). International advertising: How far can it fly? In J. P. Jones (Ed.), *International advertising: Realities and myths* (pp. 29-40). Thousand Oaks, CA: Sage.

Introduction to

The Role of Culture in Persuasive Presentations:
An Israeli and New Zealand Student Video Exchange

By Prue Holmes and Nurit Zaidman

Holmes and Zaidman note that much of the business world is relationship driven and, as a consequence, intercultural communication is a vital international competitive advantage. It is, therefore, necessary to adapt products or services to local cultures. Holmes and Zaidman tested the influence of culture on the perception of visual messages and discovered that culture does have a strong influence on the interpretation and evaluation of videos. Their study revolved around student groups who were enrolled in business degree programs in Israel and New Zealand. These business students were also enrolled in intercultural communication courses so that they had been sensitized, to some degree, to cultural differences. The purpose of the project was twofold: To raise students' intercultural communication knowledge and skills awareness as they communicated with students who shared a different culture and language, and to encourage students to explore how people from another culture experience and understand one's own culture.

Student participants produced two videos each of their own university and business program as a promotional video designed to interest students from the other school in their home institution. After the videos had been produced, they were sent for evaluation to the other group of students. Their responses were evaluated by Holmes and Zaidman who then also shared the results with their respective students. All groups employed linguistic and iconic messages to help audiences achieve a better understanding of their respective studies. Language appeared to be the most vital tool in achieving successful communication and, thus, mutual understanding between people from two different cultures. This factor, however, was underestimated by all four groups, Holmes and Zaidman discovered. It is very important, the authors note, that the messages are clear. This may be achieved by minimizing accent, speaking slowly, and using visual cues such as subtitles and titles. The use of iconic messages can be problematic when national symbols are used that are not understood by the target audience; demonstrating that symbolic imagery does not help sell the product, Holmes and Zaidman point out. That is why it is important to carry out audience analyses and market research so that iconic and symbolic differences are uncovered as well as the values and belief systems of the target audience. And finally, Holmes and Zaidman's study also revealed that editing techniques were considered important; but styles seemed to vary and had an impact on how the overall production was evaluated.

All in all, this study should prove to be of interest to business organizations and marketing agencies in that it proves that even business students who are participating in an intercultural communication course, i.e. people who have been sensitized to cultural differences, still encountered difficulties in decoding messages correctly that they received from another culture. One can only imagine what the results would be if the involved parties have not been sensitized to cultural divergence.

Michael B. Hinner

Prue Holmes is Senior Lecturer in the Department of Management Communication, University of Waikato, Hamilton, New Zealand. She teaches business writing and intercultural communication. Although a New Zealander, she has spent time abroad, teaching and studying in Italy and China. Her research has focused on the communication experiences of international students, in particular, ethnic Chinese in tertiary education and in the wider community. More recently, her research activities have explored intercultural communication competence in the pluricultural classroom; she also researches the use of ICTs in literacy development, intercultural communication, and among immigrant groups for socio-cultural adaptation and development. She has also been engaged in research commissioned by the Ministry of Education and Education New Zealand to investigate the learning and communication experiences of international students in New Zealand secondary and higher institutions.

Nurit Zaidman is currently a Senior Lecturer at the Department of Business Administration, Ben-Gurion University, Israel. Her research interests include knowledge transfer and communication in multi-nationals; intercultural communication in business; cross-cultural comparisons of behavior in organizations; consumption and marketing of sacred commodities; new age; spirituality in organizations.

The Role of Culture in Persuasive Presentations: An Israeli and New Zealand Student Video Exchange

Prue Holmes
Nurit Zaidman

As students enter the global marketplace, they must learn how to connect with their multicultural customers, stakeholders, and employees. Much of the business world is relationship driven, and, as a consequence, intercultural communication is at the heart of international competitive advantage. We cannot hope to be successful if we try to standardize our products and fail to adapt to local cultures. At the macro level, the company reaches into the multicultural marketplace to communicate with and understand its customers and other stakeholders. At the micro level, the challenge is to increase person-to person cross-cultural understanding (Brake, Walker, & Walker, 1995). As both student groups were enrolled in business degrees, this knowledge is of critical importance to them in their future work, for example, in business transactions, and where sales personnel expect to engage people from another culture into purchasing a product or service. Thus, they require two key skill sets: 1) communication—an ability to connect with others in business and the community as well as with emerging social developments; and 2) connectedness—an awareness and understanding of their role as responsible citizens in an increasingly globalized world (Guilherme, 2003).

In seeking to develop these skill sets in our students, we undertook a project—a video exchange—between students in two university business schools, one in Israel and New Zealand. The purpose of the project was twofold: to raise students' intercultural communication knowledge and skills awareness as they communicated with students who shared a different culture and language; and to encourage students to explore how people from another culture experience and understand our own culture. The project thus provided a global environment through which students can experience and learn from real life interactions.

The chapter begins by explaining the importance of the project in developing the above two skill sets. It then provides an introduction to the context of the study, the questions the study addresses, and the methodology applied. Next, Israeli and NZ students' experiences of the other culture's communication are presented. The chapter finishes with a discussion of the implications—theoretical, methodological, and pedagogical—in conducting a video exchange.

Culturally and geographically, Israel and NZ have little in common, except perhaps in the size of their populations. Thus, this disjunction provided a useful basis for the study between the two groups. A background to the two societies demonstrates the cultural distance shared by each of the countries, and therefore, the importance of understanding the other's culture in producing a persuasive sales presentation.

Israel has become a plural society composed of distinctive religious, ethnic, and national communities as a result of its war for independence and major waves of immigration. Relations among these groups have been marked by various levels of tension and conflict. Serious divisions exist between Jews of Middle Eastern and North African origin and those of European origin, between religious and secular Jews, and between Arab Israelis and Jewish Israelis (Harrison, 2001). These groups communicate on a daily basis in Israel and compose its workforce. Yet, the varied cultural heritage has created differences in general perceptions, attitudes, behavioral patterns and work values. In addition, there is a growing number of foreign workers. Thus, intercultural communication is a daily conduct in Israel. Furthermore, intercultural communication competence has become critical for people in large sectors of Israeli society who work in multinational companies, and who communicate with colleagues, and trading and business people as part of their job. Similarly, NZ's population growth and changing policies towards immigration in the past 20 years have resulted in a pluricultural society (Zodgekar, 2005). NZ's bicultural foundation of Maori and European people (from the United Kingdom and Ireland) has been influenced by recent waves of immigrants from East and South-east Asia (particularly of ethnic Chinese origin) and the Pacific, and more recently, refugees from Africa and the Middle-east. Now, one in five persons in a population of four million is born overseas (Ward & Lin, 2005). This pluricultural evolution has impacted on the learning environment, the workplace, and community. Yet, many New Zealanders, including students, have been reluctant to embrace this cultural dynamic.

Another factor contributing to the value of this project is the diversification occurring within student populations in educational institutions. With the marketization of higher education, universities have developed rigorous advertising campaigns to recruit international (Newman, Couturier, & Scurry, 2004). Consequently, students now require understanding in and experience of the processes of interculturalization within the classroom (Jiang, 2005). They could also be recipients of these advertising messages; or part of the team creating them. Thus, the project required students to respond to this challenge by developing their own campaign to recruit international students into their university.

We chose the context of an intercultural communication class in a business school because we considered it the ideal forum for students to acquire an understanding of how people from another culture perceive their own communication. Further, the choice of a video "sales" presentation of an academic program provided students with an ideal medium to investigate how sales personnel expect to engage people from another culture into purchasing a product or service.

Therefore, the research question that guided the investigation into the video exchange were: How do people from another culture experience and understand our own culture? In addressing this question we were then able to explore the implications of the two-way exchange.

Method

Methodology

The video exchange project is grounded in a methodology developed by Pan, Scollon and Scollon (2002). Pan et al. argue that, because the international workplace is now so complex, we cannot assume that there are only two cultures involved in an intercultural interaction. Although the exchange is between Israel and NZ, their pluricultural societies embody a range of possibilities for communication. Further, the co-operation required in the project is practically oriented. Students are able to get the information they need directly from their counterparts without recourse to intercultural communication textbooks or training programs.

In their project "professional communication across cultures" Pan et al. (2002) designed a program by which people in business organizations or governmental agencies could exchange professional communication portfolios across different regional and cultural offices. In each site they asked people to develop portfolios of their own best professional communications—resumes, videos of presentations, business cards—which they then sent to two other sites. In each site they led focus groups to look at and respond not only to their own portfolios, but also to the portfolios of those from the other sites. In a second round they asked them to respond to the responses from the other sites. Through this process they were able to let members of these groups: 1) provide their own best communicative products; 2) discover how those communicative products were interpreted by others; 3) discover how their own perceptions of differences were interpreted by others; and 4) reflect on how they might change their own communicative practices to account for these differences in perception and interpretation (Scollon & Scollon, 1995). It is this process that informs and guides our exchange project.

Research Design

The research design involved the making and in-class analysis of four videos. Two groups (of four to five members) in NZ and two groups in Israel each constructed a video of a sales presentation—an academic program within the students' respective business schools. The purpose of the video was to encourage students from the target culture to enrol in the program. The groups were not given any instructions about the production of the video, except a time limit of seven minutes.

The videos were then exchanged between the Israeli and NZ classes. The Israeli class consisted of only eight students enrolled in an MBA degree who were participating in a module on culture and international business. The 45 NZ students, in their final year of an undergraduate business degree, were enrolled in an intercultural communication paper. After viewing the two videos, the class separated into small groups to discuss their responses to the following seven questions (except for questions one and seven which they answered individually):

1. What is my first impression of this video tape? (Write your response individually.)
2. What worked well in the presentation?
3. What seemed confusing or unclear?
4. What was missing?
5. What was there in the video but seemed to be unnecessary?
6. What changes would you make to improve the video?
7. What grade (out of 10) would you give the video? (Write your response individually.)

Each student then emailed their word-processed responses to their teacher. All the Israeli responses were grouped for each question, and similarly, the NZ responses. We analysed the student responses to these seven questions and identified the major themes emerging which are presented in the findings section. Certain findings are presented more fully, while in other parts, we use one or two examples to illustrate our points.

Limitations

Notwithstanding the geographic difficulties of co-ordinating the exchange, there were some limitations to this study. First, students volunteered for the project and formed their own groups. Thus, through this self-selection process, one New

Zealand group consisted of all (Chinese) international students. In the Israeli class, all eight class members opted to participate.

Students, aware that their counterparts in the other country would critique their video, got professional help in the production stages. We did not discourage this practice as production techniques were not intended for evaluation. Yet, as students' feedback indicates, their judgements about the effectiveness of the communication were influenced by production techniques, so we included these themes in the findings.

A further consideration is the ethnic diversity and business experience of students in the classes. Students in the Israeli class were part-time and already had considerable experience in the business sector. Their average age was about 28. By contrast, the NZ student group consisted of undergraduate students with little experience in the workforce, apart from part-time student employment. Also, the class consisted of about one third international students, especially from China; there were also students from Europe, the Pacific, NZ Maori, and other minority groups living in NZ. Thus, the responses attributed to the NZ class cannot be considered representative of all NZ people.

Results

This section is divided into two parts. First, a brief synopsis of the four videos is provided. The two Israeli videos are described first, followed by the two NZ videos. In the second part, the major emergent themes (findings) are presented and discussed: first, the Israeli and then the NZ students' responses.

Part One: Video Synopses

Video one: Israeli students' production. The video, entitled "Welcome to the promised land," promoted the full-time honours MBA degree. At just over 4 minutes, the video had a fast pace and detailed information about the degree and institution. The title appeared as a white caption over panned aerial images of the Negev dessert—flora, landscape, a waterfall, an eagle, and the sun setting over the sea. Then came the white caption on a black background "and the promise," followed by images of the adjacent flags of Israel and the university and the university's name in both English and Hebrew. Next, topics covered in the MBA were then shown in black and white captions and narrated, followed by a series of clips showing the university learning environment—contemporary buildings, students on campus, an LCD display of the stock market, classrooms, computer rooms, gardens and accommodation. Simultaneously, the narrator described these images, focusing on the advantages of studying at the university, the benefits to students, the qualification's value, links to top universities in the United States, the quality of the professoriate, the state of the art knowledge and facilities, and Israel's global connectedness. Further images of multinational companies demonstrated Israel's links with leading international and domestic markets. These images were accompanied by soft, calm music beneath the narration. The narrator then concluded (which included a caption "To conclude") by showing two famous people receiving their honorary degrees—the former French President, François Mitterand, and a famous Italian actor who spoke of his pleasure in receiving the award. Finally, a white caption showed the Web site for further information for viewers, set against the backdrop of the main building showing the University's logo and name (in both English and Hebrew).

Video two: The full-time honours MBA – Israeli students' production. The video began with the title of the program it promoted, the MBA, in white captions on a black screen with no music. At eight minutes long, the presentation was at a slower pace, and interspersed with blackness between scenes. Then the narrator welcomed viewers, and described the university's geographical location and its global connectedness, accompanied by pans of the city and university. Next, a teacher from NZ appeared, greeted the audience in Maori ("Kia ora"), and warmly welcomed NZ students to study there. He enthusiastically reinforced the quality of the program and university, its financial links to the United States, and also invited viewers to come. The next scene was a blurred blue panned image of a computer room. The narrator, reading out the white captions that simultaneously scroll over the screen, described links with a prestigious business school in the United States through the university's advisory board, and assistance in job placement on completion of the degree. The following scene panned university buildings, classrooms, computer suites, cafes, shops, and campus gardens. The scenes were accompanied by calm music—a female singing. Next, a recent male graduate, seated in front of a computer, described in serious tones his experience of the program and the outcome—a top job in industry. He endorsed the quality of the program and invited viewers to enrol. The video closed with an image of the university's name in English and Hebrew, followed by a close-up of the gold logo. These images were accompanied by calm music.

Video three: The MBA degree – NZ students' production. This video, promoting the MBA degree, was produced by a group of four Chinese international female students. The video began with a selection of images—the university logo, business school buildings, university accommodation set among trees, a classroom showing a young male teacher, students sitting under a tree, a group playing basketball. Background music was energetic, accompanied by a steady drum beat. The narrator, a Chinese international student, previewed the contents of the video. A Maori carving stood behind her. She described the culture of the school for viewers. During the description the scene cut to four MBA students lunching and discussing their learning. The scene then switched to an interview between the narrator and Director in his office. He explained the advantages of studying an MBA, emphasizing safety, the value of an international student body (from India, China, the USA, Europe) in sharing the learning, and the competitive advantage students gained. He also emphasized the global nature of the professoriate. The next scene showed a Chinese MBA student endorsing the advantages of the MBA program and the quality of his learning experience. The video then switched to the classroom where a teacher described his international MBA teaching experience. The camera then panned the classroom with its computers, and students interacting with the teacher. Next, the same teacher endorsed the quality of the program, focusing on its practice relevance, action learning, and entrepreneurial activities. The narrator then switched to the facilities available for students on campus; the camera panned images of the library, computer rooms, clubs, accommodation, shops, banks, and the security centre. The background music was calm and soft. Then came an interview with an Israeli teacher in her office. She began with "shalom" and endorsed the program—the teaching support, research environment, and quality of the program. She closed in Hebrew, inviting students to come. The narrator then ended the video by thanking the viewers and welcoming them as prospective students. Behind her were trees among building rooftops. The camera then panned scenes of the university environment—the green campus, the school itself, MBA students in discussion, a church with a cross, and lakes. The video ended as is had begun, with the university logo.

Video four: The undergraduate business degree – NZ students' production. The video, promoting the undergraduate management degree, was produced by five female students (three international and two NZ). White captions on a black screen induced viewers to think about studying at the school. The captions were accompanied by a traditional Maori war chant – the haka. A series of promotional still images of NZ followed, including the All Blacks, Maori people, NZ symbols, and the NZ flag. Two young Maori male students introduced the video, welcomed viewers to the University of Waikato, and offered to guide them through the campus. The remainder of the video consisted of a series of presentations. Three of these were with teachers in their offices who spoke about the benefits and quality of the degree. A fourth presentation was with a public relations teacher from Israel who spoke in Hebrew. Each presentation included a pop-up caption stating the School's number one rating in NZ. Two further presentations came from the International Student Consultant who spoke of the support services available—mentoring, pastoral care, and advice on health, safety, and driving, and from the receptionist at the main desk, who also endorsed the quality of the degree and the international opportunities it provided. The remainder of the presentations were of teachers and students (NZ and international) who spoke of the enjoyment of studying in the school and the benefits of the degree. These were filmed outside on campus. Other interspersed clips showed the two Maori guides walking through the campus in fast forward motion and with a shaky effect, and pan shots inside the library. These scenes were accompanied by energetic music. The two Maori guides then concluded the video. A series of white captions on a black screen reappeared, promoting the safe and supportive learning environment, and indorsing the viewer's choice in choosing the school as a study destination. The captions were interspersed with pans of the school, a graduation ceremony, and students socialising in a café. The music was calming, but powerful and inspirational. Film credits appeared, and finally, the university logo and a website for further information.

Part Two: Major Responses from Students

The Israeli Students' Responses to the NZ Students' Videos

Israeli students' responses focused on four key themes: spoken accent and written communication, interpersonal communication, the message of safety and other iconic messages, and editing techniques. These themes are discussed below.

Accent and written communication. Most Israeli students had difficulty in understanding the NZ accent because they found it "hard to follow" and "unclear," and therefore affected their understanding of the marketing purpose of the video. Israeli students suggested that NZ students needed to be more aware that English is not the Israeli audience's mother tongue; nor do they have a high degree of fluency. Therefore, the NZ students and actors in the video should speak more clearly and slowly. Furthermore, they felt that NZ students should know that, in Israel, the American accent is prevalent, and thus, NZ students' should demonstrate their awareness of some of the major differences between the American accent and the NZ one.

Besides accent, Israeli students thought that subtitles were missing. Subtitles would help the audience to understand the identity of participants, the meanings of the images portrayed, and the geographical location of the places in the video. They advised the NZ producers to add subtitles and insert translations of interviews with important people to overcome this knowledge gap.

Overall, Israeli students' comments suggested that they regarded language, both spoken and written, as the most important precondition to ensure successful communication between people in the two cultures.

Interpersonal communication. All of the Israeli students believed that the effective use of interpersonal communication, through interviews with students, teachers, and administrative personnel, helped to overcome communication barriers between the two cultures. Some students described the positive effects in showing interviews with students, in particular, international students:

> It was good to show students from all over the world living and studying in the university. It was also good to listen to their words about enjoying studying in the university and about the integration level that exists in the university.

And:

> These things help the audience to lower their anxiety level and overcome the fears of studying and succeeding in a foreign university so far away from home.

These interviews helped to increase Israeli students' interest in joining this happy environment, and therefore, served to decrease the anxiety they might expect to feel in a foreign context. Images of international students also promoted the theme of a culturally-diverse campus, vital in promoting a cultural exchange between different countries.

Further, interviews with teachers, advisors, and administrative staff promoted a sense of security for the audience if they required help. Some Israeli students pointed out the effectiveness of using an Israeli representative in the video. For instance, one student explained that an interview with a teacher in Hebrew increased feelings of connectivity:

> Hearing an Israeli talking in Hebrew about the university makes a great difference and really helps connect to the viewer, especially when Israel is such a little place, and suddenly, we see that even from our little country there are representatives in such [a] place.

This emotional affiliation served to build a bridge between the NZ university and the Israeli students, reducing their anxieties. Thus, interpersonal communication through interviews, and through the use of Hebrew, helped eliminate barriers by shortening the distance between university experiences in Israel and NZ and by building trust between the host culture and the target audience.

The NZ students' focus on study abroad as a life-enriching experience led the Israeli students to comment that the interviews failed to convey all-important information, such as a description of modules, and the benefits in enrolling in the program. By contrast the Israeli videos had focused on the added value of the program on the economic and commercial world stage.

Communicating the specific message of safety. Israeli students showed a strong, negative view towards NZ students' portrayal of NZ as a "safe" place to study. They inferred that NZ students must perceive Israel as unsafe, and consequently, they became defensive. One Israeli student summed up this perception:

> In talking about New-Zealand as a safe place is very unnecessary and harmful. Israel, [despite] its present situation with the Palestinians, it isn't less safe than any other place in the world. Terrorist acts are happening today all over the world (USA, Spain, Turkey, etc.) and saying that Israel isn't safe is wrong, unnecessary, and annoying.

This response indicates the importance of researching values and perceptions of another culture. The NZ students needed to research their audience more in these areas, as well as the historical and cultural situation in Israel, thereby avoiding erroneous assumptions. The response shows the problem of the producers in assuming that their Israeli audience held the same or a similar perception. Instead, the NZ message created antagonism in the Israeli audience.

The use of iconic messages: symbolism, the campus. Two forms of iconic messages, NZ symbols and campus life, were identified as important by Israeli students. With regard to NZ symbols, students' responses were varied. Some argued that symbols at the beginning—a buzzy bee (a common child's wooden toy in NZ), and a drink can (a famous NZ drink)—carried no meaning. Some, confused the bee for a bird, and wanted to know its significance, and others assumed the drink was a fruit drink, and wanted to know the kind of fruit. They failed to understand the relevance of these symbols to either the program of study or campus life. Alternatively, a few students asserted that the beginning of the video was both powerful and impressive. They claimed that "the photographs of New-Zealand's famous symbols, with its native music [Maori war chant] made a great impression and generated a great anticipation to continue seeing the video". Thus, these opposing responses demonstrate that we cannot assume that people within a culture hold the same values and beliefs.

The second iconic message—images of life on campus—was considered important by Israeli students. For example, a few students wanted to see more of the university's facilities, such as classrooms, sports and recreational facilities, living accommodation, and the "emergency" centre (perhaps for health or safety). Such images would enable them to discern whether the learning and living environment within the university was conducive to study.

However, most students claimed that images of life in NZ itself were missing. Although their main objective was to study in the university, they felt that gaining more detailed information about the university and the country was vital, to help them understand the general atmosphere of the campus and community beyond, and to motivate them to choose NZ as a study-abroad destination.

Video editing techniques. Besides the use of different communication channels and the construction of detailed messages, Israeli students differed in their responses to the NZ students' editing techniques (such as the accompanying music and strong rhythmic theme). For example, "the music is very loud and aggressive," and "[it's] not clear what is the connection to the movie's content." Where NZ students had used the fast-forward device, one response was: "the fast forward rhythm of the movie was very confusing and diminished the capability to understand the messages." Thus, rhythm, volume, and pace are important elements which either facilitate or impede message effectiveness. The Maori war chant clearly did not resonate with all Israeli students' expectations of accompanying music to a promotional video. By contrast, their choice of music was lyrical and calm, conveying a sense of peace and stability.

Overall, most Israeli students believed that the NZ video was attractive and interesting, exemplified in the use of vivid images of interviews with students, teachers, and administrative staff. These images also enabled effective communication about the staff and students in NZ. However, they felt that both videos lacked detailed information about the program. The producers put all their efforts into marketing their product through iconic images and interviews with people. The Israeli students suggested that the presentation should also include images of the country of NZ, as well as information about the program and university facilities. They regarded this information as critical in persuading them to study in NZ. The Israeli students also specified that unclear language and accent impeded their understanding of the verbal commentary.

The NZ Students' Responses to the Israeli Students' Videos

Similar to the Israeli students, the NZ students' responses drew attention to message communication: the use of language, and the presentation of iconic messages such as symbols; and editing techniques.

Written and spoken language. Although the NZ class had about one-third international students, it was those NZ-born students who commented on the difficulty in understanding the narration, specifically in the "Promised Land" video. They felt that the narrator spoke too quickly: "I could not comprehend what he was saying and didn't get much information, which defeated the purpose of the video clip—promoting its fulltime MBA". Some students were also critical of the lack of professionalism of the narrator, "He couldn't pronounce 'multidisciplinary' where there was a bit of a giggle which came across as lacking in professionalism." This led one student to comment: "He should have practiced his speech better during the voice over." Others commented that the commentators lacked a passion in their speeches, and had little enthusiasm for the MBA program. Thus, the narrator's role is important in delivering the message to the audience in a clear and lively manner. Students' comments indicate that the voice of the narrator influences the audience's attitude towards the video presentation in that it may either motivate or reduce a favorable response. In this video the incongruence between the voice of the narrator and the message content helped to promote feelings of skepticism in the NZ students.

The students appreciated the use of titles and subtitles during the narration. One student commented: "I appreciate[d] the titles of the various speakers shown on the video whereby I know their credentials and what area they are commenting on in the MBA program." Further, students concurred that the use of slides (written titles between scenes in the third video) helped to emphasize the focus of the promotion. The placement of subtitles with each speaker's presentation in both videos enabled them to fully understand the roles of the speakers and the content of the MBA program. Therefore, slides, titles, and subtitles were important in ensuring the audience understood the message. These devices were missing in the NZ videos, and hence, the Israeli student audience had difficulty in understanding the content of the message, thereby diminishing its persuasive effect.

The use of iconic messages: the promised land, celebrities, the campus. Similar to the Israeli students, the NZ students interpreted symbols quite differently from their intended meaning. In particular, the biblical reference to Israel as the "promised land," in the opening scene of the first Israeli video was unclear. They felt that the use of an unknown symbol would prevent the audience from understanding the relevance of the promotion about to be introduced. Further, one student pointed out that a religious reference might suggest that there is intolerance towards other (religious) views in Israel:

> By having the biblical message, it showed that you are a very religious country but it might scare some students as they are not religious. And a message like that might create the feeling that a person is not free to express his or her own religious values.

Thus, the Israeli producers needed to engage in more careful market research to realise that NZ has a high regard for its status as a secular country, where discrimination on the grounds of religion is not permitted. However, for one student, the "promised land" symbol created an emotional response in her as she wanted to better understand what was special about this symbolic reference.

A second iconic message was the use of cultural ambassadors. The first video chose celebrity endorsement of the MBA program. However, none of the NZ students knew the famous Italian movie star shown, and some did not recognise the former president of France. Once the teacher had explained who these people were, some students commented that displaying the celebrities receiving honorary degrees helped to increase their understanding of the university's international reputation, which they viewed positively. The second video chose a New Zealand teacher to promote the MBA. The Maori greeting helped to make the students to connect with the promotional message.

A third iconic message was images of prominent international corporations such as Intel and AMDOCS. Students felt that these images were highly persuasive in that they showed the connectedness of the university with global business.

The final iconic message that received prominent comment from the NZ students was images of the campus and the countryside beyond the campus. Students enjoyed watching the natural beauty of the Israeli landscape shown at the start (the dessert and hillsides, the panned images of the city, and the flora and fauna). They also enjoyed the scenes of the university buildings, showing the contemporary architecture, and scenes of students walking around campus. One student commented:

> I was amazed by the sceneries shown at the start of the clip, the architectures of the university and the cultural diversity amongst the students filmed. All these generate a sense of peace and order, which was not what I had expected. This is because prior to watching the film, I thought that there had been constant religious tensions in Israel whereby ruins could be seen everywhere.

Thus, these images decreased the audience's anxiety about how people live and study in Israel, and increased their interest in knowing more about the society.

However, students commented on images that were missing, namely, scenes of the students' lifestyles at the university, for example, accommodation, centers for socializing and communal areas, and cafes. Students were interested to know more about the social aspects of the university as this knowledge could influence their decision to choose Israel as a study-abroad destination. They also strongly noted the absence of information on how to contact the university in order to give feedback and gain more detailed information about the MBA program. For example, one student suggested that a university Web site and email address would enable prospective students to go to the Internet to get more information. This two-way communication between the subject of the promotion—the university—and the audience were important in enabling the audience to follow up on the promotion, thereby increasing the likelihood of its success in attracting international students.

Video editing techniques. .Although both the Israeli and NZ teachers did not specify to the students to use editorial and technical support, both groups felt that their credibility was at stake; they wanted to produce a quality video for their respective audiences. Nonetheless, NZ students were critical of the Israeli students' video production, namely, a shaking camera while videoing, and in the second Israeli video, long gaps between sections, both of which distracted attention from the message. Thus, the students felt that editing and technical expertise were important in creating a convincing promotional message.

In summary, NZ students valued the use of titles and subtitles in creating a clear message, the use of celebrities to endorse the international recognition of the qualification, and images of campus life and the surrounding countryside. They also believed that the Israeli videos were informative and persuasive, and transmitted the idea of a friendly and interesting environment. These attributes shortened the distance between the product and the audience's expectations, resulting in the NZ students generally being favourably disposed to the promotional message. By contrast, students felt the message was weakened by the lack of professionalism in narration in the second Israeli video, and the missing images of the social life on campus.

Discussion

Both the Israeli and NZ students tried hard to achieve successful intercultural communication through the creation and promotion of their video products. Their responses indicate that the (student) producers put effort into presenting and conveying a meaningful and positive message to their target audience. All groups employed linguistic and iconic messages to help the audience achieve a better understanding of their respective degree programs. Language appeared to be the most vital tool or precondition in achieving successful communication, and thus, mutual understanding between people from the two cultures. A further measure of success was in the grade given to the video promotion, awarded by each student in the audience. When the scores were averaged out across all four videos, each scored 7 to 8 out of 10.

Where iconic messages were concerned, both the Israeli and NZ groups employed their national symbols to attract their audience's attention. However, in each case, the audience failed to understand the meaning of the symbols as they lacked knowledge of the other country's culture. Therefore, symbolic imagery did not help sell the product. This unexpected outcome resulted from the producers' lack of research on their target audience. This knowledge gap was also apparent in the NZ video, produced by the Chinese international students. They focused on NZ as a safe place to live and study, perhaps epitomising their views of what is important for international students. The resultant displeasure from the Israeli audience was unexpected. Clearly, the NZ producers had relied on the NZ media representations of the violence in Israel, and not on their own research of how Israeli people themselves feel about security in their country.

Further, the Israeli and NZ producers approached their promotions from different perspectives. Both of the NZ videos focused on the peaceful and quality living conditions, environment, and study atmosphere within the university. They focused on presenting messages of campus life through images of scenery, perhaps playing on the ideals of NZ as clean and green, and as a South Pacific paradise; they also focused on interviews with smiling students, and positive endorsements from teaching and administrative staff. On the other hand, the Israeli producers primarily promoted the quality of their program and the university's position and global connectedness. Both Israeli videos focused on delivering messages about the strength and quality of the teaching and research through connections with top universities in North America, the international reputation of the MBA, the success of its graduates in finding top jobs in international companies, and the university's links with global corporations. These two opposing foci indicate the respective values of each culture. In the case of the NZ students, they emphasized student life as being both relaxing and enjoyable, with international students including NZ as a safe place to study. By contrast, the Israeli students stressed the added value their degree offered, and the need to have competitive advantage through both the qualification and international connectedness. Ironically, the NZ students attend the top business school in NZ, and yet, they did not promote this accolade, except indirectly, as in one video where interviews were accompanied by a pop-up subtitle: "No 1 business school in NZ."

Yet, there was also alignment among the four groups in the use of emotional appeals to motivate the audience into participating in the sales promotion. All four groups used a cultural ambassador—an interview with a teacher from the target culture in three cases, and the use of celebrities receiving an honorary degree in the forth case. In the case of the teachers, these cultural ambassadors served as an endorsement of the program and the living and study environment; they also helped to lower the audience's anxiety and fears of studying in a foreign culture. A further emotional appeal used by all four groups was the use of the target culture's language. In one NZ video, the teacher spoke in Hebrew; in the other, some of the interviewees used the greeting "Shalom." In the second Israeli video, the NZ teacher used the Maori greeting "Kia ora." The use of a common language helped create feelings of welcome and familiarity for both audiences. These appeals promoted the idea of two-way communication, between the producers and their audience, thereby engaging the audience and creating a mutual understanding.

Implications of the Two-way Video Exchange Project

The value of engaging in a two-way video exchange between countries both geographically and culturally diverse has been demonstrated in the experiences of the students, both as producers and audience. Their responses (presented in the findings above) reveal the different ways in which people in each culture experience and understand the communication of those in the other culture. The project has implications on multiple levels: at the level of the student learning experience; and theoretically, methodologically, and pedagogically.

Implications for Experiencing and Understanding the Communication of another Culture

The findings suggest three key outcomes for students, as both as producers and audience in developing persuasive sales promotions. First, all four groups underestimated the importance of spoken and written communication. English was not a lingua franca among the audiences. Therefore, they needed to provide clearer messages by minimising accent, speaking slowly, and using visual cues such as subtitles and titles. Second, all groups needed to do more audience analysis and market research. The use of culturally-specific icons, unrecognisable by those in the other culture, resulted in audience confusion rather than appreciation of what the host culture had to offer. A second part of the market research should acknowledge that Israeli and NZ students hold different values about education and promotional messages should therefore be developed accordingly. Israeli students value an internationally recognised qualification that provides a competitive edge and connectedness on the world stage; instead, the NZ student audience placed value on study as a relaxed and enjoyable experience in a safe, peaceful, and beautiful environment. Finally, production and editing techniques were considered important. While all groups sought assistance here, NZ students were more critical of their Israeli counterparts' efforts.

Theoretical Implications

Making sense of how people from another culture understand and experience our own culture allows for a range of theoretical applications. The culture in context approach—how contextual variables such as age, gender, context of interaction, and nonverbal communication influence communication—provides a basic starting point. Many of these elements were applied by the students in their responses as they attempted to interpret the other culture's communication. Another approach, applied by the Israeli teacher, is Scollon and Scollon's (1995) discourse systems, where students identify the relevant systems in a specific interaction and analyze distance on three levels: basic assumptions, data organization and communication style. Further possibilities include the "global culture approach," for example, Hofstede's (1997) four dimensions of cultural difference, and Hall's (1976) high-low context approach. The pluricultural societies from which each student audience derives, and the cultural differences in the New Zealand class with its high ratio of international and Chinese students, may provide the basis for a rich critique of these grand theories that attempt to essentialize understandings of cultural differences.

Theories of intercultural communication competence (ICC), for example, Chen and Starosta's (1996) comprehensive model, and understandings of cultural identity (Collier, 1998), also lend themselves. Chen and Starosta defined an interculturally competent person as having the "ability to negotiate cultural meanings and to execute appropriately effective communication behaviors that recognize the interactant's multiple identities in a specific environment" (p. 359). The definition, in addition to its focus on competence, highlights the importance of identity. Both groups failed to sufficiently consider the other's cultural identity and the processes (cognitive, behavioral, affective) that underpin their communication, or why people communicate in the way that they do (Starosta & Chen, 2003). Further, Byram's (1997) notion of "s'engager" appeals to promoting the skill set of connectedness, identified at the outset, where intercultural speakers are critically aware of themselves and their own values, as well as those of people from other cultures with whom they are communicating. In these respects, are the student producers in each group sufficiently competent to engage the cultural other into accepting the sales promotion?

Methodological and Pedagogical Implications

Co-ordinating the exchange of videos, and collating and emailing students' responses between Israel and NZ provided its own logistical challenges for us as teachers. Yet, the project used only a part of Pan et al's (2002) methodology—a video presentation (of a sales promotion). Further areas of business communication could be explored, for example, resumes, business cards, business letters, or any documents that are highly persuasive in nature.

The exchange allows for a range of methodological and pedagogical applications. We tried to organise a synchronised video conference between the two classes, but the time difference prevented this exchange. Further tools might include the use of Web cameras where Israeli and NZ students pair and engage in dyadic interaction.

We attempted three additional processes not reported here. First, The two NZ groups were required to write a report where they reflected on the video production process and the feedback received from Israeli students. They identified the strengths and weaknesses in their own video, and what they would do better and/or differently next time. They also reflected on their learning experience. A second requirement was make a group presentation to their classmates of the learning experience the exchange afforded. Third, the Israeli students analysed the NZ students' responses in light of the theories they had learned in their class, noting advantages and barriers to the communication. Further applications might include building a bank of videos from the exchanges, which are placed on a Web site for students to analyse, applying the same method.

In conclusion, all the students were highly positive and enthusiastic about the production, exchange, and feedback processes. The video production groups found the experience highly satisfying, and the students in both classes regarded the exchange as a valuable learning tool for finding out how people in another culture perceived their own communication. As the findings and implications suggest, the project provided an effective means of engaging students in meaningful learning.

References

Brake, T., Walker, D.M. & Walker, T. (1995). *Doing Business Interally: A Guide to Cross-cultural Success*. Princeton: Training Management Corporation.

Byram, M. (1997). *Teaching and Assessing Intercultural Communicative Competence*. Clevedon: Multilingual Matters.

Chen, G.M., & Starosta, W. (1996). Intercultural communication competence: A synthesis. In S. Deetz (Ed.), *Communication Yearbook 19* (pp. 353-383). Thousand Oaks, CA: Sage.

Collier, M. J. (1998). Researching cultural identity: Reconciling interpretive and post-colonial perspectives. In D. V. Tanno & A. Gonzales (Eds.), *Communication and Identity across Cultures* (pp. 122-147). Thousand Oaks, CA: Sage.

Guilherme, E. (2002). *Critical Citizens for an Intercultural World*. Cleveland: Multilingual Matters.

Hall, E. (1976*). Beyond Culture*. New York: Anchor Press.

Harrison, J. (2001). Developing intercultural communication and understanding through social studies in Israel. *The Social Studies, 92*, 252-260.

Hofstede, G. (1997). *Cultures and Organizations: Software of the Mind*. New York: McGraw-Hill.

Jiang, X. (2005). Interculturalisation for New Zealand universities in a global context. *Policy Futures for Education, 3*(2), 223-233.

Newman, F., Couturier, L., & Scurry, J. (2004). *The Future of Higher Education: Rhetoric, Reality, and the Risks of the Market*. San Francisco, CA.: Wiley, Jossey-Bass.

Pan, Y., Scollon, S., & Scollon, R. (2002). *Professional Communication in Intenational Settings*. Oxford, Blackwell.

Scollon, R., & Scollon, S. (1995). *Intercultural Communication: A Discourse Approach*. Oxford: Blackwell.

Starosta, W. & Chen, G. M. (2003). "Ferment," an ethic of caring, and the corrective power of dialogue. In W. Starosta & G. M. Chen (Eds.), *Ferment in the Intercultural Field: Axiology/Value/ Praxis* (pp. 3-23). Thousand Oaks, CA: Sage.

Ward, C., & Lin, E.Y. (2005). Immigration, acculturation and national identity in NZ. In J.H. Liu, T. McCreanor, T. McIntosh, & T. Teaiwa (Eds.), *NZ Identities: Departures and Destinations* (pp. 155-173). Wellington, NZ: Victoria University Press.

Zodgekar, A. (2005). The changing face of NZ's population and national identity. In J.H. Liu, T. McCreanor, T. McIntosh, & T. Teaiwa (Eds.), *NZ Identities: Departures and Destinations* (pp. 140-154). Wellington, NZ: Victoria University Press.

Introduction to

Pragmatic Diversity, Pragmatic Transfer, and Cultural Identity

By Yuxin Jia

Jia points out that today many people from around the world use English as the language of communication. However, they will interpret and evaluate what is said in English from their own cultural perspective. This is so because cultural values, norms, or conventions shape the way people speak or program what is appropriate behavior and what is not in a given situation. However, values, norms, or conventions differ from culture to culture; and this kind of diversity leads to the tendency for people from different cultural groups to judge or evaluate the behavior of others by their own cultural standard. This kind of diversity is called the cultural difference which Jia prefers to call pragmatic diversity. It is the unawareness of this pragmatic diversity that leads to intercultural misinterpretations and misunderstandings, Jia notes, when people are using English in their communication and both or some of the participants are of different cultural background.

Jia observes that while the social functions of language or communication as well as the tasks that are to be accomplished may be universal, the pragmatic norms or conventions underlying the performance and realization of these functions and tasks may differ from culture to culture. Thus, Jia points out, every language in the world may perform the functions such as greeting, apologizing, but each culture selects norms or conventions or linguistic strategies unique to its own culture to accomplish each of these tasks in given situations. It is these culturally based pragmatic norms or conventions that shape how a pragmatic meaning is conveyed in a given context and how this pragmatic meaning should be interpreted. Jia, therefore, notes that when people of different cultural background come into contact with one another, pragmatic diversity is transferred to the English message which will lead to difficulties of interpretation or misunderstandings even though all speak English with one another. This is demonstrated by Jia in a number of cases involving Chinese and Americans interacting with one another in English. These cases clearly demonstrate that the Chinese prefer to imply or express their requests indirectly or implicitly while Americans are direct with their requests. Jia states that when people use English as a second or foreign language, they tend to transfer the pragmatic norms or conventions of their first language to the second or foreign language which is used for intercultural interactions. People also tend to judge or evaluate the other's English on the basis of their own personal cultural standards. This is a very important insight especially since so much international communication is carried out in English by people who are not native speakers of English and of different cultural background. Using English, therefore, does not automatically translate into better business understanding.

Michael B. Hinner

Yuxin Jia is Professor of Sociolinguistics and Intercultural Communication at Harbin Institute of Technology, Harbin, China. He is concurrently Vice President of the China Association for Intercultural Communication Studies and a member of the Board of Directors of the China Association for English Education Study. He has acted as Vice President and President of the International Association of Intercultural Communication Studies and now is member of the Board of Directors of the International Association of Intercultural Communication Studies and a member of the Editorial Board. Professor Jia taught intercultural communication at Illinois State University at Springfield in the years from 1987 to 1989. He is widely appreciated as one of the founders in the field of intercultural communication in China. His monograph, *Intercultural Communication,* has been used either as a textbook or reference book in almost all the foreign language departments and colleges in China. At the international level, Professor Jia has been dedicating his conscientious efforts to the building of bridges between different cultures.

Pragmatic Diversity, Pragmatic Transfer, and Cultural Identity

Yuxin Jia

We would like to begin 'Pragmatic Diversity' and its influence on intercultural communication with some illustrative facts or examples from the personal experiences of my friends in their interaction with their American friends during their stay in America. The point of giving the examples is to illustrate that the English spoken by the Chinese diverges from Anglo-American English as it has different cultural norms or conventions operating at the pragmatic level. As a result, misinterpretations of the speakers' intentions of either side occur. And hence, misunderstandings and even worse consequences are inevitable. We will examine what is odd or (systematically) deviant from the so called Anglo-American standard at the pragmatic level and what problems of understanding these oddities may present.

The first example comes from one of my friend's experience when he was teaching the graduate students in a communication program in one of the universities in the States.

One Friday afternoon, Professor Larry Smith, dean of the Communication Program where my friend had been teaching sociolinguistics called to ask if he was free that evening. He knew that it was a signal of invitation. So, he said yes as he was free and would like to relax a little bit. Larry told him that the movie "The Last Emperor" was on and he asked him if he would like to go and see it with him. So, Larry came over and took him in his car to the cinema. Arriving at the cinema, they got off and went to book the tickets. Then, my friend offered, "*Let me buy the tickets,*" which is obviously a typical Chinese way of being polite. However, out of his expectation, Larry replied, "*OK, if you insist.*" Hearing this, he was more than puzzled, as he had never expected that a person being invited would pay for what he was invited to do. Did he have to pay for being invited? Or, should he say that he was not insisting? Apparently, he could not say it. If he had, he would have certainly lost face. "Is that the American way of inviting people to see a movie?" he asked himself even long after this incident. The film was good but he kept wondering about what Americans were like as persons.

Several days later, my friend was going to hold a farewell party on the forthcoming Saturday, as he was finishing his teaching in the university and was going back to China. He intended to invite several American colleagues and friends to the party and say goodbye to them. However, when he invited Dr. Larry Smith, Larry said, *"Oh, I am sorry. I have already had an appointment on Saturday."* Again my friend felt more than puzzled. He was in fact very disappointed. This kind of rejection seldom happens in China as saying good-bye to good friends in a way like this is regarded as an important event. More than that, he regarded the presence of Larry Smith as the most important thing at the party as he was the dean of the program and also one of his closest friends. Larry's direct rejection to his invitation certainly caused him to lose face. His self-esteem was deeply hurt. However, this seems not enough. When he was inviting Doug Woken, a professor of linguistics, what he said just as much hurt his feeling. He said, *"I have to check my schedule and then I will let you know if I can come or not."* It seems to my friend that what he regarded as very important may just seem trivial to his American friends. He had been studying and teaching in the States for a couple of years. His friendship with them now seemed not important to them at all. "Will they forget me, or remember me just as much as I will remember them?" My friend asked himself. He doubted if they were really his friends. "If they invited me to a farewell party like this in China, I would give up whatever I was doing on hand and accept their invitation without any hesitation," my friend thought.

Pragmatic Diversity, Cultural Norms, and Pragmatic Transfer

The cultural facts or experiences such as these mentioned above point to possible cultural differences in values, norms or conventions that operate in the process of communication and at the same time they may in one way or another, highlight the possible tendency for people of different cultures to react emotionally to unexpected behavior.

The cultural values, norms, or conventions shape the way we speak or program what is appropriate behavior and what is not in a given situation. However values, norms or conventions differ from culture to culture and this kind of diversity leads to the tendency for people from different cultural groups to judge or evaluate the behavior of others by their own cultural standard. This kind of diversity is called the cultural differences in sociopragmatic and pragmalinguistic conventions or what the author prefers to call socio-cultural pragmatic diversity, or pragmatic diversity for short. It is the unawareness of this pragmatic diversity that leads to intercultural misinterpretation and misunderstanding.

Although in dealing with interpersonal relationship and communication, the social functions of language or communication, as well as tasks that are to be accomplished may be universal, the pragmatic norms or conventions underlying the performance and realization of these functions and tasks may differ from culture to culture. For example, every language in the world may perform the functions such as greeting, complimenting, apologizing, refusing, requesting, invitation, etc. However, each culture selects norms or conventions or linguistic strategies unique to its own culture, to accomplish each of them in given situations. What or which options or strategies will be in favor depends on culturally-based pragmatic preferences.

It is these culturally-based pragmatic norms or conventions that shape how a pragmatic meaning is conveyed in a given context and how this pragmatic meaning should be interpreted.

Facts and examples from experiences of interaction across cultures are far too many to demonstrate this point. For example, at the pragmatic level, the Chinese culture selects the *humble-self-and-respect-others* in everyday interactions as the norm or convention, due to the value of harmony and relationship or interpersonal connection, while some cultures in the West may select what is called the norm of *being-honest* or *autonomy/independence* and hence *no-imposition*. In terms of facework, the Chinese culture favors not only the interactional aspect of face but on many occasions, they also emphasize the *moral* and *relational* aspect of face while the Americans favor the *interactional* aspect. Obviously, when people from these different cultures come to interact with each other, due to the cultural influences, differences in norms or conventions that underlie communication will lead to difficulties of interpretation or misunderstandings even though they may all speak English.

Let us have a close look at the speech behavior of invitation mentioned in the first section of the paper and discover where differences lie and why misinterpretation and misunderstanding occur.

In the Chinese cultural context, when being invited (to a film, dinner, etc.), the potential guest may often be expected to offer to pay just for being polite, even though he or she may not in fact wants to pay at all as, according to the Chinese norm or convention, the inviter on such occasion is in general expected to politely decline the offer. However, following what is called *honest* norm or convention, Americans may likely take such polite behavior for a true and sincere offer and to respect the autonomy and independence of the speaker's decision, he or she would very likely say, "Yes, please," "OK, if you want to/ would like to," or "OK, if you insist," which is certainly the last thing a potential Chinese guest would expect. The American cultural selection of norm of *being-*

honest and *autonomy-and-independence/ no-imposition* norms or conventions may hence constitute face threatening act to a potential Chinese guest. In fact, a Chinese on such occasions, would expect the American to 'insist' on paying for the ticket himself or herself as a Chinese usually does so in the Chinese cultural context.

The hierarchical nature of the Chinese society predisposed a complex social network of unique hierarchical interpersonal relationships. It defines complex and different norms or conventions for appropriate conduct and behavior for every social member in their social interaction according to his or her social position. The expected behaviors include, among others, those that are asymmetrical or hierarchically complementary, reciprocally obligatory and so on. In the hierarchical interpersonal relationship, what is appropriate behavior to one party in the pair is not identical to what is appropriate for the other party. This kind of asymmetry constitutes the complementary nature of the hierarchical society. In the relationship of such vertical dyad order is often realized in the submission of the individual identity of the inferior to the superior and according to the Confucian ethic, though the superior and inferior are unequal in their status, they are interdependent, complementary, and obligatory and are equally essential in function for the establishment of harmonious relationship in social interactions.

It is just this asymmetry that predisposes the differences and specifics of the norms or conventions for the invitation behavior. In general, at least three kinds of options of norms or conventions operate in the process of invitation behavior. First, in the interaction of the unequal interpersonal relationship, an invitation from a person of a higher or superior position (in terms of social position, authority, seniority, profession, wealth, sex, etc.) to a person of lower or inferior social position, the invitation is usually considered to be an act of granting face or to be an honor to the person being invited. Second, in the interaction of the equal interpersonal relationship, when the invitation act involves significant event such as to a wedding ceremony or farewell party from either party, it is generally considered to be reciprocally obligatory, and when involving an informal event, it is not generally considered to be obligatory, that is, either side may have the freedom to accept or reject the invitation and either side will take it for granted. Then, in the interaction of the unequal interpersonal relationship, when an invitation is issued from the person of lower social position to the person of higher social position, it would be considered to be an act of asking the other side to grant face or favor and whether to accept or reject the invitation is the job of the person in power. And when the invitation from a person of inferior social position is rejected for whatever reason, the inferior would take it for an act of having no face and in contrast, the invitation rejecter would just take it for granted due to the power distance. And if the invitation is accepted, the person of socially lower or inferior position would take it for an act of enhancement of his or her face or being given an honor.

However, in the interaction with a foreigner, from North America in particular, the performance of giving or declining invitation seems to be a little bit more complex. The invitation from either side would be possibly considered to be sort of formal event by the Chinese, as in usual cases, the foreigner is usually considered to be a person in a special social position. The invitation could usually be considered to be an invitation like the one between persons of the equal relationship and may sometimes be like the one between persons of unequal interpersonal relationship with the foreign friends somewhat located at a special or superior position or looked at as a special guest. The invitation from either side, especially for an important event, could be considered to be sort of formal and hence important by the Chinese.

Examined from this analysis, we can see easily why the author's friend felt sad and considered it to be a loss of face when his invitation to his American friend to his farewell party was rejected. And when the other American said he would check his schedule to see if he could come or not, he was even more hurt, as the importance of his invitation was neglected and belittled. In the Chinese context, as a friend, he or she would feel it obligated to accept the invitation to an important occasion. He or she is in general expected to rearrange or postpone his or her appointments. And as a special guest, the Americans' rejection of the invitation could be even more face frustrating. If the Chinese could have understood the American norms or conventions embedded in the individualism orientation and if the Americans had understood the Chinese norms or conventions embedded in the principle of Li or propriety of Confucian ethics, such frustration would have been avoided.

It may be just as important to know some other aspects regarding the differences in norms or conventions and cultural values that are involved in the behavior of invitation. In the American cultural context, to invite others to a party, several other cultural norms or conventions should be taken into account. For example, for the Americans, to invite others to a party is considered to 'borrow' other's time or simply to 'borrow' other's money (as time is regarded as money), hence to respect other's autonomy or independence is pretty close to respecting other's time and this is certainly an important American norm for giving invitation. That is why we often hear an American host/hostess say, "Thanks for your time" to the guests who are saying goodbye at a party. In this light the Chinese way of imposing an invitation upon a friend and forcing him or her to accept the unwanted invitation is really odd, strange, and even offensive. The Americans are seldom aware that it is almost an unscripted norm or convention for the Chinese to urge a friend or a well-acquainted person or keep on pinning others down to accept the invitation. Likewise, as Wolfson (1989, 17) has noted, an American often extends an invitation to a social gathering by indicating when and where it will take place and then adds some sort of phrase like "Come if you want to / you like." Potential guests like Chinese and Japanese when given an invitation like this would no doubt be embarrassed or even offended as they cannot make it sure whether they are sincerely invited or not. They may think that the Americans do not want them to go to the gathering at all.

Obviously, these cross-cultural misunderstandings arise from the fact that when people from different cultural backgrounds interact with each other, either side, being unaware of the cultural or pragmatic norms or conventions of the other side, tends to transfer his or her own cultural norms or conventions that operate in the use of his or her first language. This is in general what is called pragmatic transfer. The other aspect of transfer theory is that people, without being aware of pragmatic diversities, are very likely to judge or evaluate the behavior of a person from a different culture according to the cultural standard or criterion of their own culture. No doubt the transfer of the norms or conventions from the first language culture to the target language inevitably leads to breakdowns in intercultural communication and the misjudgment and mis-evaluation of the behavior of the person from a different cultural background may make the breakdowns even worse.

It is true that a second or foreign language learner or an advanced speaker of a second language can be influenced by the second language cultural norms or conventions. However, due to long years of the formal instruction in the first language culture, very few of them, can speak and write like a native speaker because explicit instruction in their own culture cannot take the place of the socialization process (Scollon & Scollon, 1995). Culture in the socialization process, creates people as social beings and it hence becomes part of themselves. Sociocultural frameworks including values, beliefs, presuppositions, assumptions, norms, conventions, expectations, behaviors, etc. are culture bound and people are committed to the sociocultural frameworks of their own culture and cannot easily deny or step out of such cultural frameworks.

English has become an international language, however, *"We simply cannot internationalize things and ideas without having them accommodated to the customs of people who are supposed to use them for their own purposes"* (Honna, 2002). English is being internationalized. However, it is difficult for the cultural norms or conventions of native English speakers to be internationalized. The internalization of English can only prompt the diversification of English. Pragmatic diversity is the cost of the internationalization of English (Honna, 2002).

Obviously, pragmatic transfer is unavoidable in our intercultural communication. We have to admit that people from different cultural backgrounds speak English in different ways even though they share the same or similar purpose of the interaction, because we often encounter differences in terms of expectations, norms or conventions that underlie the process of communication. The different ways of speaking just reveal who the speakers are. When the Chinese speak English, they cannot but demonstrate that they are Chinese. The different ways of speaking, and writing as well, can be markers of cultural identity.

Pragmatic Norms or Conventions as Cultural Identity

We all know that the main function of language is communication. However, we seldom know that a crucial function of language is to provide identity (Kirkpatrick, 2005, 164). According to Le Page (1964), while communication is an obvious function of language, the primary function of language is to allow people to act as members of a speech community.

When we communicate with people in English as a second or foreign language, the English we use also reveal which sort of cultural group we come from. To be more specific, the English we use reveal our cultural and social identity.

The English we use reveal who we are, just like our first language does. The way we pronounce the words, the way we organize sentences, and so on all allow the people that we are interacting to know who we are. When Americans speak English, they sound Americans. When Australians speak English, they sound Australians. Likewise, when Singaporeans speak English they sound Singaporeans, and when Chinese speak English they sound Chinese. When we speak a second or foreign language we not only reveal who we are in terms of pronunciation but we also reveal who we are in terms of pragmatic norms or conventions. That is, we transfer the pragmatic norms or conventions of our first language to the use of English, for example, as a second or foreign language, as a lingua franca. However, *"While it is easy to learn that different cultures use different forms of greeting, it can be much more difficult to learn that different cultures have different pragmatic norms in many other fields, such as requesting and receiving compliments"* (Kirkpatrick, 2005,162). As mentioned earlier, the Chinese and American cultures select different norms or conventions for the behavior of invitation. Hence, the Chinese may tell the Americans that they are Chinese and vice versa, the Americans may tell the Chinese that they are Americans.

It is just as important that, in turn, the norms or conventions underlying our behavior can in one way or another help unpack our culture. Through understanding how people from different cultures communicate with each other, how people verbally perform the act of invitation, for example, we may likely come to know how politeness as an important norm operates in the interpersonal communication in the Chinese context. And more than that, the norms or conventions of politeness may help us know some aspects of Chinese culture as the norm of politeness in the Chinese context stems from the Li maxim or what may be called propriety in English. Li in fact constitutes an important aspect of Chinese Confucian culture that underlies the Chinese interpersonal relationship and interaction.

Communication is a symbolic system and symbols have meaning only in relation to cultural and social environment. Thus, communication including language as social and cultural act cannot be studied in isolation. Communication itself is culture and culture is communication. It is part of cultural values and beliefs. Culture in terms of values and beliefs, etc. does enter into face-to-face (intercultural) communication to create *"an interactional space in which the subconscious and automatic sociolinguistic (pragmatic, the author) processes of interpretation and inference can generate a variety of outcomes and make interpretations subject to question"* (Gumperz, 1982, 3). In such intercultural encounter, our most cherished expectations, assumptions, and ways of thinking cannot travel across cultural boundaries. What is customarily expected and understood becomes incomprehensible in a diverse culture. Therefore, communication cannot be studied as value-free phenomenon and as cultural and social act, must be looked at as a product of the interplay of culture and social realities.

Communication can be defined as culturally constructed act because it is not only influenced by but also enacts cultural values, beliefs, and cultural and social conventions. Or stated differently, the differing cultural values, beliefs, worldviews in one way or another impose different norms or conventions for the use of language or other modes of communication in comparable social situational context. They are enacted in a variety of manners of communication. *"Thus, the norms and values which inform speakers' knowledge as to what is appropriate to say to whom, and under which conditions show considerable variation from community to community around the world, not only from one language group to another but within language groups as well"* (Wolfson, 1989, 14). So, *what* we do and *how* in intercultural communication may in different extent reveal significant differences of identity in terms of values and beliefs because values and beliefs themselves are constitutive of communicative reality.

However, the interlocutors in the course of intercultural communication are expressing these differences without their realizing of doing so—they are not aware of them. They are enacting these differences in a natural manner. It is just this unawareness of "*being ourself and acting according to our deepest instincts, human beings reveal fundamental differences in what we all tend to think of as normal behavior*" (Storti, C., 1997).

Indirect Request as an Identity Marker for the Chinese

Research on the speech act of requests for information has been under scrutiny in recent years. Most of it however, focuses on *who* asks the question, *what* is asked, *when* it is asked, *where* it is asked, and to whom it is asked (Lin-Mei Huang, 2000, 107). Although '*what*' is asked, '*who*' asks the question and '*how*' the question is asked may determine "whether the answer is forthcoming and truthful" (Johnson, 1992, 42), few scholars examine '*how*' the question is asked in terms of cultural norms or conventions. As some scholars pointed out, '*how*' is just as important as '*what*', as '*how*' to say is often regarded as part of '*what*' to say by many scholars. It could be more important if we examine it as cultural norms and conventions in revealing who the speakers are. This section addresses this particular '*how*'. To be specific, it addresses the popular practice of indirect request, which the authors regard as a pragmatic norm and a marker of Chinese cultural identity as well.

As we probably know, requesting for information or questioning for truthful answers in interactions is a universal phenomenon. In the same token, people of almost all cultures may express requests either directly or indirectly. However, the strategies for requesting behavior vary from culture to culture. Holtgraves and Yang (1992) and Tannen (1981) stated that cultures differ in normative social styles of making requests. Previous studies, especially pragmatic studies demonstrate that there are not only differences between direct and indirect ways of requests but also differences among social and cultural factors that influence this speech behavior. And these social factors are constrained by cultural values and beliefs, particularly ideologies and social factors in turn constrain the pragmatic meaning of different forms of directives.

According to the model of high- versus low-context by Hall & Hall (1985) and scholars such as Gudykunst (1984), Stella Ting-Toomey (1988) and Yuxin Jia (1998), East Asians prefer to reveal their intention indirectly whereas Americans prefer to reveal their intentions directly through explicit requests due to the collectivism versus individualism orientations. In the collectivism oriented cultures, harmonious relationship is regarded as the most important goal in interpersonal interactions and as an immediate and most direct result of this orientation, indirectness comes to be the most cherished and hence most predominant norm or conventions for everyday interaction. It may function as a mechanism to prevent disagreement or conflict among interactants. At least, indirect request and indirect rejection to or indirect disagreement with the request may help tone down embarrassment of rejection in the process of interpersonal interactions as it may leave the relationship and the face of each interactant intact (Yum, 1988) and cultivate mutual understanding and interpersonal harmony.

According to Hall & Hall (1987), directness and indirectness constitute one of the major differences in interpersonal communication between low context and high context (e.g. East Asian cultures) in verbal expression. People from low context cultures prefer to use a direct verbal expression style, and people from high context cultures prefer to use indirect verbal expression style. Hall & Hall also point out that the direct verbal expression style consists of four features: (1) the situational context is not emphasized; (2) important information is usually carried in explicit verbal messages; (3) self-expression, verbal fluency, and eloquent speech are valued; and (4) people tend to directly express their opinions and intend to persuade others to accept their viewpoints.

The indirect verbal expression styles, according to Hall & Hall, consist of four features: (1) explicit verbal messages are not emphasized (not as much emphasized as it is in the western culture, the author); (2) important information is usually carried in contextual cues (e.g., place, time, situation, and relationship); (3) harmony is highly valued, with a tendency toward using ambiguous language and keeping silent in interactions; and (4) people tend to talk around the point, and to avoid saying 'no' directly to others . According to Stella Ting-Toomey (1999),

> "The direct and indirect approaches in communication differ in the extent to which interlocutors reveal their intentions through their tone of voice and the straightforwardness of their content message. In the direct verbal style, statements clearly reveal the speaker's intentions and are enunciated in a forthright tone of voice. In the indirect verbal style, on the other hand, verbal statements tend to camouflage the speaker's actual intentions and are carried out with more nuanced tone of voice. For example, the overall U.S. American verbal style often calls for clear and direct communication. Phrases such as 'say what you mean,' 'don't beat around the bush,' and 'get to the point' are some examples. The direct verbal style of the larger U.S. culture is reflective of its low-context communication character" (1999, 103).

The straightforward way of requests of the Americans often leaves the impression of being 'rude,' 'blunt,' 'pushy,' 'arrogant,' and 'insincere' on the Chinese listeners whereas the indirect way of requests of the Chinese often leaves the impression of being 'insincere and untrustworthy' on the Americans (Stella, 1999). In the interaction between the Americans and the Chinese, the roundabout or indirect way of making requests of the Chinese and the forthright way of making requests of the U.S. Americans may often lead to misunderstandings, hurt feelings and break friendship.

To testify whether or not the indirect / direct request can serve as a marker of the Chinese cultural identity, I select four pairs of factual interlocutions involving the behavior of requests and responses to these requests from the personal experiences of my friends either in the Chinese or American contexts and I also used these pairs of interlocutions as material (with all the names and other cues that may explicitly reveal the interlocutors' identity omitted) to test on 33 graduate students of English linguistics and applied linguistics to see if they are able to tell exactly whether the requestors and the responders are Chinese or Americans and between whom these interlocutions could possibly occur. The interlocutions are respectively between two Chinese female graduate students of English; an American professor and a Chinese graduate student of English; two Americans; a Chinese female graduate student and her American friend. The premises of the test is that if the majority of the students can tell exactly through the stylistic mode of speaking the cultural membership of the speakers in these interlocutions, we may suppose that the style, that is, the indirect style may serve as a marker of Chinese cultural identity and the direct style may serve as a marker of American cultural identity. Obviously, this kind of test may seem to be too simple for us to come to any exclusive conclusion. Anyhow, it may at least tell us something close to truth.

As the author had expected, the result turned out to be consistent with his assumption, that is, the majority of the students (over 90 per cent) can exactly tell who is who in these interlocutions merely by examining the mode of speaking. They can even tell how the indirectness is expressed by the Chinese in their request. The request, for example, could be hinted, implied, etc. according to their explanation. What is more, while providing reasons why the Chinese tended to choose the indirect style while the Americans the direct style, they traced their answers to cultural sources on the pragmatic level.

The four pairs of interlocutions with comments and cultural notes are presented and analyzed as follows.

Scene 1

Both Huamin Wang and Min Song were graduate students studying linguistics for Ph. D in the United States. They came back to China to attend an International Conference on language and culture. They could stay at home only for about a week. In these seven days they were both busily engaged in the conference activities. So, they seldom stayed at home with their parents. This dialogue happened between these two Chinese graduate students.

Min Song asked Huamin Wang to accompany her to go shopping. But Huanmin Wang had just gone shopping the day before and right now she was busy preparing her paper which she was presenting at the conference.

Min Song:	You know I have to buy a lot of things to take to the States. I am going shopping tomorrow. [Comment: A Chinese way for request or habitual hint for a request] (*I am giving her a hint of asking her to go shopping with me.*)
Huamin Wang :	(*She was asking me to accompany her to go shopping. I hope she would not as I have just gone shopping and I would like to stay with my parents tomorrow.*) Well, I have bought a lot of things already. Things here are much cheaper. [comment: a polite hint of rejection of the request]
Min Song:	By the way, you may want to buy something else. [comment: reasons to justify the request, again an implied hint of request]
Huaming Wang:	You know I have already bought a lot of things and I was shopping for the whole Sunday. [comment: refusing to say no, but giving reasons to justify her rejection] (*I hope she may understand why I don't want to go with her.*)
Min Song:	But you may need to buy something else. (*I hope she can understand that I need her company.*)
Huamin Wang:	(*It is rather frustrating, but I should give her face.*) ...Ah... O.K., I'll go with you... [comment: Chinese are considerate for others or other's face]

Scene 2

However, a similar dialogue occurred between Huamin Wang and Dr. Richard Patrick, an American professor of linguistics. He was invited as keynote speaker at the conference. It happened on the evening, just when the conference was over. Huamin Wang had only one day left for her stay at home and was planning to have a party to say goodbye to her family and friends. Obviously, this one day was important for her. However, Richard came up to her during the intermission of the conference and asked if she would like to take him to go around places in the city the next day.

Dr. Patrick: Hi, Huamin, will you be free tomorrow? [comment: a hint of request]

Huamin Wang: (*Oh, my goodness. He is asking me to accompany him. I wish he would rather not.*) Well, have you ever been to Sophia Church. That is a very nice architecture. Many foreign friends would like to visit that place...

Dr Patrick: Good. I will go to see that place first. ...Would you accompany me then? I know you have just one day left before you go back to the States and time is very precious for you. (*She will say no if she cannot manage.*)

Huamin Wang: (*Feeling frustrated. Why? That is the last thing I would expect to do as I am leaving the day after tomorrow. I have so many things to do and I am giving a party tomorrow. But if I say no, it would be impolite to a foreign friend.*) ...Well, it will be my pleasure. When shall we meet? [comment: The American left an unfavorable impression of being inconsiderate on her.]

Dr. Patrick: How about ten in the morning at the Hotel Lobby?

Huamin Wang: (*Oh, dear me! Why not earlier. Another morning will be lost.*) OK. See you then. [comment: she was disappointed. The Americans are not considerate to her.]

Scene 3

Let's look at what may happen when an American requests an American for a favor.

American 1: Hi, Bob, I am leaving the day after tomorrow. But I will be free tomorrow. I would like to go sightseeing the city. Do you have any place to recommend?

American 2:	Yeah, a lot of places you should go to. How about the Church. That's a famous attraction of the city. I would go to see that place if I were you. (*He would ask me for a ride if he wants to. But I can't as I am going to another place on business tomorrow.*)
American 1:	I wonder if you can give me a ride there? (*He will say no directly if he doesn't want to.*)
American 2:	I am afraid I can't. You know, I am leaving the day after tomorrow for Chicago on business ...
American 1:	Oh, no problem. I may ask somebody else. Thank you just the same. [The American friend is not likely to be hurt as he understands that his friend means what he said.]

Scene 4

Now let's see what happens between a Chinese female student and her American friend in a similar situation.

Chinese:	Hi, Linda, I am leaving the day after tomorrow. I will be free today. I would like to go sightseeing. Would you recommend me some places? [comment: an implied request and the request is well justified] (*She would most probably offer me a ride as she did last time as she knows that I don't have a car.*)
American:	Wonderful. There are a lot of interesting places in this city. If I were you I would first go to the Flower Street. That's a really nice place. Then, you may visit the Roman Church. A very nice Roman style architecture. And then…(*She would ask me for a ride if she wants to.*)
Chinese:	(*Why didn't she offer to give me a ride? Perhaps she needs some more hints.*) Would you tell me how I can get to these places?
American:	Why don't you get a Tour Guide? Things will be easier if you have one. (*It is funny. Why didn't she go and buy a Tour Guide?*)

Chinese: (*I have got a Tour Guide already. I am merely asking you for a ride.*) Oh, well. Thanks. Bye. [comment: she was disappointed for her friend's inconsideration.]

American: Have fun. See you later. [comment: the American did not know that the feeling of her Chinese friend was hurt.]

Here in these dialogues, cultural differences are fully manifested. In Scene 1 of the Chinese culture (between two Chinese friends) Min Song implied her request and re-requested while Huamin Wang implied her refusals or stated her refusal implicitly. She didn't even say no. Min Song, while understanding very well her friend's implicit rejection, requested her indirectly and implicitly again. Huamin Wang, like other Chinese, hated saying no. She had to give face to her friend and maintain good relationship, therefore she suffered—wasting a whole day accompanying her friend. As a result, her mother blamed her as she lost another day that she might have spent together with her at home. More often than not, the Chinese have to be indirect both in requesting other people to do things and in rejecting others' request. They hate saying no directly. Indirect style is an important mechanism for the Chinese to maintain harmonious or friendly relationship in the society. At least it may help avoid embarrassment of rejection and disagreement between the interactants and hence leaving the face of the other person and the relationship intact.

In contrast, in Scene 2, Dr. Richard Patrick stated his request directly and forthrightly, thinking she would say no if she did not want to. Huamin Wang, however, did not expect such a request as she hoped that Richard would know from the contextual cues (she was leaving the day after tomorrow and she would prefer to stay at home packing up and being together with her parents). And when requested, she could not but say yes as it would be very impolite to reject his request, especially to a foreign friend. She obviously acted according to Chinese cultural standard. As a result, she spent the whole morning with Richard and by doing so she had to give up some precious time that she might have been together with her parents and friends at home. Some Chinese would attribute the American behavior as being inconsiderate and even blunt. We also have to remember that the Americans tend to believe what the Chinese say (the 'honest' norm), that is they tend to believe that the Chinese say what they mean. As a matter of fact, the Chinese may mean no when they say yes.

Scene 3 manifests the directness and forthrightness of the American way of requests and rejections to the requests and the fact that they take the rejection for granted which would otherwise strike the Chinese as impolite and inconsiderate, even rude in similar situations. This direct way of saying no to a request from a friend would of course leave the impression of being unfriendly and untrustworthy upon the Chinese.

Scene 4 is a very good example to demonstrate how the Chinese implicitly and roundaboutly stated their request, thinking that Americans would probably get their intention from the contextual cues like the Chinese. And when she failed to achieve her implied request, the Chinese even hinted her intention for a second time but she could not get her intention across the cultural barrier either. Are the Americans so impolite and inconsiderate? That is the impression left on the Chinese mind when asking favor from their American friends and being rejected in such a way. In fact their feeling is often hurt and injured. They are often disappointed by their American friends.

As mentioned earlier, the Chinese prefer to imply their requests or express them indirectly or implicitly so that they can save other's face and establish harmony between them, or at least they can prevent embarrassment of rejection or disagreement among interactants, hence leaving the relationship and the face of the other person intact (Yum, 1988). However, this requires the listener to guess the request according to the contextual cues and then decide either to grant or reject the request. As a matter of fact, as mind readers (Jia, 1998) the Chinese are inclined to share mutual understandings in regard to what they may imply in what they say. And it is this mutual understanding that helps maintain the harmonious relationship between / among them. What should call for our attention is that differences in expectations in any interactional situation may quite likely cause misunderstanding or even worse consequence to happen. In some cases, the Chinese indirect approaches and the Americans' direct approaches often come to clash. Embarrassments are not uncommon when these two different approaches meet. Once, for example, when an American teacher, who had been teaching English at Heilongjiang University in the north of China for a couple of years, was holding a fare-well party as he had finished his teaching and was going back to America. He invited quite some Chinese fellow teachers and students to join the party. However, some teachers, out of politeness according to the Chinese custom, said to him that it would be too troublesome for him to hold a party and they would not like to give him the trouble of hosting a party. More than that, they told him that they might not come since their coming might bring about a lot of inconvenience. The American took it for granted and believed that many of his potential guests would not come to the party. Thinking so, he prepared less food and drinks than he had planned. However, to his great surprise, when time was due, almost all of his Chinese friends including those who had hinted that they would not come appeared at the party and this was obviously out of his expectation. To meet such unexpected 'incident', he had to go out to buy extra food and drinks. The Chinese friends by doing so really brought a lot of inconvenience to their American friend. The American had to pay for his loyalty to the American principle of respecting other's autonomy and independence and no-imposition or honestly interpreting others' words. The American had to suffer from strictly following his cultural norms. He just could not read the Chinese mind.

Similar facts or incidents do often occur in intercultural communication. To people who are perfectly competent in using and interpreting of their own language and who can speak English but know little about the cultural interactional norms or conventions of this target language, these incidents may sometimes seem amusing, sometimes puzzling, but more often than not, they lead to misunderstandings. Even worse, misunderstandings may lead to unexpected emotional and practical consequences. To intercultural communication scholars, however, they are their interest of study as they provide a window through which they may see the interplay of language, society, and culture in intercultural settings.

Conclusion

We may use the following assumptions to conclude this paper:

1) Different cultures may select different assumptions about situations and different pragmatic conventions or norms as to what is appropriate behavior in a given situation or context.

2) Pragmatic conventions or norms as to what is appropriate behavior and what is not in a given situation may either have to do with cultural values, beliefs, or with situational factors.

3) When we use English as a second or foreign language, we tend to transfer the pragmatic norms or conventions of our first language to the second or foreign language we use in intercultural interactions. We also tend to judge or evaluate the other's English by our own cultural standard.

4) Pragmatic norms or conventions such as the indirect way of requesting and rejection to the requests may serve as a marker of cultural identity.

5) Pragmatic diversities may lead to misunderstandings and communication breakdowns in the course of intercultural communication. Misunderstandings may lead to unexpected emotional or practical consequences or even worse.

References

Bond, M. and Spencer-Oatey, H. (1999). Culture as an explanatory variable: problems and possibilities. In H. Spencer-Oatey (Ed.), *Culturally speaking: Managing rapport through talk across cultures* (pp. 27-40). London: Assell Academic.

Gudykunst, W. B. & Kim, Y. Y. (1984). *Communicating with strangers: an approach to intercultural communication.* McGraw-Hill, Inc.

Gumperz, J. J. (1982). *Language and social identity* (pp. 1-21). Cambridge University Press.

Hall, E.T. (1976). *Beyond culture.* Anchor Books.

Hall, E. T., & Hall, M. R. (1985). *Hidden differences: doing business with Japanese.* Garden City, NY: Anchor.

Hall, E.T., & Hall, M. R. (1987). *Beyond culture* (pp. 105-116). Garden City, NY: Anchor.

Holtgraves, T., & Yang, J.N. (1992). Interpersonal underpinnings of request strategies: General principles and differences due to culture and gender. *Journal of Personality and Social Psychology, 62,* 246-256.

Honna, N. (2002). *English as an international language and Japan's ELT.* Paper presented at the Third International Symposium on ELT in China, Beijing.

Huang, L. M. (2000). The Chinese way of requesting information in intercultural negotiation. *Intercultural Communication Studies, 9:2,* 107.

Jia, Y. X. (1998). *Intercultural Communication.* Shanghai Foreign Language Education Press.

Johnson, R.A. (1992). *Negotiation basics: Concepts, skills, and exercises.* Newbury Park: Sage.

Kirkpatrick, A. (2005). English across Cultures: identity and communication. In Honna (Ed.), *English as an international language* (pp. 161-182). Aoyama Gakuin University.

Le Page, R & A. (1964). *The national language question: Linguistic probvlems of newly independent states.* Oxford: Oxford university Press.

Scollon, R. & Scollon, S.W. (1995). *Intercultural communication: A discourse approach* (pp. 148-154). Blackwell.

Spencer-Oatey, H. (1999). Rapport management: A framework for analysis. In Spencer-Oatey (Ed.), *Culturally speaking: Managing rapport through talk across cultures* (pp. 7-26). London: Assell Academic.

Stella, T.T. (1999). *Communicating across cultures.* The Guilford Press.

Storti, C. (1997). *The art of coming home.* The Yarmouth, ME: Intercultural Press.

Tannen, D. (1981). Indirectness in discourse: Ethnicity as conversational style. *Discourse Processes.*

Wolfson, N. (1989). *Perspectives: Sociolinguistics and TESOL* (pp. 14-33). Newbury House Publishers.

Yum, J. O. (1988). *The impact of Confucianism in interpersonal relationship and communication in East Asia, Cross-cultural adaptation*. Newbury Park, Ca: Sage.

Introduction to

Hispanic Ad Agencies: Taking the Pulse of Their Market

By Felipe Korzenny and Maria Gracia Inglessis

Korzenny and Inglessis note that Hispanic ad agencies in the USA are perceiving an increased sophistication of the market since the degree of acculturation is becoming more varied among Hispanics. The authors also point out that it is no longer universally true that Hispanic immigrants to the USA come to the country totally unaware of how to adapt to US society. Even humble immigrants from Latin America have an idea of the products they will find in the USA. And while Hispanics used to cling to a few well known brands, they now seem to be more analytic in their approach as they have more access to information and consumer literacy. Likewise, the market is changing in its geographic distribution with Hispanics dispersing all over the country. Similarly, the English language is becoming more accessible to US Hispanics which in turn is changing the way marketers need to reach them. At the same time, continuous immigration contributes to the maintenance of the Spanish language. Thus, the messages directed at Hispanics needs to be in both English and Spanish media and need to be consistent across the two languages.

Korzenny and Inglessis found that generally four main categories of clients exist for Hispanic ad agencies: Learners, ROI seekers, old foxes, and stereotypists. Learners are those first entering the Hispanic market and needing to rely heavily on consultants and ad agencies to understand their opportunities. ROI seekers are pragmatists who address the Hispanic market as long as they can anticipate an important return, usually in the short term. Old foxes have learned to work with the Hispanic market and have dedicated major efforts to it. Stereotypists still use the family and other traditional images of Hispanic culture to reach Hispanics.

The authors note that as the market becomes more complex, it is increasingly important to understand the nuances of diverse subgroups within the Hispanic population. Consequently, agencies are approaching segmentation beyond the traditional formulation based on country of origin, acculturation, language preferences, and regions in the USA. They are adding factors like cultural identity, product usage, brand preferences, buying habits, social networks, etc. And agencies are conducting more in-house research, in particular qualitative research in form of focus groups, ethnographies, youth panels, and participant observation. Insights that might also prove of interest to other countries having ethnic minorities and/or migrant groups.

Michael B. Hinner

Felipe Korzenny is Professor and Director of the Center for Hispanic Marketing Communication at Florida State University, and Director of Graduate Studies of the Department of Communication at Florida State University. The Center is the first of its kind in the USA. This Center prepares students to serve the Hispanic marketing industry, conducts research projects, and produces publications to enhance the knowledge of Hispanic consumer behavior. Korzenny is also Senior Consultant and co-founder of Cheskin. Until he merged his company with Cheskin in 1999, he was President and CEO of Hispanic & Asian Marketing Communication Research. Within Cheskin he led a multicultural practice with emphasis on the Hispanic market. He continues to conduct research and consults with major US corporations interested in reaching the US Hispanic market and other culture specific markets. He has established research traditions and trained many researchers in ethnographic, qualitative, and most quantitative methodologies. He has published six books and almost one hundred research publications dealing with communication and culture. His latest book, written with Betty Ann Korzenny, is entitled *Hispanic Marketing: A Cultural Perspective* (Butterworth/Heinemann Elsevier, 2005). He is an Outstanding and also a Distinguished Alumni of Michigan State University. Korzenny is also the first recipient of the Hill Library HispanSource 2005 Award for Outstanding Achievement in Hispanic Marketing Research.

Maria Gracia Inglessis is a Fulbright scholar from Venezuela and a doctoral student in the Department of Communication at Florida State University. She has a strong background in classical philology, linguistics, and semiotics which she studied at the University of Los Andes, Venezuela, and the Eberhard-Karls Universität, Germany. She worked for several years for the film and TV industry in Venezuela producing international award winning films. Currently, she is an assistant researcher in the Center for the Study of Hispanic Marketing Communication at Florida State University. She is one of the leading researchers of the ongoing study on trends in the Hispanic TV commercials. Her research interests in Hispanic marketing and communication include art and cultural industries marketing, and fashion and apparel. Ms. Inglessis is recipient of the Outstanding Research Assistant Awards, College of Communication, Florida State University, 2006.

Hispanic Ad Agencies:
Taking the Pulse of their Market

Felipe Korzenny
Maria Gracia Inglessis

Who knows the Hispanic market better than those that communicate with it continuously? Hispanic ad agencies perceive their world according to their successes and failures. Their lifeline is the accuracy with which they predict the behavior of the consumer. This study was designed to understand the evolution of the Hispanic market from the viewpoint of Hispanic Ad Agencies in the US.

In the Fall of 2004 Dr. Felipe Korzenny and two graduate students, Maria Gracia Inglessis and Nadia Saavedra, conducted a study of US Hispanic advertising agencies to find out their perceptions of:

a) How the Hispanic market is changing
b) How clients that work with the Hispanic market are evolving, and
c) How these agencies are adapting to these changes, if any

Almost all the approximately 70 members of the Association of Hispanic Advertising Agencies (AHAA) were contacted requesting an interview to answer the above main questions. Eighteen agencies cooperated with this research effort. The collaborating agencies are located in major US Hispanic markets, and were about equally distributed between larger and smaller agencies according to net revenues based on the classification in the Hispanic Fact Pack of Advertising Age, 2004.

Fifteen in-depth interviews that lasted from 30 to 90 minutes were conducted by phone, and 3 interviews were done by e-mail. All the interviews were done with high-level managers or agency owners. The interviews were recorded, transcribed and analyzed between September and December 2004. The results are summarized below.

Perceptions of a Changing Market

Agencies perceive that the sophistication of the market is increasing according to indicators of acculturation, e.g. length of time in the US, information about life in the US, understanding or products and services in the US.

It is no longer universally true that Hispanic immigrants to the US come here totally unaware of how to adapt to US society. Because of NAFTA, increasing business internationalization, and access to US cable programming, even humble immigrants from Latin America have an idea of the products they will find in the US. Those that come to the US without prior information now are more likely to benefit from family members or friends that have been longer in the US. "Hispanics are no longer isolated, they have somebody to ask and have a better sense of what to do in this country in terms of institutions, housing, transportation and so forth".

In a similar vein, Hispanic consumers have learned about how to achieve a better status in the United States via education and political participation. Hispanics are evolving into a more demanding constituency that are aware of opportunities and obstacles in this their new society. The political passivity that characterized Hispanics in the past appears to be dissipating in favor of a proactive stance.

Increasing Hispanic economic power contributes now to a more demanding attitude towards products and brands. Hispanics aspirations for products and services are climbing at a fast pace. It used to be the case that Hispanics would cling on to a few well know brands. Now they seem to be more analytic in their approach as they have more access to information and consumer literacy.

The market is also changing in its geographic distribution. Hispanics have dispersed in the United States. Agencies pointed out how traditional concentrations areas are becoming less homogenous. For example, Mexicans are moving from the west coast to the East coast and Miami is becoming a more "Argentinean" city. New emergent markets include Chapel Hill, North Carolina, Minneapolis, Minnesota and other areas where Hispanics were not abundant in the recent past. Moreover, Hispanics are migrating from urban to rural settings. This dispersion is creating a marketing dynamic that requires more widespread efforts to reach Hispanics. Marketers and Hispanic media need to anticipate this trend towards dispersion to reach Hispanics in ways that were not contemplated just a few years ago.

The English language is becoming more accessible to US Hispanics and that is changing the way in which marketers need to reach them. At the same time, continuous immigration contributes to the maintenance of the Spanish language. Spanish and English are becoming equally important and used in everyday life. Now the messages directed to Hispanics need to be in both English and Spanish media and need to be consistent across the two languages.

Because of the influence of marketers and politicians, the self-esteem of Hispanics has been elevated so that now it is truly "cool" to be Hispanic in the US. This means that marketing to non-Hispanics can be more effective with a "Hispanic touch." One can think of a hybridization of the Hispanic culture and that of the rest of the non-Hispanic population. That has also important implications for marketing in both Spanish and English and with cultural sensitivity to diverse constituencies.

Perceptions of Changing Clients

Based on the interviews with ad agencies, their clients fall into four main categories:

a) Learners
b) ROI seekers
c) Old foxes, and
d) Stereotypists

Learners are those first entering the Hispanic market and heavily relying on consultants and ad agencies to understand their opportunities. Learners read reports and articles about the complexity of the market. They are open to suggestions and education. More importantly, these clients are willing to dedicate resources and develop specific products for Hispanics. These are a very important segment of the client landscape.

ROI seekers are pragmatists that address the Hispanic market as long as they can anticipate an important return, typically in the short term. They expect from ad agencies to be a strategic partner that is able to offer a plan to demonstrate the impact of advertising.

Old foxes tend to be the large and successful companies. These have learned to work with the Hispanic market and have dedicated major efforts to it. Since these clients are leaders and have been in the market for a long time, usually they understand its dynamics. However, these clients can also represent a challenge to ad agencies when it comes to innovation because they are perceived to have fixed ways of doing things.

Stereotypists are those who still use the family and other traditional images of Hispanic culture to reach Hispanics. Even if they recognize the financial opportunity the market offers, they do not seem to understand its cultural nuances. They insist on using "la abuelita" (the grandma), "la cocina" (the kitchen), and "los labios rojos" (the red lips) as the only way to appeal to the market.

Ad agencies indicate that with the exception of the "old foxes" the other types of clients request education about the market. The tendency is for many agencies to rely heavily still on ad agencies in order to obtain cultural insights to position and communicate their products and services.

What Are Agencies Doing to Adapt to These Changes and Tendencies?

Agencies report they are adapting to the increasing sophistication of the market, and also to the requirements of their clients. Some of the interviewees pointed out that allocation of resources to the Hispanic Market continues to lag in comparison to the spending power of Hispanics and their population size. This discontinuity continues to make education efforts by agencies important.

Some interviewees indicated that audiovisual documentation efforts are important to persuade clients to abandon demographic thinking and move more towards cultural thinking.. With audiovisual materials, in the style of ethnographic documentaries, some agencies help clients to understand the cultural differences, purchasing patterns and other variables relevant to successful marketing efforts. Flexible clients allow agencies to recommend relevant and different communication approaches, and also strategies that involve new product development.

Many ad agencies, particularly smaller ones, are forming their own media divisions in order to complement their offerings. Agencies that outsource media buying accentuated their active participation with ideas and opinions in the media planning. In some cases media planning is influenced by the fact that larger clients many times have a well established relationship with media outlets. This tendency limits the autonomy of agencies in the process of media selection.

Agencies are capitalizing on the growth and diversification of Hispanic Media. This diversification includes a new a array of print outlets, radio stations, TV channels, and internet offerings. There is an increasing presence of product placements in media directed to Hispanics in order to sidestep advertising fatigue. One example is the use of "embedded scripts" in "telenovelas", were products become part of the story.

In addition, there is an increasing reliance on non-broadcast media and a proliferation of personal marketing efforts. Examples of one-on-one communication efforts include examples of interpersonal outreach to Hispanic sorority and fraternity students. Also, these efforts include marketing campaigns at the community level that include concerts, demonstrations,

In recognition of increasing sophistication on the part of Hispanics, Internet advertising and websites are proliferating. It is estimated that about 65% of US Hispanics access the Internet. That is a figure that is bound to grow very fast because Hispanics see the internet as a means to leapfrogging stages of economic and social wellbeing.

When addressing the issue of media and language, agencies admitted their preference for Spanish language media. Spanish language media are more affordable and many clients have strong budget limitations. Moreover, some conservative clients only perceive efficiency in Spanish language marketing. However, and perhaps more importantly, agencies perceive that the Spanish language will continue to be relevant to the Hispanic population for the foreseeable future. Agencies indicate that the first reason for the endurance of the Spanish language is continuous immigration to the US from Latin America. Second, even later generation Hispanics have an emotional connection to the Spanish language. Third, these later generations use Spanish media as a language-learning tool. And fourth, Spanish language is the ultimate unifier: no matter country of origin, years in the US or generation. The Spanish language is believed to keep Hispanics together.

Nevertheless, an increasing number of ad agencies are incorporating the English language in their repertoires. This used to be Taboo in the industry just a few years ago. Now there is an increasing recognition of the fact that bilingualism is a trend of the future. Placing Spanish language ads in English media was not possible in the past. Nowadays, there are many examples of cross-media advertising. Some agencies indicated in their interviews that if Spanish broadcasting companies would allow it, they would place English ads in Spanish broadcast media. Furthermore, the use of Spanglish and Code-switching are gaining acceptance and have become relevant alternatives to appeal to younger, urban segments.

Sophisticated segmentation schemes are in the process of development by many ad agencies and the industry in general. As the market has turned more complex, it is increasingly important to understand the nuances of diverse subgroups within this population. Agencies are approaching segmentation beyond the traditional formulation based on country of origin, acculturation, language preference, and region in the US. They are adding factors like cultural identity, product usage, brand preferences, buying habits, social networks, and so on. Agencies recognize the importance of lifestyle segmentation and a more holistic approach. More agencies are conducting in-house research, particularly qualitative research in the form of focus groups, ethnographies, youth panels, and participant observation. In many cases this tendency to conduct in-house research contributes to proprietary research schemes and strategic platforms.

Account planning based on consumer insights is a growing trend in Hispanic ad agencies. The account planner is the bridge between the consumer and the different ad agency functions. It is the key to strategy. Account planners are still very scarce in Hispanic marketing and in the industry in general.

Conclusion

There is an active effervescence taking place in US Hispanic marketing and ad agencies are taking note of that. Many see that they need to adapt to these changes rapidly and some also fear that the niche they have occupied is being threatened by large competitors that have created or purchased Hispanic divisions.

The key changes in the market have to do with consumer savvy and language evolution. The Spanish language, however, will continue being the language of the heart for a long time to come. Still, ignoring that Hispanics are exposed to English language content is no longer tenable. Marketing in-culture is now more important than marketing exclusively in-language.

Further insights about how to market to Hispanics from a cultural perspective can be found in the new book *Hispanic Marketing: A Cultural Perspective* by Felipe Korzenny and Betty Ann Korzenny, Elsevier, 2005.

Introduction to

Brand-Building in the Chinese Social and Cultural Contexts: Characteristics, Trends and Problems

By Junhao Hong and Xianhong Chen

The text chronicles the efforts and development of brand building in China. While China has opened its market and liberalized its economy for more than a quarter of a century, which resulted in rapid economic development, Chinese products still tend to be associated with cheap quality. Most Chinese brands are also not well known throughout the developed world as studies indicate. While Chinese companies initially assumed that they could quickly establish brand identity with investments in ad campaigns, it turned out that this did not materialize. So it was only recently that Chinese companies shifted their strategy to work long term on the cultivation of their brands and the recognition of their brands throughout the world. Efforts that are also vigorously supported by the Chinese government.

Interestingly, this initial assumption of Chinese companies seems to run counter to the long term orientation which is usually associated with Chinese culture. In fact, Hofstede's cultural model shows China with the highest (i.e. longest) value in the dimension Long Term Orientation. Hence, indicating and illustrating that cultural stereotypes could be misleading, especially in a business context. But it also shows that Chinese businesses are set to cater to the needs and requirements of consumers from around the globe; thus, clearly indicating that Chinese companies are very market oriented.

Michael B. Hinner

Junhao Hong is Associate Professor of Communication at the University at Buffalo. His primary research focus is on International Communication, Intercultural Communication, Media and Society, and Communication and Information Technology. He is also a Research Associate of the Fairbank Center for East Asian Research at Harvard University. Major publications: an authored book *The Internationalization of Television in China: The Evolution of Ideology, Society, and Media since the Reform* (Praeger, 1998), a number of chapters in edited books, and dozens of articles in various refereed journals, including *Telematics and Informatics*, *Media, Culture & Society*, *Telecommunications Policy*, *Gazette-The International Journal for Communication Studies*, *Media Development*, *Asian Journal of Communication*, *Asian Survey*, and *American Journal of Chinese Studies*. He has received various awards for research and teaching and was interviewed by the *New York Times* on media and social change in China.

Xianhong Chen is from Huazhong University of Science and Technology in China.

Brand-Building in the Chinese Social and Cultural Contexts: Characteristics, Trends and Problems

Junhao Hong
Xianhong Chen

Today, one of the most important aspects of market competition is the brand competition among the same kinds of goods and products, and brand-building and brand management has become one of the most important strategies of enterprises and corporations that especially target at the global market. According to research, countries across the world can be categorized into two groups: the group of "brain countries" and the group of "body countries." The so-called "brain countries" can earn high profits by exporting a variety of invisible intelligent goods and products abroad, such as knowledge, culture, management experience, and patterns and brands, while the so-called "body countries" can only earn meager profits by doing assembling and processing work or by exporting visible goods and products abroad, such as raw materials, labor service and so on (Kotler, 2004). Likewise, enterprises and corporations can also be categorized into the group of "brain enterprises and corporations" and the group of "body enterprises and corporations." One of the criteria to distinguish the two groups is whether they are able to produce name brand goods and products and how they build and manage name brands of goods and products both in the domestic and international market.

Most of those established enterprises and corporations had already experienced the stages of goods or product management and capital management, and many of them have either already entered or have been moving toward the brand-building and brand management stage. Brand-building and brand management of goods and products has become a crucial factor for business success particularly in the era of economic globalization. According to the statistics from UN, worldwide, name brands of goods and products only occupy less than three percent of the total brands of goods and products. But the sale volume of the goods and products of name brands accounts for 50 percent of the total sale volume of the goods and products of all brands (Huang & Hu, 2005). In other words, the goods and products of name brands are at the monopolistic position in the global market and maintain a leading role and strong momentum in the world economy. As some critics observe, now some developed countries intentionally use brands as a new economic weapon to exploit the international market by a "trilogy-phase" strategy: first, to export goods and products; next, to export capital; and third, to export brand concepts and brands. Compared with the first two phases, exporting brands is the most concealed "economic plunder," because it can receive the highest returns but costs the least yet brand affects can last a much longer period of time. Because of these reasons, brand-building has become a common strategy of many enterprises and corporation in both developed and developing countries.

However, brand-building in China has had a very short history. It did not become an issue for enterprises and corporations only until about 10 years ago, despite the fact that the country started its economic reform from a state economy to a market economy more than 25 years ago. Nevertheless, in the last ten years or so in China brand consciousness and brand-building has experienced a very fast development. Moreover, the development bears some unique Chinese characteristics and reflects some important trends. This article reviews the history of brand-building in China and examines the characteristics and trends of brand-building in the Chinese social and cultural contexts. This research also analyzes the problems and challenges that brand-building have been facing in China and discusses its prospects.

A Short History with a Swift Development

For nearly 30 years between 1949 when The People's Republic of China was founded and 1978 when the economic reform began, neither the enterprises nor the people in the country had a strong brand consciousness. Under the state-planned economic system, enterprises were ordered by the state to manufacture certain types of goods and products, goods and products were ordered to sell in certain places, and people purchased and consumed goods and products based on the quotas allocated by the government. Regardless of what kinds of goods and products—from agricultural, industrial to food, daily life and medical ones, most of them were often named as "People Brand," "Red Flag Brand," "Revolution Brand," "Workers Brand," "Peasants Brand," and "Good Students Brand," etc. Brands of goods and products usually contained a strong political and ideological connotation than an economic and commercial connotation (Chen, 2002).

Nowadays, the domestic market competition in China has already entered the phase of brand competition comprehensively. In the last two decades or so since the economic reform embarked in the late 1970s, the Chinese market has experienced three stages in regard to the development of brand-building. The first stage is the tangled warfare during the 1980s, in which inferior brands fought inferior brands. The second stage is the elimination war during the 1990s, in which famous brands fought inferior brands. The third stage is after entering the

21st century, a new period that shows a bitter war between famous brands and famous brands.

In the 1980s, the Chinese market was just restored. Neither enterprises nor consumers had brand consciousness. During this period of time, the consumer market was still basically marked by a state-planned economy. Department stores across the whole country were all named in numerical orders without names, such as "The First Department Store," "The Second Department Store," "The Third Department Store," "The Fourth Department Store," and so on. Likewise, majority enterprises across the nation were also named in numerical orders without names of their products, such as "The First Textile Mill," "The Second Textile Mill," "The Third Textile Mill," "The Fourth Textile Mill," and so on (Yu & Shu, 2002). Largely, the newly emerged market economy in the late 1970s and the early 1980s was still unknown to most people and was not clearly reflected in the consumer market. For the majority consumers, because of their limited financial capability and the society's limited economic condition, their first need was to buy the goods they needed regardless of what brands they were. Brand recognition was not a priority for most people and brand building was not a priority for most enterprises as well.

Around the mid-1980s, a great deal of imported goods entered China's market. Their coming brought many famous international brands to the Chinese people. Hundreds of millions of Chinese consumers began to gain brand consciousness. But, at that time most Chinese people had little knowledge about brands, especially about foreign brands. Many could only identify whether they are Japanese goods or American goods, and few could have a good understanding of the history, culture, position and characteristics of the imported brands.

At the beginning of 1990s, as the market was turning from a seller's one to a buyer's one, a deficiency economy was also moving towards a surplus economy. Enterprises started building up their brands and consumers also began to identify brands when they were shopping for goods. Thus, brands became a magic weapon to reign the market and brand-building became a priority of many enterprises in China. Goods and services of name brands were pursued by many people as a way for showing a higher social status and personal differences from others. Consequently, major and medium cities were full of brand-goods chains and retail stores, and consuming by brand-identity and brand loyalty started to become a popular trend among urban people.

In the mid-1990s, a nationwide elimination war between famous brands and inferior brands arose. Crushing opposite parties, cleaning the gateway with the aid of brand, scale, and network, and changing the brands' status was a necessity and symbol of mature environment. However, nearly all that had been eliminated were the small brands from small- and mid-scale enterprises, while the strong brands and big enterprises were still growing fast. Take the electrical appliances as an example. Before 1995, there were more than 200 brands in the market, but now only about 20 exist. The market is centralized to just a few brands, and 60% to 90% of the market shares concentrate to the top three to five brands . The brand centralization was so apparent. As a result, many enterprises started to cultivate the brand value consciously. In 1995, the average advertisement investment of some famous Chinese brands were more than 55 million Chinese yuan (about seven million U.S. dollars). In 2000, the figure reached 250 million Chinese yuan, showing the enterprises' increasing realization of the brand value (Tang & Schultz, 2004). Competition among Chinese brands has thus entered a fierce period.

After entering the 21 century, brand building has been experiencing many new challenges. Established brands are now fighting for more market shares. Especially, after China joined the WTO and obtained the right to hold 2008 Olympic Games, the brand competition has entered a new run and is becoming increasingly important to a company (Deng, 2003). It has become a common idea among Chinese enterprises that whoever posses a name brand will be the winner of the market. With this new philosophy, a number of new trends have emerged in the brand-building efforts in China.

New Trends in Brand-Building

Several new trends in brand-building in China can be identified, but the following three ones are worth-noting.

Chinese Brands Going International

It was not until the late 90s, some good Chinese brands like Haier, Medi, and Chuangwei began to enter the international market, gradually making Chinese brand-name products also popular abroad. For example, TCL set up a joint stock company in Vietnam and Indian, Changhong set up stock companies in Russian, Mexico and Indonesia, and 999 Company and Haier set up image advertising brand in the United States and France. In the meantime, many companies carried out a logo change movement to make their brands more eye-catching and unique. Meidi, Haixin, TCL, Kenlon and Chunlan all had a new logo to make their brands look more internationally appealing (Ogilvy, 2005).

Currently, Chinese enterprises' world strategy for brand-building has two approaches. One approach is: if the brands are already internationally known and well established, such as Haier, the enterprises will try to enter the European and American countries first to occupy the heap of the international market, and then to radiate to other countries market. Another approach is first to enter the developing countries' market, and after obtaining experiences and establishing themselves in the international market, then to enter the developed countries.

Integrating Brand-Building Means

For a period of time, brand building in China went to extremes: many enterprises blindly believed the power of advertising in achieving the results of brand-building. They mistakenly thought that as long as enough money is put in the advertisement for a product, the brand of the product would be established. Thus, they neglected other necessary means for brand-building. As a result, companies competed for putting more money into advertising, keeping a myth that advertisement alone can unilaterally make a high market distribution of a product. They assumed that the more money they spend on advertising, the louder the voice would be, and the louder the voice is, the larger the market shares a product would get (Ma, 2003). Unfortunately, this is not really true. Brand-building is not just based on advertisement. Instead, brand-building needs many other elements.

In the mid-1990s, companies in China started to integrate various communication means for brand-building. Instead of solely relying on advertising, now they also use other means or systems to enhance the market impact of brands. Now, the brand-building strategy of most corporations displays conformity of communication means. Consequently, they make full use of various kinds of communication tools to influence the target consumers in the way of "multi-tools, one voice" for better brand-building and enterprise recognition (Keller, 2003).

In China, the cost for creating a new brand is twice than the cost for maintaining an established brand. Therefore, in order to cut down the cost and reduce the risk, many corporations now use the established brands as a base to develop related brands. For instance, Haier launched the Little Prodigy brand washers and the Little Prince brand refrigerators, and Medi launched the Xiaokang Star brand microwave ovens and the Nutrition brand microwave ovens (Tang & Schultz, 2005). This strategy has made brand extensions successful. This brand extension strategy has become a vigorous trend among Chinese enterprises.

Since the Chinese market is still in the low-level competition, brand extensions would have more opportunities to succeed in China than in Western developed countries. As it has been seen, through this way some companies, such as Haier,

Wahaha, Robust, have expanded very fast and have won big successes. For example, in three years after the brand extension, sales of Robust reached 200 million Chinese yuan, compared to only 40 million Chinese yuan before the brand extension (Ries & Trout, 2004).

Shifting from Short-Term to Long-Term Brand-Building Efforts

Before the 1990s, many companies' brand-building efforts were based on short terms. They expected a quick success, hoping a brand to become popular and famous overnight. From the wine-war to the VCD war, from the beverage war to the shampoo war, and from the keep-warm-underwear war to the health-food war, all of them were short-term brand-building actions. But most of these short-term actions did not achieve long-term brand-building effects. Many brands were powerful in the market yesterday, but became little powerful shortly. This problem demonstrates that in the early years many Chinese corporations only had the enthusiasm for brand-building but lacked the persistence for brand-building, and they only had short-term efforts but lacked long-term perspectives and strategies.

However, after the 1990s the competition for market shares has become much more intensive. Many enterprises have realized that short-term efforts would not achieve the goals for brand-building and market penetration. They must develop long-term strategies for brand-building efforts. During 1980s, spending some money on advertisement would guarantee a repayment in a short term; during the 1990s, spending big money on advertisement would still guarantee some repayment in a short term; but since the beginning of the 21st century, even if spending huge money on advertisement would not guarantee a repayment, let alone in a short term. For example, Qin Chi Corporation spent 320 million Chinese yuan on advertising but it did not get what they had expected in a certain period of time (Deng, 2003). This symbolized that now Chinese brands had left the guaranteed market competition but had entered a somewhat more genuine market competition. They must make every effort first to survive and then to develop. This takes long-term and persistent efforts. Enterprises must have the preparation for a long-term brand-building process and brand war.

Challenges and Prospects

Inspite of all the progress, there is still a long way for China to build its name brands both in the domestic market and in the global market as well. Thanks to China's continuing rapid economic growth in the last 15 years or so with an annual rate of about 10 percent, the country's overall economic strength has ranked number six in the world, and its total trade volume has ranked number four among all countries. Yet, brand-building in China has not developed as fast as its economic growth. Among the top 100 most valuable name brands, 62 of them are from the United States, Japan, France, Germany and Britain each has about six or seven, while China has none. Because of the lack of namebrand products in the global market, the competitiveness of China's economy has ranked number 29, far behind the ratings of many much smaller countries (Huang & Hu, 2005). In the global market, it is sad that in most cases Chinese brands still mean cheap and low quality products. Most "Made in China" goods are usually being sold in stores like Walmart, regardless of the value of their brands.

Doubtlessly, China is quickly becoming an economic giant. On the other hand, however, the country is still very weak in terms of brand-building. So far, China has about 200 goods and products that have the highest production volume in the world, but none of China's goods and products has even entered the world's top 500 brands (Ogilvy, 2004).

There are a number of factors that have contributed to this situation. Several of them particularly reflect China's historical, social and cultural contexts. First, the market economy in China has just started for a few years, which has a much shorter history than the history of the market economy in Western developed countries. As a result of the market economy, brand-building in China is a new thing that also has a much shorter history than the one in Western developed countries. Second, China's market economy is still at the initial phase, and the system is not matured yet. Many of the things under this new system still need to learn and develop, including brand-building, both consciousness-wise and practice-wise. Third, in the last two decades China has in fact made many significant achievements in brand-building. Brand-building has experienced from zero to being a long-tern strategy for most enterprises. However, the gap between Western developed countries and China in regard to brand-building is too huge, which makes China's achievements not so noticeable and look insignificant. Finally, brand-building needs endless investment and capital, yet most Chinese enterprises do not have the desirable amount of money for brand-building.

Overall, China is facing an unprecedented opportunity for economic development. In 2005, for the first time ever in China's history, the government set the goal of helping enterprises for brand-building and made it one of the country's important economic strategies. The strategy has two aims: 1) within three to five years to make several Chinese brands enter the list of the world's top 500 namebrands; and 2) by the year 2010, to create a few Chinese namebrands in the global market (Deng, 2003). There are good reasons to expect that many Chinese enterprises will make vigorous efforts to reach these goals.

References

Chen, X. (2002) Principles of Consumer Guiding in Brand Communication. *Contemporary Communication,* No. 1, pp.36-44.

Deng, D. (2003) The Key To Brand Positioning. *Sales and Market,* No. 1, pp. 15-22.

Huang, J., & Hu, J. (2005) Ponder of Brand Connotation. *Commercial Research,* No. 312, pp. 106-116.

Keller, K. (2003) *Strategic Brand Management.* Beijing, China: The People's University of China Press.

Kotler, P. (2004) *Management of Selling: Analysis, Plan, and Control.* Shanghai, China: Shanghai People's Publishing House.

Ogilvy, D. (2005) *Advertisement.* Beijing, China: Mechanical Publishing House.

Ogilvy, D. (2004) *Principles of Brand Management: How To Build Name Brands.* Hulter, Inner Mongolia: Inner Mongolia People's Publishing House.

Ma, Y. (2003) Management of Selling: The Selling Patterns of Brand Arrangement Communication. *Quantity Economic Technology Economy Research,* No. 2, pp. 31-39.

Ries, G., & Trout, B. (2004) *Positioning.* Beijing, China: China Financial & Economic Publishing House.

Tang, C., & Schultz, F. (2005) *Brand Communication.* Beijing, China: China People's Post and Telecommunication Publishing House.

Tang, C., & Schultz, F. (2004) *Arrange Marketing Communication.* Beijing, China: China Price Publishing House.

Yu, M., & Shu, Y. (2002) On Brand Communication. *International News Field,* No. 3, pp. 24-28.

Introduction to

Is the Chinese Self-Construal in Transition?

By Nagesh Rao, Arvind Singhal, Li Ren and Jianying Zhang

The authors note that Chinese culture seems to be undergoing changes so that new ways of relating to others and one's self are emerging in China as are individual perceptions of authority, hierarchy, group cohesiveness, and family responsibility - all of which are in flux. That is why, the authors argue, it is important to understand how the Chinese view themselves, i.e. construe their "self," especially in relation to others. It is also important to discover to what degree they see themselves as being separate, i.e. independent, from others, or as connected, i.e. interdependent with others. Consequently, the authors investigated the independent and interdependent self-construals of the Chinese. Self-construals refer to the constellation of thoughts, feelings, and actions concerning one's relationship to others, and the self as distinct from others. The study of self-construals gained in prominence because cultural level variables, such as individualism and collectivism, while useful conceptual tools, have limited explanatory power for why individuals in certain cultures display both individualistic and collectivistic traits. Thus, the conceptualization of the self as being independent and interdependent represents an important individual level intervening as a variable between cultural dimensions like individualism/collectivism and human behavior.

The study undertaken by the authors included also socio-demographic factors such as age, gender, and rural-urban residence. The study was conducted in form of a quantitative questionnaire in China that was followed up with a set of qualitative interviews to enrich the quantitative findings. The results suggest that the Chinese self-construal varies across age, gender, and urban-rural residence, and is also influenced by the changing political, economic, and socio-cultural context in China. At a cultural level, collectivism is still predominant in Chinese society, and the traditional self-concept is still deeply rooted in the collective Chinese memory. However, a sense of self-awareness has arisen among the Chinese since the reformist era of Deng Xiaoping (post 1978), especially among the younger generation. The authors conclude that Chinese society as a whole is much more tolerant of individualism today than in the past. Indeed, the

Chinese find themselves in a mix of Confucian tradition, communist ideology, and a newly-emerging Westernized individualism. That is, in a state of flux. Therefore, most Chinese seem to have adopted a flexible value system to adjust to the changing environment. And this, in turn, just demonstrates once again that culture is rarely static.

This conclusion of the study should be of interest to the international business community since it has relevance to anyone doing business with China – whether it be looking for a potential production site or a potential market for one's products. Because these changes in self-awareness could influence the negotiation style, motivation, and purchase decisions.

Michael B. Hinner

Nagesh Rao is Associate Professor of Communication and Interim Director of the School of Communication Studies at Ohio University. He is the recipient of the University Professor Award at Ohio University and the Outstanding Teacher of the Year Award at the University of New Mexico in addition to numerous other awards and honors. Rao was also awarded the Franklin H. Knower top publication award in 1995. He has published many journal articles, book chapters, conference papers, reports, and a training manual. Rao also acts as advisor to various health care agencies and hospitals.

Arvind Singhal is Professor and Presidential Research Scholar in the School of Communication Studies, Ohio University, where he teaches and conducts research in the areas of diffusion of innovations, mobilizing for change, design and implementation of strategic communication campaigns, and the entertainment-education communication strategy. He is author or editor of eight books: *Communication of Innovations: A Journey with Everett M. Rogers* (Sage Publications, forthcoming), *Organizing for Social Change* (Sage Publications, 2006), *Entertainment-Education Worldwide: History, Research, and Practice* (Lawrence Erlbaum Associates, 2004), *Combating AIDS: Communication Strategies in Action* (Sage Publications, 2003), *The Children of Africa Confront AIDS: From Vulnerability to Possibility* (Ohio University Press, 2003), *India's Communication Revolution: From Bullock Carts to Cyber Marts* (Sage Publications, 2001), *Entertainment-Education: A Communication Strategy for Social Change* (Lawrence Erlbaum Associates, 1999), *India's Information Revolution* (Sage Publications, 1989). Two of Singhal's books, *Combating AIDS: Communication Strategies in Action* and *Entertainment-Education: A Communication Strategy for Social Change,* received the National Communication Association's Applied Communication Division's Distinguished Book Award for 2004 and 2000 respectively. Furthermore, his book *India's Communication Revolution:*

Bullock Carts to Cyber Marts received the CHOICE 2002 Outstanding Academic Title Award.

Li Ren received her Ph.D. in interpersonal communication at Ohio University in 2003.

Jianying Zhang is currently a master's student in the Department of Statistics at the University of Idaho.

Is the Chinese Self-construal in Transition?[1]

Nagesh Rao
Arvind Singhal
Li Ren
Jianying Zhang

The present article investigates the Chinese peoples' interdependent and independent self-construals, including how these self-construals are influenced by socio-demographic factors such as age, gender, and rural-urban residence. A modified version of Singelis' (1994) self construal scale was administered to 237 Chinese respondents' in an urban and a rural area of Shandong Province, China, and qualitative data (focus group and in-depth interviews) were collected to enrich the quantitative findings. Our results suggest that the Chinese self-construal varies across age, gender, and urban-rural residence and is also influenced by the changing political, economic, and sociocultural context in China. The theoretical and practical implications for the field of intercultural communication are outlined in the discussion section.

> In the past, in the Chinese socialist society, you were only a brick or a screw, and were used wherever you were needed. You had no self. You were only one part of a whole machine and couldn't be independent as a separate self. .. You had to put yourself in the big collectives, and belonged to your country, your work unit, your parents, or your own family. Now it's different. You are still a brick, but you are a very independent and personal brick. Suddenly the country does not take care of you anymore, and you are on your own. (Ms. Yang, a 39 year old woman respondent in our focus group interview).

Chinese society, comprising some 1.2 billion people, is in transition. The proverbial Great Wall, symbolizing the insularity of the Chinese people, is 'in ruins' (Chu & Ju, 1993). In present-day China, the lines between Confucianism and capitalism, and communes and corporations, are blurring. From 'being wealthy is pariah' during Mao's time, the prevailing doctrine in today's China is 'being rich is glorious'. As new political and economic ideologies impinge on old ones, new 'mind-sets' emerge and mix with old ones. New ways of relating to others

---

Arvind Singhal and Motoko Nagao, Is the Chinese Self-construal in Transition?, In *Asian Journal of Communication 11(1)* pp. 68-95, Copyright 2001, Reprinted by permission of the publisher and of the authors;

and one's self are emerging (Fitzgerald, 1993). Individual perceptions of authority, hierarchy, group cohesiveness, and family responsibility, while important, are now in flux (Chu, 1985; Chen, 1995). Greater contextual clarity that existed previously about what constituted appropriate or inappropriate social behaviour is not so clear now. Whether or not to squeak loudly in order to get more grease, or whether or not to stick one's neck out, is less clear in the new political, economic, cultural, and social landscape of China. For this reason, it is important to understand how the Chinese people view themselves (i.e. construe their 'self') especially in relation to others? To what degree do they see themselves as being *separate* (independent) from others or as *connected* (interdependent) with others?

The purpose of the present study is to investigate the Chinese peoples' independent and interdependent self-construals (Markus & Kitayama, 1991), and to see how their self-construals are influenced by socio-demographic factors such as age, gender, and ruralurban residence in a changing society. The concepts of independent and interdependent self-construal are explained, and the key historical, religious, and socio-cultural factors that influence the Chinese peoples' self-construals are analyzed. Our quantitative and qualitative data-collection procedures are detailed, and our findings presented. Finally, we draw theoretical and practical implications of our findings for the field of intercultural communication.

Independent and Interdependent Self-construal

Several scholars view an individual's conception of their self as an integral part of their behaviour (Geertz, 1975; Triandis, 1989). Markus and Kitayama's (1991) definition of the self explored the extent to which a person's identity is seen as separate from others (independent) or connected with others (interdependent). Drawing upon Markus and Kitayama's seminal work, Singelis (1994: 581) defined *self-construal* as a 'constellation of thoughts, feelings, and actions concerning one's relationship to others, and the self as distinct from others'. Since Markus and Kitayama's article on independent and interdependent self-construals, there has been considerable interest in exploring the role of self-construal in different contexts (Cross, 1995; Cross & Madson, 1997; Gudykunst et al., 1996; Kim et al., 1996; Kim, Sharkey, & Singelis, 1994; Oetzel & Bolton-Oetzel, 1997; Park & Levine, 1999; Singelis, 1994; Singelis & Brown, 1995). The concept of self-construal gained in prominence because cultural-level variables like individualism and collectivism, while useful conceptual tools, have limited explanatory power for why individuals in certain cultures display both individualist and collectivistic traits (Singelis & Brown, 1995). Markus and Kitayama's (1991) conceptualization of the self as being independent and interdependent, thus represented an important individual-level intervening variable between cultural dimensions like individualism/collectivism and human behaviour.

Markus and Kitayama (1991) noted that most Western cultures placed a high value on an individual's *independence*. Language use in Western cultures often reflects the positive attributes of being individualistic. For example, 'pull yourself by your boot straps', 'God helps those who help themselves', or 'self-help is the best help' are cherished notions. Achieving this cultural goal of independence requires individuals to construct themselves in ways that their 'behavior is organized and made meaningful primarily by reference to their own internal repertoire of thoughts, feelings, and action, rather than by reference to the thoughts, feelings and action of others' (Markus & Kitayama, 1991: 226). People with an independent self-construal value 'individualism, achievement, self direction, competition, and hedonism' (Oetzel & Bolton-Oetzel, 1997: 294). In general, people in individualistic cultures (like the United States) tend to primarily have an independent selfconstrual, that is, a conception of the self 'as an autonomous, independent person' (Marcus & Kitayama, 1991: 226).

In many non-Western cultures, however, the cultural norm is to maintain *interdependence* among members of a culture. Marcus and Kitayama (1991: 226) explain that:

> on certain occasions, the *individual* in the sense of a set of significant inner attributes of the person, may cease to be the primary unit of consciousness. Instead, the sense of belongingness to a social relation may become so strong that it makes better sense to think of the *relationship* as the functional unit of conscious reflection.

Thus one's actions, thoughts and feelings are influenced significantly by the specific context/situation and the key members involved in the situation. For example, to decide whether or not to come to the United States to pursue higher education, one of the present authors (who belongs to a non-western culture) held several discussions with parents, siblings, uncles, aunts, and friends before his parents suggested that it was a good idea to go to the US. Those with an interdependent self-construal learn to control their own feelings and reactions to be seen as a mature member of society (Marcus & Kitayama, 1991; Singelis, 1994). This interdependent construal of the self 'has been variously referred to, with somewhat different connotations as, sociocentric, holistic, collective, connected, and relational' (Marcus & Kitayama, 1991: 227).

There is a growing body of literature on how independent and interdependent self-construals impact human communication behaviour (Oetzel, 1998; Yamada

& Singelis, 1999). For instance, Oetzel and Bolton-Oetzel (1997) investigated the relationship between self-construal and group effectiveness and found that while task effectiveness was positively correlated with independent selfconstrual, relational effectiveness was strongly and positively related to interdependent self-construal. They concluded that a person with a strong interdependent self-construal will see building and maintaining relationships as key to task accomplishment, while those with an independent self-construal will view task outcomes as the means to build good relationships. Cross (1995) studied how the self-construal of East Asian and American students influenced their coping behaviours related to stress during cross-cultural adaptation. East Asian students with higher scores on the interdependent self-construal reported higher levels of stress and difficulty in adapting to the more individualistic US culture. However, East Asian students who scored higher on their independent self-construal used more direct coping strategies, and indicated lower levels of stress. In a study on conversational strategy, Kim, Sharkey and Singelis (1994) found that participants scaring higher on independent self-consturals were more likely to focus on conversational clarity (straight talk, linear patterns of communication, etc.), and participants with higher scores on interdependent self-construals were more likely to focus on face-related issues and used a more indirect style of communication. Results of a follow-up study by Kim et al. (1996) were consistent. Cultural individualism greatly influenced the independent self-construal, while cultural collectivism greatly influenced the interdependent self-construal. Other recent studies have reinforced the importance of self-construal as an important mediating individual-level variable in explaining cultural effects on people's communication behaviours. For instance, Gudykunst et al. (1996) hypothesized that while individualism-collectivism had direct effects on highcontext and low-context communication styles, self-construals had an indirect impact on communication styles. Results indicated that the impact of individualism-collectivism on low-context communication was mediated by independent self-construal. Similarly, the impact of individualism-collectivism on high-context communication was mediated by interdependent self-construal. Singelis and Brown (1995) argued that culture influences individual-level variables like self-construal, which, in turn, influences a person's communicative behaviour. Results indicated that culture, self-construal, and people's communication behaviours were theoretically and empirically linked in a way such that collectivism correlated positively with interdependent self-construal, and negatively with independent self-construal. In all, research suggests that individual-level factors are better predictors of behaviours than cultural-level variables.

Self-construal in China

Most past research suggests that the interdependent self-construal is stronger and more dominant than the independent self-construal in China (Yang, 1981; Hsu, 1981). In his classic work, Hofstede (1984: 151) offered a historical/political perspective to explain the collective or interdependent nature of the Chinese: 'For Mao Tsetung, individualism is evil. Individualism and liberalism, for Mao, are manifest in the selfishness and aversion to discipline characteristic of the petty bourgeoisie'. In contrast, Bond, Leung and Wan (1982) found that individualistic Americans focused more on task accomplishment, whereas the collectivistic Chinese focused more on relational maintenance (interdependence) issues. McCrae and John (1992) (cited in Bond, 1994) also found that the Chinese community (in Hong Kong of China) were much more likely to focus on agreeableness and conscientiousness (collectivistic relational issues) than Australians, for instance. Schwartz's (1994: 111) study was instrumental in pointing out that Chinese people can show individualistic traits within a collectivistic context: China 'is not a prototypical collectivistic society, if *collectivism* refers to a conception of the person as deeply embedded in the collectivity without legitimate autonomous interests'. The Chinese respects hierarchical differences, and private entrepreneurship is undertaken within tightly integrated relationships.

Several historical, political, economic, social, and cultural factors influence the self-construal of the Chinese people. Here we detail some of the key influences, including the Confucius ideal that individuals should be first concerned with their place in the scheme of human relations (Stipek, 1998). The dominant tenets of Confucianism include an attention to harmony, hierarchy (social position), face (self-image), shame, *Buoying* (reciprocation), and Guanxi (relationship maintenance) (Liu, 1997). Confucianism views family relations as the basis of society in which wives are generally subordinate to their husbands, children are subordinate to their parents, subjects are loyal to the king, the young respect the elders, and friends help each other sincerely (Chang & Holt, 1991).

After the founding of the People's Republic of China in 1949, political ideology became a key influence on the Chinese people's self-identity. The Chinese identity was shaped by several political and cultural upheavals. First, Maoism was antithetical to the hierarchical principles of Confucianism, which insisted on equality for everyone. As a part of a collective enterprise, the Chinese people were ordained to obey the decision of the collective at all times. The 'self' in this context was subordinated to others (Chen, 1995). During the turbulent Chinese Cultural Revolution (1966 to 1976), everything reminiscent of the old was rejected as 'feudal'. Temples were destroyed; children were urged to scream at their parents; students actively condemned their teachers; and officials and scholars were publicly humiliated. In 1978, the responsibility system, in which farmland was distributed to every household, was carried out in rural areas (Bernstein, 1981). The responsibility system linked income with the quantity and quality of work, so farmers were intrinsically motivated to boost their productivity, improving their self-confidence (Bernstein, 198 1). Later, in Deng Xiaoping's era (post-1978) economic reform led to the opening of China to the outside world. A strong wave of self-awareness emerged among the Chinese people during this time. 'Following your own path' has become a more and more popular motto among Chinese people. On one hand, with the opening of the society and the decline of political movements, there is less social and political pressures on people's pursuit of personal happiness. The Chinese people, it seems, have learned to mind their own business, and not to press others for certain kinds of social rules. On the other hand, Chinese people have realized that they themselves deserve a better life, and they are very determined to reach their changed goals in life.

In the past several decades, several key changes seem to have occurred in the attitude of the Chinese people toward long-held Confucian principles, which are also integral to understanding their evolving self-construal (Chu, 1985; Chu & Ju, 1993). First, it seems that there has been an erosion of the importance of 'age' and 'authority' in China. Distinctions between superiors and subordinates are weakening. While family relationships are still valued, disagreeing with parents or elder siblings is not uncommon. In most situations, people do not hesitate to express their opinions. Relative to the past, children are more independent of their parents' control, and exercise more freedom of choice, such as in the selection of marriage partners, In the work place, managers, increasingly, tend to consult subordinates for ideas and opinions when making a decision (Chu & Ju, 1993). Second, the Chinese women have experienced a sea-change in their personal, professional, and familial lives. The most remarkable achievement during Mao's era was that it liberated Chinese women from Confucian tenets. Women worked together with men. Female iron-ore workers, train drivers, and pilots appeared (Chen, 1995). Increasingly, women select their husbands by themselves. Remarkably, in present day China, some 70 per cent of divorces are initiated by women (Bullough & Ruan, 1994). Third, while family ties remain stable, social relations are becoming increasingly superficial. The kinship structure of the traditional Chinese family, especially in urban areas, has either been disbanded or destroyed. However, blood and clan relationships are still important, and Chinese people still care a great deal about siblings and relatives. Relatively, family relationships are more stable than other social relationships (Chu, 1985; Chu & Ju, 1993). People with a higher level of education, or under Western cultural influences develop more social relations outside the kinship structure, but these human ties are more superficial than family relations. Moreover, the purpose of extending social relationship networks is for personal success and interest, not just for friendship (Chang & Holt, 1991). In rural areas, on the other hand, the kinship-based network still remains a fairly strong influence, perpetuating traditional interdependent relations toward significant others, especially to ensure enduring social support (Chu, 1985).

Our above analysis suggests that the Chinese self-construal is in flux. Various political, economic, and socio-cultural events, especially of the past few decades, seems to have exerted an influence on how the Chinese people view themselves as being separate from others (independence) and in relation to others (interdependence). There is also reason to believe that socio-demographic actors such as age and authority, gender, and rural-urban residence exert an influence on the Chinese peoples' self-construal. We thus pose the following two research questions:

Research Question # 1: To what extent is the Chinese peoples' self-construal independent and interdependent? That is, do the Chinese people see themselves as being separate from others or as connected with others?

Research Question #2: How is the Chinese people's self-construal influenced by age, gender, and urban/rural residence?

Methodology and Data-collection

We collected both quantitative and qualitative data to help answer our research questions. The quantitative survey data were collected in China in mid-1998, and the qualitative focus-group and in-depth interview data were gathered from US-based Chinese respondents in late-1998 and early-1999. The primary purpose of the qualitative data-gathering was to shed further light on the quantitative findings.

The quantitative data-gathering centred on the adaptation and administration of the 24-item Singelis (1994) scale to measure a Chinese individual's independent and interdependent selfconstrual. These two distinct dimensions of the scale were supported in confirmatory factor analyses of two multiethnic samples of college students in the US, and the scale was found to have high reliability and validity (Singelis, 1994). However, since the scale was designed in the United States, we took several steps to ensure that the scale was comparable in meaning in China. The scale, comprising of 12 questions that measured an individual's 'independent' self-construal and another 12 questions measuring the individual's 'interdependent' self-construal, was first translated into Mandarin under the close supervision of two of the present paper's four authors, both of whom are Chinese nationals. The translated questionnaire was discussed in-depth with a team of about one-dozen survey interviewers and supervisors, graduate students and professors from a major Chinese university, and then pre-tested in a field-setting with several rural respondents in Yanqing County, 80 kilometers outside of Beijing.

Based on the pre-test results, and the ensuing debriefing of the survey interviewers, the questionnaire was modified for use in the Chinese context. Four items out of the original 24-item Singelis (1994) scale were dropped because they were strongly perceived by both the respondents and the survey interviewers as being 'redundant'. Additionally, rural respondents found it difficult to comprehend these four items. Further, two items of the remaining 20 items were translated into Chinese in a somewhat non-literal manner to preserve the original contextual meaning of the statement. For instance, the item on 'I should have the hope of living long enough to see my grandchildren grow up' was translated as 'I hope I could live under the same roof with my grand children', which is a common Chinese colloquial expression to signify the same meaning. Further, the number of response categories for gauging the respondents' agreement with each question was reduced to a 3-point Likert-type format (1 = Agree; 2 = Neither Agree nor Disagree; 3 = Disagree), from a 5-point response format. While a 5-point response format can tap a broader spectrum of variance in responses, our pre-test experience, and the ensuing in-depth debriefing with survey interviewers strongly suggested that in the rural Chinese field context, respondents find it easier to respond in a 3-point response format.

The 20-item self-construal scale was administered through personal interview surveys in mid-1998 to a total of 237 respondents in Shandong Province of China. Using a stratified random sampling procedure (stratifying according to age, gender, and urban/ rural residence), and drawing upon the support of local officials and local citizens' lists, some 116 respondents were selected in Dongying City, and another 121 respondents were selected from eight villages in Linqu County, Shandong Province. A profile of the respondents is provided in Table 1. The data were entered into SPSS in China by the two Chinese co-authors of this paper, checking for accuracy. The quantitative data was subsequently analyzed in the US.

After carrying out the quantitative data-analyses (the results of which are detailed later), it was felt that a more enriched qualitative understanding of the quantitative results was desirable. Many of our survey respondents had neither agreed nor disagreed with several questionnaire items. So we conducted two focus group discussions (including one eight-person all male group, and an eight-person all female group) and two in-depth interviews with two Chinese couples, giving us a respondent count of an additional 20 individuals. These Chinese respondents were students, spouses, and visiting scholars at our US-based Midwestern university, and ranged in age from 22 to 40 years. For this qualitative portion, we purposely selected respondents who had spent less than a year in the US, so that they were 'in tune' with current-day Chinese lifestyles. In fact, 18 of our 20 respondents had spent less than 3 months in the US. In the focus groups and in-depth interviews, they reacted to a range of questions and scenarios associated with how they construed their self, both independently and in relation to others, in the context of family life, parenting, work, gender relations, and other realms. Each focus group interview and indepth interview was translated and transcribed, and we will draw upon them to illuminate our quantitative findings.

Table 1
Demographic Profile of the Participants

	Variable	*Number (Percentage) N= 237*
Sex:	Female	122 (51%)
	Male	115 (49%)
Location:	City	116 (49%)
	Village	121 (51%)
Age:	14 to 24 years	75 (32%)
	25 to 39 years	124 (52%)
	40 to 50 years	38 (16%)
Average age:	29.4 years	

Results

Research Question #1 asked: *To what extent is the Chinese peoples' self-construal independent and interdependent? That is, do the Chinese people see themselves as being separate from others or as connected with others?* We subjected our 20-item self-construal scale, a modified version of Singelis' (1994) scale, to a principal components factor analysis using varimax rotation. Items with a minimum factor loading of 0.40 with no cross-loadings of over 0.20 were included. Eleven of the 20 items loaded on one of two factors, specifying, respectively, an interdependent and independent self-construal dimension. In this sense, the validity of the modified Singelis' scale was reinforced in a non-Western context. The reliability for the interdependent self-construal was reasonable (Cronbach's alpha = 0.71); however, the reliability for the independent self-construal was low (Cronbach's alpha =0.42).

Table 2
Factor Loadings for Singelis' Self-construal Scale in China.

Self-construal items	Factor 1	Factor 2
Interdependent items:		
1. I will sacrifice my for the benefit of the group I am in.	0.55	-0.11
2. I often have the feeling that my relationships with others are more important than my own accomplishments.	0.69	-0.13
3. I should take into consideration my parents' advice when making education/career plans.	0.50	-0.18
4. It is important to me to respect decisions made by the group.	0.54	-0.00
5. I will stay in a group, if they need me, even when I am not happy with the group.	0.58	-0.26
6. If my brother or sister fails, I feel responsible.	0.48	-0.18
7. Even when I strongly disagree with group members, I avoid an argument.	0.56	0.00
Independent items:		
8. I feel comfortable using someone's first name after I meet them, wen though they are much older than me.	0.00	0.54
9. I prefer to be direct and forthright when dealing with people I have just met.	0.24	0.59
10. Being able to take care of myself is a primary concern for me.	0.00	0.48
11. I enjoy being unique and different from others in many respect.	-0.10	0.48

The first factor, which included seven items assessing the interdependent self-construal (for example, 'I will sacrifice my self-interest for the benefit of the group I am in', 'I often have the feeling that my relationships with others are more important than my own accomplishments', etc.) had an eigen value of 3.1 and explained 16 per cent of the variance. The second factor, which included 4 items assessing the independent self-construal (for example, 'I feel comfortable using someone's first name after I meet them, even though they are much older than me', 'I prefer to be direct and forthright when dealing with people I have just met', etc.) had an eigen value of 1.7 and explained nine per cent of the variance. A comparison of the mean scores suggested that there was no significant difference [$t(224)=-2.70$; $p>0.05$] between independent self-construal (M = 9.13; SD=2.01) and interdependent self-construal (M=9.71; SD=2.41).

Table 3
Factor Loadings for Singelis' Self-Construal Scale in China across the three Age Groups

Self-construal items	(15-24 years)		(25-39)		(40-50)	
	F1	F2	F1	F2	F1	F2
Interdependent items:						
1. I have respect for authority figures with whom I interact.	.00	.72	.58	.14		
2. I often have the feeling that my I relationships with others are more important than my own accomplishments.	.81	.11	.00	.65	.78	.00
3. If my brother or sister fails, I feel responsible.	.56	.00			.74	.23
4. Even when I strongly disagree with group members, I avoid an argument.	.46	.00	.52	.23	.65	.00
5. My happiness depends on the happiness of those around me.			.77	.00		
6. I will stay in a group if they need me even when I am not happy with the group.			.51	.20		
7. I respect people who are modest about themselves.			.00	.77		
8. I will sacrifice my self-interest for the benefit of the group I am in.					.76	.21
9. I should take into consideration my parents' advice when making education career plans.					.72	.00
10. It is important to me to respect decisions made by the group.					.62	.34
Independent items:						
11. I'd rather say no directly, than risk I being misunderstood.					.74	.10
12. I feel comfortable being singled out.	.00	.73				
13. I value good health above everything.					.00	.81

N=237

Research Question #2 asked: *How is the Chinese peoples' self-construal influenced by age, gender, and urban/rural residence?* The modified version of Singelis' (1994) self-construal scale comprising 20 items was subjected to a principal components factor analysis using varimax rotation. Items with a minimum factor loading of 0.40 with no cross-loadings of over 0.20 were included. We did not restrict the number of factors allowed in our solution.

Influence of age

To look at the influence of age on self-construal, we divided our sample into three groups: Respondents between (1) 14 to 24 years, (2) 25 to 39 years, (3) and 40 to 50 years. Results from our factor analyses indicated that our Chinese respondents between 14 and 24 years of age did not display a clear sense of interdependent or independent self-construal (see Table 3). Only three of the interdependent self-construal items ('I often have the feeling that my relationships with others are more important than my own accomplishments', 'If my brother or sister fails, I feel responsible', and 'Even when I strongly disagree with group members, I avoid an argument') had a factor loadings of 0.40 or above with no crossloadings more than 0.20. Also, only one of the items measuring independent self-construal loaded on factor *#2* ('I feel comfortable being singled out') along with one of the interdependence self-construal items ('I have respect for authority figures'). The first factor had an eigen value of 3.18 and explained 16 per cent of the variance; the second factor had an eigen value of 1.84 and explained 10 per cent of the variance.

Analysis of the age group 25 to 39 years indicated that none of the items measuring independent self-construal had a factor loading of 0.40 or above (Table 3) suggesting that the interdependent self-construal is stronger in China. Six of the items measuring interdependence had factor loadings of 0.40 or above with no cross loadings more than 0.20. Four of these six 'interdependence' items loaded on factor #1 (for example, 'I have respect for authority figures with whom I interact', 'Even when I strongly disagree with group members, I avoid an argument', and other items), and two of the items loaded on factor #2 ('I often have the feeling that my relationships with others are more important than my accomplishments', and 'I respect people who are modest about themselves'), indicating two dimensions of interdependence. The first interdependence factor had an eigen value of 2.9 and explained 15 per cent of the variance; and the second interdependence factor had an eigen value of 1.97 and explained nine per cent of the variance.

Analysis of those between 40 to 50 years of age showed the strongest indication of the role of interdependence in China. Six of the items measuring interdependence had factor loadings of 0.60 or higher (for example, 'I often have the feeling that my relationships with others are more important than my accomplishments', 'if my brother or sister fails, I feel responsible', and other items) with no cross loadings more than 0.20. The interdependent self-construal factor had an eigen value of 5.4 and explained 27 per cent of the variance. The independent self-construal factor had an eigen value of 2.1, and explained 11 per cent of the variance. Interestingly, one of the items measuring independent self-construal ('I'd rather say no directly, than risk being misunderstood') loaded strongly on the interdependence factor. Since the elders in Chinese society have authority and respect, it is likely that they speak more directly than youngsters. Only one item ('I value good health above everything') loaded on factor #2 signifying independent self-construal. Again, this seems logical given older age respondents are more likely to be experiencing health problems.

Further, a one-way analysis of variance assessing the impact of age on interdependent self-construal (see Table 6) suggested that there was a significant difference between the three groups [$F(2,225)=3.68$; $pe0.051$]. The 14 to 24 year old respondents ($M110.32$; $SD=2.45$) demonstrated a lower level of interdependence than the 40 to 50 year-olds ($M=9.13$; $SD=2.66$), and this difference was statistically significant (Scheffe's $t=1.49$; $p<0.05$). In essence, the sense of an interdependent self-construal is stronger among the older Chinese respondents than the younger ones. A one-way analysis of variance assessing the impact of age on independent self-construal suggested that there was no significant difference between the three groups [$F(2,226) = 0.39$; $p > .05$].

Influence of gender

Similar analyses were conducted to assess how the Chinese self-construal varied with the respondents' gender. Results from the principal components factor analyses with varimax rotation indicated the interdependent self-construal was strong for both men and women in China (see Table 4).

For the female respondents, six items measuring interdependence loaded relatively strongly on factor #1 (for example, 'I have respect for authority figures with whom 1 interact', 'It is important to me to respect decisions made by the group', and other items). Interestingly, like the older age respondents in our sample, the women felt that they would prefer to say no directly than risk being misunderstood. The interdependence self-construal factor had an eigen value of 3.4 and explained 17 per cent of the variance. Three items measuring independence loaded strongly on factor #2 (for example, 'I prefer to be direct and forthright', 'I enjoy being unique, and another item). The independent self-construal factor for our female respondents had an eigen value of 1.87 and explained nine per cent of the variance.

For male respondents (see Table 4), once again, six items assessing interdependent self-construal loaded above 0.50 on the first factor, which had an eigen value of 3.3 and explained about 17 per cent of the variance (for example, 'It is important for me to respect decisions made by the group', 'I will stay in a group if they need me, even when I am not happy with the group', and other items). Only two items measuring the independent self-construal had factor loadings of 0.40 or above ('I am the same person at home and outside', and 'being able to take care of myself is my primary concern for me'). The factor had an eigen value of 1.9 and explained about 10 per cent of the variance.

An assessment of sex on independent and interdependent self-construals suggested that there was no difference between our male and female respondents on these two dimensions. A comparison of the means suggested that there was no significant difference [t(226)=0.76; p>0.05] between men's (M=9.85; SD=2.54) and women's (M=9.61; SD=2.28) interdependent self-construal. Mean score comparisons also showed no significant differences [t(227) =-1.76; p>.05] between men's (M=8.88; SD= 1.87) and women's (M=9.34; SD=2.17) independent self-construal.

In essence, our findings suggest that both Chinese women and men have strong interdependent self-construals, and relatively weaker independent self-construals. Interestingly, different items comprised the women's and men's independent self-construals, While women showed a preference for being unique and using a direct and forthright communication style, men preferred to take care of themselves and be the same person both inside and outside the home.

Influence of rural-urban residence

Interestingly, for both rural and urban respondents, the items assessing independent self-construal did not load on any one factor, and were distributed randomly across several factors (see Table 5). For rural respondents, there appeared to be two dimensions of interdependent self-construal. The first factor, which had an eigen value of 3.6 and explained 19 per cent of the variance, included three items (for example, 'I often have the feeling that my relationships with others are more important than my own personal accomplishments', 'I respect modest pople', and another item). The second factor, which had an eigen value of 1.8 and explained nine per cent of the variance, included two items ('It is important for me to respect decisions made by the group', and 'If my brother or sister fails, I feel responsible').

Two dimensions of interdependent self-construal also emerged for our urban respondents (see Table 5). The first factor, which included two items ('I often have the feeling that my relationships with others are more important than my own personal accomplishments', and another item) had an eigen value of 2.8 and explained 14 per cent of the variance. The second interdependent self-construal factor also had two items ('I respect modest people' and another item); it had an eigen value of 2.0 and explained 10 per cent of the variance. None of the items measuring independent self-construals met our factor loading criterion for both

Table 4
Female versus Male Respondents on Singelis' Self-Construal Scale in China

Self-construal items	(Female) F1	F2	(Male) F1	F2
Interdependent items:				
1. I have respect for authority figures with whom I interact.	.51	.31		
2. I often have the feeling that my I relationships with others are more important than my own accomplishments.	.56	.00	.75	.00
3. It is important to me to respect ecisions made by the group.	.58	.00	.53	.00
4. I will stay in a group if they need me, even when I am not happy with the group.	.56	.21	.62	.20
5. If my brother or sister fails, I feel Responsible.	.52	.00		
6. Even when I strongly disagree with group members, I avoid an argument.	.54	.00	.58	00
7. I will sacrifice my self-interest for the benefit of the group I am in.			.62	.12
9. I should take into consideration my parents' advice when making education career plans.			.55	.11
Independent items:				
10. I'd rather say no directly, than risk being misunderstood.	.45	.11		
11. I feel comfortable using someone's first name soon after I meet them, even when they are much older than me.	.17	.54		
12. I prefer to be direct and forthright.	.21	.47		
13. I enjoy being unique.	.00	.66		
14. I am the same person at home and out with others.			.14	.68
15. Being able to take care of myself is a primary concern for me.			.00	.61

N =237

rural and urban Chinese respondents. Further, while it appears that rural and urban respondents have stronger interdependent self-construals, there are multiple dimensions of interdependence.

A comparison of the mean scores suggested that there was a significant difference [t(226)=2.84; p>0.051 between the urban (M= 10.19; SD=2.29) and rural respondents' (M=9.30; SD=2.45) interdependent self-construal. Also, a comparison of the means suggested that there was no significant difference [t(227) =0.04; p>0.05] between the urban (M=9.12; SD= 1.77) and rural respondents' (M=9.11; SD=2.19) independent self-construal. In essence, it appears that rural respondents have a slightly higher level of interdependence than our urban respondents.

Interpretation with qualitative data

In this section, we draw upon the qualitative data to shed further light on the extent to which the Chinese peoples' self-construal (1) is independent and interdependent and (2) is influenced by age, gender, and urban/rural residence.

Table 5
Village versus City Respondents on Singelis' Self-Construal Scale in China

Self-construal items	(Rural) F1	F2	(Urban) F1	F2
Interdependent items:				
1. I often have the feeling that my relationships with others are more important than my own accomplishments.	.71	.18	.63	.40
2. I respect modest people.	.71	.00	.00	.71
3. I will sacrifice my self-interest for the benefit of the group I am in.	.71	.00		
4. It is important to me to respect decisions made by the group.	.31	.75		
5. If my brother or sister fails, I feel responsible.	.00	.77	.25	.72
6. Even when I strongly disagree with group members, I avoid an argument.			.61	.32

N=237

Independent and interdependent nature of self-construal

A recurring theme in the focus group and in-depth interviews was that utilitarian, contextual, and situational factors mediate how independent and interdependent self-construals impact communication behaviours. Whether in the context of work or family relationships, respondents showed a tendency to preface their statenients with a 'it depends' monotone.

Table 6
Impact of Age on Interdependent Self-Construal

Age	N	Mean	Std. Deviation
14 to 24 years	71	10.3286	2.4538
25 to 39 years	120	9.5667	2.2482
40 to 50 years	38	9.1316	2.6628
Total	229	9.7281	2.4125

Table 7
Impact of age on independent self-construal

Age	N	Mean	Std. Deviation
14 to 24 years	71	9.2817	1.7170
25 to 39 years	120	9.0833	2.1947
40 to 50 years	38	8.9474	1.8592
Total	229	9.1223	1.9984

For instance, in the context of professional work relationships, respondents showed a strong willingness to maintain harmonious relationships, despite considerable self-effacement. For instance, when asked if he would argue with co-workers because of a stark difference in opinion, Dong (M, 31) said he would prefer to be silent in order to maintain a harmonious work relationship, especially if his immediate interests were not in jeopardy.

Yang (F, 39) reiterated that one should not argue for small matters as that makes 'one seen as being hard to get along with, but one should stand up for one's strong feelings'. Most respondents agreed that while self-accomplishment was very important, a harmonious working relationship represented a highly integral part of one's self accomplishment. As Li (M, 24) stated: 'Once a person has harmonious relationships with others, he can accomplish a lot. Nobody can put others behind and go on to success by himself'. In the context of family relationships, respondents alluded to the importance of situational factors in mediating how independent and interdependent self-construals impact communication behaviours. For instance, Wang (F, 31) explained how the self-construal of parents and their grown-up children may be influenced by whether or not they live together: 'It is very conditional. Many couples can't move out after marriage, because they have no houses. They have to live together with their parents. Either the parents and their children become highly dependent on each other; or they get tired of each other. The habit of every family is so different'.

Influence of age, gender, and urban/rural residence on self-construal

Intergenerational (age) differences: Our focus group interviews and in-depth interviews suggest that in spite of the social, political, and socio-cultural changes in China during the past decades, the family still remains the core unit in society, and parents and children are still to a large extent mutually dependent. Interestingly, most of our respondents talked about the influence of inter generational (age) differences on self-construal in the context of family life.

Most of our focus group respondents echoed the sentiment that it is the children's obligation to take care of the parents, and parents' sacrifice for their children is viewed as natural, but nevertheless highly appreciated. Yang (F, 39) said: 'I feel we have responsibility to take care of our parents. Our parents bring us up, and when we have the capabilities, we should give them a better life'. Even among the relatively younger set of parents, the notion of 'sacrificing' one's aspirations for children's development was palpable. As Li (F, 28) stated: 'I would definitely sacrifice my education and career for the good of my kids'.

The relatively strong family bond leads to a willingness among the younger people in China to still consult their parents' opinion while making personal decisions about education, career, or marriage. As one respondent said: 'Even if we do not follow what our parents may say, such consultation is a good strategy to please the parents'. Most respondents agreed that in present-day China, most parents do not force the children to do things their way: 'Because of the open-mindedness of the parents, considerable freedom is given to the children for their personal decision-making'. Several respondents noted that if, however, conflicts arose between the parents and children about career or marriage, most children would follow their own wishes.

Zhang (F, 32) explicitly noted certain reasons for differences in self-construal between her parents' generation and her own. As her parents grew up during Mao's socialist campaigns, they did not 'think about solely following their own path as that meant being politically incorrect'. However, our respondents noted that times have changed: 'The recent awakening of the self in China has brought a tension between parents and children'. While most young people want to live by themselves for an independent and free life, most parents like to insist on living together. As one of our male respondent's said: 'We felt obligated to live with her parents, though we had an apartment of our own. We were quite relieved when we came to the US to study and finally had a life of our own'. Li (M, 24) mentioned that 'nowadays a lot of young people would live by themselves as soon as they could afford to, and just visit their parents during the weekends'. Our respondents reported their dislike for criticism and interference from their parents. Tian (F, 25) felt strongly about the inconvenience of living with her parents because she had to report her activities to them. Yang (F, 39) claimed that 'I feel my mother's love is so meticulous that it has become a burden for me'.

Zhao (M, 32) eloquently summarized the intergenerational (age) differences among the Chinese people in the context of the growing proclivity among young people to pursue their own personal and career goals:

Previously one took into consideration others' opinion. If you were looking for a life partner, you considered how your parents, relatives, and friends thought about the person. If you were thinking about quitting your job and setting up your own business, you had to consider your parent's attitudes about the social status of being a private businessmen. But now such is not the case. I would marry whoever I think is suitable for me. As for my career, as long as I like it, or I can make a lot of money, I do not care what other people think about it. For me, it is all about pursuing personal happiness.

Our respondents also emphasized that in traditional Chinese society, submission to age and authority was key. However, during the Cultural Revolution (1966-1976), people were encouraged to openly criticize authority figures. As a result, a newly found assertiveness is apparent among the younger generation Chinese. They do not submit to persons of authority simply because of their high positions in the way that their elders did in the past. Li (M, 24) claimed that his respect for the authorities did not come automatically with the high positions they held: 'Some of the authorities, I respect them, but some of them, I do not'. Deng (M, 28) also reiterated that his respect for authorities depended on the specific person and in specific situations.

In essence, our respondents remarks suggest that young people in China are looking for a subtle balance between independence of the self and interdependence with others.

Gender differences: Our focus group and in-depth interviews suggest that women's status in Chinese society and their concept of the self changed a great deal during Mao's time, when gender equality was pushed politically. Several focus group respondents commented on the changing role of women in Chinese society. As Zhang (F, 32) noted:

> In our grandparents' generation, traditional rules applied ... Men were in charge of social affairs and women of domestic affairs. Men were superior to women. Our parents grew up with the concept of men and women are equal, share housework, and child-care. Today's women are very independent, and they make money to support the family too.

Wang, (F, 31) echoed a similar sentiment: 'In the past, women had no courage to speak out, but now they can speak out'. Zhang (E 32), an editor of a women's association magazine, maintained that today's 'women had the same opportunity for promotion and same dedication for their works as men'. Such underlying sentiments may explain why our quantitative results did not demonstrate significant differences between men and women in their self-construal.

While most of our female respondents agreed 'that economic independence gave Chinese women strength to pursue their selves, some respondents believed that Chinese women are caught between the traditional family role and the newly-emerging professional one. As Zhao (MI 32) noted: 'Women still are more inclined to sacrifice their self interest for the family than men'. Some women respondents' expressed concern with the societal trend of viewing independent career women 'as unsuccessful mothers and wives'. Some others disagreed: 'If you want to be an independent person, it won't be contradictory to your role as a family member, mother, or wife'. Many respondents felt that both men and women in China were seeking a subtle balance between their personal careers and family responsibilities.

Rural-urban differences: Our focus group and in-depth interview respondents made a rural-urban distinction with respect to women's self-construals and family kinship structures. Many respondents noted that women in cities are perceived to have a much stronger independent self-concept than women in rural areas, because rural women are more dependent on the family socially and economically. Several respondents noted that in cities 'more women filed a divorce than men because women were self-reliant and can live independently without relying on men'.

Many respondents felt that in rural areas interdependent, kinship- based network structures remain relatively stronger than in urban areas. As Dong (M, 31) noted: 'In the cities, people care less about extended family members ... They try not to stick to each other too often to avoid conflicts. In the countryside.. .people have to live together'. Shi (M, 29), whose family members live in a rural township, noted: 'When any family member is in need, they can count on the help from other relatives'. However, the migration of people from the countryside to cities is gradually dispersing the traditional kinship network. For instance, most of our city-bred respondents said that the 'physical distance among family members is altering family traditions'. Also with the implementation of the one-child policy in China since 1978, many respondents felt, the number of nuclear families has been growing, and kinship structures are eroding.

In essence, our respondents' comments support our quantitative findings of relatively higher levels of interdependence among our rural respondents than the urban respondents.

Conclusion

Our investigation suggests that at the cultural level, collectivism is still predominant in Chinese society, and the traditional self concept is still deep-rooted in the collective Chinese memory. However, a sense of self-awareness has arisen among the Chinese people since the reformist era of Deng Xiaoping (post 1978) especially among the younger generation. Chinese society, as a whole, is much more tolerant today of individualism. The individual has far more economic and social opportunities for self-accomplishment. Our findings support Chu's (1985) claim that a transient 'self' is represented in the younger generation of Chinese people, who are more assertive, less accommodating, and less submissive to authority figures than were previous generations. The 'it depends' responses (as noted previously) by our respondents, with respect to valuing the 'self' versus the 'other', can be better understood within the historical context of the changing political, economic, and social climate in China. After the formation of the Peoples' Republic of China in 1949, the Communist Party initiated a series of political campaigns to attack traditional cultural values and beliefs, and to foster a collectivist spirit to build the new socialist state. The traditional kinship based 'self-other' relationship was replaced by a socialist collective self-concept. During the devastating Cultural Revolution (1966-1976), quite a lot of the Chinese people lost this collectivist belief, unsure of the relationship between the self and the collective. The post-1978 open-door policy and the economic reforms have not completely filled the vacuum created by the Cultural Revolution. While the well-defined social rules of the past do not exist anymore, the Chinese people find themselves in a mix of Confucian tradition, communist ideology, and a newly-emerging Westernized individualism: That is, in a state of flux. Therefore, most Chinese people seem to have adopted a flexible value system to adjust to the changing environment.

Compared to previous studies, our approach to studying self-construal offers several advantages. First, unlike much of the previous research on self-construal, we focused on a non-college student population in a naturalistic setting; this allowed us to draw broader generalizations. Second, we combined quantitative and qualitative approaches to study self-construal from multiple perspectives. Third, an active involvement of Chinese colleagues in the conceptualization, implementation, and writing of this project led us to interpret our findings within the contextual nuances of China's cultural, political and social history.

What implications does our present study have for the study of intercultural communication? Our study reinforces the previous findings of Markus and Kitayama (1991), Singelis (1994) and Oetzel and Bolton-Oetzel (1997) that individual-level factors (like independent and interdependent self-construals) provide a richer understanding of the depth and variability associated with a person's self-identity. Our study points to the importance of conducting further research on how a person's self-identity may not be just bipolar (i.e. independent versus interdependent self-construal), but may be more hybrid (i.e. include dimensions of both types of self-construal).

Further, our study points to how a person's self-construal influences their attitudes and behaviours in a variety of communication contexts. For example, Kim et al. (2000) found that a patient's self-construal influences her participation in a doctor-patient interaction. The more independent her self-construal, the more likely she is to actively participate while interacting with a doctor. Kim et al. (2000) discussed the implications of their findings on improving the effectiveness of doctor-patient communication.

Our future research aims to address several important areas of intercultural communication. We wish to create a self-construal scale that is 'emic' oriented and can be used in China and in other cultures. We also plan to study how self-construal influences Chinese peoples' communication styles during cross-cultural negotiations, joint venture business decision-making, or in the educational system. We hope the present research will lead to further macro and micro-level analysis of factors that influence the independent and interdependent self-construal of the Chinese people.

¹Endnote

[1] A previous version of this article was recognized as the Top Three Paper by the International and Intercultural Communication Division of the National Communication Association, Chicago, 1999. We thank our colleagues at the Center for Integrated Agricultural Development (CIAD), Beijing Agricultural Univer-

sity, for assisting us with the field data-collection activities in China. We also thank Drs. John Oetzel, Theodere Singelis. Min-sun Kim, and our anonymous reviewers for their invaluable suggestions in revising this manuscript.

References

Bernstein, R. (1981, Nov 23). Revolution down to the farm. *Time,* p. 51.

Bond, M. H. (1994). Into the heart of collectivism: A personal and scientific journey 66-84 in U. Kim, H. C. Triandis, C. Kagitcibasi, S. Choi, & G. Yoon (eds.) *Individualism and collectivism: Theory, methods and applications.* Newbury Park, CA: Sage Publications.

Bond, M. H., Leung, K., & Wan, K. C. (1982). How does cultural collectivism operate? The impact of task and maintenance contributions on reward distribution. *Journal of Cross-Cultural Psychology,* 13, 186-200.

Bruce, R. (1998). The return to Confucius? *History Today.* 48(1), 7-8.

Bullough, V.L., Ruan, F.F. (1994). Marriage, divorce and sexual relations in contemporary China. *Journal of Comparative Family Studies.* 25(3), 383-393.

Chang, H.C., & Holt, G.R. (1991). More than relationship: Chinese interaction and the principle of Kuan-His. *Communication Quarterly* 39(3), 251-271.

Chen, C.C. (1995). New trends in rewards allocation preferences: Sino-US. *Academy of Management Journal.* 38(2), 408-430.

Chu, G. C. (1985). The changing concept of self in contemporary China 67- 81 in A. J. Chu, G.C. Chu, & Y.N. Ju (eds). *The Great Wall in ruins: Communication and cultural change in China.* Albany, NY: State University of New York Press.

Chu, G. C. and Ju, Y.N. (1993). *The Great Wall in ruins: Communication and cultural change in China.* Albany, NY: State University of New York Press.

Cross, S. E. (1995). Self-construals, coping, and stress in crosscultural adaptation. *Journal of Cross-cultural Psychology,* 26(6), 673-697.

Cross, S. E., & Madson, L. (1997). Models of the self: Self-construals and gender. *Psychological Bulletin,* 122(1), 5-37.

Emerson, J. (1996). Yang Chu's discovery of the body. *Philosophy East and West,* 46(4), 533-566.

Fan, H. (1995). The socio-historical framework for the study of women and sport in China. *Women in Sport & Physical Activity Journal.* 4(1), 17-19.

Fitzgerald, J. (1993). The invention of the modern Chinese Self 48-69 in M.Lee & A. D. Sarokomla-Stefanowska (eds.) *Modernization of the Chinese past.* Wild Peony PTY LTD.

Geertz, C. (1975). On the nature of anthropological understanding. *American Scientist,* 63, 47-53.

Gudykunst, W. B., Matsumoto, Y., Ting-Toomey. S., Nishida, T., Kim, K., & Heyman, S. (1996). The influence of cultural individualism-collectivism, self-construals, and individual values on communication styles across cultures. *Human Communication Research*, 22(4), 510-543.

Hofstede, G. (1984). *Culture's consequences.* Newbury Park, CA: Sage Publications.

Hsu, F. L. K. (1981). *Americans and Chinese: Passage to differences.* Honolulu: University of Hawaii Press.

Kim, M., Hunter, J. E., Miyahara, A., Horvath, A., Bresnahan, M., & Yoon, H. (1996). Individual-vs. culture-level dimensions of individualism and collectivism: Effects on preferred conversational styles. *Communication Monographs,* 63, 29-49.

Kim, M., Klingle, R. S., Sharkey, W. F., Park, H., Smith, D. H. & Cai, D. (2000). A test of a cultural model of patients motivation for verbal communication in doctor-patient interactions. *Communication Monographs,* 67(3), 262-283.

Kim, M., Sharkey, W. E, & Singelis, T. M. (1994). The relationship between individuals self-construals and perceived importance of interactive constraints. *International Journal of Intercultural Relations,* 18(1), *117-*140.

Liu, *Y.* (1997). Relationship in Chinese negotiation (unpublished). College Park, Maryland, United States: University of Maryland.

Markus,H. R., & Kitayama, S. (1991). Culture and the self: Implications for cognition, emotion, and motivation. *Psychological Review,* 98(2), 224-*253.*

Nunnally, J.C. (1978). *Psychometric theory.* New York: McGraw-Hill Book Co.

Oetzel, J. (1998). Explaining individual communication processes in homogeneous and heterogeneous groups through individualism-collectivism and self-construal. *Human Communication Research, 25* (2), 234-25 1.

Oetzel J., & Bolton-Oetzel, K. (1997). Exploring the relationship between self-construal and dimensions of group effectiveness. *Management Communication Quarterly,* 10(3), 289-3 15.

Park, H. S. & Levine, T. R. (1999). The theory of reasoned action and self-construal: Evidence from three cultures. *Communication Monographs,* 66 (3), 214232.

Schwartz, S. H. (1994). Beyond individualism/collectivism: New cultural dimensions of values 85-122 in U. Kim, H. C. Triandis, C. Kagitcibasi, S. Choi, & G. Yoon (eds.) *Individualism and collectivism: theory, methods and applications.* Newbury Park, CA: Sage Publications.

Singelis, T. M. (1994). The measurement of independent and interdependent self-construals. *Personality and Social Psychology Bulletin; 2D,* 580-591.

Singelis, T. M.. & BRown, W. J. (1995). Culture, self, and collectivist in a communication: Linking culture to individual behavior. *Human Communication Research, 21* (3), 354-389.

Stipek, D. (1998). Differences between Americans and Chinese in the circumstances evoking pride, shames, and guilt. *Journal of Cross-Cultural Psycho-logy,* 29(5), 616-629.

Triandis, H.C. (1989). The self and social behavior in differing cultural contexts. *Psychological Review,* 96, 506-520.

Yamada, A. & Singelis, T. M. (1999). Biculturalism and self-construal. *Internatronal lournal of intercultural Relations,* 23 (5).

Yang, K. S. (1981). A social orientation and individual modernity among Chinese students. *The Journal of Social Psychology, 1 1 3,* 159-170.

Introduction to

Touring Culture(s): Intercultural Communication Principles and International Tourism

By Sundae R. Bean and Judith N. Martin

In this last text, Bean and Martin take a closer look at the one sector of the business world which would seem to be an obvious choice for intercultural studies, i.e. international tourism. Yet surprisingly, the authors note that it is the one area of international business that has not really been analyzed from an intercultural perspective. Consequently, Bean and Martin have set out to undertake such an analysis. Since tourism is such a large sector, the authors have decided to focus specifically on cultural and heritage tourism.

Tourism, Bean and Martin note, has become the largest industry in the world. And more people than ever are now in a position to travel to other countries than ever before in human history, and actually do so. Hence, for most people a trip to another country can become the first contact with other cultures. And it seems that such visits more often than not actually reinforce cultural stereotypes and affirm that one's preconceived worldview is "correct;" thereby perpetuating ethnocentrism. This goes so far as to result in the recreation of "authentic" ethnic encounters that actually distort cultural reality. In fact, many parts of the Third World in particular view such situations as disgraceful. However, the power dominance of such encounters, i.e. rich tourists paying to experience a "primitive" culture, makes the situation difficult because if the tourists fail to experience what they seek, they may decide to go elsewhere to find what they are looking for.

But international tourism has also positive aspects in that it makes people realize that cultural differences do exist. Awareness is important. This might then result in more mindful communication which in turn might make people more empathetic and, hence, less rude and unintentional in intercultural encounters. Likewise, people might become more self-reflecting which also results in learning more about oneself. Consequently, intercultural communication offers valuable insights to improving tourism for both visitors and hosts. An insight that should have come earlier since international tourism seems to be a natural choice for intercultural communication.

Michael B. Hinner

Sundae R. Bean is a recent graduate of the Hugh Downs School of Human Communication at Arizona State University, holding a master's degree in communication. Ms. Bean specializes in intercultural communication with an emphasis on tourism. Her master's thesis concentrates on tourism as a site of intercultural contact, examining tourist and host narratives as a means to better understand how identity is negotiated in the tourism context. Ms. Bean recently moved to Switzerland.

Judith N. Martin is Professor of Communication in the Hugh Downs School of Human Communication at Arizona State University. Her research interests include the role of communication in international transitions, white identity and interracial relationships, and intercultural communication pedagogy. She has published more than 40 articles and book chapters on the topic of culture and communication. She, along with her coauthor Thomas K. Nakayama, has written three undergraduate textbooks in intercultural communication as well as edited *Whiteness: The Communication of Social Identity* (Sage Publications). She has taught undergraduate and graduate courses at the University of Minnesota and the University of New Mexico, in traditional classroom contexts as well as online format.

Touring Culture(s): Intercultural Communication Principles and International Tourism

Sundae R. Bean
Judith N. Martin

Intercultural communication scholars have researched and made contributions to various areas of international business: global media (Boyd-Barrett, 2002; Comor, 2002), computer mediated commerce (Olaniran, 2004), and intercultural adaptation of overseas business personnel (Kim 2005a, 2005b), to name only a few. One area that has been less studied but is equally important is the business of international tourism. In this essay we explore the importance of tourism in the global business world and describe significant contributions of intercultural communication theory and research to scholars and practitioners in a specific area of tourism: *cultural and heritage tourism*.

In the next section, we describe the rationale for studying this area of intercultural communication: the economic importance of tourism in the global context, the potential negative effects on host cultures and the unique communication characteristics of tourist-host encounters.

The Global Importance of Tourism

Tourism is now the largest industry in the world (Smith & Brent, 2001) and it continues to grow. Since 1950, the number of international arrivals has increased from 25 million to an estimated 763 million in 2004 (World Tourism Organization, 2005). In 2000, it provided jobs for an estimated 192 million people and made up 10.8% of the world's Gross Domestic Product (GDP) (Smith & Brent, 2001). In Europe specifically, tourism is directly responsible for 5% of the GDP, and 10% indirectly. Today over 20 million Europeans are employed as a result of tourism (European Travel Commission, 2006). It is estimated that by 2015, one in every 11.2 jobs worldwide will be in tourism, for a total of over 269 million jobs (World Travel and Tourism, 2002).

In 2004 there were over 415 million tourist arrivals in Europe, making up over 50% of the world's tourism arrivals (European Travel Commission, 2006). Global forecasts for 2020 predict that there will be an annual 1.56 billion international tourist arrivals worldwide (World Tourism Organization, 2005). At this time, it is predicted that East Asia and the Pacific will surpass the Americas as second only to Europe in market share at 45.9%. The market shares for Africa, South Asia, and the Middle East are also projected to increase by 2020 (World Tourism Organization, 1997, p. 4). It is expected that 77.3 million international tourists annually will arrive on the African continent by 2020, four times the 20 million recorded in 1995 (World Tourism Organization, 2005). This continued increase contributes to "the tourist's 'shrinking world'" and is projected to result in more and more tourists searching for areas that are not overly touristed (World Tourism Organization, 1997, p.28).

There are many different kinds of tourism including ecotourism, sex tourism, legacy tourism, thanatourism[1], long-haul tourism, seaside tourism, cultural and heritage tourism, psychocentric tourism[2], camper tourism, sports tourism, and adventure tourism . One of the fastest growing segments of the travel industry, and the focus of this essay, is Cultural and Heritage Tourism--defined as "travel directed toward experiencing the arts, heritage and special character of a place" (Craine, 2005, p. 2). In addition to including experiences with present-day cultural events, rituals, traditions, festivals, celebrations, and visiting unique communities such as the Aborigines or Native American pueblos, this tourism experience may include travel to any location associated with the past, such as museums, transportation attractions, historic districts, historically-based theme parks, re-enactments of historical events, battlefields, statues, monuments, craft centers, cathedrals, countryside festivals, sites commemorating well-known people, or shrines (Richter, 2005; Timothy & Boyd, 2003; Ward, Bochner & Furnham, 2001). For some travelers, learning something of the cultural and historical backgrounds of the peoples and places visited enhances their enjoyment of their travels and increases the likelihood that they will return. Others, weary of the homogenization resulting from globalizing forces, actively seek out authentic cultural experiences in their tourist destinations (Craine, 2005).

For example, in 2004, more than 10 million tourists participated in cultural and heritage activities in the United States. Europeans are high on the list of countries most interested in cultural and heritage tourism: United Kingdom, Japan, Germany, France, and Australia (Craine, 2005). This kind of tourism is different from the "mass market" travel and as such presents great learning opportunities for tourists, but also presents important challenges for all involved: the tour operators[3] and site managers, tourists themselves, and the local hosts. Recent research on cultural tourism in Europe suggests that competition among cultural tourism destinations is on the rise (Hodes, 2005). This presents those in the industry with the challenge of using 'culture' (ethically and responsibly) in a way that the destination can be set apart from the competition. The field of intercultural communication offers a strong contribution in meeting these challenges.

Potential Negative Sociocultural Impacts on Host Communities

Tourism is an industry that is interlinked with an endless array of other industries, including agriculture, transportation, hotel, recreation, construction, gastronomy, media and entertainment, health, retailing, and banking. Consequently, its success or failure in a region has far-reaching effects – touching countless businesses. Therefore, better understanding the impacts of tourism on a local community is important for a wide-range of individuals and businesses.

The economic and sociocultural benefits of tourism on local communities are well documented. Local economies flourish because of tourism and interaction with tourists can promote a sense of cultural pride and provide a window to the outside world for local residents (Dyer, Aberdeen, & Schuler, 2002; Furnham, 1984; Manning, 1979; Pearce, 1982; Smith & Brent, 2001; Yea, 2002). However, the negative sociocultural impacts must also be addressed. For example, results from a study in the Austrian Alps showed that while tourism in this area is generally well received due to the added economic benefit to the community; the drawbacks include: increased competition among community members, gradual loss of the local dialect and several local traditions, and a disruption of family life (Kariel & Kariel, 1982). Residents of Nadi, Fiji, similarly, enjoy positive impacts of tourism in their area: money, work, and cultural pride. However, they also note negative impacts of alcohol and drug problems, crime, a growing openness to sex, and poor traffic conditions (King, Pizam, & Milman., 1993).

On the whole, there is a greater impact on the host community when the community is "small, unsophisticated and isolated" (Pearce, 1982, p. 207). For example, although there are positive outcomes of cultural tourism for the Djabugay indigenous community in Australia, including an increased feeling of pride and a cultural revival, tourist contact in that area has not reaped large economic or sociocultural benefits. Some negative effects include limited tourist/host interaction, displacement of local residents, lack of power to enforce agreements, resentment, and exploitation of the community, the local arts, and its culture (Guyette & White, 2003; Pearce, 1982). Two detrimental effects of tourism development that largely affect poorer residents of growing tourist destinations are the rise in the cost of living and disputes over land ownership (World Travel Organization, 2002). These negative outcomes are especially troubling for the poorer residents and can lead to frustrations, which then may result in crime or political unrest.

Negative outcomes often result from local identities (often minorities or indigenous groups) being seen as a tourist product merely to be consumed (Burns, 2004). These negative effects can disrupt one's sense of self, including loss of autonomy, the commodification of one's culture, and a disruption of the area's social rhythm (Berno, 1999; Cohen, 1984; Dyer, Aberdeen & Schuler, 2002; King, Pizam & Milman, 1993; Pearce, 1982; Yea, 2002). One unfortunate example of local identity being affected by intercultural contact occurred when the introduction of luxury tour groups and young travelers resulted in local New Guineans reframing their status (in synch with Westerners' perspective) as "native" and "backwards". This caused them to question their previously held conceptions of their identity and reconceptualize their past by incorporating a "retrospective understanding of the inadequacy of their previous condition as not yet civilized" (Bruner, 1991, p. 245).

This research challenges the claims prevalent in cultural tourism marketing that tourists are the ones who undergo great change. As illustrated, these New Guineans' incorporated the tourists' fantasies of the community's identity as 'primitive' into their own constructions of their collective history and cultural identity (Bruner, 1991). A negative outcome of this intercultural contact was that the host community members 'read' the tourist imagination during their interactions, incorporating into their talk and self-conceptions that could be argued as a more negative sense of collective identity.

In a similar study, Laxon (1991) reports that contact between Native Americans and their Anglo visitors can result in a reinforcement of cultural stereotypes and affirmation that one's worldview is 'correct,' thereby perpetuating ethnocentrism. This comes in stark contrast to the belief that intercultural contact through tourism can promote understanding. Although Native Americans welcome the economic benefits from tourism, many report that turning their culture into a tourist attraction is "dehumanizing" (Laxon, 1991, p. 370). In the United States during the 1970s and 1980s, promotion of Native American culture to attract tourism resulted in many feeling that their American Indian culture had been "used" (Guyette & White, 2003, p. 166). Witnessing the economic benefits to pass through their fingers and into the hands of those outside of their cultural group was difficult in light of the fact that 50-80% of their tribal communities were suffering from poverty and unemployment. When tourists arrive to host communities, locals may experience additional mistreatment.

Laxon (1991) observed that when tourists visited the pueblos of the Native Americans, several negative outcomes resulted from contrasting notions of personal space (proxemics), and time and value orientations. One example is when tourists violated the pueblo residents' boundaries for personal space by touching them, or picking up residents' babies without permission. In addition, tourists oftentimes grew impatient with the Native Americans' approach to time; for example, lamenting the lack of adherence to a strict schedule during a Hopi special event since it clashed with their rushed tourist schedule. This point of tension reveals the clash between the Anglo value of efficiency with the Hopi commitment to a less linear, more 'in the moment' approach to time (Hall, 1981).

It is widely known that tourists often enact a "high play component," while on vacation (Gartner, 1996, p. 162; see also Urry, 2002) and this play attitude and behavior were apparent and inappropriate in Laguna Pueblo on Feast Day, in San Jose, New Mexico—with tourists laughing and joking during the ceremonial dances and imitating the performers by drumming and letting out "war whoops" (Laxon, 1991, p. 372). This behavior is highly problematic in light of the sanctity of this day for the performers and pueblo members.

In order to better understand how these negative impacts come about, it is useful to examine the unique characteristics of communication in tourism contexts. The next section identifies and describes three such unique characteristics and then presents challenges that arise for interactants, in light of these characteristics.

Characteristics of Host-Tourist Encounters

Tourism encounters are a unique form of communication. First, they are fleeting in nature (Cohen, 1984; Cohen & Cooper, 1986; Katriel, 1995; Pearce, 1982; Urry, 2002). In these fleeting moments, long-lasting impressions can be made based only on the tourists' "anecdotal experiences" (Ooi, 2002). Since many tourists are in the visited country for a limited time, they lack both knowledge of local customs and the motivation to gain a deep understanding of the destination's culture. Therefore, their impressions are based on superficial knowledge (de Kadt, 1979; Ooi, 2002) and have the potential to perpetuate stereotypes or misperceptions.

Second, the interaction between the host and the guest is centered on commercialized hospitality. Berno (1999) claims that the introduction of tourism has resulted in the "commercializing interpersonal relationships" (p. 671). Developing countries in particular have been affected by large-scale tourism, where "goods and/or services that used to be part of people's personal and social lives have been commercialized and offered as commodities" (Berno, 1999, p. 691). This aspect of their interaction sets these guests apart from more traditional guest-host relationships.

A final unique aspect of this type of intercultural contact is that the nature of the host-tourist relationship is asymmetric in several ways (Katriel, 1995). First is that the host and tourist have very different meanings attached to tourism. For tourists, 'tourism' means playtime, a break from the normal work routine, a quest for novelty, and an escape from the everyday troubles of home (Ooi, 2002;

MacCannell, 1973; Nettekoven, 1979; Smith & Brent, 2001; Urry, 2002). However, for many of the hosts whose jobs rely on tourism it can mean hard work in menial jobs, the cause of family breakdown and the commercialization of culture (Kariel & Kariel, 1982; King et al., 1993). Also, the tourist and locals are in asymmetric power positions vis-à-vis one another. While the tourists may be at a disadvantage in not knowing the local language, in general, they are in the privileged position of "buying" the hosts' services. Depending on the robustness of the local economy, the locals' very survival may depend on the moneyed visitors who may or may not purchase their products and services.

One aspect that is important to keep in mind is that communication between powerful and less powerful is always constraining for the less powerful (Allen, 2004). For example, hosts are often in a position of accommodating tourists: they must learn the tourists' language(s) or risk losing out on economic benefits (Cohen & Cooper, 1986); they might feel pressure to deliver the most desirable products and services. But perhaps most important, they may experience a feeling of being patronized, of not being recognized as on the same level with tourists—in all aspects of the tourist encounter, from the language they speak, to the way they are treated in the commercial transactions involving souvenirs, lodging, and other goods and services. To what extent tourists and hosts are affected by the power differential depends on many factors, including socioeconomic status, historical context, and centrality of tourism to the economy. For example, contact between a middle-class Italian businessperson on holiday in Spain with a local restaurant manager does not present a dramatic power differential. However, the relationship is still asymmetrical due to the commodified hospitality and service aspect of the interaction.

The extremes of asymmetrical relationships are represented in tourism encounters in third world countries, or in previously colonized countries. One way to view these encounters is through the lens of Postcolonialism–an intellectual, political, and cultural movement that calls for the independence of colonized states and liberation from colonialist mentalité or ways of thinking (Said, 1978). Postcolonial scholars point out that the legacy of colonization often lasts much longer than the political relationship; and tourism scholars concur, that the legacy of colonialism is manifest in many of the structures and practices of contemporary tourism (Aitchison, Macleod & Shaw, 2000; Mowforth & Munt, 1997). Third World tourism is often characterized as touristic encounters involving members of the 'First World' (i.e. developed Western nations) traveling to the Third World (i.e. less economically developed countries). Some scholars suggest that Third World tourism is a form of neocolonialism that bears symptoms of "domination and subjugation" (Chung 1994, p.21). They explain that the power struggle in these tourist encounters goes beyond the interactions of hosts who work directly with guests (including hostel and restaurant owners, street vendors, and local residents), and reaches also to the "brokers" such as hotel owners, tour guides, vendors, and travel agency consultants. These points of contact represent and contribute to the "multiple productions of relations of power...in different localized settings with their own rationalities, histories, and mechanisms" (Cheong & Miller, 2000, 376).

For example, using a postcolonial perspective, Teo and Leong (2006) explore backpacking in Asia—showing the neocolonial power wielded by Western backpackers in determining which places are brought into the tourism economy, and their ability to commodify and set the terms of their relationship with the "Other". [The 'Other' is a term used by postcolonial scholars to emphasize the importance of historical power relations on perceptions between people from privileged and less privileged regions of the world. Specifically, the more powerful tend to perceive the less powerful in objectified, negative, ways (Said, 1989). For example, when the 'Westerners' encounter the 'Thais', the Westerners' perception of the Thai 'Others' is inevitably based on stereotypes or preconceived notions—resulting from the historical asymmetric power relations between nations of the West and East.] Teo and Long (2006) suggest that backpacking is often "a European colonial encounter with its Third World Other" (Pratt, 1992, pp. 29-30) – with backpackers collecting "places" in their quest for exotic experiences (p. 113). From a postcolonial perspective, then, backpackers are not interested in authentic relations with people in countries they visit, but rather see them only as a generalized "other" who happen to inhabit a place they are "collecting." This can be seen in real-life conversation when you hear people ask travelers, "So how many countries have you been to?"

Teo and Leong's (2006) postcolonial analysis reveals the power relations among Western backpackers, the tour brokers, and the Asian hosts and Asian backpackers—a situation where Thai brokers cater to Western backpackers at the expense of Asian backpackers, who then resist and create their own spaces and backpacking network. From a business perspective, this finding is important since it represents a loss of a market segment that is forecasted to increase in the coming years. From a cultural perspective, these imbalanced encounters have the potential to alienate those who are native to the area.

For another example, postcolonial scholars point to the Caribbean islands, where neo-colonial relationships are still being played out in tourist-host encounters — even though the islands are no longer European colonies. Locals still speaking the colonizers' language and serving European tourists are portrayed in the marketing material as smiling and submissive. As Echtner and Prasad (2003) suggest, while these material conditions are essential for catering to the tourist's indulgence, it reawakens memories of the colonial past and so has the potential to perpetuate resentments and antipathy. In effect, these types of representations reproduce the asymmetrical relationships between the former colonizers and colonized, relationships often characterized by the power divisions between master and servant. Applying a postcolonial perspective is helpful in shedding light on problematics that may lie dormant in these types of intercultural relationships.

In sum, the tourism industry—particularly cultural and heritage tourism—is an important communication context to investigate because it:

- holds enormous economic implications for both global and local economies,

- may have negative sociocultural impacts on local, particularly indigenous and third world communities and

- involves communication encounters that are short-term, often tinged with power imbalances between members of diverse cultures, and in the form of commercialized hospitality.

Given these characteristics, the tourist context provides great challenges for communication and tourism scholars and practitioners. Before identifying intercultural communication contributions to this important context, we outline the foundation of our approach: Socially Responsible Tourism—a recent tourism management strategy that emphasizes striving for positive economic, social, cultural, and environmental impacts in tourist industry planning management, product development and marketing. And specifically for tour operators and site managers, it means providing rewarding holiday experiences while enabling local communities to enjoy a better quality of life and conserving the natural environment (Greening the WSSD, 2003).

According to South Africa's Department of Environmental Affairs and Tourism (DEAT) (2002), this shift has come from various sources: 1) a growing tendency to define economic performance in general in terms of growth that is economically, socially and environmentally sustainable. 2) Tourists themselves are becoming more vigilant consumers. In addition to simply enjoying travel, many want to learn more about the host country, meet local people and reduce environmental impact of their visit; 3) Socially responsible tourism may be a matter of survival for many communities. They need to be involved to perceive and manage the benefits. Responsible tourism can create jobs, simulate entrepreneurship and boost local economies.

Contributions of Intercultural Communication Scholarship

Examining cultural and heritage tourism through a socially responsible lens requires that great attention is paid to intersection of tourism and intercultural communication: authenticity, representation, and effective, ethical communication. First, these cultural experiences for tourists are unique, one of a kind, and *authenticity* is a key value. For many tourists, it is important to feel that they are experiencing the "real" cultural traditions—not a simulated or a "Disneyfied" experience. Secondly, these tourist encounters need to be as successful as possible. We interpret this to mean the communication in these encounters is competent and ethical—particularly given the power differentials in tourist-host encounters. Thus, in the following sections we explore two central questions: 1) What challenges does "authenticity" present for those involved in tourism?; and 2) What are guidelines for competent, ethical communication in a socially responsible tourist context?

Authenticity

The issue of authenticity raises challenges for site managers, local hosts, and tourists. The average historic attraction visitor stays at a destination for an average of 4.9 days (Bergeron, 2004). Although most tourist visits are relatively brief, these short-lived moments have the potential to make long-lasting impressions. Authenticity is particularly relevant when considering heritage tourism's connection to representations of the past and of the cultural "others" (Wang, 1999). Some of the first theorizing about authenticity asserted that the search for authenticity is the result of a tourist's desire to obtain a stark contrast to his/her mundane life while simultaneously gaining insight into the lives of locals (MacCannell, 1973). This quest was likened to a pilgrimage because both are in pursuit of authentic experiences, the difference being that pilgrims aim to be part of an important religious event, while tourists are interested in destinations that are of cultural, social or historical import. For example, research suggests that part of the appeal of having an authentic experience for some tourists is 'discovering' the "primitive frozen in time" while others are eager to see a 'traditional' culture before it is destroyed (Bruner, 1991, p. 243). This desire is reminiscent of Otherizing – or objectifying - the host culture and sets up a situation in which the host culture is seen not as a group to interact with but rather one to be 'gazed' upon (Urry, 2002).

What is more, tourists are motivated to "see life as it is [or was] really lived" (MacCannell, 1973, p. 592) which means going beyond the façade that separates tourists from their hosts. MacCannell (1973) asserts that this unmet quest for authenticity leads to a feeling of alienation. Cohen (1988) critiques this modern notion of 'authenticity' by stating that what is seen as 'authentic' might differ from one tourist to the next and likewise may differ greatly from what a social analyst deems to be 'authentic.' Moreover, he suggests that authenticity is not a static concept but rather a process of negotiation between new and old meanings, becoming what he calls "emergent authenticity" (p. 380). This concept emphasizes the dynamic nature of culture and suggests that what may have at one time been seen as 'inauthentic' may become 'authentic' with time. One prominent example is Disneyland, which was originally seen as a theme-park and now is considered to be an important element of American culture.

What is important for destinations centered on a theme, such as heritage parks, is that "the objects observed must *seem* real and absolutely authentic" in order for them to be accepted by the tourists (Urry, 2002, p. 131[italics added]). McKercher & du Cros (2002) succinctly state that "tourists want 'authenticity' but not necessarily reality" (p.40). This means that there is contentment with experiencing a more idyllic and pristine version of the past rather than facing the pollution and oppression from yesteryear. In an effort to satisfy tourists, oftentimes the sites become "more real than the original," resulting in the tourist constructing images of what is authentic based on hyper-notions of a group's culture or a time period (Urry, 2002, p. 131).

Since MacCannell's introduction of the concept in the mid-seventies, scholars have classified and reclassified authenticity into several dimensions, including objective and constructive authenticity, symbolic authenticity, as well as existential authenticity (Wang, 1999). The latter has shifted the concern for authenticity of the destination or host culture to notions of an authentic self. Existential authenticity is defined as "a special state of Being in which one is true to oneself, and acts as a counterdose to the loss of 'true self' in public roles and public spheres in modern Western society (Berger 1973)" (Wang, 1999, p.358). This authentic self can be found in the *doing* of tourist activities, more so than in touring 'objectively' authentic objects. These activities are usually free from one's work norms and routine, therefore are seen as an effective space in which to pursue the authentic self or self-realization. Wang (1999) refers to this as "self-making" and defines it as "an implicit dimension underlying the motivation for tourism"(p. 363).

In an exploration of landscapes of memory (such as historically-based tourist destinations), Dickenson (1997) suggests that these sites are opportunities to do the "self-making" referred to by Wang (1999). These landscapes of memory "respond to the fragmentation of memory created by contemporary culture" (Dickenson, 1997, p.1). Dickenson (1997) utilizes classical rhetorical concepts of memory to analyze a landscape and theorize in new ways about memory and the performance of identity. In short, memories are used not only to "authenticate" the landscape but also the identity of those who visit (p.1). What one chooses to consume at these destinations, Dickenson (1997) argues, is constitutive of the self. Memory places have the power to "trigger intertextual relations that motivate, stabilize, secure, and provide the resources of identity" (p.21) thus consumption of these sites offer opportunity for both memory and the self to be constructed. This linkage between memory and identity is valuable in understanding how some individuals use heritage sites to reconcile a sense of loss of stability, tradition, and community in contemporary culture.

The above discussion on authenticity illustrates that it plays a central role in tourists' experiences. Authenticity is a social construction that is negotiated by what 'seems' to be real. Finally, notions of authenticity add meaning to one's experience and even offer a sense of a more stable self. It seems the centrality of meaningful experiences is recognized by those in the tourism industry as well. At a conference examining the role social science has in regard to tourism development, tourism scholars debated whether authenticity really matters. They concluded that it was "the *quality of visitor experience* that mattered to the tourism industry, not the authenticity of the attraction" (Shackley, 1994, p. 397, [italics added]). In light of the tourists' desires for authenticity and the destinations' goal to deliver quality experiences, those who manage heritage destinations need to find a balance between 'authenticity' and catering to the tourists' desired experience. In light of the previous discussion, we must next consider: What are the challenges related to authenticity for site managers, locals, and tourists?

Challenges for Site Managers

Recognizing that job titles and responsibilities vary greatly depending on the size, scope, and type of cultural heritage destination, we use the term 'site managers' in this section to address generally those who are responsible for either presenting a cultural product/performance or interpreting a heritage site. For example, in heritage tourism the site manager's job is to interpret events, places, and artifacts "authentically" for the audience. This means the management is responsible for interpreting the lives of all those involved and the conditions in which they lived. In this sense, we do not look at a 'real' past but rather a constructed heritage that is both created in and interpreted using the present. Moreover, these interpretations may be for a range of purposes, be it economic, social or political (Graham, Ashworth & Turnbridge, 2005). For example, Colonial Williamsburg is a cultural heritage site located in the southern state of Virginia that aims to preserve and interpret the events and people of the 18th century United States to today's visitors. This location has been criticized for interpreting the lives of those who lived in Colonial Williamsburg in such a way that poverty and class oppression is swept out of the streets and replaced by a more sanitary or "antiseptic" version of the past (Gable & Handler, 2004, p. 170). This version essentially erased minority groups and focused on the White founding fathers. The management defended this 'clean' version of the past by saying that it offers what the public wants. Later, responding to assertions that what was presented was 'too-clean,' they incorporated actual dirt. Not only did this insufficiently address the lack of depth in the representation, this helped support, what is called, the "primitivizing of the past" (Gable & Handler, 2004). Adding actual dirt to the scene primitivizes the past by providing a stark contrast to our more 'civilized' ways of living today.

Another problematic feature of presenting this version of history is that it presents a past that is "frozen" in time when, in reality, the people represented were ever-changing (Graham et al., 2005, p. 31). This presentation also reinforces a "nostalgia for a simpler past" by drawing attention the way things were done independent of our modern-day technology (Gable & Handler, 2004, p. 178). Presentation of a simpler, more-sanitized past illustrates that conflict, class divisions, poverty and slavery are often addressed in what Gable & Handler (2004) refer to as a "comforting" rather than "critical" history at heritage sites (p.180). These authors challenge this softer version of history by saying that since no one has ever presented the 'too dirty', we have not been able to find out what learning, reactions, or impressions would come of it.

Since the control of the representation lies with the heritage site management, much of this burden lies on the shoulders of the site management. The challenge, then for site managers is to provide tourists with experiences that interprets history as accurately as possible and/or presents contemporary culture in a way that is congruent with the local communities view of their identities, customs and traditions—while at the same time making a profit. This can be a delicate balancing act and requires working closely with locals. Suggestions for gaining this cooperation is discussed in more detail in the next section.

Challenges for the Host Members

As noted, cultural tourism can cause frustrations in local communities, particularly in those less economically robust (Dyer et al., 2003; Katriel, 1995; Yea, 2002). Dyer et al. (2003) warn that cultural tourism is not "the panacea for indigenous disadvantage and dependency" (p. 93). This exploitation comes in many forms, including the pressure to meet tourists' expectations of authenticity and the commoditization[4] of culture. MacCannell (1973) suggests that host cultures can feel pressure from the tourists' quest for 'authentic experiences.' This quest for authenticity can be seen as a means of providing a contrast from their mundane lives and gaining insight into locals' real lives. The hosts might react to this goal by moving the sought-after private sphere of their lives (e.g. religious ceremonies or the structure of their homes) to the forefront for tourist consumption, turning the authentic into the 'staged'. One prime example took place in Malaysian Borneo where the hosts were required to make substantial adjustments to their longhouses[5] in order to help them meet tourists' expectations of being 'authentic' (Yea, 2002).

Host communities are increasingly being faced with a tourist appetite for experiences that are more exotic and spectacular than the reality (Timothy & Boyd, 2003). For example, cultural productions in New Guinea were (com)modified to adapt to tourist expectations and wishes. This entailed shortening performances to meet their entertainment needs, scheduling the performances during times when light was suitable for photography, and crafting objects that were small enough for tourist to pack away for their return trip home (Bruner, 1991).

Perhaps one of the most famous examples of culture being commodified for tourist consumption took place in Fuenterrabia, Spain. The Alarde celebration served as a central celebration of their history for approximately 350 years. When the municipal government insisted that the locals put on the celebration twice to attract more tourists, the local residents' passion for the celebration quickly diminished. Within only two years, locals had to be paid to participate because their former celebration had become an obligation (Greenwood 1989, as discussed in Timothy & Boyd, 2003).

The above examples illustrate one particular challenge for host communities that engage in cultural heritage tourism - maintaining a balance between presenting their craft, performance, or tradition in a way that its value can be maintained among the community members while still appealing to tourist tastes. As mentioned earlier, a similar balance needs to be found at heritage sites. Recall that the management of Colonial Williamsburg defended the 'antiseptic' version of the past, claiming it is what the tourists want. Support for this claim can be found in the following: "if faced with truly authentic experiences, [many tourists] would cease visiting heritage sites, for they would appear in conditions most people would find tasteless, dirty, and otherwise unimaginable and unacceptable. This is because people can only see the past through the eyes of the present" (Timothy & Boyd, 2003, p. 251). This presents yet another challenge for host communities. How can heritage sites be presented in way that reflects the actual lived experiences and conditions of the time while still remaining profitable for the local community?

Working with site managers, community members' can insist upon a representation that reflects the multiple perspectives and diversity of the community and its history. Additionally, site managers can provide context for the tourists. This is particularly important for heritage tourism since, as previously mentioned, history is always interpreted from the present. Borrowing from key questions regarding ethics posed by communication scholar De la Garza (published as Gonzalez, 2003), the heritage destination could provide to its visitors provisional responses to the following: "What were the political, social, environmental, physical, and emotional surroundings of [the representation of history put forth]"? and "What was happening in the lives of the people about whom the story is told?" (p. 84). If an effort in this direction is made to answer such questions, it is possible that the sanitization of heritage tourism could be kept to a minimum.

Challenges for Tourists

The search for authenticity in tourist destinations involves challenges for the tourists themselves. One potentially problematic outcome is that after a brief visit, tourists' confidence in their beliefs about the locals may mistakenly increase (Laxson, 1991; Pearce, 1982). This could potentially reinforce stereotypes. Laxson (1991) states that the very short-term nature of an intercultural interaction can serve only to reinforce one's previously held views and one's perception that his/her worldview is correct. This can be particularly sensitive considering that tourists are searching for authenticity to some extent (MacCannell, 1973). The dilemma can be seen in the analysis of Bornean longhouses' guest books in Yea's (2002) study described above. This content analysis of guest books revealed that 'unique' made up 28% of the comments; 'traditional culture,' 20.5%; and 'don't change' was mentioned 18.5% of the time (p. 182). This is an indication of the tourists' interest in authenticity and desire for things to remain the same as to not destroy this 'authenticity'. Ironically, the community's effort to adapt to the tourists preferences is characteristic of MacCannell's (1973) 'staged authenticity'. Due to the nature of the tourists' short visits, they may leave feeling they have seen how the locals 'really live' but nevertheless walk away with inaccurate notions of the locals' social reality. This results in an indirect negative impact on the host community since they are forced to offer a representation of themselves that is contrived. This includes major changes in appearance, daily routine, dress, and community roles in order to appear 'more authentic' and thereby maintaining their status as one of the tour operator's selected destinations. Unknowingly, the tourist's quest for authenticity can create the very conditions that he/she was trying to avoid an "inauthentic" cultural experience. When tourists feel that they may have been duped, they can leave the destination feeling disappointed, and even resentful toward the host community members.

It is clear from the challenges outlined above that there are no easy solutions that would ensure automatic entrance into ethical, balanced, and mutually beneficial relationships; however, these challenges are not insurmountable. The next section discusses how intercultural communication offers an entrée into understanding how host members and tourists can engage in more socially responsible tourism.

Successful Intercultural Communication in Tourism Contexts

How can tourists and local hosts communicate successfully, in a way that facilitates cultural learning for the tourist and is congruent with socially responsible tourism? How can site managers promote effective intercultural communication between tourists and hosts? As Hinner (2005) points out, any international business transaction (e.g. tourism) involves reciprocal relationships and the key to successful relationships is successful intercultural communication. Intercultural communication scholars contribute three areas of investigation that could lead to more successful tourist encounters: communication competence, emphasis on contextual influences, and guidelines for ethical communication.

There is a long tradition of research on intercultural communication competence (Bradford, Allen, & Beisser, 2000; Chen & Starosta, 1996; Collier, 1989; Martin, 1993; Wiseman, 2002). Scholars have suggested that competent communication is both effective and appropriate. Effective communication suggests that people are able to achieve desired personal outcomes—i.e., individuals must be able to control and manipulate their environment to achieve these outcomes. Appropriate communication involves the use of messages that are expected in the situation—i.e., individuals must have an adequate understanding of the expectations of acceptable behavior in a given situation (Wiseman, 2002). Scholars have also suggested three conditions for competent communication—motivation, knowledge and skills (see, for example, Ting-Toomey, 1999). Motivation to communicate interculturally is probably the most important; without it, knowledge and skills are irrelevant. Second, individuals must have some knowledge (awareness and understanding) about what it takes to communicate competently across cultures. This may entail linguistic knowledge, understanding of the communication rules and norms etc. required in the situation. Skills refer to the actual performance of the behaviors one believes to be effective and appropriate (Wiseman, 2002).

Early research--primarily focused on North American Caucasian, middle-class, college-educated populations in university settings--identified communication *behaviors* perceived to be competent in a variety of intercultural contexts. That is, researchers developed scales measuring intercultural communication competence in various social contexts, such as US students going abroad, international students coming to the United States, and US students and their interactions with international students (Hammer, Gudykunst & Wiseman, 1978; Koester & Olebe, 1988; Martin & Hammer,1989; Ruben, 1976). One cross cultural study investigated German, U. S. and French tourists' perceptions of the communication competences of tour guides (Leclerc & Martin, 2004).

More recent scholarship, however, questioned the generalizability of this early research. For example, Martin, Hecht & Larkey (1994) discovered significant differences between African American and U. S. Whites' perceptions of effectiveness in interethnic encounters. For African Americans, the issue of power/powerlessness played an important role in their perceptions of the effectiveness of interethnic conversations—a dimension never included in extant competence frameworks. These and other research results points to the important role of power and power differentials in communication encounters, and leads to the question: who gets to judge whether communication is competent in a particular encounter (Collier, 1998, 2005)? The interactant with the most power? Applied to a tourist encounter-- if a tourist bargaining with a local vendor purchases a souvenir at the lowest possible price, is this competent communication? Using early definitions and frameworks, one might argue yes—the tourist achieved her goal of obtaining a cheap souvenir and communicated appropriately enough to accomplish the transaction. However, if in the interaction, the local vendor feels exploited, powerless and demeaned as a result of the communication, perhaps this should not be called competent communication.

Recent critical scholarship[6] suggests that power is involved in every communication interaction, and more importantly, those in power establish the definitions and norms for communication competence. Those in society who have less power violate the established norms at their own peril (Orbe, 1998). However, this practice becomes more complicated in tourist encounters when host members navigate the intricacies of holding a high power status in their own community while simultaneously holding a lower status vis-à-vis their more affluent tourist clients. In an intercultural tourist encounter power relations may be less obvious, yet more complex. Postcolonial communication scholars are interested not only in theorizing colonial conditions but "why those conditions are what they are, and how they can be undone and redone" (Shome & Hegde, 2002, p. 250). One might argue, then, that while one (site managers, hosts, and tourists) can *strive* for competent communication in intercultural tourist contexts and consider one's motivation, knowledge and skills, it is important to recognize that these may not be sufficient to ensure a mutually satisfying encounter.

A second contribution of intercultural communication scholarship is the emphasis on contextual influences on communication (Katriel, 1995). As noted earlier, a postcolonial perspective reminds us that tourist encounters may be heavily influenced by prior historical, geo-political relations. An understanding of any tourist encounter must also consider current economic and political influences. For example, French speaking tourists in Belgium may be treated less well by locals than German—given the current political configuration of Flemish and French relations. In the United States, Muslims tourists have been harassed as a result of to the U. S. involvement in Iraq.

Finally, successful communication must also be ethical communication. Communication scholars have long struggled with the issue of ethics in cross-cultural interactions (Barnlund, 1979; Casmir, 1997; Johannesen, 1990; Asuncion-Lande, 1979; Jaska & Pritchard, 1994); most addressing the problem of how persons from different cultures can successfully interact with each other in ethical ways. In an early essay titled "Intercultural Arena: An Ethical Void," Barnlund (1979) specifically called for a new metaethic which he hoped would provide a superordinate set of guidelines to govern intercultural interaction. While no such agreed-upon metaethic has been established, scholars have provided some guidelines, including 1) the humanness principle; 2) the dialogic principle and 3) the Principle of speaking "to" rather than "for" or "about" (Martin, Flores, & Nakayama, 2002).

First, the humanness principle stresses that our communication should be guided by a respect and tenderness toward others, that individuals be responsive in their communication to the impact they might have on the humanity of those affected by the act (Johnstone, 1981; Kale, 1994). This principle has implications for the tourism industry, particularly the tour operators, site managers, and tourists. What impact do their actions and communication have on locals with whom they interact?

The dialogic principle (Evanoff, 2003) stresses the centrality of relationships and discourse, a call for people to try to understand and share the lived experience of another, developing empathy with others, through a dialogical process in which the participants attempt to critique existing norms and arrive at a more adequate set of norms which are capable of resolving the specific problems they face. Broome (1991) points out that "provisional empathy" is the best one can do when reaching across vast cultural differences. Again, what are the implications for tourist encounters for hosts and tourists?

A third and related guideline for ethical communication is the principle of speaking "with" and "to" rather than "for" or "about" others (Alcoff, 1991/1992). This is particularly relevant to the tourism context—as cultural heritage managers are in the business of interpreting cultural attitudes, patterns, and traditions. Alcoff and others point out that when scholars or those in relatively powerful positions speak for (or describe) cultural patterns of less privileged people, they sometimes reinforce the oppression of the group spoken for (Shugart, 2003). The alternative is listening to others and engaging in conversations that are mutually engaging and satisfying.

In an effort to bring to light a more ethical approach to cultural heritage tourism, Taylor (2000) offers, "sincerity" as an alternative to authenticity. 'Sincerity' serves as a lens from which one can shift the focus from objectification and static historicizing to one that allows for "experiences in culture...to become tied to selves in the present, both local and tourist" (p.23). Shifting to an emphasis on sincerity admittedly does not circumvent the issues surrounding authenticity but it does open the tourist encounter to a more reciprocal cultural exchange, allowing for the practice of speaking 'with' and 'to' others. One Maori community's efforts toward a more respectful, less objectifying cultural tourism illustrates this shift. In this instance, Maori Heritage Tours incorporated tourist involvement into a treaty ceremony. The tourists themselves sign the treaty, which also mentions their involvement in this experience. This serves as both a re-enactment and a "symbolic contractual agreement based on principles of equality [where] tourists are encouraged to recognize their own positions as consumers of culture" (Taylor, 2001, p. 24). This not only allows for self-reflexivity[7] on the part of the tourist but also encourages the tourists to share more of themselves, enabling the 'gaze' (Urry, 2002) to be returned rather than only cast upon the visited culture.

Given the importance of the tourism industry, the unique communication characteristics of tourism encounters, and intercultural communication scholars call for competent, ethical communication, how can those involved in tourism promote successful intercultural interaction? We offer the following challenges and suggestions.

Challenges and Suggestions for Site Managers

Site managers play an important role in setting the context for interaction between tourists and locals. Their challenge is to promote the kind of tourism encounters that respects the local culture, offers authenticity to the tourists, and still makes a profit. This means offering tourist experiences are consonant with the cultural members' view of themselves and their history. A key component then is working with members of the local community, engaging in the kind of dialogue that promotes speaking "with" and "to" and not only "about" the cultures. Specifically, they ask host communities the extent to which they feel comfortable commodifying or "selling" their culture. What would they like tourists to understand and learn about their culture? They should negotiate the notice required for tourist visits, what activities are acceptable for tourist consumption and what size groups are suitable. They might also ask whether it is appropriate for tourists to visit people's homes.

The following are suggestions for site managers:

- Inform guests about local history, customs, and appropriate communication behavior, both verbal and nonverbal. Ensure that tourists follow norms and laws regarding photography and videotaping.

- Educate guests about the sanctity of religious ceremonies and ensure that they do not damage, mishandle, or remove religious artifacts.

- Encourage guests to reflect on their own quests for authenticity--to consider the notions described earlier (that all cultures evolve constantly and it is unfair to expect any to stay frozen in time).

- Encourage guests to strengthen their observation skills, interact with local people when appropriate, and learn about local culture and traditions in a variety of ways.

The Responsible Tourism Handbook (Greening the WSSD, 2003) suggests that site managers ask themselves the following questions in evaluating their performance in promoting socially responsible tourism:

- How are you raising local awareness about tourism and increasing local residents' access to your tourism products?

- What efforts have you made to improve education, health and infrastructure for local residents?

From an intercultural perspective, the following questions are also important to consider:

- Is the way in which the host culture is presented congruent with their preferred public identity? Does this presentation reflect the diversity among the community members?

- To what extent to the host community members feel comfortable in commodifying their cultural products or performances?

Challenges and Suggestions for Host Members

It should be noted that host communities cannot be expected to reach consensus on the most appropriate strategies for dealing with tourism. There may be a range of opinions—depending on individual stakes in the tourism business. Those who stand to gain financially may be supportive of incorporating tourism in the local economy; there may be others who see little gain and may retreat from or even resist tourism encounters (Bossevain, 1996). Moreover, one should not get the impression that host communities are powerless in the face of more affluent, more industrialized societies. While there are many and disparate challenges to ensuring a viable solution for host communities, local communities can organize and potentially have access to important decision-making processes. The ways in which a host community gets involved in the tourism development can greatly affect the manner their culture is presented and to what extent they benefit from the touristic presence (Guyette & White, 2003). One important issue central to tourism development is the preferred boundaries the community wants to retain between themselves and the tourists.

Another challenge is to find the delicate balance between presenting the community's history, craft, performance, or tradition in a way that its value can be maintained among the community members while still appealing to tourist tastes. The most important aspect to emphasize here is that the best suggestions will come from the community itself – since it is the best informed about the values it holds most dear and is best able to tap the creativity necessary to maintain this while appealing to tourists. Thus, community collaboration and planning are central to establishing this balance and inviting tourism into their community on their own terms. Drawing upon experiences from several Native American communities involved in tourism in the western United States, Guyette & White (2003) suggest the following for host communities to consider when working to re-establish an equitable and mutual relationship vis-à-vis tourism:

- Consider "form", "scale", and "timing" (p. 169). *Form* refers to the importance of integrating aspects of the traditional economy into tourism development (e.g. the arts). *Scale* refers to the fact that small-scale development is more sustainable. Third, *timing* reminds us that future planning and gradual development is key to creating regional networks of support.

- Identify key issues – What are the community's primary concerns?

- Protect the privacy of the community – Which areas are tourist welcome to explore? Which areas are 'off-limits'?

- Establish cultural boundaries - Which ceremonies or artifacts are not permitted for tourist consumption?

- Define tourist-host relationship and appropriate etiquette – How do the locals view tourists (e.g. 'guests,' 'visitors,' or 'consumers')? Are the ceremonies viewed as a 'performance' for tourist enjoyment or is it seen as a 'sacred ceremony'? What behavior is expected at these events or locations?

- Determining community needs, goals, and objectives – How is culture, kinship, religion, the environment, politics, and the environment predicted to be affected by tourism? What are the potential negative impacts to each area? What are the likely positive gains?

All of the above assist host communities in planning for more equitable and mutual tourism-host relationships. Intercultural scholars emphasize the importance of host community members engaging in a dialogue with their fellow community members on the topics mentioned above in an effort to understand the diverse perspectives and needs of the community. Additionally, it has become clear that tourists could also benefit from more communication regarding the host community's practices, values, traditions, and relationship to the tourism industry. This could include providing ample communication (in the form of brochures, announcements, personal communication, etc.) to tourists about the values and traditions that are behind the craft or performance. In situations where cultural ceremonies are performed in the presence of tourist audiences, a visitor's guide could be provided which educates them on the importance of the ceremony and the proper conduct that is required. These efforts are small steps in preventing inappropriate tourist behavior in host communities, communicating the cultural worth and meaning (cultural) products or performances hold for the community while also appealing to the tourists' desire for 'authenticity.' In short, host community members can work toward "effective tourism development [that] involves engaging in dialogue, defining and communicating needs, planning and managing" (Guyette &White, 2003, p. 181).

Challenges and Suggestions for Tourists

In German the concepts of *Fernweh*[8] and *Wanderlust*[9] encompass the tourist desire for and joy of travel. The long list of tourist typologies available in the extant literature is illustrative of the fact that tourists have varying motivations. Since tourists come to holiday destinations with certain motivations and divergent expectations, it is no surprise that the effects of guest and host interactions extend to tourists as well.

Extant research suggests that tourists' beliefs about their own culture and that of the host can be influenced by intercultural contact. One positive outcome intercultural contact may have on the tourist is an increased awareness of the communication problems associated with such encounters (Pearce, 1982). And this awareness is important. When one is more aware of the difficulties intercultural communication presents, one is in a position to be more mindful of his/her communication. Mindful communication is oftentimes characterized by active engagement in interpreting another's message and Langer (1989) emphasizes that mindful communication involves a greater sensitivity to context and the ability to consider multiple perspectives. Research suggests that increased mindfulness during communication encounters can reap substantial benefits. If conflict should arise, the most competent communicators are mindful of the (intercultural) differences and are more likely to consider unarticulated assumptions and be aware of conflicting preferences or approaches (Burgoon, Berger & Waldron, 2000). Thus, the first step for tourists striving for more successful communication with locals is to practice mindfulness when communicating.

Although most (cultural) tourists want to behave in a manner that is appropriate, they may not have the knowledge to do so and may unintentionally do something that is considered rude or inappropriate in the host culture (Guyette & White, 2003). Therefore, a second important step for tourists striving for competent, ethical communication with local hosts is to gather knowledge about the culture they will visit, even if it is for a short time. Knowing some words of the local language goes a long way in avoiding negative interactions and in communicating respect. Also, finding out about local customs that may relevant during the visit, such as knowing the major religious holidays. For example, Rhamadan, a Muslim holiday, falls on different days each year and is a time of fasting by day and feasting at night. In some areas, eating in public during daylight hours in Rhamadan is considered extremely rude. Likewise, knowing something of the local norms for public dress, behavior and comportment is very important. In terms of skills, one cannot be communicatively competent in all the communication rules of every society and a useful skill here is to observe. There's a piece of advice for travelers to Africa that could apply almost anywhere "Keep quiet. Listen and observe before offering an opinion" (Richmond & Gestrin, 1998).

Another suggestion is to engage in self-reflexivity. If a tourist takes the time to learn about the cultural practices of the host community, he/she is likely also to learn much about him/herself. With this greater awareness of different and similar approaches to time, family, work, play, and/or interpersonal relationships, one is in a better position to interpret touristic encounters. Self-reflexivity also allows one to recognize the importance of one's own "location" in the historical, geopolitical tourist context. This may enable tourists to recognize and resist the tendency for what anthropologist Rosaldo (1989) terms "imperialist nostalgia" — the notion that individuals from technologically advanced countries often see technological development as necessary for their own society but prefer that "others" in less developed countries remain in a less technologically advanced and "pure" state.

As noted earlier, it might be helpful for tourists to remember that all societies evolve and change; no group (including their own) is static nor ahistorical (Casteñeda, 1996). Shepard (2002) explains: "In other words, there is no original moment; there are no ethnic Others who have existed in a never-never land, segregated in both time and space. Instead, there have always been those who have come before – if not always tourists, then missionaries, traders, political agents, explorers, and anthropologists (Oakes, 1997: 36)." (p. 193). Shepard (2002) illustrates the dynamic, ever-changing, and historically-contextual nature of society with the following, "Trains, once decried as a symbol of modern society's destruction of the past, have been transformed into examples of a lost age of 'real,' 'authentic,' transportation" (p. 193). Bruner (1991) too reminds us that it is important to keep in mind that "for generations of tourists…primitive peoples have always been seen as on the edge of change, to be experienced or described before they disappear" (p. 243).

When we, as tourists, are interested in seeing a "primitive culture," and yearn for these cultures to 'stay traditional,' as we saw in the Bornean long-house example – we must interrogate why this is. Are we interested in cultures maintaining their traditional ways and not joining our fast-paced way of life? Or could it partly be due to the fact that modern communities are less interesting to those of us who belong to the high-tech, highly industrialized Western world? This view, while pervasive, is limiting for both the host and the tourist.

A static conceptualization of culture does not reflect the lived experiences of many host communities that engage in tourism. Taking a static approach prevents tourists from appreciating this special balance that is maintained and negotiated by developing communities. Taking a dialectic – more complex – view of culture allows tourists to see how communities are both modern and traditional, static and dynamic, and privileged and disadvantaged.

Conclusion

Much of the contested nature of tourism centers on issues of culture, identity, power, representation, and communication, all of which areas central to the intercultural communication discipline. For this reason viewing the interplay between tourists and host communities from an intercultural communication lens may shed light on the points of conflict and offer a first step in alleviating some of the negative impacts of tourism. It is our hope that these suggestions will be useful for those whose work involves tour operators, tour guides, marketing, advertising, promotion of cultural products, and those who are or have contact with host community members and international tourists.

Endnotes

[1] Thanatourism, sometimes known as 'dark tourism,' is a form of tourism that involves visiting sites of tragedy. One example of this would be the Dachau Concentration Camp (Richter, 2005, p. 266).
[2] Psychocentric tourism is directed at people who are not venturesome and prefer mass tourism and organized package tours. For example, they may rather view the Alps from the comfort of their own vehicle or from a tour bus rather than actually climbing in the mountains (Plog, 1974).
[3] A tour operator is responsible for selling tours (including tours and accommodation) to travel agencies (McIntosh, Goeldner & Richie, 1995).
[4] 'commoditization' here refers to making culture or cultural elements a product for sale.
[5] Longhouses are "a unique form of communal dwelling comprising a number of family owned apartments (*bileks*) joined by a common verandah (*ruai*)" (Yea, 2002).
[6] Critical scholarship is noted for its emphasis on power and how it functions in our everyday lives, and the historical context of communication (Martin & Nakayama, 1999).
[7] This is a process of reflection where you come to understand yourself and your position in society (Martin & Nakayama, 2000).
[8] This translates into English literally as "distance pain" meaning the rough equivalent of "having the travel bug" or "itchy feet."
[9] This translates into English roughly as "the passion for travel."

References

Asuncion-Lande, N.C.(Ed.) (1979), *Ethical perspectives and critical issues in intercultural communication*. Falls Church, VA: Speech Communication Association.

Barnlund, D. C. (1979). The cross-cultural arena: an ethical void. In L.A. Samovar, & R. E. Porter (Eds.), *Intercultural communication: a reader*, (4th ed.) (pp. 394–399). Belmont: Wadsworth.

Bergeron, J. M. (2004). Travel to historic attractions in South Carolina and the United States: Market trends. Retrieved June 26, 2005, from the world wide web.

Berno, T. (1999). When a guest is a guest: Cook islanders view of tourism. *Annals of Tourism Research, 26*(3), 656-675.

Boissevain, J. (Ed.). (1996). *Coping with tourists: European reactions to mass tourism.* Providence, RI: Berghahn Books.

Boyd-Barrett, O. (2002). Global communication orders. In W. B. Gudykunst & B. Mody (Eds.), *Handbook of international and intercultural communication 2nd ed* (pp. 325-342). Thousand Oaks, CA: Sage.

Bradford, L., Allen, M., & Beisser, K. (2000). An evaluation and meta-analysis of intercultural communication competence research. *World Communication, 29,* 28-51.

Broome, B. J. (1991). Building shared meaning: Implications of a relational approach to empathy for teaching intercultural communication. *Communication Education, 40,* 235-249.

Bruner, E. (1991). Transformation of self in tourism. *Annals of Tourism Research, 18,* 238-250.

Burgoon, J. K., Berger, C. R., & Waldron, V. R. (2000). Mindful and interpersonal communication. *Journal of Social Issues.* 56, 105-127.

Burns, P. (2004). Introduction: Tourism and social identities. *Tourism, Culture & Communication, 5,* 1-2.

Casmir, F.L.(Ed.) (1997), *Ethics in intercultural and international communication.* London: Lawrence Erlbaum.

Castañeda, Q. (1996). *In the museum of Maya culture: Touring Chichen Itza.* Minneapolis: University of Minnesota Press.

Chen, G. M. & Starosta, W. J. (1997). Intercultural communication competence: A synthesis. In B. Burleson (Ed.), *Communication yearbook 19* (pp. 353-383). Thousand Oaks, CA: Sage.

Cheong, S., and Miller, M. (2000). Power and tourism: A Foucauldian observation. *Annals of Tourism Research, 27,* 371–390.

Chung, H. (1994). Peoples' spirituality and tourism. *Contours, 6,* 19–24.

Cohen, E. (1988). Authenticity and commodification in tourism. *Annals of Tourism Research, 15*(3), 371-386.

Cohen, E. (1984). The sociology of tourism: Approaches, issues, and findings. *Annual Review of Sociology, 10,* 373–392.

Cohen, E., & Cooper, L. (1986). Language and tourism. *Annals of Tourism Research, 13,* 533-563.

Collier, M. J. (2005). Theorizing cultural identification: Critical updates and continuing evolution. In W. B. Gudykunst (Ed.). *Theorizing about intercultural communication* (pp. 235-256). Thousand Oaks, CA: Sage.

Collier, M. J. (1998). Reconciling interpretive and postcolonial perspectives. In D. V. Tanno & A. Gonzalez (Eds.), *Communication and identity across cultures* (pp. 122-147). Thousand Oaks, CA: Sage.

Collier, M. J. (1989). Cultural and intercultural communication competence: Current approaches and direction for future research. *International Journal of Intercultural Relations, 13*, 287-302.

Comor, E. (2002). Media corporations in the age of globalization. In W. B. Gudykunst & B. Mody (Eds.), *Handbook of international and intercultural communication 2nd ed* (pp. 309-323). Thousand Oaks, CA: Sage.

Craihe, K.(Ed.). (2005). *Cultural & heritage tourism in the United States*. A position paper prepared for the 2005 U. S. Cultural & Heritage Tourism Summit, Washington, D.C.

de Kadt, E. (1979). *Tourism—passport to development? Perspectives on the social and cultural effects of tourism in developing countries*. New York: Oxford University Press.

De la Garza, S.A. (2000) *See Gonzalez, M.C.*

Department of Environmental Affairs and Tourism, (2002). National responsible tourism development guidelines for South Africa: Provisional guidelines, March 2002. Retrieved on October 27, 2005 from the world wide web.

Dickinson, G. (1997). Memories for sale: Nostalgia and the construction of identity in old Pasadena. *The Quarterly Journal of Speech, 83*(1), 1-27.

Dyer, P., L., A., & Schuler, S. (2002). Tourism impacts on an Australian indigenous community: A djabugay case study. *Tourism Management, 24*, 83-95.

Echtner, C. N. & Parsad, P. (2003). The context of third world tourism marketing. *Annals of Tourism Research, 30*, 660–682.

Evanoff, R. J. (2004). Universalist, relativist and constructivist approaches to intercultural ethics. *International Journal of Intercultural Relations, 28*, 439–458

Furnham, A. (1984). Tourism and culture shock. *Annals of Tourism Research, 11*, 41-57.

Gable, E., & Handler, R. (2004). Deep dirt: Messing up the past at Colonial Williamsburg. In Y. Rowan & U. Baram (Eds.), *Marketing heritage: Archaeology and the consumption of the past* (pp. 167-181). Oxford: Altamira Press.

Gartner, W. C. (1996). Tourism development. Principles, processes, and policies. New York: John Wiley & Sons, Inc.

Gonzalez, M.C., (2003). An ethics for postcolonial ethics. In Clair, R. P. (2003). *Expressions of Ethnography: novel approaches to qualitative methods*. (pp.77-86). Albany, NY: SUNY Press.

Guyette, S. & White, D. (2003). Reducing the impacts of tourism through cross-cultural planning. In H. K. Rothman (Ed.), *The culture of tourism, the tourism of culture : selling the past to the present in the American Southwest.* (pp. 164 – 184). Albuquerque: University of New Mexico Press.

Glasson, J., Godfred, K., & Godfred, B. (1995). *Towards visitor impact management: Visitors impacts, carrying capacity and management responses in Europe's historic towns and cities.* Brookfield, VT: Ashgate Publishing Company.

Graham, B., Ashworth, G. J., & Turnbridge, J. E. (2005). The uses and abuses of heritage. In G. Corsane (Ed.), *Heritage, museums and galleries: An introductory reader* (pp. 26-37). New York: Routledge.

Greening the WSSD (2003). *Responsible Tourism Handbook: a guide to good practice for tourism operators.* Retrieved on February 07, 2006 from the world wide web.

Hall, E. T. (1981). *Beyond culture.* Garden City: Anchor Press.

Hammer, M. R. Gudykunst, W. B. & Wiseman, R. L (1978). Dimensions of intercultural effectiveness: An exploratory study. International Journal of Intercultural Relations, 2, 382-392.

Hinner, M. B. (2005). General Introduction: Can quality communication improve business relationships. In M.B. Hinner (Ed.). *Freiberger Beiträge zur interkulturellen und Wirtschaftskommunikation* (pp. 219-248). Frankfurt am Main, Germany: Peter Lang.

Hodes, S. (2005). City Tourism and Culture: The European Experience. *In European Travel Commission.* Research Highlights. No. 2, April 2005. Retrieved February 04, 2006, from the world wide web.

Jaksa, J. A., & Pritchard, M. S. (1994). *Communication ethics: Methods of analysis* (2nd ed.). Belmont, CA: Wadsworth.

Johannesen, R. (1990) *Ethics in human communication.* Prospect Heights, IL: Waveland.

Johnstone, C. L. (1981). Ethics, wisdom, and the mission of contemporary rhetoric: The realization of human being. *Central states Speech Journal, 32,* 177-188.

Kale, D.W. (1994).Ethics in intercultural communication. In L.A.Samovar, & R. E. Porter (Eds.), *Intercultural communication: a reader* 7th ed. (pp. 435–441). Belmont, CA: Wadsworth.

Kariel, G. H., & Kariel, P. E. (1982). Socio-cultural impacts of tourism: An example of the Austrian alps. *Human Geography, 64*(1), 1-16.

Katriel , T. (1995). From "context" to "contexts" in intercultural communication research. In R. L. Wiseman (Ed.), *Intercultural communication theory* (pp. 271-284). Thousand Oaks, CA: Sage.

Kim, Y. Y. (2005a). Adapting to a new culture: An integrative communication theory. In W. B. Gudykunst (Ed.) *Theorizing about intercultural communication* (pp. 375-400). Thousand Oaks, CA: Sage.

Kim, Y. Y. (2005b). Adapting to a new culture: An interdisciplinary overview. In M.B. Hinner (Ed.). *FreibergerBeiträge zur interkulturellen und Wirtschaftskommunikation* (pp. 343-361). Frankfurt am Main, Germany: Peter Lang.

King, B., Pizam, A., & Milman, A. (1993). Social impacts of tourism: Host perceptions. *Annals of Tourism Research, 20*, 650-665.

Koester, J. & Olege, M. (1988). The behavioral assessment scale for intercultural communication effectiveness. *International Journal of Intercultural Relations, 12*, 233-246.

Langer, E. J. (1989). *Mindfulness*. Reading, MA: Addison-Wesley.

Laxson, J. D. (1991). How "we" see "them" tourism and Native Americans. *Annals of Tourism Research, 18*, 365-391.

Leclerc, D. & Martin, J. N. (2004). Tour guide communication competence: French, German and American tourists' perceptions. *International Journal of Intercultural Relations, 28*, 181-200.

MacCannell, D. (1973). Staged authenticity: Arrangements of social space in tourist settings. *The American Journal of Sociology, 79*(3), 589-603.

McKercher, B., & du Cros, H. (2002). *Cultural tourism: The partnership between tourism and cultural heritage management*. New York: The Haworth Hospitality Press.

Manning, F. E. (1979). Tourism and Bermuda's black clubs: A case of cultural revitalization. In E. de Kadt (Ed.) *Tourism: Passport to development?: Perspectives on the social and cultural effects of tourism in developing countries* (157–176). New York: Oxford University Press.

Martin, J. N. (1993). Intercultural communication competence: A review. In R. L. Wiseman & J. Koester (Eds.), *Intercultural communication competence* (pp. 16-32). Newbury Park, CA: Sage.

Martin, J. N., Flores, L. A. & Nakayama, T. K. (2002). Ethical issues in intercultural communication. In J. Martin & T.K. Nakayama & L. A. Flores (Eds.). *Readings in intercultural communication: Experiences and contexts* 2nd ed (pp. 363-373). Boston: McGraw Hill.

Martin, J. N. & Hammer, M. R. (1989). Behavioral categories of intercultural communication competence: Everyday communicators' perceptions. *International Journal of Intercultural Relations, 13*, 303-332.

Martin, J. N., Hecht, M. L., & Larkey, L. K. (1994). Conversational improvement strategies for interethnic communication: African-American and European perspectives. *Communication Monographs, 61*, 236-255.

Martin, J. N. & Nakayama, T. K. (2000). *Intercultural communication contexts*. Boston: McGraw Hill.

Mowforth, M., and Munt, I. (1997). *Tourism and sustainability: New tourism in the Third World*. London: Routledge.

Nettekoven, L., (1979). Mechanisms of cultural interaction. In de Kadt, E., (ed.) *Tourism—Passport to development? Perspectives on the social and cultural effects of tourism in developing countries.* New York: Oxford University Press.

Olaniran, B. (2004). Computer-mediated communication in cross cultural virtual teams. In G-M Chen & W. J. Starosta (Eds.), *Dialogue among diversities* (pp. 142-166). Washington, D.C.: National Communication Association.

Ooi, C.-S. (2002). *Cultural tourism and tourism cultures: The business of mediating experiences in Copenhagen & Singapore.* Herndon, VA: Copenhagen Business School Press.

Orbe, M. (1998). *Constructing co-cultural theory: An explication of culture, power, and communication.* Thousand Oaks, CA: Sage.

Pearce, P. (1982). Tourists and their hosts: Some social and psychological effects of inter-cultural contact. In S. Bochner (Ed.), *Cultures in contact: Studies in cross-cultural interaction* (pp. 199–218). New York: Pergamon Press.

Plog, S. (1974). Why destination areas rise and fall in popularity? *Cornell Hotel and Restaurant Quarterly, 14,* 55 – 58.

Pratt, M. (1992). *Imperial eyes: travel writing and transculturation.* London: Routledge.

Richter, L. K. (2005). The politics of heritage tourism development. In G. Corsane (Ed.), *Heritage, museums and galleries: An introductory reader* (pp. 257-271). New York: Routledge.

Richmond, Y. & Gestrin, P. (1998). *Into Africa: Intercultural insights.* Yarmouth, ME: Intercultural Press.

Rosaldo, R. (1989). *Culture and Truth: The remaking of social analysis.* Boston: Beacon Press.

Ruben, B. D. (1976). Assessing communication competence for intercultural adaptation. *Group and Organization Studies, 2,* 470-479.

Said, E. (1978). *Orientalism: Western conceptions of the Orient.* London: Penguin.

Shackley, M. (1994). When is the past? Authenticity and the commoditization of heritage. *Tourism Management, 15(5),* 396-397.

Sheperd, R. (2002). Commodification, culture and tourism. *Tourist Studies,* Vol. 2, No. 2, 183-201.

Shome, R. & Hegde, R. (2002). Postcolonial approaches to communication: Charting the terrain, engaging the intersections. *Communication Theory, 12,* 249-270.

Shugart, H. A. (2003). An appropriating aesthetic: Reproducing power in the discourse of critical scholarship. *Communication Theory, 13,* 275-303.

Smith, V. L., & Brent, M. (2001). *Hosts and guests revisited: Tourism issues of the 21st century.* Elmsfond, NY: Cognizant Communication Corporation.

Taylor, J. (2000). Authenticity and sincerity in tourism. *Annals of Tourism Research, 28*(1), 7-26.

Teo, P. & Leong, S. (2006). A postcolonial analysis of backpacking. *Annals of Tourism Research, 33*, 109–131, 2006

Timothy, D. J., & Boyd, S. W. (2003). *Heritage tourism* (1st ed.): Pearson Educational Limited.

Ting-Toomey, S. (1999). *Communicating across cultures.* New York: Guilford Press.

Urry, J. (2002). *The tourist gaze* (2 ed.). Thousand Oaks, California: Sage Publications.

Wang, N. (1999). Rethinking authenticity in tourism experience. *Annals of Tourism Research, 26*(2), 349-370.

Ward, C., Bochner, S., & Furnham, A. (2001). *The psychology of culture shock.* Routledge. London.

Wiseman, R. L. (2002). Intercultural communication competence. In W. B. Gudykunst & B. Mody (Eds.), *Handbook of international and intercultural communication* 2nd ed (pp. 207-224). Thousand Oaks, CA: Sage.

World Tourism Organization. (1997). *Tourism 2020 vision: Executive summary* (Executive Summary). Madrid, Spain.

World Tourism Organization. (2002). Microtourism: A view from the grassroots: Presentation by Sarah l. Timpson, global manager, small grants programme at the WTO side event on tourism and poverty alleviation, Johannesburg, 30 august 2002. Retrieved May 7, 2005, from the world wide web.

World Travel and Tourism Council. (2005). World report. Travel & tourism. Sowing the seeds of growth: The 2005 travel & tourism economic research. Retrieved May 11, 2005, from the world wide web.

Yea, S. (2002). On and off the ethic tourism map in Southeast Asia: The case of Iban longhouse tourism, Sarawak, Malaysia. *Tourism Geographies, 4*(2), 173-194.